ONTARIO

CAROLYN B. HELLER

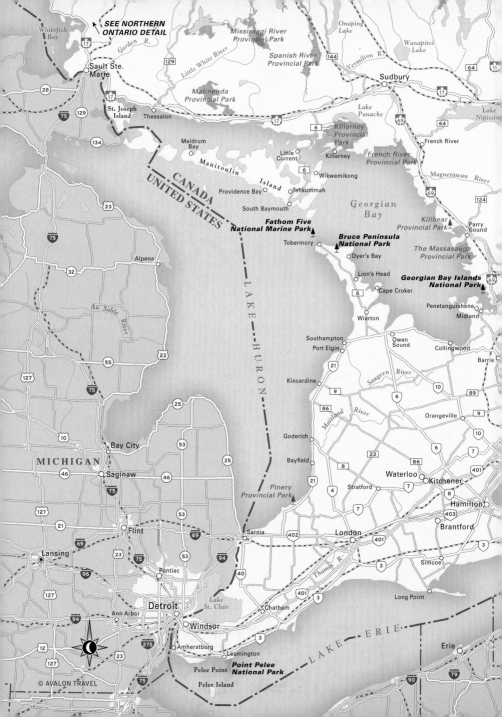

Contents

DISCOVER
Ontario

Buzzing urban centers with hip nightspots and eclectic shops. Creative chefs, international eateries, and plenty of local food. Historic sites and modern museums. A relaxing getaway with outdoor adventures and activities for the kids. And all at a good value, too? That's Ontario.

Toronto is Canada's most multicultural city. Then there's Niagara Falls, Canada's most-visited tourist attraction; Ottawa, the grand national capital; and theater festivals at Stratford and Niagara-on-the-Lake.

Beyond these well-known attractions, Ontario offers much more. Bordering four of the five Great Lakes as well as Hudson Bay, Ontario has more than 3,000 kilometers (2,300 miles) of shoreline. This vast forested province stretches from the southernmost point in Canada nearly to the Arctic.

With all that space, Ontario has countless options for outdoor adventures. You can skate along the world's largest ice rink, hike Canada's longest hiking route, or swim in the country's biggest "swimming hole." You can go cycling, canoeing, white-water rafting, cross-country skiing, even dogsledding. And while you may not think of Canada as a diving destination, you can even scuba-dive or snorkel among shipwrecks on the floor of the Great Lakes.

Clockwise from top left: Killarney East Lighthouse; Grundy Lake Provincial Park; float plane readies for a flightseeing tour in Thunder Bay; Toronto's Nathan Phillips Square; urban beach in downtown Toronto; Niagara's Whirlpool Aero Car.

Yet Ontario—home to Canada's most diverse population—delivers plenty of cultural adventures as well. More than half of Toronto's residents were born outside Canada, giving the city a vibrant multicultural buzz. You could breakfast on French croissants, lunch on Japanese *okonomiyaki,* and end your day with Italian, Greek, or Caribbean fare.

In central Ontario, Old Order Mennonites still travel by horse and buggy and sell homemade preserves at local farmers markets. Roughly 25 percent of Canada's aboriginal population lives in Ontario, where you can hike through the wilderness with an aboriginal guide or watch a performance at a First Nations-run theater. You can also follow the Underground Railroad, which sheltered people fleeing slavery during the U.S. Civil War.

Ontario has laid-back college towns, Canada's first oil well, and scores of wineries, maple syrup makers, and apple orchards. You can take in a hockey game or take the train to an eco-lodge in a remote aboriginal community. You'll find the Thousand Islands and far more than a thousand things to do.

Clockwise from top left: West Montrose Covered Bridge; Canadian Museum of History; Thunder Bay, Lake Superior; Hornblower Niagara Cruise.

Planning Your Trip

Where to Go

Toronto

Canada's largest city is home to one of the most multicultural populations on the planet. The country's cultural hub, Toronto is a major center for **film** and **theater,** with a wide range of **museums,** eclectic **boutiques,** and ethnic neighborhoods. The reclaimed waterfront along Lake Ontario has **performance spaces** and **art galleries,** along with a lakeside **walking and cycling trail.** This diversity has made Toronto one of North America's most exciting cities for eating, shopping, and simply exploring.

The Niagara Region

Niagara Falls is a must-see attraction, and whether it's your first visit or your 50th, feeling the spray and watching the cascading curtains crash into the river below is still a thrill. Yet Niagara is more than just the falls. Here in Ontario's **major wine-producing region,** you can sip new vintages or sample local produce, while the well-preserved town of Niagara-on-the-Lake stages the **Shaw Festival,** one of North America's premier summer theater festivals.

Lake Erie to Lake Huron

West of Toronto, sprawling suburbs give way to university towns with nascent arts scenes, wide-open farm country, and sandy beaches. Theater fans flock to the **Stratford Festival,** while in St. Jacobs, **Mennonite communities** preserve their traditional customs. You can tour Ontario's newest **wine district,** visit Canada's southernmost point, or explore the region's dramatic history as the terminus of the **Underground Railroad.** Finally, you reach **Lake Huron,** where you can sit by the shore and watch the sun go down.

Eastern Ontario

Water, water, everywhere—that's what you'll find in Eastern Ontario. Along Lake Ontario (home to the **Prince Edward County** wine and a hotbed of local food), in the **Kawartha** region around the city of Peterborough, among the **Thousand Islands** in the St. Lawrence River, and along the **Rideau Canal** between Kingston and Ottawa, lakes, rivers, and inland waterways mean beaches, boats, or just relaxing by the water. Yet this region has plenty for the history buff, too, from **aboriginal culture** to Canada's early development.

Ottawa

Canada's national capital combines history, culture, and outdoor activities. You can tour **Parliament** and numerous **grand museums,** then skate on the **Rideau Canal** (the world's largest rink), or hike through sprawling **Gatineau Park.** For foodies, Ottawa has a branch of **Le Cordon Bleu** culinary school, a variety of food tours, and plenty of innovative restaurants. This bilingual city knows how to party, too, hosting the nation's biggest **Canada Day celebrations** and dozens of **festivals** year-round.

Cottage Country, Algonquin Park, and the Northeast

Getting away to "the cottage" is a long-standing Ontario summer tradition, and even without a cottage of your own, you can escape to this lake district. The highlight is **Algonquin Provincial Park,** one of the province's largest protected green spaces.

Cottage Country and Northeastern Ontario are prime **canoe trip** destinations, with an extensive network of lakes. For a more culturally focused trip, ride the *Polar Bear Express* train north to James Bay to experience the culture of one of Canada's largest aboriginal groups.

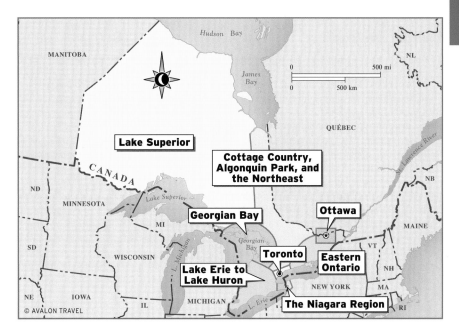

Georgian Bay

Spectacular scenery surrounds Georgian Bay, where more than 30,000 islands dot the waters. Besides **three national parks,** several beautifully remote **provincial parks,** and sections of the **Bruce Trail** (Canada's longest hiking route), you'll find dramatic rock formations, Caribbean-blue water, and a network of **lighthouses** standing guard along the coast.

Ontario's earliest European pioneers built a settlement near Georgian Bay, which is now a fascinating **historic village.** On Manitoulin Island, the **Great Spirit Circle Trail** is a leader in aboriginal tourism, offering numerous ways for visitors to experience First Nations culture.

Lake Superior

Craving more eco-adventure? Head north to Lake Superior. **Hiking trails** crisscross rocky cliffs, while **spectacular beaches** line Lake Superior's shores, and you can **canoe, kayak,** or **sail** to remote inlets and islands. Yet even if you're just doing a **driving tour** along the lake, the views seem to get better around every turn.

When to Go

Summer is Ontario's busiest season, especially in the lake regions, the wine country, and around Niagara Falls. The weather is warm—often hot—and everything is open. Many summer theaters, beach destinations, and parks operate only between May and October.

If you don't need to travel in July and August, though, you'll often find better weather (sunny skies, moderate temperatures, and lower humidity) in early **autumn.** October is the peak of the foliage season, when weekend leaf peepers flock to the Ontario countryside. Fall visitors can avoid the crowds by staying in the cities on weekends and heading for the country during the week.

Late **spring,** from May to early June, is also a good time to travel in Ontario. Although you'll need to be prepared for some rainy days, it's relatively quiet, with fewer travelers and moderate shoulder-season lodging prices. Avoid late spring in the north or if you're planning to hike, canoe, or camp; it's black fly season, and the mosquitoes can be fierce, too. You'll encounter fewer pests in late summer or fall.

Ontario's **winter,** which begins in November and can continue into April, is cold and snowy—the season for skiing, snowshoeing, and skating. If you dress for the weather, it's not a bad time for a city break; in Toronto and Ottawa the cultural calendars are full, and you can often find excellent lodging deals.

autumn views from the Agawa Canyon Tour Train

Before You Go

Passports and Visas

United States citizens need a valid **passport, passport card,** or **Enhanced Driver's License** for travel to Canada.

All other visitors need a valid passport and may need a visa. **Visas** are not required for citizens of the United States, United Kingdom, Australia, New Zealand, Mexico, Singapore, Japan, South Korea, Israel, and most Western European countries for stays in Canada of less than six months.

Vaccinations

No special immunizations or vaccinations are required to visit Canada, but it's always smart to ensure that your **routine immunizations** are up-to-date, particularly if you're traveling with children.

Transportation

Ontario's largest airport is **Toronto's Pearson International Airport,** with flights from across Canada, the United States, Europe, the Caribbean, Latin America, and Asia. **Ottawa** is another air gateway, with flights from major Canadian cities, along with several U.S. and some European destinations.

VIA Rail, Canada's national rail carrier, can bring you to Ontario from across the country, whether you're starting from Vancouver, Jasper, Edmonton, Saskatoon, Winnipeg, Montreal, or Halifax. From the United States, **Amtrak** has train service from New York City to Niagara Falls and Toronto. **Bus** travel is a reasonable option, too, from the northeastern United States or eastern Canada.

Toronto's comprehensive **public transportation system** makes a car unnecessary if you'll be staying in the city. Ottawa and Niagara Falls are also easy to navigate without a vehicle. Otherwise, outside the province's urban areas, you'll have more flexibility if you drive or rent a car.

The Best of Ontario

This itinerary takes you through Southern Ontario's highlights, from Toronto to Niagara Falls, the Muskoka Lakes, Algonquin Provincial Park, and Ottawa, the nation's capital. It's easiest to do if you have a car, or pick up a rental car when you leave Toronto (you won't need it in the city).

Day 1

Fly into **Toronto.** Visit the **CN Tower** for great views across the city and Lake Ontario. If you dare, take the **EdgeWalk,** a thrilling walk suspended outside the tower, 116 stories above the ground. Back on earth, stroll along the harbor front, then stop for lunch at **St. Lawrence Market** on your way to the galleries and shops in **The Distillery District.** Catch the ferry to the **Toronto Islands** for a late-afternoon walk or bike ride. Wrap up your day with dinner downtown or in the **Entertainment District.**

Day 2

Spend today continuing to explore Toronto. Tour the Frank Gehry-designed **Art Gallery of Ontario** or the massive **Royal Ontario Museum.** After checking out the entertaining **Bata Shoe Museum,** have lunch in **Chinatown** or **Kensington Market,** or linger over afternoon tea at the deluxe **Shangri-La Hotel.** Wander along **Queen Street West** for shopping and gallery-hopping, have dinner at one of the eclectic restaurants, and stop for a nightcap at one of the clubs.

Day 3
250 KILOMETERS (155 MILES), 4 HOURS ROUND-TRIP

You're going to **Niagara Falls** for the day; either rent a car or book a day tour. Don't miss the *Hornblower Niagara Cruise,* a boat tour under the falls. Niagara Falls has plenty of other attractions, including the **White Water Walk** and the **Whirlpool Aero Car;** for the most dramatic Falls views, take a **Niagara Helicopters Flightseeing Tour.** From the falls, it's a

The Distillery District, Toronto

half-hour drive to **Niagara-on-the-Lake,** where you can wander the historic downtown and tour local **wineries.** Have an early dinner, then see a play at the **Shaw Festival** before returning to Toronto.

Day 4

250 KILOMETERS (155 MILES), 3.5-4 HOURS

Today you'll make a leisurely drive northeast to Muskoka **Cottage Country,** but your first stop en route is just outside Toronto at the excellent **McMichael Canadian Art Collection.** Continuing north, visit **Muskoka Wharf** in **Gravenhurst** to cruise on a restored steamship and tour a heritage boat museum. In **Bracebridge,** browse the shops in the cute downtown and sample a butter tart at one of the cafés. Continue to **Huntsville** to have dinner and spend the night.

Day 5

120 KILOMETERS (75 MILES), 2 HOURS

From Huntsville, you'll enter **Algonquin Provincial Park** through the West Gate. Algonquin measures over 7,500 square kilometers (nearly 3,000 square miles), so there's plenty to explore. Go for a **hike** or rent a **canoe** at the Portage Store. Walk through the exhibits at the **Algonquin Visitors Centre;** there's usually an interesting nature program happening, as well.

Try to schedule your visit for a Thursday to join in the evening **Wolf Howl.** Spend the night at one of the park lodges.

Day 6

250 KILOMETERS (155 MILES), 3.5-4 HOURS

Drive out the park's East Gate, following Highway 60 east toward **Ottawa.** Your first Ottawa-area stop will actually be across the Ottawa River in **Gatineau** at the massive **Canadian Museum of History,** where you can learn almost anything about Canada's history and culture. After checking into your Ottawa hotel, browse the shops and galleries in the **ByWard Market** neighborhood. Stay for dinner and catch some music at one of the clubs.

Day 7

Get to the **Parliament Buildings** first thing in the morning to take a tour. If you're visiting in July or August, watch the **Changing the Guard,** complete with red-coated, fur-hat-wearing guards. For a dose of culture, go to either the **National Gallery of Canada** or the **Canadian War Museum,** then take an afternoon stroll or cycle along the **Rideau Canal.** Have dinner in Chinatown, Little Italy, or Wellington West. Wrap up your Ontario week with a concert or play at the **National Arts Centre** or the **Great Canadian Theatre Company.**

Sipping and Supping

Attention, food lovers! Ontario has plenty of gourmet getaways and scrumptious side trips for culinary tourists. From cooking classes and wine tastings to market excursions, food tours, and more, here are some of the province's food- and wine-touring highlights.

WHERE TO WIELD YOUR WHISK

Impress a special someone with some serious short-term culinary training. Spend a day honing your skills in Ottawa at **Le Cordon Bleu** (www.lcbottawa.com). On the Niagara Peninsula, both **The Good Earth Food and Wine Co.** (www.goodearthfoodandwine.com) in Beamsville and the **Wine Country Cooking School** (www.winecountrycooking.com) on the grounds of the Strewn Winery in Niagara-on-the-Lake offer recreational cooking classes. Self-described "fat guy" Stefan Schuster has a more irreverent approach to food, offering **"Trust the Fat Guy"** cooking workshops at the Hillcrest House B&B (www.hillcresthouse.ca) that he runs with his wife, Wendy, in Waterloo.

A popular destination for a learn-to-cook holiday is Prince Edward County, where **From the Farm Cooking School** (www.fromthefarm.ca), the **Waring House Cookery School** (www.waringhouse.com), and **Chef Michael Hoy** (www.chefmichaelhoy.com), all offer courses based on the region's bounty.

RAISE A GLASS

Ontario has three major wine-producing regions: the Niagara Peninsula, **Prince Edward County**, and the **north shore of Lake Erie.** The Niagara region is further subdivided into the **Niagara-on-the-Lake** and the **Twenty Valley** wine districts. These wine-making regions are great eating destinations, too. Restaurants both at the wineries and in the nearby towns pair local wines with creative dishes. During your wine tour, sample some **ice wine,** Ontario's signature dessert wine.

Ontario isn't all about the grape, though. The province has numerous microbreweries that welcome visitors, including Toronto's **Mill Street Brewery** (www.millstreetbrewery.com); the **Niagara College Teaching Brewery** (www.niagaracollegebeer.ca), Canada's first teaching brewery; and **Creemore Springs Brewery** (www.creemoresprings.com) in the Blue Mountains. In Ottawa, you can explore the city's booming craft beer scene on a **Brew Donkey** Tour (www.brewdonkey.ca). Toronto's first sake brewery, the **Ontario Spring Water Sake Company** (www.ontariosake.com), has a tasting bar at its shop in the Distillery District.

TO MARKET, TO MARKET

Many Ontario cities and towns have regular farmers markets, where you can purchase local fruits and vegetables, cheeses, jams, honey, and baked goods directly from the producers. Some of the largest are in Toronto, at the **St. Lawrence Market** and at **Evergreen Brick Works;** in **St. Jacobs,** west of Toronto, which has Canada's largest year-round farmers market; and in Ottawa at the **ByWard Market.** Other markets with lots of local variety include the year-round **Barrie Farmers Market** and the **Thunder Bay Country Market** up north. **Farmers Market Ontario** (www.farmersmarketsontario.com) lists farmers markets around the province.

Toronto also has several market districts with a multiethnic flavor. Spend an afternoon exploring **Kensington Market, Chinatown, Greektown,** or **Koreatown. Urban Adventures** (www.urbanadventures.com) leads tours of Kensington Market, while **A Taste of the World** (www.torontowalksbikes.com) explores Chinatown and other neighborhoods. If you have a sweet tooth, book an excursion with **Tasty Tours** (www.tastytourstoronto.com) to sample from bakeries, chocolate shops, and other sweet spots in several Toronto neighborhoods. In Ottawa, **C'est Bon Epicurean Adventures** (www.cestboncooking.ca) leads food tours of the ByWard Market district, Chinatown, and Little Italy.

Toronto's Art Gallery of Ontario

Toronto for Culture Vultures

A long weekend in Toronto will give you time to enjoy the city's museums, galleries, and theaters. Base yourself at the arty **Drake** or **Gladstone** Hotels, or choose a lodging in the Entertainment District, like the **Hotel Le Germain, Soho Metropolitan,** or **Thompson Toronto.** Plan a day trip to see a show in either Stratford or Niagara-on-the-Lake.

Day 1

Start your museum meandering at the **Art Gallery of Ontario,** which has an extensive collection of Canadian and International art in a striking building designed by Frank Gehry. Next door, you can't help notice the **Sharp Centre for Design**—it's the checkered box floating in the sky supported by yellow, blue, and purple "pencils."

Head east to **The Distillery District** to browse more galleries, including the **Artscape Building,** which houses more than 60 artist studios. After lunch in one of the district's cafés, go downtown to see what's happening at the always-bustling

Harbourfront Centre. Check out the **Power Plant Gallery** and the **Museum of Inuit Art,** and watch the artists at work in **The Craft Studio.**

Have dinner in the **Entertainment District,** then catch a concert at **Roy Thompson Hall,** a performance of the **National Ballet of Canada,** or a play at one of the city's many theaters.

Day 2

A tour of the **Elgin and Winter Garden Theatre Centre** takes you through Toronto stage history in Canada's only "double-decker" theater. Then get a dose of world culture and natural history at the **Royal Ontario Museum.** Nearby is the eclectic **Bata Shoe Museum,** which houses more than 10,000 shoes—from doll-like slippers worn by Chinese women with bound feet to singer Elton John's sky-high platforms.

Catch the streetcar to **Queen Street West** to see what's on at the small **Museum of Canadian Contemporary Art.** Wander into whichever galleries and boutiques catch your eye. Detour along Ossington Avenue for the newest galleries, shops, and restaurants. After dinner, see what's screening at the **TIFF Bell Lightbox.**

Day 3

From Toronto, it's an easy day trip to either the Shaw Festival in Niagara-on-the-Lake or the **Stratford Festival** in Stratford. Take a behind-the-scenes tour of the theater before lunch, then see an afternoon matinee. You'll be back in Toronto in time for a nightcap to top off your weekend of art and culture.

Georgian Bay Coastal Route

The best time for this tour, which takes in the striking natural scenery around Georgian Bay, is late summer or early fall. The autumn is especially lovely, as the leaves put on their vibrant color show. Just wrap up the trip before Canadian Thanksgiving, the second weekend in October, when the ferry to Manitoulin Island stops running and many of the region's attractions close for the season.

Day 1
300 KILOMETERS (190 MILES), 4-4.5 HOURS

From Toronto, drive northwest to the **Bruce Peninsula.** Check into a hotel in **Tobermory** or set up camp in **Bruce Peninsula National Park,** then stop into the **National Park Visitors Centre** to learn more about the region. Climb the **Lookout Tower** to take in the views, then hike to **The Grotto** and the beautiful **Indian Head Cove,** with its turquoise waters and intricate rock formations. Back in town, have dinner in a café on **Little Tub Harbour.**

Day 2

Pack a picnic and take the boat to **Flowerpot Island** to explore **Fathom Five National Marine Park,** one of only three national marine conservation areas in Canada. It's a short hike from the ferry dock to the distinctive "flowerpot" rock formations. When you return to the mainland, take a **lighthouse tour,** then hike along the **Bruce Trail,** go **kayaking,** or book a **snorkeling tour** among the shipwrecks just off-shore. Walk along broad **Singing Sands Beach** and watch the sun set over Lake Huron.

Day 3
FERRY, 2 HOURS

Take the morning ferry to **Manitoulin Island.** Enjoy a leisurely lunch at **Garden's Gate Restaurant,** then spend the afternoon at **Providence Bay Beach** or splash under **Bridal Veil Falls.** Spend the night on the Aundeck Omni Kaning First Nations Reserve at **Endaa-aang "Our Place,"** where you can rent a comfortable cottage or sleep in a teepee.

Day 4

Today you're exploring Manitoulin's aboriginal heritage with the **Great Spirit Circle Tour.** Arrange a workshop on traditional First Nations dance, drumming, or crafts. You can also take their **Mother Earth Nature Hike,** where an aboriginal guide will help you identify local plants and understand how they're used in aboriginal medicine and cooking, as you climb the **Cup and Saucer Trail.** In the evening, see a production by the aboriginal **Debajehmujig Theatre Group.**

Day 5
225 KILOMETERS (140 MILES), 3-3.5 HOURS

Get an early start today to drive to **Killarney Provincial Park,** a vast and dramatic provincial park with rugged white dolomite ridges, pink granite cliffs, pine forests, and crystal-clear lakes. You'll want to reach Killarney in time for a swim at **George Lake** and an afternoon of **hiking** or **canoeing.** You can camp in the park or stay in one of the lodges in town. Enjoy a fish-and-chips dinner at **Herbert Fisheries** while you take in the sunset over the harbor.

A hiker enjoys the view in Killarney Provincial Park.

resting on the Chikanishing Trail, Killarney Provincial Park

Day 6
200 KILOMETERS (125 MILES), 3 HOURS

In the morning, take another hike or paddle before driving south toward **Parry Sound**, stopping for a picnic or a stretch-your-legs hike at **Grundy Lake Provincial Park** along the way. Once you arrive in Parry Sound, arrange a **flight-seeing tour**, the most thrilling way to take in Georgian Bay's 30,000 Islands region; if you're with a special someone, schedule a romantic sunset flight—complete with champagne. If you'd rather stay close to the ground, explore the islands with a sightseeing cruise on the *Island Queen*. In the evening, see a play, concert, or lecture at the **Charles W. Stockey Centre for the Performing Arts.**

Day 7
150 KILOMETERS (95 MILES), 2 HOURS

Your first stop today is **Killbear Provincial Park,** about 45 minutes' drive from Parry Sound. While it's less known than Ontario's larger "destination" parks, its dramatic granite cliffs and quiet sandy beaches are well worth

exploring. Later in the day, drive south to **Honey Harbour** or **Port Severn,** where you'll spend the night.

Day 8
55 KILOMETERS (35 MILES), 1 HOUR

Of the thousands of islands that dot Georgian Bay, 63 are protected in the **Georgian Bay Islands National Park.** Your destination today is **Beausoleil Island** for a full day of hiking, mountain biking, swimming, picnicking, and exploring. Back on the mainland, drive south to **Midland** for dinner and check in to a hotel, where you'll stay for the next two nights.

Day 9

Travel back in time to the 1600s at **Sainte-Marie Among the Hurons,** a historic village that reimagines the first European settlement in Ontario, where French Jesuits lived and worked with the indigenous Wendat (Huron) people. In the afternoon, go canoeing at **Wye Marsh Wildlife Centre,** take a cruise around the offshore islands on the **MS** *Georgian Queen* from nearby

Penetanguishene Harbor, or go for a hike or swim at **Awenda Provincial Park.**

Day 10
200 KILOMETERS (125 MILES), 3 HOURS
As you begin your drive south, stop for a stroll along **Wasaga Beach,** the world's longest freshwater beach. Another worthwhile detour is the small town of **Creemore,** where the main street is lined with art galleries, cafés, and shops. After you've had your fill of browsing, have a bite to eat before making your way back to Toronto.

Niagara is for Lovers

Oh, the lovers come a thousand miles,
They leave their home and mothers,
Yet when they reach Niagara Falls
They only see each other.

Dating back to the 1840s, this song suggests that, even in the 19th century, Niagara Falls was already a popular destination for honeymooners. And why not? What's more romantic than canoodling with your beloved in view of the rushing falls?

While you'll no longer don your top hat or crinoline in preparation for a Niagara Falls visit, the Niagara region is still an excellent place for a romantic getaway. Whether you're planning your honeymoon or just planning to enjoy each other's company, here are some tips for a Niagara trip for two.

Romantic Sleeps
Book a room with a view of the falls, perhaps at the **Sheraton on the Falls** or the **Marriott Niagara Falls Fallsview Hotel and Spa.** Alternatively, choose a smaller upscale property, like the **Sterling Inn & Spa,** that will pamper the two of you.

For more luxurious accommodations, consider staying in Niagara-on-the-Lake at the elaborately appointed **Prince of Wales Hotel** or the deluxe modern **124 on Queen.** You could spend time at the falls during the day and retreat to this more peaceful village in the evenings.

Adventures for Two
When you've had your fill of strolling hand-in-hand in front of the cascading falls, you might want to escape from Niagara Falls's hustle and bustle. Rent bicycles—perhaps a bicycle built for two—and **cycle** the riverside path along the Niagara River Parkway, or book a private half-day wine and cycling tour to the nearby **Twenty Valley.**

Plan time for wine touring in Niagara-on-the-Lake; visit the luxurious tasting room at **Stratus Vineyards** or reserve a Taste of Gold experience at **Peller Estates Winery** to sample their top wines. The **Peller Estates Winery Restaurant** is one of the area's best lunch stops, or have your midday meal among the vines at **Ravine Vineyard Bistro** or on the patio at **Treadwell Farm-to-Table Cuisine.** Stop to lick each other's gelato at **Il Gelato di Carlotta** in Niagara-on-the-Lake.

Head back to the falls for an aerial tour with **Niagara Helicopters Flightseeing,** an experience that's even more dramatic at sunset. Or take a sunset trip to the base of the falls on the **Hornblower Niagara Cruises.** For dinner, choose somewhere upscale and romantic like **Windows by Jamie Kennedy** or the old-world **Casa Mia Ristorante.**

Wrap up your day by watching the **Fireworks over the Falls,** then head back to your hotel to spark your own fire.

More Amorous Inspiration
Need more inspiration to plan your romantic falls getaway? The **Niagara Falls Public Library** (www.nflibrary.ca) has collected letters from couples who honeymooned in Niagara Falls throughout the 1900s. Browse the sweet letters from these lovers past—they're available online on the library website—to motivate your own escape to Ontario's most romantic destination.

With five national parks, two national marine conservation areas, and more than 300 provincially protected green spaces, Ontario has plenty of destinations for outdoor activities. Trying to figure out which adventures are for you? Start here.

GRAB YOUR HIKING BOOTS

Whether close to the cities or deep in the wilderness, Ontario has hiking trails that suit all levels of experience. Canada's longest hiking route, the **Bruce Trail,** extends 845 kilometers (525 miles) from the Niagara region to the tip of the Bruce Peninsula. **Algonquin Provincial Park** has forested trails for everyone from kids to seasoned backpackers; just outside of Ottawa, **Gatineau Park** has plenty of day-hiking options. In **Killarney Provincial Park** and **Lake Superior Provincial Park,** your rewards for climbing The Crack and the Top of the Giant trails are spectacular mountain or lake views.

PICK UP A PADDLE

For canoe-tripping or kayaking, **Algonquin** is a prime Ontario destination, while farther north, you can paddle for days in the wilderness surrounding **Temagami** or along the rocky shores and islands of **Lake Superior.** Just getting started with your paddle? Head for the inland lakes at provincial parks like **Grundy Lake** or **Arrowhead,** or paddle along Georgian Bay at **Killarney** or **Killbear.** You can also find gentle paddling along the **Grand River** from Elora to St. Jacobs to Brantford.

TAKE OFF ON TWO WHEELS

Crisscrossed with cycling paths, the **Niagara** region is one of Ontario's best destinations for bicycling. For longer trips, there's Ontario's epic **Waterfront Trail,** which follows the shores of Lake Erie, Lake Ontario, and the St. Lawrence River for roughly 1,400 kilometers (870 miles) from Windsor all the way to the Quebec border. Unique two-wheeled Ontario tours include **Windsor Eats Wine Trail Rides,** where you cycle and wine-taste in the Lake Erie North Shore wine district, and **Grand Experiences' "The Path Less Travelled,"** where you explore the Mennonite countryside by bike, visiting local homes and shops around St. Jacobs.

GO FOR A SWIM

Surrounded by four of the five Great Lakes, with over 200,000 inland lakes of all sizes, Ontario has plenty of places to swim. Popular beaches include **Sandbanks** on Lake Ontario in Prince Edward County, the **Pinery** and **Sauble Beach** on Lake Huron, and **Wasaga Beach**—the world's longest freshwater beach—on Georgian Bay. There's **Providence Bay Beach** on Manitoulin Island, **Pancake Bay** on Lake Superior, and the striking aqua waters of **Elora Quarry.** Even **Toronto** has urban beaches on its Lake Ontario shore and less developed sands on the Toronto Islands.

IT'S NOT TOO COLD FOR SNORKELING AND SCUBA DIVING

You may not think of Ontario, with its chilly northern waters, as a destination for snorkeling or scuba diving. But with the Great Lakes and the St. Lawrence River claiming many ships over the decades, the region offers interesting shipwreck sites that you can explore from the deep. Prime diving destinations include the waters of **Bruce Peninsula,** where close-to-shore wrecks are accessible to snorkelers, too, the **Thousand Islands,** and **Lake Superior.**

LET IT SNOW

While Ontario's hilly regions pale in comparison to Western Canada's mountains, the province has several destinations for downhill skiing and snowboarding; the largest is the **Blue Mountain Resort** near Collingwood. One don't-miss winter experience is ice-skating on the **Rideau Canal** in Ottawa, which in the colder months freezes to become the world's largest outdoor skating rink. You can cross-country ski or snowshoe pretty much anywhere there's snow; several parks have extensive winter trail systems, including **Arrowhead, Wasaga Beach,** the **Pinery,** and **Gatineau Park.** To try your hand at dogsledding, head for **Algonquin** or **Temagami.**

With adventures like these across Ontario, there's no reason to stay inside.

Cochrane's polar bear welcomes visitors to this northern town.

Northern Exposure

An excellent way to see the highlights of Ontario's near north is by combing a road trip with train travel. In fact, as you travel toward James Bay, you have to leave your car behind—no roads run this far north. This itinerary begins in Toronto, stops off for canoeing and hiking in the Temagami lake lands, and continues north to Cochrane, where you catch the *Polar Bear Express* train to the Cree First Nations communities of Moosonee and Moose Factory Island. The best time to make this trip is in July or August, when the weather is warm, and the *Polar Bear Express* runs Sunday to Friday.

Day 1
455 KILOMETERS (285 MILES), 5.5-6 HOURS

Get an early start from Toronto on your drive north to **Temagami;** allow at least an extra hour to stop to eat in Bracebridge, Huntsville, or North Bay. You'll arrive at the **Smoothwater** Wilderness Lodge in time for a late afternoon paddle on the property's lake and a leisurely family-style dinner; the lodge is the best place to eat in the area, and a bonus is the travel tips you'll get from the other guests.

Day 2

Spend the day outdoors around Temagami. Ask the Smoothwater staff to organize a canoe, kayak, or hiking trip in **Lady Evelyn Smoothwater Provincial Park.** Return to the lodge for dinner and spend the evening relaxing in the Gathering Hall.

Day 3
275 KILOMETERS (170 MILES), 3.75-4.5 HOURS

You'll have time for a brief early-morning hike or paddle in Temagami before driving north to **Cochrane.** Arrive in time to visit the **Polar Bear Habitat,** and even swim with the bears, before checking into your hotel.

calm lake shore at Algonquin Provincial Park

Day 4

Today you're going where no roads go—north toward James Bay on Ontario Northland's *Polar Bear Express* train. You'll arrive in **Moosonee** by mid-afternoon; walk to the docks to catch the water taxi to **Moose Factory Island.** Spend the night at the **Cree Village Ecolodge,** run by the Cree First Nation, and have dinner (with traditional aboriginal ingredients) in the lodge's lovely dining room.

Day 5

You'll spend most of the day on Moose Factory Island. Visit the **Cree Cultural Interpretive Centre** to learn more about Cree culture, language, traditional medicine, and food. Walk over to the **Moose Cree Complex;** part shopping mall, part community center, it's the hub of the First Nations reserve, so you can glimpse what local life is like on this remote island. After lunch, take a **boat tour to James Bay.**

The *Polar Bear Express* heads south in the late afternoon and will take you as far as **Cochrane,** where you'll need to spend the night.

Day 6
720 KILOMETERS (450 MILES), 9-10 HOURS

In the morning, begin your long drive back to Toronto. If you have time, add a stopover in Huntsville and a visit to **Algonquin Provincial Park.**

Following the Underground Railroad

Several recent Oscar-winning films—*Lincoln, Django Unchained, and 12 Years a Slave*—focus on the period surrounding the U.S. Civil War, when thousands of enslaved African Americans fled north toward Canada. These refugees traveled along the Underground Railroad, a network of safe houses that provided them with shelter. But what happened to these former slaves once they reached Canada's promised land?

Many crossed into Canada into what are now the Southwestern Ontario communities of Windsor, Amherstburg, Chatham, Dresden, and Buxton. At sights throughout this region, you can explore the African Canadian Heritage Route, tracing the history of the former slaves and their new life in Canada. In Dresden, the **Uncle Tom's Cabin Historic Site** (www.uncletomscabin.org) tells the story of former slave and abolitionist Reverend Josiah Henson, whose memoirs may have been part of the inspiration for Harriet Beecher Stowe's historic antislavery novel, *Uncle Tom's Cabin*.

Farther west, the Buxton Settlement became the largest black settlement in Canada, with one of North America's first integrated schools. Many descendants of these early settlers still live in the region, and you can learn more about their heritage at the **Buxton National Historic Site and Museum** (www.buxtonmuseum.com).

Built and operated by descendants of formerly enslaved people who traveled here on the Underground Railroad, the **John Freeman Walls Historic Site and Underground Railroad Museum** (www.undergroundrailroadmuseum.com), outside Windsor, brings the fugitive slave experience to life. As you walk into the nearby woods,

Ring the bell for freedom at the John Freeman Walls Historic Site and Underground Railroad Museum.

you hear hound dogs attempting to track you down (fortunately, it's just a recording). You also learn more about the family who settled here and tour the 1846 log cabin, where they raised nine children.

Before you set out along these routes, have a look at the useful resources for exploring Ontario's black history that the **Ontario Heritage Trust** (www.heritagetrust.on.ca) provides on the "Slavery to Freedom" section of their website. Also check out **Black History Canada** (www.blackhistorycanada.ca) from the Historica-Dominion Institute.

Toronto

Look for ★ to find recommended
sights, activities, dining, and lodging.

Highlights

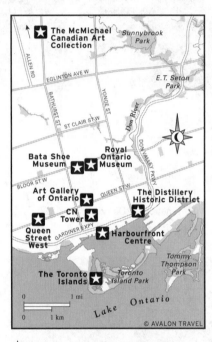

★ **CN Tower:** Toronto's tallest building has two observation levels and a revolving restaurant, all with great views across the city and the lake. Daredevils can even take the "EdgeWalk," a thrilling walk suspended *outside* (yes, outside!) the tower, 116 stories above the ground (page 31).

★ **Harbourfront Centre:** There's always something happening in this waterfront arts complex. Watch artists at work in their studios, browse gallery exhibits, take in a play or a lecture, go canoeing or ice-skating, or stroll the walkways along the lake (page 33).

★ **The Toronto Islands:** Only a 10-minute ferry ride from downtown, these small islands in Lake Ontario are the city's backyard, where you can lounge at the beach, ride a bike, or have a picnic. The awesome views of the city skyline are a bonus (page 36).

★ **The Distillery Historic District:** Where whiskey was once king, the Victorian-era brick buildings that housed the world's largest distillery have been converted into a cool arts district full of galleries, artist studios, shops, cafés, and theaters (page 42).

★ **Royal Ontario Museum:** Inside this massive museum of natural history and world cultures, you'll find everything from Egyptian mummies to British neoclassical dining rooms, Buddha statues to medieval armor—and scads of kid-pleasing dinosaur skeletons (page 43).

★ **Bata Shoe Museum:** This quirky—and fun—gallery of footwear traces the history and culture of a wide swath of humanity by showcasing what people wore on their feet (page 44).

★ **Art Gallery of Ontario:** In a striking Frank Gehry-designed building, Toronto's art museum is one of the largest in North America, with significant collections of Canadian, Inuit, African, and Oceanic art. The architecture alone merits the price of admission (page 47).

★ **Queen Street West:** Lined with art galleries, funky shops, eclectic eateries, and happening bars, the west end of Queen Street is one of the city's "in" arts districts (page 48).

★ **The McMichael Canadian Art Collection:** It's worth the trip to these forested grounds north of the city for this excellent all-Canadian art museum, with significant works by Canada's Group of Seven, noteworthy early 20th-century landscape painters (page 51).

C anadians may typically be modest about their country's attractions, but Toronto has plenty to boast about. With more than 5.9 million people living in the metropolitan area, it's the country's largest city and Ontario's provincial capital. As Canada's cultural hub, it's home to one of the most multicultural populations on the planet.

About half of metropolitan Toronto's residents were born outside Canada, hailing from China, India, Italy, the Caribbean, the Philippines, the Middle East, Portugal—name a country and Toronto probably has residents who used to call it home. This diversity has made Toronto one of North America's most exciting cities for eating, shopping, and exploring. You can wander through Little India, Koreatown, Greektown, and at least five Chinatowns.

Toronto is often called "Hollywood North" for the number of movies made here; every September the city hosts the Toronto International Film Festival, one of North America's major film fests. Toronto is also a center for English-language theater, with dozens of theaters and repertory companies. A significant event on the city's calendar is the annual Pride Week, one of the world's largest gay and lesbian pride celebrations.

Set on the shore of Lake Ontario, Toronto is reclaiming its waterfront, which now houses performance spaces and art galleries, along with a lakeside walking and cycling trail. Skyscrapers stand side by side with Victorian-era buildings downtown, while farther afield museums and eclectic shops satisfy culture- and couture-seekers alike. Whether you want to wrap up your day with a contemporary dinner from one of the city's hottest chefs or unwind over a drink in a neighborhood club, you'll find it all in Toronto.

PLANNING YOUR TIME

Toronto is a year-round destination. Summer is the most popular time to visit, particularly if you're traveling with kids. Everything is open, and you'll find plenty of festivals and special events. Just be prepared for hot, humid weather.

Previous: Toronto's Old City Hall and Nathan Phillips Square; Toronto's Sugar Beach. **Above:** dim sum at Luckee Restaurant and Bar.

Toronto

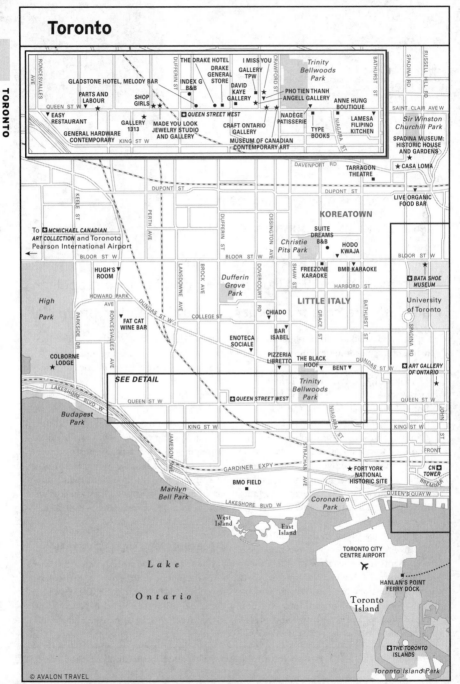

THE DRAKE HOTEL
DRAKE GENERAL STORE
I MISS YOU
GALLERY TPW
Trinity Bellwoods Park
GLADSTONE HOTEL, MELODY BAR
INDEX G B&B
DAVID KAYE GALLERY
PHO TIEN THANH
ANGELL GALLERY
ANNE HUNG BOUTIQUE
PARTS AND LABOUR
SHOP GIRLS
QUEEN ST W
Queen Street West
NADÈGE PATISSERIE
LAMESA FILIPINO KITCHEN
EASY RESTAURANT
GALLERY 1313
MADE YOU LOOK JEWELRY STUDIO AND GALLERY
CRAFT ONTARIO GALLERY
TYPE BOOKS
GENERAL HARDWARE CONTEMPORARY
KING ST W
MUSEUM OF CANADIAN CONTEMPORARY ART

RONCESVALLES AVE
DUFFERIN ST
CRAWFORD ST
BATHURST ST
SPADINA RD
RUSSELL HILL RD

SAINT CLAIR AVE W

Sir Winston Churchill Park

SPADINA MUSEUM: HISTORIC HOUSE AND GARDENS ★

★ CASA LOMA

DAVENPORT RD
TARRAGON THEATRE

DUPONT ST
DUPONT ST

LIVE ORGANIC FOOD BAR

KOREATOWN

To ★ MCMICHAEL CANADIAN ART COLLECTION and Toronto Pearson International Airport ←

KEELE ST
PERTH AVE
DUFFERIN ST
OSSINGTON AVE

SUITE DREAMS B&B
Christie Pits Park
HODO KWAJA

BLOOR ST W
BLOOR ST W
BLOOR ST W

★ BATA SHOE MUSEUM

HUGH'S ROOM ▼
HOWARD PARK AVE
LANSDOWNE AVE
BROCK AVE
DOVERCOURT RD
SHAW ST

FREEZONE KARAOKE
BMB KARAOKE

HARBORD ST

High Park

Dufferin Grove Park

LITTLE ITALY
BATHURST ST

University of Toronto

PARKSIDE DR
RONCESVALLES AVE
DUNDAS ST W

FAT CAT WINE BAR

COLLEGE ST
CHIADO
GRACE ST

SPADINA RD

COLBORNE LODGE ★

ENOTECA SOCIALE
BAR ISABEL
★ ART GALLERY OF ONTARIO ★

PIZZERIA LIBRETTO
THE BLACK HOOF
BENT ▼
DUNDAS ST W

SEE DETAIL

QUEEN ST W
QUEEN STREET WEST
Trinity Bellwoods Park
QUEEN ST W
JOHN ST

Budapest Park

KING ST W
NIAGARA ST
KING ST W

FRONT ST

JAMESON AVE
STRACHAN AVE

GARDINER EXPY
★ FORT YORK NATIONAL HISTORIC SITE

CN TOWER
BREMNER

BMO FIELD

Marilyn Bell Park
LAKESHORE BLVD W
Coronation Park

QUEEN'S QUAY W

Lake Ontario

West Island
East Island

TORONTO CITY CENTRE AIRPORT ✈

HANLAN'S POINT FERRY DOCK

Toronto Island

★ THE TORONTO ISLANDS

Toronto Island Park

© AVALON TRAVEL

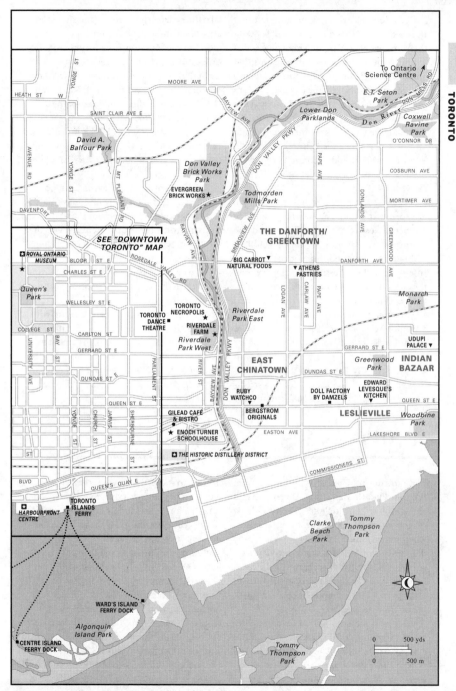

Torontonians are quick to point out that the "lake effect" that dumps piles of snow on their upstate New York neighbors has a different result in their city. Toronto's position on Lake Ontario's northern shore moderates the winter weather, and the city averages 115 centimeters (45 inches) of snow per year—less than Buffalo can get on a single day. Sure, it's cold and often snowy in winter, but Toronto has great museums, the cultural season will be in full swing, and accommodations are often less expensive than at other times of the year.

The best seasons for a Toronto trip, though, are spring and fall. The weather should be temperate, especially in autumn, and the cultural calendar will be full. If you'll be in town in September during the Toronto International Film Festival, a major event on the city's cultural agenda, book accommodations well in advance.

How much time do you need to explore Toronto? You could visit for a weekend and catch the city's highlights or stick around for weeks and still have plenty to do. Start with a visit to the **CN Tower** to get an overview of what's where, and then catch the streetcar east to **St. Lawrence Market** and the **Distillery District.** Browse the shops, and after lunch, head back downtown for one (or more) of the museums: the **Royal Ontario Museum** if you're into world cultures and natural history; the **Art Gallery of Ontario** for contemporary art (and a striking Frank Gehry-designed gallery building); or the **Bata Shoe Museum** for, well, shoes—but shoes as you've never seen before. Have dinner in the Entertainment District or in the West End, take in a concert or a film, or see what's happening in the clubs.

The next day, visit the lavish **Casa Loma** (the city's "castle on the hill"), have lunch in **Chinatown,** and then poke around the **Kensington Market** district or spend the afternoon browsing the galleries and shops along **Queen Street West.**

Alternatively, if the weather is fine, you could catch the ferry to the **Toronto Islands,** or just walk or cycle along the Harbourfront, stopping into the galleries at **Harbourfront Centre.** If you're traveling with kids, you might want to add the **Ontario Science Centre** to your itinerary. Toronto is also close enough to **Niagara Falls** that you can take a day trip there and still be back in town for supper.

Sights

Toronto's downtown core is just inland from the Lake Ontario waterfront. Downtown and the Harbourfront include the city's oldest neighborhoods and its newest developments, where narrow streets laid out in the city's early days are a short walk from water-view skyscrapers. The city's landmark CN Tower is here, and you can catch a ferry to the Toronto Islands, a waterfront green space a quick cruise from downtown.

Like most major cities, Toronto has noteworthy museums of art, science, and natural and cultural history. The city has some less typical museums, too: galleries of textiles and ceramics, a hockey museum, even a museum devoted to shoes. You can tour the city halls—old and new—and visit the provincial legislature, the fort where the city was first settled, a high-tech aquarium, and the only "double-decker" theater in Canada.

Beyond the museums and sights, Toronto's lure is its diverse neighborhoods, including several Chinatowns, an Indian district, and communities that have Greek, Korean, and Portuguese roots. There's bohemian, multicultural Kensington Market, with its cheap eateries and offbeat shops, and Cabbagetown, with well-manicured Victorian homes. For art and shopping, head for the Distillery District, Queen Street West, or Leslieville on the city's

Toronto for a Toonie (or Less)

On a budget? Don't worry: Toronto has plenty of free and low-cost attractions. Here's how to stretch your dollars while exploring Toronto.

- There's no charge to wander the **St. Lawrence Market, the Distillery District, Kensington Market,** or any of the city's multicultural neighborhoods—although you may want to budget for snacks along the way.

- Walk along the Harbourfront or browse the galleries and shops along **Queen Street West,** all for free.

- Tours of the **Ontario Legislative Assembly** are free, and there's no charge to explore the grounds at the **Evergreen Brick Works.**

- A trip to the **Toronto Islands** will cost a small ferry fare, but once you're there, you can stroll, picnic, and lounge on the sand without spending a penny.

- Many of Toronto's museums offer free or discounted admission at certain times. The **Royal Ontario Museum** has reduced admission on Friday after 4:30pm. The **Art Gallery of Ontario** is free on Wednesday 6pm-8:30pm. The **Bata Shoe Museum** offers "pay what you can" admission on Thursday 5pm-8pm. Admission to the **Gardiner Museum** is half-price on Friday 4pm-9pm.

- Take one of the city's free walking tours. Locals lead free guided walks of their neighborhoods or other favorite places around town on the **Toronto Greeter** tours. The **Heritage Toronto Walks,** highlighting a neighborhood's architectural, cultural, or natural history, are free as well.

east side. And then there's the Harbourfront, with its galleries, gardens, and green spaces to enjoy on a sunny city day.

If you're planning to visit several of Toronto's major attractions, consider purchasing a **CityPass** (www.citypass.com, adults $69.50, ages 5-12 $44.75), which includes admission to the CN Tower, Royal Ontario Museum, Casa Loma, Ontario Science Centre, and Toronto Zoo. In addition to discounted admission, the pass lets you bypass the ticket lines at most attractions. Buy a CityPass online or at any of the included attractions; it's good for nine days beginning with the first day that you use it.

THE HARBOURFRONT

In mild weather, the Lake Ontario shore is one of Toronto's loveliest areas, with walking paths along the waterfront, parks, and lots of things to see and do. While the lakeshore is only a short walk from downtown, the Gardiner Expressway, the elevated highway that bisects the city, cuts off the Harbourfront from the rest of the city. Several streets, including Bay, York, and Lower Simcoe Streets, pass underneath the expressway, so you can walk from downtown.

★ CN Tower

If you've seen photos of the Toronto skyline, you've seen the iconic **CN Tower** (301 Front St. W., at John St., 416/868-6937, www.cntower.ca, subway: Union, 9am-10:30pm daily, adults $32, seniors and ages 4-12 $24, family $99). At 457 meters (1,500 feet) high, the tower, which opened in 1976 to provide telecommunications capabilities for the city, held the record for the world's tallest building for many years. Even if loftier skyscrapers have taken away its title, this is still one tall building.

At ground level, you'll find a 3-D movie, a surround-sound theater, and a game arcade, but the real reason to visit the tower is to go up. Once you've boarded the glass elevators and rocketed 113 stories to the LookOut level (the elevator ride takes only 58 seconds), the views stretch out over the city and Lake Ontario.

The next thrill is a walk across the see-through **Glass Floor;** it's 346 meters (1,136 feet) straight down. If you want to get even higher, go up to the **SkyPod,** the next observation level, at 447 meters (1,465 feet), 34 stories above the LookOut. Sky Pod access is an additional $12.

For extreme thrill-seekers, there's the **EdgeWalk** (www.edgewalkcntower.ca, mid-Apr.-mid-Nov., $175, including admission to other tower attractions), where you walk outside (yes, outside!) around the roof of the tower restaurant, 116 stories (356 meters, 1,168 feet) above the ground. You're harnessed to a safety rail, but the daring can lean out over the edge. When you're suspended outside the building, it's probably not the time to tell you that lighting strikes the tower an average of 75 times per year, but don't worry: The Edgewalk closes during high winds and electrical storms.

The tower has three on-site restaurants. The revolving **360 Restaurant at the CN Tower** (416/362-5411, 11am-2pm and 4:30pm-10:15pm daily) makes a complete revolution every 72 minutes, giving you great views over the city. Though meal prices are high, they include access to the LookOut level and Glass Floor, and you can bypass the ticket line. On the LookOut level is an upscale bistro, **Horizons Restaurant** (11am-9pm daily), and at the base of the tower is casual **Le Café** (8:30am-7pm daily).

With two million people visiting the tower every year, ticket lines can be long, and visitors must pass through airport-style security checkpoints. Arrive before 11am or after 3pm, and buy your tickets online in advance, to minimize your wait time. Purchasing a CityPass, which includes CN Tower admission, also lets you skip the box office line-ups.

Ripley's Aquarium of Canada

Housing more than 16,000 marine animals

The landmark CN Tower rises over the downtown waterfront.

in 5.7 million liters (1.5 million gallons) of water, Toronto's modern aquarium, **Ripley's Aquarium of Canada** (288 Bremner Blvd., 647/351-3474, www.ripleyaquariums.com, subway: Union, 9am-11pm daily, adults $30, seniors and ages 6-13 $20, ages 3-5 $10) has North America's biggest collection of sharks, along with all manner of other aquatic creatures.

The aquarium's galleries each highlight a different aquatic habitat or type of marine life. The Canadian Waters gallery showcases eels, lobsters, gigantic octopi, and other creatures who inhabit the Great Lakes and the country's coastal regions. The colorful Planet Jellies exhibit surrounds you with graceful jellyfish, while in the Dangerous Lagoon, which you pass through on a moving walkway, sharks, stingrays, and other fearsome-looking fish swim all around. "Please touch" exhibits let the kids get their hands wet, and interactive shows are offered in different galleries throughout the day.

Adjacent to the CN Tower, the aquarium

is generally open nightly till 11pm but occasionally closes earlier to host private events; check the website or phone before making an evening visit.

Rogers Centre

Toronto's professional baseball team, the Blue Jays, and Canadian Football League team, the Argonauts, play in the **Rogers Centre** (1 Blue Jays Way, 416/341-1000, www.rogerscentre. com, subway: Union), a massive arena that also hosts megaconcerts, performances, and other events by luminaries ranging from U2 to the Dalai Lama. Opened in 1989 adjacent to the CN Tower, the building's claim to fame is its roof; it's the world's first fully retractable roof, which can open or close in 20 minutes. The **Rogers Centre Tour Experience** (416/341-2771, adults $16, seniors and ages 12-17 $12, ages 5-11 $10) offers sports fans a one-hour guided tour of the facility.

You can buy tickets for Rogers Centre events online or at the **box office** (Gate 9, Bremner Blvd., 10am-6pm Tues.-Sat.).

★ Harbourfront Centre

Harbourfront Centre (235 Queens Quay W., 416/973-4000, www.harbourfrontcentre. com, hours vary) is activity central for arts and literary events and for enjoying the outdoors. Inside this four-hectare (10-acre) lakeside complex of buildings are numerous art galleries, artist studios, theaters, and shops. A walkway wends along the waterfront, and you can canoe on a small lagoon (or skate in winter). Stop at the center's information desks, or check the comprehensive website, to find out what's on the current event schedule.

On the east side of the complex, **Queen's Quay Terminal** (207 Queens Quay W.) houses the **Museum of Inuit Art** (416/640-1571, www.miamuseum.ca, 10am-6pm daily, adults $5, seniors and kids $3), packed with works by artists from across the arctic regions. In summer, **Queen's Quay Terminal Farmers Market** (3pm-7pm Wed. June-mid-Oct.) sets up outside, and there's a ticket booth for **boat tours.**

Look for the smokestack to find the **Power Plant Gallery** (231 Queens Quay W., 416/973-4949, www.thepowerplant.org, 10am-5pm Tues.-Sun., 10am-8pm Thurs., free), a contemporary art gallery in a former 1920s power station. The eclectic exhibits change regularly, so there's always something new to see.

Inside **Bill Boyle Artport** (formerly York Centre Quay) are other small art galleries, and

Ripley's Aquarium of Canada has plenty for kids to see and do.

Downtown Toronto

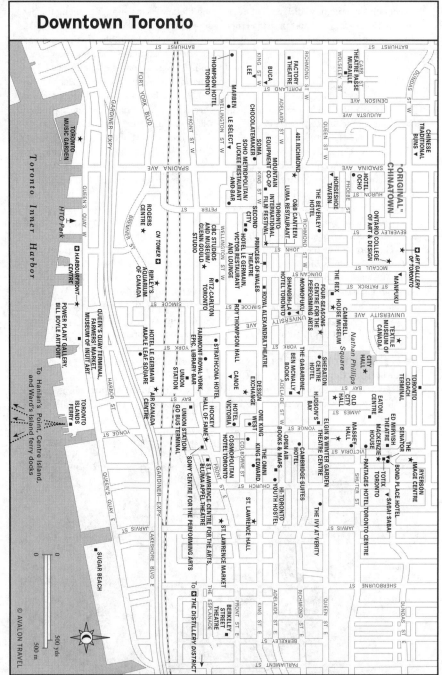

© AVALON TRAVEL

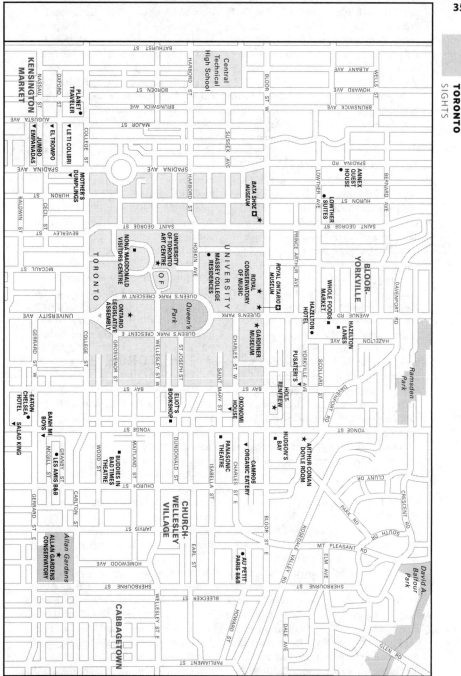

you can watch artists at work in **The Craft Studios** (10am-8pm Mon.-Sat., 10am-6pm Sun.). **The Centre Shop** (416/973-4993, 11am-6pm Sat.-Wed., 11am-8pm Thurs.-Fri.) sells cool, arty stuff, from jewelry to craft supplies to housewares.

To get to Harbourfront Centre, take the subway to Union Station, then walk (about 10 minutes) or catch the no. 509 Exhibition streetcar west to Lower Simcoe Street.

Toronto Music Garden

What do a cellist and a garden designer have in common? In Toronto, they have a garden: the **Toronto Music Garden** (475 Queens Quay W., www.harbourfrontcentre.com, dawn-dusk daily year-round, free). Renowned cellist Yo-Yo Ma collaborated with garden designer Julie Moir Messervy to create this waterfront green space inspired by J. S. Bach's "First Suite for Unaccompanied Cello." In Messervy's design, each movement within the piece corresponds to a different section of the garden.

Perhaps the best way to appreciate the music garden is to come for the music. **Summer Music in the Garden** (416/973-4000, www.harbourfrontcentre.com, 7pm Thurs., 4pm Sun. late June-mid-Sept.) is a series of free one-hour classical and world-music concerts.

From Union Station to the garden, take the no. 509 Exhibition streetcar west to Spadina Avenue.

Fort York National Historic Site

As you stand next to the restored 19th-century barracks, surrounded by condo and office towers, with the hum of city traffic buzzing in the background, it's hard to imagine that this urban pocket was once the first significant settlement in the Toronto area. In 1793, the lieutenant governor of Upper Canada, John Graves Simcoe, and his troops began building a garrison at Fort York, now the **Fort York National Historic Site** (250 Fort York Blvd., 416/392-6907, www.fortyork.ca, 10am-5pm

daily mid-May-early Sept., 10am-4pm Mon.-Fri., 10am-5pm Sat.-Sun. early Sept.-mid-May., adults $9, seniors and ages 13-18 $4.50, ages 6-12 $4.25), which would become the territory's new capital. Upper Canada's original capital had been in Niagara, dangerously close, Simcoe thought, to the U.S. border.

Moving the capital north didn't keep it safe, though. During the War of 1812, American troops attacked and burned Fort York. The British quickly began to rebuild, and many of the buildings now standing—including two blockhouses, several barracks, and two powder magazines—date to this period of reconstruction, between 1813 and 1815. It's the largest collection of original War of 1812 buildings in Canada.

From Union Station or the Harbourfront, take the no. 509 Exhibition streetcar west to Fort York Boulevard, and follow the signs to the fort. You can also take the subway to Bathurst station (Bloor-Danforth line), then catch the no. 511 Bathurst streetcar southbound; it stops on the fort's eastern side.

★ THE TORONTO ISLANDS

A short ferry ride across the harbor from downtown, the **Toronto Islands** (415/397-2628, www.toronto.ca or www.torontoislands.org) are the city's backyard, where both residents and visitors go to lounge at the beach, cruise around by bike or kayak, or have a picnic. The awesome views of the skyline, from the ferries and from the islands themselves, are a bonus; take those picture-postcard city snapshots here.

The "Toronto Islands" consist of several small islands connected by bridges. Ferries dock at Centre Island, Ward's Island to the east, and Hanlan's Point to the west.

Restrooms and drinking water are available on the islands, and there are several places to eat, including the year-round **Rectory Cafe** (102 Lakeshore Ave., Ward's Island, 416/203-2152, www.therectorycafe.com, 11am-5pm Mon.-Thurs., 11am-8pm Fri.-Sun. late May-mid-Oct., 11am-5pm Wed.-Sun. mid-Oct.-late

May, $12-18) or the more touristy **Shopsy's Island Deli Bar and Grill** (416/203-0405, www.centreisland.ca, 11am-8pm daily mid-June-early Sept., $9-16), next to the Centre Island docks.

Centre Island

Centre Island is the entertainment hub, with an amusement park, gardens, bicycle and boat rentals, and beaches. If you have young kids, head for the **Franklin Children's Garden,** with play structures, a tree house, and a theater with summer storytelling events. There's a beach by the pier on Centre Island, but if you walk or cycle either direction from there, you'll find prettier, less populated sand.

You can rent bikes at **Toronto Islands Bike Rentals** (416/203-0009, www.torontoislandbicyclerental.com, May-Sept., $8 per hour, tandems $15 per hour, cash only) near the Centre Island pier, across the island from the ferry dock. You can also rent fun "quadricycles," four-wheeled pedal bikes seating two ($17 per hour) or four ($30 per hour) people. It takes about an hour to cycle a loop of the islands. You can take bicycles over from the mainland, except on the Centre Island ferry on busy summer weekends.

In summer, the **Boat House** (416/397-5166) rents **canoes, kayaks,** and **pedal boats.** From the Centre Island docks, follow the main path past the amusement park, cross the bridge near the fountains, then bear left (east) toward the Boat House.

A big draw for the kids is **Centreville Amusement Park** (604/203-0405, www.centreisland.ca, 10:30am-8pm daily July-early Sept., call or check the website for hours May-June and mid-late Sept.), with a 1907 carousel, a Ferris wheel, bumper boats, a roller coaster, and other old-time carnival attractions. If you arrive on the Centre Island ferry, it's hard to sneak past the amusements without the kids noticing; the park is a short walk from the ferry dock.

Admission to the amusement park is free, but you'll pay to ride the rides. A sheet of 25 ride tickets costs $25, or you can buy an all-day pass. Individual passes are based on height; one-day passes for adults and kids over four feet tall are $37, under four feet tall $26. Family all-day passes are $112. Passes are discounted if you buy them online.

Ward's Island

Ward's Island looks like an urban cottage colony, with the islands' only community of permanent residents, a beach, and a playground.

view from the Toronto Islands

Wander past the lakeside homes and imagine living here yourself. The mostly sandy **Ward's Island Beach** can be less crowded than some of the others.

Toronto Island SUP (416/877-4668, www. torontoislandsup.com, May-Sept., 1st hour $30, $10 per additional hour) rents stand-up paddleboards from Ward's Island Beach. They're on the beach every weekend, but call first if you're coming on a weekday.

Hanlan's Point

If you see airplanes coming in over the harbor, so low that you think they're going to land on your ferry, it's because they're headed to the Toronto Island Airport, near Hanlan's Point, which also has parks and beaches, including **Gibraltar Beach,** west of the pier. Nearby, the stone **Gibraltar Point Lighthouse,** built in 1808-1809, is the oldest surviving lighthouse on the Great Lakes and the second oldest in Canada. There's a **clothing-optional beach** at Hanlan's Point.

Getting There and Around

Catch the **ferry** (9 Queens Quay W., at Bay St., 416/397-2628, round-trip adults $7, seniors and students $4.50, ages 3-14 $3.50) to the islands from the docks west of the Westin Harbour Castle Hotel.

From downtown, ferries run to Centre Island, Hanlan's Point, and Ward's Island. You can disembark at one and return from another. The schedules for the three ferries are different, however, so be sure to check. While schedules vary seasonally and by time of day, Centre Island boats (mid-Apr.-mid-Oct.) run most frequently, with summer departures every 15-30 minutes. Boats to Hanlan's Point (mid-Apr.-mid-Oct.) and Ward's Island (year-round) typically operate every 30-60 minutes in summer. Only the Ward's Island ferry runs year-round.

Cars are not allowed on the islands, so you'll need to get around on foot or by bicycle. Cycling is a good way to tour these flat islands, which are crisscrossed with pathways.

In summer, 35-minute **tram tours** leave from Centre Island, a short walk south of the ferry docks.

DOWNTOWN AND THE FINANCIAL DISTRICT
Canadian Broadcasting Corporation Studios and Museum

If you're interested in the history of radio and TV, or if you're nostalgic for the programs of your childhood (do you remember *Mr. Dressup?*), stop into the **CBC Studios and Museum** (250 Front St. W., 416/205-5574 or 866/306-4636, www.cbc.ca/museum, subway: Union, 9am-5pm Mon.-Fri., free) in the network's Toronto headquarters. Even if you're not Canadian, you can still learn about the Canadian counterpart to the long-running children's show *Sesame Street* (it was called *Sesame Park*) and other interesting tidbits about TV and radio in Canada.

Hockey Hall of Fame

Are you a hockey fan? Then make the pilgrimage to the **Hockey Hall of Fame** (Brookfield Pl., 30 Yonge St., 416/360-7735, www.hhof.com, subway: Union, King, 9:30am-6pm Mon.-Sat., 10am-6pm Sun. late June-early Sept., 10am-5pm Mon.-Fri., 9:30am-6pm Sat., 10:30am-5pm Sun. early Sept.-late June, adults $18, seniors $14, ages 4-13 $12), a museum devoted to the sport and its star players, located on the lower level of the Brookfield Place office tower. In addition to all manner of hockey memorabilia, two theaters show archival footage of hockey game highlights and the "be a player" zone lets you wield your own stick.

Design Exchange

The former Toronto Stock Exchange, a 1937 art deco building with a limestone and pink granite facade, now houses the **Design Exchange** (234 Bay St., 416/363-6121, www. dx.org, 11am-6pm daily), a gallery space devoted to Canadian design. Admission prices vary by exhibition. Ask the staff if you can take a peek at the well-preserved former trading floor on the second level.

Elgin and Winter Garden Theatre Centre

The only "double-decker" theater in Canada, and one of less than a dozen ever built worldwide, the **Elgin and Winter Garden Theatres** (189 Yonge St., 416/314-2901, subway: Queen) are two full-size theaters—stacked one on top of the other. Constructed as a vaudeville house, the Elgin opened in December 1913 on the main level; the Winter Garden upstairs opened two months later. While the Elgin is traditional in style, with detailed gold plasterwork and red upholstered seats, the Winter Garden was designed to resemble a garden. Its walls are painted with floral murals, and real leaves hang from the ceiling, like a garden arbor.

As the vaudeville era ended, the lower-level theater became a popular movie house in the 1930s and 1940s, but by the 1970s, it had become a porn palace. The Winter Garden, shuttered in 1928, was all but abandoned. In 1981, the Ontario Heritage Foundation purchased the building and launched a multiyear restoration project.

While the Elgin had been renovated repeatedly over the years (the lobby had been painted 27 times), the Winter Garden was essentially preserved from the 1920s, hidden under decades of grime. The restoration team couldn't use water or other liquids to clean the wall murals, which had been created with water-soluble paint. Instead, they used more than 385 kilograms (850 pounds) of raw bread dough, rolling it over the murals to lift off the dirt. The team also harvested more than 5,000 beech branches to replace the crumbling leafy ceiling.

Since the restored theaters reopened in 1989, they've been used primarily for touring productions—dramas, musicals, ballets, and operas—as well as various special events. For an event calendar and tickets, contact Ticketmaster (855/622-2787, www.ticketmaster.ca) or phone the theater directly.

The **Ontario Heritage Trust** (www.heritagetrust.on.ca) runs fascinating 90-minute **tours** (5pm Thurs., 11am Sat. year-round, adults $12, seniors and students $10, cash only) of the theater complex that take you through both theaters and tell you more about the building's history and restoration. Arrive at the theater 15 minutes before the scheduled tour time.

Old City Hall

Toronto architect Edward James Lennox (1854-1933), who later designed the even more ornate Casa Loma, crafted the intricately carved Romanesque Revival stone building now known as Toronto's **Old City Hall** (60 Queen St. W., www.toronto.ca, subway: Queen, 8:30am-4:30pm Mon.-Fri.). When it opened in 1899, it was the largest municipal building in North America.

On the building's exterior, Lennox included stone caricatures that represented politicians of his era. At the main entrance on Queen Street, marked by three stone archways, look closely at the top of the columns on the west side of the center arch and you might spot a face with a handlebar mustache—that's Lennox himself.

Old City Hall was actually the Toronto's third city hall building. The first, which burned down in 1849, was on the current site of the St. Lawrence Market. The St. Lawrence Market building was the second city hall from 1845 to 1899.

Surrounding skyscrapers now dwarf the landmark 103-meter (300-foot) clock tower adorning the structure that housed city offices and council chambers until the mid-1960s. Today, Old City Hall is used as a court building. Visitors can walk around inside (after you clear the security check), taking in the finely detailed mosaic floors and marble walls, but no interior photos are allowed.

Toronto City Hall

Two curved towers flanking a spaceship-style pod? Finnish architect Viljo Revell designed the distinctive complex of buildings that is the **Toronto City Hall** (100 Queen St. W., www.toronto.ca, subway: Queen, Osgoode), which opened in 1965. (Sadly, the architect died 10 months before the building's opening ceremony.)

When you enter City Hall from the plaza, you can't miss the massive white column in the center of the rotunda; it's the support structure for the **City Council Chambers** that sit above it. If you'd like to attend a council meeting, check the city website (www.toronto.ca) to see when the council is in session.

To the right of the main entrance (on the east wall) is the **"nail mural,"** a wall sculpture called *Metropolis* that artist David Partridge (1919-2006) crafted from 100,000 nails. Other artwork is on view around the building's first and second floors; feel free to browse.

To the left of the entrance is a **scale model of the city.** The buildings in the model that are colored pink are those designated as historically or architecturally significant.

There are no public tours of City Hall, but ask at the lobby reception desk for a free **self-guided tour booklet,** which points out many of the building's noteworthy features. The tour booklet is also available online on the city website.

Free concerts and festivals frequently take place on **Nathan Phillips Square,** the plaza in front of City Hall, which is named for the former Toronto mayor who was in office from 1955 to 1962. The plaza's reflecting pool, a pleasant spot for a rest or picnic in summer, becomes a **skating rink** in winter. The arches that span the pool are the **Freedom Arches,** dedicated in 1991 "to the millions who struggled, including Canadians, to gain and defend freedom and to the tens of millions who suffered and died for the lack of it."

Four Seasons Centre for the Performing Arts

Both the National Ballet of Canada and the Canadian Opera Company perform at the **Four Seasons Centre for the Performing Arts** (145 Queen St. W., www.fourseasonscentre.ca, subway: Osgoode), where the main auditorium seats more than 2,000. To learn more about the building and its resident companies, take a 90-minute **Four Seasons Centre tour** (adults $20, seniors and students $15), which takes you backstage, into the dressing rooms, the wardrobe and wig rooms, the orchestra pit, and the ballet rehearsal studio. You'll get some theater trivia, too, like the fact that the 2006 building houses the world's longest free-spanning glass staircase, or that the center has 103 restrooms, two-thirds of which are for women. Call or check the website for tour schedules. You can buy advance tickets online or purchase tickets at the lobby welcome desk.

Campbell House Museum

Built in 1822 when the Toronto area was still a frontier outpost, the Georgian-style **Campbell House Museum** (160 Queen St. W., at University Ave., 416/597-0227, www.campbellhousemuseum.ca, subway: Osgoode, 9:30am-4:30pm Tues.-Fri., noon-4:30pm Sat. late Sept.-Dec. 24 and Feb.-late May, 9:30am-4:30pm Tues.-Fri., noon-4:30pm Sat., noon-4:30pm Sun. late May-late Sept., adults $6, seniors and ages 13-18 $4, ages 5-12 $3) is the oldest remaining house from the original Town of York. On the 30- to 45-minute guided tours, you'll learn about early Toronto history and about the lives of Judge William Campbell—the sixth chief justice of Upper Canada—and his wife Hannah, who built and resided in the house. Although few original furnishings remain, the house is outfitted with elegant period pieces that reflect the Campbells' well-to-do status.

Campbell House was originally located 1.5 kilometers (0.9 miles) to the southeast. After being threatened with destruction in 1972, it was moved to its current location, one block west of City Hall.

Mackenzie House

Illegitimate children, mental illness, political intrigue, sibling rivalry, even suicide are all part of the history of William Lyon Mackenzie (1795-1861) and his family, who moved to this Georgian row house in 1859, just two years before his death. Yes, when you take a 45-minute tour of **Mackenzie House** (82 Bond St., 416/392-6915, www.toronto.ca, subway: Dundas, noon-5pm Sat.-Sun. Jan.-Apr., noon-5pm Tues.-Sun. May-early Sept., noon-4pm Tues.-Fri., noon-5pm Sat.-Sun. early Sept.-Dec., adults $5.71, seniors and ages 13-18 $2.62, ages 5-12 $2.38), two blocks east of Dundas subway station, you'll learn about Mackenzie's official biography as a journalist, political reformer, and politician who became the first mayor of the city of Toronto. Yet the guides also share personal details about his life that make a visit here more than just a historic house tour.

Mackenzie published a reform-minded newspaper, the *Colonial Advocate,* and one section of the house is now a working 1850s replica of Mackenzie's Toronto print shop, with an original 19th-century printing press.

Ryerson Image Centre

Interested in contemporary photography? Then visit this cutting-edge gallery, **Ryerson Image Centre** (33 Gould St., 416/979-5164, www.ryerson.ca/ric, subway: Dundas, 11am-6pm Tues. and Thurs.-Fri., 11am-8pm Wed., noon-5pm Sat.-Sun., free), on the Ryerson University campus. You'll recognize the modern glass-and-steel building by the larger-than-life photos of Gloria Steinem, Albert Einstein, and other notables on the exterior. Exhibits in the three exhibition spaces change several times a year; complimentary tours of the current shows are offered at 2:30pm Tuesday-Sunday.

Textile Museum of Canada

Quilts, clothing, carpets, kimonos, pillow covers, and hats—you'll find all these and more at the **Textile Museum of Canada** (55 Centre Ave., www.textilemuseum.ca, 11am-5pm Thurs.-Tues., 11am-8pm Wed., adults $15, seniors $10, over age 4 $6, families $30; 5pm-8pm Wed. pay what you can). The museum's permanent collection includes more than 12,000 objects that come from 200 regions around the world and span almost 2,000 years. They're shown in rotating exhibits, along with changing exhibitions of contemporary and historical textiles from Canada and abroad. Free **guided tours** of the galleries are offered at 2pm Sunday.

The subway station closest to the museum is St. Patrick; you can also take the no. 505 Dundas streetcar to Chestnut Street.

St. Lawrence Market

From the Town of York's earliest days, the area bounded by Front, Jarvis, King, and Church Streets was a market district. In 1845, the town built a city hall nearby on Front Street, which housed the mayor's office, council chambers, the police station, and the jail, as well as a produce and poultry market. When the city again outgrew these quarters and constructed a new municipal building on Queen Street, the structure now known as Old City Hall, in 1899, the market began to take over the former city offices, evolving into the **St. Lawrence Market** (Front St. E., between Market St. and Jarvis St., 416/392-7219, www.stlawrencemarket.com).

The St. Lawrence Market is four blocks east of Union Station. You can also take the no. 504 King streetcar to Jarvis Street.

South Market

The main St. Lawrence Market building, the **South Market** (93 Front St. E., 8am-6pm Tues.-Thurs., 8am-7pm Fri., 5am-5pm Sat.), is packed with market stalls selling cheeses, meats, and produce as well as prepared foods. Not all of it is locally produced, but some is, so look hard if you're into local goodies.

On the South Market's second floor, the city-run **Market Gallery** (10am-4pm Tues.-Fri., 9am-4pm Sat., free) mounts changing exhibitions that reflect the city's art, culture, or history. The gallery space housed the Toronto City Council Chamber in the late 1800s.

For a detailed history of the market district, book a 90-minute **St. Lawrence Market History Walking Tour** (647/393-8687, bruce.bell2@sympatico.ca, www.brucebelltours.ca,

10am Tues.-Sat., adults $25) with guide Bruce Bell. Reservations are required; book by phone or email.

The **Market Kitchen** (416/860-0727, www.themarketkitchen.ca), on the mezzanine level of the South Market, offers cooking classes (2-3 hours, $40-85 pp) on topics ranging from baking scones to cooking with beer to preparing Spanish tapas. Book in advance on the website.

Note that the South Market is closed Sunday-Monday.

North Market

Across Front Street from the South Market building, the North Market has been a place for area farmers to sell their wares since 1803. It is still a year-round Saturday **farmers market** (5am-3pm Sat.) and Sunday **antiques market** (dawn-5pm Sun.). At the time of this writing, a new North Market building was being constructed, and these weekend markets had relocated to 125 The Esplanade, south of the South Market building, during construction.

St. Lawrence Hall

The stately cupola-topped building at the corner of King and Jarvis Streets is **St. Lawrence Hall** (157 King St. E., www.stlawrencemarket.com/hall). Built in 1850, the hall was once one of the city's social hubs, hosting concerts, lectures, and balls. The hall also played a role in the abolitionist movement, when the North American Convention of Coloured Freemen, an abolitionist group, met here in 1851 to discuss the issue of former slaves fleeing the United States. After debating whether to encourage these refugees to start new lives in Canada, the Caribbean, or Africa, the 53 delegates concluded that Canada was the best destination.

St. Lawrence Hall is now primarily a city office building, but visitors can go up to the **East Room,** on the third floor, to see the small exhibit about the notables who lectured, performed, or visited here, from Canadian politician and journalist William Lyon Mackenzie to abolitionist leader Frederick Douglass to circus impresario P. T. Barnum.

★ The Distillery Historic District

Toronto was once home to the world's largest distillery, the Gooderham and Worts Distillery, founded in 1832. Though the stills have long been stilled, the five-hectare (13-acre) site east of downtown has been redeveloped into **The Distillery Historic District** (55 Mill St., 416/364-1177, www.thedistillerydistrict.com), where the Victorian-era brick industrial buildings now house galleries, shops, cafés, and theaters, as well as high-end condominiums.

The Distillery Historic District is bounded by Parliament, Mill, and Cherry Streets. From downtown, take the no. 504 King streetcar to Parliament Street, then walk two blocks south. You can also follow a **walking path** along the Esplanade between the St. Lawrence Market and the Distillery District, bordering David Crombie Park.

Galleries and Artist Studios

The **Artscape Building** (15 Case Goods Lane, www.torontoartscape.on.ca, noon-5pm Wed.-Sun.) houses more than 60 artist studios, many of which are open for browsing, and you may be able to watch the artists at work.

The **Corkin Gallery** (7 Tank House Lane, 416/979-1980, www.corkingallery.com, 10am-6pm Tues.-Sat., noon-5pm Sun.) has one of the coolest art spaces in the Distillery District, displaying contemporary works amid the brick columns, steel girders, and soaring ceilings of the building's original structure.

While you may think about multicultural Toronto in terms of its various ethnic populations, you can learn about a different sort of community at the **Deaf Culture Centre** (34 Distillery Lane, 416/203-0343, www.deafculturecentre.ca, 11am-6pm Tues.-Sat., noon-5pm Sun., free). The center has a small museum about the deaf community and about technological innovations and communications tools for the deaf. It also offers resources for deaf individuals and their families.

Breweries

Toronto's first sake brewery, the **Ontario Spring Water Sake Company** (51 Gristmill Lane, 416/365-7253, www.ontariosake.com, 11am-7pm Mon.-Sat., noon-6pm Sun.) has a retail store and tasting bar.

The **Mill Street Brewery** (21 Tank House Lane, 416/681-0338, www.millstreetbrewpub. ca, store 11am-8pm Mon.-Thurs., 11am-10pm Fri.-Sat., 11am-6pm Sun., brewpub 11am-11pm Mon.-Tues., 11am-midnight Wed., 11am-1pm Thurs., 11am-2am Fri., 10:30am-2am Sat., 10:30am-10pm Sun.) produces more than a dozen varieties of beer in this Distillery District microbrewery. You can take a tour of the brewery (4pm Mon.-Fri., 3pm and 5pm Sat.-Sun., $10), which includes tastings; check in 15 minutes before the tour time.

Enoch Turner Schoolhouse

Near the Distillery District, the **Enoch Turner Schoolhouse** (106 Trinity St., 416/327-6997, www.heritagetrust.on.ca, 10am-4pm Mon.-Tues., 10am-noon Wed., free) housed Toronto's first free school. Funded by a well-to-do local brewer, Enoch Turner, the school opened in 1849. Its pupils were the children of the immigrants, most of whom were Irish, who settled the surrounding Corktown neighborhood. Look inside the one-room school to learn more about life and learning in mid-19th-century Toronto.

You can walk to the school from the Distillery District, or take the no. 504 King streetcar to Trinity Street. The schoolhouse is located behind the Little Trinity Anglican Church.

BLOOR-YORKVILLE AND THE ANNEX

Bloor Street bisects the city from west to east, and its central section, between Yonge Street and Avenue Road, is the **Bloor-Yorkville** (www.bloor-yorkville.com) neighborhood. An upscale shopping destination, Bloor-Yorkville also houses several of the city's top cultural attractions, including the Royal Ontario Museum and the Bata Shoe Museum.

West along Bloor Street between Avenue Road and Bathurst Street, **The Annex** (www. bloorannexbia.com) is more residential and more bohemian, with a mix of cafés, shops, and bed-and-breakfasts. Many of its businesses cater to students and staff at the nearby University of Toronto.

★ Royal Ontario Museum

A visit to the venerable **Royal Ontario Museum** (ROM; 100 Queen's Park, 416/586-8000, www.rom.on.ca, subway: Museum, St. George, 10am-5:30pm Sat.-Thurs., 10am-8:30pm Fri., adults $16, seniors and students $14.50, ages 4-14 $13, discounted admission after 4:30pm Fri.) is like a stroll through the history of the world. In this massive museum of natural history and world cultures, you'll find everything from Egyptian mummies to British neoclassical dining rooms, Buddha statues from China and India, armor from medieval Europe, and, of course, lots and lots of kid-pleasing dinosaur skeletons.

Approach the museum building on the Queen's Park side and you'll see an imposing stone face with arched windows that dates back to the early 1900s. But when you come around to Bloor Street, it looks like an altogether different structure. Architect Daniel Libeskind designed this contemporary addition, the **Michael Lee-Chin Crystal,** a series of five interlocking glass and steel prisms that appear to hang off the building's Bloor Street facade.

Take a free 45-minute **tour** (daily, times vary) to get your bearings—either an introduction to the museum's highlights or a more in-depth look at a particular aspect of the collection. The ROM also offers lectures, children's programs, and lots of other special events; check the website for schedules. Avoid lines at the ticket counter by buying your tickets online in advance ($2 service fee).

Gardiner Museum

Exhibiting ceramics from ancient times to the present, the **Gardiner Museum** (111 Queen's Park, 416/586-8080, www.gardinermuseum.on.ca, subway: Museum, 10am-6pm Mon.-Thurs., 10am-9pm Fri., 10am-5pm Sat.-Sun., adults $15, seniors $11, students $9, under age 12 free, half-price 4pm-9pm Fri.) shows pieces like a Zapotec funerary urn (created AD 500-700), porcelain from Japan and China, and English delftware from the 17th and 18th centuries. To learn more about the museum's exhibits and collections, take a free guided **tour** (2pm daily).

If ogling all these fine ceramics pieces inspires you to get your own hands dirty, try a two-hour drop-in **clay class** (6pm Wed. and Fri., 1pm Sun., adults $15, seniors and students $12, under age 13 $5). Sign up at the museum's front desk 30 minutes before each session.

★ Bata Shoe Museum

If you think that a museum devoted to shoes would appeal only to foot fetishists or footwear-fixated fashionistas, think again. The quirky **Bata Shoe Museum** (327 Bloor St. W., 416/979-7799, www.batashoemuseum.ca, subway: St. George, 10am-5pm Mon.-Wed. and Fri.-Sat., 10am-8pm Thurs., noon-5pm Sun., adults $14, seniors $12, students $8, ages 5-17 $5, families $24-35) traces the history and culture of a wide swath of humanity by showcasing what people wore on their feet.

Inside the asymmetrical building, designed by architect Raymond Moriyama to resemble a shoebox with its lid askew, the museum's collections include more than 10,000 shoes—from doll-like slippers worn by Chinese women with bound feet (there's even an overshoe version for wearing while working in the fields) to singer Elton John's sky-high platform shoes. They even have British Queen Victoria's silk stocking and a pair of socks that Napoleon wore at Elba. Exhibits include captions with fascinating snippets about the people who wore them.

From 5pm to 8pm Thursday, admission is pay-what-you-can (suggested donation $5).

University of Toronto

With more than 75,000 students and over 15,000 faculty and staff, the **University of Toronto** (www.utoronto.ca, subway: St. George, Museum) is Canada's largest university. The main St. George campus is roughly bounded by Bloor, Bay, and College Streets and Spadina Avenue.

Royal Ontario Museum

As you're wandering the leafy grounds, see what's on at the **University of Toronto Art Centre** (15 King's College Circle, 416/978-1838, www.utac.utoronto.ca, noon-5pm Tues. and Thurs.-Sat., noon-8pm Wed. Sept.-June, free), which shows wide-ranging exhibits in a Romanesque Revival building. It's off Hoskin Avenue, between St. George Street and Queen's Park Crescent.

Prospective students and visitors can take a 90-minute **general campus tour** (http://discover.utoronto.ca, 11am and 2pm Mon.-Fri., free) to learn more about the university. Tours depart from the **Nona Macdonald Visitors Centre** (25 King's College Circle, 416/978-5000).

Ontario Legislative Assembly

Although Toronto is Canada's largest city, it's not the national capital; Ottawa has that distinction. But it is the capital of the province of Ontario, which, like all Canadian provinces, has its own provincial government. Ontario's seat of government is the august **Ontario Legislative Assembly** (111 Wellesley St. W., 416/325-7500, tour information 416/325-0061, www.ontla.on.ca, subway: Queen's Park, tours 9:30am-5:30pm Mon.-Fri., 9am-4pm Sat.-Sun. mid-May-June, 9am-5:30pm Mon.-Fri., 9am-4:30pm Sat.-Sun. July-early Sept., 9:30am-5:30pm Mon.-Fri. early Sept.-mid-May, free) in Queen's Park.

On the free 30-minute **tours** of the building, which opened in 1893, you'll get a brief history of the building and the structure of Ontario's government. Guides share interesting tidbits about members of the provincial parliament (though they're more historical than scandalous). Tour schedules vary depending on what's happening in the building, so it's a good idea to phone ahead.

Visitors are welcome to observe the provincial parliament in action, which, during the legislative session, is typically 10:30am-6pm Monday and 9am-6pm Tuesday-Thursday. Pick up a free access pass from the Special Constable at the legislature's south basement entrance. Staff at the information desk in the main lobby can also answer questions about tours and parliament sessions.

Arthur Conan Doyle Room

Are you a fan of Sherlock Holmes? On the fifth floor of the Toronto Reference Library, the **Arthur Conan Doyle Room** (789 Yonge St., 416/395-5577, www.torontopubliclibrary.ca, subway: Bloor-Yonge, 9am-8:30pm Mon.-Fri., 9am-5pm Sat., 1:30pm-5pm Sun. Sept.-June, free), modeled after the study at 221B Baker Street (the mythical sleuth's residence), is full of books by and about the author of the Sherlock Holmes mysteries. Also on display is a variety of Holmes memorabilia, from his trademark pipe to comic books based on Holmes's (fictional) life, as well as Doyle's letters and papers. The collection doesn't circulate, but visitors are welcome to browse, and the helpful staff can tell you about the materials.

Casa Loma

You don't have to travel to Europe to tour a castle; Toronto has **Casa Loma** (1 Austin Terrace, at Spadina Rd., 416/923-1171, www.casaloma.org, 9:30am-5pm daily, adults $24, seniors and ages 14-17 $18, ages 4-13 $14, parking $3 per hour or $9 per day Mon.-Thurs., flat-rate $10 Fri.-Sun.). This opulent "House on the Hill" overlooking the city took three years (1911-1914) to build and contains enough grand salons, towers, and elaborate gardens to satisfy most castle buffs. While kids may not care about the architecture or plush furnishings, they might enjoy climbing the twisty spiral staircase to the turret, finding secret passageways, or following the creepy underground tunnels to the horse stables (where mahogany paneling lines the deluxe stalls).

The ticket price includes a self-guided audio tour with all sorts of details about the house, its owners, and its various furnishings, as well as admission to a documentary film about Canadian financier Sir Henry Pellatt, who built the castle.

From downtown, the most direct route to

the castle is to take the subway to Dupont station (Spadina-University line). Exit the subway, walk north two blocks on Spadina Road, and climb the Baldwin Steps (a 110-step staircase) to the castle.

Spadina Museum: Historic House and Gardens

Across the road from Casa Loma, the large but decidedly more modest historic house that now houses the **Spadina Museum** (285 Spadina Rd., 416/392-6910, www.toronto.ca, noon-5pm Sat.-Sun. Jan.-mid-Apr., noon-5pm Tues.-Sun. mid-Apr.-early Sept., noon-4pm Tues.-Fri., noon-5pm Sat.-Sun. early Sept.-Dec., adults $8, seniors and ages 13-18 $5.75, ages 6-12 $5) is more typical of an upper-class family home from the early 20th century. Built in 1886, the house belonged to the well-to-do Austin family, and nearly all the furnishings, from the ornate art deco wallpaper to the billiards table, are original to the home.

Kensington Market

Like Casa Loma, the Spadina Museum is at the top of the Baldwin Steps, a short walk (but a steep climb up) from Dupont station.

THE WEST END

West of downtown, Toronto's diverse neighborhoods include some of the city's hippest districts, filled with galleries, restaurants, and funky boutiques, as well as several ethnic neighborhoods—fun to explore when you're hungry.

Kensington Market

Kensington Market isn't a market building. Rather, it's a market neighborhood, filled with vendors' stalls and international eateries that span the globe. There's a Chilean empanada place near a Mexican taco joint, an Indian spice vendor opposite a Latino meat market, and a plethora of fruit sellers, bakeries, nut vendors, cheese shops, and inexpensive clothing outlets. On a mild evening, sidewalk cafés are packed, and people spill out of restaurants and bars onto the streets. Most of the action takes place along Augusta Avenue, Baldwin Street, and Nassau Street, west of Spadina Avenue between Dundas and College Streets.

Generations of immigrants have settled in the Kensington Market area, which gives it its multicultural vibe. In the second half of the 19th century, working-class immigrants from England and Ireland made the neighborhood their home. Then, between 1905 and 1930, Jews fleeing persecution in Europe settled here, many opening small shops that resemble those still lining the narrow streets today. After World War II, Caribbean, Chinese, South Asian, and Latin American newcomers joined the European settlers in the market district.

To get to Kensington Market, take the no. 506 Carlton streetcar to Major Street or Augusta Avenue, or take the no. 510 Spadina streetcar and get off anywhere between Dundas and College.

"Original" Chinatown

Toronto's first Chinatown, settled in the early 1900s, was originally located along

Elizabeth Street, near Dundas Street, behind the current Toronto City Hall. When the city began appropriating land in the neighborhood during the late 1940s and early 1950s, with a plan to build a new city hall and public square, many Chinatown businesses closed, but many others moved west into the district now known as Toronto's original Chinatown. Chinese groceries, herbalists, and restaurants line Spadina Avenue and Dundas Street, extending north to College Street and south toward Queen Street. The neighborhood has grown increasingly multiethnic, too, with Vietnamese and other Southeast Asian businesses joining the Chinese vendors. It's a fun place to browse and, of course, eat.

To get to Chinatown, take the no. 505 Dundas or no. 506 Carlton streetcar to Spadina Avenue. You could also take the no. 510 Spadina streetcar and get off anywhere between Dundas and College.

★ Art Gallery of Ontario

Born Frank Owen Goldberg in Toronto in 1929, the internationally acclaimed architect now known as Frank Gehry grew up not far from the **Art Gallery of Ontario** (AGO, 317 Dundas St. W., 416/979-6648 or 877/225-4246, www.ago.net, subway: St. Patrick, 10am-5:30pm Tues. and Thurs.-Sun., 10am-8:30pm Wed., adults $19.50, seniors $16, students and ages 6-17 $11, families $49; free admission 6pm-8:30pm Wed.). The Art Gallery is one of North America's largest museums, with more than 80,000 works, so perhaps it's fitting that Gehry designed the gallery's dramatic building, which opened in 2008. While Gehry has constructed buildings all over the world—from the Guggenheim Museum Bilbao in Spain and the Experience Music Project in Seattle to the Walt Disney Concert Hall in Los Angeles—the AGO was his first project in Canada.

Among the highlights of the museum's collection, beyond the building itself, are its Canadian collections, which include significant works by the Group of Seven (early 20th-century landscape artists) and by contemporary Inuit artists. The AGO has the largest collection of African and Oceanic art in a Canadian art museum, the largest public collection of work by the British sculptor Henry Moore (1898-1986), and a major European Old Masters collection that's particularly strong in Italian and Dutch painting from the 1600s, and French impressionist works from the 1800s.

The best way to get an overview of the museum's extensive collection is to take the 60-minute **AGO Highlights Tour** (11am, noon, 1pm, and 3pm Thurs.-Tues., 11am, noon, 1pm, and 3pm, and 7pm Wed., free).

When you need a break, you can get coffee and pastries in the second floor Galleria Italia espresso bar. For sandwiches, salads, and light meals, there's **caféAGO.** The museum's flagship dining room is the upscale **FRANK** (lunch 11:30am-2:30pm Tues.-Fri., brunch 11am-3pm Sat.-Sun., dinner 5:30pm-10:30pm Tues.-Sat., lunch $14-24, dinner $19-26), which serves contemporary fare.

The museum is three blocks west of the St. Patrick subway station. The no. 505 Dundas streetcar stops at McCaul or Beverly Streets are both in front of the AGO.

Ontario College of Art & Design

If you can imagine a black- and white-checkered box floating in the sky, supported only by yellow, blue, and purple pencils, then you can begin to envision one of Toronto's most distinctive buildings, the Sharp Centre for Design at the **Ontario College of Art & Design** (OCAD, 100 McCaul St., 416/977-6000, www.ocad.ca, subway: St. Patrick).

The floating box, or tabletop, section of the building is 9 meters (29.5 feet) tall, 31 meters (102 feet) wide, and 84 meters (275 feet) long and houses studios and classrooms. Twelve colorful hollow steel legs, each measuring 30 meters (100 feet)—or roughly the equivalent of a 10-story building—support the "tabletop." British architect Will Alsop, in partnership with the Toronto-based Robbie/Young

Family-Friendly Toronto

Toronto has plenty of activities to engage children of all ages.

- Ride to the top of the **CN Tower** and let your little daredevils jump on the Glass Floor, 112 stories above the ground.

- Check out the sharks, jellyfish, and more than 16,000 other aquatic creatures at **Ripley's Aquarium of Canada.**

- The dinosaurs and mummies at the **Royal Ontario Museum** have lots of kid appeal, as do the hands-on exhibits at the **Ontario Science Centre** and the animals at **Riverdale Farm.** Young hockey fans won't want to miss the **Hockey Hall of Fame.**

- If it's a nice day, take the ferry to the **Toronto Islands,** especially if your youngsters love amusement parks. You can also rent bikes and go exploring.

- Older kids might enjoy a family version of an **Urban Quest** walking tour, where you follow a series of clues through the city.

- When it's time to eat, wander the **St. Lawrence Market** and let everyone pick out their favorite bites. In Chinatown, have dim sum or watch the dumpling makers at work at **Mother's Dumplings.**

- If you don't mind venturing farther afield, several attractions in suburban Toronto are popular with the kids, including **Canada's Wonderland** (Canada's Wonderland Rd., Vaughan, 905/832-8131, www.canadaswonderland.com), an amusement park that's home to Canada's tallest and fastest roller coaster; **LEGOLAND Discovery Centre** (1 Bass Pro Mills Dr., Vaughan, 855/356-2150, www.legolanddiscoverycentre.ca/toronto), for kids ages 3-10 who love colorful LEGO blocks; and the **Toronto Zoo** (Meadowvale Rd., Toronto, 416/392-5929, www.torontozoo.com), which has more than 5,000 animals, including giant pandas.

- Toronto's most family-friendly place to stay is the **Eaton Chelsea Hotel,** a mega-size property (it's Canada's largest lodging) with an indoor pool with a 40-meter (130-foot) water slide, a "Kid Centre" for games, arts, and crafts, and a regular roster of family activities.

+ Wright Architects, designed this unusual structure, which opened in 2004.

The building is most remarkable from the exterior. There are no public tours of the interior, but you can go inside to view exhibitions at **Onsite [at] OCAD U** (11am-7pm Tues.-Fri., noon-6pm Sat., free), a small contemporary gallery space.

401 Richmond

Just south of Queen Street at Spadina Avenue is **401 Richmond** (401 Richmond St. W., 416/595-5900, www.401richmond.net), a rehabbed brick heritage building that's home to artists, galleries, art shops, and other cultural businesses. Poke around and see what's happening, or check out some of these art spaces: **Musideum** (416/599-7323, www.musideum.

com, noon-6pm Tues.-Sat.) carries musical instruments from around the world and also hosts performances; **Open Studio** (416/504-8238; www.openstudio.on.ca, noon-5pm Tues.-Sun.) is an artist-run printmaking center; and **Swipe Design|Books+Objects** (416/363-1332, www.swipe.com, 10am-7pm Mon.-Fri., noon-6pm Sat.) sells design books and lots of cool design stuff.

★ Queen Street West

As you head west from downtown through the Entertainment District along Queen Street, the shops and eateries change from chains and mainstream brands to smaller, independent businesses. Farther west, this funky neighborhood gets a mouthful of a moniker: West Queen West. Though it still has a grunge feel in parts, this "in" arts district is packed with eclectic shops and galleries, arty hotels, and hip bars.

Run by the Ontario Crafts Council, the small **Craft Ontario Gallery** (990 Queen St. W., 416/925-4222, www.craft.on.ca, 11am-6pm Mon.-Sat., noon-5pm Sun.) shows work by Ontario craftspeople. At the **David Kaye Gallery** (1092 Queen St. W., at Dovercourt Rd., 416/532-9075, www.davidkayegallery.com, 11am-6pm Wed.-Fri., 11am-5pm Sat.-Sun.), you'll find paintings, objects, and jewelry by a mix of up-and-coming and more established artists. Housed in a former police station, **Gallery 1313** (1313 Queen St. W., 416/536-6778, www.g1313.org, 1pm-6pm Wed.-Sat.) is an artist-run space that shows contemporary Canadian art. **General Hardware Contemporary** (1520 Queen St. W., 416/516-6876, www.generalhardware.ca, noon-6pm Wed.-Sat.), in a former hardware store west of Lansdowne Avenue, exhibits contemporary art by Canadian and international artists.

On Ossington Avenue, just north of Queen Street West, there's another emerging gallery district. Look for the **Angell Gallery** (12 Ossington Ave., at Queen St. W., 416/530-0444, www.angellgallery.com, noon-5pm Wed.-Sat.), which shows contemporary art, and **Gallery TPW** (56 Ossington Ave., at Queen St. W., 416/645-1066, www.gallerytpw.ca, noon-5pm Tues.-Sat.), which exhibits photography.

Museum of Canadian Contemporary Art

The small **Museum of Canadian Contemporary Art** (952 Queen St. W., 416/395-0067, www.mocca.ca, 11am-6pm Tues.-Sun., free), just east of Ossington Avenue, shows cutting-edge creations by Canadian, and some international, artists, working in many different media.

High Park

On the far west side of the city, Toronto's largest public park, **High Park** (1873 Bloor St. W., 416/397-2628, www.toronto.ca/parks, subway: High Park, dawn-dusk daily, free) has Grenadier Pond, hiking trails, playgrounds, gardens, and even a small **zoo** (Deer Pen Rd., 7am-dusk daily) with cows, sheep, bison, llamas, peacocks, and deer.

To see what's where in the park, you can catch the "trackless train" (10:30am-dusk Sat.-Sun. Apr. and Sept.-Oct., 10:30am-dusk daily May-Aug; adults $4.50, seniors and kids $3.50), which makes a 30-minute tour of the park grounds.

Another park attraction is the 1837 **Colborne Lodge** (11 Colborne Lodge Dr., 416/392-6916, www.toronto.ca, noon-5pm Tues.-Sun. May-Aug., call for off-season hours, adults $6.20, seniors and ages 13-18 $3.60, ages 4-12 $2.65), the former home of John and Jemima Howard, who founded High Park.

To reach most park sights, take the Bloor subway, which runs along the park's northern border, to High Park station. If you're going to Colbourne Lodge, on the south side of the park, it's easier to take the no. 501 Humber/Long Branch streetcar to Colborne Lodge Drive; from there, it's a short walk up the road.

THE EAST END

Exploring Toronto's east side is less about seeing "sights" and more about exploring different neighborhoods and communities.

The area surrounding Church and Wellesley Streets may officially be **Church-Wellesley Village** (www.churchwellesleyvillage.ca), but as the hub of Toronto's large gay and lesbian community, its unofficial name is the Gay Village.

East of Parliament Street, between Gerrard and Wellesley Streets, lies **Cabbagetown.** According to legend, the immigrants who settled here in the 1800s could afford to eat only the cabbage they grew themselves—giving rise to the Cabbagetown name. Nowadays, you might still have to eat cabbage to afford the pricey, meticulously preserved Victorian homes in what is now a well-to-do corner of town. This urban district has several outdoor attractions (all accessible via the no. 306 Carleton streetcar), including **Allan Gardens Conservatory** (19 Horticultural Ave., 416/392-1111, www.toronto.ca, 10am-5pm daily, free), greenhouses with more than 1,500 square meters (16,000 square feet) of plants; **Riverdale Farm** (201 Winchester St., 416/392-6794, www.toronto.ca, 9am-5pm daily, free), a kid-friendly farm and gardens; and the 1850 **Toronto Necropolis** (200 Winchester St., 416/923-7911, 8am-8pm Apr.-Sept., 8am-dusk daily Oct.-Mar.), a leafy, park-like cemetery where a number of notable Torontonians are interred.

Stretching east along Danforth Avenue between Chester and Pape Avenues is The Danforth, the neighborhood also known as **Greektown** (www.greektowntoronto.com), since it was historically the center of Toronto's Greek community. You'll still find souvlaki shops, traditional cafés, and baklava-filled bakeries, but the Danforth is becoming a trendy district popular with hip young families who shop in the organic market and frequent the local yoga studio.

Around Broadview Avenue and Gerrard Street is one of Toronto's smaller Chinatowns. This **East Chinatown** actually has a significant Vietnamese population, which means lots of *pho* and *bánh mì* shops line the streets. The no. 506 Carlton streetcar will take you to this community.

Farther east along Gerrard are the sari shops and curry-scented dining rooms of Little India, in the neighborhood called the **Indian Bazaar** (www.gerrardindiabazaar.com). Take the no. 506 Carlton streetcar and get off when you begin to see Indian shops.

Ride the no. 501 Queen Street streetcar east from downtown, and you'll reach the gentrifying neighborhood of **Leslieville,** which is drawing the artistically inclined to its galleries, cafés, and increasingly hip restaurants and shops. Continuing east is the residential neighborhood known as **The Beaches.** It borders Lake Ontario, with lakefront walkways and, yes, beaches, making it a pleasant spot for a day's excursion.

GREATER TORONTO
Evergreen Brick Works

For more than 100 years, the Don Valley Brick Works made many of the bricks that built Toronto, including notable buildings like Old City Hall and Massey Hall. When the brick works ceased operations in 1986, this complex of buildings northeast of downtown fell into disrepair. Graffiti artists began using its huge brick walls as their canvases, and performance artists held underground raves in the abandoned factory.

In 1991, the site took on a new identity with the launch of **Evergreen Brick Works** (550 Bayview Ave., 416/596-7670, www.evergreen.ca), whose mission was to restore the 16 buildings and create a new environmental design and education center. Since then, Evergreen Brick Works has started a variety of "green" programs to bring nature back into the city. If you're interested in green design, local food, cycling and alternative transportation, or a host of environmental issues, pay a visit here.

To get your bearings in this sprawling complex, stop into the **Young Welcome Centre** (9am-5pm Mon.-Fri., 8am-4pm Sat., 11am-4pm Sun.) and see what's on for the day or learn more about the various offerings. As you wander through the former factory buildings, notice that much of the graffiti—artistic and otherwise—still adorns the walls.

On weekends, a large **Farmers Market** (8am-1pm Sat. late May-Oct., 10am-3pm Sun. late June-Oct., 9am-1pm Sat. Nov.-late May) sets up shop, with vendors selling local produce, cheeses, honey, maple syrup, baked goods, and a variety of prepared foods. In mild weather, it's in the outdoor pavilion; in winter, it moves into the Welcome Centre. You can also sit down for a meal at **Café Belong** (416/901-8234, www.cafebelong.ca, 11:30am-9pm Mon.-Fri., 10am-10pm Sat., 10am-9pm Sun., lunch $13-29, dinner $22-44), which emphasizes local foods.

Hiking trails wend through the property, and in winter, there's free **ice-skating** (4pm-9pm Thurs., 11am-4pm Fri.-Sun.). Workshops, exhibits, and other special events take place throughout the year; a calendar is posted on the website.

To get here, take the subway (Bloor-Danforth line) to Broadview station, where you can catch a free shuttle to the Brick Works. The shuttle stop is next to the park on Erindale Avenue, on the east side of Broadview Avenue, just north of the station. The shuttles run every 30-45 minutes.

Ontario Science Centre

"Please touch" exhibits are common at science museums these days, but at the well-designed **Ontario Science Centre** (770 Don Mills Rd., at Eglinton Ave. E., www.ontariosciencecentre.ca, 10am-4pm Mon.-Fri., 10am-5pm Sat.-Sun., adults $22, seniors, students, and ages 13-17 $16, ages 3-12 $13, IMAX film $6 extra, parking $10), the exhibits go beyond button-pushing and computer-based games to promote real explorations of the material. Besides the expected displays about space, the human body, and the earth, you can investigate prejudice, stereotyping, and racism in the thought-provoking exhibit called "A Question of Truth." While a play area will entertain the little ones, the museum is especially interesting to older children, and even jaded teens can find cool stuff here. In the Innovation Centre, older kids and teens can choose from activities ranging from creating and testing their own paper airplane designs to constructing a pair of shoes.

Located northeast of downtown Toronto, this sprawling museum is built into a hillside in the Don Valley. From downtown, take the subway (Yonge line) to Eglinton Station. Then take the no. 34 Eglinton East bus to Don Mills Road. The museum is a short walk south on Don Mills Road.

Alternatively, you can take the Bloor-Danforth line to Pape Station, in the Danforth (Greektown) neighborhood. From there, catch the no. 25 Don Mills bus north to St. Dennis Drive; it stops directly in front of the Science Centre.

★ The McMichael Canadian Art Collection

You wouldn't expect to find a major museum of Canadian art way out in the woods. Yet this 6,000-piece collection of works by Group of Seven, First Nations, Inuit, and contemporary artists sits on 40 hectares (100 acres) of forested land in the village of Kleinburg, north of the city.

What is now **The McMichael Canadian Art Collection** (10365 Islington Ave.,

the grounds at The McMichael Canadian Art Collection

Kleinburg, 905/893-1121 or 888/213-1121, www.mcmichael.com, 10am-5pm daily, adults $18, seniors and children over age 5 $15, family $36, parking $5) got its start when Robert and Signe McMichael began collecting Canadian art in their rural home. In the 1960s, they donated their collection and residence to the province of Ontario to become a public museum.

You can easily spend several hours exploring the McMichael, which has significant holdings of works by the Group of Seven among its all-Canadian galleries; six of these artists are buried on the property in the Artist Cemetery, which you can visit. There's also a sculpture garden and a network of walking trails.

The McMichael is 45 kilometers (28 miles) north of downtown Toronto, a 40- to 60-minute drive. If you are traveling from Toronto to the Muskoka region, Georgian Bay, or other points north of the city, you can detour to the McMichael along the way.

Using public transit, reaching the McMichael is doable but complicated; routings involve connecting from Toronto's subway and buses to the **York Region's public transit system** (www.yorkregiontransit.com), where Bus no. 13 runs along Islington Avenue to the gallery.

Entertainment and Events

Toronto is not only Canada's largest city, it's the country's cultural capital, home to many of Canada's premier cultural institutions: the Toronto Symphony Orchestra, the National Ballet of Canada, the Canadian Opera Company, and the Canadian Stage Company. But the city has a more contemporary side, too. Toronto hosts an annual fringe festival in July and an international writers' fest in October. Among the liveliest summer events are a popular carnival celebrating Caribbean culture and annual Pride Week, one of the world's largest gay and lesbian pride celebrations.

The acclaimed Second City comedy company has a Toronto branch, and the city has a range of professional and local theater groups. Don't forget the nightclubs, the jazz bars, and the sports pubs broadcasting all hockey, all the time.

If you're looking for theaters, concert halls, and clubs, you'll find some near Dundas Square while others cluster in the Entertainment District, on and around King Street, west of the downtown core.

To find out what's going on, the best sources are the free arts and entertainment publications. *Now* (www.nowtoronto.com) is available online and at cafés and bookstores. The **City of Toronto** website (www.toronto.com) also includes an event calendar.

NIGHTLIFE

The neighborhood known as the Entertainment District, around King Street West from St. Andrew station west to Bathurst Street, has lots of clubs and bars, as does West Queen West (Queen Street from Ossington to Gladstone). For hotel bars and lounges, you'll find plenty of options in the Entertainment District and around downtown.

The **Gay Village** (around Church St. and Wellesley St., www.churchwellesleyvillage.ca) has long been the center of the city's gay and lesbian scene, although there's an up-and-coming west-side district, dubbed **Queer West** (along Ossington Ave. and Queen St. W., www.queerwest.org).

Since bars and clubs go in and out of fashion, it's always best to check locally to see what's going on.

Rock, Jazz, and Blues

Jazz club **The Rex** (194 Queen St. W., 416/598-2475, www.therex.ca, subway: Osgoode) hosts 1,000 gigs a year. Two bands play nightly

Around the World in a Toronto Day

In this city there are Bulgarian mechanics, there are Eritrean accountants, Colombian café owners, Latvian book publishers, Welsh roofers, Afghani dancers, Iranian mathematicians, Tamil cooks in Thai restaurants, Calabrese boys with Jamaican accents, Fushen deejays, Filipina-Saudi beauticians, Russian doctors changing tires; there are Romanian bill collectors, Cape Croker fishmongers, Japanese grocery clerks, French gas meter readers, German bakers, Haitian and Bengali taxi drivers with Irish dispatchers.

Toronto writer Dionne Brand in her novel *What We Long For*

Although Brand included this description of Toronto in a work of fiction, there's nothing fictional about the city's multicultural makeup. About half of metropolitan Toronto's residents were born outside of Canada, hailing from nearly every part of the globe. And throughout the city, you'll find ethnic enclaves where you can explore the food and culture of Toronto's various communities.

Perhaps the most visible of these neighborhoods are Toronto's Chinatowns—and Toronto has several of these predominantly Chinese districts, not surprisingly, since the Chinese are one of Toronto's largest visible-minority groups. Downtown, the **"original" Chinatown,** extending outward from the intersection of Spadina Avenue and Dundas Street, is a traditional immigrant neighborhood, where you'll find Chinese groceries, herbalists, and plenty of modest—and tasty—restaurants. The smaller **East Chinatown** is located around Broadview Avenue and Gerrard Street; it has a significant Vietnamese population as well.

Toronto has several large Chinese communities in the suburbs of Scarborough east of downtown, Mississauga to the west, and Richmond Hill and Markham to the north. The northern suburbs, in particular, are wealthier communities than the central-city Chinatowns, with higher-end restaurants and shops, many concentrated in malls, catering to this more upscale demographic. The **Pacific Mall** (4300 Steeles Ave. E., Markham, www.pacificmalltoronto.com) is one of the largest Asian malls in North America.

Like the Chinese, the South Asian community is a significant visible minority. Many South Asian immigrants once made their homes in Toronto's **Little India** neighborhood, also known as the Indian Bazaar, in the city's East End along Gerrard Street East. While Indian residents—and restaurants—have moved throughout Toronto, you'll still find a concentration of eateries, jewelers, and clothing shops here that cater to the Indian community.

Many of Toronto's Greek immigrants settled along Danforth Avenue, particularly between Chester and Pape Streets, in the district called The Danforth, or **Greektown.** The neighborhood has gentrified and lost some of its Greek character as younger families and trendier shops have moved in, but Toronto's Greek community, one of the largest outside Greece, still shops in the markets and traditional bakeries, lingers over coffee and pastry in the cafés, and dines on classic dishes like dolmades (grape leaves) and souvlaki.

Although Toronto's Korean community isn't as concentrated in one neighborhood as some other ethnic groups, the city does have a **Koreatown,** on Bloor Street West, around Christie Street. Markets, restaurants, and karaoke bars cater both to Koreans and others who enjoy the lively district's vibe.

In the early 20th century, many European immigrants settled on the west side of Toronto, including large numbers of Italians and Portuguese. **Little Italy,** primarily along College Street, west of Bathurst, and **Little Portugal,** on Dundas Street, near Ossington, today seem to have a lot of overlap, with Italian restaurants on the "Portuguese" streets and Portuguese bakeries on the "Italian" ones. And increasingly, hip contemporary eateries are moving in alongside the more traditional businesses. No matter; there's still good eating in these districts.

The streets on and around Roncesvalles Avenue, in the city's West End, were settled by Polish immigrants, giving the community the nickname **Little Poland.** This neighborhood still has Polish businesses, primarily bakeries, delis, restaurants, and travel agencies, although the district no longer has a predominantly Polish population. In a recent census, Polish was the second most widely spoken language in the neighborhood. The first? Chinese.

Monday-Thursday, there are three shows on Friday, and at least four groups take the stage on Saturday and Sunday, beginning most weekends at noon. A range of live music acts perform at **Hugh's Room** (2261 Dundas St. W., 416/531-6604, www.hughsroom.com, subway: Dundas West), with the emphasis on folk and blues artists. Bands from Willie Nelson to the Talking Heads to the Tragically Hip have all taken the stage at the **Horseshoe Tavern** (370 Queen St. W., 416/598-4753, www.horseshoetavern.com) since the club first opened in 1947. These days, they're going for an indie vibe, booking up-and-coming new music acts. Take the no. 501 Queen streetcar to Spadina Avenue, or the no. 510 Spadina streetcar to Queen Street. All kinds of events happen at **The Underground at the Drake Hotel** (1150 Queen St. W., 416/531-5042 or 866/372-5386, www.thedrakehotel.ca), from DJ dance parties and indie band concerts, to film screenings and comedy shows. Get there on the no. 501 Queen streetcar. The events at the Gladstone Hotel's **Melody Bar** (1214 Queen St. W., 416/531-4635, www.gladstonehotel.com) are as eclectic as the hotel itself, including TV trivia and all sorts of indie music shows.

Big-name rock and pop concerts perform at the city's two sports and entertainment arenas: **Air Canada Centre** (40 Bay St., 416/815-5400, www.theaircanadacentre.com, box office 9:30am-6pm Mon.-Fri., 9:30am-5pm Sat.) and **Rogers Centre** (1 Blue Jays Way, 416/341-1000, www.rogerscentre.com, box office 10am-6pm Mon.-Sat.). For online or phone sales for events at either venue, contact **Ticketmaster** (416/870-8000, www.ticketmaster.ca).

Bars, Pubs, and Lounges

The classic dark wood-paneled **Library Bar** (100 Front St. W., 416/368-2511, www.fairmont.com, noon-1am Mon.-Fri., 5pm-1am Sat.) at the venerable Fairmont Royal York Hotel feels ever so sophisticated, particularly when you're savoring one of their famous martinis. Afternoon tea is served here

on weekends, with seatings at noon, 12:30pm, and 2:30pm Saturday-Sunday. A chic spot for a drink is the Thompson Toronto Hotel's **Lobby Lounge** (550 Wellington St. W., 416/640-7778, www.thompsonhotels.com, 5pm-2am daily), where the bar glows with white light and the wall mural is a whimsical interpretation of the Toronto skyline. In the Entertainment District, meet for a pre- or post-theater libation at the **Victor Restaurant and Lounge** (30 Mercer St., 416/883-3431, www.victorrestaurant.com, 5pm-11pm daily), a stylish lounge in the lobby of Hotel Le Germain. If you're looking for serious karaoke, head for Koreatown along Bloor Street West where crooners take the mike at spots like **BMB Karaoke** (593 Bloor St. W., 416/533-8786) and **Freezone Karaoke** (721 Bloor St. W., 416/530-2781).

Comedy

The Toronto branch of the Chicago-based sketch comedy club **Second City** (51 Mercer St., 416/343-0011 or 800/263-4485, www.secondcity.com, shows 8pm Mon.-Thurs., 7:30pm and 10pm Fri.-Sat., 7:30pm Sun., $20-30) has cabaret-style shows every night.

THE ARTS

For discounted day-of-show tickets to theater, music, and other cultural events (as well as regular-price advance tickets), visit the **TOtix Toronto** ticket booth (Dundas St. W. at Yonge St., www.totix.ca, noon-6:30pm Tues.-Sat.) in Dundas Square.

Theater

Toronto is one of the world's hubs of English-language theater, with more than 90 theater venues in the metropolitan area. A number of professional repertory companies are based here, many of which focus on Canadian plays. The city's large theaters also host major musicals and other touring productions.

The **Canadian Stage Company** (416/368-3110, www.canadianstage.com), one of Canada's largest not-for-profit theater companies, produces contemporary Canadian and international plays. Their main stage is the **Bluma Appel Theatre** (St. Lawrence Centre for the Arts, 27 Front St. E., 416/366-7723 or 800/708-6754, www.stlc.com, subway: Union). They also perform at the smaller **Berkeley Street Theatre** (26 Berkeley St.); from downtown, take the no. 504 King streetcar east to Ontario Street. In the summer, the company goes outdoors for the **Canadian Stage in High Park** (High Park Amphitheatre, 1873 Bloor St. W., late June-early Sept.), a pay-what-you-can outdoor production; bring a picnic.

The **Factory Theatre** (125 Bathurst St., 416/504-9971, www.factorytheatre.ca) produces a full season of all-Canadian plays, including many world premieres. Founded in 1970, the Factory was the first company to present only Canadian works. The no. 511 Bathurst streetcar stops at Adelaide Street, right near the theater. You can also take either the no. 501 Queen or no. 504 King streetcars to Bathurst Street. Another long-standing local company, the **Tarragon Theatre** (30 Bridgman Ave., at Howland, 416/531-1827, www.tarragontheatre.com, subway: Dupont) has been producing a mix of new plays, Canadian works, and classic and contemporary international theater since 1970. Since 1969, the **Theatre Passe Muraille** (16 Ryerson Ave., 416/504-7529, www.passemuraille.ca) has produced edgy contemporary works. The small Queen West theater space is two blocks from the no. 501 Queen streetcar's Bathurst Street stop. The professional **Soulpepper Theatre Company** (www.soulpepper.ca) stages the classics, including Tolstoy, Tennessee Williams, David Mamet, and more contemporary works, at the **Young Centre for the Performing Arts** (50 Tank House Lane, 416/866-8666, www.youngcentre.ca) in the Distillery District.

Buddies in Bad Times Theatre (12 Alexander St., 416/975-8555, www.buddiesinbadtimes.com, subway: Wellesley) is a not-for-profit professional company that has been producing queer theater since 1979. Its plays focus primarily on gay, lesbian, bisexual, and transgendered identity issues. You never know

quite what you'll find on the **World Stage at Harbourfront Centre** (235 Queens Quay W., 416/973-4000, www.harbourfrontcentre.com), but expect creative contemporary Canadian and international performances.

Canada's oldest continuously operating legitimate theater (built in 1907), the beaux arts **Royal Alexandra Theatre** (260 King St. W., between Simcoe St. and Duncan St., 416/872-1212 or 800/461-3333, www.mirvish.com, subway: St. Andrew) hosts a variety of plays and musicals. The 2,000-seat **Princess of Wales Theatre** (300 King St. W., at John St., 416/872-1212 or 800/461-3333, www.mirvish.com, subway: St. Andrew), which opened in the Entertainment District in 1993, is one of Toronto's newer stages. Large-scale musicals, including *Miss Saigon, The Lion King,* and *The Sound of Music,* are a mainstay of the theater. Opened in 1920 as a vaudeville house, the **Ed Mirvish Theatre** (244 Victoria St., 416/872-1212 or 800/461-3333, www.mirvish.com, subway: Dundas) was once Canada's largest movie theater; it originally had 3,373 seats. These days, it stages major musicals, like *Billy Elliot,* as well as other theater and dance productions. The **Elgin and Winter Garden Theatre Centre** (189 Yonge St., 416/314-2901, subway: Queen), the only "double-decker" theater in Canada, houses two full-size theaters. Drama, musicals, ballet, and opera, as well as various special events, go on stage here. For an event calendar and tickets, contact **Ticketmaster** (855/622-2787, www.ticketmaster.ca) or phone the theater directly.

Only the facade of the **Panasonic Theatre** (651 Yonge St., 416/872-1212 or 800/461-3333, www.mirvish.com, subway: Bloor-Yonge) was saved when the building, which began life in 1911 as a private residence, was rebuilt in 2005. It's now a venue for live theater and concerts.

Live Music
The **Toronto Symphony Orchestra** (416/593-4828, www.tso.ca), one of Canada's major orchestras, performs at **Roy Thompson Hall** (60 Simcoe St.,

416/872-4255, www.roythomson.com, subway: St. Andrew), the 2,600-seat concert hall with a distinctive curved facade designed by noted Canadian contemporary architect Arthur Erickson (1924-2009). You can purchase symphony tickets at the Roy Thompson box office, by phone, or online at the website. Opened in 1982 in the Entertainment District, the theater hosts other concerts as well as the TSO events.

Built in 1894, the venerable **Massey Hall** (178 Victoria St., at Shuter St., 416/872-4255, www.masseyhall.com, subway: Dundas, Queen) was once Toronto's most important venue for classical concerts, opera, jazz, and other events, hosting appearances by Enrico Caruso, George Gershwin, Glenn Gould, Oscar Peterson, Bob Dylan, Gordon Lightfoot, and the Dalai Lama. These days, in addition to big-name popular concerts, the theater also stages the annual **Jazz @ Massey Hall** concert series, as well as the **Sing-Along Messiah,** an audience participation version of the Handel classic that's become a Toronto December tradition. The Massey Hall Box Office is open on performance days only, from noon to showtime; otherwise, you can buy tickets for Massey Hall events online or at the **Roy Thompson Theatre Box Office** (60 Simcoe St., 416/872-4255, www.roythomson.com).

Located on the main floor of the Canadian Broadcasting Centre, the 341-seat **Glenn Gould Studio** (250 Front St. W., information 416/205-5000, tickets 416/872-4255, www.cbc.ca/glenngould, subway: Union) is part concert hall and part recording studio, hosting classical and contemporary music concerts. It's named for Toronto pianist Glenn Gould (1932-1982), who performed and recorded extensively until his sudden death from a stroke at age 50. The **Roy Thompson Theatre Box Office** (60 Simcoe St., 416/872-4255, www.roythomson.com) sells tickets for events at the Glenn Gould Studio.

Canada's largest opera troupe is the Toronto-based **Canadian Opera Company** (416/363-8231 or 800/250-4653, www.coc.ca).

They perform at the **Four Seasons Centre for the Performing Arts** (145 Queen St. W., www.fourseasonscentre.ca, subway: Osgoode). Buy tickets by phone or in person from the Four Seasons Centre box office, or online at the opera website. From the Bolshoi Ballet to the Soweto Gospel Choir, the 3,191-seat **Sony Centre for the Performing Arts** (1 Front St. E., 855/872-7669, www.sonycentre.ca, subway: Union) presents international dance, music, and theatrical productions. Tickets are available online through Ticketmaster (www.ticketmaster.ca) or at the theater box office.

The **St. Lawrence Centre for the Arts** (27 Front St. E., 416/366-7723 or 800/708-6754, www.stlc.com, subway: Union), has four music organizations in residence. **Music Toronto** (www.music-toronto.com) presents traditional and modern chamber music, while **Opera in Concert** (www.operainconcert.com) produces operas that are rarely seen in Canada. The professional **Toronto Operetta Theatre** (www.torontooperetta.com) presents operetta, light opera, and musical theater featuring Canadian performers. The **Hannaford Street Silver Band** (www.hssb.ca), a professional brass band, performs several concerts throughout the year. Visiting musicians and other performers also take to the stage at the St. Lawrence Centre. Contact the St. Lawrence box office for tickets, or order online. At the **Royal Conservatory of Music** (273 Bloor St. W., 416/408-0208, www.rcmusic.ca, subway: St. George) in the Bloor-Yorkville neighborhood, notable Canadian and international musical acts, including those working in classical, chamber, early music, and world music, perform at the 1,135-seat **Koerner Hall.**

Dance

The **National Ballet of Canada** (416/345-9595 or 866/345-9595, www.national.ballet.ca), one of the world's top dance companies, works its artistic magic at the **Four Seasons Centre for the Performing Arts** (145 Queen St. W., www.fourseasonscentre.ca, subway: Osgoode). Tickets are available online from the ballet company website, or from the Four Seasons Centre box office in person or by phone.

One of Canada's leading contemporary dance companies, the **Toronto Dance Theatre** (416/967-1365, www.tdt.org), established in 1968, performs several Toronto shows a year, either at Harbourfront Centre or at their own Winchester Street Theatre (80 Winchester St.) in Cabbagetown, a short walk from the Parliament Street stop on the no. 506 Carlton streetcar. On the upper level of the Queen's Quay Terminal at Harbourfront Centre, the **Fleck Dance Theatre** (207 Queens Quay W., 416/973-4000, www.harbourfrontcentre.com) plays host to a variety of local, national, and international dance performers.

Cinema

If you're interested in film, don't miss visiting the **TIFF Bell Lightbox** (350 King St. W., 416/599-8433 or 888/599-8433, www.tiff.net). The distinctive contemporary glass building is not only headquarters for the annual Toronto International Film Festival, it's also home to the **TIFF Cinematheque,** which screens a wide range of movies throughout the year, and a **gallery** that shows film-related exhibits.

The lazy days of summer mean outdoor movies, right? The **Free Flicks** series (Harbourfront Centre, 235 Queens Quay W., 416/973-4000, www.harbourfrontcentre.com, July-Aug., free) screens films on some summer Wednesday nights; call or check the website for the schedule.

Literary Events

The **International Festival of Authors** (235 Queens Quay W., 416/973-4760 or 416/973-4000, www.ifoa.org) hosts weekly readings and other literary events from September to June at Harbourfront Centre. **Pages Unbound** (www.pages-unbound.com) runs a series of periodic literary evenings at the **Gladstone Hotel** (1214 Queen St. W., 416/531-4635, www.gladstonehotel.com).

FESTIVALS AND EVENTS

Spring

Photography buffs should schedule a Toronto visit during the **Scotiabank CONTACT Photography Festival** (416/539-9595, www.scotiabankcontactphoto.com, May), which showcases the work of more than 1,000 local, national, and international artists at more than 200 venues around town. During the last weekend in May, more than 150 museums, historic buildings, art spaces, condos, and religious institutions—including many that aren't usually open to the public—welcome visitors during **Doors Open Toronto** (www.toronto.ca/doorsopen, May, free). The **Toronto Jewish Film Festival** (416/324-9121, www.tjff.com, May) typically screens 90-100 movies from many different countries, some by Jewish filmmakers, others with themes of Jewish interest.

Summer

Luminato (416/368-3100, www.luminato.com, June) is a 10-day arts fest, featuring theater, dance, music, literature, food, visual arts, film, and even magic. Many events are free, although others require a ticket; the website has a schedule and ticketing information. Though it may not be as well known as the similarly named SXSW (South by Southwest festival in Austin), Toronto's **North by Northeast Music Festival** (NXNE, 416/863-6963, www.nxne.com, June) presents Canadian and international new and indie music, as well as avant-garde film and digital media. One of the world's largest gay-lesbian pride celebrations, **Toronto Pride Week** (416/927-7433, www.pridetoronto.com, June-July) features 10 days of marches, parades, and entertainment as well as a street fair and family activities. The annual Pride Parade is a highlight.

Jazz aficionados converge on the city for the annual **Toronto Jazz Fest** (416/928-2033, www.torontojazz.com, June-July), featuring more than 350 performances at locations around the city. The Beaches neighborhood gets into the jazz act, too, with the long-running **Beaches Jazz Fest** (416/698-2152, www.beachesjazz.com, July). All events are free. You never quite know what you'll see at the **Toronto Fringe Festival** (416/966-1062, www.fringetoronto.com, July), an eclectic lineup of more than 150 plays and other theatrical performances. The **Scotiabank Caribbean Carnival Toronto** (416/391-5608, www.torontocaribbeancarnival.com, July), formerly known as Caribana, is a three-week celebration of all things Caribbean, with music, dance, street parties, food, and a whopper of a parade.

Toronto's Greek community welcomes visitors to Danforth Avenue during the annual **Taste of the Danforth** (416/469-5634, www.tasteofthedanforth.com, Aug.), a weekend of food, music, kids' activities, and more that make this one of Canada's largest street festivals. For many Torontonians, it's not summer till you've been to the **Canadian National Exhibition** (416/393-6300, www.theex.com, Aug.-Sept.), a waterfront fair with carnival rides, a sand sculpture contest, a dog show, farm animals, a garden show, and all sorts of concerts and special events.

Fall

The city's premier cultural event is the **Toronto International Film Festival** (www.tiff.net, Sept.), which screens more than 300 movies from around the world and draws celebrities from across the globe. Advance ticket sales generally begin in July, although the detailed festival lineup isn't announced until about two weeks before opening night. Contact the **TIFF Bell Lightbox** (350 King St. W., 416/599-8433 or 888/599-8433) to find out when tickets go on sale. Stay up all night for Toronto's annual **Nuit Blanche** (www.scotiabanknuitblanche.ca, Oct.), a sundown-to-sunrise celebration of the contemporary arts. A major literary festival, the **Toronto International Festival of Authors** (www.ifoa.org, Oct.) is 11 days of readings, discussions, and interviews with authors from across Canada and abroad. Most events take place at **Harbourfront Centre** (235 Queens Quay W., information 416/973-4760, tickets 416/973-4000, www.harbourfrontcentre.com).

Winter

Get your holiday shopping done, or pick up a unique souvenir, at the **One of a Kind Show and Sale** (416/960-3680, www.oneofakindshow.com, Nov.-Dec.), an annual arts and crafts market. During the **Cavalcade of Lights** (www.toronto.com), the city lights its official Christmas tree in Nathan Phillips Square, outside City Hall. The tree-lighting ceremony, complete with concerts and outdoor ice-skating, takes place the last weekend of November; the Square remains illuminated through December. The smaller winter sibling of the Toronto Fringe Festival, the **Next Stage Theatre Festival** (www.fringetoronto.com, Jan.) presents a lineup of new plays.

Shopping

Toronto is a Canadian art center with a good mix of galleries, craft shops, and arts-oriented shops. The city also has a growing cohort of homegrown fashion designers, so it's worth browsing the boutiques. You'll also find many of the same chain stores that populate the malls across North America.

SHOPPING DISTRICTS

The largest mall in the downtown area, **Eaton Centre** (220 Yonge St., 416/598-8560, www.torontoeatoncentre.com, subway: Dundas or Queen, 10am-9pm Mon.-Fri., 9:30am-9:30pm Sat., 10am-7pm Sun.) has more than 230 stores, extending along Yonge Street from Queen to Dundas Streets. Most are Canadian or international chains, including Abercrombie & Fitch, H&M, Lululemon Athletica, and Roots.

In the **Bloor-Yorkville** neighborhood (subway: Bloor-Yonge, Bay, St. George), Bloor Street is lined with a mix of mid-range and upscale chain stores, from the Gap to Gucci; on some of the side streets, you'll find independent boutiques. Elsewhere in Yorkville, **Hazelton Lanes** (87 Avenue Rd., at Yorkville Ave., 416/968-8680, www.hazeltonlanes.com) houses a collection of high-end boutiques, including Jacadi, Marina Rinaldi, and Cop. Copine.

Galleries, clothing shops, and design studios populate the restored industrial buildings in the **Distillery District** (www.thedistillerydistrict.com), east of downtown. If you continue east into funky **Leslieville,** along Queen Street East, you'll find more independent designers and vintage furniture shops. Along **Queen Street West,** there's a mix of chains and independent shops, with the more creative independents winning out as you continue west to the district known as **West Queen West** (from Bathurst Street to Gladstone Avenue and continuing west to Roncesvalles Avenue). Just off Queen Street,

Ossington Avenue is a mini hub for cool shops and restaurants.

DEPARTMENT STORES

Founded in 1670 as a fur-trading company, the **Hudson's Bay Company**—Canada's oldest corporation—has grown to become the country's largest retailer. Its flagship chain of department stores, with locations across Canada, is known as The Bay. Among the many Toronto branches, there's one downtown near **City Hall** (176 Yonge St., 416/861-9111, www.thebay.com, subway: Queen, 10am-9:30pm Mon.-Fri., 9:30am-9:30pm Sat., 10am-7pm Sun.) and another in the Bloor-Yorkville neighborhood (44 Bloor St. E., 416/972-3333, subway: Bloor-Yonge, 10am-7pm Mon.-Wed., 10am-9pm Thurs.-Fri., 10am-7pm Sat., 11am-6pm Sun.).

The upscale fashion emporium **Holt-Renfrew** (50 Bloor St. W., 416/922-2333, www.holtrenfrew.com, subway: Bloor-Yonge, 10am-8pm Mon.-Wed., 10am-9pm Thurs.-Fri., 10am-8pm Sat., 11am-7pm Sun.) boasts top international designers and personal service. And the prices? Well, as the saying goes, if you have to ask, you can't afford it.

BOOKS AND MAGAZINES

A classic independent bookstore that's a lovely spot to browse downtown, **Ben McNally Books** (366 Bay St., 416/361-0032, www.benmcnallybooks.com, 10am-6pm Mon.-Fri., 11am-5pm Sat.) also hosts readings and other literary events. The no. 501 Queen streetcar stops at Bay Street, a block from the shop. **Eliot's Bookshop** (584 Yonge St., 416/925-0268, subway: Wellesley, 11am-8pm Mon.-Sat., noon-8pm Sun.) has three floors crammed full of good-quality used books—a browser's delight.

You'll need a map to find **Open Air Books & Maps** (25 Toronto St., 416/363-0719, www.openairbooksandmaps.com, subway: King,

10am-6pm Mon.-Fri., 10am-5pm Sat.), a downtown travel bookshop that's packed with guidebooks, travel narratives, and maps to destinations worldwide. It's behind a heavy black door on the lower level, at the corner of Adelaide and Toronto Streets downtown. The independently owned **Type Books** (883 Queen St. W., 416/366-8973, www.typebooks. ca, 10am-6pm Mon.-Wed., 10am-7pm Thurs.-Sat., 11am-6pm Sun.) not only has a good selection of all types of books, they also sponsor readings and literary events. Take the no. 501 Queen streetcar to Strachan Avenue.

CLOTHING, SHOES, AND ACCESSORIES
Queen Street West
Local designer Anne Hung sells pretty party frocks at her **Anne Hung Boutique** (829 Queen St. W., 416/364-7251, www.annehung. com, 12:30pm-7pm Tues.-Fri., 12:30pm-6:30pm Sat., noon-5pm Sun.). Work by more than 100 local jewelry designers is on view at the **Made You Look Jewelry Studio and Gallery** (1338 Queen St. W., 416/463-2136, www.madeyoulook.ca, 10am-8pm Mon.-Fri., 10am-6pm Sat., noon-5pm Sun.). They'll also custom-design special pieces. Part boutique and part art gallery, **Shop Girls** (1342 Queen St. W., 416/534-7467, www.shopgirls. ca, 11am-7pm Mon.-Wed., 11am-8pm Thurs.-Fri., 10am-6:30pm Sat., noon-5pm Sun.) is a collective that sells clothing, jewelry, and artwork by Canadian designers. Just north of Queen Street, **I Miss You** (63 Ossington Ave., 416/916-7021, noon-6pm Tues.-Wed., noon-7pm Thurs.-Sat., noon-6pm Sun.) stocks good-quality vintage designer labels and other clothing and accessories, including lots of 1960s cocktail dresses.

Distillery District
For beautifully crafted jewelry, handbags, and other accessories, peruse the wares—many by Toronto-based artisans—at **Corktown Designs** (5 Trinity St., 416/861-3020, www. corktowndesigns.com, 10am-7pm Mon.-Wed., 10am-8pm Thurs., 10am-9pm Fri.-Sat.,

11am-6pm Sun.). More than 200 Canadian designers created the distinctive clothing, jewelry, ceramics, glass, and other works at the **Distill Gallery** (24 Tank House Lane, 416/304-0033, www.distillgallery.com, 11am-7pm Mon.-Wed., 11am-8pm Thurs.-Fri., 10am-8pm Sat., 11am-6pm Sun.), for both browsing and buying.

Leslieville
Designer Christina Bergstrom creates the unique, vibrantly colored women's clothes she sells in her Leslieville shop, **Bergstrom Originals** (781 Queen St. E., 416/595-7320, www.bergstromoriginals.com, 11am-7pm Tues.-Wed., 11am-8pm Thurs.-Fri., 11am-7pm Sat., noon-6pm Sun.). Bergstrom complements her own pieces with shoes and accessories by other designers near and far. To get here from downtown, take the no. 501 Queen streetcar eastbound to Saulter Street. Playful contemporary and vintage-inspired dresses are ready to rock and roll at **Doll Factory by Damzels** (1122 Queen St. E., www.damzels.com, 11am-6pm Tues.-Sat., noon-5pm Sun.). Designers Kelly Freeman and Rory Lindo sell their own line, *Damzels in This Dress,* along with other clothing, gifts, and accessories. Take the no. 501 Queen streetcar to Caroline Avenue.

GIFTS AND NOVELTIES
Design geeks could lose themselves for hours at cool **Bergo Designs** (28 Tank House Lane, 416/861-1821, www.bergo.ca, 10am-8pm Mon.-Wed., 10am-9pm Thurs.-Sat., 11am-6pm Sun.) in the Distillery District. Alvar Aalto, Philippe Starck, and other international designers are represented, but you'll find quirky jewelry, toys, and gifts for your artsy friends, created by up-and-coming craftspeople.

Pawing through the assortment of stuff in the **Drake General Store** (1144 Queen St. W., 416/531-5042, ext. 101, www.drakegeneralstore.ca, 10am-9pm Mon.-Sat., 11am-6pm Sun.) is like visiting a cool friend who has a collection of weird and wonderful things. Need a stick-on mustache? Check. A classic CBC radio bag? Check. Croissant-shaped earrings, Canadian Mountie cock-tail napkins, or same-sex cake toppers? Check, check, and check. In addition to the Queen West location, they have stores in the Hudson's Bay store downtown (176 Yonge St., lower level, 416/861-6009, 10am-9:30pm Mon.-Fri., 9:30am-9:30pm Sat., 10am-7pm Sun.) and at Yonge and Eglinton (2607 Yonge St., 416/966-0553, 10am-7pm Mon.-Sat., 11am-6pm Sun.).

OUTDOOR GEAR

For clothing, boots, or camping supplies, visit **Mountain Equipment Co-Op** (MEC, 400 King St. W., 416/340-2667, www.mec.ca, 10am-7pm Mon.-Wed., 10am-9pm Thurs.-Fri., 9am-6pm Sat., 11am-5pm Sun.), the Toronto branch of Canada's largest outdoor retailer. The store rents out tents, sleeping bags, canoes, kayaks, cross-country skis, and snowshoes. You must become a co-op member to make a purchase; anyone can join by paying a lifetime membership fee of just $5.

Sports and Recreation

Whenever the sun shines, residents flock to the lakefront, the Toronto Islands, or the city's many parks, and there are numerous paths for walking and cycling. When winter comes, ice-skating keeps Toronto folks busy (unless they head north to the downhill ski and snowboard resorts). And year-round, Toronto is Canada's hub for professional sports, especially hockey, baseball, and basketball.

PARKS AND BEACHES

The city's best beaches are on the **Toronto Islands** (ferry: 9 Queens Quay West at Bay St., 416/397-2628, www.toronto.ca, round-trip adults $7, seniors and students $4.50, ages 3-14 $3.50). The south shore has several narrow but sandy stretches on Lake Ontario. There's also Ward's Island Beach, Gibraltar Beach, even a clothing-optional beach at Hanlan's Point. For a more urban beach experience, head for the pink umbrellas at **Sugar Beach** (25 Dockside Dr., at Queen's Quay E., www.toronto.ca, dawn-dusk daily, free). Part of Toronto's on-going waterfront redevelopment, this stretch of sand at the foot of Lower Jarvis Street faces Lake Ontario in the shadow of the Redpath Sugar Factory. You can't swim here, but it's a popular spot to sit in the sun. **HTO Park** (339 Queens Quay W.), a similar urban beach, is downtown west of Harbourfront Centre. The city's most beautiful parkland is **High Park**

(1873 Bloor St. W., 416/397-2628, www.toronto.ca/parks, subway: High Park, dawn-dusk daily, free). The park is in the city's west end, south of Bloor Street, with a large pond, playgrounds, hiking trails, and even a small zoo.

Note that the Lake Ontario waters are not always clean enough for safe swimming, so check on the water quality before you dive in. Phone the city's **Beach Water Quality Hotline** (416/392-7161) or check the Beach Water Quality page on the city website (www.toronto.ca). City staff will also post signs at the beach if bacteria levels are too high for healthy swimming.

BICYCLING

Toronto has hundreds of kilometers of bike lanes on city streets. However, if you're not an experienced urban cyclist, you may want to stick to one of the off-road cycling trails. The 56-kilometer (35-mile) **Martin Goodman Trail** runs along the Toronto lakeshore. It's part of the 1,400-kilometer (870-mile) **Waterfront Trail,** which follows the shores of Lake Erie and Lake Ontario from Windsor to the Quebec border. The **Toronto Islands** (ferry: 9 Queens Quay W. at Bay St., 416/397-2628, www.toronto.ca, round-trip adults $7, seniors and students $4.50, ages 3-14 $3.50) are another popular cycling spot. You can rent

Canada's First Urban National Park

Rouge National Urban Park will be Canada's first urban national park.

Imagine a "national park." Don't you think of an expansive wilderness, far from city skyscrapers, traffic jams, and noise? But on the eastern borders of metropolitan Toronto, Canada's newest nationally protected outdoor space will be the country's first urban national park: **Rouge National Urban Park** (office: 50 Bloomington Rd. W., Aurora, 905/713-6038, www.rougepark. com or www.pc.gc.ca, year-round, free).

A 47-square-kilometer (18-square-mile) parcel of land stretching from Lake Ontario in the south to the community of Markham in the north, Rouge Park has been a recreational playground for the Toronto region for many years. However, as development increasingly encroached on the parkland, many Torontonians began lobbying to provide greater protection for this natural area. In 2011, Rouge Park was approved to become part of Canada's national park system.

While Parks Canada is still sorting out the administrative details for Rouge to obtain its full national park status, the park is open to the public. Hiking trails crisscross Rouge Park's forested areas, and park staff lead periodic guided walks. You can look out over the Little Rouge Creek Valley from the **Glen Eagles Vista Trail** (7 Twyn Rivers Dr., Toronto)—a great place to take in the fall colors—or go for a swim in Lake Ontario from sandy **Rouge Beach** (195 Rouge Hills Dr., Toronto). Campers can pitch a tent or park their RV in the 125-site **Glen Rouge Campground** (7450 Kingston Rd., Toronto, 855/811-0111, www.trca.on.ca/GlenRouge, May-Oct., $25-31 tent sites, $37-43 electrical sites), the only camping spot within Toronto city limits.

Several sections of the park are accessible by public transit from downtown Toronto. To reach Glen Eagles, bus no. 85A Sheppard East from the Sheppard-Yonge subway station will drop you near the park. To Rouge Beach, you can take bus no. 54A Lawrence East from Eglinton station to the intersection of Lawrence Avenue East and Starspray Boulevard; alternatively, catch the GO Train to Rouge Hill, which is 1.3 kilometers (0.8 miles) from the beach entrance. A national park that you can reach by public transit? How cool and urban is that!

bikes ($8 per hour, tandems $15 per hour) and four-wheeled pedal bikes ("quadricycles") that seat two ($17 per hour) or four ($30 per hour) near the Centre Island pier.

To figure out the best cycling routes around Toronto, try the useful **Ride the City** (www.ridethecity.com/toronto) mapping tool, which plots the safest route between two points. You can get more information about cycling in Toronto, as well as a bike-route map, at www.toronto.ca/cycling. **Bike Share Toronto** (www.bikesharetoronto.com), a public bike-sharing system, lets you pick up a bike from one of 80 rental stations around the city, ride it to your destination, and return it to the nearest station when you arrive. The basic rental fee is $7 for 24 hours (or $15 for 72 hours); if you keep your rides short (up to 30 minutes per trip), that's all you pay. Since the service is designed for short hops, there are additional fees for each half-hour beyond the initial 30 minutes. Bikes are located throughout the downtown area (look for rental stations near the subway stops) and around the University of Toronto; there's a location map on their website.

In the Distillery District, you can rent bikes from **Segway of Ontario** (30 Gristmill Lane, 416/642-0008 or 866/405-8687, www.segway-ofontario.com, 1st hour $10, $5 per additional hour, $35 per day), which also offers Segway tours.

HIKING

The **Toronto Islands** (ferry: 9 Queens Quay W. at Bay St., 416/397-2628, www.toronto.ca, round-trip adults $7, seniors and students $4.50, ages 3-14 $3.50) and **High Park** (1873 Bloor St. W., 416/397-2628, www.toronto.ca/parks, subway: High Park, dawn-dusk daily, free) are popular hiking destinations. You can also hike the trails that wend around the property at the **Evergreen Brick Works** (550 Bayview Ave., 416/596-7670, www.evergreen.ca).

ICE-SKATING

Popular places to ice-skate are on the pond in front of City Hall, which becomes the seasonal **Nathan Phillips Square Rink** (100 Queen St. W., 416/304-1400, www.toronto.ca, 10am-10pm daily Nov.-Mar., skate rentals adults $10, kids $5), and at Harbourfront Centre's lakeside **Pond Rink** (Queen's Quay W., 416/973-4000, www.harbourfrontcentre.com, skate rentals adults $12). Skating season is weather-dependent but typically begins in

Explore Toronto's waterfront in a kayak or a traditional voyageur canoe.

late November or early December and continues until March.

KAYAKING AND CANOEING

To introduce your kids to canoeing or to try it yourself for the first time, head to the **Natrel Pond at Harbourfront Centre** (235 Queens Quay W., 416/973-4000, www.harbourfrontcentre.com, hours vary, $4) for a 15-minute paddle around the petite pond. Nearby, at the **Harbourfront Canoe and Kayak Centre** (283A Queens Quay W. at Rees St., 416/203-2277 or 800/960-8886, www.paddletoronto.com), you can rent canoes ($30 per hour, $60 per day), kayaks (single $30 per hour, $70 per day, double $40 per hour, $85 per day), and stand-up paddleboards (1st hour $30, $10 per additional hour). You can also rent canoes, kayaks, and pedal boats on the **Toronto Islands** (ferry: 9 Queens Quay W. at Bay St., 416/397-2628, www.toronto.ca, round-trip adults $7, seniors and students $4.50, ages 3-14 $3.50) during the summer. The rental shop is in the Boat House on Centre Island.

SPECTATOR SPORTS

As in most Canadian cities, hockey is Toronto's major sport, and the team to root for is the National Hockey League's **Toronto Maple Leafs** (http://mapleleafs.nhl.com).

They take to the ice at the Air Canada Centre (40 Bay St., 416/815-5400, www.theaircanadacentre.com), which is also the home court for the **Toronto Raptors** (www.nba.com/raptors), in the National Basketball Association.

The **Toronto Blue Jays** (416/341-1234 or 888/654-6529, www.bluejays.com), in Major League Baseball's American League, play their home games at the Rogers Centre (1 Blue Jays Way, 416/341-1000, www.rogerscentre.com) from spring through fall. Buy tickets online at **Ticketmaster** (www.ticketmaster.ca) or in person at the Rogers Centre **Box Office** (Gate 9, Bremner Blvd., 10am-6pm Tues.-Sat.). The city's Canadian Football League team, the **Toronto Argonauts** (416/341-2746, www.argonauts.ca), plays at the Rogers Centre, too.

Toronto has a professional men's soccer team, **Toronto FC** (416/360-4625, www.torontofc.ca). They play at BMO Field (170 Princes' Blvd.) on the Exhibition Place grounds, west of downtown. Tickets are available through **Ticketmaster** (www.ticketmaster.ca). To get to BMO field, take the no. 509 Harbourfront streetcar west from Union Station to Exhibition, or catch the no. 511 Bathurst streetcar south from Bathurst station (Bloor-Danforth line) to Exhibition. You can also take the GO train from Union Station to Exhibition.

Accommodations

Like most metropolitan areas, Toronto offers a range of lodgings from major international hotels to boutique properties to homey B&Bs. Accommodations are concentrated downtown, in the Bloor-Yorkville district, and in the Annex neighborhood around the University of Toronto, but anything within walking distance of the subway or streetcar can be convenient. If you like funky and modern, look for one of the city's "art" hotels or newer B&Bs.

If you're on a tight budget, and you're

visiting in summer, check out the residence halls on the University of Toronto campus, which offer basic but good-value rooms. Otherwise, for accommodations under $100, you're generally looking at hostels; most of Toronto's hostels have private rooms as well as dormitory beds. If you can spend a bit more ($125-175 for a double room) you'll have more choices among B&Bs and mid-range hotels. Outside the Christmas-New Year's holiday period, rates are typically lowest in winter.

Beware that most Toronto hotels,

particularly those downtown, charge for parking, which can add more than $50 per day to your tab. While free Wi-Fi has become much more common, some larger hotels still charge for Internet access.

DOWNTOWN AND THE FINANCIAL DISTRICT
Under $100

There's always something going on at the **HI-Toronto Youth Hostel** (76 Church St., subway: King, 416/971-4440 or 877/848-8737, www.hostellingtoronto.com, $31-47 dorm, $129-139 d), whether it's a pub crawl, karaoke night, or a summer barbecue. The hostel has more than 140 beds across nine floors in six-, eight-, and 10-bed dorms (male only, female only, and mixed); quad rooms with bunk beds; more spacious "deluxe" rooms with two or three single beds and a private bath; and private doubles with en suite baths. A basement café serves breakfast and dinner, or there is a common kitchen. Wi-Fi is free. The no. 504 King streetcar stops a block away at Church Street.

$100-150

One block east of busy Yonge Street, **Les Amis B&B** (31 Granby St., 416/591-0635, www.bbtoronto.com, subway: College, $95-105 s, $125-145 d), in a narrow 1870s townhouse, is on a quiet residential street. The five cozy guest rooms have wide-board floors, down duvets, and simple furnishings. On the second floor, one room has a private bath, while the other two share a bath; the two third-floor rooms share an adjacent bath. Owners Paul-Antoine and Michelle Buer serve meat-free breakfasts. Paul-Antoine is a photographer, and photos of his travels adorn the walls. The same owners also run Au Petit Paris B&B in the Bloor-Yorkville neighborhood.

Don't expect luxury at the 18-story **Bond Place Hotel** (65 Dundas St. E., subway: Dundas, 416/362-6061, www.bondplace.ca, subway: Dundas, $130-254 d), but do expect moderately priced comfort and style. The 285 guest rooms have been updated with white duvets and flat-screen TVs. The least expensive standard rooms are quite small, but some of the larger "deluxe" rooms have two separate sleeping areas—not separate rooms, but somewhat private. The building has a fitness room, and parking is available ($19 per night); there's also a charge for Wi-Fi. The no. 505 Dundas streetcar stops at Bond Street, right out front.

If you don't need a lot of space and you want a central downtown location at a moderate price, consider the **Strathcona Hotel** (60 York St., 416/363-3321, www.thestrathconahotel.com, subway: Union, $135-235 d). The rooms in this 12-story building, decorated with white duvets and red accents, cover the basics—decent beds, coffeemakers, TVs—with no extraneous frills. The street-facing rooms are noisier but bright; the interior rooms are quieter and darker. Wi-Fi is available for a fee.

$150-200

Built in the early 20th century, the 56-room **Hotel Victoria** (56 Yonge St., 416/363-1666 or 800/363-8228, www.hotelvictoria-toronto.com, subway: King, $149-229 d) is a petite but pretty boutique inn, convenient to downtown. The style starts in the art deco lobby with a black granite fireplace and marble columns, and continues upstairs, where rooms have black furniture, white duvets, and gold accents, along with iPod docks, coffeemakers, and free Wi-Fi. The standard rooms are cozy; for more space (plus a mini fridge), opt for a deluxe king or deluxe queen.

Canada's largest hotel and Toronto's most family-friendly, the 1,590-room **Eaton Chelsea Hotel** (33 Gerrard St. W., 416/595-1975 or 800/243-5732, http://chelsea.eaton-hotels.com, subway: College, $169-260 d, $285-385 suite), feels like a small city. There's always something for kids to do, including an indoor pool with a big water slide, games and crafts in the "Kid Centre," and the teen lounge, with video games, foosball, and movies. Relax in the top-floor adults-only pool and fitness room. Rooms range from 25-square-meter (275-square-foot) standards with a king, queen, or two doubles to slightly larger kitchenette units to two-bedroom "Family Fun" suites with bunk beds and a play area. Wi-Fi is free; parking is $29 (self-parking) and $39 (valet) daily.

With its colored neon lighting and sleek martini lounge, the lobby at the **Pantages Hotel Toronto Centre** (200 Victoria St., 416/362-1777 or 855/852-1777, www.pantages-shotel.com, subway: Queen, $169-299 d) has a space-age air. Upstairs, in the 89 serene suites, with hardwood floors, kings or queens topped with white duvets, kitchenettes, and washer-dryers, you'll feel like a contented Buddha. For even more relaxation, head for the Shizen Spa or the well-equipped 24-hour fitness room. One block south of Dundas Square and one block west of Yonge Street, the hotel is convenient to Massey Hall and Eaton Centre.

The **Cambridge Suites Hotel** (15 Richmond St. E., 416/368-1990 or 800/463-1990, www.cambridgesuitestoronto.com, $179-269 d) may not be as stylish as trendier boutique properties, but you get a lot of space for your money. The 229 modern units are all two-room suites with separate living and sleeping areas (with a flat-screen TV in each room), as well as kitchenettes stocked with fridges, microwaves, coffeemakers, dishes, and cutlery. The top floor of the 22-story building has a small workout room, a hot tub, and a sauna. Wi-Fi is free; parking is $27 per day.

$200-300

Built in 1929, the ★ **Fairmont Royal York** (100 Front St. W., 416/368-2511 or 866/540-4489, www.fairmont.com, subway: Union, $209-459 d) was once the tallest building in the British Empire. The solicitous staff and 1,365 rooms are gracious and welcoming, whether you're the Queen of England (yes, she's stayed here) or a regular Joe. Have a drink in the dark-paneled Library Bar or dinner in the contemporary Epic restaurant. Room rates vary significantly, so check for promotions online; to park your car overnight (valet only) adds $53. Sign up for the

Fairmont Royal York

Fairmont's frequent-stay program to get free Internet access during your stay.

As skinny as a guru, the 27-story tower of the **Cosmopolitan Hotel Toronto** (8 Colborne St., 416/350-2000 or 800/958-3488, www.cosmotoronto.com, $229-300) has a Zen feel. Each floor has only five sleek, modern guest rooms, with wood floors and kitchenettes; they even come with yoga mats. The larger Deluxe Suites, with washer-dryers, are configured either as a studio with sleeping and sitting areas or as a one-bedroom unit with a separate living room. Head for the fitness room or book a treatment in the spa. Tip: For the best views, ask for a room on the 20th floor or above.

They don't build hotels like this anymore: Retaining the elegance of a bygone era, the majestic ambience of **The Omni King Edward** (37 King St. E., 416/863-9700, www.omnihotels.com, subway: King, $229-359 d) begins in the lobby, with its ornate columns and plasterwork, soaring ceiling, and marble floors. Most of the 301 rooms aren't quite as grand, but they're comfortable, traditionally furnished retreats from the bustle of the surrounding Financial District; ask for one that's been recently renovated. Sign up for the Omni loyalty program before your stay to get complimentary Wi-Fi.

One King West (1 King St. W., 416/548-8100 or 866/470-5464, www.onekingwest.com, subway: King, $234-469 d), a deluxe centrally located condominium-hotel, caters to business travelers and couples with sleekly modern apartments for short or extended stays. The building combines the elegance of a former 1880s bank headquarters with a new tower that soars above the original structure. The suites are larger than typical hotel rooms and have kitchens with dishwashers and laundry facilities. Parking (valet only) is $40 per day; fortunately, you can leave the car at home, since you can walk to the underground PATH network and the subway.

Opposite City Hall, the **Sheraton Centre Hotel** (123 Queen St. W., 416/361-1000, www.sheratontoronto.com, subway: Osgoode, $229-489 d) has 1,377 guest rooms in two towers; the taller soars 43 stories above downtown. The rooms feel business casual, with white duvets, large desks, and leather arm chairs. The higher-priced club rooms on floors 36-42 have the best city views and provide access to the top-floor lounge, with complimentary breakfast, evening hors d'oeuvres, and Internet access (which normally costs $15 per day). There's an indoor-outdoor pool and a spacious health club. Parking is valet only ($48 per day).

Over $300

Larger-than-life photos of sports stars adorn the guest room walls of the deluxe, intimate ★ **Hotel Le Germain Maple Leaf Square** (75 Bremner Blvd., 416/649-7575 or 888/940-7575, www.germainmapleleafsquare.com, subway: Union, $369-517 d). With down duvets, espresso machines, and 40-inch flat-screen TVs, the 167 contemporary rooms have the expected luxuries. Many of the glass-walled showers open to the bedrooms;

pull the shades if you're feeling modest. The athletic artwork may inspire a visit to the well-equipped fitness room, and the expanded continental breakfast has cheeses, charcuterie, and pastries. Rates include Wi-Fi; parking (valet only) is $40 per night.

The Ivy at Verity (111d Queen St. E., 416/368-6006, ext. 300, www.theivyatverity.ca, $349-379 d) is a discreetly upscale boutique lodging inside a members-only private club for high-powered professional women. Accommodations are open to anyone, but the indoor pool, exercise room, and spa are for women only. The four deluxe guest rooms are decorated with eclectic light fixtures, balconies overlooking the pocket courtyard, and marble baths with rain showers and heated floors. Continental breakfast is served, and guests have access to the members' lounge for drinks or light meals. **George Restaurant** (647/496-8275, www.georgeonqueen.ca, lunch noon-2:30pm Mon.-Fri., dinner 5:30pm-10:30pm Tues.-Sat., lunch $18-26, dinner $21-31) shares the building, which once housed a chocolate factory, and provides room service for the Ivy's guests.

There's a lot to love at the luxurious Asian-style **Shangri-La Hotel Toronto** (188 University Ave., 647/788-8888 or 866/344-5050, www.shangri-la.com, subway: St. Andrew, Osgoode, $350-510), including always at-your-service staff, a window-lined fitness facility, a hammam spa, and an indoor pool with private cabanas and subtle lighting. And that's before you even walk into the 202 generously proportioned rooms and suites, outfitted with both terrycloth robes and kimonos, iPads to use during your stay, 46-inch flat-screen TVs, and capacious spa-like baths. Not pampered enough? Take afternoon tea (with sweets and finger sandwiches) in the lobby; the tea menu lists 75 varieties.

More than 450 original artworks decorate the deluxe, subtly Canadian-themed **Ritz-Carlton Toronto** (181 Wellington St. W., 416/585-2500 or 800/542-8680, www.ritzcarlton.com, subway: St. Andrew, $455-635 d). The 263 guest rooms are on floors

6-20; choose a south-facing high-floor room for views of the lake, or splurge on a spacious corner suite with bamboo floors and a separate living area. You can see the CN Tower from the indoor saltwater pool, and the large fitness center has the expected equipment. At the **Spa** (www.spamyblend-toronto.com), book a massage, facial, or yoga class. The restaurant **ToCa** (for "Toronto, Canada"; breakfast 6:30am-10:30am Mon.-Fri., 7am-11:30am Sat., 7am-11am Sun.; lunch 11:30am-2:30pm Mon.-Fri.; brunch 11:30am-3:30pm Sun.; dinner 5:30pm-10pm daily; lunch $19-34, dinner $24-55) serves Italian dishes with ingredients from Ontario and across the country.

THE ENTERTAINMENT DISTRICT
$150-200

Style without frills could be the slogan of **The Beverley Hotel** (335 Queen St. W., 416/493-2786, www.thebeverleyhotel.ca, $139-259 d), an 18-room European-style lodging. Decorated with black-and-white photos, guest rooms—on floors 2-4 above the hotel's restaurant—are small and simple sleeping spaces with white linens, flat-screen TVs, iPod docks, modern baths, and free Wi-Fi. The most spacious, the Queen Suites, have large street-facing windows; most other units have interior, frosted-glass windows, but if you're just here to snooze, maybe you won't care. Get here on the no. 501 Queen streetcar to John Street.

Hotel Ocho (195 Spadina Ave., 416/593-0885, www.hotelocho.com, $180-260 d) is a trendy 12-room inn in a rehabbed 1902 industrial building. In the spare but comfy rooms, the Ocho has kept many original features—exposed brick, stocky wood beams, factory-size windows—while adding flat-screen TVs, modern baths with rain showers, and contemporary art. Even if you don't stay here, stop into the espresso bar (with free Wi-Fi) or have cocktails and snacks in the lounge. The Ocho is two blocks north of Queen Street West; take the no. 501 Queen streetcar to Spadina or the no. 510 Spadina streetcar to Queen.

Shangri-La Hotel Toronto

$200-300

With 92 rooms and suites, the **Soho Metropolitan** (318 Wellington St. W., at Blue Jays Way, 416/599-8800 or 866/764-6638, www.metropolitan.com/soho, $220-475 d) feels quiet and intimate, occupying the first four floors of a condominium tower. In the bright and airy guest rooms, floor-to-ceiling windows, large walk-in closets, and marble baths with heated floors are standard. Set aside time for a workout in the health club or indoor lap pool. The hotel's **Luckee Restaurant and Bar** tempts with modern Chinese cuisine from celeb-chef Susur Lee, and **Wahlburgers** sports bar is all about the burgers. Take the no. 504 King streetcar to Peter Street, then walk two blocks south.

From the expansive lobby bar with its cartoon-style mural of the Toronto skyline, to the 102 guest rooms with sleek dark wood, white linens, and whimsical orange chairs, to the rooftop infinity pool overlooking the city, **Thompson Toronto** (550 Wellington St. W., at Bathurst St., 416/640-7778 or 888/550-8368, www.thompsonhotels.com, $265-539 d) is one stylish spot. You won't go hungry here, either: **Thompson Diner** ($12-18) is an upscale 24-hour diner and bar; window-lined **Colette Grand Café** (647/348-7000, www.colettetoronto.com, bakery 7am-6pm daily, dining room 11:30am-11pm Mon.-Fri., 5pm-11pm Sat., 10am-11pm Sun., lunch $19-36, dinner $28-44) is part French bakery and part chic Mediterranean dining destination; and **Wabora** (416/777-9901, www.waborasushi.com, 11am-11pm Sun.-Wed., 11am-midnight Thurs.-Sat., $18-42) is an eclectic fusion sushi spot imported from Bracebridge in Cottage Country. The no. 504 King streetcar stops one block away at Bathurst Street.

Over $300

Like its sister property at Maple Leaf Square, the 11-story **Hotel Le Germain** (30 Mercer St., 416/345-9500 or 866/345-9501, www.germaintoronto.com, $295-490 d), on a quiet side street one block from King, is run by a hip and helpful crew offering au courant accommodations with down duvets and large baths, many with glass showers facing the bedroom. Have a complimentary cappuccino in front of the fireplace in the lobby lounge, or head for the rooftop terrace, which has a putting green. Stylish **Victor Restaurant** (416/883-3431, www.victorrestaurant.com, 5pm-11pm daily, $14-35) serves sharing plates that work before theater or after an evening out. Wi-Fi is free; parking (valet only) is $38 per night.

BLOOR-YORKVILLE AND THE ANNEX
Under $100

From Wi-Fi-equipped "phone booths" to electrical outlets in the lockers, the little touches make **Planet Traveler** (357 College St., 647/352-8747, www.theplanettraveler.com, $31 dorm, $80 d), a privately-run hostel near Kensington Market, stand out. There's a colorful lounge, communal kitchen, coin-op laundry, and rooftop deck with views across downtown. The small dorms have six beds, a bath, and big windows. Basic private rooms share a bath with four other rooms, and there's an additional common washroom down the hall. Rates include continental breakfast and Wi-Fi. Take the no. 506 Carlton streetcar to Augusta Avenue, or the no. 510 Spadina streetcar to College Street.

$100-150

Annex Quest House (83 Spadina Rd., 416/922-1934, www.annexquesthouse.com, subway: Spadina, $105-120 d) is an ascetic but serene 18-room guesthouse, decorated with Indian-print cotton bedspreads, rag rugs on the wide-plank floors, and copper wash basins in the private baths; Wi-Fi is free. There's no breakfast, but the rooms have fridges and coffeemakers to do it yourself, or head for one of the cafés on nearby Bloor Street.

The owners of Les Amis B&B run a sister property, **Au Petit Paris B&B** (3 Selby St., 416/928-1348, www.bbtoronto.com/aupetit-paris, subway: Sherbourne, $99-105 s, $135-145 d), about a 10-minute walk from Yonge and Bloor. This homey bed-and-breakfast has four guest rooms in a narrow townhouse; rooms are decorated in bright, warm colors with wood floors, and all have private baths. There's no living room or lounge area for guests, but there is a top-floor deck, which is a lovely spot for an evening glass of wine. Vegetarian breakfast is served, and there's free Wi-Fi.

In the residential Annex neighborhood, **Lowther Suites** (88 Lowther Ave., 416/925-4600, www.lowthersuites.com, subway: St. George, Spadina, $130-395 d) has five spacious one- or two-bedroom apartments with full kitchens and washer-dryers in a renovated brick mansion. Rates include Internet access and parking. The property caters to independent travelers—there's no common area, food service, or other hotel-style services (although a caretaker is on call). It's well suited to longer-term stays.

Over $300

Toronto has plenty of luxurious lodgings, but one of the most deluxe is the intimate **Hazelton Hotel** (118 Yorkville Ave., 416/963-6300 or 866/473-6301, www.thehazeltonhotel.

com, $395-600 d). The 77 sizable, sound-insulated rooms have amenities like 47-inch flat-screen TVs, roomy rain showers, heated bath floors, and plush mattresses. There is a spa, a health club, and an indoor lap pool. The solicitous concierge service will arrange whatever you need. The hotel even has a private screening room in case you're hosting a film premiere or a playoffs party. If you're not traveling by chauffeured limousine, Bay is the most convenient subway station.

THE WEST END
$100-150

How about a stay in an art gallery? The main floor of the **Index G B&B** (50 Gladstone Ave., 416/535-6957, www.indexgbb.com, $90-95 s, $105-125 d) is a contemporary gallery space. Upstairs are five spare but arty guest rooms with original artwork on the walls. In the morning, help yourself to a simple continental breakfast (cereal, fruit, yogurt, coffee, tea) in the gallery. Wi-Fi is free. The no. 501 Queen streetcar stops at Gladstone Avenue, one block away, and the building is just a short stroll from the West Queen West action.

Personable proprietor Albert Tan welcomes guests to the **Suite Dreams Toronto B&B** (390 Clinton St., 416/538-0417, www.

suitedreamstoronto.com, subway: Christie, $150-199 d, $289 suite) in his comfortable townhome on a residential Koreatown street. The high-ceilinged top-floor suite runs the length of the house, with ample closet space. The rear-facing room on the second floor has a sleigh bed and a mini fridge; the sunny front room is a bit smaller. All have private baths, except for the basement-level garden room, which is gloomier but has direct access to the patio. Breakfasts include deliciously nutty granola from Albert's own secret recipe.

$150-200

As much a place to lounge, drink, and eat as to sleep, the arty ★ **Drake Hotel** (1150 Queen St. W., 416/531-5042 or 866/372-5386, www.thedrakehotel.ca, $189-339 d) is a cultural hub on West Queen West. Guest rooms range from the cozy Crash Pad (just big enough to crash) to the progressively larger Dens, Salons, and Suite, with hardwood floors, exposed brick walls, TVs, and original artwork. If you're staying with a special someone, you can order champagne, flowers, or something from the cheeky Pleasure Menu, from plumes of feathers to all manner of sex toys.

The Drake Hotel is a hub of activity on West Queen West.

$200-300

The funky ★ **Gladstone Hotel** (1214 Queen St. W., 416/531-4635, www.gladstonehotel.com, $199-275) is a combination art gallery and hotel in a restored 1889 building. The 37 rooms are all unique, designed by different artists. In the Teen Queen, the walls are plastered with photos of teen idols, while the Offset resembles a sleek urban loft. Most aren't large, but they are way cool, with flat-screen TVs, iPod docks, and Wi-Fi, and the hotel hosts all sorts of fun music, art, and literary events.

PEARSON INTERNATIONAL AIRPORT
$100-150

If you have an early departure or late arrival at the airport, hole up for the night at the cool, good-value **ALT Hotel Toronto Airport** (6080 Viscount Rd., Mississauga, 905/362-4337 or 855/855-6080, http://toronto.althotels.ca, $134 s or d). The 153 compact rooms in this modern 14-story tower are technology-friendly, with free Wi-Fi, lots of outlets for plugging in your devices, bedside reading lamps, flat-screen TVs, and iPod alarm clocks. In the lobby, you can shoot some pool or have a drink at the bar. When it's time to catch your flight, pick up a "grab-and-go" meal (fruit, pastries, salads, or sandwiches), then take the free Terminal Link train right to the gates.

Food

In multicultural Toronto, eating out can be a major cultural event, with choices ranging from Vietnamese, Thai, Japanese, Korean, and all manner of regional Chinese restaurants to Indian, Latino, Portuguese, Italian, Polish, Ukrainian, Caribbean, and more. You can find everything from simple noodle shops to roti stands to Indian buffets, often within a single neighborhood. And it's not all mom-and-pop joints, either; Toronto has some of Canada's top restaurants, a roster of celebrity chefs, and innovative dining rooms serving creative cuisine for every budget.

DOWNTOWN AND THE FINANCIAL DISTRICT

If you're hungry downtown, go underground. Scads of cafés and snack shops line the PATH network that runs underneath the city-center streets.

The **St. Lawrence Market** (93 Front St. E., 416/392-7219, www.stlawrencemarket.com, 8am-6pm Tues.-Thurs., 8am-7pm Fri., 5am-5pm Sat.) is a fun place to browse, whether you're looking for produce, cheeses, or a more substantial lunch. The **Nathan Phillips Square Farmers Market** (100 Queen St. W., 8am-2:30pm Wed. June-mid-Oct.) takes over the plaza in front of City Hall on Wednesday in summer and fall.

Asian

The **Banh Mi Boys** (399 Yonge St., 416/977-0303, www.banhmiboys.com, subway: College, Dundas, 11am-10pm Mon.-Fri., 11am-9pm Sat., noon-7pm Sun., $5-9) have made Vietnamese baguette sandwiches cool, serving modern versions laden with grilled pork, lemongrass tofu, even duck confit. Graffiti-inspired wall art, along with fusion tacos like kalbi beef and sides like kimchi fries, amp up the hipster quotient at this fast-food joint with style. There's a second location on the west side (392 Queen St. W., 416/363-0588). **Salad King** (340 Yonge St., 2nd Fl., 416/593-0333, www.saladking.com, subway: Dundas, 11am-10pm Mon.-Thurs., 11am-11pm Fri., noon-11pm Sat., noon-9pm Sun., $7-10) doesn't specialize in salads. It's a cheap and cheerful Thai eatery that's convenient for a quick bite downtown. They serve curries, noodles, and several choices for vegetarians.

If you do want a salad, try their green papaya version.

For more upscale Thai fare in a hipper setting, head for **Sabai Sabai Kitchen and Bar** (225 Church St., 647/748-4225, www.sabai-sabaito.ca, subway: Dundas, lunch 11:30am-2:30pm Mon.-Sat., dinner 5:30pm-10pm Mon.-Wed., 5:30pm-11pm Thurs.-Sat., $9-12), softly illuminated with dangling pendant lights. The bold-flavored dishes, designed to share, include *khao soi* (noodles with chicken or beef swimming in a rich coconut milk curry broth), grilled pork salad with fresh herbs, and garlicky stir-fried morning glory greens. Vegetarians have lots of options here.

Toronto was all abuzz when New York chef David Chang opened a branch of his uber-cool, modern Japanese **Momofuku** (190 University Ave., 647/253-8000, www.momofuku.com, subway: St. Andrew, Osgoode) in the Shangri-La Hotel. It's actually like a small city of restaurants: the casually-hip **Noodle Bar** (ground floor, 11:30am-3pm and 5pm-11pm daily, $6-18) serves ramen, pork buns, and other Asian small plates; loungey **Nikai** (2nd Fl., 5pm-11pm Mon.-Wed., 5pm-midnight Thurs.-Sat., $6-18) offers a similar menu but with a stronger cocktail focus; **Daisho** (3rd Fl., lunch 11:30am-2:30pm Mon.-Fri.,

dinner 5:30pm-10pm Sun.-Wed., 5:30pm-11pm Thurs.-Sat., $10-49) creates family-style dishes designed for groups of 4-10, including *bo ssäm* (pork and vegetable lettuce wraps) and salt-and-pepper lobster; and upscale **Shoto** (3rd Fl., dinner Tues.-Sat., $95-150 pp) crafts elaborate multicourse tasting menus.

Bakeries and Cafés

If you've never sampled the Canadian bacon known as peameal, or even if you have, a good place to try it is at the St. Lawrence Market's **Carousel Bakery** (416/363-4247), which sells the "world-famous peameal bacon on a bun" for a tasty, meaty lunch. Not a meat eater? The market's **Cruda Cafe** (647/919-5721, www.crudacafe.com, 9am-5:30pm Tues.-Thurs., 9am-6pm Fri., 7am-5pm Sat.) sells fresh juices, smoothies, raw wraps, and other vegetarian fare.

A handy spot for a snack or light meal in the Distillery District is **Brick Street Bakery** (27 Trinity St., 416/214-4949, www.brickstreetbakery.ca, 8:30am-6pm Sun.-Mon., 8:30am-7pm Tues.-Wed., 8:30am-8pm Thurs.-Sat., $5-9). Croissants, brioche, and scones pair with morning coffee; later in the day, sandwiches include lamb *kofta* (a lamb burger with fennel slaw), a chicken and bacon club,

Stop for a peameal bacon sandwich at St. Lawrence Market.

or a vegetarian combo of portobello mushrooms, zucchini, red peppers, and basil puree. Revive your flagging energy with a cookie or mini tart.

Stop into **SOMA Chocolatemaker** (32 Tank House Lane, 416/815-7662, www.somachocolate.com, 10am-8pm Mon.-Sat., 11am-6pm Sun.) in the Distillery District to sniff the chocolatey goodness and watch the chocolate makers at work. It's not easy to choose between the beautifully crafted bonbons and pastries, freshly made gelatos and sorbets, and hot chocolate drinks, including the Mayan chocolate spiced with ginger, orange peel, and chili. As their tagline says, it's "a place to eat, drink, and worship chocolate." Amen.

Contemporary

With sturdy pine tables and walls decorated with old photos, **The Gabardine** (372 Bay St., at Richmond, 647/352-3211, www.thegabardine.com, subway: Queen, 8am-10pm Mon.-Fri., $13-28) looks like it has always been in the Financial District; surprisingly, it opened in 2011. In the morning, stop in for pastries, oatmeal, or a breakfast sandwich; later in the day, it's upscale pub fare, such as sandwiches like a shrimp po' boy or Chinese barbecue pork, or larger plates: chicken pot pie, grilled skirt steak, or halibut with puy lentils. Because they cater to the office crowd, The Gabardine is closed on weekends.

Whether you're dining with a client, a special someone, or your great-aunt Tillie, the gracious staff at **Epic** (100 Front St. W., 419/860-6949, www.epicrestaurant.ca, subway: Union, 7am-10am, noon-2pm, and 5:30pm-10pm Mon.-Fri., 7am-2pm and 5:30pm-10pm Sat.-Sun., lunch $16-36, dinner $36-49), the flagship restaurant at the Fairmont Royal York Hotel, will ensure you're well cared for. The menu includes enough contemporary touches to keep things interesting while still offering options for more conservative palates. Order whatever is local and in season—whether it's a farm-fresh salad, Ontario rack of lamb, or a simple bowl of fresh strawberries to end your meal.

A long-standing special-occasion destination, **Canoe** (66 Wellington St. W., 416/364-0054, www.oliverbonacini.com, subway: King, St. Andrews, Union, 11:45am-2:30pm and 5pm-10:30pm Mon.-Fri., lunch $20-29, dinner $32-47) oversees the city from the 54th floor in the Toronto Dominion Bank Tower. Canadian ingredients predominate, at lunch in the classic *tourtière* (Quebecois meat pie), or in the evenings with the tea-smoked duck with pickled leeks or west coast halibut. You can assemble an all-Canadian cheese plate, or sample sweets like roasted Niagara peaches with yogurt mousse. The wine list also has a strong Canadian focus. Reservations are recommended; you'll feel most comfortable among the suits if you dress up, too.

Toronto's oldest restaurant, **The Senator** (249 Victoria St., 416/364-7517, www.the-senator.com, subway: Dundas, 7:30am-9pm Mon.-Fri., 8am-2:30pm and 4:30pm-9pm Sat., 8am-2:30pm Sun., lunch $7-15, dinner $14-24) certainly looks the part, with burgundy vinyl booths, a checkerboard floor, and a 1920s-style lunch counter. While the evening menu concedes to modern tastes, with house-smoked salmon, wine-braised short ribs, and burgers made of naturally raised beef, it's daytime classics like fresh-squeezed orange juice, eggs benedict, roast turkey sandwiches, and homemade meat loaf that have been bringing in the customers for decades.

THE ENTERTAINMENT DISTRICT

Centered along King Street West from University Avenue to Bathurst Street, this downtown neighborhood is home to many of the city's theaters, concert venues, and hip restaurants.

Asian

From his start as a Hong Kong kitchen apprentice to his rise as a Food Network star, chef Susur Lee has been wowing (and occasionally exasperating) the food world. His latest Toronto venture, **Luckee** (328 Wellington St. W., 416/935-0400, www.luckeerestaurant.

com, dinner 5:30pm-11pm Tues.-Sun., $12-29, dim sum brunch 11am-2:30pm Sat.-Sun., $7-12), a cool red-hued restaurant and bar at the Soho Metropolitan Hotel, takes the chef back to his Chinese roots, with uniquely Susur twists on Cantonese, Shanghai, and Sichuan dishes. Try the delicate lobster and asparagus dumplings, the unusual tofu skin and chrysanthemum leaf salad, or the black pepper beef. Lee's other Toronto restaurants are the loungey eponymous **Lee** (603 King St. W., 416/603-2205, www.susur.com) and the eclectic world-roaming **Bent** (777 Dundas St. W., 647/352-0092, www.bentrestaurant.com).

Bakeries and Cafés

SOMA Chocolatemaker (443 King St. W., at Spadina, 416/599-7662, www.somachoco-late.com, 9am-8pm Mon.-Wed., 9am-9:30pm Thurs.-Fri., noon-9:30pm Sat., 11am-6pm), an artisanal chocolate and gelato café with an original location in the Distillery District, lures those with a sweet tooth with hot choco-late, truffles, pastries, and ice cream.

Contemporary

The Oliver and Bonacini Restaurants group, which operates the high-end Canoe, among others, runs two eateries in the TIFF Bell Lightbox Theatre. Café-style **O&B Canteen** (330 King St. W., 416/288-4710, www.oliver-bonacini.com, 11am-10pm Mon., 11am-11pm Tues.-Fri., 10am-11pm Sat., 10am-10pm Sun., $7-22), in a window-lined see-and-be-seen street-level room, is perfect for a quick bite before a show, with audience favorites like pizzas, sandwiches, pastas, roast chicken, and grilled salmon. Their grab-and-go counter (8am-9pm daily) offers pastries and light meals to take out.

The more expensive seats—and more in-novative menus—are upstairs in the upscale **Luma Restaurant** (416/288-4715, www.oli-verbonacini.com, lunch 11:45am-3pm Mon.-Fri., dinner 5pm-10pm Mon.-Tues., 5pm-11pm Wed.-Sat., lunch $16-27, dinner $16-36), where you can lunch on scallops with curried cauliflower and Kamut pilaf, chicken salad with

puffed wild rice, or grilled prawn and corn fritters. In the evening, start with a cocktail like the Nighthawk (vodka, Frangelico, white chocolate, and espresso) or the Picante Violeta (tequila with prickly pear-jalapeño shrub), before digging into Oscar-worthy entrées like rabbit *cavatelli* with chard and asparagus or a roasted piglet with mustard spaetzle.

Marben (488 Wellington St. W., 416/979-1990, www.marbenrestaurant.com, brunch 11:30am-2:30pm Wed.-Fri., 11am-2:30pm Sat.-Sun., dinner 5pm-11pm Tues.-Sun., $18-26) is wildly popular for brunch, with dishes like Euro Trash (Nutella-stuffed french toast with red fruit flambé) and Stockholm Syndrome (a four-minute egg with lobster crème fraîche on flaxseed sourdough). The menu is no less interesting when the sun goes down, with salt cod *buñuelos;* smoked risotto with scallops, chorizo, and sea buckthorn; or Yucatán-style achiote-glazed beef. Get here on the no. 510 Spadina streetcar to Wellington, or the no. 504 King to Spadina or Portland.

French

Ask Torontonians to recommend a clas-sic French bistro and the name you'll keep hearing is **Le Select Bistro** (432 Wellington St. W., 416/596-6405, www.leselect.com, 11:30am-11pm Mon.-Wed., 11:30am-11:30pm Thurs.-Fri., 11am-midnight Sat., 10:30am-10:30pm Sun., lunch $13-26, dinner $16-35), an old favorite for steak frites, *choucroute garnie* (pork with sauerkraut), cassoulet, and other traditional bistro dishes. Always busy for brunch, they also offer a late-night menu—convenient for a post-theater bite. Take the no. 504 King streetcar to Spadina or Portland, or the no. 510 Spadina to Wellington.

Italian

Lounge at the long communal tables at ever-so-stylish **Buca** (604 King St. W., 416/865-1600, www.buca.ca, 11am-3pm and 5pm-10pm Mon.-Wed., 11am-3pm and 5pm-11pm Thurs.-Fri., 5pm-11pm Sat., 5pm-10pm Sun., $18-36), and start your evening with Italian shared plates like house-cured *salumi* or crispy pig ears. The unusual pastas might include handmade duck egg *bigoli* with duck-offal *ragù* or pork-blood spaghetti, and the pizzas might be topped with braised dandelions and anchovies or octopus, potatoes, and olives. The cave-like wine room has an intimate atmosphere. Take the no. 504 King streetcar to Portland Street; the restaurant entrance is down a narrow lane.

BLOOR-YORKVILLE AND THE ANNEX

Gourmet grocer **Pusateri's** (57 Yorkville Ave., at Bay St., 416/785-9100, www.pusateris.com, subway: Bay, 7:30am-8pm Mon.-Wed., 7:30am-9pm Thurs.-Fri., 7:30am-8pm Sat., 7:30am-7pm Sun.) is like a miniature Whole Foods Market, selling produce, cheeses, breads, and prepared foods. Prices are high, but so is the quality. Speaking of **Whole Foods Market** (87 Avenue Rd., 416/944-0500, www.wholefoodsmarket.com, subway: St. George, Bay, 9am-10pm Mon.-Fri., 9am-9pm Sat.-Sun.), the large natural foods retailer has a Yorkville outpost.

Asian

With its cartoon logo, red lanterns, and fast-food ambience, **Okonomi House** (23 Charles St. W., 416/925-6176, subway: Bloor-Yonge, 11am-10pm Mon.-Fri., noon-10pm Sat., $6-12) looks like a Japanese Denny's. But no matter—you're here for the *okonomiyaki*, a savory pancake that resembles a cross between an omelet and a crepe. Fried with cabbage, onions, and your choice of beef, pork, bacon, vegetables, squid, or shrimp, they're a quick, filling meal. It's worth the extra $0.50 to add salty bonito (fish flakes) and seaweed to punch up the flavor.

Vegetarian

Camros Organic Eatery (25 Hayden St., 416/960-0723, www.camroseatery.com, subway: Bloor-Yonge, 11am-7:30pm Mon.-Fri., noon-7pm Sat.) is a cheery cafeteria serving Persian-influenced vegetarian stews, rice dishes, and salads. The selection rotates, but you might find *gheyme* (yellow lentil and potato stew flavored with limes and plums), *adas polo* (brown rice with lentils, saffron, cinnamon, and raisins), or a lemony fresh kale salad. Prices depend on the number of dishes you select (2-dish combination $10.40, 3-dish $13.72, 4-dish $15.04). From Bloor-Yonge station, exit toward Hayden Street.

Live Organic Food Bar (264 Dupont St., at Spadina, 416/515-2002, www.livefoodbar.com, subway: Dupont, 11:30am-9:30pm Mon.-Thurs., 11:30am-10pm Fri., 11am-3pm and 4pm-10pm Sat., 11am-3pm and 4pm-9pm Sun., $12-20) is a vegan café near Casa Loma. This chipper orange and green space looks like one of their colorful composed salads, like the Detox, brimming with kale, parsley, kelp noodles, seaweed, and avocado. Among the many raw choices are pizza (the crust is made of walnuts) and a beet "burger" (beets mixed with nuts and sunflower seeds). Even the drinks nod to health-consciousness, in cocktails like a vodka, lime, and *kombucha* blend.

THE WEST END

Some of Toronto's most interesting eateries are along West Queen West, Ossington Avenue, and Dundas Street West—a hotbed of casually contemporary bistros, tapas joints, and fun and funky dining rooms.

Inexpensive eateries abound around Kensington Market and in Toronto's original Chinatown. Although no longer exclusively Old World Italian, Toronto's **Little Italy** (www.littleitalyintoronto.ca) district, along College Street west of Bathurst, is lively with sidewalk cafés and trattorias. Look for traditional Portuguese breads and the sweet custard tarts known as *pasteis de nata* in bakeries and cafés along Dundas Street West in **Little Portugal** (www.littleportugal.ca). If you want to sample pierogi or stuffed cabbage rolls, explore Roncesvalles Avenue, between Queen and Bloor Streets, in the community known as **Little Poland. Koreatown** (www.koreatownbia.com) is centered along Bloor Street West, between Bathurst and Christie Streets, where, in addition to restaurants serving traditional pork bone soup, spicy fried chicken, or grill-it-yourself barbecued meats, you'll find authentic Korean pastries.

Asian

West Queen West isn't only about hip cafés and funky diners. If you're craving a comforting bowl of soup, head for **Pho Tien Thanh** (57 Ossington Ave., 416/588-6997, 11am-10pm daily), which specializes in the traditional Vietnamese noodle soup called *pho*. Take the no. 501 Queen streetcar to Ossington, then walk two blocks north.

In Chinatown, watch the deft dumpling makers at work at ★ **Mother's Dumplings** (421 Spadina Ave., 416/217-2008, www.mothersdumplings.com, 11:30am-10pm Sun.-Thurs., 11:30am-10:30pm Fri.-Sat., $5-10), which specializes in *jiaozi*, steamed or boiled dumplings native to northeastern China. Order a steamer or three—filled with shrimp, egg, and chive; cabbage, mushroom, and tofu; or pork with pickled cabbage—to pair with excellent northern-style side dishes, like tofu strip salad (bean curd dressed with peppers and fragrant cilantro) or garlicky smashed cucumbers. Take the no. 510 Spadina streetcar to College or Nassau

Streets, or the no. 506 Carlton streetcar to Spadina Avenue.

A dingy basement room with about as much ambience as, well, a dingy basement room, **Chinese Traditional Buns** (536 Dundas St. W., 416/299-9011, 10am-10pm daily, $3-10) nonetheless cooks up simple, scrumptious specialties of China's western regions. Try the Xi'an cured pork sandwich (like a Chinese pork slider), or any of the hand-pulled noodles, including the ground meat-topped *dan dan mien* or the super-spicy Shanxi-style noodles. It's in Chinatown, just west of Spadina Avenue; take the no. 505 Dundas streetcar to Spadina, or the no. 510 Spadina streetcar to Dundas.

Sheltered from the busy food court in the Village by the Grange building, the surprisingly serene **Manpuku** (105 McCaul St., 416/979-6763, www.manpuku.ca, subway: St. Patrick, 11:30am-8pm Mon.-Wed., 11:30am-11pm Thurs.-Fri., noon-11pm Sat., $5-7) is a good choice for an inexpensive Japanese meal near the Art Gallery of Ontario, which is just across the street. Choose from simple *udon* noodle soups, rice plates, and curries.

Lamesa Filipino Kitchen (669 Queen St. W., 647/346-2377, www.lamesafilipinokitchen.com, dinner 5pm-10pm Tues.-Sun.,

Hodo Kwaja in Koreatown

Le Ti Colibri offers tastes of the Caribbean in the Kensington Market neighborhood.

8am-7pm Sun.) crafts luscious pastries, *macarons,* and chocolates.

It's not easy to get into the **Easy Restaurant** (1645 Queen St. W., 416/537-4893, www.easyrestaurant.ca, 9am-5pm daily, $10-19), at least on the weekends, when this funky diner has long been an all-day-breakfast favorite. The only problem with ordering the signature *huevos divorciados* (poached eggs with black beans, tortillas, salsa, guacamole, and ancho chili jam) is that you'll be hungry again in about three days. Take the no. 501 Queen or the no. 504 King streetcar to Roncesvalles Avenue.

The specialty at Korean bakery **Hodo Kwaja** (656 Bloor St. W., 416/538-1208, subway: Christie, www.hodokwaja.ca, 9am-10pm Mon.-Sat.) is walnut cake, a walnut-shaped pastry filled with red-bean paste or a slightly sweet potato mixture. Even better are the brown sugar pancakes with peanuts; check the website for current baking times, so you can eat these excellent snacks while they're hot.

brunch 11am-3pm Sat.-Sun., $7-24) aims to make this Asian cuisine more accessible, creating modern interpretations of Filipino classics in small-plate versions designed for sharing. The friendly crew running this fun restaurant, just west of Bathurst Street, is quick to tell you about dishes like sweet-tart green mango salad with corn nuts, or *halo halo sisig,* a mix of chicken, pork, and beef, topped with a fried egg, and to pour your Filipino Shandy (beer and *calamansi* juice), or Lolo Cool J (bourbon, ginger, pineapple syrup, and lemon).

Bakeries and Cafés

Craving croissants, brioche, or *pain au chocolat?* Take the no. 501 Queen streetcar to Strachan Avenue to find **Clafouti Patisserie** (915 Queen St. W., 416/603-1935, www.clafouti.ca, 8am-6pm Thurs.-Sun., 8am-5pm Mon.-Tues.), a cozy French café. One block east, **Nadège Patisserie** (780 Queen St. W., 416/368-2009, www.nadege-patisserie.com, 8am-8pm Mon.-Wed., 8am-9pm Thurs.-Sat.,

Caribbean

Escape to the islands at **Le Ti Colibri** (291 Augusta Ave., 416/925-2223, www.leticolibri.com, noon-7pm Tues.-Sun., call for extended summer hours, $8-12), a petite Kensington Market eatery serving *accras de morue* (codfish fritters), *calaloo* (a greens-filled stew), and creole-inspired sandwiches. Order at the counter, then sip a sorrel-ginger punch as you settle on the tiny back patio, where the reggae tunes and French-Caribbean flavors will almost transport you to Martinique or Guadeloupe. Take the no. 506 Carlton streetcar to Major or Augusta.

Contemporary

"Party like you're in Barcelona" could be the motto of lively **Bar Isabel** (797 College St., 416/532-2222, www.barisabel.com, 6pm-2am daily, $7-59), where the inventive tapas, accompanied by equally imaginative cocktails, have earned plenty of kudos. You might sip an Isabel Fashioned (made with bacon-infused bourbon), while you graze on cured sardines,

Serrano ham, and *pintxos* topped with salt cod and *chistorra* (sausage), or go big with a plate of razor clams or an entire grilled octopus. The signature dessert is a Basque cake topped with sherry cream. Ride the no. 506 Carlton streetcar to Shaw.

With horse tartare, beef heart with spring vegetables, and tongue on brioche, the menu at **The Black Hoof** (928 Dundas St. W., at Bellwoods Ave., www.theblackhoof.com, 6pm-1am Thurs.-Sat., 6pm-11:30pm Sun.-Mon., small plates $9-25) reads like a challenge—at least if you don't normally nibble the nasty bits. But if you're eager to embrace nose-to-tail eating, join the hordes at this mod meatery for tapas and a cocktail or glass of wine. Black Hoof doesn't take reservations, so prepare to wait, and credit cards are not accepted, either. The no. 505 Dundas streetcar will get you here.

Crowds of carnivores are cruising into **Parts and Labour** (1566 Queen St. W., at Dowling Ave., 416/588-7750, www.partsandlabour.ca, dinner 6pm-2am Wed.-Sat., brunch 11am-2pm Sun., small plates $15-22), where shattered windshields and recycled lights decorate the garage-like space. The modern meat-centric menu rumbles from beef tartare with pickles and a daily *crudo* (cured seafood) to maple-glazed pork belly with navy beans. In The Shop, on the lower level, you can listen to live music most weekends. Hop on the no. 501 Queen streetcar; it stops in front of the restaurant.

Nibbles like gorgonzola crostini with kale and raisins, Mexican flank steak salad, and shrimp baked in a *piri piri*-garlic butter sauce bring the neighbors and visitors to the **Fat Cat Wine Bar** (331 Roncesvalles Ave., 416/535-4064, www.fatcat.ca, 5pm-10pm Mon.-Thurs., 5pm-11pm Fri.-Sat., small plates $5-12) to unwind over a glass of wine and inventive small plates. The no. 506 Carlton streetcar toward High Park stops at Roncesvalles Avenue, a few blocks north of the restaurant.

Italian

Every neighborhood needs a sociable wine bar and Italian eatery like ★ **Enoteca Sociale** (1288 Dundas St. W., 416/534-1200, www.sociale.ca, 5pm-11pm daily, $13-18), where you can bring the family, a pal or two, or a special someone to sample from the large selection of wines and Roman-style plates. There are several pastas, like orecchiette with squid and semi-cured tomatoes, or a simple spaghetti, an albacore tuna *conserva*, and heartier plates like sea bream with cauliflower *ragù*. Book ahead—the restaurant is small and frequently busy—and get here on the no. 505 Dundas streetcar to Dovercourt, just west of Ossington.

Always-packed **Pizzeria Libretto** (221 Ossington Ave., at Dundas, 416/532-8000, www. pizzerialibretto.com, 11:30am-11pm daily, pizzas $11-17) tames the hungry hordes with Neapolitan-style pizza, paired with interesting salads like arugula with pears, walnuts, and piave cheese, or antipasto platters laden with cured meats and regionally made cheeses. Take the no. 505 Dundas streetcar to Ossington Avenue.

Mexican and Latin American

The only thing "jumbo" about this tiny Kensington Market shop may be the appetites of the patrons who flock here for the signature stuffed pastry. **Jumbo Empanadas** (245 Augusta Ave., at Nassau, 416/977-0056, 9am-8pm Mon.-Sat., 11am-8pm Sun., $5-6) serves tasty Chilean empanadas filled (more traditionally) with beef or chicken with olives and hard-boiled egg, or (more Toronto) with vegetables, including a spinach-mushroom-pepper mélange. Take the no. 510 Spadina streetcar to Nassau Street, or the no. 506 Carlton streetcar to Major or Augusta.

Tacos are the specialty at lively Mexican café **El Trompo** (277 Augusta Ave., 416/260-0097, www.eltrompo.ca, 11am-8pm Tues.-Thurs., 11am-9pm Fri.-Sat., 11am-6pm Sun., $6-13) in the Kensington Market district. They come in plates of four or five, so ask for a combination: pork *al pastor* with pineapple and cilantro, slightly spicy chorizo, grilled beef with onions, or chipotle-sauced chicken.

Other choices include *queso fundido* (like a cheese fondue) and quesadillas. If you're not drinking beer or a margarita, try cinnamon-scented *horchata* or fruity *jamaica*. Get off the no. 506 Carlton streetcar at Major or Augusta, and walk one block south.

Portuguese

When you tire of grunge waitstaff, warehouse-bare rooms, and hipper-than-thou pig ear-filled menus, retreat to Old World **Chiado** (864 College St., 416/538-1910, www.chiadorestaurant.com, noon-2:30pm and 5pm-10pm Mon.-Fri., 5pm-10pm Sat.-Sun., lunch $16-23, dinner $30-48), where dignified waiters wear crisp white aprons and candlelit tables are dressed in starched white cloths. The menu is "progressive Portuguese"; the salt cod is grilled, then roasted with olive oil and garlic, and traditional *piri piri* sauce glazes the pan-seared monkfish. If the prices seem rich, come for lunch or a selection of tapas ($5-12). Take the no. 506 Carlton streetcar west to Ossington Avenue.

THE EAST END

What to eat in Toronto's East End? Head to the Danforth, also known as Greektown, for Greek food, Little India (the Indian Bazaar) for food from South Asia, and Leslieville for fine contemporary fare in laid-back neighborhood settings.

Big Carrot Natural Foods (348 Danforth Ave., 416/466-2129, www.thebigcarrot.ca, subway: Chester, 9am-9pm Mon.-Fri., 9am-8pm Sat., 11am-6pm Sun.) is a well-stocked natural foods market in the Danforth neighborhood.

Contemporary

One of the pioneers of Leslieville's foodie renaissance, **Edward Levesque's Kitchen** (1290 Queen St. E., 416/465-3600, www.edwardlevesque.ca, lunch noon-3pm Thurs.-Fri., dinner from 5:30pm Tues.-Sat., brunch 9am-3pm Sat.-Sun., lunch $9-16, dinner $18-32) is perpetually packed for their just-creative-enough weekend brunch. But with entrées like spaghettini with smoked chicken

and roasted olives, spice-crusted salmon with kale and quinoa tabbouleh, or wild scallops served with sweet potato mash, this laid-back French-influenced bistro is a worthy choice for dinner, too. Take the no. 501 Queen east to Leslie, then walk two blocks farther east.

At neighborhood bistro ★ **Ruby Watchco** (730 Queen St. E., 416/465-0100, www.rubywatchco.ca, dinner Tues.-Sat., $49 prix-fixe), wildly imaginative chef and co-owner Lynn Crawford, of Food Network Canada's *Pitchin' In,* and her team serve a four-course prix fixe menu that changes every night. Examples of Crawford's wow-worthy locally sourced spreads include fried chicken served with cheesy polenta, grilled broccoli, and carrots with arugula pesto, or raw-milk cheese paired with charred grapefruit, orange jelly, almonds, and watercress. Peruse the weekly dishes on the restaurant's website, but phone for reservations. From downtown, take the no. 501 Queen streetcar east to Broadview.

Down a lane near the Distillery District, ★ **Gilead Café and Wine Bar** (4 Gilead Pl., at King St. E., 647/288-0680, www.jamiekennedy.ca, breakfast 8am-11am Mon.-Sat., lunch 11am-3pm Mon.-Sat., brunch 10am-3pm Sun., dinner 5:30pm-10pm Tues.-Sat., breakfast $3-6, lunch $9-17, brunch $6-14, dinner $12-23) is a casual contemporary café run by celebrity chef Jamie Kennedy. Arty types hang here for coffee, pastries, and free Wi-Fi; later in the day are soups, salads, and entrées like Moroccan-spiced chickpea and vegetable stew made from locally sourced ingredients. In the evenings the space morphs into an upscale wine bar. Reservations are accepted for evenings only.

Greek

The menu is simple at **Athens Pastries** (509 Danforth Ave. at Logan Ave., 416/463-5144, www.athenspastries.com, subway: Chester, Pape, 9am-11pm Sun.-Thurs., 9am-midnight Fri.-Sat., $4-6), a Greek café in the Danforth neighborhood. Spinach-, cheese-, or meat-filled pies wrapped in a flaky phyllo dough, as well as a few sweets, including *loukoumades* (honey doughnuts) that pair beautifully with a strong cup of coffee.

Indian

A long-established restaurant in the Little India neighborhood, **Udupi Palace** (1460 Gerrard St. E., 416/405-8189, www.udupipalace.ca, noon-10pm Sun.-Thurs., noon-11pm Fri.-Sat., $6-10) specializes in south Indian vegetarian and vegan dishes, including a lengthy list of *dosas,* crisp pancakes that come stuffed with combinations of potatoes, onions, vegetables, or *paneer* (a cheese). Don't expect much ambience in the cavernous space; it's all about the food. Take the no. 506 Carlton streetcar to Ashdale Avenue.

Information and Services

VISITOR INFORMATION

Tourism Toronto (416/203-2500 or 800/499-2514, www.seetorontonow.com), the city's convention and visitors association, has loads of information on their website to help you plan a Toronto visit, including a detailed calendar of events around town. At Union Station, the provincial **Ontario Travel Information Centre** (65 Front St. W., 416/314-5899, www.ontariotravel.net) can provide information about travel around Toronto and elsewhere in the province.

MEDIA AND COMMUNICATIONS

Canada's two national newspapers, the **Globe and Mail** (www.theglobeandmail.com) and the **National Post** (www.nationalpost.com), are headquartered in Toronto, and the city has two other daily newspapers, the **Toronto Star** (www.thestar.com) and the **Toronto Sun** (www.torontosun.com). **Toronto Life Magazine** (www.torontolife.com), published monthly in print and available online, covers the arts, restaurants, and things to do, as does **Now** (www.nowtoronto.com), **Where Toronto** (www.where.ca), **blogTO** (www.blogto.com), and **Post City News** (www.postcity.com).

Transportation

GETTING THERE

As Canada's largest city, Toronto has flights from many parts of the world, as well as train and bus connections from around Ontario, from major Canadian cities, and from many U.S. points as well.

Air
Toronto's Pearson Airport

Toronto's **Pearson International Airport** (YYZ, 6301 Silver Dart Dr., Mississauga, 416/247-7678 or 866/207-1690, www.torontopearson.com) is Canada's largest, with flights from across Canada, the United States, Europe, and Asia. The airport is 24 kilometers (15 miles) northwest of downtown in the suburb of Mississauga. Most major Canadian and U.S. carriers and many international airlines fly into Toronto.

Pearson Airport has two terminals, Terminal 1 and Terminal 3. Check with your airline or the airport website to confirm which terminal you need. The free **Terminal Link Train** runs between the two terminals and to Viscount Station, where some rental car shuttles pick up customers and where the ALT Hotel Toronto Airport is located. Slated to begin operating in 2015, the **Union-Pearson Express** (www.upexpress.com, one-way adults $27.50, seniors and students $23.40, ages 6-12 $13.75, families $55), a rail link between Union Station downtown and Pearson Airport, will include stations at Terminal 1, the Weston and Bloor GO stations, and at Toronto's Union Station. It should cut travel time between downtown and the airport to about 25 minutes.

You can also travel between downtown and the airport by public transit; it's slower but cheaper than the Union-Pearson Express. From the airport, catch the **no. 192 Airport Rocket bus** ($3) to the subway. It runs to Kipling station, on the Bloor-Danforth line, which goes from west to east across the city. Get a transfer on the bus, so you don't have to pay another fare to board the subway. The first no. 192 bus leaves the airport at 5:40am Monday-Saturday and at 8am Sunday; the last departure from the airport is at 2am. Service runs every 10 to 20 minutes.

You need exact change to pay your fare on the bus. You can also purchase a single-fare ticket from a **TTC ticket machine** inside Terminal 1. There are two ticket vending machines on the Ground Transportation level, just inside from where the TTC buses stop. The machines accept cash or credit cards. Once you're on the subway, you'll need to transfer again from the Bloor-Danforth line if you're headed to the Union Station area, the Harbourfront, or other points downtown. Get off at St. George Station, and change to the Yonge-University-Spadina line heading southbound. Between 2am and 5am, when the no. 192 Airport Rocket isn't running, you can instead take the **no. 300A Bloor-Danforth bus** ($3), which operates from the airport into the city along Bloor Street and Danforth Avenue, essentially following the route of the Bloor-Danforth subway line. Buses run about every 30 minutes.

A taxi from Pearson airport to downtown Toronto costs $45-60 and generally takes 30-45 minutes, depending on traffic conditions and the destination.

Toronto City Airport

Toronto has a second, smaller airport on the Toronto Islands, the **Billy Bishop Toronto City Airport** (YTZ, www.torontoport.com). **Porter Airlines** (416/619-8622 or 888/619-8622, www.flyporter.com) is the main carrier serving this airport. Porter flies from Toronto to the Ontario cities of Ottawa, Windsor, Sudbury, Sault Ste. Marie, and Thunder Bay. It also flies to Montreal, Quebec City, Halifax, Moncton, and St. John's in Canada and to Boston, Chicago, Newark, and Washington Dulles in the United States. **Air Canada** (514/393-3333 or 888/247-2262, www.aircanada.com) flies from Toronto City Airport to Montreal.

For an airport on an island, the Toronto City Airport is surprisingly easy to get to, in part because it's so close to downtown. A **free ferry** (5:30am-midnight daily) runs between the airport and the foot of Bathurst Street about every 15 minutes. One of the world's shortest ferry routes, the crossing takes just a few minutes. As this book went to press, a new underground pedestrian tunnel between the airport and the mainland was under construction, so you will be able to walk to and from the island.

Once you're on the mainland, you can take Porter Airlines' free **shuttle bus** downtown, which departs approximately every 15 minutes. The downtown shuttle stop is at the Fairmont Royal York Hotel (100 Front St. W.), opposite Union Station. Alternatively, you can catch the no. 509 streetcar to Union Station or the no. 511 streetcar to the Bathurst subway station.

Buffalo-Niagara International Airport

If you're traveling to Toronto from the United States, you may find lower fares to **Buffalo-Niagara International Airport** (BUF, 4200 Genesee St., Cheektowaga, NY, 716/630-6000 or 877/359-2642, www.buffaloairport.com). Flying into Buffalo can also be convenient if you're planning to visit the Niagara region as part of your trip, since you can stop in Niagara between Toronto and Buffalo.

The cheapest way to travel between Toronto and the Buffalo airport is **Megabus** (705/748-6411 or 800/461-7661, www.megabus.com, 3-3.5 hours, $10-23), which runs two buses a day in each direction. **Greyhound** (www.greyhound.ca, 3.5-4.5 hours, $20-48) also runs several times a day between Toronto and Buffalo airport, with a 30-minute layover in downtown Buffalo. Several other shuttle and limo services operate between Toronto and Buffalo airport; check the Buffalo airport website for a complete list.

Train

Toronto's rail depot is **Union Station** (65 Front St. W., www.toronto.ca/union_station) downtown. VIA Rail, Amtrak, and GO Transit trains all run to Union Station, which is also a stop on the Toronto subway (Yonge-University-Spadina line).

VIA Rail

Toronto is a hub for the **VIA Rail** (888/842-7245, www.viarail.ca) trains that travel across Canada. Trains from the east travel to Toronto from Ottawa, Kingston, and Montreal; you can connect in Montreal for Quebec City, Moncton, and Halifax. Trains traveling west go to Winnipeg, Saskatoon, Edmonton, Jasper, and Vancouver. Shorter routes within Ontario operate between Windsor, London, and Toronto; between Sarnia, London, and Toronto; and between Niagara Falls and Toronto.

From Montreal to Toronto (5-6 hours, one-way economy adults $50-111, ages 2-11 $50-60), VIA Rail runs six trains a day in each direction Sunday-Friday and four on Saturday. From Ottawa to Toronto (4-4.5 hours, one-way adults $49-144, ages 2-11 $49-72), seven trains run in each direction Monday-Friday, four on Saturday, and six on Sunday. Most of the Montreal and Ottawa trains stop at Kingston en route to Toronto. There are several daily trains between Windsor and Toronto (4-4.5 hours, one-way economy adults $50-80, ages 2-11 $36-40) and one a day between Sarnia and

Toronto's Union Station is the city's transportation center.

Toronto (4.5 hours, one-way economy adults $44-99, ages 2-11 $36-50). Both the Windsor and Sarnia trains travel via London. VIA Rail runs one train daily in each direction between Toronto and Niagara Falls (2 hours, one-way adults $23-46, ages 2-11 $22-23).

VIA's flagship route, *The Canadian,* crosses Canada from Vancouver to Toronto via Jasper, Edmonton, Saskatoon, and Winnipeg. If you do the trip nonstop, it takes 3.5 days. There are departures three times a week in each direction May through mid-October and twice a week the rest of the year. Fares vary by class of service; choose from options that include a seat, a bunk, or a private cabin. Within Ontario, you can catch *The Canadian* to Toronto from Sudbury or Parry Sound, although the train stops in both those communities in the middle of the night.

Amtrak

The **Amtrak *Maple Leaf*** (800/872-7245, www.amtrak.com, 12.5 hours, adults $121-153, ages 2-12 $61-92) travels from New York

City's Penn Station to Toronto's Union Station (65 Front St. W., 311/392-2489). The train runs once a day, with major stops at Poughkeepsie, Albany, Syracuse, Rochester, Buffalo, Niagara Falls (New York), Niagara Falls (Ontario), St. Catharines, Grimsby, Aldershot (in Burlington), and Oakville en route to Toronto.

If you're coming from Detroit, you can cross the border to Windsor and catch the VIA Rail train from there. From Chicago and U.S. points farther west, there's no direct rail service to Toronto. You can either take the Amtrak *Wolvervine* train from Chicago to Detroit (6.5 hours), where you can cross the border and transfer to VIA Rail; or take the Amtrak *Lake Shore Limited* train from Chicago to Buffalo (10.5 hours). From Buffalo, change to the *Maple Leaf* or catch a bus on to Toronto. On any of these routings, be prepared for long layovers.

GO Trains

GO Transit (416/869-3200 or 888/438-6646, www.gotransit.com) operates a network of trains and buses that travel between the suburbs and surrounding communities and Toronto's city center. It's primarily a commuter option, so most schedules are optimized for business days, with lots of service into Toronto in the mornings and out of the city in the evenings, and less frequent service on the weekend. Seven GO Train lines link Toronto with nearby cities, including Oakville, Burlington, Hamilton, Milton, Brampton, Georgetown, Barrie, Richmond Hill, Markham, Lincolnville, and Oshawa. GO also provides seasonal service to Niagara Falls, running weekends and holidays from late May through mid-October.

Bus

The **Toronto Coach Terminal** (610 Bay St., 416/393-7911, www.torontocoachterminal.com) is the city's main long-distance bus depot, located one block north of the corner of Dundas and Bay. The closest subway station is Dundas, two blocks east. You can also take the no. 505 Dundas streetcar to Bay Street.

Greyhound

Greyhound (www.greyhound.ca) reaches Toronto from many Canadian and U.S. cities, although many routes involve a change of buses along the way. Greyhound runs frequent buses between Toronto and Ottawa (5-6 hours, one-way adults $35-84, ages 2-11 $35-64); from Montreal (8-9 hours), passengers change buses in Ottawa; from Quebec City, Halifax, and points farther east, transfers are in both Montreal and Ottawa. From the west, Greyhound reaches Toronto from Calgary (52 hours) and Winnipeg (32 hours), stopping in Thunder Bay, Sault Ste. Marie, and Sudbury en route. From Vancouver, passengers change buses in Calgary; from Edmonton, transfers are in either Calgary or Winnipeg.

From the United States, Greyhound runs buses to Toronto from New York City (10-11.5 hours, one-way adults $45-85, ages 2-11 $45-64), with stops in Syracuse and Buffalo. To Toronto from Boston (13.5-17.5 hours), transfers are in Buffalo or Syracuse; from Philadelphia (14-17.5 hours) and Washington DC (16-19 hours), transfers are in New York City. Greyhound has several daily buses to Toronto from Detroit (5.5-6 hours), with stops in Windsor and London, and twice a day from Chicago (12 hours).

Ontario Northland

Ontario Northland (800/461-8558, www.ontarionorthland.ca) runs buses between Toronto and Northeastern Ontario, including the Muskoka Lakes, Parry Sound, Sudbury, Temagami, and Cochrane.

Megabus

Megabus (705/748-6411 or 800/461-7661, www.megabus.com) has some of the best fares to Toronto from Niagara Falls (2 hours, one-way $12-18), Kingston (3 hours, one-way $15-59), Montreal (6 hours, one-way $19-64), New York City (12 hours, one-way $30-85), Syracuse (5.25-5.75 hours, one-way $21-55), Washington DC (15 hours, one-way $45-63), Baltimore (13.5 hours, one-way $45-63), and Philadelphia (11.5 hours, one-way $45-63). On some routes, one-way sale fares may drop as low as $1.50, so check the website for deals, particularly if you have flexible travel dates.

GO Buses

In addition to a commuter train network, **GO Transit** (416/869-3200 or 888/438-6646, www.gotransit.com) runs buses between surrounding communities and downtown Toronto. GO Transit buses arrive and depart from the **Union Station GO Bus Terminal** (141 Bay St., at Front St. W.), not from the Toronto Coach Terminal. Among the main GO bus routes to and from Toronto are routes from Niagara Falls, St. Catharines, Hamilton, Kitchener, Waterloo, Cambridge, Guelph, Orangeville, Barrie, and Peterborough.

Car

Toronto is 450 kilometers (280 miles) from Ottawa, 558 kilometers (349 miles) from Montreal, 2,115 kilometers (1,322 miles) from Winnipeg, 1,926 kilometers (1,204 miles) from Halifax, and a long-haul 4,550 kilometers (2,844 miles) from Vancouver.

Several major highways run in and around the Toronto area. The **Gardiner Expressway** follows the lakeshore into downtown Toronto. West of the city, it connects with Queen Elizabeth Way (known as the QEW), which despite its noble-sounding name is a traffic-clogged multilane highway that continues around Lake Ontario to Hamilton and the Niagara Region. East of downtown, the Gardiner meets the Don Valley Parkway, a main route from the eastern and northeastern suburbs. **Highway 401** crosses the region north of Toronto proper. It's the main east-west route across Southern Ontario, extending east to Quebec and west to Windsor. **Highway 407** (www.407etr.com), an electronic toll highway, parallels Highway 401 farther north. Tolls are charged automatically by distance and time of travel; the end-to-end charge is $21-25. Even if you've driven from out of the province, or from the United States, your license plate information will be recorded and you'll receive a bill.

From the United States

From the United States, Toronto is 160 kilometers (100 miles) from Buffalo, New York; 808 kilometers (505 miles) from New York City; 906 kilometers (566 miles) from Boston; 378 kilometers (236 miles) from Detroit; and 854 kilometers (534 miles) from Chicago. The nearest highway border crossings from the United States are at the Peace, Rainbow, Whirlpool, and Queenston-Lewiston Bridges near Niagara Falls; the Blue Water Bridge on Highway 402 and I-69/94 at Sarnia/Port Huron on the Michigan border; the Ambassador Bridge or the Detroit-Windsor Tunnel between Detroit and Windsor; or via the Thousand Islands Bridge east of Gananoque.

GETTING AROUND

Toronto is built on the shores of Lake Ontario. Beginning at the lake and heading north, downtown Toronto includes the Harbourfront, the Financial District, and a mix of residential and commercial neighborhoods. Downtown extends north to Bloor Street, a main east-west street that borders the University of Toronto campus. North of Bloor is Midtown, where you'll find many of Toronto's residential neighborhoods alternating with commercial developments.

Yonge Street, Toronto's main north-south artery, bisects the city, beginning at the lakeshore and continuing north well beyond the city limits. "East" addresses are east of Yonge; "west" addresses are west of Yonge. Pay careful attention to the "east" and "west" designators, since 1200 Queen Street East would be in Leslieville in the city's far east end, while 1200 Queen Street West is eight kilometers (five miles) away on the city's west side.

Toronto has a comprehensive public transit system, including a subway, streetcars, and buses, so it's easy to get around the city without a car. The **Toronto Transit Commission** (TTC, 416/393-4636, www.ttc.ca) runs the transit network within the city. Use the online Trip Planner (www.ttc.ca) to figure out the best way to get from one point to another.

The TTC website also has detailed maps of the streetcar and bus routes.

Transit Fares and Passes

The fare structure is the same for the TTC subways, streetcars, and buses. The most expensive way to ride any of these public transit options is to pay cash for a single ride (adults $3, seniors and ages 13-19 $2, ages 2-12 $0.75). In the subway stations, pay your fare at the ticket collector's booth; they'll make change if you need it, but they don't accept credit or debit cards. On buses or streetcars, pay your fare when you board; you will need exact change.

Cheaper than the individual cash fares are **tickets** or **tokens** (adults $8.10 for 3 or $18.90 for 7, seniors and students $9.25 for 5 or $18.50 for 10, children $6 for 10 only), good for the subway, streetcars, and buses. Buy tickets or tokens (cash only) from the fare collectors when you enter any of the subway stations, or purchase them from grocery stores, convenience stores, and drugstores around the city. The **TTC website** (www.ttc.ca) lists sales outlets, or contact **TTC Customer Service** (416/393-4636) for the nearest location.

To transfer between the subway, bus, or streetcar, get a "transfer" (a paper ticket) that allows you to connect without paying an additional fare. Transfers are valid only for the next available bus or streetcar and only at locations where the two routes intersect. In the subway stations, get a transfer from the automated transfer machine near the turnstiles. On the bus or streetcar, ask the driver.

If you expect to ride public transit frequently, consider purchasing a pass. The TTC **Day Pass** (adults $11) offers unlimited rides on subways, streetcars, and buses in a single day. Purchase the day pass from the fare collectors in the subway stations, then simply show the pass to the fare collector when you board the subway (enter next to the collector booth, not through the regular turnstiles), or to the driver when you board a streetcar or bus. On Saturday, Sunday, and holidays, the day pass is an even better deal, particularly for families. One pass is good for unlimited one-day travel for up to six people, including up to two adults and up to four children age 19 and under.

For a longer stay, consider purchasing a **Weekly Pass** (adults $39.25, seniors and students $31.25). Weekly passes are good for seven days, beginning on Monday and continuing through the following Sunday. However, if you arrive in Toronto on Wednesday and plan to stay a week, a weekly pass doesn't make sense, since you could use it for only three days (Mon.-Wed.). The fare collectors in the subway stations sell weekly passes, as do a variety of grocery and other stores. You can buy a weekly pass between the previous Thursday until the Tuesday of the week in which you'll travel. If you're using a daily or weekly pass, you don't need a transfer; simply show your pass each time you board.

Subway

The Toronto subway has four lines: two main lines that are most useful to visitors and two shorter "spur" lines that extend service into the suburbs. The two main lines are the **Bloor-Danforth line,** which runs east-west across the city, following Bloor Street and Danforth Avenue, and the **Yonge-University-Spadina line,** which runs on a roughly U-shaped route. From its southernmost point at Union Station, a section of the Yonge-University-Spadina route runs north along Yonge Street to Finch station in North Toronto. The other section follows University Avenue in the downtown area, and then continues northwest to Downsview station, also in North Toronto. You can transfer free of charge between the two lines at Spadina, St. George, and Bloor-Yonge station.

The subway operates from 6am to 1:30am Monday-Saturday and from 9am to 1:30am Sunday. Trains generally run every few minutes, slightly less often late at night and on Sunday.

Streetcar

The TTC operates a network of streetcars that

run along major streets downtown and beyond. Most streetcars run 6am-1am Monday-Saturday and 9am-1am Sunday. Among the more useful routes for visitors are:

- **No. 501 Queen:** The system's longest route travels along Queen Street from the West End through downtown to Leslieville and the Beaches.

- **No. 504 King:** Operates from Dundas West station along Roncesvalles Avenue in the West End, along King Street through downtown, continuing east past the Distillery District, then turning north along Broadview Avenue, and connecting to the Bloor-Danforth subway at Broadview station.

- **No. 505 Dundas:** Travels west-to-east along Dundas Street.

- **No. 506 Carlton:** From High Park in the West End, runs along College Street, Carlton Street, and Gerrard Street, and connects to Main Street station on the Bloor-Danforth subway line.

- **No. 509 Harbourfront:** Travels between Union Station and Exhibition Place, passing Harbourfront Centre and Fort York en route.

- **No. 510 Spadina:** Runs between Spadina station (on both the Bloor-Danforth and Yonge-University-Spadina subway lines) and Union Station, via Spadina Avenue and Queen's Quay along the harbor.

Between 1:30am and 5am, the **Blue Night Network,** an overnight bus service, operates along some streetcar routes. Stops are marked with a blue band, and service runs at least every 30 minutes. Blue Night service runs along the Queen and Carlton streetcar routes as the no. 301 Queen and no. 306 Carlton.

Bus

In downtown Toronto, you can reach most places by subway or streetcar. As you venture farther from the city center, buses become more convenient. To figure out if buses travel to your destination, enter your starting and ending point into the **TTC's online Trip Planner** (www.ttc.ca). The website also maps all the bus routes in the city. Buses typically run 6am-1am Monday-Saturday and 9am-1am Sunday. After 9pm, women traveling alone on Toronto city buses can ask to be let off between stops, so you don't have to walk as far to your destination.

From 1:30am to 5am, the overnight **Blue Night Network** runs buses along the Bloor-Danforth and Yonge subway routes. The no. 300 Bloor-Danforth bus operates along Bloor Street and Danforth Avenue between Pearson Airport to Victoria Park Avenue, while the no. 320 Yonge bus follows Yonge Street from Union Station north to Steeles Avenue. Blue Night buses also run along many regular bus routes. Stops are marked with a blue band, and service runs at least every 30 minutes. The **TTC website** (www.ttc.ca) has maps and schedules of all Blue Night buses.

The PATH Network

Underneath downtown Toronto, the PATH is a 30-kilometer (19-mile) network of interconnected underground walkways. You can walk from building to building, protected from the weather. You'll often find more stores and services underground along the PATH walkways than you will at street level; in fact, the PATH is the largest underground shopping complex in the world. The PATH extends from Union Station north to City Hall, Eaton Centre, and the Toronto Coach Terminal, bounded roughly by Yonge Street to the east and University Avenue to the west, with a couple of spurs continuing west into the Entertainment District. Multicolored directional signs mark the walkways.

Following the PATH can be confusing for newcomers, because you don't have the landmarks you see at street level. Many signs direct you to particular buildings, rather than streets, and you may not know whether you want to go, for example, toward the Canadian Pacific Tower or First Canadian Place. Come up to the street, or ask someone, if you can't figure out where you are. Tourism Toronto's website (www.seetorontonow.com) has a useful PATH map; pick up a copy at hotels, museums, and other city attractions.

Taxi

Toronto taxis are metered, so make sure the driver uses the meter. Rates include an initial charge of $4.25, with an additional charge of $1.75 for every kilometer traveled. Short trips around the downtown area can cost $10-15. You can hail taxis on the street, although it's often easier to find them in front of hotels, train or bus stations, shopping centers, and attractions such as museums. Call **416/TAXICAB** (416/829-4222, www.416-taxicab.com) from anywhere in Toronto and you'll be connected to local taxi services.

Car

Unless you plan to explore the suburbs or take day trips out of town, it's easier to get around Toronto without a car. Traffic can be heavy, with rush hours extending at least 7am-9am and 4pm-6pm Monday-Friday. Many downtown streets are one-way, and turns, both left and right, are often restricted from major arteries. While right turns are allowed at red lights in Ontario, they're often prohibited in downtown Toronto; look for signs at the intersection.

Drivers must yield to streetcars. When a streetcar stops, the cars behind it must stop at least two meters (six feet) behind and wait for passengers to board or unload.

Parking

There's metered on-street parking throughout Toronto, but the rate varies by location ($1.50-3.50 per hour), so be sure to check the meter or ticket dispenser. Some streets have single-space meters that take coins only. Others have ticket dispensers that take either coins or credit cards and give you a ticket to put on your car's dashboard. The city also operates 160 parking lots containing about 20,000 spaces. The **Toronto Parking Authority** (www.greenp.com) has a useful parking lot finder that shows the location and rates at all municipal parking lots. When booking a hotel reservation, ask about the cost and availability of parking if you're planning to bring a car. Daily parking charges can add significantly to your costs.

Car Rentals

All the major North American car rental companies have outlets at Toronto's **Pearson Airport** (YYZ, 6301 Silver Dart Dr., Mississauga, 416/247-7678 or 866/207-1690, www.torontopearson.com), and most have offices downtown as well:

- **Alamo** (877/222-9075, www.alamo.ca)
- **Avis** (800/879-2847, www.avis.ca)
- **Budget** (800/268-8900, www.budget.ca)
- **Dollar** (800/848-8268, www.dollarcanada.ca)
- **Enterprise** (800/261-7331, www.enterpriserentacar.ca)
- **Hertz** (800/654-3131, www.hertz.ca)
- **National** (877/222-9058, www.nationalcar.ca)
- **Thrifty** (800/847-4389, www.thrifty.com)

A number of smaller car rental agencies have offices near Pearson Airport, and it's worth checking to see if their rates are lower than the major companies. They provide shuttles to their locations from the terminals or from the airport's Viscount Station, which you can reach on the free **Terminal Link Train** from either Terminal 1 or Terminal 3.

- **Advantage Car Rentals** (905/687-2834 or 866/893-5882, www.advantagecarrentals.com)
- **Discount Car Rentals** (416/249-5554 or 800/263-2355, www.discountcar.com)
- **Fox Rent-A-Car** (800/225-4369, www.foxrentacar.com)
- **Payless Car Rental** (416/675-2000 or 800/729-5377, www.paylesscar.com)
- **Zoom Rent-A-Car** (905/670-7368 or 888/317-9666, www.zoomrentals.com)

Note that most rental-car companies do not allow you to drive on Highway 407; if you do, they'll charge you a premium over the basic toll charges.

Tours
Walking Tours

One of the best ways to get to know a city is to meet local residents. **Toronto Greeters** (aka TAP into TO!, 416/338-2786, www.toronto.ca/tapto, year-round, free) offers free two- to three-hour tours of a Toronto neighborhood led by a local "greeter," an enthusiastic resident and volunteer tour guide. Choose which neighborhood to visit and note whether you have a specific interest (such as architecture or food), or let the greeter select a favorite area. Request a greeter at least a week in advance; sign up or get more information on the program website.

Heritage Toronto Walks (416/338-3886, www.heritagetoronto.org, May-Oct.) are free walking tours that highlight a neighborhood's history, whether architectural, cultural, archaeological or natural. Check their online schedule or phone the information line for walk times and locations. Reservations aren't required; just show up a few minutes before the walk's departure.

A unique way to explore Toronto—and go home with great photographs—is with **Live Toronto Walking Tours** (647/637-0832, www.livetoronto.ca, adults $75, ages 7-16 $25). On these private one-hour tours, designed for 1-8 people, your guide will photograph you in front of iconic city sights, essentially creating digital postcards with you in them. You can request particular stops, but tours normally visit photogenic downtown locations like City Hall, Eaton Centre, Roy Thompson Hall, the CN Tower, and the Lake Ontario waterfront.

Urban Adventures (800/691-9320, www.urbanadventures.com) offers several different walking tours, including "Beer Makes History Better" (3.5 hours, $43) that combines a walking tour through the St. Lawrence Market and Distillery District with stops at several pubs for a brew; a tour of Kensington Market and Chinatown (2 hours, $30); and When Pigs Fly (3 hours, $59), where you'll learn why Toronto is nicknamed "Hogtown" and taste bacon, sausage, and other pork snacks along the way.

The Urban Adventures guides also run free walking tours as **The Tour Guys** (647/230-7891, www.tourguys.ca, June-mid-Oct.), including several different 90-minute guided walks downtown. Although there's no charge

sweet samples from Toronto's Tasty Tours

for these tours, you're encouraged to tip your guide. Check their website for a current schedule. On an **Urban Quest** (www.urbanquest. com, year-round, $10), you solve a series of clues that lead you from place to place around town. Typically lasting around 1.5 hours, the quests end at a mystery restaurant where you can have lunch or dinner (not included in the quest fee). You can do a quest with any number of people, but most are designed for two to four.

The **West Queen West Art + Design Tour** (www.artinsite.net, noon-2:30pm Sat., $25) gives an insider's look at the artists, galleries, and other denizens of this arty neighborhood. Meet in the Gladstone Hotel lobby (1214 Queen St. W, 416/531-4635). The Royal Ontario Museum runs **ROM Walks** (416/586-8097, www.rom.on.ca/programs, usually 2pm Sun. and 6pm Wed. May-Sept., free), guided walks that highlight the history and architecture of particular neighborhoods. Check the website for the weekly schedule.

Boat Tours

Take a two-hour sail around Toronto Harbour on a traditional 50-meter (165-foot) three-masted schooner with the **Toronto Tall Ship Boat Cruises** (416/260-6355 or 800/267-3866, www.tallshipcruisestoronto.com, May-Sept., adults $24, seniors $22, ages 5-15 $13).

Want to see Toronto from a traditional voyageur canoe? **Canoe Toronto** (283 Queens Quay W., 416/993-4224, www.canoetoronto.com, May-Sept.) runs a 30-minute paddling tour around Toronto Harbour ($10), a 90-minute paddle around the Toronto Islands ($20), and a 2.5-hour Islands paddle with a stop on Centre Island. Canoes can accommodate 6-20 paddlers each.

Food Tours

A Taste of the World (416/923-6813, www. torontowalksbikes.com, adults $50, seniors and students $45, under age 13 $35) leads 3.5-hour food-centric walking tours in Chinatown, Kensington Market, and other neighborhoods, with snacks along the way. Chinatown tours frequently run during the Lunar New Year or other festivals. **ChowBella Taste and Travel** (416/483-8030, www.chowbella.ca) offers a three-hour Chocolate and Cheese Crawl walking tour (11am Fri.-Sat., $69), an edible exploration of the Queen and King West neighborhoods, and "Global Bites" (noon Sun., $69), an international food tour along Queen Street West.

Indulge your sweet tooth as you explore Kensington Market, Trinity-Bellwoods, or other districts with **Tasty Tours** (www. tastytourstoronto.com, adults $31-36, ages 7-12 $18-23), which offers guided 2- to 2.5-hour neighborhood walks with snacking stops at bakeries, chocolate shops, and other sugary destinations. Check their website for tour schedules and locations.

The Niagara Region

Niagara Falls, an easy drive south of Toronto or across the border from New York State, is one of the most-visited destinations in Canada. Families, honeymooners, tour groups, and everyone in between make their way to this iconic must-see attraction. Whether it's your first falls visit or your 50th, feeling the spray on your face, watching the cascading curtains tumble and crash into the river below, or glimpsing a rainbow arching over the torrents, is still a thrill.

Yet Niagara is more than just the falls. Beyond the town of Niagara Falls, with its quirky mix of stunning natural beauty and honky-tonk tourist lures, the Niagara region offers plenty of attractions. The Niagara Peninsula is Ontario's major wine-producing region, and a prime destination for a wine country getaway. Wine tasting and touring lures visitors to Niagara-on-the-Lake, home to more than two dozen wineries. Many more are clustered in the Twenty Valley area, in the towns of Beamsville, Vineland, and Jordan—a popular day trip from Niagara Falls. Niagara-on-the-Lake is also home to one of North America's premier theater festivals—the Shaw Festival, which produces works by noted Irish playwright George Bernard Shaw along with more contemporary playwrights.

The towns along the Welland Canal, from St. Catharines south to Port Colborne, attract boat enthusiasts as well as vacationers seeking a quiet getaway that's still convenient to the peninsula's other attractions. Built back in the 1820s, the canal provides a shipping route between the Great Lakes. Freighters, barges, and pleasure craft continue to navigate the canal's eight locks, and you can watch megaships up close as they lock through.

Outdoors lovers can explore an extensive network of cycling paths that crisscrosses the Niagara Peninsula, or set out on the Bruce Trail, an 800-kilometer (500-mile) hiking route that extends to the tip of the Bruce Peninsula. History lovers will find numerous historic sites that date to the War of 1812.

From wine-tastings to places to unwind, Niagara is much more than just the falls.

Previous: Niagara's Horseshoe Falls; staff dressed as 19th-century soldiers at Fort George National Historic Site. **Above:** bottles on display at The Niagara College Teaching Winery.

Highlights

★ **Visiting Niagara Falls:** No matter how many times you've seen these thundering waterfalls—the Horseshoe Falls on the Ontario side of the Niagara River and the American Falls on the New York banks—they're still spectacular (page 96).

★ **Hornblower Niagara Cruises:** Since the 1840s, ferry boats have taken visitors to the base of the falls, so put on your rain poncho and climb aboard. A cruise aboard these modern ships is still the best way to hear the crashing waters and feel the spray (page 96).

★ **Niagara Glen Nature Reserve:** The window-lined Nature Centre at this park north of the falls has great views of the Niagara River Gorge. Take a guided hike through the reserve, or hit the trails on your own (page 100).

★ **Shaw Festival:** From April through October, the town of Niagara-on-the-Lake hosts one of North America's major theater festivals, devoted to the works of Irish playwright George

Bernard Shaw, along with more contemporary plays (page 115).

★ **Niagara-on-the-Lake Wineries:** With more than two dozen wineries clustered in this small region, you can easily stop at many producers—and sample many varieties—in a short visit (page 117).

★ **Fort George National Historic Site:** An important battleground during the War of 1812, this restored fort overlooking the Niagara River is now a national historic site. Learn about the Niagara region's early history and watch staff demonstrate traditional weaponry, cook on an open hearth, and perform fife and drum music (page 120).

★ **Twenty Valley Wineries:** This growing wine-producing district includes the towns of Beamsville, Vineland, and Jordan. You can sample ice wine, Ontario's distinctive dessert wine, as well as other varietals (page 127).

The Niagara Region

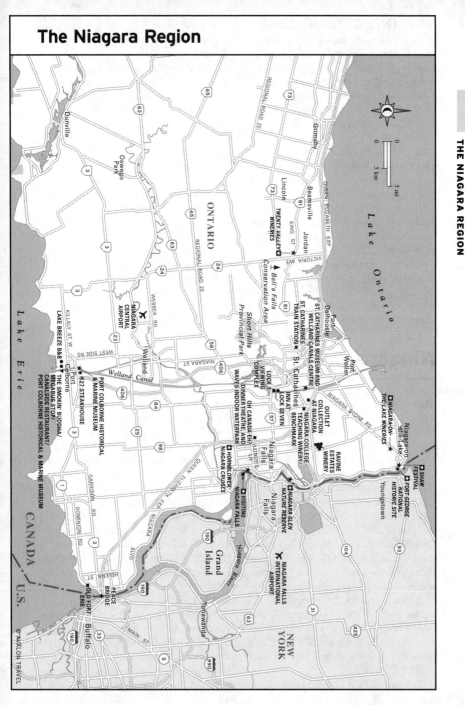

PLANNING YOUR TIME

You can easily visit Niagara Falls on a day trip from Toronto or upstate New York, but there's plenty to do around the Niagara Peninsula to occupy a long weekend. Plan at least a day or two at Niagara Falls, another day in Niagara-on-the-Lake, and a third touring either the Twenty Valley Wine Country or the Welland Canal.

Summer is peak season in the Niagara region. From late June through early September, everything is open, and most attractions keep long hours, from 9am until at least 7pm-8pm. The Shaw Festival begins with preview productions in April and shows run through October, with June through September its prime time.

Weekends are busiest in both Niagara Falls and Niagara-on-the-Lake, especially in summer and early fall, so you'll find more accommodations options (and often lower prices) if you can visit midweek. Look for lodging in some of the less-touristed towns along the nearby Welland Canal—St. Catharines, Thorold, Port Colborne—if you have trouble finding a room in your price range.

At Niagara Falls, many attractions open for the season in April or May and close in late October or early November. Visiting the falls during the spring or fall "shoulder" periods outside the June-August peak can mean fewer crowds. September and October are harvest season for the region's vineyards, making it a popular wine-touring time. The falls themselves are, obviously, still there year-round, and you can save significantly on accommodations by visiting midwinter, when far fewer tourists are around. Just prepare for snow and cold temperatures.

Whenever you visit, check attractions' opening hours before you set out, since many Niagara-area sights change their hours with the seasons.

Niagara Falls

The city of Niagara Falls is home to about 83,000 people and hosts more than 10 million visitors every year—all because of the spectacular torrents of water that cascade down the Niagara River. Long popular as a honeymoon destination, Niagara Falls has plenty of appeal for everyone from kids to seniors.

The Niagara River connects two of the Great Lakes—Lake Ontario and Lake Erie—and also separates Canada from the United States. That means that there are actually two cities named Niagara Falls—one in Ontario, the other across the river in New York State—and two main waterfalls: the Horseshoe Falls on the Canadian side and the American Falls on the New York side. The Ontario side of the river is more developed, with numerous attractions in addition to the falls, mixing history, green space, and, unfortunately, plenty of tacky tourist traps.

The area along the Niagara River closest to the Horseshoe Falls is known as **Table Rock,** where a large visitors center houses several attractions. The **Fallsview** area, with lots of skyscraping hotels, is atop the Niagara Escarpment, a steep climb up the hill above Table Rock.

To the north of Table Rock along the river is **Queen Victoria Park** and the departure point for **Hornblower Niagara Cruises,** a deservedly popular boat ride that takes you under the falls. Up the slope just north of the Hornblower docks is **Clifton Hill,** with numerous places to stay, as well as the flashing neon of arcades, wax museums, and other kitschy attractions.

North along the river is the **Whirlpool** area, where the river makes a 90-degree turn. A number of parks and natural attractions are clustered between the Whirlpool and **Queenston,** a historic district 12 kilometers (7.5 miles) north of the falls. The **WEGO**

Niagara Falls

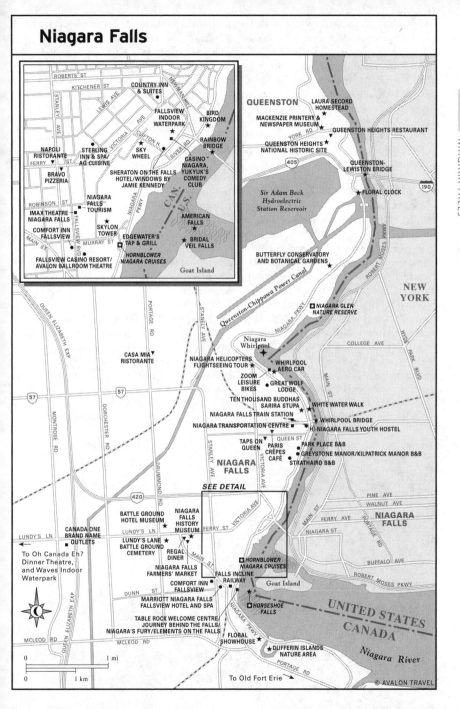

© AVALON TRAVEL

bus runs along the Niagara Parkway to all the major attractions and has other routes to take you around the city of Niagara Falls.

Away from the river, Queen Street is the main business route through "downtown" Niagara Falls, although there's actually more development along Ferry Street and Lundy's Lane, which run east-west from the river across the city to the Queen Elizabeth Way (QEW), the highway that connects Toronto with the Niagara region.

★ VISITING NIAGARA FALLS

Niagara's Falls aren't the world's tallest or widest falls, but they certainly rank among the most spectacular. The Niagara Falls began forming during the last ice age, more than 12,000 years ago, and they have actually moved 11 kilometers (7 miles) during that period. They originally began north of their present location, near the Niagara Glen.

The best free vantage point for viewing the falls is near the **Table Rock Visitors Centre** (6650 Niagara Pkwy., www.niagaraparks.com), adjacent to the Horseshoe Falls. Be prepared for some spray to mist around you, even as you walk or stand nearby.

The larger **Horseshoe Falls,** often called the Canadian Falls (on the Ontario side of the Niagara River), are 670 meters (2,200 feet) wide and curve in a semicircular "horseshoe" from bank to bank. While the Horseshoe Falls measure only 57 meters (188 feet) from top to bottom, more than 168,000 cubic meters (44 million gallons) of water crash over the falls every minute during daylight hours.

On the New York shore, the **American Falls** have a gentler curve. In fact, unless you see them from above, they look like a straight curtain of water stretching 260 meters (850 feet) wide and 21 to 34 meters (70-110 feet) tall, depending on where you measure.

A third narrow waterfall, known as **Bridal Veil Falls,** almost looks like part of the American Falls, since it's just beside it, separated from the American Falls by Luna Island. The Bridal Veil Falls measure 17 meters (56 feet) across.

★ Hornblower Niagara Cruises

Boat tours to the base of the falls have been running since the 1840s, when the *Maid of the Mist* ferry began operating as a sightseeing boat; over the years, the *Maid* transported such notable passengers as Princess Diana and her sons, U.S. presidents Theodore Roosevelt and Jimmy Carter, Soviet president Mikhail

The Hornblower Niagara Cruises take you right under the spray.

Gorbachev, and the actor Marilyn Monroe. In 2014, **Hornblower Niagara Cruises** (Queen Victoria Park, 5920 Niagara Pkwy., 905/642-4272, www.niagaracruises.com, daily May-mid-Nov., check the website for seasonal schedules; peak times adults $20, off-peak $18, ages 5-12 $12.25) took over the tour routes from the Canadian side of the falls, and they're still the best way to hear the thundering waters and feel the spray.

Departing every 15 to 30 minutes from early-morning sunrise trips on into the evening, the Hornblower catamarans, which accommodate up to 700 passengers, cruise past the American Falls and into the Horseshoe Falls basin. The ride lasts about 30 minutes, and yes, you will get wet; you can protect yourself from the spray, but you'll want to get as close as you can to the falls views. Tours are slightly cheaper during off-peak hours (before 10:30am). Hornblower also offers 40-minute Falls Illumination tours and Fireworks tours (adults $35, ages 5-12 $31.50), departing at 9:30pm, with a bar and music onboard.

The *Maid of the Mist* still runs from the American side of the falls, leaving from Prospect Point in the **Niagara Reservation State Park** (716/284-8897, www.maidofthemist.com, adults US$17, ages 6-12 $9.90).

Journey Behind the Falls

The walk, **Journey Behind the Falls** (Table Rock Welcome Centre, 6650 Niagara Pkwy., www.niagaraparks.com, daily year-round, check the website for seasonal schedules; adults $16, ages 6-12 $11, mid-Apr.-mid-Dec., adults $11.25, ages 6-12 $7 mid-Dec.-mid-Apr.), lets you see the waterfalls from a different perspective. You start your journey in an elevator that descends 45 meters (150 feet) through the rock beside the Horseshoe Falls. Then you walk through underground tunnels to two observation decks, where the falls crash beside you. The spray on the observation platforms can be drenching, so protect your camera gear, your guidebook, and anything else that you don't want waterlogged. Allow about 30 minutes to explore, longer if you're with kids who relish the falls' chilly shower.

Save this attraction for a warm day if you can; the spray can feel frigid. From mid-December through mid-April, the lower observation deck, which gives you the best falls view, is closed (it's too icy), so admission prices are reduced.

Niagara's Fury

A two-part multimedia show, *Niagara's Fury* (Table Rock Welcome Centre, 6650 Niagara Pkwy., www.niagarasfury.com, daily year-round, check the website for seasonal schedules, adults $13.50, ages 6-12 $8.80) tries to explain how the falls were created, starting with a short cartoon. Then you move into a circular theater, where lightning flashes, the earth shakes, and water pours from the ceiling as you "experience" the birth of the falls.

Older kids may think *Niagara's Fury* is cool, but the crashing thunder and shaking floor may frighten younger ones. Although the entire show lasts less than 20 minutes, give it a miss if you're short on time; the real falls are far more dramatic.

White Water Walk

As you go north of Horseshoe Falls, the Niagara River bucks and churns through a section known as the whirlpool rapids. Rated as Class VI white water—defined as "extremely difficult to successfully maneuver . . . usually considered unrunnable"—the rushing rapids slicing through the deep gorge are impressive, even from the shore, where the **White Water Walk** (4330 Niagara Pkwy., www.niagaraparks.com, daily early Apr.-late Oct., call for seasonal hours, adults $11, ages 6-12 $7) gives you an up-close look.

After taking an elevator 70 meters (230 feet) into the gorge and walking through a tunnel to the riverbank, you follow a 300-meter (0.25-mile) boardwalk along the Niagara River rapids. Stairs lead to two observation areas at the river's edge. A small exhibit area near the elevators profiles some of the daredevils who attempted various stunts

The American Side of the Falls

spring flowers at the American Falls

There are two cities named Niagara Falls—one on the Ontario side of the Niagara River and another on the opposite bank in New York State. On the New York side, the Falls area is part of the **Niagara Reservation State Park** (716/278-1796, www.niagarafallsstatepark.com). You'll find the best views of the Falls at **Prospect Point,** right next to the American Falls. The overall views of the American Falls are more majestic from the Canadian shore, but you're closer to the spray on the U.S. side. The historic *Maid of the Mist* tour boats (716/284-8897, www.maidofthemist.com, mid-May-Oct., call or check the website for seasonal schedules, adults US$17, ages 6-12 US$9.90), which take you right under the falls and which formerly ran from both the Canadian and American sides, now operate only from Prospect Point.

If you want to feel the spray full in your face, head for **Goat Island,** where you can descend alongside Bridal Veil Falls on the **Cave of the Winds** (716/278-1730, 9am-9pm Sun.-Fri., 9am-9pm Sat. mid-May-mid-June, 9am-9pm Sun.-Thurs., 9am-10pm Fri.-Sat. mid-June-early Sept., 9am-7pm Sun.-Fri., 9am-9pm Sat. early Sept.-mid-Oct., 9am-5pm daily mid-late Oct., adults US$12, ages 6-12 US$9), which follows a wooden walkway to a platform just six meters (20 feet) from the falls. You'll receive a rain poncho, but should still expect to get wet.

The **Visitors Center** (8am-6pm Sun.-Thurs., 8am-9pm Fri.-Sat. May-late June and early Sept.-mid-Oct., 8am-9pm Sun.-Thurs., 8am-10pm Fri.-Sat. late June-early Sept., 8am-6pm daily Oct.-Apr., free) has exhibits about the Falls, as well as coffee, ice cream, and snacks.

The **Rainbow Bridge** connects Niagara Falls, Ontario, with Niagara Falls, New York. You can cross the bridge by car, on foot, or by bike, but remember: Even if you're just strolling across for the afternoon, this is an international border and you need to *bring your passport.*

For more information, contact **Niagara USA** (10 Rainbow Blvd., Niagara Falls, NY, 716/282-8992 or 877/325-5787, www.niagara-usa.com). *Moon Niagara Falls* (www.moon.com), by Joel A. Dombrowski, has lots more details about exploring the American side of the Falls.

on the Niagara River or over the falls—just don't try these tricks yourself. Not only is stunting extremely dangerous (only a few of the adventurers survived), it's now illegal, and trespassers can face hefty fines.

The White Water Walk is four kilometers (2.5 miles) north of Horseshoe Falls, on the WEGO bus route. You follow the walk at your own pace, but most people find that 30-45 minutes is enough time.

Whirlpool Aero Car

Over thousands of years, the Niagara River slowly eroded a path through the Niagara Escarpment, creating a deep canyon called the Great Gorge. North of the falls, as the river wends through the gorge, it makes a sharp right-angle turn, which forces the water into a counterclockwise spin. This unusual churning water formation, the Niagara River Whirlpool, is difficult to see from shore (without a long, steep hike), but it's easily visible from above, aboard the **Whirlpool Aero Car** (3850 Niagara Pkwy., www.niagaraparks.com, daily early Apr.-early Nov., call for seasonal hours, adults $13.50, ages 6-12 $8.50).

The unusual-looking Aero Car, designed by Spanish engineer Leonardo Torres Quevedo, has been transporting passengers over the whirlpool since 1916. You stand in the red cable car, which is attached to the overhead cables by a sunshine-yellow contraption that looks like half of a giant bicycle wheel. As you ride across the gorge and back, the views extend up and down the river.

The Aero Car is 4.5 kilometers (3 miles) north of Horseshoe Falls, on the WEGO bus route. Although the ride itself takes just 10 minutes round-trip, the Aero Car accommodates only 35 people and tickets are issued for specific times, so be prepared to wait.

Skylon Tower and Sky Wheel

For an aerial view of the falls, take the "yellow bug" elevators—they do resemble yellow beetles—that scoot up the outside of the **Skylon Tower** (5200 Robinson St., 905/356-2651 or 888/975-9566, www.skylon.com,

8am-midnight daily summer, 9am-10pm daily winter, adults $13.91, ages 2-12 $8.11) to the observation deck 236 meters (775 feet) in the sky. You can also buy a combination ticket that includes a show in the 3-D/4-D theater (adults $25.50, ages 2-12 $15.06). Tickets are discounted if you buy them online in advance.

Yet another vantage point for viewing the falls is the 10-minute whirl on the **Sky Wheel** (4950 Clifton Hill, 905/358-4793, www.sky-wheel.ca, call or check the website for seasonal hours, adults $11, under age 13 $7), a 53-meter (175-foot) Ferris wheel.

SIGHTS
Museums

Lundy's Lane, which runs east-west across the city of Niagara Falls, was the site of a major battle between American and British troops in the War of 1812. Both sides suffered some of the heaviest casualties of the war during the Battle of Lundy's Lane on July 25, 1814. Neither side won the battle, but American troops withdrew south to Fort Erie, setting the scene for the Battle of Fort Erie later that summer.

Along Ferry Street and Lundy's Lane (Ferry changes its name west of Main St.), several sights help you learn more about Lundy's Lane and Niagara's 19th-century history. In an 1874 stone building with a modern glass-walled addition, the **Niagara Falls History Museum** (5810 Ferry St., 905/358-5082, www.niagarafallshistorymuseum.ca, 10am-5pm Tues.-Sun., 10am-9pm Thurs., adults $5, ages 6-19 $4) houses more than 25,000 artifacts about the region's history, with featured exhibits about the history of the falls, including the daredevils who've tried to cross them, and about the War of 1812. Additional exhibitions in the temporary gallery change several times a year. Kids can try on soldiers' uniforms or walk a tightrope over the "falls."

A short walk farther west, the **Lundy's Lane Battle Ground Cemetery** (6110 Lundy's Lane), also known as the Drummond Hill Cemetery, is on the site where the Lundy's Lane Battle was fought. The cemetery has a mix of historic and more recent graves, including a monument honoring Laura Secord, a Canadian heroine during the War of 1812, who is buried here. Pick up a guide to the cemetery at the Niagara Falls History Museum.

On the 30-minute guided tours of the **Battle Ground Hotel Museum** (6151 Lundy's Lane, 905/358-5082, www.niagara-fallshistorymuseum.ca, 11am-5pm Fri.-Sun. late May-Aug., donation), a restored wood-frame tavern, you'll learn about life in Niagara Falls from the 1830s to the 1850s, when the falls were already a tourist attraction and travelers gathered in taverns such as this one. The museum also houses some artifacts from the War of 1812.

Ten Thousand Buddhas Sarira Stupa

One of Niagara's most incongruous sights might be the peaceful **Ten Thousand Buddhas Sarira Stupa** (4303 River Rd., 905/371-2678), also called the Cham Shan Buddhist Temple, built in the 1990s, which looks as if it were transported directly from Asia. The seven-story pagoda houses Buddhist arts and artifacts (Sat.-Sun. June-mid-Oct.), while a smaller Buddhist temple (9am-5pm daily) is in an adjacent building. A walk around the property may help you recover your Zen state after Niagara's tourist frenzy.

★ Niagara Glen Nature Reserve

Some of the best views of the Niagara River and gorge are from the window-lined—and free—Nature Centre at the **Niagara Glen Nature Reserve** (3050 Niagara Pkwy., 905/354-6678, www.niagaraparks.com, mid-May-mid-Oct., call for seasonal hours, free). Inside the **Nature Centre,** a small exhibit area includes a Touch Table to explore rocks, fossils, and animal skulls found in the gorge, as well as displays about the area's flora and fauna.

The Glen has about four kilometers (2.5 miles) of hiking trails that descend into the Niagara Gorge. The **River Path** is a

When Niagara feels too crowded, tour the peaceful Ten Thousand Buddhas Sarira Stupa.

particularly scenic route that follows the Niagara River all the way to the Whirlpool. This trail has lots of steep climbs and descents, so Parks staff recommend allowing at least three hours round-trip. Pick up a trail map at the Nature Centre or get one online at the Niagara Parks website (www.niaga-raparks.com).

Park naturalists lead one-hour guided hikes (11am and 2pm daily summer, $6), where you learn more about the area's history, geology, plants, and wildlife as you explore the walking paths. Because some of the terrain is quite steep, these guided walks are best suited for adults and older children.

Niagara Glen is eight kilometers (five miles) north of Horseshoe Falls, on the WEGO bus route.

Butterfly Conservatory and Botanical Gardens

More than 2,000 butterflies flit around the **Butterfly Conservatory** (2405 Niagara Pkwy., 905/356-8119, www.niagaraparks.com, daily year-round, call or check the website for seasonal hours, adults $13.50, ages 6-12 $8.80), alighting on the tropical flowers and on visitors' arms and heads. Start your visit with a six-minute video about butterflies and their habits, from which you learn, among other things, that butterflies smell with their antennae and taste with their feet. The family-friendly conservatory is a good choice for a chilly day, since inside it's warm year-round.

The Butterfly Conservatory is on the grounds of the **Niagara Parks Botanical Gardens** (2565 Niagara Pkwy., 905/356-8554, www.niagaraparks.com, dawn-dusk daily year-round, free, parking $5), a 40-hectare (100-acre) expanse of manicured grounds, ornamental flowers, and herb gardens, crisscrossed with walking paths. Among the flowering highlights are rhododendrons and irises, which typically peak in June, and roses that bloom from mid-June into September; check the website for a detailed bloom schedule.

The Gardens and Butterfly Conservatory are nine kilometers (six miles) north of Horseshoe Falls, on the WEGO bus route, opposite the Niagara Glen Nature Reserve.

Floral Clock

As you're traveling along the Niagara Parkway between the falls and Queenston, stop to check the time at this 12-meter-wide (40-foot-wide) working **Floral Clock** (14004 Niagara Pkwy., www.niagaraparks.com, dawn-dusk daily, free), inlaid with more than 15,000 plants. Ontario Hydro, the regional power company, originally created this floral attraction back in 1950. Its hour hand measures 4.5 meters (14.5 feet); the minute hand is 5.3 meters (17.5 feet). Niagara Parks staff change the clock's botanical design twice a year.

The Floral Clock is 11.5 kilometers (7 miles) north of Horseshoe Falls, on the WEGO bus route.

Bird Kingdom

Housed in a former corset factory, the world's largest free-flying indoor aviary, **Bird Kingdom** (5651 River Rd., 905/356-8888 or 866/994-0090, www.birdkingdom.ca, 9:30am-5pm daily, adults $17, seniors $15, ages 4-1' $12, parking $3 per hour), is fun for children, especially on a bad-weather day. In the small aviary, more than 40 species of tiny birds flit about, while in the main glass-walled sanctuary, nearly 400 birds representing approximately 80 species, including brilliant orange-red scarlet ibis, African royal starlings, and multicolored macaws, fly all around you as you wander the paths.

Animal encounters and activities, from bat feeding to snake handling, are held throughout the day; check the schedule on the website or at the admission desk to time your visit to the activities that most interest you and your family. Inside the main aviary is a surprise: a traditional **Javanese tea house.** This intricately hand-carved teak structure houses a snack bar, though unfortunately it serves pizza, hot dogs, and coffee rather than more exotic Indonesian fare.

The Bird Kingdom is 2.5 kilometers (1.5 miles) north of the Horseshoe Falls, just north of the Rainbow Bridge.

ENTERTAINMENT AND SHOPPING
Nightlife

Jay Leno, Aretha Franklin, Olivia Newton-John, Sean Penn, and Ringo Starr have all performed at the 1,500-seat **Avalon Ballroom Theatre** (6380 Fallsview Blvd., 888/325-5788, www.fallsviewcasinoresort.com), in the Fallsview Casino Resort, which has a regular lineup of concerts, Broadway-style musicals, comedians, and other shows. Children under age 19 are not permitted in the theater. Buy tickets through the theater box office or from **Ticketmaster** (www.ticketmaster.ca).

As long as you don't mind a few corny jokes about Mounties and beavers, the dinner theater *Oh Canada Eh?* (8585 Lundy's Lane, 905/374-1995 or 800/467-2071, www.ohcanadaeh.com, 6:15pm Mon.-Sat. mid-Apr.-mid-Oct., adults $60-80, ages 3-16 $40-80) is an evening of rollicking good fun. As you tuck into a hearty multicourse meal featuring dishes from across Canada, enthusiastic performers take you on a cross-country journey of Canadian music, from Newfoundland sea shanties to songs by Joni Mitchell, Neil Young, k.d. lang, and Leonard Cohen. Kids under age 12 enter free with the purchase of certain adult tickets; check the website or call for details. Show-only tickets without dinner are also available (adults $40-50, kids $20-30).

Among the many places where Niagara Falls can separate you from your money are its two casinos: **Casino Niagara** (5705 Falls Ave., 905/374-3598 or 888/325-5788, www.casinoniagara.com) and the **Fallsview Casino** (6380 Fallsview Blvd., 888/325-5788, www.fallsviewcasinoresort.com), Canada's largest gaming facility. At Casino Niagara, **YukYuk's Comedy Club** (5705 Falls Ave., 877/968-5233, www.casinoniagara.com, $12-17) has four stand-up comedy shows every week (Thurs.-Sat.). Both casinos are open 24 hours daily; guests must be at least 19 years old to enter.

Cinema

The **IMAX Theatre Niagara Falls** (6170 Fallsview Blvd., 905/358-3611 or 866/405-4629, www.imaxniagara.com, shows on the hour 9am-9pm daily June-Aug., 9am-8pm daily May and Sept.-Oct., 10am-4pm daily Nov.-Apr., adults $14.50, kids $10.50) screens "you are there" films about the falls and the daredevils who've tried to plummet over the rushing water. Also on-site is the **Daredevil Gallery** (adults $9.30, kids $7.50), which tells the stories of the falls-plunging thrill seekers. Combination tickets for the IMAX movie and gallery (adults $24, kids $18) are available, as are packages that include the movie, the gallery, and admission to the nearby Skylon Tower (adults $38, kids $27). Buy your tickets online for discounts of 20 to 45 percent.

Festivals and Events

The **Fireworks over the Falls** (www.niagaraparks.com) illuminate the night sky at 10pm on Fridays, Sundays, and holidays early May-November, with additional shows at 10pm on summer Wednesdays (mid-June-Aug.). From mid-May to mid-October, there are free concerts at 8pm in Queen Victoria Park before the fireworks begin.

During the **Winter Festival of Lights** (www.wfol.com, Nov.-Jan., free), the falls are illuminated nightly, and fireworks over the falls continue weekly. Additional light displays are at the Dufferin Islands Nature Area.

Shopping

What would a mega tourist attraction be without an outlet mall? Just off the QEW, west of the falls, the 40 stores at the **Canada One Brand Name Outlets** (7500 Lundy's Lane, 905/356-8989, www.canadaoneoutlets.com, 10am-9pm Mon.-Sat., 10am-6pm Sun.) carry a variety of North American brands such as Levi's, Guess, Mexx, Coach, Reebok, and Nike.

SPORTS AND RECREATION
Parks

At the peaceful **Floral Showhouse** (7145 Niagara Pkwy., 905/354-1721, www.niagaraparks.com, 9:30am-5pm daily, adults $5, ages 6-12 $3.75), floral displays change with the seasons, including geraniums in June, begonias in the early autumn, and poinsettias, cyclamen, and azaleas in December. In summer, you can stroll through the gardens surrounding the showhouse, which is 500 meters (0.3 miles) south of Horseshoe Falls, on the WEGO bus route.

Dufferin Islands Nature Area (Niagara Pkwy., www.niagaraparks.com, dawn-dusk daily, free) is crisscrossed with walking trails to explore the region's natural side. You can follow the paths and bridges that connect several small islands. From November to January, lighting displays illuminate the islands as part of the annual **Winter Festival of Lights** (www.wfol.com). The nature area is 750 meters (0.5 miles) south of the falls, between the Floral Showhouse and the Rapidsview Parking Lot.

Biking

Zoom Leisure Bikes (3850 Niagara Pkwy., 905/468-2366 or 866/811-6993, www.zoom-leisure.com, 9am-7pm daily June-Aug., 9am-7pm Sat.-Sun. late-May and early Sept., half-day $20, full-day $30) rents bikes from their location near the Whirlpool Aerocar. Zoom also offers cycling tours, including a 4-hour **afternoon parkway winery tour** ($89), where you ride from Niagara Falls to Niagara-on-the-Lake, stopping for samples at 2-3 wineries; they'll shuttle you back to Niagara Falls at the end of the tour.

Hiking

Ontario's premier hiking route, the 800-kilometer (500-mile) **Bruce Trail** (www.niagarabrucetrail.org), which runs all the way to the northern tip of the Bruce Peninsula, begins in Queenston. Throughout the year, the **Niagara Bruce Trail Club** offers frequent hikes of varying lengths and levels of difficulty; nonmembers are welcome. If you'd like to participate in more than one or two hikes, the club will ask you to become a member ($50/year).

The **Greater Niagara Circle Route** (www.niagararegion.ca) includes more than 140 kilometers (87 miles) of paved walking or cycling trails. It loops around the Niagara Peninsula, following the Niagara River south from Niagara-on-the-Lake, to Niagara Falls, to Fort Erie, turning west to Port Colborne, north along the Welland Canal to St. Catharines, and east to return to Niagara-on-the-Lake.

Ice-Skating

At the open-air **Rink at the Brink** (www.wfol.com, 4pm-9pm Mon.-Thurs., noon-10pm Fri.-Sat., noon-9pm Sun., Dec.-Feb.), near the Table Rock Centre, you can skate in view of the falls. Skate rentals are available.

Waterparks

Sixteen waterslides, a huge wave pool, and a water play area keep families splashing at the **Fallsview Indoor Waterpark** (5685 Falls Ave., 888/234-8408, www.fallsviewwaterpark.com, call or check the website for seasonal hours, day pass $45). The park offers accommodations packages with several nearby hotels, including the Sheraton on the Falls, Crowne Plaza Niagara Falls-Fallsview Hotel, Skyline Inn, and Clifton Victoria Inn at the Falls.

The **Waves Indoor Waterpark** (8444 Lundy's Lane, 905/356-8444 or 866/707-0030, www.americananiagara.com, call or check the website for seasonal hours, $27 pp), located at the Americana Resort on the west end of Lundy's Lane, also has a wave pool, water slides, a kiddy play structure, and whirlpools.

ACCOMMODATIONS

Niagara Falls has thousands of rooms, in everything from barebones motels to homey B&Bs to glitzy hotel towers. In general, the closer you are to the falls, the higher the price, and any room with even a partial falls view will cost more than a viewless lodging.

Accommodations are clustered in several main areas. The Fallsview area, on the Niagara Escarpment above Horseshoe Falls, has predominantly high-end hotel towers and some of the best falls views. A mix of basic chain hotels and more upscale properties lines the streets surrounding Clifton Hill. North of the falls, along River Road and the surrounding residential streets, are numerous bed-and-breakfasts. Along Ferry Street and Lundy's Lane west of the falls, you'll find a mix of old-fashioned roadside motels and more modern chains. Some of the cheapest rooms are on the west end of Lundy's Lane (which, despite its picturesque name, is a busy multilane boulevard), near the entrance to the QEW; just budget for parking near the falls or plan to take the bus, since it's too far to walk.

Rates are generally highest in July-August and during holiday weekends. Fall weekends, when the leaves are in full color, are also busy. Room rates can fluctuate wildly, even within the same month, so check different travel dates if your plans are flexible. Outside the summer season, you can often find great deals, with the budget-price to mid-range chain properties around the falls advertising rooms in the $59-99 range.

Under $100

Near the bus and train stations and the Queen Street downtown district, **HI-Niagara Falls Youth Hostel** (4549 Cataract Ave., 905/357-0770 or 888/749-0058, www.hostellingniagara.com, $33-37 dorm, $79 d) provides cheap beds, space to hang out, and activities ranging from barbecues to pub crawls. Sleeping options include cramped four- and six-bed dorms, two-bed "deluxe" dorms ($45)—basically a shared twin room—and tiny double-bed private rooms, all with shared baths. Linens and towels are included, as is a light continental breakfast. You can prep your own meals in the communal kitchen or play pool in the basement lounge. Wi-Fi is free.

Staying at **Strathaird Bed & Breakfast** (4372 Simcoe St., 905/358-3421, www.strathairdinn.com, May-Oct., $80-105 d) is like visiting a favorite aunt and uncle. Owners Tom and Val Jackson offer a warm Scottish welcome to their modest but comfortable home, encouraging you to have a cup of tea or relax on the porch. The three guest rooms upstairs cover the basics: queen beds, en suite baths, air-conditioning, and Wi-Fi, and you'll fuel up with a full Scottish breakfast of eggs, bacon, beans, tomatoes, and fruit. Rates include parking, or if you phone ahead, they'll pick you up at the train or bus station. The WEGO bus stops one block away.

$100-150

A full hot breakfast is served in the formal dining room at **Greystone Manor B&B** (4939 River Rd., 905/357-7373 or 877/237-4746, www.greystone-manor.ca, $115-135 d), but the atmosphere in this restored 1908 home is anything but formal. The double-size living room has plenty of space for lounging, yoga, or dancing (owner Barbara Grumme, who's a wealth of local information, teaches Latin dance, and you can arrange a lesson). Upstairs, the four queen-bed air-conditioned guest rooms (three en suite, one with a private bath across the hall) are simple but cozy. Wi-Fi, phone calls within North America, and parking are free.

Among Clifton Hill's many family-friendly midrange chains, a good choice is the **Country Inn & Suites** (5525 Victoria Ave., 905/374-6040, www.countryinns.com, $139-209 d, parking $8 per day). Though there's nothing especially country-like about this seven-story motel, it's got what families need, including standard rooms with two queen beds, an indoor pool, a games room, complimentary buffet breakfast, and Internet access; kids under 18 stay free. Rates drop significantly outside the July-August high season.

Across the street from the Fallsview Casino, the **Comfort Inn-Fallsview** (6645 Fallsview Blvd., 905/358-9353 or 800/463-1938, www.comfortinnfallsview.ca, $109-219 d) gives you a Fallsview location for moderate rates. The rooms are standard chain-motel style, but the kids will appreciate the indoor and outdoor pools. If you need more space, ask about the slightly larger family rooms, with two queen beds and a sleep sofa, or the two-bedroom family suites. Wi-Fi is free.

$150-200

Owners Carolyn and Gary Burke have lived in their 1886 heritage home—with its own turret—for more than 30 years, and they share their local knowledge with their guests at the **Park Place B&B** (4851 River Rd., 905/358-0279, www.parkplaceniagara.com, $160-185 d). Each of the two upstairs guest rooms has a king bed, a fireplace, and a large bath with a whirlpool tub; a third suite is in the carriage house. You can choose breakfast delivered to your room or served by candlelight in the Victorian-style dining room. The WEGO bus stops one block away.

Occupying a 1928 former dairy, the boutique ★ **Sterling Inn & Spa** (5195 Magdalen St., 289/292-0000 or 877/783-7772, www.sterlingniagara.com, $165-270 d) has a three-story milk bottle above its entrance. Inside, the 41 contemporary guest rooms are spare but spacious, with couple-courting features like king beds, fireplaces, and large steam showers or whirlpool baths for two. Overall, the feel is upscale, if not deluxe, but pampering touches include a breakfast tray delivered to your room. Wi-Fi and parking are included.

$200-300

The prime rooms at the contemporary **Sheraton on the Falls Hotel** (5875 Falls Ave., 905/374-4445 or 888/229-9961, www. sheratononthefalls.com, $179-549 d, parking $20-35 per day), a 669-room mirrored tower opposite the American Falls, are those overlooking the waterfalls, of course. You'll pay a significant premium for falls-view rooms, but the upcharge is smaller midweek and outside summer high season. Facilities include indoor and outdoor pools, a fitness center, and a spa overlooking the falls; Casino Niagara is nearby. A daily resort fee ($10) covers Wi-Fi, phone calls within Canada and to the United States, and two WEGO bus tickets.

Another top choice for falls-view rooms is the 23-story **Marriott Niagara Falls Fallsview Hotel and Spa** (6740 Fallsview Blvd., 905/357-7300 or 888/501-8916, www. niagarafallsmarriott.com, $189-599 d, parking $35 per day). Of the 432 guest rooms, the higher-floor units have the best perspective of the falls; the suites, including a two-level loft unit with floor-to-ceiling windows, have some of the most dramatic vantage points. Even the indoor pool overlooks Horseshoe Falls. Wi-Fi is $10 per day.

Your kids may not care about seeing the falls once they're at **Great Wolf Lodge** (950 Victoria Ave., 905/354-4888 or 800/605-9653, www.greatwolf.com, $250-350 d), a resort that features a wave pool and several water slides. Amenities include several eateries and snack bars, a spa for adults, a spa for preteens, and a nightly story hour for little ones. The standard family suite has two queens or one queen plus a sleep sofa, or choose a fun themed suite. Rooms have microwaves and mini fridges. Room rates include waterpark access, which is limited to hotel guests. The lodge is seven

kilometers (4.5 miles) north of the Horseshoe Falls.

A 30-story tower, the **Fallsview Casino Resort** (6380 Fallsview Blvd., 888/325-5788, www.fallsviewcasinoresort.com, $269-349 d) feels like a small city. The lobby, with its art deco-style ceiling, checkerboard floor, and Doric columns, channels the French belle epoque, while the 374 guest rooms are more spare, perhaps to avoid competing with the views of the falls from most rooms. There's an indoor pool, a spa, a collection of shops and boutiques, 18 restaurants and fast-food outlets, and the casino itself, Canada's largest gaming facility. The 1,500-seat theater hosts concerts, comedy shows, and other big-name entertainment.

FOOD

If you're at home in chain restaurants, you'll be happy eating in Niagara Falls. The chains are cheek by jowl on the streets surrounding the falls, particularly along Clifton Hill. However, if you're looking for decent quality or independent eateries, you'll have to look a little harder. Queen Street, the still-reviving downtown district, is worth checking out, as is the area on Ferry Street near Stanley Avenue. It's also a short drive to Niagara-on-the-Lake, where you'll find more dining options.

The Niagara Parks agency runs convenient restaurants and snack bars at several of the visitors centers around Niagara Falls. Meals range from basic sandwiches to high-end fare; expect crowd-pleasing, rather than spectacular, cuisine. Hours vary seasonally. **Elements on the Falls** (6650 Niagara Pkwy., 905/354-3631, lunch $17-23, dinner $25-37) has great views of the Horseshoe Falls; if you'd rather be grazing while gazing out at the falls, come for afternoon tapas (3pm-6pm daily, $9-14). Other Parks restaurants include the **Queenston Heights Restaurant** (14184 Niagara Pkwy., Queenston, 905/262-4274, lunch $16-22), and **Edgewaters Restaurant** (6345 Niagara Pkwy., 905/262-4274, $12-32) at Queen Victoria Place.

The small **Niagara Falls Farmers**

Market (5943 Sylvia Pl., 905/356-7521, www.
niagarafalls.ca/farmersmarket, 6am-noon
Sat.) operates year-round near the intersection of Main and Ferry Streets.

Fallsview

Designed by the Toronto celebrity chef,
Windows by Jamie Kennedy (5875 Falls
Ave., 866/374-4408, www.windowsbyjamiek-
ennedy.com, 6pm-10pm daily, $25-38), on the
14th floor of the Sheraton on the Falls Hotel,
pairs falls views with a locally focused menu
to create a special evening. Start with a crab-
filled California roll or squash and chorizo
soup, and continue with mustard-crusted rack
of lamb or salmon paired with olive and tomato quinoa. Kennedy is known for his fries;
consider a side order. Finish with an all-Canadian cheese plate or a dark chocolate cake
with espresso cream. To drink? Ontario wine,
of course.

You'd be unlikely to stumble into ★ **AG
Cuisine** (Sterling Inn, 5195 Magdalen Ave.,
289/292-0005, www.agcuisine.com, 5:30pm-
9:30pm Tues.-Sun., $24-37), but this stylish
restaurant on the lower level of the Sterling
Inn earns kudos for its creative cuisine. With
retro white banquettes, red drapes, and twinkling chandeliers, the dining room channels
the Rat Pack, while the food is ever so au courant. Executive chef Cory Linkson favors
regional ingredients in his artfully plated
dishes, perhaps locally raised beef tenderloin with an almond-Brie crust or rainbow
trout with pollen-roasted fennel. The well-
constructed wine list emphasizes Niagara
producers.

Want to eat above it all? In the Skylon
Tower's **Revolving Dining Room** (www.
skylon.com, 11:30am-3pm and 4:30pm-11pm
daily, lunch $25-49, dinner $41-77), which
makes a complete rotation every hour, even
a hamburger will set you back $25, but tower
admission is free when you ride up for a meal.
For families, the **Summit Suite Buffet
Dining Room** (11:30am-3pm and 5pm-10pm
Mon.-Sat., 10:30am-2:30pm and 5pm-10pm
Sun., lunch adults $27.50, children $12.50,

dinner adults $40, children $15), which also
includes tower admission, is a better value.

Ferry and Main Streets

For good food, moderate prices, and a family-
friendly feel, all within walking distance from
Clifton Hill, **Bravo Pizzeria** (5438 Ferry St.,
905/354-3354, www.bravopizzeriagrill.com,
11:30am-midnight daily, $11-21) specializes
in pizzas cooked in the wood-fired oven, from
Greek-style with feta, olives, and spinach to
the *arrabbiata*, loaded with spicy sausage,
hot calabrese salami, and peppers. The overstuffed sandwiches include chicken parmi-
giana and prosciutto with fresh mozzarella,
Montreal smoked meat, and other deli favor-
ites. Soups, salads, and pastas round out the
menu. The beer selection features brews from
70 countries; parking is free.

Italian classics done well have kept the
traditional family-run **Napoli Ristorante**
(5485 Ferry St., 905/356-3345, www.napolir-
istorante.ca, 4pm-close daily, $12-32) in busi-
ness since 1962. Start with the *aranchini* (rice
balls stuffed with prosciutto and arugula),
or a freshly made Caesar salad. Then share
a pizza; tuck into a pasta, such as the orechi-
ette abruzzese (shaped like "little ears" and
tossed with rapini and homemade sausage);
or fuel up with the grilled veal chop or the
chicken stuffed with butternut squash. The
wines include both Niagara and Italian labels.
Parking is free.

An old-fashioned lunch counter with
an updated menu and hipster vibe, **Regal
Diner** (5924 Main St., 905/351-2524, www.
theregaldiner.com, 8am-3pm Thurs.-Mon.,
$5-12) serves breakfast all day, including
omelets, first-rate home fries, and a "sausage butty" (homemade sausage on a bun).
Mushroom burgers, BLTs, and grilled cheese
sandwiches are on the menu midday.

Queen Street and North

France's loss became Niagara's gain after chef-
owner Thierry Clement left his homeland and
opened **Paris Crêpes Café** (4613 Queen St.,
289/296-4218, www.pariscrepescafe.com,

lunch 11am-2pm Mon.-Fri., dinner 5pm-8pm Sun.-Thurs. and 5pm-9pm Fri.-Sat., brunch 10am-2:30pm Sat., 10am-3pm Sun., $9-25), a French bistro and *crêperie* in downtown Niagara Falls. The classic crepes are the must-haves, particularly savory buckwheat versions like the Sud Ouest (stuffed with duck confit, onion jam, Swiss cheese, and a sunny-side-up egg); sweet varieties include dark chocolate, chestnut, and salted caramel.

The full-bodied Red Cream Ale, lighter Charleston Lager, and creamy Vanilla Wheat are among the brews on tap at **Taps on Queen** (4680 Queen St., 289/477-1010, www.tapsbeer.ca, noon-10pm Sun.-Tues. and Thurs., noon-midnight Wed. and Fri.-Sat., $10-17), a local microbrewery and pub with a sidewalk patio. To go with your beer, choose pizza, sandwiches like the giant meatball sub, or comfort fare like macaroni and cheese or fish-and-chips.

Gracious Old World ★ **Casa Mia Ristorante** (3518 Portage Rd., 905/356-5410, www.casamiaristorante.com, lunch 11:30am-2:30pm Mon.-Fri., dinner 5pm-10pm daily, $20-58) feels light-years away from the whirl of the falls. The traditional Italian offerings include cannelloni fiorentina (stuffed with ground veal and spinach) or rack of lamb, alongside beet gnocchi with gorgonzola cream sauce. Choose among 30 wines by the glass and hundreds more by the bottle. The lunch menu is simpler, with pizzas, sandwiches, pastas, lemon chicken, and a catch of the day. Casa Mia, about a 15-minute drive north of Horseshoe Falls, offers free transportation to and from area hotels.

INFORMATION AND SERVICES
Visitor Information

A good source for guidance about things to do and places to stay in Niagara Falls is **Niagara Falls Tourism** (905/356-6061 or 800/563-2557, www.niagarafallstourism.com), the city's Visitor and Convention Bureau.

The **Niagara Parks Commission** (877/642-7275, www.niagaraparks.com) operates several seasonal information offices that can help you once you're in town. Their objective is to encourage you to visit Niagara Parks attractions (and sell tickets), but they provide information as well. They open at 9am daily June-August:

- **Table Rock Welcome Centre** (6650 Niagara Pkwy., near Horseshoe Falls)
- **Grand View Marketplace Welcome Centre** (outside the Hornblower Niagara Cruises ticket booths)
- **Clifton Hill Welcome Centre** (Clifton Hill at Falls Ave.)
- **Murray Street Welcome Centre** (near Queen Victoria Pl.)
- **Rapidsview Welcome Centre** (south of the Falls at the Rapidsview parking lot)

Discounts and Passes

Niagara Parks sells passes that offer discounts for various attractions. The **Niagara Falls Adventure Pass Classic** (www.niagaraparks.com, May-mid-Nov., adults $50, ages 6-12 $37) includes admission to the Hornblower Niagara Cruises, Journey Behind the Falls, *Niagara's Fury,* and the White Water Walk, along with two days' transportation on the WEGO buses. If you plan to see all these attractions, the pass will save you about 30 percent off the individual ticket prices.

For the same price, you can choose the **Niagara Falls Adventure Pass Nature,** which covers admission to Hornblower Niagara Cruises, Whirlpool Aero Car, Floral Showhouse, and Butterfly Conservatory, as well as two days of WEGO rides. The Adventure Passes are available online, at the Niagara Parks Welcome Centres, or at any of the included attractions.

GETTING THERE

The main commercial airports serving the Niagara region are in Toronto and Buffalo. Niagara Falls has train service from Toronto and Buffalo, with connections to other Canadian and U.S. cities, and you can get

Bridges to Niagara

To travel between the United States and Canada in the Niagara region, you have to cross the Niagara River on one of four bridges. All are toll bridges; you pay the toll when you're *entering* Canada. The bridges can get clogged with traffic, so before you choose your route, check the border lineups online or by phone through the **Niagara Falls Bridge Commission** (800/715-6722, www.niagarafallsbridges.com). You can also get border crossing updates from the **U.S. Customs and Border Protection** (http://bwt.cbp.gov) and the **Canadian Border Services Agency** (www.cbsa-asfc.gc.ca).

The **Peace Bridge** (www.peacebridge.com, 24 hours daily, CAD$3.25 or US$3) is the southernmost crossing, linking I-190 from the Buffalo area with the QEW in Fort Erie.

The **Rainbow Bridge** (www.niagarafallsbridges.com, 24 hours daily, CAD$3.75 or US$3.50) directly connects Niagara Falls, Ontario, with Niagara Falls, New York. The main highway routes to this bridge are the QEW on the Canadian side and I-190 on the U.S. side.

You must have a NEXUS card to cross the **Whirlpool Bridge** (www.niagarafallsbridges.com, 7am-11pm daily, CAD$3.75 or US$3.50), north of the Rainbow Bridge. NEXUS is a pre-screened traveler program designed to expedite border crossings for frequent travelers between the United States and Canada. To get more information about NEXUS, contact the **U.S. Customs and Border Protection** (www.cbp.gov) or the **Canadian Border Services Agency** (www.cbsa-asfc.gc.ca).

North of the falls, the **Queenston-Lewiston Bridge** (www.niagarafallsbridges.com, 24 hours daily, CAD$3.75 or US$3.50) connects Queenston, Ontario, and Lewiston, New York. This is the closest bridge to Niagara-on-the-Lake. Choose another crossing if you have a NEXUS card, though, since there's no NEXUS lane on this bridge.

---

there by bus from a variety of destinations as well. By car, it's about two hours' drive from Toronto and less than an hour from Buffalo, traffic and border crossings permitting.

If you're traveling between Niagara and Buffalo or other U.S. points, remember that you must cross an international border. Allow extra time for border formalities, and make sure you have your passport.

Air

Toronto

Toronto's **Pearson International Airport** (YYZ, 6301 Silver Dart Dr., Mississauga, 416/247-7678 or 866/207-1690, www.toronto-pearson.com) has flights from across Canada, the United States, and overseas. All the chain car rental agencies, and several local rental companies, have offices at Pearson airport.

The most direct way to travel from Pearson to Niagara Falls is to take the **Niagara Air Bus** (905/374-8111 or 800/206-7222, www.niagaraairbus.com, 2 hours, one-way $92), a door-to-door airport shuttle. Book online

at least three days in advance for a 5 percent discount. If you're stopping off in Toronto anyway, it's much cheaper to catch a bus to Niagara Falls from downtown Toronto than from the airport.

Buffalo

Flying from the United States, you may find cheaper flights into the **Buffalo-Niagara International Airport** (BUF, 4200 Genesee St., Buffalo, NY, 716/630-6000, www.buffalo-airport.com). All the major North American car rental agencies operate at the Buffalo airport.

The cheapest way to reach Niagara Falls from the Buffalo airport is by bus. Both **Megabus** (866/488-4452, www.megabus.com, 1.5-2 hours, one-way $3-10) and **Greyhound** (800/661-8747, www.greyhound.ca, 1.25-2 hours, one-way $11.50-17) run two daily buses in each direction between Buffalo airport and the **Niagara Transportation Centre** (4555 Erie Ave., Niagara Falls).

Several taxi, shuttle, and limo services offer

more frequent, but more expensive, service between Buffalo airport and Niagara Falls. The most economical carrier will depend on the number of people in your party. Check the airport website (www.buffaloairport.com) for additional transportation information.

- **Buffalo Airport Express** (716/472-8580 or 800/604-1570, www.buffaloairportexpress.com): Scheduled shuttle service to or from major Niagara Falls hotels.
- **Buffalo Airport Shuttle** (716/685-2550 or 877/750-2550, www.buffaloairportshuttle.com): Scheduled shuttle service to or from major Niagara Falls hotels.
- **Buffalo Airport Taxi** (716/633-8294 or 800/551-9369, www.buffaloairporttaxi.com, 8am-8pm daily, one-way $65 pp): Scheduled shuttle service to or from major Niagara Falls hotels.
- **Gray Line Niagara Falls** (716/285-2113 or 877/285-2113, www.graylineniagarafalls.com, one-way $85 per car, up to 3 people): Private car service to or from any Niagara Falls address.
- **Niagara Air Bus** (905/374-8111 or 800/206-7222, www.niagaraairbus.com, one-way $93 pp, 5 percent discount for 3-day advance online booking): Door-to-door service to or from any Niagara Falls address.

Train

VIA Rail, GO Trains, and Amtrak all provide service to the **Niagara Falls Train Station** (4267 Bridge St.), which is north of the falls, one block from the Queen Street downtown district. **VIA Rail** (888/842-7245, www.viarail.ca, 2 hours, one-way adults $22-46, ages 2-11 $22-23) runs one train daily in each direction between Toronto's Union Station (65 Front St. W., 311/392-2489) and Niagara Falls.

From late May through mid-October, **GO Transit** (416/869-3200 or 888/438-6646, www.gotransit.com, Fri.-Sun., one-way adults $20.65, seniors and ages 6-12 $10.35) runs weekend and holiday train service from

Toronto's Union Station; the trip takes two hours. On weekends and holidays, these seasonal GO trains run as the **bike train** (www.gotransit.com), with coaches specifically designed to carry bicycles.

The **Amtrak *Maple Leaf*** (800/872-7245, www.amtrak.com) travels from New York City's Penn Station to Toronto's Union Station, stopping in Niagara Falls. The train runs once daily, with major stops at Poughkeepsie, Albany, Syracuse, Rochester, Buffalo, and Niagara Falls (New York) before crossing into Canada. The New York City-Niagara trip (one-way adults $88-119, ages 2-12 $44-75) takes 9.5 hours.

Bus

Long-distance buses, including those from Toronto and New York City, arrive at and depart from the **Niagara Transportation Centre** (4555 Erie Ave., 905/357-2133), across the street from the Niagara Falls Train Station. **Megabus** (www.megabus.com) has frequent service between Toronto's Central Bus Station (610 Bay St.) and Niagara Falls. The trip takes about two hours, and fares can be as low as $1.50 each way (yes, really), although more typical one-way fares are $12-18. Megabus also travels between Niagara Falls and Hamilton (1.5-1.75 hours, one-way $10) and between Niagara Falls and Beamsville (50 minutes, $5-6) in the Twenty Valley.

GO Transit (416/869-3200 or 888/438-6646, www.gotransit.com, 2-2.75 hours, one-way adults $17.65, seniors and ages 6-12 $8.85) operates several daily buses from Toronto's Union Station to Niagara Falls, but note that you have to change buses at Burlington en route. From the United States, **Greyhound** (www.greyhound.ca, 10-11 hours, one-way adults $75-145) has several daily buses from New York City to Niagara Falls.

Car

Niagara Falls is 130 kilometers (80 miles) southeast of Toronto. From downtown Toronto, you can take the Gardiner Expressway west to the QEW. Follow the

Niagara on Two Wheels

The Niagara region is one of Ontario's most bicycle-friendly areas, crisscrossed with bike routes and cycling paths. To get yourself and your bike to Niagara, take the **Bike Train** (www.biketrain.ca), operated by **GO Transit** (416/869-3200 or 888/438-6646, www.gotransit.com). From late May through mid-October, bike trains running between Toronto's Union Station and Niagara Falls on Saturday, Sunday, and holidays have coaches specifically designed to carry bicycles.

For more information about bicycling in the Niagara region, check the website for **Regional Niagara Bicycling Committee** (www.rnbc.info), which has regional cycling maps and resources. The Niagara Region website (www.niagararegion.ca, click on "Maps and Trails") has an online regional cycling route planner that allows you to specify your starting point, the approximate distance you want to ride, the level of difficulty, and types of sights you might like to see along the way. They also have a bike map app that you can download to a mobile device.

While many accommodations will provide places for you to store your bike, **Cycle and Stay Niagara** (www.cycleandstayniagara.com) is a network of B&Bs located on or near a bike route that are particularly cyclist-friendly. If your Niagara cycling adventures whet your appetite for seeing more of Ontario by bike, explore **Ontario By Bike** (www.ontariobybike.ca), which can help you plan cycling trips across the province.

THE GREATER NIAGARA CIRCLE ROUTE

The Greater Niagara Circle Route (www.niagararegion.ca) includes more than 140 kilometers (87 miles) of mostly paved cycling trails, which lets you cycle to many of the area's highlights. The trail loops around the Niagara Peninsula, following the Niagara River south from Niagara-on-the-Lake to Niagara Falls and on to Fort Erie. It then turns inland between Fort Erie and Port Colborne, running along the Welland Canal from Port Colborne to St. Catharines before returning to Niagara-on-the-Lake.

The circle route is actually made up of a number of shorter trails, so if you don't want to cycle the whole loop, you can choose one or more of the following routes:

· The **Niagara River Recreational Trail** (www.niagaraparks.com) follows the Niagara River 56 kilometers (35 miles) from Fort George in Niagara-on-the-Lake past Niagara Falls

QEW south as it skirts the Lake Ontario shore, then passes Hamilton and St. Catharines. Exit onto Highway 420 east, which will take you into Niagara Falls.

Coming from the United States, Niagara Falls is 40 kilometers (25 miles) from Buffalo, New York. Interstate 190 from Buffalo goes north to the four bridges over the Niagara River, which separates New York from Ontario.

Tours from Toronto

Many tour companies offer one-day excursions from Toronto to Niagara Falls. Prices and services vary widely, from barebones backpacker trips to deluxe limousine tours. In general, you'll save money exploring on your own, but the convenience of a tour may be worth the extra money.

· **Chariots of Fire** (www.tourniagarafalls.com, $77) runs good-value Niagara Falls day tours that include either the Hornblower Niagara boat tour or the Skylon Tower, a winery stop, and round-trip transportation. They have three pickup points in Toronto: one near Pearson Airport (7am), one at 33 Yonge Street near Front Street downtown (7:30am), and one at 279 Yonge Street near Eaton Centre (8am). You'll arrive in Niagara by 10am, and you'll be back in Toronto between 5pm and 5:30pm.

· Departing from downtown Toronto hotels

to Fort Erie. The section of the trail between Niagara-on-the-Lake and the falls is one of the region's most popular.

- Crossing the southern end of the Niagara Peninsula, parallel to the Lake Erie shore, the paved **Friendship Trail** (www.friendshiptrail.forterie.ca) runs 16 kilometers (10 miles) from Seaway Park in Port Colborne to Fort Erie, where it joins the Niagara River Recreational Trail.

- The **Welland Canals Trail** (www.welland.ca) is a 42-kilometer (27-mile) north-south cycling path that connects St. Catharines and Port Colborne, running along the Welland Canal.

LAKE ONTARIO WATERFRONT TRAIL

The Niagara region is at the western end of the Lake Ontario Waterfront Trail (www.waterfronttrail. org), which follows the shores of Lake Erie, Lake Ontario, and the St. Lawrence River from Windsor all the way to the Quebec border. Extending for roughly 1,400 kilometers (870 miles), the trail includes a mix of dedicated off-road cycling paths and on-road routes, typically on less trafficked residential streets, although some sections do run along the shoulder of major roads.

On the Niagara Peninsula, the waterfront trail connects the towns of Port Colborne, Fort Erie, Niagara Falls, Niagara-on-the-Lake, St. Catharines, Lincoln, and Grimsby, continuing on to Hamilton and then north to Toronto.

NEW YORK TO NIAGARA

If you want to ride your bike from New York State to the Niagara region, you can. Cyclists are allowed to cross the Peace Bridge between the Buffalo area and Fort Erie. You don't have to pay the toll, but you do need the same documents (including your passport) as you do if you're coming by other means of transportation. You can pick up the Niagara River Recreation Trail or the Friendship Trail on the Ontario side of the bridge.

Cyclists can also cross the Rainbow Bridge ($0.50). If you're in Niagara Falls—either Ontario or New York—and you want to cross over to the other Niagara Falls, the Rainbow Bridge is the most direct route. Again, passports are required. Cyclists and pedestrians are not allowed on the Queenston-Lewiston Bridge.

between 8am and 9am, and returning to Eaton Centre between 5pm and 6pm, **Queen Tour** (www.tourstoniagarafalls. com, adults $79, under age 12 $71) includes a Hornblower Niagara boat tour; time to explore Niagara Falls; quick stops at the Floral Clock, the Whirlpool Rapids, and a winery; and round-trip transportation from Toronto. You can also choose the same tour without the boat ride (adults $59, kids $53).

- **GrayLine Tours** (www.grayline.ca, adults $138, seniors $124, ages 5-11 $91, families $397) runs daily 9.5-hour trips from Toronto that include a buffet lunch, a Hornblower Niagara boat tour, and stops at the Whirlpool Rapids, the Floral Clock, and a winery. Their "Freedom Tour" (adults

$110, seniors $96, ages 5-11 $73, families $318) includes the same stops without meals. Both include return transportation from many Toronto hotels, departing around 10am.

- **HI-Toronto Youth Hostel** (416/971-4440 or 877/848-8737, www.hostellingtoronto. com) sells a Discovery Package ($75) that includes a Niagara Falls day tour, a visit to the Steam Whistle Brewery, a Toronto city tour, and a two-hour bike rental; you must be a Hostelling International member to qualify for this package rate.

GETTING AROUND

You can easily walk along the river near the falls, between Table Rock and the

Hornblower Niagara cruise docks, and up to Clifton Hill, where many hotels are located. You can also walk between Horseshoe Falls and the Fallsview hotel district, although it's a fairly steep climb up the hill. Cycling is another good option; you can pedal the 56-kilometer (35-mile) Niagara River Recreation Trail between Niagara-on-the-Lake and Fort Erie.

Bus

Operated in partnership by the City of Niagara Falls and the Niagara Parks Commission, the **WEGO bus** (www.wegoniagarafalls.com, check the website for seasonal hours, day pass adults $7, ages 6-12 $4) is a convenient year-round shuttle bus. Its several useful routes converge at the Table Rock Visitors Centre and transport you around Niagara Falls. The **Niagara Falls Adventure Pass** (www.niagaraparks.com) includes two free days of WEGO bus rides.

The WEGO Green Line travels along the Niagara Parkway, stopping at all the major Niagara Parks attractions. If you've driven to the falls area, you can park your car for the day in the Rapidsview lot ($10) and catch the WEGO bus to the falls and other points of interest.

The Blue Line loops through the Fallsview and Clifton Hill districts, and the Purple Line will take you to Queen Street downtown, including stops at the bus and train station. The Red Line runs through Clifton Hill and continues out along Ferry Street and Lundy's Lane—handy if you'd like to visit the Niagara Falls History Museum or if you're staying at a Lundy's Lane hotel.

Daunted by the steep hill between the Fallsview district and the falls themselves? The **Falls Incline Railway** (www.niagaraparks.com, one-way $2.50, all-day pass $6, kids under 5 free) transports passengers up and down the 30-meter (100-foot) embankment between the Table Rock Visitors Centre and Fallsview Boulevard, near the Fallsview Casino and the Skylon Tower. The ride is quick—about one minute.

Car

Parking near the falls is quite limited. If you can leave the car at home, you'll save yourself some parking hassles. The least expensive long-term parking near the falls is at the **Rapidsview Parking Lot** ($10 per day), on the Niagara Parkway 1.5 kilometers (one mile) south of the falls. From here, you can take the WEGO bus to Table Rock and Horseshoe Falls. The parking area is open

Getting around Niagara Falls is easy on the WEGO buses.

Saturday-Sunday mid-May-late June, and daily late July-early September.

Other parking lots include the **Falls Lot,** directly behind the Horseshoe Falls, which has daily parking rates; the **Floral Showhouse Lot,** with parking by the hour; and **Queen Victoria Place,** which also has hourly parking. You can park for free at Niagara Parks's locations outside the central falls area, including the White Water Walk, Whirlpool Aero Car, Niagara Glen, and Old Fort Erie.

When driving around the falls, watch out for pedestrians. Many become captivated by the waterfalls and thus completely oblivious to traffic.

Tours

It lasts only 12 minutes, but **Niagara Helicopters Flightseeing Tour** (3731 Victoria Ave., 905/357-5672, www.niagarahelicopters.com, 9am-sunset daily, adults $137, couples $264, kids $85) is an exciting way to see the falls from a different perspective. Aboard a six-passenger Bell 407 helicopter, your flight path takes you along the Niagara River, over the Whirlpool, past the American Falls, and around the Canadian Horseshoe Falls; their semicircular horseshoe shape is most apparent from the air. You don headphones to listen to narration about the sights along the way.

VICINITY OF NIAGARA FALLS
Queenston

Located 13 kilometers (8 miles) north of Niagara Falls and 11 kilometers (6.8 miles) south of downtown Niagara-on-the-Lake, the quiet village of Queenston houses several historic sites.

Queenston Heights National Historic Site

British and Canadian troops clashed with the American invaders in the Battle of Queenston Heights, one of the early skirmishes of the War of 1812 fought on Niagara soil. Through the British won the battle, the British commander, Major General Isaac Brock, was killed.

The battle site is now the **Queenston Heights Park** (www.niagaraparks.com), with gardens and picnic tables, as well as **Brock's Monument,** a national historic site honoring the fallen British military leader. Parks Canada runs **interpretive programs** (905/468-4257, www.pc.gc.ca, 10am-5pm daily May-Aug., 11am-4pm Wed.-Fri. and 10am-5pm Sat.-Sun. Sept.-mid-Oct., adults $4.50, ages 6-16 $3.50) at the monument, or you can follow a self-guided tour.

Mackenzie Printery and Newspaper Museum

In 1824, political reformer and journalist William Lyon Mackenzie (1795-1861) began publishing a newspaper, the *Colonial Advocate,* in this Queenston house. This ivy-covered stone building, which dates to the late 1700s, is now the **Mackenzie Printery and Newspaper Museum** (1 Queenston St., 905/262-5676, www.niagaraparks.com or www.mackenzieprintery.org, 10am-5pm daily May-early Sept., adults $5, ages 6-12 $3.75) devoted to Mackenzie's life and work, the early history of the Niagara-York (now Toronto) region, and the development of printing technology from the 18th century to the present. The museum also houses Canada's oldest printing press, a wooden device built in Britain in 1760, which was used to print Ontario's first newspaper, the *Upper Canada Gazette,* in 1793.

Guided tours run 30-45 minutes and include plenty of hands-on activities. You can set your name in movable type—and learn how hard it was to be a printer's apprentice. The Printery is 13.3 kilometers (8.3 miles) north of Horseshoe Falls.

Laura Secord Homestead

During the War of 1812, Laura Ingersoll Secord and her husband, James, were ordered to billet several American soldiers in their Queenston home. One night, they overheard the American officers planning an attack on British forces at nearby Beaverdams. Since James had been injured several months earlier during the Battle of Queenston Heights, Laura decided that she would go warn the British commander, based near Thorold, of the impending American assault. Her 32-kilometer (20-mile) journey on foot through the dense woods took 18 hours. As a result of Secord's information, the British set up an ambush and defeated the Americans in the Battle of Beaverdams on June 24, 1813.

Secord is often called "Canada's Paul Revere," after the man who made a similar journey during the American Revolution to warn that British troops were arriving in Boston. The home where she and her husband lived, the **Laura Secord Homestead** (29 Queenston St., 905/262-4851, www.niagaraparks.com, 10am-5pm daily May-early Sept., 10am-4pm Wed.-Sun. early Sept.-mid-Oct., adults $9.50, ages 6-12 $6.25) is now a museum, where guides in period dress lead 30-minute tours, providing information about Secord's life and times. Also on the property is the gothic-style **Queenston Chapel,** a Methodist church built in the 1860s and subsequently moved to the Secord Homestead site.

The Homestead is 13.3 kilometers (8.3 miles) north of Horseshoe Falls, a short walk from the Mackenzie Printery.

Old Fort Erie

In 1764, at the Niagara Peninsula's southeastern point, a short hop across the river to the New York shore, the British built their first fort in Ontario. The fort became a base for an alliance of British, Loyalist, and Iroquois soldiers during the American Revolution (1775-1783), but it took its place in history during the War of 1812 when it became Canada's bloodiest battlefield. During the six-week Siege of Fort Erie in 1814, more than 3,000 troops were killed or wounded. Later that year, as American troops were withdrawing to Buffalo, they destroyed what remained of the fort.

It wasn't until the 1930s that **Old Fort Erie** (350 Lakeshore Rd., Fort Erie, 905/871-0540, www.niagaraparks.com, 10am-5pm daily mid-May-mid-Oct., adults $12.25, ages 6-12 $8) was restored and opened to the public. You can tour the fort, wandering into the soldiers' barracks, officers' quarters, kitchens, and other buildings, where costumed staff tell you about the history of the fort and the region.

Old Fort Erie is 19 kilometers (12 miles) south of Niagara Falls. It's a pretty drive along the Niagara Parkway, although it's a bit faster to take the QEW.

Laura Secord, Canada's "Paul Revere," is buried in Lundy's Lane Cemetery.

Niagara-on-the-Lake

Although it's just 20 kilometers (12.5 miles) up the road from Niagara Falls, the small town of Niagara-on-the-Lake (NOTL) feels like it's on a different planet. While the city of Niagara Falls teeters between brash, honky-tonk, and naturally spectacular, NOTL is more reserved, with a cute (perhaps excessively so) main street, historic attractions that date primarily from the War of 1812, a peaceful lakeshore, and hundreds of B&Bs. The town's main attractions are theater and wine. It's home to the highly regarded Shaw Festival, which runs from April through October, as well as more than two dozen wineries.

Niagara-on-the-Lake is divided into several different sections. The historic downtown is centered along Queen Street, bounded by Lake Ontario and the Niagara River. The village of Virgil, along Niagara Stone Road (Highway 55), is the commercial hub, while the more rural village of St. Davids to the south is where you'll find several of the wineries.

★ SHAW FESTIVAL

"You see things; and you say 'Why?'
But I dream things that never
were; and I say 'Why not?'"

Perhaps Shaw Festival founder Brian Doherty had these words from George Bernard Shaw's 1921 play *Back to Methuselah* in mind when he conceived the idea of a summer festival devoted to Shaw's work. Whatever his inspiration, Doherty, a lawyer, playwright, and Shaw fan, launched the **Shaw Festival** (10 Queen's Parade, 905/468-2172 or 800/511-7429, www.shawfest.com, Apr.-Oct.) in the summer of 1962, when he produced eight performances of Shaw's *Don Juan in Hell* and *Candida*.

Author George Bernard Shaw (1856-1950) had no connection to Niagara-on-the-Lake. Born in Dublin, Ireland, in 1856, he wrote 63 plays, five novels, numerous essays, and more

than 250,000 letters during his 94-year life, most of which he lived in England. The festival's original mandate was to perform plays by Shaw and his contemporaries, who include Chekhov and Tennessee Williams. More recently, directors have expanded this mission to include plays about the period when Shaw lived, as well as works by contemporary playwrights who are controversial or political in the same way that Shaw was during his lifetime.

The Shaw Festival operates as a repertory theater, with plays running simultaneously on four stages. The festival company typically includes 65-70 actors per season, many of whom return year after year—as do many patrons.

Tickets

The festival typically announces the lineup for its upcoming season at the end of the previous summer. You can order tickets (adults $35-113) online, by phone, by fax (905/468-3804), by mail (Box 774, Niagara-on-the-Lake, ON L0S 1J0), or in person at any of the festival theaters.

You can save money on tickets by attending discounted preview performances before a play's official opening, as well as Sunday-evening shows. Discounted tickets are available at certain performances for students ($24-29), patrons under age 30 ($30-40), and seniors (from $40). Families can purchase one or two youth tickets (under age 18) for $30 with each regular adult ticket.

Theaters

The Shaw Festival stages its productions at four theaters in Niagara-on-the-Lake. Its flagship venue is the 869-seat **Festival Theatre** (10 Queen's Parade), which opened in 1973 on the east end of downtown. The building also houses the 200-seat **Studio Theatre.** Parking in the Festival Theatre lot costs $10 during performances.

Niagara-on-the-Lake

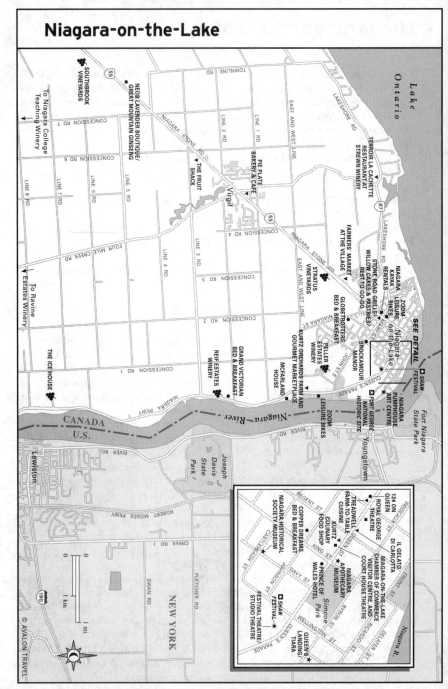

© AVALON TRAVEL

the Shaw Festival's Royal George Theatre

only $5 if you also purchase a ticket to a performance.

Lectures and Workshops

The festival offers a variety of talks, readings, and special events throughout the season. Look for the following events, and get more information about these and other activities on the website (www.shawfest.com):

- **Pre-show Chat:** Before many evening performances mid-May-August at the Festival Theatre, a company member hosts a free introduction to the evening's play at 7:30pm.

- **Continue the Conversation:** After select matinees, join a free moderated discussion about the afternoon's production. The event is free, but reservations are required; call the box office (905/468-2172 or 800/511-7429) for details.

- **Tuesday Q & A:** Following most Tuesday evening performances in all the theaters, you can stay for a free question-and-answer session with company members.

★ WINERIES

Niagara-on-the Lake has more than two dozen wineries. You'll find them along Highway 55 (Niagara Stone Rd.); on York Road in St. Davids, toward Queenston; along the Niagara River Parkway and the concessions (rural roads) parallel to the parkway; and on Lakeshore Road skirting Lake Ontario.

Most NOTL wineries are open year-round and charge a small fee ($2-5) for tastings; if you purchase wine, you may get credit for your tasting fee. Larger wineries offer regularly scheduled tours, but smaller facilities may offer tours only by appointment or not at all. The **Wineries of Niagara-on-the-Lake** (www.wineriesofniagaraonthelake.com) has more details about the region's winemakers and a downloadable touring map.

The Niagara College Teaching Winery

The Niagara College Teaching Winery is Canada's only licensed teaching winery, where

The festival's other two stages are on NOTL's main downtown street: the 327-seat **Court House Theatre** (26 Queen St.) and the similar-size **Royal George Theatre** (85 Queen St.), a former vaudeville house with 328 seats. There's a metered parking lot (Market St., at Regent St.) near the Court House Theatre; for the Royal George, the closest parking is on the surrounding streets.

Tours

For a fascinating behind-the-scenes experience, take the hour-long **backstage tour** (11am Sat.-Sun. Apr.-May; 11am Tues.-Wed. and Sat.-Sun. June-Oct., $10) of the Festival Theatre. You'll learn about the festival's history; visit the rehearsal hall (staff estimate that actors rehearse one hour for each minute they spend on stage); tour the dressing rooms; walk through the wardrobe shop, which occupies a staff of 40 (nearly three-quarters of the costumes used on stage are new every year); and find out more about set design and construction. Tours are

Niagara Food and Wine Events

With so many wineries and local food producers around the Niagara Peninsula, it's no surprise that several festivals and events showcase the area's wine and food. The Niagara region's more than 100 wineries kick off the summer tasting season at the **Niagara New Vintage Festival** (www.niagarawinefestival.com, June) with two weeks of food and wine events.

Every Wednesday in summer, local food trucks, craft brewers, and wine makers join forces for **The SupperMarket** (Market at the Village, 111 Garrison Village Dr., Niagara-on-the-Lake, www.marketatthevillage.ca, 4:30pm-dusk Wed. mid-May-mid-Sept.), a festive alfresco food fair. Look for popular trucks like **El Gastrónomo Vagabundo** (www.elgastro.com), **Yellow Pear** (www.farmtotruck.ca), and **Tide & Vine Oyster Company** (www.tideandvine.com).

Wouldn't running be more fun if you could stop for chocolate along the way? That's the philosophy behind **The Chocolate Race** (905/932-6356, www.thechocolaterace.com, May), a 5K, 10K, and 10-mile walk and run with a chocolate-dipping stop en route and more chocolate treats at the finish line.

In the fall, the **Niagara Wine Festival** (www.niagarawinefestival.com, Sept.) celebrates the harvest with tastings, concerts, and other special events, while the **Niagara Food Festival** (www.niagarafoodfestival.com, Sept.) in Welland serves up tastes of local food. It's worth braving the winter weather for the **Niagara Ice Wine Festival** (www.icewinefestival.com, Jan.), where the tastings, winery tours, a gala party, and other festivities highlight the region's distinctive dessert wines. You can also sample ice wines and more at the **Twenty Valley Winter WineFest** (www.20valley.ca, Jan.).

students study wine making, viticulture, and marketing and staff a working winery on 15 hectares (38 acres) of vineyards. Stop into the college-run **Wine Visitor and Education Centre** (135 Taylor Rd., 905/641-2252, www.niagaracollegewine.ca, 10am-6pm daily May-Oct., 11am-5pm Sun.-Fri., 10am-5pm Sat. Nov.-Apr.) for information about area wineries and tastings of the college's wines, including the reserve wines known as the Dean's List.

The college doesn't neglect beer, either: the **Niagara College Teaching Brewery** (www.niagaracollegebeer.ca) is Canada's first teaching brewery—a two-year program where students learn all aspects of the beer business. Sample the students' brews in the retail shop (10am-6pm daily May-Oct., 11am-5pm Sun.-Fri., 10am-5pm Sat. Nov.-Apr.).

Ravine Estates Winery

The tasting room at the small family-owned **Ravine Estates Winery** (1366 York Rd., St. Davids, 905/262-8463, www.ravinevineyard.com, 10am-6pm Sun.-Thurs., 10am-8pm Fri.-Sat.) is in a historic clapboard home built in the early 1800s. They make merlot, cabernet franc, chardonnay, and sauvignon blanc, among others, and offer several types of tours. Stop here if you're hungry, too; there's a market-inspired bistro and bakery on-site.

Southbrook Vineyards

You can't miss the striking azure wall—200 meters (650 feet) long and three meters (10 feet) high—that slices across the fields at **Southbrook Vineyards** (581 Niagara Stone Rd., 905/641-2548 or 888/581-1581, www.southbrook.com, 10am-6pm daily summer, call for off-season hours), marking the entrance to Canada's first certified biodynamic winery. Inside, you can sample wines in the sleek glass-walled tasting pavilion; they're known for chardonnays and cabernet-merlot blends. Tours of the vineyards and winery are offered on weekends; call for a schedule. The farm-to-table **Vineyard Bistro** (noon-5pm Fri.-Sun. late May-mid-Oct., $8-16) serves pizzas outside on the patio.

Stratus Vineyards

With a marble bar, library-style shelves lined with wines, and views across the fields, the tasting room at **Stratus Vineyards** (2059 Niagara Stone Rd., 905/468-1806, www.stratuswines.com, 11am-5pm daily May-Dec., noon-5pm Wed.-Sun. Jan.-Apr.) feels like a luxurious lounge, rather than a muddy-boots winery. Tasting flights of four wines ($10) are served in crystal stemware, and special events, including cheese tastings, concerts, and upscale picnics, take place throughout the season. Their signature wines are blends, labeled simply Stratus White and Status Red. It's also the first winery in the world to receive Leadership in Energy and Environmental Design (LEED) certification, a green-building stamp of approval.

Peller Estates Winery

Best known for chardonnay, riesling, and ice wine, the winery in a grand château at **Peller Estates Winery** (290 John St. E., 905/468-4678 or 888/673-5537, www.peller.com, 10am-7pm Sun.-Thurs., 10am-9pm Fri.-Sat.) produces several lines of wines, from the affordable Family Series to the mid-priced Private Reserve and the high-end Signature Series. They offer multiple options for tastings and tours, and their restaurant is one of the area's most deluxe.

Reif Estates Winery

Opened in 1982, the German-style **Reif Estates Winery** (15608 Niagara Pkwy., 905/468-7738, www.reifwinery.com, tastings 10am-6pm daily Apr.-Oct., 10am-5pm daily Nov.-Mar., tours 11:30am and 1:30pm daily Apr.-Oct., $5) specializes in gewürztraminer and riesling, but they also make chardonnay, pinot noir, cabernet merlot, cabernet franc, and other wines. In addition to the standard tastings, you can book a variety of special options, including a blind tasting of either a red or white flight ($15). Ask about the wine gelato.

The Ice House

On a hot summer afternoon, the sign for "ice wine slushies" may lure you down the lane to **The Ice House** (14774 Niagara Pkwy., 855/331-6161, www.theicehouse.ca, 11am-6pm daily May-June, 10:30am-7pm daily July-Oct., 11am-5pm daily Nov.-Apr.), a small producer of, yes, ice wine. They make several ice wine varieties: white vidal, riesling, and a more unusual cabernet sauvignon. Sample them in their tasting room as you learn more about how ice wine is made. If only every slushie shop could make their chilled treats with ice wine!

SIGHTS

Stop into the **Niagara Historical Society Museum** (43 Castlereagh St., 905/468-3912, www.niagarahistorical.museum, 10am-5pm daily May-Oct., 1pm-5pm daily Nov.-Apr., adults $5, seniors $3, students $2, kids $1) to learn more about the history of the Niagara region. Housed in the first building in Ontario built specifically as a museum (the original structure dates to 1907), the museum today has more than 40,000 historical artifacts, and its exhibits trace Niagara's history from the early aboriginal communities to the founding of Upper Canada through the War of 1812 and into the present day.

A pharmacy that operated on the town's main street for more than 140 years, the **Niagara Apothecary Museum** (5 Queen St., 905/468-3845, www.niagaraapothecary.ca, noon-6pm daily mid-May-June, noon-6pm Mon.-Fri. and 11am-6pm Sat.-Sun. July-Aug., noon-6pm Sat.-Sun. Sept.-mid-Oct., donation) is still filled with many of its original medicine jars and bottles.

One of Niagara-on-the-Lake's oldest buildings, **McFarland House** (15927 Niagara Pkwy., www.niagaraparks.com, noon-5pm daily early May-early Sept., noon-5pm Sat.-Sun. early Sept.-mid-Oct., adults $5, ages 6-12 $3.75) is also one of the town's few structures to have survived the War of 1812. Scottish immigrant John McFarland settled here when the British crown granted him 246 hectares (608 acres) of land to reward his services as a boat builder to King George III.

McFarland and his descendants lived in this 1800 Georgian-style house for more than 140 years. As you tour the restored home, you can learn more about life in the area from 1800 to 1830. Afternoon tea is served in the garden in summer.

The small gallery in the **Niagara Pumphouse Art Centre** (247 Ricardo St., 905/468-5455, www.niagarapumphouse.ca, noon-4pm Mon.-Fri., 1pm-4pm Sat.-Sun. Apr.-Dec., noon-4pm Mon.-Fri. Jan.-Mar., free) shows work by local artists. It's worth a look at the building itself, a Victorian structure overlooking the Niagara River that supplied the town's water from 1891 to 1983.

★ Fort George National Historic Site

Between 1796 and 1799, British troops built a fort to protect the Niagara River—an important supply route to the Great Lakes—as well as the growing town of Newark (now Niagara-on-the-Lake). When the Americans attacked the Niagara region during the War of 1812, U.S. troops bombed Fort George and forced the British to withdraw in May 1813. The Americans occupied Fort George until December 1813, when the British forced them

to retreat to Fort Niagara, on what is now the New York side of the river. British troops once again took control of Fort George and held it through the duration of the war. By the 1820s, however, the British had built a new stronghold nearby at Fort Mississauga (on the grounds of what is now the Niagara-on-the-Lake Golf Club), and Fort George was abandoned.

Today, at the **Fort George National Historic Site** (51 Queens Parade, 905/468-6614, www.pc.gc.ca or www.friendsof-fortgeorge.ca, 10am-5pm daily May-Oct., 10am-5pm Sat.-Sun. Apr. and Nov., noon-5pm Sat.-Sun. Dec.-Mar., adults $11.70, seniors $10.05, ages 6-16 $5.80, families $29.40, parking $5.90), visitors can tour the restored fort's buildings and grounds, including two blockhouses that served as soldiers' quarters, the 1796 powder magazine (the only structure to survive the War of 1812), the officers' quarters, and the kitchen, where costumed guides often cook snacks for visitors on the open hearth. Guides staff many of the buildings and can tell you about the history of the period. Fife and drum corps periodically perform, and staff demonstrate how to operate muskets like those used during the War of 1812.

the Niagara Historical Society Museum

ENTERTAINMENT AND EVENTS

The **Shaw Festival** (10 Queen's Parade, 905/468-2172 or 800/511-7429, www.shawfest.com, Apr.-Oct.) is obviously the main entertainment in town, but beyond the theaters, you'll find other arts events as well. **Music Niagara** (905/468-5566 or 800/511-7429, www.musicniagara.org, mid-July-mid-Aug., $25-50) is a summer festival of classical, jazz, blues, and choral music concerts at wineries, churches, parks, and other venues around town. Established by the founders of the Toronto International Film Festival, the **Niagara Integrated Film Festival** (NIFF, 416/944-8105, www.niagarafilmfest.com, June) combines several days of movie screenings with food and wine events.

SHOPPING

Queen Street is the main downtown shopping street, lined with boutiques, galleries, and restaurants. Most seem designed for visitors. For Shaw books and other memorabilia, visit **Bernard's** (10 Queen's Parade, 905/468-2172 or 800/511-7429, 9am-8pm daily May-Oct., 9am-6pm daily Nov., 9am-5pm Mon.-Sat. Dec., 9am-6pm Mon.-Sat. Jan.-Apr.), the gift shop in the Festival Theatre lobby. Outside downtown, Niagara Stone Road (Hwy. 55) is the region's commercial hub, particularly around the village of Virgil, midway between the QEW and the historic district.

Husband-and-wife team Robert and Melissa Achal founded the **NEOB Lavender Boutique** (758 Niagara Stone Rd., 905/682-0171, www.neoblavender.com, 10am-6pm daily), and they readily share their passion for their 8,000 lavender plants and other flowers and herbs. Their shop is stocked with oils, lotions, and other body products, as well as lavender cookies and even lavender-scented coffee. Tours of the fields and greenhouse ($5) are offered 10am-5pm May-October.

Another crop grown in Niagara is ginseng, which many Asian cultures use to make tea or herbal remedies. Find out more about ginseng's uses at **Great Mountain Ginseng** (758 Niagara Stone Rd., 905/685-7328 or 866/900-0527, www.greatmountainginseng.com, call for hours), which also sells a variety of ginseng products.

Part farm stand and part gourmet food emporium, **Kurtz Orchards Farm and Gourmet Marketplace** (16006 Niagara Pkwy., 905/468-2937, www.kurtzorchards.com, 9am-6pm daily Apr.-Nov.) sells fresh produce, cheeses, baked goods, and sandwiches. You can take an **Orchard and Vineyard Tour** with lunch on the grounds ($22-25); call for schedules. They're known for their jams, jellies, and salsas, which they also sell at the **Kurtz Culinary Food Shop** (38-40 Queen St., 905/468-3815, 10am-5pm daily) downtown.

Banana Republic, Forever 21, J. Crew, and Kate Spade are among the discounted brand names sold at the large **Outlet Collection at Niagara** (300 Taylor Rd., 905/687-6777, www.outletcollectionatniagara.com, 10am-9pm Mon.-Sat., 10am-6pm Sun.), just off the QEW.

SPORTS AND RECREATION

Both walkers and cyclists enjoy the 56-kilometer (35-mile) **Niagara River Recreation Trail,** which begins in Niagara-on-the-Lake and follows the Niagara River south to Niagara Falls and on to Fort Erie. You can rent bicycles from **Zoom Leisure Bikes** (431 Mississauga St., 905/468-2366 or 866/811-6993, www.zoomleisure.com, 8:30am-7pm daily Apr.-Oct., half-day $20, full-day $30). They have an additional rental location on the Niagara River trail (16052 Niagara Pkwy.). They also offer cycling tours, including a 3.5-hour winery tour ($69), which visits several local wineries.

Contact **Niagara Kayak Rentals** (496 Mississauga St., 905/328-1048, www.niagarakayak.com) to get out on the water. They offer several kayaking options, including a two-hour paddle along Lake Ontario (single $35, double $60) or a two-hour paddle in the Niagara River from Queenston Heights to NOTL (single $50, double $85).

ACCOMMODATIONS

The **Niagara-on-the-Lake Chamber of Commerce** (www.niagaraonthelake.com) can book rooms for you at more than 200 area lodgings. You can also search for lodging availability and prices on their website. For bed-and-breakfast listings and bookings, contact the **Niagara-on-the-Lake Bed-and-Breakfast Association** (905/468-0123, www.niagarabedandbreakfasts.com).

$100-150

Owners Donna and Fernando Vieira are avid travelers (and Donna edits *Dreamscapes,* a glossy travel magazine), so it's no surprise that **Globetrotters Bed & Breakfast** (642 Simcoe St., 905/468-4021 or 866/835-4446, www.globetrottersbb.ca, $135-150), a guesthouse on a suburban cul-de-sac, is filled with original art and mementos from their journeys. Draped with colorful sheer curtains, the Sultan's Tent suite feels seductive, although its attached twin-bed room could accommodate a family or friends. The compact Crystal Palace room, on the main floor, has bright blue walls and a hand-painted headboard. Rates include a full breakfast, Wi-Fi, and parking.

$150-250

Just a short walk from Queen Street and the theaters, the **Copper Dreams Bed & Breakfast** (28 Johnson St., 905/468-7097, www.copperdreams.ca, $180-220 d) was originally built in the 1870s to house military officers and their families. You won't feel confined to your quarters here in the three updated guest rooms, each with a queen bed, fireplace, and modern bath. The largest, the Newark Room, has a whirlpool tub. A three-course breakfast, Wi-Fi, and parking are included in the rates.

Built in the 1860s as a summer "cottage," this stately ★ **Grand Victorian Bed & Breakfast** (15618 Niagara Pkwy., 905/468-0997, www.grandvictorian.ca, $185-245 d) has a large wraparound porch and regal architectural details—12-foot ceilings, original woodwork, stained-glass windows, and numerous fireplaces. The six guest rooms have four-poster or canopy beds, antique wardrobes, and other period details; one has a private sun deck. Rates include Wi-Fi and a complimentary tour and tasting at the Reif Estates Winery next door. You can play tennis on the courts out back—at least if you can rouse yourself from that fantastic porch.

You'll want to wake up for the elaborate four-course breakfasts that welcoming owners Colleen and Rick serve promptly at 9am at ★ **Brockamour Manor** (433 King St., 905/468-5527, www.brockamour.com, $199-269 d). Seasonal fruit, freshly baked pastries, and a hearty hot dish will start your day right as you trade travel tips and theater reviews with fellow guests. Wander into the billiards room to work off your meal with a round of pool or lounge over the newspaper. The six guest rooms are spacious, with classic furnishings and modern touches like gas fireplaces, DVD players, and Wi-Fi.

$200-300

In several buildings in the historic district, **124 on Queen** (124 Queen St., 905/468-4552 or 855/988-4552, www.124queen.com, $250-460 d) is a plush place to lay your head. The least expensive rooms have a king or queen bed with a flat-screen TV, Keurig coffeemaker, and mini fridge; up the price scale, added amenities include fireplaces and kitchenettes. The one- and two-bedroom villas ($400-650) have full kitchens and laundry facilities. You can work out in the small fitness room 24-7, and the spa offers massages and facials. Room rates include Wi-Fi, unlimited North American phone calls, parking, and a local shuttle service.

Queen's Landing (155 Byron St., 905/468-2195 or 888/669-5566, www.vintagehotels.com, $270-410 d), a majestic Georgian-style brick inn that looks like it's been on the lakeshore for generations, was actually built in 1990. While the furnishings are classic, it doesn't have the creakiness of an old-fashioned hotel. Some of the 142 rooms have fireplaces or jetted tubs; the best have views over Lake Ontario. There's also an indoor pool. The hotel hosts lots of business events, but you won't be out of place on a weekend escape.

Built in 1864, the refined ★ **Prince of Wales Hotel** (6 Picton St., 905/468-3246 or 888/669-5566, www.vintage-hotels.com, $270-460 d) wows with its elaborately decorated public spaces, from the lobby's ornate inlaid wood floor to the classic drawing room, where afternoon tea is served daily. There is an indoor pool and the Secret Garden spa. The decor varies in the 110 traditionally appointed guest rooms; some have antique four-poster beds, Tiffany lamps, or fireplaces, but all have modern amenities, from rain showers to heated towel racks. The location couldn't be better, right in the town center.

FOOD

Queen Street downtown is lined with places to eat, although you'll often find better value in other parts of town. Several wineries have excellent restaurants, too.

Bakeries and Cafés

Amid the scones and croissants that lure morning lingerers, and the gorgeous-looking cakes and tarts (including mini ones, just right for a picnic), **Willow Cakes and Pastries** (242 Mary St., 905/468-2745, www.willowcakes.ca, 8am-6pm daily mid-Oct.-late May, 8am-6pm Mon.-Thurs., 8am-7pm Fri.-Sun. late May-mid-Oct.), a petite café just outside downtown, bakes quiche, pork pies, and other savory dishes for a light lunch.

Sandwiches, tacos, and creative pizzas are all fine choices at the country-style **Pie Plate Bakery and Café** (1516 Niagara Stone Rd., Virgil, 905/468-9743, www.thepieplate.com, 10am-7pm Tues.-Thurs., 10am-9pm Fri.-Sat., 10am-7pm Sun.), but remember, you're here for the pie: strawberry in June-July, blueberry June-September, peach July-September, and pumpkin in the fall. Whole pies will feed the family; you can eat the individual mini pies right now.

NOTL's latest taste sensations are the frozen treats from ★ **Il Gelato di Carlotta** (59 Queen St., 905/468-8999, www.gelatodicarlotta.com, 11am-10pm Mon., 11am-11:30pm Tues.-Sun. mid-Apr.-mid-Oct; call or check the website for off-season hours), an Italian-style ice cream parlor. Their signature flavor is Crema di Carlotta, a citrus cream, though the rich dark chocolate is pretty irresistible.

It looks like a strip-mall fast-food joint, but

Find the best gelato in Niagara at Il Gelato di Carlotta.

Rest to Go-Go (Garrison Plaza, Mary St. at Mississauga St., 905/468-4685, 11:30am-9pm Sun. and Tues.-Thurs., 11:30am-10pm Fri.-Sat., $7-20), under the same ownership as the upscale Stone Road Grille next door, turns out seriously tasty pizzas and sandwiches. You can concoct your own sandwich, choosing your protein, cheese, and fixings, or select from options like Thai chicken salad with peanut sauce. The pizzas range from traditional to innovative, too; the Ringo is topped with pancetta, cheddar cheese, and potatoes.

Contemporary

Benchmark (135 Taylor Rd., 905/641-2252, ext. 4619, www.niagaracollege.ca, lunch 11:30am-2pm Tues.-Sat., dinner 5pm-9pm Wed.-Sat., lunch $11-14, dinner $18-28), the student-run restaurant room at Niagara College, is teaching its students about local, seasonal cuisine. Your bitter greens salad might come with an ice wine vinaigrette, and the chicken, served with fingerling potato *poutine*, may have been raised nearby. The wine list draws from the college's own labels and other Niagara producers. For a lighter bite, stop into **Bench to Go** (8:30am-2:30pm Mon.-Fri. June-Aug., 8am-4pm Mon.-Fri. Sept.-May, $4-6), which sells good-value salads, sandwiches, and a daily hot dish, plus pastries and coffee.

Look for the sign saying "Rest" to find the ★ **Stone Road Grille** (Garrison Plaza, 238 Mary St., www.stoneroadgrille.com, lunch 11:30am-2pm Tues.-Sun., dinner 5pm-9pm Sun. and Tues.-Thurs., 5pm-10pm Fri.-Sat., lunch $15-22, dinner $17-28) in a nondescript strip mall. This locally lauded restaurant serves some of the area's most interesting fare. At midday, you might find a smoked chicken-cheddar melt on cornbread or mussels and french fries, while in the evening, the kitchen might create duck confit with raisin-caper compote, vegetarian pasta in a white wine-basil syrup, or grilled pork chops with house-made *choucroute*.

Overlooking Lake Ontario, this pretty **Tiara** (Queen's Landing Hotel, 155 Byron St., 905/468-2195 or 888/669-5566, www.vintage-hotels.com, 11am-2pm and 5pm-9pm daily, brunch prix-fixe $32, lunch $16-25, dinner $34-49) sparkles for its views. The midday menu includes seafood, grilled dishes, and interesting sandwiches, like smoked pork with kimchi. Dinner is more formal, with entrées like "100-Mile Fish" with snow crab cannelloni and bacon foam or prosciutto-wrapped turkey with bulgur salad and candied figs. A five-course tasting menu ($85) is available, and Tiara is also popular for a refined Sunday brunch.

An early promoter of local food in the Niagara region, the classy **Treadwell Farm-to-Table Cuisine** (114 Queen St., 905/934-9797, 11:30am-3pm and 5pm-10pm daily spring-summer, call for off-season hours, lunch $16-22, dinner $26-36) continues to feature regional products in dishes like house-cured duck with locally grown strawberries and mustard greens or handmade orecchiette with Ontario asparagus and ricotta from Stratford cheese-maker Monforte Dairy. The wine list highlights Ontario labels, and the beers are mostly Ontario craft brews. Reserve in advance for this dining destination.

Winery Restaurants

Ice wine lobster linguini. Charred wild boar loin with bitter greens. Soy-glazed duck with quinoa and warm four-pea salad. These are just a few of the imaginative, locally focused dishes you might find at **Peller Estates Winery Restaurant** (290 John St. E., 905/468-6519 or 888/673-5537, ext. 2, www.peller.com, lunch noon-3pm Mon.-Fri., brunch noon-3pm Sat.-Sun., dinner 5:30pm-8:30pm Sun.-Fri., 5pm-8:30pm Sat., lunch $23-30, dinner $28-48), a splurge-worthy dining room in the winery's grand château. Can't decide what to order? Choose a lavish tasting menu, offered at lunch (4 courses $58, wine pairing $29; 5 courses $70, wine pairing $35) and dinner (5 courses $89, wine pairing $35; 7 courses $109, wine pairing $45).

Set amid the vines at the Ravine Vineyard

Estate Winery, the casual-chic **Ravine Vineyard Bistro** (1366 York Rd., St. Davids, 905/262-8463, www.ravinevineyard.com, 11am-3pm and 5pm-9pm, lunch $18-22, dinner $27-30) serves modern bistro fare with Niagara ingredients. Going hyper-local, they raise their own pigs, grow organic vegetables, and bake their own bread. Look for dishes like blackened pickerel paired with a kale, corn, and chorizo fricassee, or roast lamb with blue cheese bread pudding.

Combining local ingredients with French Provençal flavors, **Terroir La Cachette Restaurant** (Strewn Winery, 1339 Lakeshore Rd., 905/468-1222, www.lacachette.com, lunch from 11:30am and dinner from 5pm daily mid-June-mid-Oct., Wed.-Sun. May-mid-June, Thurs.-Sat. mid-Oct.-Apr., lunch $15-21, dinner $15-33) serves such dishes as fennel seed-crusted salmon with roasted pepper aioli or pork medallions with cabernet jus. Pizzas, pastas, and salads round out the menu at both lunch and dinner.

Groceries and Markets

Produce, prepared foods, and baked goods are available at the **Farmers Market at the Village** (111 Garrison Village Dr., www.farmersmarketatthevillage.ca, 8am-1pm Sat. late May-mid-Oct.), just off Niagara Stone Road (Hwy. 55). **The Fruit Shack** (1267 Niagara Stone Rd., Virgil, 905/468-9821, www.thefruitshack.com, 9am-6pm daily mid-June-mid-Oct., 9am-6pm Thurs., 9am-5pm Fri.-Sat. mid-Oct.-June) sells local produce, meats, and homemade baked goods. Their butter tarts are particularly delicious.

INFORMATION AND SERVICES

The **Niagara-on-the-Lake Chamber of Commerce** (26 Queen St., 905/468-1950, www.niagaraonthelake.com, 8:30am-6pm daily mid-May-mid-Oct., 8:30am-5pm daily mid-Oct.-mid-May) runs a visitors center downtown on the lower level of the courthouse. They can also help you find a place to stay.

Cooking Classes

On the grounds of the Strewn Winery, the **Wine Country Cooking School** (1339 Lakeshore Rd., 905/468-8304, www.winecountrycooking.com, mid-Jan.-Nov.) offers recreational cooking classes on Saturday. Most classes, in which you cook and eat a seasonal meal with wine pairings, are taught 10am-3pm, but evening classes (4pm-9pm) are available. Call or check their website for a detailed schedule.

GETTING THERE

Niagara-on-the-Lake is on the northeast tip of the Niagara Peninsula, bordering both Lake Ontario and the Niagara River. It's 135 kilometers (85 miles) southeast of Toronto and 20 kilometers (12.5 miles) north of Niagara Falls.

Air

Toronto's **Pearson International Airport** (YYZ, 6301 Silver Dart Dr., Mississauga, 416/247-7678 or 866/207-1690, www.torontopearson.com) and **Buffalo-Niagara International Airport** (BUF, 4200 Genesee St., Buffalo, NY, 716/630-6000, www.buffaloairport.com) are the commercial airports closest to Niagara-on-the-Lake. The **Niagara Air Bus** (905/374-8111 or 800/206-7222, www.niagaraairbus.com), a door-to-door airport shuttle, can take you from either Pearson (one-way $105) or Buffalo (one-way $89) to Niagara-on-the-Lake; book online at least three days in advance for a 5 percent discount.

Train

Niagara-on-the-Lake does not have direct train service, but on summer weekends, **GO Transit** (416/869-3200 or 888/438-6646, www.gotransit.com) runs trains from Toronto to St. Catharines, where you can pick up a connecting shuttle bus to NOTL.

Car

From Toronto to Niagara-on-the-Lake, take the QEW south, passing Hamilton and St. Catharines. At exit 38B, follow the Niagara-on-the-Lake signs to Highway 55, which is also Niagara Stone Road. Go northeast on Highway 55 for 12 kilometers (7 miles) until it ends at Queen Street. Turn right toward the downtown business district and the Shaw Festival Theatre.

From Buffalo and points south in the United States, take I-190 north to the Queenston-Lewiston Bridge. Once you've crossed to the Ontario side, the most scenic route is to follow the Niagara River Parkway into Niagara-on-the-Lake.

Shuttle from Niagara Falls

From May to late October, you can take a **Niagara Parks shuttle** (www.wegoniagarafalls.com, one-way adults $5, ages 6-12 $3) between the Floral Clock in Niagara Falls and Fort George in Niagara-on-the-Lake. It makes several stops in Queenston en route. The shuttle operates once an hour in each direction and connects with the Niagara Falls WEGO buses.

GETTING AROUND

You can easily walk around the downtown heritage district, between the theaters, the shops, and the lake, and many accommodations are also within walking distance. Few of the wineries are within an easy walk of downtown, though, so you'll need to have a car or bicycle—or book a wine tour—to get out to the tasting rooms. **Niagara-on-the-Lake Transit** (905/468-3266, www.notl.org, $3) provides limited bus service around the downtown area and between downtown, Niagara College, and the Outlet Collection at Niagara.

Niagara-on-the-Lake has plenty of pleasant cycling routes. Follow the Niagara River Recreation Trail south toward Niagara Falls, and you can reach many of the wineries by bicycle—at least if you don't drink too much en route.

Parking around town is somewhat limited, particularly on Queen Street and around the theaters. The town website (www.notl.org) has an online parking map, which shows parking lots, meter rates and durations, and free parking locations.

Walking Tours

The **Niagara Historical Society** offers one-hour walking tours of Niagara-on-the-Lake (11am. Sat. June, 11am Sat.-Sun. July-Aug., $10). The price includes admission to the Niagara Historical Society Museum.

Old Town Tours (289/292-3532 or 888/492-3532, www.oldtowntours.ca, 10:30am daily May-Sept., 10:30am Sat.-Sun. Apr. and Oct., adults $20, ages 7-12 $10) runs 90-minute walking tours through the town's historic district that also include a wine tasting.

Winery Tours

If you want to leave the driving to someone else (a good idea if you're drinking), or combine cycling and wine touring, consider these winery day tours:

- **Crush on Niagara Wine Tours** (905/562-3373 or 866/408-9463, www.crushtours.com, $89-129)
- **Grape Escape Wine Tours** (905/468-9959 or 866/935-4445, www.tourniagarawineries.com, $49-129)
- **Niagara Getaway Wine Tours** (905/468-7367, www.niagaragetaways.com, $59-139)
- **Niagara Wine Tours International** (905/468-1300 or 800/680-7006, www.niagaraworldwinetours.com, $65-139)

The Twenty Valley

The Twenty Valley lies in the north-central section of the Niagara Peninsula, west of Niagara Falls and Niagara-on-the-Lake. This wine region is centered around the towns of Beamsville, Vineland, and Jordan, yet it is close enough to Toronto, Niagara Falls, and Niagara-on-the-Lake for a day of wine touring or a getaway weekend.

★ TWENTY VALLEY WINERIES

At last count, the Twenty Valley had close to 40 wineries, and new ones crop up regularly. The peak season for wine touring is during the fall harvest, generally mid-September through early October; summer (particularly July and August) is popular, too, with the vineyards full and lush and the weather hot. Most wineries remain open year-round, though many reduce their hours from November to April.

Most wineries charge a small fee ($2-5) for tastings, which may be credited toward any wine purchases. Larger wineries typically offer regular tours, while smaller facilities may offer them only by appointment or not at all.

Beamsville

Owner Nicolette Novak grew up on the property that now houses **The Good Earth Food and Wine Co.** (4556 Lincoln Ave., 905/563-6333, www.goodearthfoodandwine.com, winery 11am-5pm daily, restaurant 11am-4pm Mon.-Fri., 11am-5pm Sat.-Sun.), where she and her staff make riesling, rosé, cabernet franc, and pinot noir, among others, which Novak describes as "good for food." Sample these for yourself in the tasting room, buy snacks, jams, and other gourmet goodies in the seasonal "pantry shed," or sit down for lunch in the bistro. They also run a recreational **cooking school,** offering two- or three-hour cooking classes and

demonstrations that focus on local ingredients; check the website or call for schedule and prices.

The striking wood-and-stone building that houses the family-owned **Fielding Estate Winery** (4020 Locust Lane, 905/563-0668 or 888/778-7758, www.fieldingwines.com, 11am-6pm daily June-Sept., 11am-5:30pm daily Oct.-May) overlooks the fields and vineyards, a particularly lovely setting for wine tasting. The winery is known for aromatic whites, especially riesling and pinot gris. You can book a private tour and tasting (2pm daily, $10).

On the 32-hectare (80-acre) property at **Peninsula Ridge Estate Winery** (5600 King St. W., 905/563-0900, www.peninsularidge.com, 10am-6pm daily June-Oct., 10am-5pm daily Nov.-May), the winemakers produce cabernet sauvignon, merlot, syrah, chardonnay, sauvignon blanc, and viognier. Tours ($5) are available at 11:30am daily from June through the fall harvest.

The beehives behind **Rosewood Estates Winery and Meadery** (4352 Mountainview Rd., 905/563-4383 or 866/633-3248, connect@rosewoodwine.com, www.rosewoodwine.com, tasting daily 11am-6pm Mon.-Sat., 11am-5pm Sun. June-Oct., 11am-5pm Thurs.-Mon. Oct.-May) provide raw materials for Niagara's first mead (honey wine), as well as several varieties of honey. They make wine, too, including pinot noir and riesling. You can drop in for tastings, but to take a tour ($5), call or email in advance.

Vineland

Vineland Estates (3620 Moyer Rd., 905/562-7088 or 888/846-3526, www.vineland.com, 10am-6pm daily May-Oct., 11am-5pm daily Nov.-Apr., tours noon and 4pm daily June-Oct., noon Sat.-Sun. Nov.-May, $9) released their first vintage back in 1983, which makes them an old-timer in these parts. The

The Twenty Valley

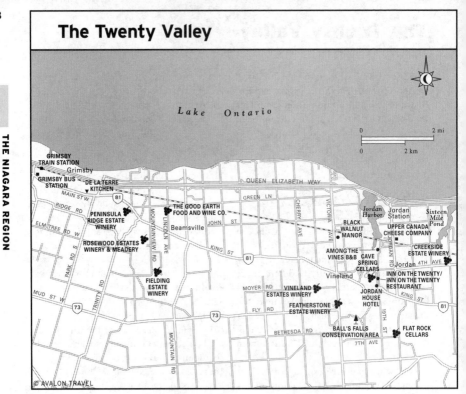

© AVALON TRAVEL

signature wines are cabernet franc and riesling, and Vineland makes a distinctive drink called Vice, a blend of their Vidal ice wine and vodka. A small market above the spacious tasting room sells cheeses and offers cheese tastings. The winery restaurant serves lunch and dinner, and the property has two guesthouses.

Not only are the grapes used at the **Featherstone Estate Winery** (3678 Victoria Ave., 905/562-1949, www.featherstonewinery.ca, Apr.-Dec.) grown without pesticides, the winery relies on sheep to graze in the vineyards as a natural way to prune the vines. The fleecy animals give their name to the Black Sheep Riesling; the winery also produces merlot, pinot noir, and cabernet franc, among others. On mild days, you can sit on the veranda for a light lunch with a glass of wine. Hours for the tasting room and veranda

vary seasonally, so call or check the website before visiting.

Jordan

Think wine tasting can be staid, even snooty? Stop into laid-back **Flat Rock Cellars** (2727 7th Ave., 905/562-8994, www.flatrockcellars.com, 10am-6pm Sun.-Fri., 10am-7pm Sat. May.-Oct., 10am-5pm Sun.-Fri., 10am-6pm Sat. Nov.-Apr.) where you can tour ($5) the vineyards and cellars, learn about their "gravity flow" production process, and sample their wines, which include riesling, chardonnay, and pinot noir.

The winery building at **Cave Spring Cellars** (3836 Main St., www.cavespringcellars.com, 905/562-3581 or 888/806-9910; 10am-6pm daily June-Sept., 10am-5pm Sun.-Thurs., 10am-6pm Fri.-Sat. Oct.-May, tours 1:30pm daily June-Sept., 1:30pm Fri.-Sun.

Oct.-May), in Jordan Village, was built in 1871 and houses Ontario's oldest functioning wine cellar. The current winery, founded in 1986, specializes in riesling, including ice wines, and also makes well-regarded pinot noir, chardonnay, and cabernet franc.

The tagline for **Creekside Estate Winery** (2170 4th Ave., 905/562-0035 or 877/262-9463, www.creeksidewine.com, 10am-6pm daily May-Oct., 10am-5pm daily Nov-Apr., tours 2pm daily May-Oct.) is "serious wine from an irreverent bunch," so stop in for a seriously irreverent sampling of their sauvignon blanc, cabernet shiraz, or other varieties. **The Deck @ Creekside** (11:30am-4pm Sat.-Sun. late May-mid-Oct., $8-16) sates weekend visitors with salads, mussels, burgers, and other light meals.

BALL'S FALLS CONSERVATION AREA

The Twenty Valley isn't entirely about wine touring. Beyond the wineries are several conservation areas where you can go hiking, and the rolling hills make pleasant cycling. Billing itself as "Niagara's Other Falls," the **Ball's Falls Conservation Area** (3292 6th Ave., Jordan, 905/562-5235, www.ballsfalls.ca, grounds 8am-8pm daily May-Oct., 8am-4pm daily Nov.-Apr., adults $5.75, seniors and students $4.25) has 10 kilometers (six miles) of hiking trails, including routes that lead to two waterfalls: the 27-meter-tall (90-foot) Lower Falls, and the 11-meter-tall (35-foot) Upper Falls. The falls run strongest in the spring, and the grounds are a pretty picnic spot.

In a modern, environmentally sensitive building, the **Ball's Falls Centre for Conservation** (9am-4pm daily) has exhibits about the plants and animals that live in the region. Also on the site is a collection of **heritage buildings** (10am-3pm daily May-Oct.), including a flour mill, a church, a blacksmith shop, and the home that belonged to the Ball family, who settled here in 1807. Guides take you around the buildings and demonstrate milling, weaving, and other 19th-century skills.

SHOPPING

Jordan Village (www.jordanvillage.com) has a small collection of boutiques and galleries clustered near the Inn on the Twenty and the Cave Spring Winery. **Native Arts Niagara** (3845 Main St., Jordan, 905/562-8888 or 800/646-2848, www.nativeartsniagara.com, 10am-6pm daily) shows works by Canadian aboriginal artists, while the **Jordan**

Cave Spring Cellars houses Ontario's oldest functioning wine cellar.

Art Gallery (3836 Main St., Jordan, 905/562-6680, www.jordanartgallery.com, 10am-5pm Sun.-Thurs., 10am-6pm Fri.-Sat. late May-mid-Oct., call for off-season hours) exhibits contemporary paintings, prints, sculpture, drawings, and photography, primarily by Niagara artists.

ACCOMMODATIONS
Vineland

Though the **Black Walnut Manor** (4255 Victoria Ave., 905/562-8675 or 800/859-4786, www.blackwalnutmanor.com, $175-210 d) was built in 1911, this smart-casual B&B is far from Victorian kitsch. The three second-floor bedrooms have polished oak floors and modern furnishings—no knickknacks here—while the airy attic suite (available Apr.-Nov. only) has sunny nooks under the sloped ceilings. Guests settle around the glass-topped table for family-style breakfasts, lounge by the fireplace, or relax by the pool. A bit of daytime traffic noise—the house is set back from a busy road—is the only minor blemish.

At the entrance to the **Vineland Estates Winery** (3620 Moyer Rd., 905/562-7088 or 888/846-3526, www.vineland.com) are two self-contained lodgings. The cozy one-bedroom B&B Cottage ($175 d) is designed for a couples escape. The staff provide a complimentary bottle of wine and provisions for a make-your-own breakfast, but you might not see another soul during your stay. The larger Estate Guesthouse ($295) looks like a suburban home and can accommodate a family or group of friends. It has three bedrooms, a living room, and kitchen facilities; breakfast provisions and a bottle of wine are included here, too.

Jordan

"You get fed like you're a farmer," says Carollynn Desjardins, the owner of **Among the Vines B&B** (4055 19th St., 905/562-7080, www.amongthevines.ca, $100-130 d), who serves guests a full breakfast (including dessert) in the dining room or on the deck facing a five-hectare (12-acre) vineyard. Her comfortable family home overlooking the fields has three airy guest rooms with air-conditioning and Wi-Fi. The largest, the Gamay Suite, has black grape-hued furnishings and a private bath. The other two rooms are rented together to a family or two couples traveling jointly (they share a bath); otherwise, you'd have the room and bath to yourself.

Owned by the proprietors of Cave Spring Cellars and the more upscale Inn on the

Inn on the Twenty is also a fine-dining destination.

Twenty, the **Jordan House Hotel** (3751 Main St., 905/562-9591 or 800/701-8074, www.jordanhouse.ca, $129-199 d, with breakfast $149-219 d) is an excellent choice for moderately priced wine-country accommodations. It's an upscale two-story motel attached to a historic tavern, with contemporary chocolate-brown and royal-blue linens, flat-screen TVs, coffeemakers, and simple but functional baths. Expect no frills, done well.

Looking for a romantic wine-country escape? The ★ **Inn on the Twenty** (3845 Main St., 905/562-5336 or 800/701-8074, www.innonthetwenty.com, $239-389 d) has the region's most deluxe accommodations, staffed by an attentive team. The 27 spacious rooms, all more than 500 square feet, are all different, furnished with a mix of antiques and contemporary pieces; some have a separate sitting area and sleeping alcove, some have private terraces, while others are two-level lofts, with a living room and upstairs bedroom. Most have fireplaces and whirlpool tubs. The spa, in an adjacent 1840s building, offers massage, facials, reflexology, and other services.

FOOD
Grimsby

On your way to or from the Twenty Valley, stop for the top-notch sandwiches and baked goods at **De La Terre Kitchen** (270 Main St. E., 289/235-8952, www.delaterrekitchen.ca, 8am-5pm Mon.-Fri., 8am-4pm Sat., $5-9). Try the Grimsby smoke (house-smoked meat with sauerkraut) or the vegan version with smoked tofu, or opt for a simple grilled cheese with tomato chutney. Cookies, brownies, butter tarts, scones—how do you choose? Get more than one, of course. There are just a few seats, so plan for take-out.

Beamsville

A salad of seasonal vegetables. A cheese or charcuterie platter to share. An open-face pulled pork sandwich. That's the simple, fresh fare on offer at the **Good Earth Food and Wine Company** (4556 Lincoln Ave., 905/563-6333, www.goodearthfoodandwine. com, 11am-4pm Mon.-Fri., 11am-5pm Sat.-Sun., $9-20), where you can lunch on the patio overlooking the vineyards (or inside the dining room).

Housed in an 1885 Queen Anne revival manor house, **The Restaurant at Peninsula Ridge** (5600 King St. W., 905/563-0900, ext. 35, www.peninsularidge.com, noon-2:30pm and 5pm-9pm Wed.-Sat., 11:30am-2:30pm Sun., lunch $13-22, dinner $25-34) bills its style as "casual fine dining." That means that at lunch, your choices will range from a simple vegetable focaccia to duck confit with bacon mashed potatoes, while you might sup on chicken with *chimichurri* and cheesy polenta, pickerel in a chardonnay lemon butter sauce, or a grilled rib-eye.

Vineland

In a former farmhouse overlooking the vineyards, **Vineland Estates Winery Restaurant** (3620 Moyer Rd., 905/562-7088 or 888/846-3526, www.vineland.com, 11:30am-3pm and 5pm-9pm daily May-Dec., 11:30am-3pm and 5pm-9pm Wed.-Sun. Jan.-Apr., lunch $20-26, dinner $22-34) serves upscale wine-country fare. At midday, you might choose citrus-cured rainbow trout with a warm bulgur salad or waffles topped with duck confit and blueberries. For dinner? Perhaps tortellini with pork belly and locally made ricotta, or Ontario rack of lamb with ratatouille. Multicourse tasting menus are available at lunch ($35) and dinner ($75), with optional wine pairings.

Jordan

Need some cheese for your wine-country picnic? Visit the **Upper Canada Cheese Company** (4159 Jordan Rd., 905/562-9730, www.uppercanadacheesecompany.com, 10am-5pm daily), which produces several cheeses, including the Camembert-style Comfort Cream and the semi-soft Niagara Gold, from the milk of local Guernsey cows.

After a hard day of wine touring, maybe you just want to kick back with a burger and a beer. Then the **Jordan House Tavern** (3751

Main St., 905/562-9591, www.jordanhouse. ca, 11:30am-9:30pm Sun.-Thurs., 11:30am-10:30pm Fri.-Sat., $8-15) is your joint. In the homey room with a stone fireplace and timbers from the original 1840s saloon that stood on this site, the unfussy, well-executed menu includes straightforward sandwiches, salads, and bar snacks. The star attractions are the hearty burgers; try the curried lamb burger with feta cheese for a flavorful variation. There's live music most Friday and Saturday nights.

The formal, white-tablecloth **Inn on the Twenty Restaurant** (3836 Main St., 905/562-7313, www.innonthetwenty.com, 11:30am-3pm and 5pm-9pm daily, lunch $12-20, dinner $22-39), with a wall of windows looking across the countryside, is a special-occasion spot. An early adopter of the Niagara regional food movement, the kitchen creates contemporary cuisine that draws on local products. In the evening, starters might include cured scallops with heirloom tomatoes or a local beet salad with figs, while the entrée could be organic chicken served with kohlrabi-leek gratin. The wine list includes labels from Cave Springs Cellars (under the same ownership), and other Ontario producers.

INFORMATION AND SERVICES

For information about the Twenty Valley region, contact the **Twenty Valley Tourism Association** (905/562-3636, www.20valley. ca). The **Wine Council of Ontario** (905/562-8070 ext. 221, www.winecountryontario. ca) can provide more details about the area wineries.

GETTING THERE AND AROUND

To explore the Twenty Valley, you'll either need to have a car or arrange for a tour.

Cycling is another option, although it's hilly terrain.

Train or Bus

For rail service to the Twenty Valley, the closest **VIA Rail** (888/842-7245, www.viarail.ca) stations are in Grimsby (99 Ontario St.) or St. Catharines (5 Great Western St.). **Megabus** (www.megabus.com) runs frequent buses from Toronto to Grimsby (36 Main St. W., 1 hour, $6-11) and St. Catharines (70 Carlisle St., 1.25-1.5 hours, $7-11).

Car

Highway 81 is the main east-west route across the Twenty Valley, running between Grimsby and St. Catharines. From Toronto, take the QEW south toward the Niagara Peninsula. It's 95 kilometers (59 miles) to Beamsville (exit 64, Ontario St.), 100 kilometers (62 miles) to Vineland (exit 57, Victoria Ave.), and 102 kilometers (64 miles) to Jordan (exit 55, Jordan Rd./Hwy. 26).

From Niagara Falls, the simplest route is to take the QEW north. To Jordan it's 34 kilometers (21 miles), to Vineland 36 kilometers (22 miles), and to Beamsville 41 kilometers (25 miles).

Winery Tours

For tours that stop at several Twenty Valley wineries, or for cycling tours through wine country, contact the following tour operators:

- **Crush on Niagara Wine Tours** (905/562-3373 or 866/408-9463, www.crushtours. com, $89-139)

- **Grape Escape Wine Tours** (905/468-9959 or 866/935-4445, www.tourniagarawineries.com, $49-129)

- **Niagara Wine Tours International** (800/680-7006, www.niagaraworldwinetours.com, $65-139)

St. Catharines and the Welland Canal

The Great Lakes are part of an extensive shipping route that extends from Lake Superior to the Atlantic Ocean. But until the 1800s, a significant natural obstruction—Niagara Falls—blocked the passage between Lake Ontario and Lake Erie. William Hamilton Merritt (1793-1862), a St. Catharines entrepreneur, proposed the idea of a canal across the Niagara Peninsula, connecting the two lakes. He began raising money, and in 1824, construction began on the first Welland Canal.

Building the canal involved finding a way for ships to "climb the mountain," otherwise known as the Niagara Escarpment, since Lake Erie is roughly 100 meters (326 feet) higher in elevation than Lake Ontario. The solution was a series of locks that lift up ships traveling south through the canal and let them descend the same distance when they journey from Lake Erie to Lake Ontario. After the first Welland Canal opened in 1829, it was rebuilt three times, refining the route and improving the lock technology. The current, fourth canal opened in 1932.

At 43.5 kilometers (27 miles), the Welland Canal is about half the length of the Panama Canal. On the Lake Ontario side, the canal starts in St. Catharines, the peninsula's largest city. It heads south through Thorold and Welland before reaching the town of Port Colborne, where it meets Lake Erie on the Niagara Peninsula's south shore. Ships transit the canal between April and December. It takes roughly 9-10 hours for a boat to make the journey between the two lakes.

SIGHTS

You can bicycle the entire length of the Welland Canal if you follow the **Welland Canals Trail** (www.welland.ca), a 42-kilometer (27-mile) cycling path that runs from St. Catharines to Port Colborne.

St. Catharines Museum and Welland Canals Centre

The exhibits in the well-designed **St. Catharines Museum and Welland Canals Centre** (1932 Welland Canals Pkwy., St. Catharines, 905/984-8880 or 800/305-5134, www.stcatharines.ca, 9am-5pm daily,

Learn about the Welland Canal at St. Catharines Museum.

donation $4), located at Lock 3 on the canal, illustrate the history of the Welland Canal and the St. Catharines area. One section of the museum houses the **Ontario Lacrosse Hall of Fame,** devoted to Canada's official summer sport (the official winter sport is hockey).

A highlight is behind the museum, where you can climb up to the **viewing platform** to watch the massive ships pass through the locks. The museum posts a schedule showing when the next ships expect to arrive, and also sends out these details on its Twitter feed (www.twitter.com/StCMuseum).

Port Colborne Historical and Marine Museum

The **Port Colborne Historical and Marine Museum** (280 King St., 905/834-7604, www.portcolborne.ca, noon-5pm daily May-Dec., free) is a complex of several historic buildings, including an 1835 log schoolhouse (one of the region's oldest), an 1880s blacksmith shop, and a Victorian-era home that now houses **Arabella's Tea Room** (2pm-4pm June-Sept.), which serves homemade biscuits and jam to visitors. Also on the property is the 1901 **Neff Steam Buggy,** thought to be the oldest surviving Ontario-made automobile.

ACCOMMODATIONS

Sit on your balcony at the **Inn at Lock Seven** (24 Chapel St. S., Thorold, 905/227-6177 or 877/465-6257, www.innatlock7.com, mid-Mar.-mid-Dec., $110-125 d) and watch the ships travel through the Welland Canal; if you were any closer, you'd be in the canal yourself. Though this modest motel looks right out of the 1960s, with floral bedspreads and pink bath tiles, the owners have done updates where it counts; the beds are firm, and there's free Wi-Fi. The location is convenient for cyclists, just off the Welland Canals Trail.

Owner Gloria Simon, an interior decorator who relocated to Port Colborne from Toronto, has done extensive renovations on the 1904 farmhouse that's now the comfortable **Lakebreeze B&B** (234 Steele St., Port Colborne, 905/834-1233 or 877/834-1233,

a ship in the locks on the Welland Canal

www.lakebreezeniagara.com, $120-135 d, 2-bedroom suite $150-210). She's created three large eclectic suites, each with its own keyless private entrance, Wi-Fi, and central air-conditioning. An enthusiastic booster for Niagara's south shore, she's happy to suggest things to see and do nearby (and she cooks a fine breakfast, too). The house is a short walk to the Lake Erie shore, the town center, or the Welland Canal.

FOOD

Searching for enlightenment, or at least dinner, from the far corners of the globe, **The Smokin' Buddha** (265 King St., Port Colborne, 905/834-6000, www.thesmokinbuddha.com, 4:30pm-10pm Tues., 11:30am-10pm Wed.-Sat., $9-15) cooks up small plates, curries, and noodles that take inspiration from Asia, Latin America, India, and the Middle East. Try the Japanese-style *sobo* pockets, sweet tofu stuffed with smoked salmon, sprouts, rice, and wasabi mayo, or go global with Korean beef noodles, Thai curries, or chicken enchiladas. The location in the town's old train station, with exposed brick walls and wooden benches, puts you in the mood for your journey.

Stop in for a beer or a bite at the friendly **Canalside Restaurant** (232 West St., Port Colborne, 905/834-6090, www.canalside.ca, lunch and dinner daily, lunch $10-17, dinner $10-25) facing the Welland Canal. Canalside carries a long list of brews from Canada and abroad, including its own Lock 8 Lager, and the crowd-pleasing pub menu runs from burgers and sandwiches to pastas, seafood, and steaks.

The **@27 Steakhouse** (27 Main St., Port Colborne, 905/835-2700, www.attwentyseven.com, lunch 11:30am-1:30pm Tues.-Fri., dinner 5pm-8pm Tues.-Thurs., 5pm-8:30pm Fri.-Sat., lunch $10-16, dinner $16-29), the area's most upscale dining room, occupies a bright yellow house near Lock 8. The updated surf-and-turf fare includes steaks, ribs, grilled fish, and pastas.

INFORMATION AND SERVICES

The **St. Catharines Tourism Information Centre** (1932 Welland Canals Pkwy., St. Catharines, 800/305-5134, www.tourismstcatharines.ca), inside the St. Catharines Museum and Welland Canals Centre, has information about the canal and the surrounding region. **Thorold Tourism** (50 Chapel St., Thorold, 905/680-9477, www.thorold.com) has a year-round information office inside the Lock 7 Viewing Complex.

For information about Port Colborne and the Niagara Peninsula's south shore, contact the **Port Colborne Visitor Information Centre** (76 Main St. W., Port Colborne, 905/834-5722 or 888/767-8386, www.experienceportcolborne.com).

GETTING THERE AND AROUND

Unless you're planning to bicycle around the Welland Canal region, you really need a car, as public transit is limited. **VIA Rail** (888/842-7245, www.viarail.ca) trains run to St. Catharines (5 Great Western St.), where you could rent a car to continue your explorations, or head off on your bike.

If you're going only to Port Colborne, taking the bus is an option. **Megabus** (www.megabus.com) runs two daily buses from Toronto to Port Colborne (King St. at Clarence St., 800/461-7661, 2.25-2.5 hours, one-way $9-15). Once you're in Port Colborne, you can easily walk around town. Megabus also has frequent service between Toronto and St. Catharines (70 Carlisle St., 1.25-1.5 hours, $7-11).

Lake Erie to Lake Huron

Bounded by two Great Lakes, the triangle of Ontario stretching west from Toronto includes arty university towns, great theater, traditional Mennonite communities, African Canadian historical sights, a wine district, and plenty

of lakeside beaches and parks. Most are close enough to Toronto for a weekend getaway.

Midway between Toronto and Niagara Falls, the gritty steel town of Hamilton has gradually reinvented itself, and its cool arts and shopping districts and worthwhile museums can easily occupy a day or more. In nearby Brantford, a large First Nations community operates several heritage sights. Farther west are the twin cities of Kitchener-Waterloo, where high tech has reshaped this formerly industrial region and launched a fledgling arts scene. As Kitchener-Waterloo embraces technology, St. Jacobs and the surrounding farm country are home to Mennonite communities that hold fast to their traditional ways, while the nearby villages of Elora and Fergus are among Ontario's most beautiful small towns.

Theatergoers make regular pilgrimages to Stratford for its namesake theatre festival with doses of Shakespeare and more contemporary

playwrights. Like its British namesake (yes, it's on the River Avon), the town also has plenty of high-end restaurants and browseworthy shops. While considerably smaller than its UK counterpart, the city of London is Canada's 10th largest metropolitan area. Its large student population has given rise to culture, shops, and pubs.

Many towns in Southwestern Ontario were the last stop on the Underground Railroad, the network of safe houses that sheltered slaves escaping plantations in the U.S. South. In Windsor, Amherstburg, Buxton, and Chatham, sights from that era dramatically illustrate this history. Along Lake Erie's shores you can tour an emerging wine district, visit the southernmost point on the Canadian mainland, or hop the ferry to laid-back Pelee Island. To the west, the Lake Huron shore is lined with beachfront vacation towns and plenty of places to unwind, sit by the shore, and watch the sun set.

Previous: Mennonite buggies near St. Jacobs; last stop on the Underground Railroad, Southwestern Ontario. **Above:** costume on view at the Stratford Perth Museum.

Look for ★ to find recommended sights, activities, dining, and lodging.

Highlights

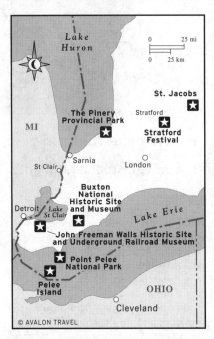

★ **St. Jacobs:** This small town outside Kitchener-Waterloo is a base for learning more about the region's traditional Mennonite community. You can see farmers driving horse-drawn buggies, and purchase homemade jams, quilts, and other handcrafted items from Mennonite families (page 153).

★ **Stratford Festival:** Running annually from April through October, North America's largest classical repertory theater has been producing plays by William Shakespeare and more contemporary playwrights since 1953 (page 160).

★ **Buxton National Historic Site and Museum:** This museum and its adjacent historic buildings recount the fascinating story of the Buxton Settlement, which became the largest 19th-century African Canadian community in Canada (page 177).

★ **Point Pelee National Park:** On a spit of land jutting into Lake Erie, the southernmost tip of Canada's mainland is a major stopover point for migrating birds, particularly in spring (page 178).

★ **Pelee Island:** A peaceful getaway for a day, a week, or more, this rocky island in Lake Erie is the southernmost point in Canada. Bring your bike (or rent one on the island); it's a good spot for cycling (page 181).

★ **John Freeman Walls Historic Site and Underground Railroad Museum:** Built and operated by the descendants of escaped slaves, this open-air museum illustrates the arduous journey north on the Underground Railroad to freedom in Canada (page 188).

★ **The Pinery Provincial Park:** The 10-kilometer (six-mile) powdery sand beach at this popular park is one of the loveliest on the Lake Huron shore (page 192).

Lake Erie to Lake Huron

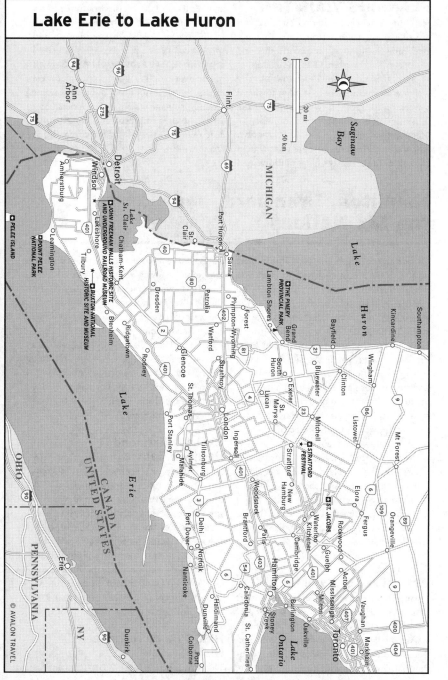

© AVALON TRAVEL

PLANNING YOUR TIME

Hamilton, Kitchener-Waterloo, and Stratford are all an easy day trip from Toronto. For a weekend getaway, tour the historic sites and wineries of Southwestern Ontario, or hang out in one of the Lake Huron beach towns.

For a more complete tour, plan to spend a week to 10 days. Start by exploring the museums in Kitchener-Waterloo and the Mennonite communities around **St. Jacobs.** Allow a day to browse the shops and swim in the quarry in the pretty village of **Elora,** and another day or two to visit Stratford and see at least one play at the **Stratford Festival.** From Stratford, drive to Lake Huron and spend a couple of days relaxing in **Bayfield** or at **The Pinery Provincial Park.** Stop off in **London** as you make your way southwest to visit the African Canadian heritage sights around Chatham, wine-tour in Amherstburg, and sightsee in Windsor. If you have time, head over to **Pelee Island** to cycle, walk, or just unwind.

Hamilton, Brantford, and the Six Nations

Canada's ninth-largest city, Hamilton hitched its star to the steel industry, and when you pass through town along certain routes, you can still see the smoke-belching legacy of the steel plants. Yet gritty Hamilton, midway between Toronto and Niagara Falls, has an arty, edgy side. Artists are opening studios in its brick storefronts, young families are finding the city more affordable than nearby Toronto, and funky shops are luring both locals and visitors. In fact, the motto of one local art store is "Art is the New Steel." Hamilton may not have the world's prettiest face, but it's definitely worth a second look.

West of Hamilton, the Brantford area's draws are its First Nations heritage sights (the region encompasses the traditional territory of the Six Nations of the Grand River) and a historic home that featured in the development of a now-ubiquitous technology: the telephone.

SIGHTS
Art Gallery of Hamilton

Surprise: Ontario's third-largest public art gallery is in Hamilton. The **Art Gallery of Hamilton** (123 King St. W., 905/527-6610, www.artgalleryofhamilton.com, 11am-6pm Tues.-Wed. and Fri., 11am-8pm Thurs., noon-5pm Sat.-Sun.) has a wide-ranging collection, emphasizing 19th-century European and Canadian historical works, African sculpture, and contemporary art from Canada and abroad. Every Saturday and Sunday at 2pm, you can take a free tour of some aspect of the gallery's collection.

The Level Two Gallery upstairs is always free, but there's a charge to visit the Level One Gallery (adults $10, seniors and students $8, ages 6-17 $4, families $25). On the first Friday of every month, admission to the entire museum is free 4pm-8pm.

Workers Arts and Heritage Centre

Since industry was such an important component of Hamilton's development, it's fitting that the city has a museum devoted to working people. The **Workers Arts and Heritage Centre** (51 Stuart St., 905/522-3003, www.wahc-museum.ca, 10am-4pm Wed.-Sat., donation), in the 1860 Custom House, has changing exhibits that might focus on Hamilton's steel industry, labor protests, or the history of office work. And yes, it's far more absorbing than punching the clock.

HMCS *Haida* National Historic Site

The **HMCS *Haida*** (Pier 9, 658 Catharine St.,

Hamilton

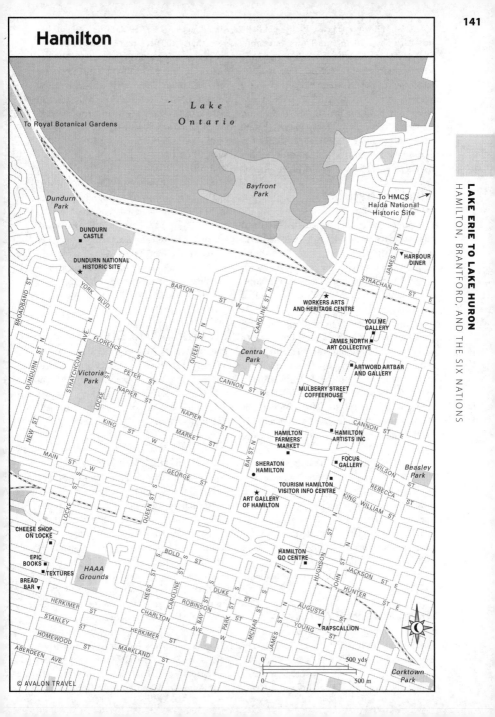

Lake Ontario

To Royal Botanical Gardens

Dundurn Park

Bayfront Park

To HMCS Haida National Historic Site

DUNDURN CASTLE

DUNDURN NATIONAL HISTORIC SITE

HARBOUR DINER

STRACHAN ST E

BROADBAND ST

YORK BLVD.

BARTON ST W

STRATCHCONA AVE. N

FLORENCE ST

QUEEN ST N

CAROLINE ST N

WORKERS ARTS AND HERITAGE CENTRE

YOU ME GALLERY

JAMES NORTH ART COLLECTIVE

Central Park

ARTWORD ARTBAR AND GALLERY

DUNDURN ST N

Victoria Park

PETER ST

NAPIER ST

CANNON ST W

MULBERRY STREET COFFEEHOUSE

LOCKE

KING ST

NEW ST

NAPIER ST

MARKET ST

CANNON ST E

NAPIER ST

HAMILTON ARTISTS INC

MAIN ST S

HAMILTON FARMERS' MARKET

BAY ST N

FOCUS GALLERY

WILSON ST

Beasley Park

LOCKE ST S

GEORGE ST

SHERATON HAMILTON

REBECCA ST

QUEEN ST S

TOURISM HAMILTON VISITOR INFO CENTRE

KING WILLIAM ST

ART GALLERY OF HAMILTON

CHEESE SHOP ON LOCKE

EPIC BOOKS

TEXTURES

BREAD BAR

HAAA Grounds

BOLD ST

HAMILTON GO CENTRE

JACKSON ST E

HUGHSON ST N

JOHN ST N

HUNTER ST E

HERKIMER ST

HESS ST

CAROLINE ST

DUKE ST

ROBINSON ST

BAY ST

AUGUSTA ST

STANLEY ST

CHARLTON AVE

PARK ST

MCNAB ST

YOUNG ST

RAPSCALLION

HOMEWOOD ST

HERKIMER ST

JAMES ST

ABERDEEN AVE.

MARKLAND ST

0   500 yds

0   500 m

Corktown Park

© AVALON TRAVEL

905/526-6742, www.pc.gc.ca, 10am-5pm daily July-early Sept., 10am-5pm Thurs.-Sun. mid-May-June and early Sept.-mid-Oct., adults $3.90, seniors $3.40, ages 6-16 $1.90, families $9.80) served the Canadian navy from World War II until 1963. One of 27 Tribal Class destroyers built for Britain, Australia, and Canada, it's the only one that remains (13 were sunk, and 13 more were scrapped). Clamber around the ship and learn about its operation, the Canadian navy, and history in the process.

Dundurn National Historic Site

Dundurn Castle, at **Dundurn National Historic Site** (610 York Blvd., 905/546-2872, www.hamilton.ca, noon-4pm Tues.-Sun., adults $11.50, seniors and ages 13-17 $9.50, ages 6-12 $6, families $30), has a connection to the contemporary British royals. Camilla, Duchess of Cornwall, who is the second wife of Charles, Prince of Wales, is the great-great-great-granddaughter of Sir Allan Napier MacNab (1798-1862) and his wife, Mary, who built and lived in this stately mansion with their daughters, Sophia and Minnie. A lawyer, entrepreneur, and politician, MacNab served as premier of the United Province of Canada (the pre-Confederation union of what would become the provinces of Ontario and Quebec).

Completed in 1835, the home has more than 40 rooms restored to the Victorian era, from grand public spaces to modest servants' quarters (the family had eight live-in servants). Visits are by one-hour guided tour only. To learn more about life in the castle, read *The Diary of Sophia MacNab*, which the older MacNab daughter wrote when she was 13, the year her mother died. It's available in the gift shop.

Royal Botanical Gardens

Located northwest of downtown on the Hamilton-Burlington line, the **Royal Botanical Gardens** (680 Plains Rd. W., Burlington, 905/527-1158, www.rbg.ca, 10am-8pm daily, adults $12.50, seniors and students

$10.50, ages 5-12 $7.50, families $30.50) has more than 1,100 hectares (2,700 acres) of flowers, plants, and trees, and more than 30 kilometers (19 miles) of walking trails. There are roses and magnolias, cherry trees and tulips, and one of the most extensive collections of lilacs in the world. The gardens are open year-round; some exhibits are indoors.

Waterfalls

Hamilton is sometimes called the "City of Waterfalls" for the more than 100 streams that cascade down slopes around the region. In the Dundas area west of downtown, the 22-meter (72-foot) **Webster's Falls** (Fallsview Rd., off Short Rd.) and the narrower but taller (41-meter, 135-foot) **Tew's Falls** (Harvest Rd.) have a short walking trail between them. The **Hamilton Conservation Authority** (www.waterfalls.hamilton.ca) lists more waterfalls to explore.

ENTERTAINMENT

The **Artword Artbar and Gallery** (15 Colbourne St., at James St. N., www.artword.net, from 6pm Wed.-Sat. events from 7:30pm or 8pm Wed.-Sat.) is part art gallery and part club, with live blues, jazz, and roots music several nights a week.

SHOPPING
James Street North

Just north of downtown, the **James Street North Gallery District** (www.jamesstreet-north.ca) is an emerging arts community. It's still a bit rough around the edges, but that's what gives it a pleasantly edgy feel. Most neighborhood galleries are open Wednesday-Saturday afternoons.

Some galleries to look for include: **Focus Gallery** (66 James St. N., 905/218-9557, www.thefocusgallery.ca, noon-5pm Wed.-Sat.), **Hamilton Artists Inc.** (155 James St. N., 905/529-3355, www.theinc.ca, noon-5pm Wed.-Sat.), **James North Art Collective** (328 James St. N., 289/426-5785, www.james-northartcollective.com, noon-5pm Wed.-Sat., noon-4pm Sun.), and **You Me Gallery** (330

James St. N., 905/523-7754, www.youmegallery.com, noon-5pm Wed.-Sun.).

The liveliest time to explore James Street North is during the monthly **ArtCrawl,** the second Friday of every month, when you can visit galleries up and down the street. The biggest crawl of them all is September's **SuperCrawl** (www.supercrawl.ca), which adds music, dance, and theater events for a weekend-long arts festival.

Locke Street

Hamilton's other up-and-coming shopping district is on Locke Street (http://lockestreetshops.com), with trendy boutiques, bookstores, and food shops. Check out **Epic Books** (226 Locke St. S., 905/525-6538, www.epicbooks.ca, 10am-6pm Tues.-Thurs., 10am-9pm Fri., 10am-6pm Sat., noon-4pm Sun.), an independent bookstore, and **Textures** (236 Locke St. S., 905/523-0636, 11am-5:30pm Mon.-Fri., 11am-5pm Sat.-Sun.), a local artists' cooperative.

Nearly three-quarters of the products at the **Cheese Shop on Locke** (190 Locke St. S., 289/389-7000, www.cheeseshoppeonlocke.com, 10am-6pm Mon.-Thurs. and Sat., 10am-7pm. Fri., 11am-5pm Sun.) are Canadian. Look for cheeses from Ontario and nearby Quebec, and other local gourmet fare. They host regular wine and cheese pairings, cheese tastings, and other special events.

ACCOMMODATIONS

If you want to stay right downtown, **Sheraton Hamilton** (116 King St. W., 905/529-5515, www.sheratonhamilton.com, $169-299 d) has all the standard business-class amenities. Otherwise, Hamilton has a couple of lovely B&Bs outside the city center.

Grand ★ **Osler House B&B** (30 S. St. W., Dundas, 289/238-9278, www.oslerhouse.com, $155-180 d) feels like a place you might have inherited if your relations were minor royalty. Owners Gary Fincham and Sara Burnet-Smith bought, designed, and furnished this 1848 Georgian-style home, with high ceilings, a grand staircase, spacious rooms, oriental rugs, antiques, and capacious baths with heated floors in the three guest rooms upstairs. Enjoy the gracious parlor or the more casual billiards room; breakfast may include beautifully carved fresh fruit, apricot scones with homemade jam, and a carefully rolled omelet.

On a rural road between Hamilton and Brantford, owner Shane Burry has transformed a suburban home into **Serenity**

Webster's Falls, Hamilton

Ranch B&B (2171 Wilson St. W., Ancaster, 289/346-0278 or 800/659-3714, www.serenityranchbb.com, $99-179 d). Each of the five traditionally furnished guest rooms, with pillow-top mattresses and remote-controlled lights, has a fridge with complimentary beverages, a microwave with free popcorn, and a flat-screen TV with a DVD player. Rates include continental breakfast, and you can use the guest kitchen to prep other meals. There's a complimentary guest laundry and a lovely porch overlooking the fields.

FOOD

More than 70 vendors sell produce, meat, and prepared foods at the year-round indoor **Hamilton Farmers Market** (35 York Blvd., 905/546-2096, www.hamilton.ca, 8am-6pm Tues. and Thurs.-Fri., 7am-5pm Sat.). Note the historic Birks Clock in the center of the market that's more than five meters (17 feet) high.

When browsing the galleries on James Street North, stop for coffee, pastries, or sandwiches at the cool **Mulberry Street Coffeehouse** (193 James St. N., 905/963-1365, www.mulberrystreet.ca, 7am-10pm Mon.-Wed., 7am-11:30pm Thurs.-Fri., 8am-11:30pm Sat., 8am-8pm Sun.). Laptop-toters appreciate the free Wi-Fi.

Before James Street began to get trendy, there was the **Harbour Diner** (486 James St. N., 905/523-7373, www.harbourdiner.com, 8am-8pm Tues.-Thurs., 8am-10pm Fri.-Sat., 8am-3pm Sun., lunch $6-9, dinner $8-22), which is both down-home and hip. Besides eggs, bacon, and pancakes (popular for weekend brunch), the comfort-food menu includes oversized sandwiches and hearty dinners, like meatloaf or shepherd's pie. If you're missing Thanksgiving, try the turkey dinner sandwich: turkey, mashed potatoes, and stuffing, all smushed onto an overflowing bun.

The guiding principle at **Bread Bar** (258 Locke St. S., 905/522-2999, www.breadbar. ca, 11:30am-4:30pm and 5pm-close Mon.-Fri., 8am-4:30pm and 5pm-close Sat.-Sun., $9-30), a neighborhood bakery by day and mellow pizzeria by night, is that "good ingredients matter." Those good ingredients make mighty fine pizzas, whether topped with brie, roasted garlic, and arugula; beef brisket and smoked potatoes; or other flavorful combinations. Wheel in your stroller, bring in your date, or roll in with your pals, and you'll feel equally at home.

In a snug downtown storefront, eclectic **Rapscallion** (61 Young St., 905/522-0088,

a plush guest room at Hamilton's Osler House B&B

www.rapscallionrestaurant.com, from 5pm daily, $5-15) gets imaginative with its meat, concocting a changing assortment of sharing plates like Tongue and Cheek (confit tongue with braised veal cheek) or Brent's Balls (meatballs stuffed with foie gras). But don't fret, plant-lovers: the kitchen gets equally creative with vegan "charcuterie," red pepper stew topped with fried avocado, and other veggie-friendly fare on its periodic Meatless Mondays.

Serving inventive contemporary fare, ★ **Quatrefoil Restaurant** (16 Sydenham St., Dundas, 905/628-7800, www.quatrefoil-restaurant.com, noon-2:30pm and 5pm-close Tues.-Sat., lunch $15-24, dinner $32-42), west of downtown, put Hamilton on the fine-dining map. At lunch, try the pan-seared rainbow trout with lemon risotto, or the classic eggs benedict. In the evening, halibut might be paired with charred cabbage and smoked bacon, while the locally raised beef might be served with wild mushrooms and a potato-parsnip purée. It's straightforward, stylish, and scrumptious.

INFORMATION AND SERVICES

The **Tourism Hamilton Visitor Information Centre** (28 James St. N., 905/546-2666 or 800/263-8590, www.tourismhamilton.com) can provide information about things to see and events around the region.

GETTING THERE AND AROUND

Hamilton International Airport (YHM, 9300 Airport Rd., 905/679-1999, www.flyhi.ca) is 14 kilometers (nine miles) south of downtown. **WestJet** (888/937-8538, www.westjet.com) is the airport's main carrier, with nonstop flights to Calgary year-round, and spring through fall flights to Edmonton, Halifax, and Moncton. Toronto's **Pearson International Airport** (YYZ, 6301 Silver Dart Dr., Mississauga, 416/247-7678 or 866/207-1690, www.torontopearson.com),

just over an hour away, has many more flight options.

Buses and trains arrive and depart from the **Hamilton GO Centre** (36 Hunter St. E., 416/869-3200, www.gotransit.com), an art deco-style building downtown. There's frequent service to Toronto's Union Station (1-1.25 hours, one-way adults $11, seniors and kids $5.50). **Megabus** (www.megabus.com) can take you to Niagara Falls (1.5-1.75 hours, one-way $10).

Hamilton is midway between Toronto and Niagara Falls. It's 65 kilometers (40 miles) southwest of Toronto, a straight shot down the Queen Elizabeth Way (QEW). To Niagara Falls, continue south on the QEW south for another 70 kilometers (44 miles). You can explore downtown Hamilton without a car. It's a short walk from the train-bus station to the Art Gallery and Farmers Market; the James Street North Gallery District is also within walking distance. To visit other attractions, you can get around on the city's bus system, the **Hamilton Street Railway** (905/527-4441, www.hamilton.ca, one-way $2.55).

BRANTFORD AND THE SIX NATIONS

West of Hamilton, the city of Brantford claims the invention of an indispensable modern technology: the telephone. The surrounding region has several interesting First Nations heritage sites, home to the Six Nations of the Grand River Territory, comprising the Onondaga, Cayuga, Seneca, Mohawk, Oneida, and Tuscarora.

Sights and Activities

Alexander Graham Bell (1847-1922) lived with his family in this 1858 farmhouse, now the **Bell Homestead National Historic Site** (94 Tutela Heights Rd., 519/756-6220, www.bellhomestead.ca, 9:30am-4:30pm Tues.-Sun., adults $6.25, seniors $5.25, children over age 7 $4.50), which they purchased in 1870 after immigrating from Scotland. Sitting by the river behind the house in what he called his "dreaming place," Bell reportedly had the inspiration that led him to develop his most famous invention. Guides in period costume tell you about the Bell family's life, Bell's research, and the history of the telephone. As you travel rural roads in this part of Ontario, be on the lookout for **barn quilts** (www.barnquilttrails.ca), replicas of colorful fabric quilts painted on the sides of area barns. There's one on the Bell Homestead property.

Her Majesty's Royal Chapel of the Mohawks (301 Mohawk St., 519/756-0240, www.mohawkchapel.ca, 10am-5pm Tues.-Sun. mid-May-mid-Oct.) was the first Protestant house of worship in Upper Canada and remains Ontario's oldest surviving church. Built by the British in 1785, it was given to Loyalist First Nations who supported the British during the American Revolutionary War. One of two Royal Chapels in North America, this simple wood-frame structure is the only such chapel located on First Nations land; services are still held at 10:30am Sunday in summer. Thayendanegea, the Mohawk chief, soldier, and statesman more commonly known as Joseph Brant, for whom the present-day city is named, is buried in a tomb beside the chapel.

The **Woodland Cultural Centre** (184 Mohawk St., 519/759-2650, www.woodland-centre.on.ca, 9am-4pm Mon.-Fri., 10am-5pm Sat.-Sun. late May-Dec., 9am-4pm Mon.-Fri., 10am-5pm Sat. Jan.-late May, adults $7, seniors $5, ages 5-18 $5, cash only) houses a museum exhibiting archeological, historical, and cultural artifacts from the Six Nations communities, as well as periodic First Nations art shows.

Writer and poet E. Pauline Johnson (1861-1913) was born to a Mohawk father and English mother in the 1853 manor house that's now **Chiefswood National Historic Site** (1037 Hwy. 54, Ohsweken, 519/752-5005, www.chiefswood.com, 10am-3pm Tues.-Sun. late May-early Sept., 10am-3pm Sat.-Sun. early Sept.-mid-Oct., donation $8). She became one of the earliest First Nations author to earn wide recognition in Canada. On the 30-minute tours, you can learn more about her life, work, and family that spanned two cultures.

Southern Ontario's longest river, the Grand, flows 266 kilometers (165 miles) from its source near the town of Dundalk to Lake Erie, passing through the Brantford area. **Grand Experiences** (888/258-0441, www.grand-experiences.com, Apr.-Nov.) offers several guided half-day, full-day, and longer canoe and kayak excursions on the

Bell Homestead National Historic Site

Grand, including the Mohawk Run, a gentle four-hour paddle that starts from the Brant Conservation Area, and a 2.5- to 3-hour Moonlight Paddle.

Events

Visitors are welcome at the **Grand River "Champion of Champions" Powwow** (Chiefswood Park, off Hwy. 54, Ohsweken, 519/445-4061, July), held every summer on the Six Nations territory.

Accommodations and Food

Brantford has the usual assortment of chain motels, including the nicely updated **Best Western Plus Brant Park Inn** (19 Holiday Dr., 519/753-8651 or 877/341-1234, www.best-westernbrantford.com). Hamilton has more lodging options.

On the Six Nations reserve, the **Burger Barn** (3000 4th Line, Ohsweken, 519/445-0088, www.burgerbarn.ca, 8am-9pm daily, $6-20) should be your destination, if you like big meaty patties with imaginative toppings. The Smokey Mountain is piled high with Canadian bacon, cheddar, and BBQ sauce, the Luau with monterey jack, grilled pineapple, ham, and hot peppers, and there's even a Mac & Cheeseburger, topped with, yes, macaroni and cheese. You can order breakfast, sandwiches, *poutine,* or steak, but it's called the *Burger* Barn for a reason.

Practicalities

The **Brantford Visitor and Tourism Centre** (399 Wayne Gretzky Pkwy., 519/751-9900 or 800/265-6299, www.discoverbrantford.com, 9am-6pm Mon.-Fri., 10am-6pm Sat., 10am-5pm Sun. mid-May-Sept., 9am-5pm Mon.-Fri., 10am-4pm Sat. Oct.-mid-May) dispenses information about the region. The **Six Nations Tourism** office (2498 Chiefswood Rd., Ohsweken, 519/758-5444 or 866/393-3001, www.sixnationstourism.ca) has a small exhibit area about Six Nations' heritage; staff also answer questions about local First Nations attractions and culture.

Brantford is 105 kilometers (65 miles) from Toronto and 40 kilometers (25 miles) west of Hamilton via Highway 403.

Look for barn quilts as you travel through rural Ontario.

Kitchener-Waterloo and Vicinity

Billing itself as "Canada's technology triangle," the formerly industrial communities of Kitchener-Waterloo (a.k.a. "K-W") and nearby Cambridge have reinvented themselves with high tech. Much of the area's rebirth was due to BlackBerry, which put Waterloo on the innovation map after launching its smart phone back in 1999. Other high-tech companies, including Google, Open Text, and Christie, have since established K-W offices, and graduates of University of Waterloo's well-regarded computer science, mathematics, and engineering programs start up technology ventures in the region.

This high-tech development is slowly triggering a renaissance in other areas, notably the arts. The region has several excellent small museums and galleries, clustered in downtown Kitchener or uptown Waterloo (the city's central area), and an increasingly robust calendar of arts events. Like many gentrifying communities, K-W has its ragged patches, with pawnshops next to hipster coffeehouses, but there's a feeling of excitement here that makes it worth exploring.

Well before the high-tech boom, many early settlers arrived from Germany, and a wildly popular event remains the annual Oktoberfest, the largest such festival outside of Germany. The most visible day-to-day legacy of this Germanic heritage is in the countryside around K-W, particularly in the village of St. Jacobs, where many residents are traditional Old Order Mennonites, whose simple buggy-driving, technology-shunning lifestyle contrasts sharply with the smart phone-toting, online-obsessed world of their more urban neighbors. See it while you still can.

SIGHTS
Kitchener-Waterloo Art Gallery

Compact yet cool, the region's art museum, the **Kitchener-Waterloo Art Gallery** (101 Queen St. N., Kitchener, 519/579-5860, www.kwag.ca, 9:30am-5pm Mon.-Wed., 9:30am-9pm Thurs., 9:30am-5pm Fri., 10am-5pm Sat., 1pm-5pm Sun., free), shows contemporary Canadian and international works from the 4,000-piece permanent collection and in changing exhibits. Located in the Centre in the Square theater building, the gallery stays open late before performances.

THEMUSEUM

Part children's museum and part "museum of ideas," **THEMUSEUM** (10 King St. W., Kitchener, 519/749-9387, www.themuseum.ca, 10am-4pm Wed.-Fri., 10am-5pm Sat.-Sun., over age 14 $12, ages 3-13 $9, everyone $5 Wed.) has plenty of things for kids to do, but as you climb to the higher floors in the open, multitiered space, exhibits become more sophisticated, like the recent *Science of Sexuality* or *Rethinking Art and Machine,* which showcased artists working with the interaction of art and technology.

Waterloo Region Museum

Starting with its striking, multicolored glass exterior, the **Waterloo Region Museum** (10 Huron Rd., Kitchener, 519/748-1914, www.waterlooregionmuseum.com, 9:30am-5pm daily May-early Sept., 9:30am-5pm Mon.-Sat., 11am-5pm Sun. early Sept.-Apr., adults $10, seniors and students $8, ages 5-12 $5, families $25) isn't your ordinary historical museum. Multimedia exhibits trace the region's roots from its aboriginal inhabitants to today's high-tech businesses. Behind the museum, travel back to 1914 in the **Doon Heritage Village** (9:30am-5pm daily May-early Sept., 9:30am-4pm Mon.-Sat., 11am-4pm Sun. early Sept.-mid-Oct., 9:30am-5pm Mon.-Fri. mid-Oct.-Dec.), where costumed staff recreate early-20th-century life.

The museum and heritage village are nine

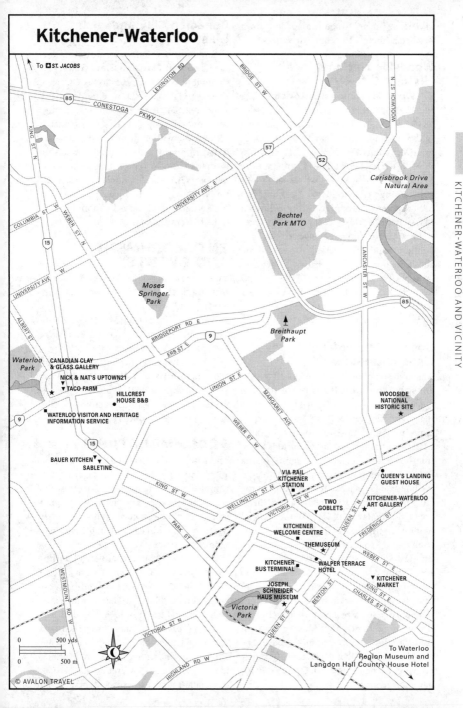

Kitchener-Waterloo

To ✚ ST. JACOBS

85
CONESTOGA PKWY

KING ST N

LEXINGTON RD

BRIDGE ST W

WOOLWICH ST N

57

52

Carisbrook Drive
Natural Area

COLUMBIA ST W

WEBER ST N

UNIVERSITY AVE E

Bechtel
Park MTO

15

UNIVERSITY AVE W

Moses
Springer
Park

LANCASTER ST W

85

ALBERT ST

BRIDGEPORT RD E

ERB ST E

9

Breithaupt
Park

Waterloo
Park

CANADIAN CLAY
& GLASS GALLERY

UNION ST E

MARGARET AVE

9

NICK & NAT'S UPTOWN21
★ ▼ TACO FARM

HILLCREST
HOUSE B&B ●

WOODSIDE
NATIONAL
HISTORIC SITE
★

● WATERLOO VISITOR AND HERITAGE
INFORMATION SERVICE

WEBER ST W

15

BAUER KITCHEN ▼
SABLETINE

KING ST W

WELLINGTON ST N

VICTORIA ST W

VIA RAIL
KITCHENER
STATION
■

QUEEN'S LANDING
GUEST HOUSE ●

PARK ST

TWO
GOBLETS
★

QUEEN ST N

KITCHENER-WATERLOO
ART GALLERY
★

FREDERICK ST

KITCHENER
WELCOME CENTRE
■

THEMUSEUM
★

WEBER ST E

WESTMOUNT RD W

KITCHENER
BUS TERMINAL
■

● WALPER TERRACE
HOTEL

BENTON ST

KING ST E

▼ KITCHENER
MARKET

JOSEPH
SCHNEIDER
HAUS MUSEUM
★

CHARLES ST W

Victoria
Park

VICTORIA ST N

QUEEN ST S

HIGHLAND RD W

To Waterloo
Region Museum and
Langdon Hall Country House Hotel

0   500 yds
0   500 m

© AVALON TRAVEL

kilometers (six miles) southeast of downtown Kitchener, about a 15-minute drive.

Woodside National Historic Site

The **Woodside National Historic Site** (528 Wellington St. N., Kitchener, 519/571-5684 or 888/773-8888, www.pc.gc.ca, 1pm-5pm daily mid-May-Sept., 1pm-5pm Wed.-Sat. Oct.-mid-Dec., adults $3.90, senior $3.40, ages 6-16 $1.90) is the boyhood home of William Lyon Mackenzie King (1874-1950), Canada's longest-serving prime minister. The house has been restored to its appearance in 1891, when Mackenzie King was a teenager, and includes some furnishings that belonged to the King family. Interpreters in period costume tell you about the home and its history. To get here by public transit, take bus no. 6 (Bridgeport) from the Kitchener bus station to the corner of Lancaster and Wellington, then walk east on Wellington to the site.

Joseph Schneider Haus Museum

The oldest home in Kitchener, the 1816 **Joseph Schneider Haus Museum** (466 Queen St. S., Kitchener, 519/742-7752, www.region.waterloo.on.ca, 10am-5pm Wed.-Sat., 1pm-5pm Sun. mid-Feb.-mid-Dec., adults $2.25, seniors and students $1.50, kids $1.25, families $5) belonged to a Pennsylvania German Mennonite farm family. Although the house today is just a few blocks from the city's urban center, it once sat on a 181-hectare (448-acre) farm, and within the restored home it's still the 1800s. Costumed staff cook, put up pickles, spin, or do chores appropriate to the season, and explain about 19th-century farm life and Mennonite customs. In the Beggar's Room, families would often lodge an itinerant traveler who'd work in exchange for a bed. Another section of the building, the Doddy Haus, common in traditional Mennonite homes even today, would house the older generation after their grown children assumed the farm's day-to-day management.

Canadian Clay and Glass Gallery

Changing its exhibits several times a year, the **Canadian Clay and Glass Gallery** (25 Caroline St. N., Waterloo, 519/746-1882, www.theclayandglass.ca, 11am-6pm Tues.-Fri., 10am-5pm Sat., 1pm-5pm Sun., free) features contemporary clay and glass works, often in conjunction with multimedia, painting, and other genres, by artisans from Canada and farther afield. Do your gift shopping in the museum's first-rate boutique, which sells distinctive jewelry, stained-glass pieces, ceramics, and glass sculptures by more than 140 Canadian craftspeople.

ENTERTAINMENT AND EVENTS

The weeklong Kitchener-Waterloo **Oktoberfest** (519/570-4267, www.oktoberfest.ca, Oct.), which claims to be the largest Bavarian festival outside Munich, celebrates the region's German heritage with beer, music, beer, food, and more beer.

Part of a network of Ontario regional theaters, the **Dunfield Theatre** (46 Grand Ave. S., Cambridge, 519/621-8000, www.draytonentertainment.com) stages crowd-pleasing plays on its sleek, modern stages.

ACCOMMODATIONS

The Kitchener-Waterloo area has a mix of Victorian-style B&Bs, historic inns, and run-of-the-mill chain hotels. Prices rise and availability plummets during university graduations and other special events, but otherwise, you shouldn't have trouble finding a room.

Built in the 1920s, the **Queen's Landing Guest House** (187 Queen St. N., Kitchener, 519/576-9297, www.queenslandingguesthouse.com, $100-115 s, $110-125 d) retains many original features, including dark walnut woodwork and art nouveau stained glass. The largest room has a four-poster bed and a fireplace, while a second room, overlooking the garden, has a secret nook. Guests in the smallest room use a spacious private bath across the hall. Longtime owners Wilma and Brian Skipper can tell you all about things to do nearby. Wilma's hearty breakfasts might feature delicious oatmeal pancakes or apricot scones with homemade jam. Wi-Fi and parking are included.

Do you "Trust the Fat Guy"? At the **Hillcrest House B&B** (73 George St., Waterloo, 519/744-3534 or 866/624-3534, www.hillcresthouse.ca, $145 d), self-described "fat guy" Stefan Schuster runs this lovely B&B in an 1882 hilltop home in Uptown Waterloo with his wife, Wendy. Schuster not only cooks gourmet breakfasts—his take on eggs Benedict might include poached eggs topped with smoked salmon on a potato *rosti*—he also offers "Trust the Fat Guy" cooking workshops for couples or small groups. Of the three large Victorian-style guest rooms, two are suites with separate sleeping and sitting areas. Rates include Wi-Fi and parking.

Eleanor Roosevelt, Bob Hope, Elton John, and Lady Gaga have all stayed at the **Walper Terrace Hotel** (1 King St. W., Kitchener, 519/745-4321 or 800/265-8749, www.walper. com, $119-169 d), built in 1893 in Kitchener's downtown. The floors are a bit creaky, but the 85 guest rooms have been upgraded with a mix of old and new furnishings, flat-screen TVs, Keurig coffeemakers, and free Wi-Fi, and decorated gallery-style with original artworks.

Play tennis or croquet on the lawn or lounge by the pool at ★ **Langdon Hall Country House Hotel and Spa** (1 Langdon Dr., Cambridge, 519/740-2100, www.langdonhall.ca, $295-685 d). Enjoy afternoon tea in the conservatory or stroll the gardens. The grand 1902 brick manor was the summer house of New York-born Eugene Langdon Wilks, great-grandson of American mogul John Jacob Astor. Twelve of the 52 elegant guest rooms are in the main house, while the rest are in two separate wings, with overstuffed chairs, fireplaces, and luxurious baths with soaker tubs. The buffet breakfast is lavish.

FOOD

In the **Kitchener Market** (300 King St. E., Kitchener, 519/741-2287, www.kitchenermarket.ca, 8am-3pm Tues.-Fri., 7am-2pm Sat.), vendors sell Croatian, Caribbean, and other international food to go. On Saturday, the lower level houses a large **Farmers Market** (7am-2pm Sat.).

It's easy to pass right by **Sabletine** (203 King St. S., Waterloo, 519/568-7373, www. sabletine.com, 8am-5:30pm Tues., 8am-6pm Wed.-Fri., 9am-5pm Sat., 10:30am-4pm Sun., $6-8), but don't. This petite café bakes chocolate croissants, lemon tarts, and other fine French pastries, along with daily soups, sandwiches, and interesting salads, like a hearty wheat-berry Waldorf with apples, cranberries, and nuts.

Two Goblets (85 Weber St. W., Kitchener, 519/749-1829, www.twogoblets.com, 11:30am-2pm and 5pm-9pm Tues.-Fri., 4pm-9pm Sat., $14-20) specializes in schnitzel, with more than a dozen variations, as well as goulash, cabbage rolls, and other hearty dishes that show off K-W's Central European roots. On the walls are rustic scenes of peasants making wine; you can fill your own goblets with wine from Germany, Canada, and farther afield.

Cool little **Taco Farm** (8 Erb St., 519/208-1300, www.tacofarm.ca, 11:30am-close Tues.-Sat., $5-17) doesn't claim to serve authentic Mexican fare, but with dishes like smoked pork belly tacos topped with grilled pineapple salsa or fried chicken finished with tequila, honey, and lime, you won't care. Thirsty? Study the tequila bible, which has more than 40 varieties.

The hottest seats at casually hip bistro **Nick and Nat's Uptown21** (21 King St. N., Waterloo, 519/883-1100, www.uptown21.ca, dinner 5pm-close Tues.-Sat., $24-33) are at the "kitchen counter"—a bar facing the action in the kitchen. The hottest items on the intriguing menu? Whatever's in season. You might find smoked trout with sweet pea and potato cakes, caramelized onion and blue cheese ravioli, or milk-braised lamb shoulder paired with lamb-dandelion sausage.

For dessert? That might be a lemon tart with smoked blueberry compote or freshly made cinnamon-sugar doughnuts.

With exposed brick walls, a lengthy booze list, and lots of grazing options, always-busy **Bauer Kitchen** (187 King St. S., Unit 2, Waterloo, 519/772-0790, www.thebauerkitchen.ca, 11am-11pm Mon.-Fri., 9am-1am Sat., 9am-11pm Sun., lunch $9-19, dinner $15-38) is the kind of place where you can meet up for drinks or bring the gang for a laid-back meal. Snack on smoked fried calamari and hoisin-glazed chicken tacos, or dig into burgers, pizzas, pasta, or steaks.

Langdon Hall's **Dining Room** (1 Langdon Dr., Cambridge, 519/740-2100, www.langdonhall.ca, 7am-10:30am, noon-2:30pm, and 5:30pm-9pm Mon.-Fri., 7:30am-10:30am, noon-2:30pm, and 5:30pm-9pm Sat.-Sun., brunch $55, lunch $26-28, dinner $29-48) is a special-occasion destination with gracious staff. Using local ingredients, the chefs might concoct halibut paired with a crustacean boudin or a beef platter with roasted loin and bone marrow. Dessert options include tea-smoked melon with cashew praline. Reservations are recommended. You can also dine in the more casual but still luxe **Wilks' Bar** (lunch and dinner daily, $15-26), where menu choices include cod and chips or roast pork with mustard greens salad.

INFORMATION AND SERVICES

Waterloo Regional Tourism Marketing Corporation (519/585-7517 or 877/585-7517, www.explorewaterlooregion.com) provides information about sights, activities, events, and accommodations in Kitchener, Waterloo, Cambridge, St. Jacobs, and the surrounding towns. The **Kitchener Welcome Centre** (200 King St. W., 519/741-2200, ext. 7130, www.kitchener.ca) and the **Waterloo Visitor and Heritage Information Service** (10 Father David Bauer Dr., Waterloo, 519/885-2297, www.waterloo.ca) dispense visitor information.

GETTING THERE

Air

The **Region of Waterloo International Airport** (YFK, 4881 Fountain St., Breslau, 519/648-2256 or 866/648-2256, www.waterlooairport.ca) is located east of K-W. **WestJet** (888/937-8538, www.westjet.com) has a direct daily flight from Calgary with connections to Vancouver, Edmonton, and other Western Canadian cities. American Airlines flies non-stop daily from Chicago.

Alternatively, fly into Toronto's **Pearson International Airport** (YYZ, 6301 Silver Dart Dr., Mississauga, 416/247-7678 or 866/207-1690, www.torontopearson.com), which has many more flight options, and either rent a car or catch the bus to K-W. Airways Transit's **Toronto Airporter Bus Service** (519/886-2121, www.airwaystransit.com, 1.5-2 hours, one-way adults $56, ages 2-12 $33) runs buses three times a day between Pearson airport and several points in Kitchener-Waterloo.

Train

VIA Rail (888/842-7245, www.viarail.ca) runs trains between Toronto's Union Station and **Kitchener Station** (126 Weber St. W., 888/842-7245, 1.75 hours, one-way adults $25-36, ages 2-11 $18). **GO Transit** (416/869-3200 or 888/438-6646, www.gotransit.com) operates commuter trains between these same stations (2 hours, one-way adults and students $16, seniors and ages 6-12 $8).

Bus

GO Transit buses (416/869-3200 or 888/438-6646, www.gotransit.com, one-way adults $16, seniors and children $8) travel from Toronto to the downtown Kitchener Bus Terminal (15 Charles St. W., 1.5 hours) or to the University of Waterloo (Student Life Center, 200 University Ave. W., 2 hours). **Greyhound** (www.greyhound.ca) operates numerous daily buses from Toronto to Kitchener (1.5-2 hours, one-way adults $20-29, ages 2-12 $16-22), as well as several buses a day from Toronto to the University of Waterloo (1.75-2.5 hours, one-way adults \$20-30, ages 2-11 \$16-23). **Coach Canada** (www.coachcanada.com) runs buses from Kitchener to Hamilton (1.5 hours, one-way adults \$16.70, ages 2-11 \$8.35).

Car

Downtown Kitchener is 105 kilometers (65 miles) southwest of central Toronto, about 90 minutes (except at rush hours); take Highway 401 west to exit 278, where you'll pick up Highway 8 west. Exit onto King Street east if you're heading to central Kitchener. Uptown Waterloo is five kilometers (three miles) northwest of downtown Kitchener. From Highway 8, you can either take King Street East and continue through Kitchener and into Waterloo, or take Highway 85 north to Erb Street East and go west.

GETTING AROUND

With a little effort, you can explore K-W car-free, particularly if you're mainly interested in attractions near downtown Kitchener or Uptown Waterloo. **Grand River Transit** (GRT, 519/585-7555, www.grt.ca) runs a comprehensive network of buses around the region. Out-of-town buses arrive at the Kitchener Bus Terminal (15 Charles St. W.), a hub for GRT buses; from there, buses travel along King Street, connecting downtown Kitchener with Uptown Waterloo. Use the **EasyGO trip planner** (www.grt.ca) to plot your route.

It's much easier to explore farther afield with a car. Most major car rental agencies have offices in Kitchener-Waterloo. However you're getting around, pay particular attention to the directional and city designations in street addresses: 10 King Street East in Kitchener is not near 10 King Street North in Waterloo.

★ ST. JACOBS

This small town north of Waterloo is a base for learning more about the region's Mennonite community, who settled here in the 1800s. The Mennonites continue to observe traditional customs, traveling in horse-drawn buggies, wearing unadorned clothing, and farming, canning, and quilting as they have for generations.

St. Jacobs's attractions are in two separate areas. The Market District, where you'll find the year-round Farmers Market, as well as a collection of outlet stores, is three kilometers (1.9 miles) south of St. Jacobs Village, which houses the Visitors Centre and several smaller attractions. While both the market and village are worth a visit, they're undeniably

Ontario maple syrup at the St. Jacobs Farmers Market

touristy, so make time to explore the surrounding countryside for a clearer glimpse of Mennonite life.

The Market District

Canada's largest year-round farmers market, **St. Jacobs Farmers Market** (878 Weber St. N., 519/747-1830, www.stjacobs.com, 7am-3:30pm Thurs. and Sat. year-round, 8am-3pm Tues. mid-June-Aug., free) is like a department store of farm markets, where you can buy everything from tomatoes to T-shirts to toenail clippers. Although the market suffered a devastating fire in 2013, it quickly reopened for business in a temporary building, and on a busy day, the aisles are as packed as a carnival midway on a hot summer's night.

Many shopkeepers, particularly those selling fruits and vegetables, homemade jams and pickles, or locally produced maple syrup, are Mennonites—the men in traditional black jackets and straw hats, the women in long dresses and bonnets, with their buggies parked behind their stalls. Look for their fresh seasonal produce, homemade baked goods, and quilts and other crafts.

One of the market's most popular snack stalls is the **Fritter Company,** which turns apple slices into crispy, batter-fried apple fritters. Prepare for long lineups if you want a fritter fix.

St. Jacobs Village

Stop into the St. Jacobs Visitor Information Centre, not just for information about the region (which they have plenty of), but to see **The Mennonite Story** (1406 King St. N., 519/664-3518, www.stjacobs.com/mennonite-story, 11am-5pm Mon.-Sat., 1:30pm-5pm Sun. Apr.-Dec., 11am-4:30pm Mon.-Sat., 2pm-4:30pm Sun. Jan.-Mar., donation $4) on the lower level. This informative exhibit includes a video about the Old Order Mennonites in the St. Jacobs region, a history of the Mennonites' European roots, including a replica of a cave where their Swiss ancestors hid from their persecutors, a reproduction of a Mennonite meetinghouse, and another video that explains about life in modern Mennonite communities from Brazil to Mexico to Zimbabwe.

If you think a model railroad is just for kids or train geeks, you haven't visited the **St. Jacobs & Aberfoyle Model Railway** (1440-3 King St. N., 519/664-3737, www.stjacobsmodelrailway.com, 10am-5pm Sat.-Sun. May-Dec., adults $8, seniors $7, children $5), a fascinating miniature world

The Mennonite Story in St. Jacobs

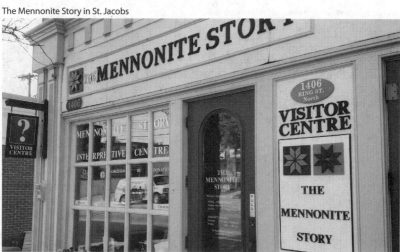

depicting Southern Ontario life in the 1950s. Yes, there are tiny trains, but this elaborate diorama, hand-built by a group of local residents over the past 40 years, comes complete with the local movie house, a Mennonite meeting house, and even a farmer in his outhouse.

At **Hamel Brooms** (1411 King St. N., 10am-6pm Mon.-Sat., noon-5:30pm Sun. Mar.-Dec., call for winter hours), you can watch the staff make straw brooms as they've done since the early 1900s. The **Country Mill** (1441 King St. N., 10am-6pm Mon.-Sat., noon-5:30pm Sun.) is primarily a collection of shops, but the building also houses the modest **Maple Syrup Museum of Ontario** (519/664-3626, 10am-6pm Mon.-Sat., noon-5:30pm Sun., free) and the **St. Jacobs Quilt Gallery** (519/664-2728, 10am-6pm Mon.-Sat., noon-5:30pm Sun., free), with changing displays of regionally crafted quilts.

When you need liquid refreshment, ask for a taste or a pint at **Block Three Brewing Company** (1430 King St. N., Unit 2, 519/664-1001, www.blockthreebrewing.com, 11am-6pm Sun.-Thurs., 11am-8pm Fri.-Sat.), a local microbrewery.

Mennonite Cultural Tour

Outfitter **Grand Experiences** (888/258-0441, www.grand-experiences.com) offers a unique pedal-powered way to explore Mennonite culture in and around St. Jacobs. On the "The Path Less Traveled" tour, you'll cycle gently rolling rural roads to visit a Mennonite-run harness shop, where you can talk with the owner about driving a horse-drawn buggy. Have lunch on a nearby farm with the gregarious family matriarch, who runs a quilting business and keeps a sizeable vegetable garden. You'll also visit a Mennonite general store and the West Montrose Covered Bridge. You can book this trip as a day tour ($120) or as a two-day, two-night package that includes a behind-the-scenes visit to the St. Jacobs Farmers Market, a half-day canoe excursion along a quiet section of the Grand River, and accommodations in St. Jacobs.

Entertainment and Events

Located near the Farmers Market, the year-round **St. Jacobs Country Playhouse** (40 Benjamin Rd. E., 519/747-7788, www.draytonentertainment.com) stages musicals and other lighter fare. At the more intimate **St. Jacobs Schoolhouse Theatre** (11 Albert St., 519/638-5555, www.draytonentertainment.com), in a stone former school dating to 1867 in St. Jacobs Village, you can watch professional theater productions with cabaret-style seating.

The annual **Quilt and Fibre Art Festival** (800/265-3353, www.stjacobs.com), typically held over several days in late May, showcases quilt work by regional artisans. Quilts are displayed in St. Jacobs, Kitchener-Waterloo, and surrounding towns. As part of the festival, quilts are auctioned off at the **New Hamburg Mennonite Relief Sale** (www.nhmrs.com), one of Canada's largest quilt auctions.

Accommodations and Food

St. Jacobs has a comfortable inn, a couple of B&Bs in the village, and several chain motels close to the Farmers Market, including the family- and business-friendly **Homewood Suites** (45 Benjamin Rd., 519/514-0088, http://homewoodsuites3.hilton.com, $159-219 d), which has modern one- and two-bedroom apartment-style units with full kitchens as well as an indoor pool. Rates include a buffet breakfast daily and even dinner (Mon.-Thurs.).

You won't go hungry at the **St. Jacobs Farmers Market** (878 Weber St. N., 519/747-1830, www.stjacobs.com, 7am-3:30pm Thurs. and Sat. year-round, 8am-3pm Tues. mid-June-Aug., free), with plenty of stalls selling snacks and more substantial meals.

In St. Jacobs Village, owner Claire Bowman keeps three neat second-floor guest rooms at **Baumann House Bed & Breakfast** (25 Spring St., 519/664-1515, www.bbcanada.com/3205.html, $95 d), and she can tell you everything about touring the region. One room has twig furniture, another has a spool bed topped with a red velvet coverlet, and a

The Old Order Mennonites

Most of the roughly 4,000 Mennonites who live in and around St. Jacobs are known as "Old Order Mennonites." The Old Order community is what many people envision when they think of Mennonites: men and women wear traditional clothing, the men in dark suits and black or straw hats, the women in simple long dresses and bonnets; and reject contemporary conveniences, like cars and computers. In this patriarchal society, women may work before they are married, but once they tie the knot, their responsibilities are at home. Large families, with an average of seven children, are common. Women don't wear makeup or jewelry and typically sew the long, plain dresses that they and their daughters wear.

Old Order Mennonites settled in Ontario in the 1800s and can trace their roots to Switzerland in the 1500s. While many of the Old Order now have electricity and telephones in their homes, they shun other technologies, from automobiles and clothes dryers to radios and TVs. Most speak a German dialect, although all learn English at school. The Old Order communities run their own schools, which children typically attend through grade 8 or age 14.

The Old Order Mennonites are private people, but you can learn more about their communities and customs if you're respectful of their beliefs and traditions. Drive along the back roads outside St. Jacobs and you'll likely see horse-drawn buggies trotting alongside your car, or black-hatted men pedaling along on their bicycles. On Sunday, you may see lines of buggies heading to the meetinghouse.

Many Mennonite families sell produce, eggs, homemade jams, and quilts from their farms in the countryside around St. Jacobs. They'll post a sign at the end of their driveway if they're open for business. You're welcome to chat while you're browsing their wares or making a purchase, but remember that they're running a business, not opening their homes to gawking travelers. Also, Mennonites frown on picture taking (they believe it can lead to the sin of pride), so don't snap photos of people, and ask permission before photographing their buggies or the products they're selling.

You can stop into the Mennonite-run **Wallenstein General Store** (7278 Hwy. 86, at Hwy. 10, 519/669-2231), about 12 kilometers (7.5 miles) northwest of St. Jacobs, which sells the traditional hats, religious books, fabrics, and farm supplies used in the Old Order community. Their homemade morning glory muffins ($1) are tasty, too.

Northeast of St. Jacobs, the **Lost Acres Variety Store** (12 Covered Bridge Dr., West Montrose, 519/669-5689) is also Mennonite-run (note the extra-large packages of Jell-O for sale). It's adjacent to Ontario's only remaining covered bridge, the **West Montrose Covered Bridge,** built in 1881; it's known as the "Kissing Bridge," since it offered couples traveling by horse and buggy a secluded spot to smooch.

To find other Mennonite-owned businesses, simply drive the country lanes—if the sign says "No Sunday Sales," it's likely run by a Mennonite family. You can also purchase the *Map Directory of Local Country Shops in Waterloo and Wellington County* ($5) at the **St. Jacobs Visitor Information Centre** (1406 King St. N., 519/664-1133 or 800/265-3353, www.stjacobs.com). Some of the listed businesses, such as those repairing buggies or shoeing horses, don't cater to outsiders, but others welcome your trade. In additional to produce vendors and quilters, look for furniture makers and other artisans.

At the **St. Jacobs Visitor Information Centre** (1406 King St. N., 519/664-1133 or 800/265-3353, www.stjacobs.com), pick up the helpful free booklet *The Plain and Simple Facts: Inside the Old Order Mennonite Community of the St. Jacobs Area,* which explains more about the community's beliefs and traditions, courtship and marriage customs, schools, and child-rearing practices. They also sell other books about Mennonite culture and traditions.

third, with twin beds, is done all in lavender; rooms share one bath upstairs and a half bath on the main level. Breakfast specialties include herb and cheese omelets and pancakes with local maple syrup.

Originally a stagecoach stop, **DH Food & Lodging** (1430 King St. N., 519/664-3731, $100-145 d), in a restored 1852 building once known as the Dominion Hotel, is again catering to weary travelers. The nine country-style guest rooms upstairs are decorated with duvet-topped beds and sturdy oak furniture. Rates include Wi-Fi and continental breakfast. In the downstairs **restaurant** (11:30am-9pm daily, lunch $12-17, dinner $17-42), expect salads, sandwiches, and heartier entrées like pork schnitzel or steak and mushroom pot pie midday; in the evening, the fare includes maple-glazed salmon, osso buco, and rack of lamb.

Pick up a Dutch apple square, butter tart, or other sweet from the **Stone Crock Bakery** (1402 King St. N., 519/664-3612, 6:30am-6pm Mon.-Sat., 11am-5:30pm Sun.). Next door, you can sit down to a full meal at the family-style **Stone Crock Restaurant** (1396 King St. N., 519/664-2286 or 886/664-2286, 7am-3pm Mon.-Tues., 7am-8pm Wed.-Sat., 11am-8pm Sun.), which sets up a buffet at lunch (Mon.-Sat., $15) and dinner (Fri.-Sun., $21); among the à la carte options are solid dishes like roast turkey, cabbage rolls, and pot roast.

Jacob's Grill (1398 King St. N., 519/664-2575, 11:30am-9pm Mon.-Wed., 11:30am-10pm Thurs.-Sat., 11:30am-5pm Sun., $12-25) tries to bridge the gap between traditional and contemporary with a menu that includes macaroni and cheese, meat loaf, barbecue ribs, lamb curry, and Thai sesame noodles. DH Food & Lodging, the Stone Crock, and Jacob's are all under the same ownership.

Information and Services

The knowledgeable staff at the **St. Jacobs Visitor Information Centre** (1406 King St. N., 519/664-1133 or 800/265-3353, www. stjacobs.com, 11am-5pm Mon.-Sat., 1:30pm-5pm Sun. Apr.-Dec., 11am-4:30pm Mon.-Sat., 2pm-4:30pm Sun. Jan.-Mar.) can offer directions, point out things to do, and answer questions about the area's Mennonite community. There's a seasonal **Visitor Information Centre** (15 Farmers Market Rd., 519/883-3953, 9am-5pm Mon.-Fri., 8am-4pm Sat., 11am-5pm Sun. May-Oct.) opposite the Farmers Market.

Getting There and Around

St. Jacobs is eight kilometers (five miles) north of Waterloo via Highway 85. King Street, the village's main street, runs between the village and the market district.

A fun way to get to St. Jacobs is aboard the heritage **Waterloo Central Railway** (www. waterloocentralrailway.com, adults $10 one-way, $15 round-trip, seniors and students $8 one-way, $12 round-trip, kids $7 one-way, $10 round-trip), which runs from Uptown Waterloo (Waterloo Station, 10 Father David Bauer Dr., off Erb St. W., 519/885-2297) to St. Jacobs Market and St. Jacobs Village (50 Isabella St.). The train operates three 20- to 25-minute trips in each direction on Tuesday (mid-June-Aug.), Thursday (mid-May-mid-Oct.), and Saturday (mid-Apr.-late Oct.).

Grand River Transit (519/585-7555, www.grt.ca) bus no. 21 runs between the Conestoga Mall (550 King St. N., Waterloo) and St. Jacobs, and also connects the Market District and St. Jacobs Village. Buses run about every 30 minutes; there's no service after 7pm Monday-Friday, after 4pm Saturday, or on Sunday. You can make connections to the mall from downtown Kitchener.

ELORA AND FERGUS

Frequently named to lists of Ontario's prettiest small towns, the communities of Elora and Fergus make enjoyable stopover destinations as you're traveling around the province or as a weekend getaway from Toronto. Scottish pioneers settled the Elora-Fergus region in the mid-1800s, building well-crafted homes from the abundant limestone quarried nearby. Many of these imposing stone structures still stand, housing galleries, shops, and inns.

Sights and Activities

Limestone was once dug from the depths of the **Elora Quarry** (319 Wellington County Rd. 18, 519/846-5234, www.grandriver.ca, 11am-8pm Mon.-Fri., 10am-8pm Sat.-Sun. June-early Sept., adults $5.75, seniors $5, ages 6-14 $3). Surrounded by stone cliffs, the quarry's deep, strikingly blue water now makes it the town's summertime swimming hole.

The Grand River rushes through **Elora Gorge** (7400 Wellington County Rd. 21, Elora, 519/846-9742, www.grandriver.ca, May-mid-Oct., adults $5.75, seniors $5, ages 6-14 $3), creating a natural tubing park (9am-7pm daily late June-early Sept., 9am-7pm Sat.-Sun. May-late June and early-late Sept., $3) in the 22-meter-deep (72-foot-deep) chasm; you can rent a tubing gear package with an inner tube, helmet, and life jacket ($25). Three kilometers (1.9 miles) of hiking trails wend along the river, where experienced canoeists and kayakers also come to run the white water. Bring a picnic, and spend the afternoon.

In a majestic building that belies its origins as a poor house, **Wellington County Museum** (536 Wellington County Rd. 18, Fergus, 519/846-0916 ext. 5221, www.wellington.ca/museum, 9:30am-4:30pm Mon.-Fri., 1pm-5pm Sat.-Sun., donation) has well-designed exhibits about the area's past. The building was constructed in 1877 as a refuge for the region's impoverished and homeless population.

You'd be unlikely to stumble on **Templin Gardens** (400 Tower St. S., Fergus, free), a series of stone terraces leading down to the Grand River. The publisher of the town's newspaper built this secret escape between 1920 and 1934, and its flowers still bloom today.

Entertainment and Shopping

See what's firing in the hot shop at **Blown Away Glass Studio** (6506 Wellington Rd., Elora, 519/846-8268, www.blownawayglassstudio.com, 10am-6pm Tues.-Fri., 10am-5pm Sat.), which sells original glass art. Looking for something crafty to do with your partner? How about "One Hot Date?" It's an introductory two-hour glass-blowing workshop for couples.

Painter Kreso Cavlovic likes to keep the door open at his **Gallery Vernissage Art Studio** (78 Metcalfe St., Elora, 519/729-5063, www.kresofineart.com), so visitors can stop in to watch him work and have a chat. His gallery is one of many along Elora's downtown streets.

The Wellington County Museum building was once a poor house.

A modern movie house inside the 1860s former Commercial Hotel, the **Gorge Cinema** (43 Mill St. W., Elora, 519/846-0191, www.gorgecinema.ca) is Canada's longest continuously running repertory cinema.

Accommodations and Food

The Elora-Fergus area has lovely B&Bs, casual cafés, and more upscale restaurants in restored historic buildings.

Welcoming owners Kathleen Stanley and Roger Dufau operate ★ **Drew House B&B** (120 Mill St., Elora, 519/846-2226, www.drewhouse.com, $125-130 d) in a historic stone farmhouse and former barn set around a lovely garden. In the coach house, six guest rooms are decorated in a French country style. The owners have filled an alcove with books to read and coffee, tea, and cold drinks. In the main house are two multiple-bedroom suites for 5-8 people ($280-340). The ample hot breakfast, served family-style, is a highlight. There's Wi-Fi in the main house but not in the coach house rooms.

In a stately stone manor, the **Breadalbane Inn & Spa** (487 St. Andrew St. W., Fergus, 888/842-2825, www.breadalbaneinn.com, $130-195), pronounced "bruh-DAHL-bun," has seven traditional rooms, with four additional suites in the carriage house. They also have two restaurants: Italian **Scozia** (519/843-4770, www.scoziarestaurant.com, 11:30am-11pm Mon.-Sat., 11:30am-10pm Sun., $13-29) serves pastas, pizzas, steak, and in a nod to the town's Scottish heritage, haggis-stuffed ravioli. The relaxed **Fergusson Room Pub** (519/843-4770, www.fergussonroompub.com, 11am-11pm Sun.-Thurs., 11am-1am Fri.-Sat., $12-20) takes the Scottish theme further, with bangers and mash and shepherd's pie alongside other pub fare; there's plenty of beer on tap, too.

Friendly **Café Creperie** (40 Mill St., W., Elora, 519/846-1618, 10am-11pm Tues., 10am-6pm Wed.-Thurs., 10am-8pm Fri.-Sat., 10am-5pm Sun.), in downtown Elora, serves coffee, salads, and both savory and sweet crepes.

Practicalities

Check the website for **Elora-Fergus Tourism** (www.elorafergus.ca) for more information about the region. Elora is 115 kilometers (70 miles) northwest of Toronto and 30 kilometers (19 miles) north of Waterloo. Fergus is five kilometers (three miles) northeast of Elora. Public transit around the region is nonexistent, so plan to come by car.

Drew House B&B in Elora

LAKE ERIE TO LAKE HURON
KITCHENER-WATERLOO AND VICINITY

Stratford and Vicinity

The main attraction in this town of 30,000 is the Stratford Festival, North America's largest classical repertory theater. Originally known as the Stratford Shakespeare Festival, it's not only works by the Bard on the stage; the festival also includes productions by other classical and more contemporary playwrights.

Even if theater isn't your thing, Stratford makes a good getaway, just two hours from Toronto. Due to the presence of the Stratford Chef School, the town has a large number of high-end restaurants, and you can entertain yourself with music, shopping, and special events throughout the year. If you're not coming for theater, visit Sunday-Tuesday, when fewer productions are staged, or outside the festival season, when accommodations are easier to find; prices and crowds both peak from July through September.

SIGHTS AND ACTIVITIES

Located in an 1880s pump house, a 10-15-minute walk from the Festival Theatre, **Gallery Stratford** (54 Romeo St., 519/271-5271, www.gallerystratford.on.ca, 10am-5pm Tues.-Sat. July-Sept., 11am-3pm Tues.-Sat. Oct.-June., adults $5, seniors and students $4) mounts changing exhibits of Canadian contemporary art.

In an 1880s Victorian home with more recent additions, exhibits at the **Stratford Perth Museum** (4275 Huron Rd., 519/393-5311, www.stratfordperthmuseum.ca, 10am-4pm Mon.-Sat., noon-4pm Sun., adults $5, seniors and students $4, children $3) showcase the Stratford Festival and other elements of the region's past.

Since 1968, local artists have been showing their work along the Avon River at **Art in the Park** (Lakeside Dr., www.artintheparkstratford.com, Wed. and Sat.-Sun. June-Sept.).

Karen Hartwick, who owns the **Tea Leaves Tasting Bar** (433 Erie St., 519/273-1201 or 800/733-0376, www.stratfordtealeaves.com,

11am-5pm Wed.-Sat. and by appointment), is a certified tea sommelier who can teach you all about blacks, greens, herbals, and more. She carries 150 different varieties in her petite shop, including her own unique blends, and offers complimentary tastings.

Buy a pass to the **Stratford Chocolate Trail** ($25) and you can sample six chocolate offerings—truffles, teas, cookies, ice cream, even chocolate martinis—at any of 20 locations around town. If beer and pork are more your style, check out the **Stratford Bacon & Ale Trail** ($25) with hoppy drinks and porcine snacks at several local purveyors. Purchase passes for either trail at the **Stratford Tourism Alliance** (47 Downie St., 800/561-7926, www.visitstratford.ca).

★ STRATFORD FESTIVAL

Stratford-born journalist Tom Patterson hatched the idea for a hometown festival devoted to William Shakespeare's works. He then convinced British actor and director Tyrone Guthrie to become its first artistic director. The inaugural production—*Richard III,* with Alec Guinness playing the lead—took to the stage in July 1953 in a giant canvas tent.

Today, the **Stratford Festival** (519/273-1600 or 800/567-1600, www.stratfordfestival.ca) has produced thousands of plays, many by Shakespeare, but many also by other classical and more contemporary playwrights. The festival typically opens with preview performances in late April-early May and continues through October. July-September are the busiest months, with multiple plays running in repertory. Beyond the plays, the festival offers theater tours, lectures, and special events. Some of the major events are listed below.

Tickets

Ticket sales (519/273-1600 or 800/567-1600, www.stratfordfestival.ca) for the upcoming

Stratford

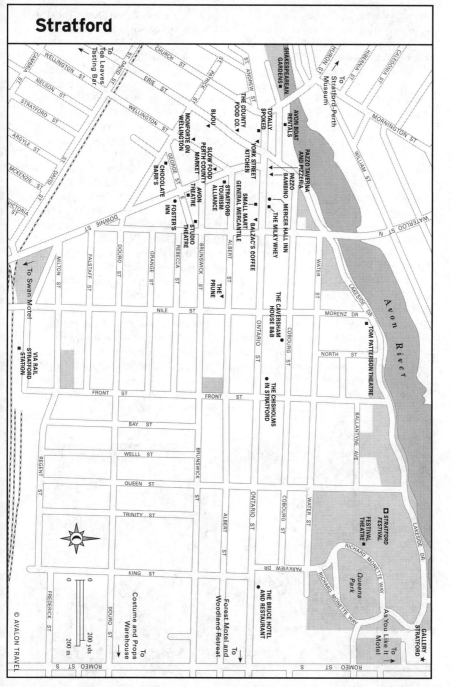

To Tea Leaves Tasting Bar

To Stratford-Perth Museum

CAMBRIA ST
WELLINGTON ST
NELSON ST
STRATFORD ST
ARGYLE ST
MCKENZIE ST
VICTORIA ST

DAVID ST
CHURCH ST
ERIE ST
ANDREW ST
PATRICK ST
WELLINGTON ST
MONFORTE ON WELLINGTON
BIJOU
THE COUNTY FOOD CO.
TOTALLY SPOKED
SHAKESPEAREAN GARDENS
AVON BOAT RENTALS

ST
ST
MORNINGTON ST
WILLIAM ST
HIBERNIA ST
CALEDONIA ST

HURON ST

To Swan Motel

DOWNIE ST
MILTON ST
FALSTAFF ST
DOURO ST
GRANGE ST
REBECCA ST
BRUNSWICK ST
ALBERT ST
WATER ST
WATERLOO ST N

GEORGE ST
CHOCOLATE BARR'S
SLOW FOOD PERTH COUNTY MARKET
AVON THEATRE
YORK STREET KITCHEN
STRATFORD TOURISM ALLIANCE
FOSTER'S INN
STUDIO THEATRE
SMALL MART GENERAL MERCANTILE
BALZAC'S COFFEE
THE PRUNE
THE MILKY WHEY
PAZZO BAMBINO
PAZZO TAVERNA AND PIZZERIA
MERCER HALL INN
THE CAVERSHAM HOUSE B&B

NILE ST
FRONT ST
BAY ST
WELLL ST
QUEEN ST
TRINITY ST
KING ST

REGENT ST
FREDERICK ST

ONTARIO ST
FRONT ST
ALBERT ST
ONTARIO ST
BRUNSWICK ST

MORENZ DR
COBURG ST
NORTH ST
LAKESIDE DR

Avon River

TOM PATTERSON THEATRE

BALLANTYNE AVE
COBURG ST
WATER ST

THE CHISHOLMS IN STRATFORD

STRATFORD FESTIVAL THEATRE

RICHARD MONETTE WAY
PARKVIEW DR

Queens Park

As You Like It Motel

GALLERY STRATFORD

DOURO ST S
ROMEO ST
ROMEO ST S

To Costume and Props Warehouse

THE BRUCE HOTEL AND RESTAURANT

To Forest Motel and Woodland Retreat

VIA RAIL STRATFORD STATION

To Swan Motel

0   200 yds
0   200 m

© AVALON TRAVEL

season typically start in January. If you're hoping to visit during a July or August weekend or any holiday period, buy tickets and book your accommodations as early as you can. Many regular patrons who return year after year reserve their lodgings for the following season before they even leave town.

Ticket prices range from $35 to more than $120, depending on the type of play, dates, and seat location. Seniors, students, and families can purchase discounted tickets, and you can sometimes buy last-minute "rush" tickets for 20-50 percent off; they're sold two hours before the performance by phone or at the box office, but not online. On some Tuesday and Thursday evenings, two-for-one tickets are available.

Theaters

The Stratford Festival plays are performed at four venues. The largest, the 1,826-seat **Festival Theatre** (55 Queen St.), built in 1957, is located east of the town center in Upper Queen's Park. The 480-seat **Tom Patterson Theatre** (111 Lakeside Dr.) is near Lake Victoria, just east of downtown, while the other two performance spaces are right downtown: the 1,090-seat **Avon Theatre** (99 Downie St.) and the 260-seat **Studio Theatre** (34 George St. E.), behind the Avon.

Tours and Talks

For a behind-the-scenes look at the Stratford Festival, take the one-hour **Festival Theatre Tour** (55 Queen St., www.stratfordfestival.ca, 9am and 9:15am Wed.-Sun. mid-June-mid-Oct., adults $8, seniors and students $6). You'll also learn more about the current season and past productions.

On the one-hour **Costume and Props Warehouse Tour** (350 Douro St., www.stratfordfestival.ca, 9:30am, 10am, 10:30am, and 11am Wed.-Sat. mid-May-mid-Oct., adults $8, seniors and students $6), you can visit the Stratford Festival's massive costume and props warehouse, one of the largest in North America; it houses over 55,000 costumes and 10,000 pairs of boots and shoes. Amid the racks of gowns, pantaloons, capes, crowns, and swords, you learn how staff create props from ordinary household objects (a foam pool "noodle" might become the foundation for an archway), how designers make a thin actor achieve the proper abdominal "jiggle" when playing a portly character, and how to remove body odor from elaborate costumes

inside the Costume and Props Warehouse at the Stratford Festival

that can't be washed. Wrap up the tour by trying on costumes.

Part of the costume-warehouse building houses the festival's archives, the world's largest performing-arts archives devoted to a single theater. If you're interested in festival history, take the **Archives Tour** (350 Douro St., www.stratfordfestival.ca, 10:45am Wed. June-Sept., adults $8, seniors and students $6).

Reservations (www.stratfordfestival.ca) are recommended for all tours. The Festival offers lectures, post-performance discussions, and other informal ways to learn more about the current productions throughout the season. Check the festival website (www.stratfordfestival.ca) for schedules.

ENTERTAINMENT AND SHOPPING

Though Stratford is known for its classical theater productions, **SpringWorks** (www.SpringWorksFestival.ca, May), the town's "Indie Theatre and Arts Festival," showcases more avant-garde music, dance, and theater performances. During the month-long **Stratford Summer Music** (www.stratfordsummermusic.ca, mid-July-mid-Aug.), more than 100 concerts, from jazz to Mozart to organ recitals, take place. The town's big foodie fest is the annual **Savour Stratford Culinary Festival** (www.visitstratford.ca/culinaryfestival, July), which includes local food samplings, celebrity chef events, wine and beer tastings, concerts, and activities for kids.

Ontario Street is downtown Stratford's main shopping street, with boutiques, galleries, pubs, and cafés. **Small Mart General Mercantile** (121 Ontario St., 519/271-6283, www.small-mart.ca, 10am-6pm Tues.-Sat., 11am-5pm Sun.) sells a quirky mix of clothing with classic Canadian logos, T-shirts, retro candies, watches, and miscellaneous cool stuff. **The Milky Whey** (118 Ontario St., 519/814-9439, www.themilkywhey.ca, 10am-5pm Tues.-Wed., 10am-6pm Thurs.-Fri., 9:30am-5pm Sat., 11am-3pm Sun.) is the place for cheese, with lots of regionally produced varieties.

Given their last name, Derek and Jacqueline Barr may have been destined to open a chocolate shop: theirs, which sells rich handmade truffles, as well as caramels and other candies, is called **Chocolate Barr's** (55 George St. W., 519/272-2828, www.chocolatebarrs.com, 9am-6pm Mon.-Sat., 10am-5pm Sun.), of course.

SPORTS AND RECREATION

The 104-kilometer (65-mile) **Avon Trail** (www.avontrail.ca) runs from St. Marys northeast to Conestogo, passing through the Stratford area. The Avon Trail Association organizes regular volunteer-led day hikes. Visitors are welcome; check the website for a schedule.

Stratford is compact enough for exploring by bike. Rent your wheels from **Totally Spoked** (29 Ontario St., 519/273-2001, www.totallyspoked.ca, 9am-5:30pm Mon.-Wed. and Fri., 9am-8pm Thurs., 9am-5pm Sat., noon-4pm Sun. spring-summer, 10am-5:30pm Tues.-Fri., 10am-5pm Sat., noon-4pm Sun. fall-winter; half-day $20, full-day $35). **Avon Boat Rentals** (30 York St., 519/271-7739, www.avonboatrentals.ca, 9am-dusk daily May-Oct.) rents canoes, kayaks, and bicycles alongside the Avon River. You can also take a 30-minute river cruise aboard the *Juliet III* pontoon boat or a two-hour guided **cycling tour**.

Many of the flowers in the **Shakespearean Gardens** (Huron St., at York St.), a pretty spot to stroll near the Avon River and the Perth County Court House, are mentioned in Shakespeare's plays.

Stratford has a large population of swans that live along the Avon River. The **Stratford Tourism Alliance** (47 Downie St., 800/561-7926, www.visitstratford.ca) occasionally offers free guided **Swan Walk** tours where you can learn more about the swans' habits and habitat.

ACCOMMODATIONS

For a fairly small community, Stratford has a large number of lodgings, including motels, inns, and many B&Bs. What you won't find are inexpensive accommodations, at least during the summer theater season. If you're on a tight budget, and you have a car, consider driving in from Kitchener-Waterloo or London; you could also come from Toronto for the day without staying overnight.

On the **Stratford Tourism Alliance** website (www.visitstratford.ca), you can search for available lodgings by date, location, and various features. The Stratford festival also runs an accommodations booking service (800/567-1600, www.stratfordaccommodations.com). If you're looking for more B&B options, try the **Stratford and Area Bed & Breakfast Association** (www.bbstratford.ca).

Under $100

One of Stratford's only budget accommodations is the **SGH Residence** (130 Youngs St., 519/271-5084, www.sgh.stratford.on.ca/residence, $67 s, $78 d), a residence hall with shared baths on the grounds of the Stratford Hospital. Rates include breakfast and parking.

$100-150

In this price range, you'll find well-maintained motels—not fancy, but comfortable. The trade-off is that you're not within walking distance of downtown. The star of the show at the old-fashioned, family-run **Swan Motel** (960 Downie St., 519/271-6376, www.swanmotel.ca, May-Oct., $108-132 d), two kilometers (1.2 miles) south of the town center, is the pretty manicured grounds, with gardens, picnic tables, and an outdoor pool. You get a warm welcome from longtime owners Peter and Colleen Pola before settling into one of 24 simple rooms with mini fridges, coffeemakers, and free Wi-Fi. Though there's no restaurant, you can stop into the lobby for complimentary morning muffins, coffee, and tea.

At the 18-room **As You Like It Motel** (379 Romeo St. N., 519/271-2951, www.asyoulikeit.on.ca, May-Oct., $114-160 d), 3.5 kilometers (2.2 miles) northeast of the town center, the updated linens and carpets, mixed with the old-time furniture, give the spaces a cool, almost midcentury-modern vibe. Rooms have mini fridges and free Wi-Fi. You can have a light continental breakfast in the dining area behind the front desk, and there's a pool out back.

Though it's less than a 10-minute drive from town, the **Forest Motel and Woodland Retreat** (2941 Forest Rd., 519/271-4573, www.forestmotel.on.ca, $139-225 d) feels like just that: a retreat into the woods. A short stroll from peaceful Lake McCarthy, the 19 motel rooms with sturdy pine furniture are simple but snug, with fridges, microwaves, coffeemakers, and free Wi-Fi. Outside, you can lounge on the waterside patios or take a canoe for a leisurely paddle. Rates include continental breakfast.

$150-200

Owners Kent and Dianne Chisholm of **The Chisholms in Stratford** (310 Ontario St., 519/273-6813 or 877/373-6813, www.thechisholmsinstratford.com, $149-194 d), a three-room B&B in an 1881 yellow-brick Victorian, give guests name cards at breakfast to encourage chatting. They also keep a database of what every guest had for breakfast, served around the antique dining table, so return visitors can come back to old favorites. Guests sip cappuccinos in the parlor or settle into wicker chairs on the expansive front porch. Upstairs, guest rooms have four-poster beds and wingback chairs as well as iPod docks, CD players, and free Wi-Fi.

Butter tart muffins and French toast with rhubarb fool are among the breakfast specialties at **The Caversham House B&B** (155 Cobourg St., 519/271-7882 or 866/998-7882, www.thecavershamhouse.com, $149-198 d), a friendly lodging in a 1917 Edwardian house, where you can read in the book-lined living room and help yourself to juice from the guest fridge. The three guest rooms aren't large, but they're well designed, with original oak floors, air-conditioning, and free Wi-Fi; the Henley suite's private balcony overlooks the garden.

Stratford has several small inns on the

Stratford Chef School

Every fall, three Stratford restaurants are reborn. **The Prune** (151 Albert St., www.theprune.com), **Rundle's** (9 Cobourg St., www.rundlesrestaurant.com), and **Rene's Bistro** (20 Wellington St., www.renesbistro.ca) close their doors to reopen with completely new staff and menus as the restaurants of the **Stratford Chef School** (68 Nile St., 519/271-1414, www.stratfordchef. com). This professional culinary institute trains 35 aspiring chefs every year, but the students spend very little time in the lecture hall. Instead, they're running the kitchens and dining rooms of these three transformed restaurants.

Every year, the school brings in international guest chefs who work with the students and oversee diners' meals. You may not have the chance to visit Melbourne or rural France to eat in the restaurants that chefs Ben Shewry (Attica) or Alexandre Gauthier (La Grenouillère) run, but you can dine on their dishes in Stratford. Diners not only get a fine-dining experience for a moderate cost but can also provide feedback that will assist in the chefs' training.

The chef-school restaurants typically open in late October and run through February. Check the school's website for a calendar of meals and guest chef appearances. And who knows? The student prepping your salad today may be the Ferran Adrià or Thomas Keller of the future.

upper floors of downtown historic buildings, including **Foster's Inn** (111 Downie St., 519/271-1119 or 888/728-5555, www.fostersinn.com, $149-199 d), with nine unfussy, loft-style guest rooms on the second and third stories. You can hang out downstairs in the friendly bar or have meals in the brightly painted restaurant; the three-cheese omelet will fuel you for the day. They don't have parking, but a free lot is two blocks away. Wi-Fi is included.

Also above a downtown restaurant, the 14 rooms at the **Mercer Hall Inn** (108 Ontario St., 519/271-1888 or 888/816-4011, www.mercerhallinn.com, $145-225 d) are all decorated differently. They're not deluxe, but they're modern, with Keurig coffeemakers and mini fridges; some have whirlpool tubs, some have fireplaces, and room 209 has a river view. Rates include parking and Wi-Fi.

Over $300

Stratford didn't have a true luxury lodging until **The Bruce Hotel** (89 Parkview Dr., 519/508-7100 or 855/708-7100, www. thebruce.ca, $500-650 d) opened near the Festival Theatre. At this upscale 25-room property, guest rooms are large, with Frette linens and deep tubs. Detail-obsessed owner Jennifer Birmingham personally laid more

than 660,000 mosaic tiles in the hotel's baths, while on the lobby wall is a hand-painted map of the world as it looked in 1564—the year Shakespeare was born. Other amenities include a small indoor pool, a fitness room, a library, a games room, and a suitably deluxe restaurant.

FOOD

With the professional Stratford Chefs School in town, as well as an audience of hungry, well-heeled theatergoers, Stratford is a great spot for a gourmet splurge. Reservations are strongly recommended during the summer, and they're essential if you're trying to have dinner before the theater. If you're watching your budget, Stratford still offers good eating, with bakeries, cafés, and locally focused bistros.

While most of Stratford's restaurants are open daily from June through August or September, many reduce their hours, or close altogether, outside the summer high season. Notable exceptions are the Stratford Chef School restaurants (Oct.-Feb.).

Bakeries and Cafés

Named for the French playwright Honoré de Balzac, **Balzac's Coffee** (149 Ontario St., 519/273-7909, www.balzacs.com, 6:30am-9pm

Mon.-Fri., 7am-9pm Sat.-Sun.) would be right at home in Paris, with its high ceilings, embossed wallpaper, and excellent coffees. Nibble pastries or sandwiches, or linger over a cup of joe. **Pazzo Bambino** (76 Ontario St., 519/273-6666, 9am-6pm Tues.-Sun.) sells Italian sandwiches, pizzas, pastries, and espresso drinks to go, handy for a picnic by the river.

Don't expect a bland assortment of lettuce and shredded carrots on the salad bar at **The County Food Co.** (38 Erie St., 519/275-2665, www.countyfoodco.com, 10am-7pm Tues.-Sat. summer, call for off-season hours, $6-13), a café and takeout shop that emphasizes local ingredients; you might find fresh kale with dried cranberries, mustard-dressed chickpeas, or beets with caramelized onions and pecans. They make sandwiches, too, including the signature stuffed pork schnitzel. Try the oversize oatmeal cookies.

Contemporary

Though relocated from their original York Street location, **York St. Kitchen** (24 Erie St., 519/273-7041, www.yorkstreetkitchen.com, 8:30am-4pm Mon.-Thurs., 8am-4pm Fri.-Sat., 8am-3pm Sun. May-Dec., 8:30am-4pm Mon.-Thurs., 8am-4pm Fri.-Sat. Jan.-Apr., lunch

$5-7, dinner $14-16) remains cheerful and unpretentious; it has been serving interesting yet inexpensive eats since the mid-1990s. Hugely popular for breakfast—the signature morning dish is the Canadiana (a BLT with peameal bacon, lettuce, and tomatoes, and an optional fried egg)—it serves sandwiches midday and stews, pastas, and pot pies come evening.

The owners of a local dairy and cheesemaker operate ★ **Monforte on Wellington** (80 Wellington St., 519/301-7256, www.monfortedairy.com, 9am-9pm daily, small plates $5-15), an informal bistro that focuses on cheese but offers so much more. At the rustic wooden tables, lit with funky dangling bulbs, you can dig into cheese and charcuterie plates, a killer grilled goat cheddar sandwich served with sweet-tart apple butter, or seasonally changing small plates ranging from creamy ricotta-topped crostini with summer-fresh pea purée to perfectly fried cheese-stuffed zucchini blossoms. Cheeselovers (and their food-focused friends) never had it so good.

★ **Bijou** (105 Erie St., www.bijourestaurant.com, lunch 11:30am-1:30pm Fri.-Sat., dinner 5pm-9pm Tues.-Sun. May-Oct.), a small bistro, pairs casual—refurbished wood floors and benches, a chalkboard menu—with

creamy ricotta crostini at Stratford's Monforte on Wellington

white tablecloths, well-informed service, and a kitchen committed to sourcing locally. Lunch is served à la carte, while dinner offers two- and three-course prix fixe options ($48-56). You might start with kombu-cured mackerel or local asparagus with pickled mushrooms before moving on to pork cheek goulash with potato dumplings. Don't neglect the desserts, perhaps chocolate and *dulce de leche* bread pudding or a peach tart with black pepper ice cream.

One of Stratford's original fine-dining restaurants, **The Prune** (151 Albert St., 519/271-5052, www.theprune.com, dinner 5pm-9pm Tues.-Sat. mid-May-mid-Oct.) is still a favorite dining destination for theatergoers. Pairing classical French techniques and local ingredients, the kitchen creates dishes like herb-crusted pickerel with baby leeks and black olives, hanger steak with northern woods mushrooms, or risotto with autumn squash. Prix-fixe meals are $49, $59, and $69 for two, three, or four courses.

The classy Bruce Hotel has an equally refined restaurant, in a soothing dining room lit with contemporary chandeliers. Aaron and Bronwyn Linley (he's the executive chef and she runs the front-of-house), who launched highly-regarded Bijou, now run **The Restaurant at the Bruce** (89 Parkview Dr., 519/508-7100, www.thebruce.ca, breakfast 7:30am-10:30am daily, lunch 11:30am-1:30pm daily, dinner 5pm-9pm Tues.-Sat., breakfast $22.50, lunch $15-24, dinner prix-fixe $58-68), serving locally focused contemporary cuisine, including a super-fresh heirloom tomato salad, pan-seared perch in a delicate vegetable broth, and veal schnitzel paired with mustardy potato salad. The wine list is strong on Ontario labels.

Italian

Pazzo Taverna and Pizzeria (70 Ontario St., 519/273-6666 or 877/440-9666, www.pazzo.ca, pizzeria 11:30am-10pm Sun. and Tues.-Thurs., 11:30am-midnight Fri.-Sat., lunch $11-14, dinner $15-20, tavern 11:30am-2pm and 5pm-10pm Tues.-Sun., lunch $16-20,

dinner $18-29) is two restaurants in one. On the lower level is a more casual pizzeria, with salads, pastas, panini, and excellent pizzas. On the main floor is a more upscale restaurant, with sleek white chairs and oversize windows, where the updated Italian classics might include slow-cooked pork shoulder with fava beans, risotto with grilled squid and scallops, or chicken cacciatore.

Groceries and Markets

Stratford has two farmers markets: the **Stratford Farmers Market** (Stratford Rotary Complex, 353 McCarthy Rd., 519/271-5130, www.stratfordfairgrounds.com, 7am-noon Sat. year-round) and the **Slow Food Perth County Market** (Market Square, behind Stratford City Hall, www.slowfoodperthcounty.com, 10am-2pm Sun. May-mid-Oct.).

INFORMATION AND SERVICES

The **Stratford Tourism Alliance** (47 Downie St., 800/561-7926, www.visitstratford.ca, 8:30am-4:30pm Mon.-Fri., 10am-6pm Sat. June, 8:30am-5pm Mon.-Fri., 10am-6pm Sat. July-Aug., 8:30am-4:30pm Mon.-Fri., 10am-3pm Sat. Sept.-May) runs a helpful visitors center stocked with information about the region. Their website lists scads of things to see and do.

GETTING THERE

Stratford is 150 kilometers (93 miles) southwest of Toronto, 45 kilometers (28 miles) southwest of Kitchener, and 60 kilometers (37 miles) northeast of London.

Air

The closest airports to Stratford are **Waterloo International Airport** (YKF, 4881 Fountain St. N., Breslau, 519/648-2256, www.waterlooairport.ca) or **London International Airport** (YXU, 1750 Crumlin Rd., London, 519/452-4015, www.londonairport.on.ca), but Toronto's **Pearson International Airport** (YYZ, 6301 Silver Dart Dr., Mississauga, 416/247-7678 or

866/207-1690, www.torontopearson.com) has flights from many more destinations. **Stratford Airporter Shuttle** (519/273-0057 or 888/549-8602, www.stratfordairporter.com, 2.5 hours, one-way $79 pp, $109 for 2 people) provides transportation from Pearson to Stratford. They also run shuttles to the Waterloo and London airports.

Train

You can catch the train to **VIA Rail's Stratford Station** (101 Shakespeare St., 888/842-7245, www.viarail.ca) from Toronto (2.25 hours, one-way adults $30-55, ages 2-11 $20-25), although the Stratford Direct Bus is less expensive and better aligned with the festival performance schedule. VIA Rail also operates between Stratford and London (1-1.25 hours, one-way adults $25-30, ages 2-11 $15-20).

Bus

The Stratford Festival runs the convenient **Stratford Direct Bus** (800/567-1600, www.stratfordfestival.ca, round-trip $20), which lets theatergoers come from Toronto without a car. In early-to-mid-May and from late September through mid-October, buses depart Toronto's Intercontinental Hotel (Front St. and Simcoe St.) at 10am daily, which brings you to Stratford in time for an afternoon matinee. The return buses depart Stratford at 5pm. From late May through late September, there are two buses a day in each direction, leaving Toronto at 10am and 3pm, and returning from Stratford at 4pm and 11pm. Book at least one day in advance.

From June through September, the Stratford Direct Bus travels from **Detroit** (round-trip $40) to Stratford on Tuesday, Friday, and Sunday. Buses depart at 8am from Kmart (40855 Ann Arbor Rd., Plymouth, MI) and 9am from Meijer's Store (30800 Little Mack Ave., Roseville, MI). Buses leave Stratford at 5pm. Reservations are required at least two days in advance. To use either bus service, you must have a ticket to a festival performance or event.

Car

From Toronto, it's about a two-hour drive to Stratford. Take Highway 401 west to exit 278 onto Highway 8 west toward Kitchener. Then follow Highway 7/8 west from Kitchener to Stratford. As you enter Stratford, Highway 7/8 becomes Ontario Street, the town's main east-west street.

GETTING AROUND

If you're staying downtown, you can easily walk to restaurants and shops. The Stratford Festival's theaters are scattered around the town center; two are right downtown, one is lakefront near downtown, and the largest, the Festival Theatre, is 1.5 kilometers (0.9 miles) east of downtown. To walk to the Festival Theatre, follow the riverfront path or go east on Ontario Street, then north on Queen Street.

Downtown street parking is metered, and while it's inexpensive, it's limited to three hours, so pull into a lot if you're parking for a meal and a show. If the free parking on the streets surrounding the Festival Theatre is full, try the large Queen Street lot near the theater ($10). The Tom Patterson Theatre has its own lot with free parking. Street parking is free on Sunday.

City of Stratford Transit (519/271-0250, www.stratfordcanada.ca, one-way adults $2.75, seniors and students $2.50) operates limited bus service around town Monday through Saturday. Buses run about every 30 minutes, but the last buses leave at 9:30pm Monday-Friday and 7:30pm Saturday, so they're not convenient for post-theater transportation. If you need a taxi, phone **City Cab** (519/272-2222) or **Radio Cab** (519/271-4242).

ST. MARYS

Known as "Stonetown" for the limestone dug from the area's quarries and the classical stone buildings that line the downtown streets, St. Marys is a small town with a big pool: **The Quarry** (Water St., www.townofstmarys.com, 1pm-5pm Sat.-Sun. June,

1pm-8pm daily July-Aug., adults $4.75, seniors $4.50, kids $3.50, families $13.25), Canada's largest outdoor swimming pool, in a former stone quarry. Swimmers can use the changing rooms in the adjacent Lind Sportsplex. Also in town is a destination for baseball fans: the **Canadian Baseball Hall of Fame** (386 Church St. S., 519/284-1838, www.baseballhalloffame. ca, 10:30am-4pm Sat., noon-4pm Sun. May, 10:30am-4pm Mon.-Sat., noon-4pm Sun. June-early Sept., 10:30am-4pm Thurs.-Sat., noon-4pm Sun. early-Sept.-mid-Oct., adults $7.50, seniors $6, ages 6-16 $3.75, families $15), crammed with memorabilia about baseball in Canada and Canadians who play baseball.

Accommodations and Food

You can stop off in St. Marys as a day trip from Stratford or London. For an overnight stay, the town's best lodging is the **Westover Inn** (300 Thomas St., 519/284-2977 or 800/268-8243, www.westoverinn.com, $140-300 d). The nicest rooms are in the main building, a Victorian stone manor built in 1867, with 11-foot ceilings, rich-hued linens, and period furnishings. The 12 modest rooms in the "terrace," a former church dormitory, lack the manor's charms but are fine if you just want to sleep. The four "cottage" rooms fall somewhere in between, more modern but without the manor's character.

The Westover Inn also houses the white-tablecloth **Dining Room** (breakfast 7:30am-10:30am, lunch 11:30am-2pm, dinner 5pm-8pm daily May-Oct.; breakfast 7:30am-10:30am Wed.-Sun., lunch 11:30am-2pm Tues.-Sun., dinner 5pm-8pm Tues.-Sun Nov.-Apr; lunch $12-15, dinner $26-31), serving dishes like duck breast with lentils and lardoons, Asian-marinated pork tenderloin, or leek and mushroom *agnolotti*. If you're dining with a special someone, book the alcove table in a secluded nook for two.

Calling itself a modern gastropub, **Little Red's Pub and Eatery** (159 Queen St. E., 226/661-2233, www.littlereds.ca, 11am-2pm and 5pm-9pm Tues.-Sat., $8-20) mixes British pub classics (shepherd's pie, fish-and-chips, beef and Guinness stew) with burgers, salads, even bison chili-topped *poutine*.

Practicalities

St. Marys is 20 kilometers (12 miles) southwest of Stratford and 45 kilometers (28 miles) northeast of London. For visitor information, call the town's **information center** (519/284-3500 or 800/769-7668, www.townofstmarys. com). Although **VIA Rail** (5 James St. N., 888/842-7245, www.viarail.ca) has train service to Toronto (2.75 hours, one-way adults $39-52, ages 2-11 $19-26) and London (40 minutes, one-way adults $23, ages 2-11 $12), you'll want a car unless the objective of your stay is to cocoon.

London

Canada's 10th-largest city makes a convenient stopover between Toronto and Lake Huron or if you're exploring Southwestern Ontario. It's home to one of Canada's major universities—the University of Western Ontario—which gives the town a youthful feel, with lots of pubs and boutiques, as well as several worthwhile museums and an interesting pioneer village.

SIGHTS

In the city center, the six-hectare (15-acre) **Victoria Park** (bounded by Dufferin Ave., Central Ave., Clarence St., and Wellington St.) is a great place for a picnic. You'll often find festivals, concerts, and other special events here. At the park's southwest corner is grand **St. Peter's Cathedral** (196 Dufferin Ave., 519/432-3475, www.cathedral.rcec.london.on.ca), built in the 1880s to resemble

London

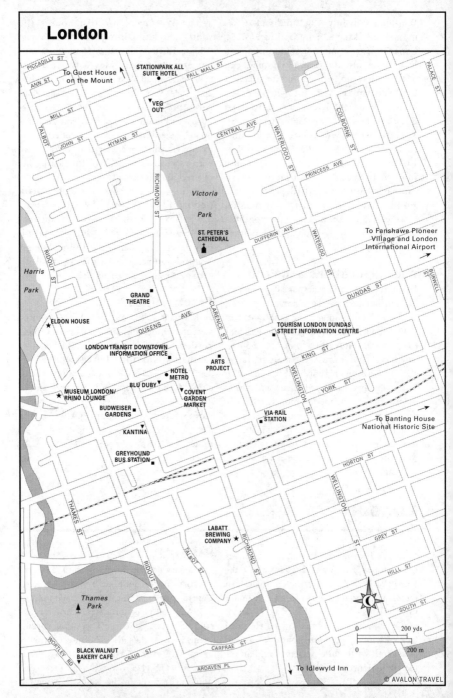

a 13th-century French Gothic cathedral. Visitors are welcome to take a peek inside or to attend mass.

Museum London (421 Ridout St. N., 519/661-0333, www.museumlondon.ca, noon-5pm Tues.-Sun., noon-9pm Thurs., donation) exhibits a mix of historical art, contemporary art, and historical artifacts. Canadian architect Raymond Moriyama, who designed the Bata Shoe Museum and the Ontario Science Centre in Toronto, as well as the Canadian War Museum in Ottawa, designed London's distinctive silvery museum. The on-site **Rhino Lounge** (519/850-5111, noon-5pm Tues.-Wed. and Fri.-Sun., noon-9pm Thurs., www.rhinolounge.ca) is a cool spot for coffee, pastries, or light bites; for lunch (Tues.-Fri., $11-15) or Sunday brunch ($25), there's the stylish **River Room** (519/850-2287, www.northmoore.ca/theriverroom), overlooking the river.

Wander through London's oldest surviving residence, the 1834 **Eldon House** (481 Ridout St. N., 519/661-0333, www.eldonhouse.ca, noon-5pm Tues.-Sun. June-Sept., noon-5pm Wed.-Sun. May and Oct.-Dec., noon-5pm Sat.-Sun. Jan.-Apr., donation), and you can imagine yourself a guest of the well-to-do Harris family, who lived in this white clapboard home for four generations. Among its idiosyncratic furnishings are an umbrella stand made from an elephant's foot, gold-embossed faux-leather wallpaper that the family brought back from Japan in 1897, and a melodeon (a miniature organ).

Founded in London in 1847, the Labatt Brewing Company still makes beer here. To learn more about the brewing process, take a two-hour **Labatt Brewery Tour** (150 Simcoe St., 519/850-8687 or 800/268-2337, londontour@labatt.com, www.labatt.com, Mon.-Fri., $10) that wraps up with a beer tasting. You must book in advance (8am and 4pm Mon.-Fri.) by phone or email.

London played an important role in medical history, when a local doctor, Frederick Banting (1891-1941), conceived the idea of extracting insulin from a pancreas as a treatment for diabetes. Thanks to Banting's research, insulin was first used successfully in a human trial in 1922, and Banting received the Nobel Prize in Medicine the following year. Banting's former home is now the **Banting House National Historic Site** (442 Adelaide St. N., 519/673-1752, www.diabetes.ca, noon-4pm Tues.-Sat., adults $5, seniors and students $4, families $12), where guides recount the history

Architect Raymond Moriyama designed the distinctive Museum London.

of his life and his discovery in 45-minute tours.

Another aspect of London's history is on view at the **Fanshawe Pioneer Village** (Fanshawe Conservation Area, 1424 Clarke Rd., 519/457-1296, www.fanshawepioneervillage.ca, 10am-4:30pm Tues.-Sun. mid-May-mid-Oct., over age 3 $7), which illustrates rural life from 1820 to 1920. Costumed interpreters staff the restored buildings, demonstrating woodworking, printing, and cooking, or working in the general store or the school. If you're visiting with school-age kids, pick up the *Village Scavenger Hunt* to guide your explorations. The village is nine kilometers (5.6 miles) northeast of the city center, near the intersection of Clarke and Fanshawe Park Roads.

ENTERTAINMENT AND SHOPPING

The downtown **Budweiser Gardens** (99 Dundas St., 519/667-5700 or 866/455-2849, www.budweisergardens.com) hosts major concerts, theatrical productions, and sporting events. The **Grand Theatre** (471 Richmond St., 519/672-8800, www.grandtheatre.com) has two stages for professional theater productions, concerts, and other events. For more experimental works, check what's on at the **Arts Project** (203 Dundas St., 519/642-2767, www.artsproject.ca), a gallery and performance space.

Performers from across Canada and farther afield converge on downtown London for the weekend-long **Sunfest** (Victoria Park, 519/672-1522, www.sunfest.on.ca, July), a free outdoor festival of world music; the organization presents additional world music concerts throughout the year at various venues. The **Western Fair** (519/438-7203 or 800/619-4629, www.westernfairdistrict.com, Sept.) is London's old-time country expo, with rides, concerts, horse shows, and more. It's on County Road 2 (Florence St.) east of downtown.

Boutiques and places to eat line **Richmond Row** (www.richmondrowlondon.com), the shopping district along Richmond Street downtown from the Grand Theatre north to Oxford Street.

ACCOMMODATIONS

London has a slew of basic chain motels south of downtown on Wellington Road. Otherwise, accommodations are clustered in the downtown area or near the University of Western Ontario campus north of the center.

Under $100

A cross between a dormitory and a hotel, the no-frills **Guest House on the Mount** (Ignatia Hall, 2nd Fl., 1486 Richmond St., 519/641-8100, www.guesthouseonthemount.ca, $39-79 s, $59-89 d) attracts guests of all ages. The spacious hotel-style rooms are simply furnished, with a bed and a TV; you can choose shared bath, half bath (with a toilet and sink), or a private bath. Facilities include a lounge, laundry, a shared kitchen, and free Wi-Fi. The guest house is north of the university campus, on the grounds of the Windermere on the Mount retirement home; follow the signs to Ignatia Hall.

$100-150

One block from Richmond Row, the **StationPark All Suite Hotel** (242 Pall Mall St., 519/642-4444 or 800/561-4574, www.stationparkinn.ca, $139-184 d) is popular with business travelers and families, who appreciate the suites with a bedroom and separate living area. The "superior" suites on floors 9-14 are a little brighter and have newer furnishings, but all rooms are equipped with mini fridges, microwaves, and coffeemakers. Continental breakfast and Internet access are included; parking is $12 per day.

$150-200

In a lane facing Covent Garden Market, **Hotel Metro** (32 Covent Market Pl., 519/518-9000, www.hotelmetro.ca, $139-199 d) is London's first "boutique" lodging, set in a former shoe factory warehouse. The best of the 20 contemporary loft-style rooms, with iPod docks, modern baths with rain showers, and Wi-Fi, are on the fourth (top) floor, where they have exposed brick walls and oversize windows. The hotel doesn't have its own parking lot, so you can park next door in the Covent Market garage ($13 per day) or hunt for parking on nearby streets.

Built in 1878 as a private home, the **Idlewyld Inn** (36 Grand Ave., 519/432-5554, www.idlewyldinn.com, $149-239 d) is a rambling mansion with bay windows, stained glass, gingerbread trim, and a turret. The original owner, Charles Smith Hyman, served as London's mayor, a federal cabinet minister, and captain of Canada's national cricket team, and you can imagine this Victorian notable receiving guests in the formal dining room (which now serves breakfast, lunch, and dinner). While retaining some of the period features, the 19 guest rooms have updated decor and amenities that include flat-screen TVs and Wi-Fi. Rates include continental breakfast.

FOOD

You can find coffee, pastries, sandwiches, soups, salads, fresh produce, Thai food, sushi, falafel, and more at **Covent Garden Market** (130 King St., 519/439-3921, www. coventmarket.com, 8am-6pm Mon.-Thurs. and Sat., 8am-7:30pm Fri., 11am-4pm Sun.). Outside on the market plaza is a seasonal **farmers market** (8am-2pm Thurs. and Sat. May-Nov.).

For scrumptious muffins, cookies, quiche, and other baked goods, head to the ★ **Black Walnut Bakery Café** (134 Wortley Rd., 519/850-2253, www.blackwalnutbakerycafe. com, 7am-6pm Mon.-Sat., 9am-5pm Sun.) in the Wortley Village neighborhood south of downtown. If you're in a savory mood, try the flaky spinach pie; they also serve sandwiches and soups midday. And if you're lucky, there'll be slices of fresh fruit pie.

In a brightly painted house along downtown's Richmond Row, vegan café **Veg Out** (646 Richmond St., 519/850-8688, www.veg-outrestaurant.com, 4:30pm-9:30pm Tues.-Wed., 11:30am-3pm and 4:30pm-9:30pm Thurs.-Sat., 11:30am-4pm Sun., $7-16) serves meat-free sandwiches, salads, smoothies, and fresh juices.

The chef at **Kantina** (349 Talbot St., 519/672-5862, www.kantina.ca, 5:30pm-10pm Tues.-Sun., $15-21) hails from Serbia, so the fare in this upscale contemporary bistro draws influences from his home country. The Serbian salad includes peppers, tomatoes, cucumbers, and feta cheese in a lemony dressing, and the "Black George" is deep-fried veal loin with ham and *kaymak,* a Serbian cheese. Tuesday and Wednesday are tapas nights, Thursday-Saturday are regular dinners, and Sunday is a fixed-price family supper ($30).

Buzzing with conversation and a friends-hanging-out vibe, **Blu Duby** (32 Covent Market Pl., 519/433-1414, www.bluduby.com, 11:30am-11pm Mon.-Thurs., 11:30am-1am Fri.-Sat., 3pm-9pm Sun., lunch $9-14, dinner $11-32), at the Hotel Metro, is fun for a drink or a light meal. On the big menu are nibbles like Moroccan chicken skewers and lamb "lollipops" and larger plates from beef short ribs to lentil cakes with yellow curry.

INFORMATION AND SERVICES

Tourism London (www.londontourism.ca) runs two helpful visitors centers that provide information about the London area: the **Dundas Street Information Centre** (267 Dundas St., 8:30am-4:30pm Mon.-Fri., 10am-5pm Sat.-Sun. late May-mid-Oct., 8:30am-4:30pm Mon.-Fri. mid-Oct.-late May) downtown, and the **London Tourist Information Centre** (696 Wellington Rd. S., 8:30am-12:30pm and 1:30pm-4:30pm Mon.-Fri., 10am-5pm Sat.-Sun.) between Highway 401 and the city center. The *London Visitors Guide* and *London's Local Flavour* restaurant guide are both available online.

GETTING THERE
Air

London International Airport (YXU, 1750 Crumlin Rd., 519/452-4015, www.londonairport.on.ca) is 10 kilometers (six miles) northeast of downtown. **Air Canada** (www. aircanada.com) flies to Toronto, Ottawa, and Montreal; **WestJet** (888/937-8538, www. westjet.com) has direct flights to Winnipeg, Calgary, and Orlando; and **United** (www. united.com) flies nonstop to Chicago and New York.

A taxi between the airport and downtown London costs $30-35. **Avis** (www.avis.com), **Enterprise** (www.enterpriserentacar.ca), **Hertz** (www.hertz.ca), and **National** (www. nationalcar.ca) have car rental offices at the London airport. **London Transit** (www.lt-conline.ca) buses can take you between the airport and downtown (Mon.-Fri.), but you have to change buses. Take bus no. 36 from the airport to Fanshawe College, where you can connect with bus no. 4 or no. 20 heading downtown.

You'll find many more flight options via **Toronto's Pearson Airport** (YYZ, 6301 Silver Dart Dr., Mississauga, 416/247-7678 or 866/207-1690, www.torontopearson. com). **Robert Q Airbus** (105 Wharncliffe Rd. S., 519/673-6804 or 800/265-4948, www. robertq.com, 2.25 hours, one-way adults $60, seniors and students $57, kids under 12 $30) runs shuttles between Pearson Airport and London.

Train

London is easy to reach by train. The Toronto-Windsor and Toronto-Sarnia trains all stop at London's **VIA Rail station**

(205 York St., 888/842-7245, www.viarail. ca) downtown. Most trains between Toronto and London (one-way adults $50-68, ages 2-11 $25-34) make the trip in 2.25-2.5 hours, but check the schedule: a couple chug along for 3.5 hours. Windsor to London (one-way adults $47-63, ages 2-11 $23-32) takes 1.75 hours.

Bus

Greyhound operates numerous daily buses from Toronto to the London **Greyhound Bus Station** (101 York St., 519/434-3250, www. greyhound.ca, 2-2.5 hours, one-way adults $30-44, ages 2-11 $23-33) downtown.

Car

London is 195 kilometers (120 miles) southwest of Toronto; it's a 2-2.5-hour drive. You can either take the QEW to Highway 403 to Highway 401 or just pick up Highway 401 directly. From Highway 401, take exit 187 and follow Wellington Road north toward downtown.

GETTING AROUND

Downtown London is compact enough to explore on foot, and the extensive bus system, run by **London Transit** (519/451-1347, www. ltconline.ca, adults $2.75, ages 5-11 $1.35) can take you farther afield; phone or stop into the **Downtown Information Office** (150 Dundas St., 7:30am-7pm Mon.-Fri., 8:30am-6pm Sat.) if you need help.

Southwestern Ontario

In the 1800s, thousands of enslaved African Americans fled from the United States to freedom in Canada. Following what was known as the Underground Railroad, a network of safe houses and churches that sheltered the refugees, the majority of those enslaved people crossed into Canada into what is now Southwestern Ontario. Many remained in the region, with significant settlements in

Windsor, Sandwich, Amherstburg, Chatham, Dresden, and Buxton, and many of their descendants live here today. A number of sites throughout Southwestern Ontario enable you to explore this African Canadian Heritage Route, tracing the history of the former slaves and their new life in Canada.

Windsor, now this region's largest city, continues to be a magnet for newcomers,

Southwestern Ontario

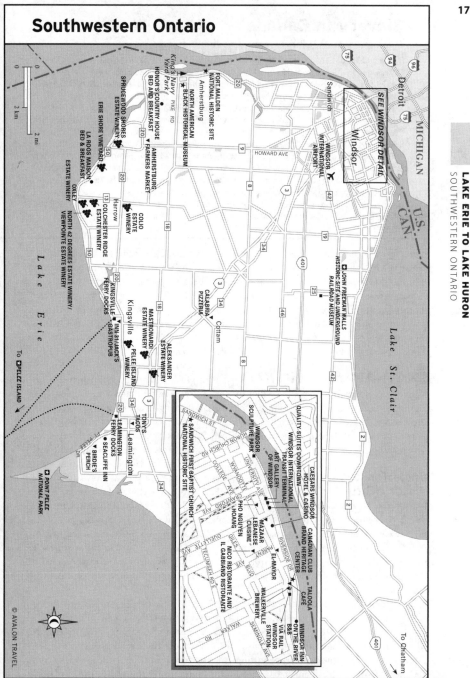

© AVALON TRAVEL

Slavery in Canada

By the mid-1800s Canada was a safe haven for enslaved people escaping north from the United States along the Underground Railroad, but unfortunately Canada had a history of slavery as well. In 1629, the first slave was transported from Africa to the colony of New France. Many of the early British and French settlers in Canada kept slaves throughout the 1600s and 1700s.

In 1793, Lieutenant Governor John Graves Simcoe prohibited the importation of slaves into the region then known as Upper Canada. By this decree, no new slaves could be brought into the province, but existing slaves were not freed. It wasn't until 40 years later, in 1833, that the British Slavery Abolition Act freed enslaved people across the British Empire, including Canada.

The migration of slaves from the United States into Canada began in earnest after the United States passed the 1850 Fugitive Slave Act, which required law enforcement officers to apprehend and return escaping slaves, even in the nonslave-holding northern states. The Underground Railroad developed to shelter fugitive enslaved people en route to Canada to prevent them from being returned to slavery in the South. Until the U.S. Civil War in the 1860s, thousands of enslaved people fled north to freedom in Canada, many of them settling in Ontario.

attracting immigrants from many nations. An industrial city, it has several worthwhile museums, and its restaurants offer up a multiethnic cornucopia. Southwestern Ontario wears another hat: It's a growing wine-making region, where you can head out for wine-tasting and exploring, particularly around the towns of Amherstburg and Harrow.

CHATHAM AND VICINITY

Many formerly enslaved people settled in Chatham and the nearby communities of Dresden and Buxton, where several sites explore the history of these African Canadian settlements.

Uncle Tom's Cabin Historic Site

The **Uncle Tom's Cabin Historic Site** (29251 Uncle Tom's Rd., Dresden, 519/683-2978, www.uncletomscabin.org, 10am-4pm Tues.-Sat., noon-4pm Sun. mid-May-June and Sept.-Oct., 10am-4pm Mon., 10am-4pm Tues.-Sat., noon-4pm Sun. July-Aug., adults $6.25, seniors and ages 13-17 $5.25, ages 6-12 $4.50, families $20) tells the story of former slave and abolitionist Reverend Josiah Henson (1796-1883), who was born on a plantation in Maryland, then sold to a slave owner in Kentucky before following the Underground Railroad north to Canada.

Settling near Dresden in 1842, he helped establish the Dawn Settlement, a community that became a refuge for formerly enslaved people. In 1852, American writer Harriet Beecher Stowe published her historic antislavery novel *Uncle Tom's Cabin*, which some historians say was based in part on Henson's memoirs.

Start your visit by watching a video introducing Josiah Henson, the history of slavery in the United States and Canada, and the settlements that former slaves set up in Southwestern Ontario. Then visit the gallery, where exhibits explore these topics in more detail. You can tour several restored buildings, including Henson House, the reverend's last residence, as well as a local church built in the 1880s. Inside the church, look for the booklet *Sounds of Freedom*, which explains that many songs that slaves sung contained coded messages. "The Gospel Train's a-Comin'," for example, would alert other enslaved people that a group was planning an escape. You can also visit the small cemetery where Henson is buried.

The Uncle Tom's Cabin Historic Site is located west of Dresden, 30 kilometers (19 miles) north of Chatham. From Highway 401, the most direct route is to take exit 101, Kent Bridge Road/County Road 15, and continue north to Highway 21. Turn left (west) onto Highway 21 toward Dresden, then turn left onto Park Street and left again onto Uncle Tom's Road. From Chatham, take Grand Avenue East which becomes Longwoods Road, turn north on Kent Bridge Road/County Road 15.

Chatham-Kent Black Historical Society

In the 1850s, as more blacks established themselves in the Chatham area, the town became a center for African Canadian intellectual life, and by 1861, Chatham had one of the largest black populations in Upper Canada. The **Chatham-Kent Black Historical Society** (177 King St. E., Chatham, 519/352-3565, www.ckblackhistoricalsociety.org, 1pm-4pm Mon.-Fri., adults $5, seniors and students $4) maintains a small museum about the region's African Canadian heritage and notable citizens from the black community from this period and beyond. The museum is located inside the W.I.S.H. Centre, a community center near downtown.

★ Buxton National Historic Site and Museum

In 1849, an abolitionist organization called the Elgin Association purchased 3,650 hectares (9,000 acres) of land south of Chatham to establish a settlement for formerly enslaved people and free blacks. The new settlers would pay $2.50 per acre to buy a parcel of land, and within five years, approximately 150 families had settled here. The community opened a school, which educated African Canadian children and began attracting white students who lived nearby, becoming one of North America's first integrated schools. By the 1860s, more than 2,000 people lived in what became known as the Buxton Settlement; at the time, it was the largest black settlement in Canada.

The **Buxton National Historic Site and Museum** (21975 A. D. Shadd Rd., North Buxton, 519/352-4799, www.buxtonmuseum.com, 1pm-4:30pm Wed.-Sun. May-June and Sept., 10am-4:30pm daily July-Aug., 1pm-4:30pm Mon.-Fri. Oct.-Apr., adults $6, seniors and students $5, families $20) tells the fascinating story of this settlement and its community. A 20-minute film introduces the settlement, and among the museum's artifacts is a berth from a slave ship, its small size illustrating the horrifically cramped conditions on board, and original slave shackles, in both adult and child sizes. Also on the site is an 1852 log

Pupils studied in Buxton's one-room schoolhouse until 1968.

cabin that was the oldest home in the settlement, a one-room schoolhouse used from 1861 until 1968, and the British Methodist Episcopal Church, built in 1866 and still in use today.

The museum is 15 kilometers (nine miles) southwest of Chatham. From Highway 401, take exit 81 onto County Road 27/Bloomfield Road south, and turn right (west) onto 8 Line/County Road 14 and left (south) onto A. D. Shadd Road.

Accommodations and Food

Chatham has one surprisingly cool place to stay—the **Retro Suites Hotel** (2 King St. W., 519/351-5885 or 866/617-3876, www.retrosuites.com, $159-249 d). In a restored block of Victorian-era buildings, the 34 rooms are wildly different, from the Easy Rider, with an antique motorcycle hanging from the ceiling, to the traditionally upscale King William. The hotel's dining room, the **Chilled Cork Restaurant and Lounge** (6:30am-9pm Mon.-Fri., 9am-9pm Sat., 9am-2pm Sun., lunch $8-22, dinner $14-36), offers an appropriately eclectic menu that travels from pastas and steaks to Australian kangaroo.

There are several basic roadside motels on Grand Avenue East, with cafés and sandwich shops on and around King Street downtown.

Practicalities

Chatham is off Highway 401, 290 kilometers (180 miles) southwest of Toronto and 110 kilometers (68 miles) from London. From Highway 401, take exit 90 and go north on Highway 40/Communication Road toward Wallaceburg; then turn left onto Park Avenue East, toward the center of town. From Windsor, 80 kilometers (50 miles) to the southwest, take Highway 401's exit 81, Bloomfield Road; follow Bloomfield Road north, then turn right (east) onto Park Avenue West. **Chatham-Kent Tourism** (445 Grand Ave. W., Chatham, 519/351-7700 or 800/561-6125, www.visitck.ca) can provide information about the region.

KINGSVILLE AND LEAMINGTON

Along the Lake Erie shore, the towns of Kingsville and Leamington are popular with bird-watchers—Point Pelee National Park is a highlight. The surrounding land is farm country, where you can visit several wineries. Leamington is known as the "Tomato Capital of Canada," both for the extensive tomato crop that grows nearby and for the large Heinz plant that once dominated the town. Ferries to Pelee Island leave from Kingsville and Leamington.

★ Point Pelee National Park

The southernmost point on Canada's mainland, the waterfront **Point Pelee National Park** (1118 Point Pelee Dr., Leamington, 519/322-2365 or 888/773-8888, www.pc.gc.ca, www.friendsofpointpelee.com, adults $7.80, seniors $6.80, ages 6-16 $3.90, families $19.60), jutting into Lake Erie, is an important stopover point for migrating birds; more than 390 species have been identified in the vicinity, with the greatest variety during the annual spring migration, typically the first three weeks of May. The **Festival of Birds** (www.festivalofbirds.ca, May) celebrates this annual migration with guided birding hikes, birding presentations, and other special events. Monarch butterflies also migrate through the Point Pelee region, although in recent years, their numbers have been less consistent. Visit from late August through early October for the best viewings.

At the park **Visitors Centre** (10am-6pm daily July-early Sept., 10am-5pm daily late May-June and early Sept.-Oct.), you can walk through exhibits about the region's flora and fauna; periodic "creature feature" presentations include live animals. Several short hiking trails start nearby. The Visitors Centre has extended hours (7am-5pm daily) during the spring bird migration.

The road between the Visitors Centre and the narrow spit of land at the park's southern end—the "Tip of Canada"—is closed to private vehicles from spring through fall. The park service runs the free **Shuttle to the Tip** (7am-5pm daily early-mid-May, 10am-6pm daily late May-late June, 10am-7pm daily late June-early Sept., 8am-6pm daily early-Sept.-mid-Oct.), which takes visitors close to the park's endpoint. From the shuttle drop-off point, there's a one-kilometer (0.6-mile) loop trail to the tip and back. Swimming is prohibited near the tip because currents can be quite strong. To swim, head for the sandy beaches along the park's western shore.

Follow the **Marsh Boardwalk Trail,** a one-kilometer (0.6-mile) loop through the cattails to experience the marshy habitat of the park's eastern side, or climb the lookout tower overlooking the marsh. To explore the marsh from the water, you can rent canoes ($17 for 1 hour, $26 for 2 hours) at the nearby **Marsh Shop** (519/322-1654, May-Sept.), which also sells snacks. The park offers one-hour guided **Freighter Canoe Tours** (July-early Sept., $7.30 pp, families $20) of the marsh in their "Cattail Cruiser" 10-person canoes. **Farm Dog Cycles** (519/551-1613, www.farmdog-cycles.com, 10am-5pm Sat.-Sun. late May-early Sept., $10 per hour, half day $20, full day $30) rents bicycles from a stand near the boardwalk.

Designated a Dark Sky Preserve, the park stays open till midnight several times a year for star-gazing during its **Dark Sky Nights.** Get the schedule from the Visitors Centre or the park website. The park, which has no camping facilities, is open year-round, although some services, including the Shuttle to the Tip, are seasonal. Park admission rates are reduced slightly from November through March.

Wineries

Canada's southernmost winery, **Pelee Island Winery** (455 Seacliff Dr./County Rd. 20, Kingsville, 519/733-6551 or 800/597-3533, www.peleeisland.com, 9am-6pm Mon.-Sat., 11am-5pm Sun., tours noon, 2pm, and 4pm daily, adults $5, seniors $4) grows its grapes on Pelee Island but makes most of its wines—pinot grigio, riesling, cabernet merlot, cabernet franc, ice wine, and more—at this Kingsville location. Tours include a video about the wine-making process, a walk through the winery, and a tasting.

Most other Kingsville-area wineries are small, family-owned properties, including **Mastronardi Estate Winery** (1193 Concession 3 E., Kingsville, 519/733-9463 or 800/320-5040, www.mastronardiwines.com, 11am-5pm daily May-Sept., 11am-4pm Fri.,

Canada's southernmost mainland point is in Point Pelee National Park.

11am-5pm Sat.-Sun. Oct.-Apr., tours by appointment) and **Aleksander Estate Winery** (1542 County Rd. 34, Ruthven, 519/326-2024, www.aleksanderestate.com, 11am-6pm Mon.-Fri., 11am-5pm Sat.-Sun., tours by appointment).

Entertainment and Events

A highlight of the three-day **Leamington Tomato Festival** (519/326-2878, www.leamingtontomatofestival.com, Aug.), which includes concerts, a parade, and, of course, tomato tastings, is the annual "tomato stomp." Don't wear white.

Accommodations

At the **Hellemsfield Inn** (2 Mill St. W., at Division St. S., Kingsville, 519/733-5250, www.bbcanada.com, $95-105 d), owners Carol and Scott Sitler created self-contained guest quarters in their 1872 Greek Revival-style home. The two bedrooms, one upstairs and one on the main level, aren't large, so the space is well suited to sociable types or couples traveling together who'd enjoy hanging out by the wood-and-stone fireplace in the cheery common living area. The owners serve a full breakfast on Saturday and Sunday, and a lighter continental spread during the week.

Built in the early 1900s, the stately brick **Inn 31** (31 Division St. S., Kingsville, 519/733-6900, www.jacksdining.com, $89-99 s, $109-129 d) houses a restaurant-pub with three guest rooms upstairs. With original dark woodwork, the rooms are furnished with antique-style pieces, mixed with modern accessories, puffy duvets on the queen beds, and flat-screen TVs. Rates include continental breakfast and Wi-Fi.

You can practically roll out of bed and onto the Pelee Island ferry (at least when it's leaving from the Leamington docks) when you stay at the **Seacliffe Inn** (388 Erie St. S., Leamington, 519/324-9266, www.seacliffeinn.com, $119-159 d). The 23 nautical-themed motel-style rooms with sturdy wooden furnishings are comfortable enough, and you can grab a beer or a bite in the downstairs lounge.

Food

Its walls decorated with local art, funky **Merlis' Coffeehouse & Eatery** (4 Main St., Kingsville, 519/733-0110, 10am-8pm Mon.-Thurs., 10am-9pm Fri.-Sat.) dishes out coffee, homemade soups, sandwiches, and vegetarian options, with occasional live music. Lively **Jack's Gastropub** (31 Division St. S., Kingsville, 519/733-6900, www.jacks-dining.com 11:30am-9pm daily, $10-18), in the building that houses Inn 31, serves pub snacks, sandwiches, burgers, pot pies, and Lake Erie perch. It stocks a decent selection of Ontario beers, too.

On your way to Point Pelee National Park, look for the "Bustaurant," a big red double-decker bus that houses **Birdie's Perch** (625 Point Pelee Dr., Leamington, 519/551-7043, www.birdiesperch.ca, 11am-11pm daily May-mid-Oct., $4-15), a restaurant and take-out shop offering fish-and-chips, tacos, sandwiches, and ice cream. Walk into **Tony's Tacos** (52 Erie St. S., Leamington, 519/326-0110) and you'll think you've wandered into a convivial cantina in small-town Mexico. The walls are bright orange, the merengue music blares, and the traditional tacos—heaped with meat—are only $2 each. Ask for the house-made green hot sauce. On weekends, hunker down over a steaming bowl of posole (soup made with corn or hominy) or *menudo* (tripe stew).

Calabria Pizzeria (123 Talbot Rd. W./ Hwy. 34., Cottam, 519/839-5611, dinner Tues.-Sun., $12-25) is a casually romantic restaurant with a serious commitment to local food, masquerading as a pizza joint. Oh, they do make fine pizzas, topped with locally sourced ingredients, but they fry up an even more excellent fresh perch dinner. The wines are local, too. Worth a drive, the restaurant is 12 kilometers (7.5 miles) north of Kingsville. From Highway 3, go north on Highway 27; at Talbot Road/ Highway 34, turn left (west) for one block.

Information and Services

Ontario's most unusual tourism office may be the **Leamington Tourist Information**

Booth (Talbot St. W. at Mill St. W., www. leamington.ca). Reflecting the town's tomato-growing and processing heritage, it's shaped like a tomato. Pick up local information and pose for tomato photos. **Tourism Windsor, Essex, and Pelee Island** (333 Riverside Dr. W., Suite 103, Windsor, 519/255-6530 or 800/265-3633, www.visitwindsoressex.com) also provides information about Kingsville and Leamington.

Getting There and Around

You'll want a car to explore the Kingsville-Leamington area. From Toronto (350 kilometers, 215 miles) or London (170 kilometers, 107 miles), take Highway 401 to Highway 77 south to Leamington. Kingsville is 15 kilometers (nine miles) west of Leamington. County Road 20, which is Seacliff Drive in Leamington and Main Street in Kingsville, connects the two towns. From Windsor, follow Walker Road south to Highway 3 east. Exit at Division Road/County Road 29 for Kingsville (40 kilometers, or 25 miles) or at Erie Street for Leamington (50 kilometers, 30 miles).

Ferries to Pelee Island (www.ontario-ferries.com) leave from Leamington (Erie St. S., 519/326-2154, Apr.-July) and Kingsville (Lakeview Ave. at Park St., 519/733-4474, Aug.-Dec.). To travel between Kingsville-Leamington and northern Ohio, you can take the Pelee Island ferry to or from Sandusky.

★ PELEE ISLAND

Canada's southernmost point is this laid-back little island in Lake Erie, where most visitors come simply to escape the mainland's hustle and bustle. In fact, the island's name, which locals pronounce "PEE-lee," comes from the French *pelée,* meaning "bare." Pelee is ringed with beaches—it's a peaceful spot for cycling and bird-watching, and there's even a winery—but otherwise, you won't find many sights. As one island innkeeper said, "There's nothing to do here, but it takes at least three days to do it."

Pelee's summer population is about 1,500,

but only 300 hardy souls live on the island year-round. Many accommodations and eateries open in April or May and close in October or November. Even during the high season, business hours can be erratic; if few visitors are around, or if the owner has something else to do, places can close unexpectedly, so call ahead.

Travel on and off the island is also weather-dependent. While Pelee has some of Canada's warmest weather, winds can whip up along Lake Erie, causing the ferry from the mainland to delay or even cancel service. Ferries run mid-March through mid-December.

Cycling is an easy way to get around the island; from the west ferry dock, it's 10 kilometers (six miles) north to the lighthouse (one-way), 1.2 kilometers (0.75 miles) south to the Pelee Island winery, and four kilometers (2.5 miles) south to Fish Point. Bring your own bike on the ferry or rent one from **Comfortech Bike Rental** (1023 West Shore Rd., 519/724-2828, www.peleebikerental.com, daily May-Oct.) near the West Dock.

Sights

Jam-packed with artifacts, photos, and fossils, the **Pelee Island Heritage Centre** (1073 West Shore Rd., 519/724-2291, www. peleeislandmuseum.ca, 10am-5pm daily May-Oct., adults $3, seniors $2.50, students $2), a small museum opposite the ferry docks, is a good place to start your island explorations. Exhibits detail the island's geology, ecology, and human history, and you can learn about shipwrecks that plagued the surrounding waters.

South of the ferry docks, at the intersection of West Shore Road, **Pelee Island Winery** (20 East West Rd., 519/733-6551 or 800/597-3533, www.peleeisland.com, 10am-4pm Mon.-Thurs., 10am-7pm Fri.-Sun. late May-late June, 10am-8pm daily late June-early Sept., 10am-4pm daily early Sept.-mid-Oct.) grows 223 hectares (550 acres) of grapes. At the Island Pavilion visitor center, find out more about the wine-making process and walk among the vines. One-hour tours (noon and

2pm daily late May-late June and early Sept.-mid-Oct., noon, 2pm, 4pm, and 6pm late June-early Sept., adults $5, seniors $4) include a wine tasting. Also on the grounds is the **Deli Hut,** serving burgers, chili, and snacks.

On West Shore Road north of the dock, be on the lookout for **Stoneman,** a massive stone *inukshuk* sculpture, designed by local resident Peter Letkeman. The kids at the Pelee Island Public School gave Stoneman his name.

On the island's northeast tip, follow the short trail in **Lighthouse Point Provincial Nature Reserve** (www.ontarioparks.com) to the 1834 limestone lighthouse. There's a small pebbly beach, but no restrooms or other facilities.

At the **Stone Road Alvar Conservation Area** (www.erca.org, dawn-dusk daily year-round, free) in the island's southeast, you can wander the rocky shore to see one of Pelee Island's distinctive natural features: alvars. Areas of limestone covered with a thin layer of topsoil, alvars allow unique vegetation to grow. Butterfly spotters have seen five rare species here, including the giant swallowtail, tawny emperor, Acadian hairstreak, hackberry butterfly, and sachem skipper. From the West Dock, take West Shore Road to East West Road, then turn south on Stone Road.

A popular bird-watching spot is the **Fish Point Provincial Nature Reserve** (519/825-4659, www.ontarioparks.com), a stopover point for migrating birds. There's a beach, but no facilities. Follow West Shore Road south until it becomes McCormick Road, then continue south to Fish Point. Other island beaches include **Sunset Beach** (West Shore Rd., north of the ferry docks) and **East Park Beach** (East Shore Rd., just north of East West Rd.).

Entertainment and Events

Birders and their friends flock to Pelee Island for the annual **Spring Song Weekend** (www.peleeislandmuseum.ca, May), which typically includes a bird-watching race and an evening banquet with a presentation by a guest author.

A major local event is the annual **Pelee Island Pheasant Hunt** (www.pelee.org, Oct.-Nov.), started in the 1900s as a way to control the island's burgeoning pheasant population. More recently, it has become a sporting event, with pheasants raised for the hunt on the Pelee Island Pheasant Farm. The hunt draws hundreds of visitors during the last two weeks of October and the first week of November; if hunting isn't your thing, visit another time.

Accommodations and Camping

Pelee Island has a few small inns and B&Bs; on busy July and August weekends, you might want to arrange a place to stay before you hop on the ferry. While most accommodations are comfortable, none are luxurious. For links to cottage rentals, check the Pelee Island website (www.pelee.org). The island has restaurants, but not many.

The Anchor and Wheel Inn (11 West Shore Rd., 519/724-2195, www.anchorwheelinn.com, Apr.-early Nov.) has a quirky variety of accommodations. Upstairs in the main building, six snug chambers ($65 s, $85 d), furnished like grandmother's guest rooms, share two baths. Out back, there's a block of basic motel rooms with private baths ($125-175 d) and a camping area (tent sites $20, electrical sites $35). They also run a restaurant and bar.

It's worth staying at **The Wandering Pheasant Inn** (1060 East West Rd., 519/724-2270, www.thewanderingpheasantinn.com) for enthusiastic owner Sandra Laranja's breakfasts, which include fresh baked muffins and good conversation. The original Victorian inn building houses several simple guest rooms ($115-125 d) with shared baths. In an adjacent cottage-style block, the rooms ($175) are larger, furnished with Victoriana (and en suite baths). You can walk to the water in less than five minutes. Guests must be over age 17.

Near the lighthouse on the island's northeast corner, **Wavecrest Bed-and-Breakfast** (79 East Shore Rd., 519/724-1111, www.

wavecrestpelee.com, May-early Nov., $160-170 d) faces a sandy beach. The Fishing Suite and Beachfront Suite are both light and airy, with white antique furniture, while the smaller Victorian Suite lives up to its name with a sleigh bed and gold-framed portraits; all three have private baths. Owners Thom Brown and Barry Wayman encourage guests to mingle in the spacious living room and serve a full breakfast.

The **East Park Campground** (1362 East Shore Rd., 519/724-2200, www.pelee.org, May-early Nov., $20) has 25 sites for tents and trailers, a short walk from East Beach. There are no electrical hookups, but there are washrooms with showers, as well as a small store.

Food

You can buy picnic supplies and groceries at the **Co-op Grocery Store** (West Pump Rd. and Centre Dyke Rd., 519/724-2910) on the island's north end. If there's something specific you want, though, bring it from the mainland.

Tiny **Conorlee's Bakery and Delicatessen** (5 North Shore Rd., 519/724-2321, http://rickolte.wix.com/bakery, 8:30am-4pm Mon.-Wed., 8:30am-9pm Thurs.-Sun. summer, 8:30am-3pm Thurs. and Sun., 8:30am-9pm Fri.-Sun. spring and fall), in a little yellow cottage, serves pastries and coffee in the mornings, deli sandwiches and pizza later in the day. On occasional summer Fridays, Conorlee's hosts their Wine and Dinner Series ($48 pp), a five-course meal with wine pairings served in the garden at the Pelee Island Winery.

Crammed with buoys, sailing flags, and other nautical gewgaws, the funky dining room at **The Anchor and Wheel** (11:30am-8:30pm daily summer, call for off-season hours, $15-35) looks like it washed ashore from a Jimmy Buffet song. You can start with a tropical drink, out in the Tiki Bar if the weather cooperates, but the real action is on the dinner plates, laden with bountiful portions of fish, prime rib, or pasta.

Your basic island bar, **Scudder Beach Bar and Grill** (North Shore Rd., 519/724-2902, www.scudderbeach.com, lunch and dinner daily May-Sept., $8-13) serves wings, wraps, fried fish, and other pub fare. Bands liven things up most summer weekends.

Information and Services

The **Municipality of Pelee Island** (519/724-2931 or 866/889-5203, www.pelee.org) is the best source of local island information. If you'd like a guide to organize your Pelee Island visit, contact **Explore Pelee: Pelee Island Tours** (519/325-8687, www.explore-pelee.com). Owner Anne Marie Fortner can tell you anything you need to know about the island and offers several bike tours ($40-60 pp), as well as van-based tours ($25 pp) that explore Pelee's geology, agriculture, or history.

Getting There

Pelee Island is located in Lake Erie, south of Kingsville and Leamington and north of Sandusky, Ohio. Between late March and mid-December, the **Pelee Island Transportation Company** (519/724-2115 or 800/661-2220, www.ontarioferries.com, one-way adults $7.50, seniors $6.25, ages 6-12 $3.25, bicycles $3.75, cars $16.50) runs 90-minute ferries to the island. Note that from the Ontario mainland, ferries leave from different points depending on the season. April through July, ferries depart from the **Leamington Docks** (Erie St. S., Leamington, 519/326-2154), while August to December, boats leave from the **Kingsville Docks** (Lakeview Ave. at Park St., Kingsville, 519/733-4474). The fare is the same from either point. Because of weather conditions, the ferry will occasionally be rerouted to the alternate dock, so it's always smart to confirm your departure and arrival points.

In summer (late June-early Sept.), ferries run 3-4 times daily in each direction. Check the website or phone for the exact schedule, for off-season hours (when departures are much less frequent), and for any unexpected schedule changes.

Travelers from the United States can catch the ferry from the **Sandusky Docks** (Jackson

St. at Shoreline Dr., Sandusky, OH, late Apr.-Sept., 1.75 hours, one-way adults $13.75, seniors $11.25, ages 6-12 $6.75, bicycles $6.50, cars $30). Call or check the website for seasonal schedules.

If you're traveling between Sandusky and Pelee, remember your passport! You're crossing an international border and must clear customs and immigration. If you're taking a car on the ferry, advance reservations (519/326-2154 or 800/661-2220) are required, whether from the Ontario mainland or from the United States.

From mid-December to March, the only way on and off the island is by air. **Pelee Island Transportation Company** (519/724-2115 or 800/661-2220) flies regularly between Windsor and **Pelee Island Airport** (Centre Dyke Rd., 519/724-2265). **Griffing Flying Service** (419/626-5161, www.griffingflyingservice.com) flies to Pelee from Sandusky.

Getting Around

Pelee Island is about 13 kilometers (eight miles) from north to south and about six kilometers (3.8 miles) across. The island has no public transportation, but there are taxis, or you can bring a car or bike from the mainland on the ferry.

AMHERSTBURG AND VICINITY

One of the oldest settlements in Southwestern Ontario, Amherstburg, on the Detroit River south of Windsor, was occupied by American forces during the War of 1812. The British burned the town's original Fort Amherstburg, when U.S. troops forced them to retreat in 1813. After the war, the British regained control of the town and built Fort Malden, which is now a national historic site.

Amherstburg is also a gateway to the wine region known as the **Essex Pelee Island Coast (EPIC) Wine Country** (www.epicwineries.com) along Lake Erie's North Shore, with wineries around Amherstburg and in the adjacent community of Harrow.

Sights

In the first half of the 19th century, the British built fortifications in a strategic setting on the Detroit River to protect the Amherstburg area from American attacks. What remains of Fort Malden, now the **Fort Malden National Historic Site** (100 Laird Ave., 519/736-5416, www.pc.gc.ca, 10am-5pm daily July-early Sept., 10am-5pm Tues.-Sat. mid-May-June and early Sept.-Oct., adults $3.90, seniors $3.40, ages 6-16 $1.90, families $9.80), dates to the 1830s. You can tour the soldiers' barracks, cookhouse, and other fort buildings; staff demonstrate musket drills, open-hearth cooking, and other elements of 19th-century military life.

Like other Southwestern Ontario communities, Amherstburg was a destination for formerly enslaved people who escaped to Canada via the Underground Railroad. The exhibits at the **North American Black Historical Museum** (277 King St., 519/736-5433 or 800/713-6336, www.blackhistoricalmuseum.org, noon-5pm Tues.-Fri., 1pm-5pm Sat.-Sun., adults $7.50, seniors and kids $6.50, families $30) illustrate this history, along with other elements of the black experience in North America. You can walk through a log cabin that belonged to a former slave family in the 1880s and explore one of the oldest surviving African Methodist Episcopal churches in Canada.

On the site of a former navy yard that dates to 1796, **King's Navy Yard Park** (Dalhousie St., www.amherstburg.ca) contains lovely manicured gardens and a riverside walking path.

Wineries

The Mitchell family planted their first grapes in 1991 and now grow nine varieties, including chardonnay, pinot noir, merlot, and cabernet sauvignon. You can drop in for tastings at their Tuscan-style **Sprucewood Shores Estate Winery** (7258 County Rd. 50 W., Harrow, 519/738-9253 or 866/938-9253, www.sprucewoodshores.com, 11am-5pm daily) overlooking the lake, but call ahead to arrange a tour (Mon.-Fri., $6 pp). In summer, enjoy live music, wine, and snacks on the expansive grounds at the weekly Sips, Sounds, and Bites events (1pm-4pm Sun. late-May-Aug.).

Vidal, riesling, chambourcin, and baco noir are among the interesting wines at the friendly **Erie Shore Vineyard** (410 County Rd. 50 W., Harrow, 519/738-9858, www.erie-shore.ca, 1pm-6pm Mon.-Fri., 10am-6pm Sat., noon-5pm Sun.). Ask about their ice wine and the unusual "cabernet ice."

Bernard and Nancy Gorski have run CREW, **Colchester Ridge Estate Winery** (108 County Rd. 50 E., Harrow, 519/738-9800, www.colchesterridge.com, 11am-5pm Sun.-Tues., 11am-6pm Wed.-Sat. late May-Sept., 11am-5pm Sun. and Wed.-Thurs., 11am-6pm Fri.-Sat. Oct.-late May), since 2006. They make a fruity gewürztraminer and big flavorful cabernet, among others.

Ann Wilson left a law career in Detroit to launch **Oxley Estate Winery** (533 County Rd. 50, Harrow, 519/738-3264, www.oxleyestatewinery.com, 11am-6pm daily) with her husband, Murray, where they began making wines, including riesling, auxerrois, and chardonnay, in 2011. On weekends, you can lunch in the lovely Wine Garden (11am-4pm Sat.-Sun., $12-19).

The **Viewpointe Estate Winery** (151 County Rd. 50 E., Harrow, 519/738-0690 or 866/372-8439, www.viewpointewinery.com, 11am-6pm daily) produces especially nice whites, including riesling and an unusual (but very good) auxerrois. The winery offers tours as well as cooking classes.

Opened in 1980, **Colio Estate Winery** (1 Colio Dr., just off Walker Rd., Harrow, 519/738-2241 or 800/265-1322, www.colio-winery.com, 10am-6pm Mon.-Sat., 11am-5pm Sun.) makes a number of different wines, from the easy-drinking Girls' Night Out line to more premium varieties like the Bricklayer cabernet merlot in their large (for this region, anyway) winery. Tours (2pm daily May-Dec.) visit the production facilities, crushing room, barrel room, and shop.

Tiny family-owned **North 42 Degrees Estate Winery** (130 County Rd. 50 E., Colchester, 519/984-2684, www.north42degrees.com, 11am-6pm Tues.-Sun.) bottled their first wines, including sauvignon blanc, riesling, gewürztraminer, pinot noir, and cabernet franc, in 2013. Also on the property is **Serenity Lavender**, (519/980-4504, www.serenitylavender.com, 11am-5pm Tues.-Sun.), where you can wander among the aromatic plants; the shop sells lavender products for bath, bed, and kitchen.

one of Canada's oldest surviving African Methodist Episcopal churches at the North American Black Historical Museum

Wine Tours

One of the best ways to explore the Lake Erie North Shore wineries and the gently rolling surrounding countryside is by bicycle. On the guided **Windsor Eats Wine Trail Rides** (www.winetrailride.ca, May-Oct., $75 pp, $95 tour plus bike rental), you cycle to several wineries, taste several wines at each stop, and have a communal multicourse meal at a winery, park, or local farm. These well-run tours, usually offered once a month and averaging 20-25 kilometers (12-16 miles) of cycling, draw groups of 30-50 people, and they're sociable experiences, whether you come alone or with companions.

Entertainment and Shopping

Concerts, dinners, food demos, and, of course, wine tastings are all part of the annual four-day **Shores of Erie International Wine Festival** (268 Dalhousie St., Amherstburg, 519/730-1001, www.soewinefestival.com, Sept.), held on the grounds of the Fort Malden National Historic Site (100 Laird Ave.).

Since the 1800s, **The Harrow Fair** (McAfee St., off County Rd. 20, Harrow, 519/738-3262, www.harrowfair.com, late Aug. or early Sept.) has been showcasing the region's produce and livestock, and showing visitors an old-fashioned good time. Besides plenty of eating, activities include horse shows, sheep shearing, and musical entertainment.

You can browse the shops and galleries along Dalhousie Street in Amherstburg. Founded by a group of local artists, the **Mud Puppy Gallery** (264 Dalhousie St., 519/736-7737, noon-8pm Wed.-Sun. spring-fall, call for winter hours) shows work by artists in the community.

Accommodations

The town of Amherstburg and the rural wine country nearby have a handful of B&Bs. For more accommodation options, consider staying in Kingsville or Windsor, which are within a short drive of the Amherstburg area.

Lake Erie wine country's most upscale accommodation is **La Roos Maison Bed & Breakfast** (309 Martin Lane, Harrow, 519/890-1657, www.laroosmaison.com, $99-189 d), with five guest rooms in a sprawling modern home directly on the lakeshore. The ceilings in the common living room soar two stories high, and three rooms have balconies facing the water, including the huge Lakefront 3, with vibrant rust-hued walls, black-and-white furnishings, and a

Colchester Ridge Estate Winery

gas fireplace. The two smallest rooms share a bath. Rates include Internet access and a full breakfast.

Robert Honor and his wife Debbie have been running ★ **Honor's Country House Bed-and-Breakfast** (4441 Concession 4 S., Amherstburg, 519/736-7737 or 877/253-8594, www.honorscountryhouse.com, $90-100 d) in their 1920 farmhouse for more than 25 years. With deep roots here, they can tell you all about the community. The B&B's common areas, including a comfy living room and a dining room with guest fridge and microwave, are done in craftsman style. Upstairs, the two simply furnished guest rooms have private baths. After a hearty breakfast, you might want to just sit on the front porch and watch the world go by.

Food

The **Amherstburg Farmers Market** (7860 County Rd. 20, Amherstburg, 519/730-1253, www.amherstburgfarmersmarket.com, 8:30am-1:30pm Sat. mid-May-mid-Oct.) takes place at the Malden Community and Cultural Center.

One of the nicest settings for a summer meal is the patio overlooking the vineyards at the ★ **Viewpointe Estate Winery Restaurant** (151 County Rd. 50 E., Harrow, 519/738-0690 or 866/372-8439, www.viewpointewinery.com, lunch noon-5pm Thurs.-Mon., dinner 5pm-8pm Fri., $10-16). In addition to salads, a charcuterie plate, and excellent pizzas, they're known for their famous fried perch. The restaurant moves indoors when the weather turns.

Along Dalhousie Street in town, you'll find several casual dining spots, including **Dalhousie Bistro** (219 Dalhousie St., Amherstburg, 519/736-0880, www.thedalhousiebistro.com, generally 8:30am-3pm Mon.-Thurs., 8:30am-9pm Fri.-Sat., 9:3am-6pm Sun.) in a Victorian house opposite King's Navy Yard Park, serving salads, sandwiches, wine-friendly platters of cheeses and charcuterie, and other light meals.

Information and Services

Amherstburg's **Tourism Office** (268 Dalhousie St., 519/730-1309, www.amherstburg.ca) provides information about things to do in the vicinity. You can also get information from **Tourism Windsor, Essex, and Pelee Island** (333 Riverside Dr. W., Suite 103, Windsor, 519/255-6530 or 800/265-3633, www.visitwindsoressex.com), the regional tourism association. The **Essex Pelee Island Coast (EPIC) Wine Country** website (www.epicwineries.com) has a listing of wineries in the region.

Getting There and Around

Downtown Amherstburg is 35 kilometers (22 miles) west of Kingsville and 25 kilometers (15 miles) south of Windsor; County Road 20 connects these three communities. Most of the wineries are on or near County Road 50, along the Lake Erie shore.

WINDSOR

If you're interested in history or in sampling international foods, make a stop in Windsor, an ethnically diverse industrial city on the Canadian side of the Detroit River facing the Detroit skyline. The region was one of Ontario's earliest settlements; it was the oldest French colony west of Montreal. In later years, its history entwined with that of the United States, first over the issue of slavery and then during the Prohibition era.

More recently, the city has become a magnet for immigrants from around the world, with nearly one-quarter of its 215,000 people born outside Canada. Windsor's Little Italy district is along Erie Street, south of the city center, and Wyandotte Street, which runs east-west across downtown, offers a snapshot of Windsor's other ethnic communities.

West of Ouillette Avenue downtown, Wyandotte Street turns toward Asia, with Vietnamese, and some Chinese, eateries and shops. Heading east, the street is Middle Eastern, lined with Lebanese restaurants, bakeries, and markets. It begins to gentrify near Walker Street, in the Walkerville neighborhood of stately brick homes and hip cafés. It's here that you'll find **Walkerville Brewing** (525 Argyle Rd., 519/254-6067, www.walkervillebrewery.com, 11am-6pm Sun.-Wed., 11am-7pm Thurs.-Sat.), with a tasting bar and tap room in a high-ceilinged former whiskey warehouse; stop for free samples of their microbrews, which include the easy-drinking Honest Lager and a flavorful India Pale Ale.

Canadian Club Brand Heritage Center

On January 17, 1920, the U.S. Congress ratified the 18th Amendment to the U.S. Constitution, which banned the manufacture, sale, and transport of alcoholic beverages, ushering in the era of Prohibition. Many Canadian provinces enforced a similar alcohol ban. In Ontario, the Liquor Control Act prohibited public drinking, but it didn't outlaw either the manufacture or export of liquor. Distilleries in the Windsor region capitalized on this loophole; more than 75 percent of the alcohol consumed in the United States during the 1920s and early 1930s traveled across the Detroit River.

Learn more about Prohibition and Windsor's role as a rum-running town at the **Canadian Club Brand Heritage Center** (2072 Riverside Dr. E., 519/973-9503, www.canadianclubwhisky.com; tours noon, 2pm, and 4pm Wed.-Sat., noon and 2pm Sun. May-Dec., noon, 2pm, and 4pm Thurs.-Sat. Jan.-Apr., adults $5, seniors $4), home of Canadian Club whiskey. Ninety-minute tours of the gorgeous 1894 building, with its dark oak woodwork and ornate marble fireplaces, include a whiskey tasting. Gangster Al Capone, who was heavily involved in the illicit liquor trade, allegedly fired a warning shot during a contentious meeting; you can still see the bullet hole in the basement wall.

Art Galleries

Showcasing Canadian art, particularly works by artists from Southwestern Ontario, the **Art Gallery of Windsor** (401 Riverside Dr. W., 519/977-0013, www.agw.ca, 11am-5pm Wed.-Sun., free) has a cool contemporary building overlooking the river. At 2pm on Wednesday and Sunday, the museum offers free gallery tours. **Windsor's Community Museum** (519/253-1812, www.citywindsor.ca), with exhibits about area history, is located on the first floor of the gallery building.

More artwork lines the Windsor waterfront in the **Windsor Sculpture Park** (along the Detroit River, between Huron Church Rd. and Church St., www.citywindsor.ca, free), with over 30 outdoor sculptures. Windsor's Community Museum (519/253-1812, www.citywindsor.ca) offers free one-hour **Art Cart Tours** (11am-5pm Sat.-Sun. May-June and Sept.-mid-Oct., 4pm-7:30pm Wed.-Fri. and 11am-5pm Sat.-Sun. July-Aug.) that cruise through the sculpture park in an electric golf cart. The tours depart from the riverbank at the foot of Ouellette Avenue.

Sandwich

Southwest of downtown, the Sandwich neighborhood is the oldest permanent European settlement in Ontario, inhabited by French pioneers in the 1700s; the City of Windsor publishes a Sandwich Walking Tour online (www.citywindsor.ca), which describes the community's historic structures. Sandwich was also important in the region's African Canadian history, as a destination for formerly enslaved people who came to Canada along the Underground Railroad. The **Sandwich First Baptist Church National Historic Site** (3652 Peter St., 519/252-4917, www.sandwichbaptistchurch.ca) is Canada's oldest active black church, beginning as a log structure in the 1820s. The current church building, which is still used for services, opened in 1851. Historians have found evidence of tunnels leading into the church cellar that were likely used by fugitive slaves.

★ John Freeman Walls Historic Site and Underground Railroad Museum

Ring! Ring! When you arrive at the **John**

Freeman Walls Historic Site and Underground Railroad Museum (859 Puce Rd., Lakeshore, 519/727-6555, www.undergroundrailroadmuseum.org, Tues.-Sat. May-Sept., call for hours), ring the Freedom Bell to call the "conductor," who will guide you around this open-air museum, built and operated by descendants of John Freeman Walls and his wife, Jane King Walls, fugitive slaves who traveled here from North Carolina on the Underground Railroad. As you walk into the nearby woods, following the path of former slaves, you hear the hound dogs attempting to track you down (fortunately, it's just a recording). You also tour the Walls's 1846 log cabin, where they raised nine children and which became a safe house for formerly enslaved people; watch a video about the family's history; and visit the family cemetery.

The museum is 35 kilometers (22 miles) east of Windsor. Take Highway 401 to exit 28, Highway 25/Puce Road, and go north to the site. Hours can be irregular, so call before visiting.

Accommodations

Windsor has a cluster of high-rise chain hotels near the riverfront and a few B&Bs around town.

Built in the 1880s east of the city center, the white clapboard home that houses the **Windsor Inn on the River Bed-and-Breakfast** (3857 Riverside Dr. E., 519/945-2110, www.windsorinnontheriver.com, $99-179 d) was once a private manor. Three of the five well-kept rooms look across the lawn to the river (a favorite, the Alexander Park Suite, has an antique queen bed, a fireplace, and an en suite bath), and a full breakfast is served in the formal dining room or on the veranda.

Though it lacks a riverside location, **Quality Suites Downtown** (250 Dougall Ave., 519/977-9707, www.choicehotels.ca, $115-145 d) is a decent value for its walk-to-everything setting. The family-friendly suites have a living room (with a sleep sofa) and a separate bedroom; all have mini fridges, and some have kitchenettes. Local calls and Wi-Fi are free; ask about costs for parking.

The city's top lodging is the glitzy **Caesars Windsor Hotel and Casino** (377 Riverside Dr. E., 519/258-7878 or 800/991-7777, www.caesarswindsor.com, $139-349 d), with 758 rooms in two riverfront towers (to stay in the Forum Tower, you must be at least 19 years old; all ages are welcome in the Augustus Tower). Riverside rooms on the upper floors have views of the Detroit skyline. In addition to the gaming rooms, the hotel has a spa, an indoor pool, a fitness facility, and several restaurants.

Food

Windsor has a large Lebanese population and several excellent Middle Eastern restaurants. Bring your family or friends to the brightly lit **El-Mayor** (936 Wyandotte St. E., 519/258-7645, www.elmayorrestaurant.com, 9am-1am Sun.-Thurs., 9am-3am Fri., 9am-4am Sat., $5-25), the better to share the overflowing platters of falafel, kebabs, *shawarma,* and salads. Another excellent Lebanese eatery is the more upscale **Mazaar Lebanese Cuisine** (372 Ouellette Ave., 519/967-9696, www.mazaar.ca, 11am-9pm Mon., 11am-10pm Tues.-Thurs., 11am-11pm Fri., noon-11pm Sat., noon-9pm Sun., $8-27), which has belly-dancing shows on Wednesday evenings and Arabic music Friday and Saturday. If you're craving a bowl of hot beef noodle soup, or other inexpensive Vietnamese classics, the friendly but barebones **Pho Nguyen Hoang** (510 Wyandotte St. W., 519/977-0852, 9am-9pm Thurs.-Tues., $4-12) can oblige.

At the cozy **Taloola Café** (396 Devonshire Rd., 519/254-6652, www.taloolacafe.com, 7:30am-10pm Tues.-Fri., 8:30am-11pm Sat., 10am-4pm Sun., $5-8), dine amid exposed brick walls and wood floors, from a menu of vegetarian-friendly salads, sandwiches, and rice bowls as well as pastries, coffees, and teas. Try the Blue Green Salad of kale, blue cheese, cranberries, walnuts, and fennel.

Local musicians often perform on Friday and Saturday nights.

In Windsor's "Little Italy," locally popular choices include **Nico Ristorante** (851 Erie St. E., 519/255-7548, www.nicoristorante. com, 5pm-9pm Tues.-Sun., $18-35) and **Il Gabbiano Ristorante** (875 Erie St. E., 519/256-9757, www.ilgabbiano.com; lunch 11:30am-2pm Mon.-Fri., dinner 4:30pm-9pm Mon.-Thurs., 4pm-10pm Fri.-Sat., 4pm-9pm Sun., lunch $19-19, dinner $18-32).

Information and Services
The website of **Tourism Windsor, Essex, and Pelee Island** (333 Riverside Dr. W., Suite 103, 519/255-6530 or 800/265-3633, www.visitwindsoressex.com, 8:30am-4:30pm Mon.-Fri.) is an excellent resource for travel planning, with listings for hotels, attractions, and upcoming events in Windsor and surroundings.

If you like beer and bicycling, explore the city on a **Windsor Eats Bikes & Beers Cycling Tour** (www.windsoreats.com, May-Oct., $60 pp, $80 tour plus bike rental). You cycle to several breweries for tours and tastings, with samples of food along the way. Tours are usually offered once a month and average 20 kilometers (12 miles) of cycling. Check their website for schedules and for other walking or cycling tours in Windsor and the surrounding area.

Getting There
Air
Windsor International Airport (YQG, County Rd. 42, 519/969-2430, www.yqg. ca) is located 12 kilometers (7.5 miles) southeast of downtown. **Porter Airlines** (www.flyporter.com) flies to Toronto's City Airport, **Air Canada** (www.aircanada.com) goes to Toronto Pearson Airport, and **WestJet** (888/937-8538, www.westjet.com) flies nonstop to Calgary. **Transit Windsor**'s (www.citywindsor.ca) no. 8 Walkerville bus runs between the airport and Riverside Drive downtown every 30-60 minutes (less often on weekends). A taxi

from the airport to most downtown points should be less than $10.

Across the U.S. border, about 40 kilometers (25 miles) from Windsor off I-94, **Detroit Metro Airport** (DTW, 734/247-7678, www.metroairport.com) has more options for flights to U.S. cities and overseas. **Robert Q Airbus** (519/673-6804 or 800/265-4948, www.robertq.com, 1.25 hours, one-way adults $46, seniors and students $44, under age 12 $23) runs a shuttle between Detroit Airport and the Windsor Holiday Inn (1855 Huron Church Rd.). **Courtesy Transportation** (519/977-9700, www.courtesytransportation.com) and **Classic Shuttle** (519/796-4634, www.classicshuttle.ca) also provide transportation between DTW and downtown Windsor.

Train
From the **VIA Rail Windsor Station** (298 Walker Rd., at Riverside Dr., 888/842-7245, www.viarail.ca), trains run to London (1.75 hours, one-way adult $38-56, kids $25-32) and Toronto (4.25 hours, one-way adult $50-80, kids $36-40). U.S. rail carrier **Amtrak** (800/872-7245, www.amtrak.com) runs trains from Chicago to Detroit, where you can cross the border into Windsor. Unfortunately, the convenient Windsor Tunnel Bus doesn't stop at the Detroit train station (11 W. Baltimore Ave.). The simplest option is to take a cab from the Amtrak station to one of the tunnel bus stops downtown. Alternatively, catch a **Detroit Department of Transportation bus** (DDOT, 313/933-1300 or 888/336-8287, www.ci.detroit.mi.us, adults US$1.50, seniors US$0.50, students US$0.75) from the train station to a Tunnel Bus stop; the ride takes about 20 minutes.

Bus
Windsor's bus station is the **Windsor International Transit Terminal** (300 Chatham St. W., 519/254-7575, www.citywindsor.ca) downtown. **Greyhound** (www.greyhound.ca) runs several buses a day

between Toronto and Windsor (5-5.5 hours, adults one-way $55-88, seniors $46-81, ages 2-11 $46-67). The same buses stop in London (2-2.5 hours, adults one-way $32-48, seniors $19-43, ages 2-11 $27-37).

Between downtown Detroit and downtown Windsor, you can catch Transit Windsor's **Tunnel Bus** (www.citywindsor. ca, 519/944-4111, 5:30am-12:30pm Mon.-Sat., 8am-midnight Sun., one-way $4.50). In Windsor, the bus arrives at and departs from the Windsor International Transit Terminal; you can also get off at the Caesars Windsor Hotel and Casino (377 Riverside Dr. E., 519/258-7878 or 800/991-7777, www.caesarswindsor.com). From Detroit, you can catch the bus at the Rosa Parks Transit Center (E. Park Pl. at State St.) or at the Detroit Tunnel Platform (Randolph St. at Renaissance Dr. N.), near the Mariner's Church opposite the Renaissance Center. Assuming no traffic or border delays, the trip takes only 15-20 minutes.

Car

Windsor has two 24-hour international border crossings (www.crossingmadeeasy.com): the **Detroit-Windsor Tunnel** (www.dwtunnel.com) and the **Ambassador Bridge** (www.ambassadorbridge.com). Tolls in the tunnel vary slightly depending on which direction you're traveling: from Detroit to Windsor (US$4.75) or from Windsor to Detroit (US$4.50). Bridge tolls (US$4.75) are the same in either direction.

Check the current border lineups online at **U.S. Customs and Border Protection** (http://bwt.cbp.gov) and the **Canadian Border Services Agency** (www.cbsa-asfc. gc.ca). Always allow extra time if you're catching a plane, or if you have a time-critical appointment, on the opposite side. Remember that passports are required for travel between the United States and Canada.

To Windsor from Toronto, 365 kilometers (225 miles) to the northeast, it's a direct drive down Highway 401. Allow 4-4.5 hours. From London, it's 185 kilometers (115 miles).

Getting Around

Ouellette Avenue is the main north-south street in the downtown area and the dividing line between "east" and "west" addresses. Riverside Drive (along the river) and Wyandotte Street cross the city from east to west. **Transit Windsor** (www.citywindsor. ca, one-way $2.75) runs buses throughout the downtown area.

You'll want to have a car for exploring Southwestern Ontario's wineries or African Canadian heritage sites. Car rental companies with Windsor offices include **Avis** (www.avis. com), **Budget** (www.budget.ca), **Discount** (www.discountcar.com), **Enterprise** (www. enterpriserentacar.ca), and **National** (www. nationalcar.ca).

Along Lake Huron

Lake Huron is famous for its sunsets. As the sun illuminates the darkening sky with streaks of gold, people come down to the beach to watch, pausing as if to say good night to the day. And even though you know the sun will rise and set again tomorrow, there's something about watching it hover over the lake that makes you want to stop and watch it one more time.

During the day, the lake and its beaches are equally compelling, since Huron is lined with lovely stretches of sand. In the lakeside beach towns, you'll find lighthouses and small museums, galleries and theaters, but it's the beach—and the sunset—that will draw you again and again to the second-largest of the Great Lakes.

From Toronto, there's no direct highway to Lake Huron, so you'll need to slow down as you meander through rural towns along the way. But that's okay—the leisurely drive gives you time to tune into the laid-back vibe of the lakeshore. Once you reach Lake Huron, Highway 21, known as the Bluewater Highway, connects lakeside towns from Sarnia north to Southampton.

GRAND BEND

Grand Bend has a long, sandy beach on Lake Huron and the honky-tonk feel of a summer tourist town. You've got ice cream stands and T-shirt shops, cheek-by-jowl rental cottages, and packs of young folks cruising the beach and the bars looking for a good time. Plenty of families return to the beach year after year. Visit outside of frenetic July and August, though, and Grand Bend quiets down into a pleasant spot for a weekend by the shore. Just outside town is a provincial park with a spectacular dune-backed expanse of sand.

★ The Pinery Provincial Park

One of the most beautiful beaches along Lake Huron is just south of Grand Bend. At **The Pinery Provincial Park** (9526 Lakeshore Rd./Hwy. 21, 519/243-2220, www.ontarioparks.com or www.pinerypark.on.ca, year-round, $17 per vehicle), the 10-kilometer (six-mile) powdery sand beach, backed by the undulating dunes topped with waving grasses, feels like it goes on forever. While the beach is wildly popular in summer, the day-use area is divided into nine sections, so you can explore till you find a spot to lay your towel.

The **Visitors Centre** (519/243-8574, 10am-5pm daily July-Aug., call for off-season hours), near the campgrounds on the park's west side, runs various nature programs in summer. Near the Visitors Centre you can rent bicycles ($10-15 per hour, $25-50 per day), or canoes and kayaks ($12-15 per hour, $25-45 per day) to paddle along the Old Ausable River Channel.

Ten short hiking trails, ranging one to three kilometers (0.6-2 miles), wend through the park. With the exception of the challenging **Nipissing Trail,** which climbs to a lookout atop the park's largest dune ridge, and the

sunset over Lake Huron

longer wilderness trail, most trails are easy enough to explore with kids. Pick up trail guides at the Visitors Centre. The 14-kilometer (8.7-mile) **Savannah Multiuse Trail** loops through the park, more or less paralleling the road, making it a more pleasant (and safer) option for pedestrians and cyclists.

In winter, you can cross-country ski or snowshoe along 38 kilometers (24 miles) of trails. You can rent skis and snowshoes (10am-4pm Sat.-Sun., adults $12 per hour, ages 6-17 $10 per hour) at the Visitor Centre.

The park entrance is eight kilometers (five miles) south of Grand Bend on Highway 21. Once you arrive, park your car and explore on foot or by bicycle. The park road is a 12-kilometer (7.5-mile) one-way loop, so to revisit a spot you just passed, it's a long way around again.

Entertainment and Events

Several plays run in repertory every summer at the **Huron Country Playhouse** (70689 B Line, off Highway 81, 519/238-6000 or

855/372-9866, www.draytonentertainment. com, mid-May-early Sept.). If you thought that old-time drive-in movies were long gone, think again. Grand Bend's **Starlite Drive-in Theatre** (36,752 Crediton Rd., 519/238-8344, www.starlitedriveintheatre.com) still screens films nightly in July and August and on weekends in the spring and fall.

Accommodations and Food

Motels, places to eat, and shops line Ontario Street (Hwy. 21) and Main Street. The **Bluewater Motel** (121 Ontario St. S./Hwy. 21, 519/238-2014, from $99 d) is a well-maintained, family-run, and family-friendly property with an outdoor pool. The 22 standard motel units cover the basics: decent beds, fridges, TVs, and included Wi-Fi. Out back are three cottages that sleep 2 to 6. It's a one-kilometer (0.6-mile) walk along Lake Road to the town's South Beach and about the same distance along Highway 21 to the town center. Farther south, the **Whispering Pines Motel** (10456 Lakeshore Rd./Hwy. 21, 519/238-2383, www.whisperingpinesmotel.org, $99-139 d) has similar rooms and facilities.

The **Grand Bend Farmers Market** (1 Main St., www.grandbendfarmersmarket. ca, 8am-1pm Wed. late May-early Oct.) sets up in the parking lot of the Colonial Hotel. The aroma of fresh baked goods may lure you into **Grandpa Jimmy's Scottish Bakery** (36 Ontario St. N., 519/238-5055 or 877/225-5907, www.grandpajimmys.com, 9am-5pm Tues.-Sun.). Don't resist; the scones have just the right amount of sweetness (try a berry one in season). For a beach picnic, pick up traditional sausage rolls, meat pies, breads, or pastries. Like any good grandfather's house, this one has toys for the kids (and magazines for the grown-ups).

Old-fashioned family dining has kept the tables full since the 1950s at friendly **Aunt Gussie's Country Dining** (135 Ontario St. S., 519/238-6786, www.auntgussies.ca, 8am-9pm Mon.-Fri., 7am-9pm Sat.-Sun., call for off-season hours, breakfast $4-9, lunch $7-11, dinner $10-17), south of the town center. Stop in for breakfast before heading to the beach; later, you can fuel up on classics like burgers, open-face turkey sandwiches with mashed potatoes and gravy, pot pies, and smoked pork chops.

Camping
The Pinery Provincial Park (9526 Lakeshore Rd./Hwy. 21, 519/243-2220, www. ontarioparks.com or www.pinerypark.on.ca, tent sites $40-44, electrical sites $46-50) has the second-largest campground in the Ontario Provincial Park system (only Algonquin is larger), with 1,000 campsites in three camping areas; 404 of the sites have electrical hookups. The Dunes and Burley Campgrounds (May-Sept.) have sites near the beach; the Riverside Campground (year-round) is inland near the river. All areas have flush toilets and showers.

The Riverside Campground has 12 **yurts** ($98), with electricity, electric heat, and a gas barbecue outside. The yurts sleep up to six, in two sets of bunk beds (one double and one single bunk). Bring sleeping bags, cooking gear, and food.

Book in advance for this popular park, especially if you plan to camp in summer or on any holiday weekend. Contact the **Ontario Parks Reservation Service** (888/668-7275, www.ontarioparks.com, reservation fee online $11, by phone $13).

Practicalities

For visitor information, contact the **Grand Bend and Area Chamber of Commerce and Tourism** (81 Crescent St., 519/238-2001 or 888/338-2001, www.grandbendtourism. com, 10am-4pm Mon.-Sat. June, 10am-6pm Mon.-Sat., 10am-4pm Sun. July-Aug., noon-4pm Mon.-Fri. Sept.-May).

Grand Bend is 220 kilometers (137 miles) west of Toronto, about a 3.5-hour drive. Follow Highway 401 west to Kitchener, then take Highway 8 west to Stratford. From there, continue west to Mitchell, then follow Highway 23 south to Highway 83, which meets Highway 21 just north of Grand Bend. Alternatively, pick up Highway 7 south from Stratford, then take

Highway 20 toward Fullarton, where you'll connect with Highway 83.

BAYFIELD

If Grand Bend is a teenager in a bikini scarfing down hot wings or soft ice cream, Bayfield is her proper hat-wearing great aunt—more about heritage buildings, luxurious inns, and art galleries than catching rays in the sand. In the mid-1800s, Bayfield became a well-to-do port, shipping grain from area farms. Although the coming of the railroad, which didn't extend to Bayfield, ended the town's shipping industry, many stately lodgings and homes date to this prosperous era.

Sights and Recreation

Bayfield's town square, **Clan Gregor Square,** is now a park surrounded by historic structures, while shops, galleries, lodgings, and restaurants line sedate Main Street, just off the square. A short walk from Main Street, **Pioneer Park** overlooks Lake Huron, with steps that descend to the lovely town beach.

The **Bayfield Historical Society** (20 Main St., www.bayfieldhistorical.ca, 1pm-5pm Wed. and Sat. mid-Apr.-mid-Dec.) runs a small museum and archives with photos, letters, and other documents about the town's history. The society also leads historical walking tours (1pm Sat. July-Aug., $10) around the town.

For more active pursuits, visit **Outside Projects** (6 Main St., 519/565-4034, www.outsideprojects.ca, 10am-7pm daily July-Aug., 10am-5pm Fri.-Mon. Sept.-June), an outdoor gear store that rents bikes (half-day $22, full-day $40), and, in winter, snowshoes. They also organize guided hikes, bike excursions, and snowshoe tours.

Entertainment and Events

The annual **Bayfield Writers' Festival** (www.bayfieldwritersfestival.com, June) brings authors to town for a weekend of readings and other events. Get tickets from the **Village Bookshop** (24 Main St. N., 519/565-5600, www.thevillagebookshop.com), which also hosts readings and literary events throughout the year.

Accommodations and Food

The old-timey **Albion Hotel** (1 Main St., 519/565-2641, www.thealbionhotel.com, $115-145 s, $125-155 d) has been taking guests since 1856. Of the four simply furnished, country-cottage guest rooms upstairs, the largest has a four-poster bed and a fireplace. Rates include continental breakfast. The pub is a popular local hangout; the dining room (11:30am-midnight Mon.-Sat., 11:30am-11pm Sun., $10-30) serves burgers, ribs, fish-and-chips, and steaks.

Ontario's longest continually operating inn, **The Little Inn of Bayfield** (26 Main St. N., 519/565-2611 or 800/565-1832, www.littleinn.com, $170-231 s, $230-308 d) was a stagecoach stop in the 1830s. The original building houses 18 traditionally appointed guest rooms, starting with the least expensive (and tiny) "original" rooms. For more space, opt for a "carriage house" room, or a more luxurious junior suite, with a whirlpool tub or gas fireplace. In the separate "guest cottage" across the street, the 10 rooms are more spacious and contemporary. The main inn houses the highly regarded **Little Inn of Bayfield Restaurant** (breakfast 8am-10am daily, lunch noon-2pm daily, dinner 5pm-8:30pm daily, lunch $13-20, dinner $26-40), where the locally sourced menu might feature Lake Huron pickerel with broccoli rabe or black Angus beef with roasted chanterelles. Rates include a full breakfast; packages including dinner are also available.

If your style is more contemporary, consider the seven deluxe guest rooms at the **Red Pump Inn and Restaurant** (21 Main St., 519/565-2576 or 888/665-2576, www.theredpumpinn.com, Apr.-Dec., $250-425). Mixing modern and traditional furnishings, the large units all have king beds, fireplaces, roomy baths, and private balconies. The restaurant (lunch and dinner Wed.-Mon. Apr.-Dec., lunch $15-19, dinner $18-39) draws inspiration from around the world, with dishes like red coconut curry, lobster pasta, or maple-glazed pork tenderloin.

The relaxed **Black Dog Village Pub and Bistro** (5 Main St. N., 519/565-2326, www.blackdogpubbistro.ca, 11:30am-close daily summer, 11:30am-close Wed.-Sun. fall-spring, lunch $11-20, dinner $13-33) serves burgers and sandwiches midday, adding pastas, curries, and steaks in the evening. There are 20 beers on tap and a large whiskey selection.

Practicalities

Bayfield is 215 kilometers (134 miles) west of Toronto. Take Highway 401 west toward Kitchener, then continue west on Highway 8. At the town of Seaforth, pick up Highway 3 west, which meets Highway 21 (the Bluewater Hwy.) just south of Bayfield. From London, 85 kilometers (53 miles) to the southwest, follow Highway 4 north to Brucefield, then take Highway 3 west to Highway 21.

You can get information about the town online from **Bayfield and Area Chamber of Commerce** (www.villageofbayfield.com).

KINCARDINE AND VICINITY

Settled by Scottish settlers in the mid-1800s, this Lake Huron town grew up from the lumber, fishing, and salt-producing industries. In 1968, a new technology changed the town's fortunes: a nuclear power plant—Canada's first commercial nuclear reactor—was built on the lakeshore north of town.

Sights and Recreation

In addition to its pretty, sandy town beach, which runs for over a kilometer (0.6 miles) along the lake, Kincardine's sights are linked to its marine past and its nuclear future.

An active lighthouse since 1859, 18 kilometers (11 miles) south of Kincardine, the light station that now constitutes the **Point Clark Lighthouse National Historic Site** (530 Lighthouse Rd., Huron-Kinloss, Point-Clark, 519/395-2494, www.pc.gc.ca) is one of six "imperial towers" that guided ships along Lake Huron and Georgian Bay. It's a 34-meter (110-foot) limestone tower, with a 12-sided lantern on top. A multiyear project to restore the lighthouse was still in progress as this book went to press; contact Parks Canada (705/526-9804) for an update before visiting.

On the harbor in the center of Kincardine, the town's octagonal lighthouse was built in 1881. Still an operating light, it's now the **Kincardine Lighthouse and Museum** (236 Harbour St., 519/396-3150 or 800/268-3838, www.brucecoastlighthouses.com, 11am-5pm daily July-early Sept.).

One of the Lake Huron shore's most unusual attractions illustrates the role that nuclear power plays in the region. At the **Bruce Power Visitors Centre** (3394 Bruce Rd. 20, Tiverton, 519/361-7777 or 866/748-4787, www.brucepower.com, 9am-4pm Mon.-Sat. July-Aug., 9am-4pm Mon.-Fri. Sept.-June, free), you can learn more about the nuclear industry and the workings of the local power plants. The exhibits have a decidedly pro-nuclear bent, but it's still educational. Outside are the spinning turbines of Ontario's first commercial wind farm (www.huronwind.com); the Visitors Centre has an exhibit about wind power, as well. The Bruce Power Visitors Centre is 20 kilometers (12.5 miles) north of Kincardine. Go north on Highway 21 to Highway 15/Main Street west toward Inverhuron; then take Highway 23 north to Concession 4 west.

Kincardine celebrates its Scottish heritage during the annual **Kincardine Scottish Festival and Highland Games** (www.kincardinescottishfestival.ca, July), with kilt-wearing pipe bands, Highland dancing, and "heavy events," a traditional athletic competition that includes stone and hammer throws and the caber toss.

Accommodations and Food

You can't get much closer to the lake than at the aptly named **Lakefront B&B** (328 Goderich St., 519/396-4345, www.lakefrontbb.com, $165-177 d). The largest unit is a cozy cabin with a sunroom facing Lake Huron and a separate bedroom. Additional rooms are available on the lower level of the main house. Co-owner Katrena Johnston, who plays bass in a local band, serves breakfast in the Crow's Nest, a nook overlooking the water.

Along Highway 21, there are a couple of newer chain motels, including **Holiday Inn Express & Suites Kincardine** (2 Millenium Way, 877/660-8550, www.ihg.com). You'll find several restaurants along Queen Street in the town center, including the peanuts-on-the-floor-casual **Hawg's Breath Saloon and Deli** (894 Queen St., 519/396-6565, 11am-midnight Mon.-Wed., 11am-1am Thurs., 11am-2am Fri.-Sat., 11am-9pm Sun. late May-early Sept., 11am-11pm Mon.-Wed., 11am-midnight Thurs., 11am-2am Fri.-Sat., early-Sept.-late May), which serves beer, sandwiches, beer, burgers, and beer.

Practicalities

Kincardine is about 225 kilometers (140 miles) northwest of Toronto. By car, you can either head toward Guelph, where you can take Highway 7 north and west to Highway 9, which goes into Kincardine, or pick up Highway 10 north to Orangeville, where you turn west. The **Kincardine Visitor Information Centre** (777B Queen St., 519/396-2731 or 866/546-2736, www.sunsets.com/kincardine) can provide more information about the area and assist with cottage rentals.

SOUTHAMPTON AND VICINITY

Summer life in Southampton revolves around the beach, and the town has a pretty, sandy one just a short walk from the laid-back downtown district. But Southampton also has a first-rate museum, and it's the starting point for an island lighthouse tour. Nearby, you can learn about the region's First Nations culture.

Sights and Recreation

You may not think about touring a museum on a sunny day in a beach town, but even if it's not raining, it's worth visiting the excellent **Bruce County Museum and Cultural Centre** (33 Victoria St. N., 519/797-2080 or 866/318-8889, www.brucemuseum.ca, 10am-5pm Mon.-Sat., 1pm-5pm Sun. summer, call or check the website for off-season hours, adults $8, seniors and students $6, ages 4-12 $4). The modern, interactive exhibits focus on the region's heritage and culture, with displays about shipwrecks, marine history, and local life. Sit around a farm kitchen table and listen to recordings recounting what it was like to live in Bruce County in the early 1900s, or learn about how ships in peril are rescued.

The **Chantry Island Lighthouse** was built in 1859 on an island off the coast of Southampton. Because the island is now a Federal Migratory Bird Sanctuary, home to nesting colonies of great blue herons, double-crested cormorants, and great egrets, among others, access is restricted. To tour the lighthouse, reserve in advance with **Chantry Island Tours** (89 Saugeen St., 519/797-5862 or 866/797-5862, www.chantryisland.com, late May-early Sept., $30 pp); the two-hour tour includes the boat ride to the island and a guided hike to the lighthouse.

The Southampton area is home to the Saugeen First Nation, who are an Ojibwa people. The nation runs the open-air **Saugeen Amphitheatre** (519/797-2781 or 800/680-0744, www.saugeenfirstnation.ca); visit during the annual **Saugeen Pow Wow** (July), for dancing, music, and traditional food. The amphitheater is 3.5 kilometers (two miles) north of Southampton on Highway 21.

Accommodations and Food

Restaurants, shops, and a few places to stay cluster along High Street, Southampton's "downtown," on either side of Albert Street (Hwy. 21). At the comfortable **Chantry Breezes Bed & Breakfast** (107 High St., 519/797-1818 or 866/242-6879, www.chantrybreezes.on.ca, rooms $150-190 d, cottages $180-220), one block from the beach, accommodations include four Victorian-style guest rooms, a two-room suite, and two small guest cottages out back. Guests gather in the large window-lined parlor, the formal dining room, or out on the porch.

Opposite the Chantry Breezes, the more basic yellow brick Victorian **Southampton Inn & Spa** (118 High St., 519/797-5915 or 888/214-3816, www.thesouthamptoninn. com, $135-155 d) is far from fancy, but the seven country-style rooms have mini fridges and private baths; three are suites with separate sitting areas. If you need a massage, facial, or pedicure, walk downstairs to the spa. Room rates include Wi-Fi and a light breakfast.

Even when it's not the middle of summer, you can savor the soups, sandwiches, coffee, and ice cream at the **Mid Summers Café** (171 High St., 519/797-1122). Old favorite **Duffy's Restaurant and Bar** (151 High St., 519/797-5972, www.duffyssouthampton.com, 11:30am-9pm Tues.-Sat., 11:30pm-8pm Sun. summer, call for off-season hours) is known for its fish-and-chips, but the pan-fried Lake Huron whitefish is a popular choice, too.

Practicalities

Saugeen Shores Tourism (800/387-3456, www.visitsouthampton.ca) provides visitor information for the Southampton area. Southampton is 225 kilometers (140 miles) northwest of Toronto. The most direct route is via Highway 10 to Owen Sound, where you can pick up Highway 21 south into Southampton. Southampton can also be a base for exploring the southern Bruce Peninsula; it's 20 kilometers (12 miles) south of Sauble Beach via Highway 13. If you're traveling along the Lake Huron coast, it's 45 kilometers (28 miles) on Highway 21 from Kincardine to Southampton. Once you get to the compact town center, you can leave the car parked. It's a short stroll from the shops to the beach or the museum.

Eastern Ontario

A s you travel along the shores of Lake Ontario, the St. Lawrence River, the network of interconnected lakes in the Kawartha region, or the Rideau Canal, you're never far from a beach or a boat. If it's an island getaway you seek,

you have literally thousands to choose from. Eastern Ontario is home to the Thousand Islands, and another island destination, Prince Edward County, has a booming food and wine scene that draws gourmets and oenophiles from Toronto and beyond.

Kingston, the region's largest city, was the first capital of Upper Canada in 1841, and many historic structures from the 1800s still dot the city. Whether at a 19th-century fort, the grand city hall, or any number of restored downtown buildings, history is very present in present-day Kingston. Kingston serves as a good base for day-trips to the Thousand Islands, to Prince Edward County, or into the backcountry at provincial parks just north of town. Eastern Ontario offers more opportunities for adventures in the Peterborough area, whether it's going back in time at a pioneer village, exploring an aboriginal community or ancient aboriginal rock carvings, or simply vacationing in a lakeside cottage. Whether

you're organizing a brief holiday or traveling across the province, the eastern districts serve up plenty of fun—and tasty—detours along the way.

PLANNING YOUR TIME

Many Eastern Ontario destinations are close enough to Toronto or Ottawa for a weekend getaway, and they also make convenient stopping points if you're traveling between Toronto and Montreal. You can easily spend a weekend at a lakeside resort around **Peterborough** or exploring the museums in **Kingston. Prince Edward County,** with its wineries, comfortable inns, and contemporary restaurants, is ideal for a couple of days of exploration, too.

If you have a week, you could travel from Toronto along **Lake Ontario,** stopping off in the lakeside towns of Port Hope or Cobourg, spend a couple of days wine touring in Prince Edward County, explore Kingston for a

---

Previous: a historic Martello Tower on Kingston's waterfront; Sandbanks Provincial Park. **Above:** wine trail, Prince Edward County.

Look for ★ to find recommended
sights, activities, dining, and lodging.

Highlights

★ **Canadian Canoe Museum:** This well-designed museum in Peterborough traces Canadian historical and cultural developments through the country's waterways and watercraft (page 202).

★ **Petroglyphs Provincial Park:** One of the largest concentrations of petroglyphs in North America, Petroglyphs Provincial Park is a sacred First Nations site with more than 900 symbols carved into a massive marble slab (page 205).

★ **Prince Edward County Wineries:** If you enjoy good wine and local food, this booming wine region is a great place for a getaway and is an easy drive east of Toronto (page 214).

★ **Sandbanks Provincial Park:** Like the beach? This expansive and popular Prince Edward County park has some lovely ones and giant sand dunes, too (page 218).

★ **Fort Henry:** There's always something happening at these 19th-century fortifications

overlooking the city of Kingston. You can tour the barracks, attend "Victorian school," and watch the Sunset Ceremonies, with military maneuvers, music, and fireworks (page 225).

★ **Thousand Islands Boat Tours:** The best way to see the Thousand Islands is by water. Choose from a variety of cruises around the islands, departing from Gananoque or from the nearby town of Rockport (page 235).

★ **Fulford Place:** George Taylor Fulford made his fortune selling "Pink Pills for Pale People," and he used the considerable proceeds to build this opulent 35-room mansion overlooking the St. Lawrence River in Brockville (page 240).

★ **Upper Canada Village:** Travel back to the 1860s at one of Ontario's largest and best-preserved historic villages. You can chat with costumed interpreters as they go about their daily business as millers, bakers, or blacksmiths, and join in a variety of traditional activities, from milking the cows to riding in a horse-drawn barge (page 242).

Eastern Ontario

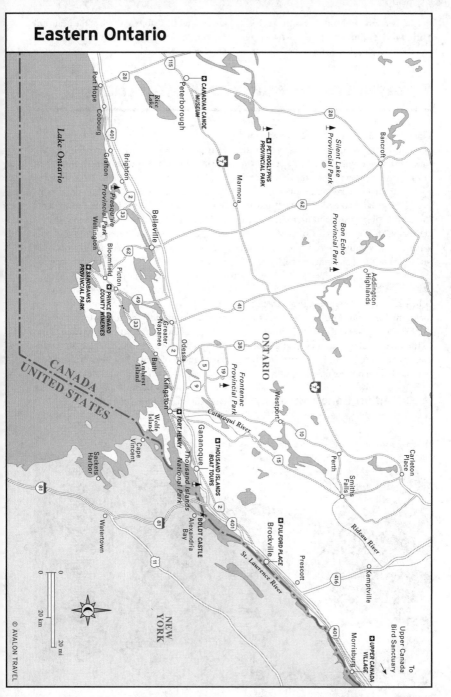

© AVALON TRAVEL

day or two, and continue east through the **Thousand Islands.** In 10 days to two weeks, you could make a loop from either Toronto or Ottawa, adding stops at some of the beautiful provincial parks in the region and time by the lakes in the Kawarthas.

Peterborough and the Kawarthas

The city of Peterborough, with a year-round population of 135,000, is the gateway to the Kawartha region. Just two hours northeast of Toronto (traffic permitting), the Kawarthas is a rural district of lakes and waterways, provincial parks, and lakeside resorts. While the Kawartha region historically hasn't had the cachet of the Muskoka Lakes "Cottage Country," it's still worth visiting, especially to explore the region's aboriginal and cultural heritage.

SIGHTS

While several of Peterborough's attractions, including the Canoe Museum, the Locks, and the Art Gallery, are within the city, others are in the surrounding countryside and lake regions. In planning your itinerary, allow time to travel between these far-flung sites.

★ Canadian Canoe Museum

If you think that a canoe museum would appeal only to boating enthusiasts, think again. The well-designed exhibits at the **Canadian Canoe Museum** (910 Monaghan Rd., 705/748-9153 or 866/342-2663, www.canoemuseum.ca, 10am-5pm Mon.-Sat., noon-5pm Sun., adults $10.50, seniors and students $8.25, families $25) aren't just about watercraft. They trace Canada's history and culture, exploring how the lakes and rivers that cross the country—and the boats that provided vital transportation links along those waterways—have influenced the nation's development. Yes, the exhibits illustrate how different peoples across Canada built and used canoes, from the West Coast First Nations' massive whaling canoes to the birchbark canoes of central and eastern Canada, but they also detail cultural developments, like how canoes became an integral part of Ontario's recreational culture.

In the summer, you can often watch

The Canadian Canoe Museum traces the country's history through its boats.

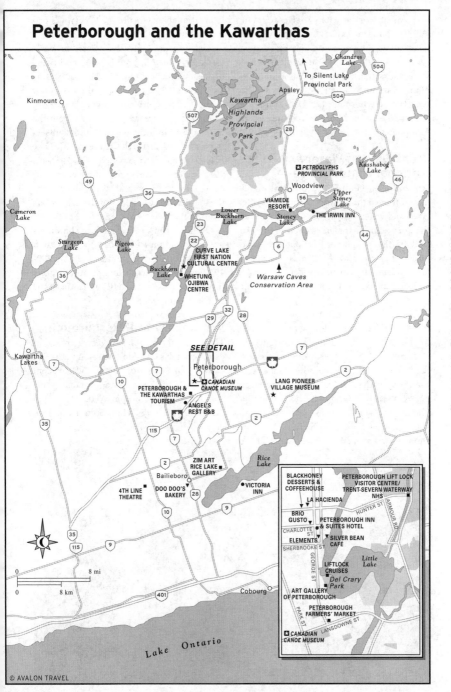

artisans at work in the galleries, carving paddles, building canoes, or doing other related crafts. The museum also offers periodic workshops where you can learn these skills yourself. The museum has announced plans to move to a new waterfront facility near the Peterborough Lift Lock, targeting their relocation for 2017; check the website for updates.

Trent-Severn Waterway National Historic Site

Since at least 9000 BC, aboriginal people have traversed the network of interconnected lakes and waterways across Ontario. When the European fur traders arrived in the 17th century, they also used these water routes to explore and trade. In the 1800s settlers lobbied for an inland canal to make water travel easier and to gain access to markets across what is now Ontario.

The first lock on this waterway was built in 1833 at the Kawartha town of Bobcaygeon; by the 1880s, additional locks made it possible to travel smoothly through several of the Kawartha Lakes. Today, the Trent-Severn Waterway, with more than 40 locks, connects Lake Ontario with Georgian Bay, running 386 kilometers (241 miles) across central Ontario.

Recreational boaters are the waterway's primary users.

The waterway's must-see is Peterborough's **Lock 21,** which opened in 1904 and is the highest hydraulic lift lock in the world; rising 19.8 meters (65 feet), it's essentially an elevator for boats. To experience going up and down in the lock, (there are great views from the top), take an informative two-hour sightseeing cruise with **Liftlock Cruises** (Little Lake Peterborough Marina, George St., 705/742-9912 or 888/535-4670, www.liftlockcruises.com, daily mid-May-mid-Oct., call or check the website for seasonal schedules, adults $22, seniors and students $20, ages 4-12 $12).

On land, you can learn about the waterway system at the **Peterborough Lift Lock Visitors Centre** (353 Hunter St. E., 705/750-4950, www.pc.gc.ca/trent, 9am-6pm daily July-Aug., 10am-5pm daily mid-May-June and Sept.-mid-Oct.).

Art Gallery of Peterborough

There's usually something new to see at Peterborough's lakeside art museum, the **Art Gallery of Peterborough** (250 Crescent St., 705/743-9179, www.agp.on.ca, 9am-5pm Mon.-Fri., 9am-8pm Wed., 11am-5pm Sat.-Sun. July-Aug., 11am-5pm Tues.-Sun.

The Art Gallery of Peterborough shows Canadian contemporary art.

Sept.-June, free). The gallery hosts four or five exhibitions every year, emphasizing Canadian contemporary art, and the shop stocks ceramics, jewelry, textiles, and other work by regional artists. The gallery also organizes the weekend-long **Kawartha Studio Tour** every September, when local artists open their studios to visitors.

Lang Pioneer Village Museum

Many settlers came to the Peterborough area in the 1800s from England, Scotland, and Ireland. To learn about the lives of these pioneers, explore the **Lang Pioneer Village Museum** (104 Lang Rd., off Hwy. 34, Keene, 705/295-6694 or 866/289-5264, www.lang-pioneervillage.ca, 10am-3pm Mon.-Fri. late May-mid-June, 10am-4pm daily late June-early Sept., adults $8, seniors and students $7, ages 5-14 $4, families $20), where more than 25 buildings date from the 1820s to the 1880s.

Newly arrived settlers would typically build a simple log cabin, like the 1820s Fife Cabin. As they became more established, they would construct larger homes, like the 1840s Fitzpatrick House or the comparatively more comfortable 1870s Milburn House. In addition to touring these restored homes, visit the general store, church, and schoolhouse, as well as the reconstructed shops of the village carpenter, tinsmith, printer, and blacksmith. The weaving shop houses two authentic Jacquard looms, rarely seen in North America. Costumed guides help bring the village to life.

In autumn (early Sept.-Oct.), the village is open weekdays for guided fall color tours, by reservation only. The village is 18 kilometers (11 miles) southeast of Peterborough. Take Highway 7 east for 10 kilometers (six miles), then turn south on County Road 34 (Heritage Line). From there, it's six kilometers (3.7 miles) to Lang Road and the village entrance.

★ Petroglyphs Provincial Park

Containing one of the largest concentrations of petroglyphs—rock carvings made by indigenous people—in North America, **Petroglyphs Provincial Park** (2249 Northey's Bay Rd., Woodview, 705/877-2552, www.ontarioparks.com, 10am-5pm daily late June-early Sept., 10am-5pm Wed.-Sun. mid-May-late June and early Sept.-mid-Oct., $14.50 per vehicle) is also an active sacred site for First Nations people.

No one knows for sure when the Algonquian people carved the more than 900 symbols onto the massive crystalline marble slab, now protected in a large glass building constructed around the rock. Experts date the carvings, which include human figures as well as snakes, turtles, and other animals, at somewhere between 600 and 1,100 years old. Park interpreters can help identify the carvings and share ideas about their traditional meanings. All park visitors must register at the **Learning Place Visitor Centre,** where you can watch a 20-minute film about the site and view exhibits about the region's aboriginal traditions, before heading for the petroglyphs.

On several evenings in July and August, park staff run a 90-minute light show, in which the glyphs are illuminated and become more visible than they are during the day. Even if you've seen the petroglyphs in daylight, it's worth returning for these special evening events. Although the park is regularly open until 5pm, arrive by 3:30pm so you have time to drive to the site, visit the Learning Place, and see the glyphs. The province's park service manages the site in partnership with the local Curve Lake First Nation. Due to the site's spiritual importance, no photos are allowed.

The park is 55 kilometers (34 miles) northeast of Peterborough. Take Water Street/Highway 29 north, continue north on Highway 28, and turn right (east) onto Northey's Bay Road, which leads to the park entrance. There are no camping facilities or other accommodations within the park.

Curve Lake First Nations Reserve

If a visit to the petroglyphs piques your

curiosity about First Nations' heritage and culture, your next stop should be the **Curve Lake First Nations Reserve** (www.curvelakefirstnation.ca). More than 750 Ojibwa people live on this reserve, with several hundred more in the surrounding communities.

At the **Curve Lake First Nation Cultural Centre** (1024 Mississauga St., 705/243-1646, www.curvelakeculturalcentre.ca, 8:30am-4:30pm Mon.-Thurs., 8:30am-4pm Fri., adults $3, seniors and kids ages 5 and older $2), curator Anne Taylor, the cultural archivist who manages the facility, or one of her staff uses the displays of drums, baskets, and beadwork to introduce visitors to the culture and history of the Curve Lake people. The staff discuss traditional teachings, explain how particular items are used, and answer your questions. The Cultural Centre is on the main floor of the nation's government offices; look for the "Curve Lake Business Centre" sign.

The **Whetung Ojibwa Centre** (875 Mississauga St., 705/657-3661, www.whetung.com, 9am-5pm daily, free) is part souvenir shop, part art gallery, and part museum. It stocks everything from inexpensive doodads to high-quality works by regional aboriginal artists. Poke around the museum room on the lower level, which is crammed with buffalo bones, arrowheads and other artifacts, photographs, and traditional craftwork.

Another way to experience First Nations culture is to attend the annual **Curve Lake Pow Wow** (www.curvelakefirstnation.ca, 3rd weekend of Sept.), a festival of traditional music and dance that's open to the public. The Curve Lake Reserve is located 35 kilometers (22 miles) northwest of Peterborough on a peninsula surrounded by lakes; the only direct road access is from the north. From Peterborough, take Water Street/Highway 29 north, then continue north on Buckhorn Road/Highway 23. At Curve Lake Road/Highway 22, turn left (west); the road (called Mississauga St.) will turn south onto the reserve.

Warsaw Caves Conservation Area

If you're claustrophobic, you might want to skip the **Warsaw Caves** (289 Caves Rd., Warsaw, 705/652-3161 or 877/816-7604, www.warsawcaves.com, caves daily mid-Apr.-Nov., park and campground daily mid-May-mid-Oct., $12 per vehicle), a series of seven narrow caverns formed in the limestone bedrock. But if you or your kids enjoy

The Whetung Ojibwa Centre is part shop and part museum.

underground exploring, you can climb, slither, and crawl through these caves that range in size from 40 meters (130 feet) to 91 meters (300 feet) long. While you don't need technical climbing skills, you do need to clamber over rocks and scoot through dark narrow passageways; it's like an underground jungle gym.

There's no light in the caves, so you'll need a flashlight—a headlamp is best to keep your hands free (you can purchase one at the gatehouse). Wear sturdy shoes and clothes that can get dirty or wet, and don't enter the caves alone. Download the park's *Spelunkers' Guide* from their website, or pick up a copy at the gatehouse; it gives tips for tackling each cave.

The conservation area also has several short hiking trails, including one that leads to the **Disappearing River,** a quirk of nature in which the Indian River disappears into the limestone, reemerging farther downstream. Beyond this underground section, the Indian River is typically a placid place to paddle. Canoe rentals ($10 per hour, 2-hour minimum, $40 per day) are available. The caves are 25 kilometers (15 miles) northeast of Peterborough via County Road 4.

Kawartha Highlands Provincial Park

Ontario's largest park south of Algonquin, the wilderness expanse of **Kawartha Highlands** (613/332-3940, www.ontarioparks.com) encompasses 37,587 hectares (92,879 acres). With a series of interconnected lakes and waterways, this is an excellent spot for canoeing. Park staff have mapped out recommended canoe routes, with stopovers at some of the 121 backcountry campsites.

The park doesn't rent canoes. For canoes and other gear, contact **Adventure Outfitters** (1828 County Rd. 18, Lakefield, 705/652-7986, www.adventureoutfitters.ca, $30 per day, $50 per weekend) or **Wild Rock Outfitters** (169 Charlotte St., Peterborough, 705/745-9133, www.wildrock.net, $45 per day, $40 per additional day).

You can reach the park's east side via Highway 28 and west side from Highway 507. From Peterborough, the park's closest entrance is about 50 kilometers (30 miles) to the north.

Silent Lake Provincial Park

For an outdoor stopover en route to Algonquin Provincial Park's East Gate, visit **Silent Lake Provincial Park** (Hwy. 28, Cardiff, 613/339-2807, www.ontarioparks.com, $17 per vehicle). The park has hiking trails, beaches, three mountain-bike routes, canoeing, and two campgrounds, including 10 yurts.

The day-use area has a sandy beach and a large, grassy picnic area. From here, you can reach the easy, 1.5-kilometer (0.9-mile) **Lakehead Loop** hiking trail, which is good for kids. Serious hikers may want to circle the lake on the 15-kilometer (nine-mile) **Lakeshore Hiking Trail** (4-6 hours, strenuous). You can rent canoes and kayaks at the **Pincer Bay** canoe launch (8:30am-5pm daily July-Aug.). In the spring and fall, rentals are available at the park gatehouse.

Silent Lake is 75 kilometers (47 miles) northeast of Peterborough, off Highway 28. For groceries and other services, head south of the park to the town of Apsley or north to Bancroft.

ENTERTAINMENT AND EVENTS

Since 1991, the excellent **4th Line Theatre** (Winslow Farm, 779 Zion Line, Millbrook; box office 4 Tupper St., Millbrook, 705/932-4445 or 800/814-0055, www.4thlinetheatre.on.ca, July-Aug.) has performed original plays with Canadian historical themes on a farm 30 kilometers (19 miles) southwest of Peterborough. The outdoor shows start at 6pm; bring a picnic to enjoy before the performance, or order one ($13) from the box office a week in advance.

The **Peterborough Musicfest** (Del Crary Park, www.ptbomusicfest.ca, late June-Aug.) presents free outdoor concerts at 8pm Wednesday and Saturday in summer.

From Zimbabwe to Ontario

One of the Peterborough area's most unexpected attractions is out in the farmland south of the city. At the **Zim Art Rice Lake Gallery** (855 2nd Line, Bailieboro, 705/939-6144, www.zimart. ca, 11am-6pm daily June-mid-Oct., by appointment mid-Oct.-May), Fran Fearnley showcases high-quality stone carvings by artists from Zimbabwe.

After doing volunteer work in South Africa, Fearnley was introduced to the stonework, known as Shona sculpture, from nearby Zimbabwe. She now returns to Africa for two or three months every winter to scout out new artworks to exhibit and sell back in Ontario. She has established an artist-in-residence program that brings a stone sculptor to her property every summer to promote their work and teach sculpting workshops to both adults and children.

For two weeks every September, Fearnley sets up a sprawling outdoor exhibition, showing more than 200 sculptures outdoors among her trees and gardens. Outside of this September period, you can view a smaller selection of sculptures around the grounds. Admission is free, but donations, which support community programs in Zimbabwe, are welcome.

The gallery is 23 kilometers (14 miles) south of downtown Peterborough, outside the town of Bailieboro. From Highway 115, take Bensfort Road south to County Road 2. Turn right and follow County Road 2 for about eight kilometers (five miles), then turn right onto 2nd Line.

ACCOMMODATIONS

Peterborough has some standard chain motels on Lansdowne Street, both east and west of the city center. Outside of town, inns and cottage resorts sit on the shores of the many lakes.

Hotels and B&Bs

Overlooking the Otonabee River, **Angel's Rest B&B** (585 River Rd. S., 705/741-0500, www.angelsrestbbsuites.com, $189-249 d) feels like a cottage country escape, though you're just a few minutes' drive from the center of town, and the three air-conditioned suites, with whirlpool tubs, gas fireplaces, and mini kitchens, are far more plush and romantic than the average cabin. Take the canoe out for a paddle or watch the sunset from the dock; in the morning, welcoming hosts Gina and Bill Stewart deliver a hot breakfast to your suite.

The **Peterborough Inn and Suites Hotel** (312 George St. N., 705/876-6665 or 866/446-4451, www.peterboroughinn.com, $130-180) has a central location downtown. The 32 rooms are fairly generic, but all have fridges and microwaves, and you get free Wi-Fi, parking, and continental breakfast.

Lake Resorts

The Irwin family opened the **Irwin Inn** (1390 Irwin Rd., Douro-Dummer, 705/877-2240 or 800/461-6490, www.irwininn.com) on the south shore of Stoney Lake in 1947, and a stay here feels like going back to summer camp. In July and August, the roster of activities includes swimming and horseback riding. Accommodations comprise old-fashioned B&B rooms ($149 d) in the main inn, more upscale lakefront units, and multiple-bedroom country-style cottages. Except for the B&B rooms, lodging rates (from $225 pp per day) include hearty breakfasts and dinners. The inn is 40 kilometers (25 miles) northeast of Peterborough via County Roads 4 and 6.

Viamede Resort (595 Mt. Julian Viamede Rd., Woodview, 705/654-3344 or 800/461-1946, www.viamede.com, $229-319 d, cottages $319-509) is a traditional lake resort with modern amenities. There's tennis, shuffleboard, kayaks, canoes, stand-up paddleboards, a small beach, and an outdoor pool and hot tub. The resort's three restaurants are a casual pub, the traditional dining room, and the elegant **Inn at Mount Julian,** in an 1875 waterfront house. The best inn rooms and cottages overlook the lake. Rates include breakfast and most activities. Viamede is on Stoney

Lake's north shore, 40 kilometers (25 miles) northeast of Peterborough, off Highway 28, near Petroglyphs Provincial Park.

On the south shore of Rice Lake, the old-timey **Victoria Inn** (5316 Rice Lake Scenic Dr., Gore's Landing, 905/342-3261, www.thevictoriainn.ca, mid-Feb.-Dec., $80-125 s, $95-175 d) has nine cozy guest rooms, including the octagonal turret room with great lake views. The 1902 building is a little creaky, but the lakefront grounds, with an outdoor pool, are lovely. Rates include full breakfast; the country-style dining room, which features local lamb, trout, and produce when available, also serves lunch and dinner. The inn is 40 kilometers (25 miles) south of Peterborough and 20 kilometers (12.5 miles) north of Cobourg.

Camping

The **Warsaw Caves** (289 Caves Rd., Warsaw, 705/652-3161 or 877/816-7604, www.warsaw-caves.com, daily mid-May-mid-Oct., $12 per vehicle, camping $40) has a wooded 52-site campground. The individual sites don't have water or electrical hookups, but there are central flush toilets and showers, and drinking water is available throughout the campground.

Kawartha Highlands Provincial Park (613/332-3940, www.ontarioparks.com, reservation fee online $11, by phone $13) has 108 backcountry campsites. You can reach the campsites only by canoe—there are no walk-in sites or car camping—and a permit is required.

Silent Lake Provincial Park (Hwy. 28, Cardiff, 613/339-2807, www.ontarioparks.com, day use $16.25 per vehicle, tent sites $40, electrical sites $46) has two campgrounds with a total of 157 campsites and 10 yurts ($98). Most of the campsites are set amid the evergreens away from the lake. Campers who don't mind carrying their gear a short distance might choose one of the walk-in sites close to the lakeshore, at the corner of the Pincer Bay Campground, but it's a longer walk from the showers. Both campgrounds

have central showers, flush toilets, and laundry facilities.

FOOD

In downtown Peterborough, restaurants cluster around George Street, while funky Hunter Street, between George and Aylmer Streets, has lots of cafés and pubs. The dining rooms at most lake resorts are open to the public. To sample Ontario's signature pastry, eat your way along the **Kawarthas Northumberland Butter Tart Trail** (www.kawarthasnorthumberland.ca), or head directly to **Doo Doo's Bakery** (187 County Rd. 28, Bailieboro, 705/939-1394, www.doodoos.ca) near Rice Lake for some of the best. The **Peterborough Farmers Market** (Lansdowne St. W. at George St. S., 705/742-3276, www.peterboroughfarmersmarket.com, 7am-1pm Sat.) operates outdoors in Morrow Park on the south end of downtown from May through October. It moves into the park's Morrow Building November through April.

If you like your coffee, pastries, salads, and sandwiches with a water view, park on the shady riverside terrace at the **Silver Bean Café** (130 King St., 705/749-0535, www.silverbeancafe.com; 8am-8pm Mon.-Fri., 9am-8pm Sat.-Sun. May, 8am-9pm Mon.-Fri., 9am-9pm Sat.-Sun. June-Aug., 8am-6pm Mon.-Fri., 9am-6pm Sat.-Sun. Sept.-mid-Oct., $3-12) in Millennium Park. At cheery little **Blackhoney Desserts and Coffeehouse** (221 Hunter St. W., 705/750-0014, www.blackhoneydesserts.com, 8am-10pm Mon.-Thurs., 8am-11pm Fri., 10am-11pm Sat., 10am-6pm Sun., $5-10), you can have a sandwich or a salad, but don't leave without sampling the sweets.

Craving enchiladas, *pollo con mole* (chicken with a chocolaty mole sauce), or traditional Mexican tacos? Say *hola* to **La Hacienda Restaurante Mexico** (190 Hunter St. W., 705/742-1559, www.lahaciendamexico.com, 11am-11pm Mon.-Sat., 4pm-8pm Sun., $8-21). Ask for their selection of salsas to spice up your dish.

The daily specials invite you to be a bit adventurous at **Brio Gusto** (182 Charlotte St., 705/745-6100, www.briogusto.com, 11:30am-9pm Sun.-Tues., 11:30am-10pm Wed.-Thurs., 11:30am-11pm Fri.-Sat., $13-24), an unfussy contemporary bistro with garage-door windows that open to the street. You might find grilled avocado stuffed with salsa and feta cheese, or soba noodles in a spicy coconut broth, though you can stay homey, too, with burgers, pizzas, or ribs. Try the "Duck 'n Greens" salad topped with snap peas, strawberries, and shredded duck confit.

Elements Restaurant (140 King St., 705/876-1116, www.elementsrestaurant. ca, 11:30am-10pm Mon.-Thurs., 11:30am-11pm Fri.-Sat., 11am-9pm Sun., lunch $9-21, dinner $18-33) has all the "elements" of a first-rate meal, starting from the garden-like dining room with sunny yellow walls. The kitchen sources locally whenever possible, and everything tastes fresh, from the delicious pear, watercress, and blue cheese salad, to the hearty sandwiches (the pulled barbecued wild boar is popular), to chicken stuffed with sun-dried tomato and olive tapenade. In the evening, you can graze a selection of tapas ($9-16), or choose larger plates.

INFORMATION AND SERVICES

Peterborough and the Kawarthas Tourism runs a year-round **Visitors Centre** (1400 Crawford Dr., 705/742-2201 or 800/461-6424, www.thekawarthas.ca, 9am-5pm Mon.-Fri., 10am-5pm Sat.-Sun.) just off Highway 115/7 south of the city center.

GETTING THERE AND AROUND

Peterborough is 140 kilometers (87 miles) northeast of Toronto. By car, the most direct route is to take Highway 401 east to Highway 115 north. **Greyhound** (www.greyhound.ca) runs frequent buses between Toronto and the **Peterborough Bus Station** (220 Simcoe St., 705/743-8045, 1.75-2.25 hours, adults $16-29, seniors $14-20, students $14-26, ages 2-11 $12-22).

You need a car to explore Peterborough and vicinity, since many attractions are outside the city proper, and even in town, sights aren't within easy walking distance. Outside of town, navigating around the Kawartha region requires careful attention to your map or GPS, since there are few direct roads and many lakes to circumnavigate. Allow more time to reach your destination than the mileage might indicate.

Lake Ontario

As you head east from Toronto along Highway 401, suburban sprawl and industrial developments give way to farms, orchards, and beaches. A string of towns along Lake Ontario—including Port Hope, Cobourg, Grafton, and Brighton—make convenient stops en route to Prince Edward County, Kingston, or points farther east, or as getaway destinations for a quick holiday.

Northumberland Tourism (600 William St., Cobourg, 905/372-3329, ext. 6257, or 866/401-3278, www.northumberlandtourism.com) provides information about the region, including details about festivals, special events, cycling routes, and other activities.

PORT HOPE

Port Hope's draw is its historic downtown, where many of the well-preserved buildings date to the late 1800s. Wander along Walton Street to browse in the boutiques, antiques shops, and bookstores, or hang out in one of the cafés. Pick up a brochure outlining self-guided walking or driving tours of the historic district at the **Municipality of Port Hope Tourism Office** (20 Queen St., 905/885-2004 or 888/767-8467, www.porthopetourism.ca). You might also check what's happening at the **Capitol Theatre** (20 Queen St., 905/885-1071, www.capitoltheatre.com), a restored 1930s theater that hosts plays, concerts, and films.

Port Hope is 100 kilometers (60 miles) east of Toronto, off Highway 401. It's just over an hour's ride on **VIA Rail** (888/842-7245, www.viarail.com, one-way adults $26-42, ages 2-11 $18-22) to Port Hope Station (Hayward St.).

Accommodations and Food

The Waddell (1 Walton St., 905/885-2449 or 800/361-1957, www.thewaddell.ca, $159-199), a traditionally furnished inn in an 1845 brick building, fits right in with downtown's historic ambience. Rates include Wi-Fi and a light breakfast downstairs in **Trattoria Gusto** (www.trattoriagusto.ca), which also serves lunch and dinner.

Stop for a beer or creative cocktail at **Black Beans Steakhouse and Lounge** (63 Walton St., 905/885-1888, www.blackbeans.ca, 4:30pm-9:30pm Sun.-Thurs., 4:30pm-10:30pm Fri.-Sat., $14-24), a popular watering hole with Southwestern flair. If you're hungry, tuck into a burger, a smoky pork empanada, salmon with mango-tomatillo salsa, or a steak.

COBOURG

Like nearby Port Hope, Cobourg has a historic downtown district, as well as a pretty sandy beach, just a short stroll from the town center. Before you get too sandy, though, explore King Street and take a peek into stately **Victoria Hall** (55 King St. W., 8am-5pm Mon.-Fri., 1pm-4pm Sat.), built in 1860. The courtroom on the first floor is a replica of London's Old Bailey. On the top floor is the **Art Gallery of Northumberland** (905/372-0333, www.artgalleryofnorthumberland.com, 10am-4pm Tues.-Fri., 1pm-4pm Sat., donation), which shows contemporary works.

The **Town of Cobourg Business and Tourism Centre** (212 King St. W.,

905/372-5481 or 888/262-6874, www.cobourgtourism.ca) can tell you more about what's happening around town.

Cobourg is off Highway 401, 120 kilometers (75 miles) east of Toronto. **VIA Rail** (888/842-7245, www.viarail.com) trains stop in Cobourg (563 Division St.) en route between Toronto (1-1.25 hours, one-way adults $28-46, ages 2-11 $19-22) and Kingston (1-1.25 hours, one-way adults $40-65, ages 2-11 $27-33).

Accommodations and Food

What do you get when you cross an upscale hotel with a jail? You get something like the weirdly fun **King George Inn and Spa** (77 Albert St., 905/373-4610, www.thekinggeorgeinn.com, $89-169 d), set inside the former Cobourg Jail, which housed prisoners as recently as 1997. Even if you don't stay here, visit a small exhibit area in the former solitary confinement cells. Many of the 26 guest rooms retain the cell bars, bunks, or original stainless-steel jail showers, although some are simply standard hotel rooms. Bring your own handcuffs.

Like pie? At **Betty's Pies & Tarts** (7380 County Rd. 2, between Port Hope and Cobourg, 905/377-7437, 8am-5pm Mon.-Fri., 9am-5pm Sat.-Sun. July-Aug., call for off-season hours), the tasty pastries come in both full-size and convenient single-serving sizes—the better to sample more varieties! The apple pies are good, but resisting the gooey butter tarts is futile.

If you're in town on a Saturday, stop into the **Cobourg Farmers Market** (Market Square, 2nd St. and Albert St., 7am-1pm Sat. May-Oct., 8am-1pm Sat. Nov.-Dec., www.cobourgfarmersmarket.ca), which has been supplying residents and visitors with locally grown produce, cheeses, meats, breads, and pastries since 1839.

GRAFTON

Grafton is 130 kilometers (80 miles) east of Toronto and 10 kilometers (6 miles) east of Cobourg. The main attraction in town—St.

Anne's Spa—is north of Highway 401; Grafton Village lies to the south.

Accommodations and Food

Set on nearly 200 hectares (500 acres) high in the hills, ★ **St. Anne's Spa** (1009 Massey Rd., Grafton, 905/349-2493 or 888/346-6772, www.spavillage.ca) feels like a secluded European health retreat, where you can settle in for a day of pampering. The sprawling property is built around the elegant stone main inn, but you may not care about the resort's heritage once you've had a shiatsu massage, mud wrap, or lymphatic drainage treatment. You can take a yoga or meditation class, go for a swim (the outdoor pool looks across the hills to Lake Ontario), rejuvenate in the eucalyptus steam room, or indulge in a wide range of other spa treatments.

Overnight guests can choose a traditionally furnished room in the main inn or one of several cottages around the property. Some cottages are quite a distance from the main inn and spa building (the hotel does offer shuttle services), so they're best for a girlfriends' getaway or for couples who want to cocoon.

Spa services start at $65 for a half-hour massage, but you can choose from a variety of packages, such as an All-Inclusive Day ($170-220 pp), which includes $120 worth of spa services, a yoga or other wellness class, lunch, afternoon tea, and use of the pools and other facilities; add round-trip transportation from Toronto on VIA Rail for $85 pp. Overnight packages, including lodging, three meals, and spa treatments, start at $299-515 per person per day. Most visitors to the spa stay put, so you don't need a car. You can arrange for spa staff to pick you up at the VIA Rail station in Cobourg.

If you're passing through Grafton and want a bite to eat, the **Grafton Village Inn** (10830 County Rd. 2, 905/349-3024, www.graftonvillageinn.ca, 9am-2:30pm Mon.-Fri. 8am-2:30pm Sat.-Sun., lunch $14-17) makes salads and excellent (if somewhat pricey) sandwiches. Try the Brie BLT (bacon, lettuce, and tomato), made richer with the addition of melted Brie cheese.

BRIGHTON

This part of Ontario is apple-growing country, and Highway 2, which parallels Highway 401 closer to the lake, is dotted with orchards and farm stands. Brighton celebrates the rosy fruit every autumn with a weekend-long **Applefest** (www.applefest.ca, Sept.).

You can pick your own apples at

When you need a butter tart, stop at Betty's Pies & Tarts.

Cricklewood Farm (27 Grandview Rd., Brighton, 613/475-4293, www.cricklewood. ca). Another highlight, especially for kids, is their **corn maze** (9:30am-4:30pm Sun.-Fri., 9:30am-6pm Sat. Aug.-early Nov.), where you have to find your way through the maze-like rows of corn. The farm is off County Road 2, about three kilometers (1.9 miles) west of Brighton.

Presqu'ile Provincial Park

As its French name suggests, **Presqu'ile Provincial Park** (328 Presqu'ile Pkwy., Brighton, 613/475-4324, www.ontarioparks. com or www.friendsofpresquile.on.ca, $14.50 per vehicle) is "almost an island." Set on a peninsula jutting into Lake Ontario, it's like two parks in one; the section closest to the mainland is lined with flat, wide beaches, while the section extending between Presqu'ile Bay and the lake has both marshes and woods.

The park sees an abundance of migrating birds in the spring and fall; May and September are particularly popular with birders. Frogs, fish, and other creatures entertain kids at the **Nature Centre** (10am-4pm daily July-early Sept.); in summer, park staff organize guided hikes, kids' programs, and evening campfires. A lighthouse stands guard at the far end of the park, and the nearby **Lighthouse Interpretive Centre** (10am-5pm daily July-early Sept., 10am-4pm Sat.-Sun. late May-June and early Sept.-mid-Oct.) has exhibits about the area's natural and nautical past.

On Wednesday and Thursday in July-August, you can hop on the free shuttle bus that runs to Presqu'ile from downtown Brighton (Chamber of Commerce office, 74 Main St., 613/475-2775), on the hour between 10am and 3pm.

Accommodations and Camping

Presqu'ile's 394 campsites in eight **campgrounds** (328 Presqu'ile Pkwy., Brighton, 613/475-4324, www.ontarioparks. com, late Apr.-mid-Oct., tent sites $40-44, electrical sites $46-50, reservation fee online $11, by phone $13) are popular with families. The most requested, particularly among RV campers, are the waterfront sites in the High Bluff campground, although they are not very shaded.

In town, a comfortable place to stay is the **Brighton Inn Bed & Breakfast** (40 Young St., Brighton, 613/475-9706 or 888/895-5807, www.brightoninn.com, $85-95 s, $105-115 d), with four guest rooms in an 1890s Victorian. Lemon crepes are one of owners Don and Nikki Parks's breakfast specialties, and they'll keep your coffee cup filled while giving you tips about the area.

Practicalities

Brighton is 160 kilometers (100 miles) east of Toronto via Highway 401. It's about a 45-minute drive to the Prince Edward County wineries. Learn more about the region at the **Brighton and District Chamber of Commerce** (74 Main St., Brighton, 613/475-2775 or 877/475-2775, www.brightonchamber.ca).

Prince Edward County

Once a predominantly agricultural area, Prince Edward County has been reborn as a wine-producing district. County farms have always raised tomatoes, apples, and other produce (more than 70 canneries once operated here), but the region has jumped on the local-food bandwagon, with numerous restaurants featuring the county's bounty. What does that mean for visitors? Wine tasting and good eating!

Prince Edward County is located along Lake Ontario between Toronto and Kingston, south of the mainland towns of Trenton, Belleville, and Napanee. Lodgings, restaurants, galleries, and shops are concentrated in the communities of Picton, Bloomfield, and Wellington. The largest group of wineries is in the Wellington-Hillier area on the county's west side, with others scattered around the region.

High season is May through mid-October, and the county is especially busy in July and August. For fewer crowds, come midweek in summer or visit in June or September. In early spring and late fall, some businesses reduce their hours (many restaurants close Tues.-Wed. off-season), and from January till March the county seems to hibernate. Some lodgings remain open for winter getaways, but if you're hoping to visit particular wineries or eateries, confirm first that they're not on holiday themselves.

Lastly, don't mistake Prince Edward *County* for Prince Edward *Island,* the province in Atlantic Canada, even though, confusingly, Prince Edward County is also on an island. Even more confusingly, the county was once a peninsula connected to the mainland by a narrow strip of land, known as "the Carrying Place." In 1889, the Murray Canal was built at the Carrying Place, linking the Bay of Quinte with Lake Ontario but severing the county from the mainland.

★ WINERIES

Wine-making is a relatively new venture in Prince Edward County. The first winery opened in 2001, and most of the more than 35 producers are still quite small. At many properties you might meet the winemaker, and tours, if offered, tend to be informal. The county is best known for its white wines, although many wineries now produce reds as well.

The **Prince Edward County Winegrowers Association** (613/921-7100, www.thecountywines.com) has additional wine-touring tips on their website. They publish a helpful wine-touring map that you can access online or pick up at visitor information offices, hotels, and wineries around the county. Most wineries charge a small fee for tastings, which they'll often waive if you purchase wine.

Wellington

Ira Chadsey, who lived in the 1800s on this property just east of Wellington, erected a series of stone cairns on the land. According to legend, Ira believed he'd be reincarnated as a white horse and the cairns would mark his way home. He needed that guidance, perhaps, because he shot and killed himself in his maple syrup shack.

So what does this legend have to do with wine? Nothing, really, except it gave its name to the **By Chadsey's Cairns Winery and Vineyard** (17432 Hwy. 33, 613/399-2992, www.bychadseyscairns.com, 11am-6pm daily June-Oct., 11am-6pm Sat.-Sun. Mar.-May and Nov.-Dec.), a laid-back producer of riesling, gamay noir, a dry rosé, and chenin blanc, among others. Their tasting room is in a brick apple storehouse, and they make wine in the former carriage barn. There are no official tours, but you're welcome to explore the property, which includes an old cemetery. If

Prince Edward County

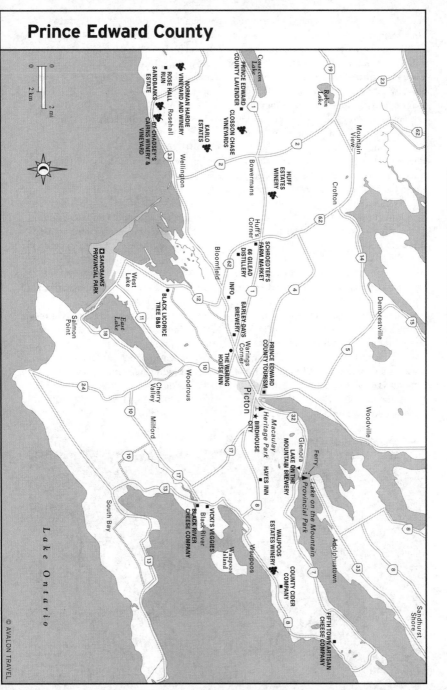

you ask, they'll tell you about the cairns and other legends.

With a tasting bar in a cool, industrial hut-like structure, the **Norman Hardie Vineyard and Winery** (1152 Greer Rd., 613/399-5297, www.normanhardie.com, 10am-6pm daily Apr.-Dec., 11am-5pm Mon.-Sat. Jan.-Mar.) specializes in pinot noir and chardonnay, and also produces pinot gris, muscadet, and cabernet franc. Tours are available, but staff suggest that you phone ahead. A wood-fired oven churns out freshly baked pizzas on their popular **Pizza Patio** (11am-6pm Thurs.-Mon. July-Aug., 11am-6pm Sat.-Sun. May-June and Sept.-Oct.).

Known for chardonnay and pinot noir, **Rose Hall Run** (1243 Greer Rd., 613/399-1183 or 888/399-1183, www.rosehallrun.com, 10am-6pm daily Apr.-mid-Oct., call for off-season hours) is a casual place where you might meet owners Dan and Lynn Sullivan in the wine shop or around the tasting bar. You can pick up cheese, bread, and other picnic fare at the on-site **Greer Road Grocer**.

Want more wine stops? Other Wellington-area wineries include **Closson Chase Vineyards** (629 Closson Rd., Hillier, 613/399-1418 or 888/201-2300, www.clossonchase.com, 11am-5pm daily. mid-Apr.-Dec., 11am-5pm Sat.-Sun. Jan.-mid-Apr.), **Karlo Estates** (561 Danforth Rd., 613/399-3000, www.karloestates.com, 11am-6pm daily May-Oct., 11am-5pm Sun.-Fri., 11am-6pm Sat. Nov.-Apr.), and **Sandbanks Estate Wintery** (17598 Hwy. 33, 613/399-1839, www.sandbankswinery.com, 10:30am-6pm daily May-Oct., 10:30am-5pm daily Nov.-Apr., tasting bar from 11am).

Bloomfield

One of the county's more established wineries is **Huff Estates** (2274 County Rd. 1, 613/393-5802, www.huffestates.com, 10am-6pm daily), which makes riesling, chardonnay, pinot gris, and pinot noir. You can drop in for a guided tasting; winery tours are available by appointment. Their sunny outdoor **restaurant** (noon-4pm Thurs.-Mon. spring-fall, weather permitting, $13-19) uses lots of locally sourced ingredients in salads, sandwiches, and seafood dishes.

Adjacent to the winery, the **Oeno Gallery** (2274 County Rd. 1, 613/393-2216, www.oenogallery.com, 10am-6pm daily) exhibits high-end contemporary art by international artists, including some with Ontario connections. Outside, you can wander among the more than 40 works on view in the Sculpture Garden (donation).

wine tasting in Prince Edward County

Waupoos

The county's oldest winery, **Waupoos Estates Winery** (3016 County Rd. 8, 613/476-8338, www.waupooswinery.com, 10:30am-6pm daily May-mid-Oct., 11am-5pm Thurs.-Mon. mid-Oct.-Dec, 11am-5pm Sat.-Sun. Mar.-Apr., call for winter hours) opened in 2001, east of Picton, on manicured grounds overlooking the water. While they produce a variety of wines, they're best known for their riesling (white) and baco (red). They also make the county's first ice wine.

Tastings and several tour options are available, including the basic tour (11am, 1pm, and 3pm daily July-Aug., 11am, 1pm, and 3pm Sat.-Sun. Apr.-June and Sept.-Oct., $5). The winery's **Gazebo Restaurant** (11:30am-9pm Wed.-Sun. May-mid-Nov., call for off-season hours, lunch $12-20, dinner $26-32) serves sandwiches, salads, pastas, and a couple of larger plates midday, with contemporary locally focused fare in the evenings.

The County Cider Company (657 Bongards Crossroad, at County Rd. 8, 613/476-1022, www.countycider.com, 10am-6pm daily May-Oct., call for off-season hours) makes both hard (alcoholic) and nonalcoholic apple cider, as well as a unique ice cider, a sweet dessert wine that's similar to grape-based ice wine. They fire up their pizza oven (11am-5:45pm daily July-Aug., 11am-5:45pm Tues.-Sun. late May-June and Sept.-mid-Oct.) spring to fall, serving pizzas, burgers, and salads outdoors with views across the vineyard to the lake.

BREWERIES AND DISTILLERIES

Lest you think the county is only about wine, there are breweries and a distillery, too. **Barley Days Brewery** (13730 Hwy. 33, Picton, 613/476-7468, www.barleydaysbrewery.com, 11am-5:30pm Mon.-Thurs., 11am-6pm Fri.-Sat., 11am-5pm Sun.) brews pale ale, lager, stout, and several seasonal varieties. You can take a tour (11am-4pm Sat.) that includes tastings.

Brown ale and cream ale are the main products at the small **Lake on the Mountain Brewery** (www.lakeonthemountain.com/brewery). Sample them across the road at **Miller House Café-Brasserie** (275 County Rd. 7, 613/476-1321, www.lakeonthemountain.com, 9am-sunset daily July-Aug., 11am-sunset daily late-May-June and Sept.-Oct.), where the terrace has spectacular views above Picton Bay.

The tasting room at **66 Gilead Distillery**

The tasting room at 66 Gilead Distillery is inside this ornate homestead.

(66 Gilead Rd., Bloomfield, 613/393-1890, www.66gileaddistillery.com, 11am-5pm Wed.-Mon. summer, call for off-season hours) is set in an ornate 1874 brick homestead, once the residence of a wealthy hops grower. You can sample vodka, gin, whiskey, and *shochu* brewed on-site in a copper still. Also on the property is the **Carriage House Cooperage** (46 Gilead Rd., Bloomfield, 613/243-3762, www.thecarriagehousecooperage.com), where owner Pete Bradford makes finely crafted barrels (he apprenticed for seven years to learn the trade) and offers tastings of his barrel-aged wine vinegars.

For more microbreweries as well as local cheese-makers in and around Prince Edward County, follow the **Bay of Quinte Cheddar and Ale Trail** (www.tourism.bayofquinte.ca). The online map directs you to more than a dozen regional producers.

SIGHTS

At **Macaulay Heritage Park** (35 Church St., at Union St., Picton, 613/476-3833, www.pecounty.on.ca, 9:30am-4:30pm Wed.-Sun. mid-May-Aug., 9:30am-4:30pm Sat.-Sun. Sept., adults $4.50, seniors and students $3.50, ages 5-12 $2.50, families $11.50), the 1820s **Church of St. Mary Magdalene** is now a museum of county history. Follow the timeline exhibit to learn about the area's settlement and development. Many of the county's earliest settlers were Loyalists, British supporters who left the United States in the late 1700s, after the American Revolutionary War. In the room adjacent to the altar is one of the county's curiosities: a tombstone belonging to a Mr. Pierce, whose stone says he died on the nonexistent February 31, 1860. Historians have never been able to unravel the source of this error. Next door to the church is the 1830 **Macaulay House,** where costumed guides will tell you about Reverend William Macaulay (1794-1874) and other settlers who lived in the county in the middle of the 19th century.

★ Sandbanks Provincial Park

With some of the best beaches on Lake Ontario, the lakefront **Sandbanks Provincial Park** (County Rd. 12, 613/393-3319, www.ontarioparks.com and www.friendsofsandbanks.org, late Apr.-mid-Oct., $17 per vehicle), one of the most visited destinations in the Ontario Park system, is also known for its giant sand dunes.

The largest of the park's beaches is the long, sandy **Sandbanks Beach,** which extends along Lake Ontario for nearly 11

the dunes at Sandbanks Provincial Park

Prince Edward County's birds nest in style at the quirky Birdhouse City.

Sandbanks is 18 kilometers (11 miles) west of Picton; take County Road 10 to County Road 11. From Bloomfield, it's 13 kilometers (eight miles) southwest on County Road 12. Coming from Bloomfield, you can bypass the park's main gate and pay your admission fee at the parking area, which may save time on busy days.

Birdhouse City

The county's birds nest in style at the quirky **Birdhouse City** (Macaulay Mountain Conservation Area, 224 County Rd. 8, Picton, 613/968-3434, www.quinteconservation.ca, dawn-dusk daily, free), a large field populated with more than 100 birdhouses designed as replicas of historic structures and other buildings from near and far. There's a log cabin, a church, and a B&B, even a McDonald's and the Leaning Tower of Pisa! The birdhouses are just east of Picton; take Union Street east, which becomes County Road 8.

Lake on the Mountain Provincial Park

If you don't know the story behind **Lake on the Mountain Provincial Park** (296 County Rd. 7, Picton, 613/393-3319, www.ontarioparks.com, dawn-dusk daily, free), you might think it's just a pretty little body of water. But what makes the lake a curiosity is that it has a constant flow of fresh water with no obvious source. Early settlers to the region assumed it must be a bottomless lake, and even modern scientists, who believe that underground springs now feed the lake, haven't been able to unravel how it formed, since the lake is 60 meters (195 feet) higher than nearby Lake Ontario.

The lake is east of Picton; follow Highway 33 to County Road 7. The parking lot overlooks Picton Bay; Lake on the Mountain is across the road.

Prince Edward County Lavender

Take a deep breath as you wander the aromatic purple fields at the 1.2-hectare (three-acre)

kilometers (7 miles). Access to the beach is only from the south end, but you can walk along the beach literally for miles. You can also hike to the dunes along the 2.5-kilometer (1.5-mile) **Dunes Trail.** The three-kilometer (1.8-mile) **Outlet Beach,** on a sliver of land between Lake Ontario and East Lake, is more sheltered, shallower, and popular with families. The famous sand dunes are at **Dunes Beach** on West Lake, where the water can be a little warmer than in Lake Ontario. The Outlet River is a good spot for **canoeing.** You can rent canoes at the Wood Yard, adjacent to the river.

The park's **Visitors Centre** (10am-4:30pm daily mid-June-early Sept.) has exhibits about the animals and plants that live in the Sandbanks area and often has snakes, fish, or other creatures on hand. In summer, the park offers **guided dunes walks,** evening campfire programs, and other activities. Because the park gets so crowded in summer, particularly on weekends, try to visit in late spring or early fall, particularly if you're camping.

Prince Edward County Lavender (732 Closson Rd., Hillier, 613/399-1855, www. peclavender.com, 11am-5pm daily mid-Apr.-mid-Oct., 11am-5pm Wed.-Sun. mid-Oct.-Dec., $3) lavender and herb farm. In their boutique, you'll find soaps, lotions, teas, and other products, all made from the farm's plants.

ENTERTAINMENT AND EVENTS

Built in the 1920s, the **Regent Theatre** (224 Main St., Picton, 613/476-8416, www. theregenttheatre.org) shows movies and hosts concerts and other special events. The region's professional summer theater, the **Festival Players of Prince Edward County** (613/476-1991 or 866/584-1991, www. festivalplayers.ca, July-Aug.) presents shows at wineries and other county venues. **Taste Community Grown** (www.tastecommunitygrown.com, Sept.) celebrates the county's local food and wine, with tastings and special events.

SHOPPING

Shops, galleries, and cafés line the Main Streets of Picton, Bloomfield, and Wellington. Farther afield, you'll find farm stands, cheese makers, and orchards. All the wineries have shops where you can buy wine and wine-related souvenirs.

Art Galleries

Numerous artists work in the county, and you can follow the **Arts Trail** (www.artstrail. ca), a self-guided tour of galleries and studios. Wellington, Bloomfield, and Picton each have clusters of galleries, while others are around the county. Access the Arts Trail guide online or pick up a brochure at county tourist offices, hotels, and galleries.

Arts on Main (223 Main St., Picton, 613/476-5665, www.artsonmaingallery.ca, 10am-5pm daily, call for winter hours), an artist cooperative, shows works by its members, who all live and work in the county. **The Red Barns** (167 White Chapel Rd., Picton,

613/476-6808, www.theredbarns.com, 10am-5pm daily May-mid-Oct.) bills itself as "an artisan's playground," and whether you want to make art, see it made by the artists-in-residence, or browse locally created works in the gallery and shop, there's something for you on this former farm. Check their website for a schedule of workshops in stained glass, glass blowing, pottery, painting, wood carving, and blacksmithing. The property is about two kilometers (1.2 miles) north of downtown Picton, off Highway 49.

Bookshops

Books and Company (289 Main St., Picton, 613/476-3037, www.pictonbookstore.com, 9am-6pm Mon.-Sat., 10am-5pm Sun.) is a large independent bookstore that hosts readings and other literary events. It's connected to **Miss Lily's Cafe** (613/476-9289, $4-8), a light and airy spot to have a coffee, pastry, or light lunch—or curl up with a book.

Gifts

An eclectic little shop whose motto is "Celebrating Canadian design and lakeside living," **Kokito** (285 Main St., Bloomfield, 613/393-2828, www.kokito.ca, 10am-5pm daily) stocks handcrafted canoe paddles, salad tongs, soaps, leather goods, cards, and more—all Canadian-made.

Gourmet Treats

You can sample handmade goat's- and sheep's-milk cheeses in the tasting room at **Fifth Town Artisan Cheese Company** (4309 County Rd. 8, Waupoos, 613/476-5755, www.fifthtown.ca, 10am-6pm daily summer, call for off-season hours). The dairy itself is a "green" building, made from more than 80 percent recycled materials.

Established in 1901, the **Black River Cheese Company** (913 County Rd. 13, Milford, 613/476-2575 or 888/252-5787, www. blackrivercheese.com, 9am-7pm daily July-early Sept., 9am-5pm daily Apr.-June and early Sept.-Dec., 11am-5pm Tues. and Thurs.-Sun. Jan.-Mar.), 11 kilometers (eight miles)

south of Picton, specializes in cheddar cheese. The aged varieties are deliciously flavorful, and the fresh curds are properly squeaky.

ACCOMMODATIONS
Wellington

The owners of Toronto's übercool Drake Hotel completely rebuilt a former lakeside lodging to create the **Drake Devonshire Inn** (24 Wharf St., 613/399-3338, www.drakedevonshire. ca, $229-599 d), where the ambiance is part country cottage and part hip boutique hotel. The guest rooms—some in the original circa-1897 inn and others in a new addition—range from the Stargazer Crash Pad (with a skylight but no windows) to the striking 658-square-foot Owner's Suite with a peaked ceiling and water views. Musicians perform in the window-lined **restaurant** overlooking the lake, which is open for breakfast, lunch, dinner, snacks, and booze.

Bloomfield

Owners Diane and Bruce Milan used to be organic farmers in Minnesota before decamping to the county's milder Canadian climate. They operate the cozy **Hillsdale House** (332 Main St., 613/393-2952, www.bbcanada.com, $135 d), a two-room B&B in their 1890s home. Diane serves a three-course hot breakfast each morning, and Bruce is also a blacksmith; stop into his **Island Forge Gallery** (www.pec. on.ca/islandforge) out back to see what he's working on.

Art and the outdoors mix at **Black Licorice Tree B&B** (1287 County Rd. 12, 613/970-3031, www.blacklicoricetree.com, $119 s, $139 d), an 1892 Victorian on a three-hectare (seven-acre) property; rates include canoes and a day pass to Sandbanks Provincial Park nearby. Owners Mark and Melanie have outfitted the three cozy guest rooms (two in the main house, one in the adjacent carriage house) with a funky assortment of furnishings. Melanie is a ceramic artist, who'll happily show you her **Mena Dragonfly Studio** (www.menadragonfly.com); breakfast is served on her handmade plates.

On the grounds of the Huff Estates winery, **Inn at Huff Estates** (2274 County Rd. 1, 613/393-1414 or 866/484-4667, www.huffestates.com, $199-269 d) is a modern building with 21 guest rooms done in a woodsy, cottage style. All have private patios; some overlook the interior courtyard, while others look onto the vineyards. Rates include a breakfast buffet.

Picton

You don't have to be an artist to stay at **The Red Barns** (167 White Chapel Rd., 613/476-6808, www.theredbarns.com, May-Oct., $90-125 d), but artist-owners Heather Watson and Peter Josic have decorated the three guest rooms in their farmhouse with original stained glass inspired by the likes of Frank Lloyd Wright and Charles Rennie Mackintosh. Families might prefer the one-bedroom coach house ($150), with midcentury modern furnishings, a kitchen, a living room with sleep sofa, and more stained glass. Rates for the farmhouse rooms, but not the coach house, include breakfast.

The former owner of the county's oldest inn moved it across the island and spent more than 40 years painstakingly putting it back together. The current owners of the **Hayes Inn** (2319 County Rd. 8, 613/476-6904, www.hayesinn.com, $175-195 d), on the road between Picton and Waupoos, finished the job, reopening this bright and airy four-room lodging with cream-colored furnishings, white duvets, flat-screen TVs, and new baths. You get a full breakfast that might include crepes with local cheeses and fruit or eggs with freshly made salsa—nothing like its early rough-hewn tavern days.

Don't want a fussy Victorian look? The **Loyalist Lofts** (56 Mary St., 613/471-1169, www.loyalistlofts.ca, $159-189 d), in a restored 1877 brick home, rents three spacious apartments furnished in a relaxed modern and old-fashioned mix. Both the first-floor Wellington suite and the upstairs Picton unit have two bedrooms, while the two-level Bloomfield suite has a sleep sofa in the living room and a bedroom above. Rates include Wi-Fi and a pass to Sandbanks Provincial Park. Breakfast isn't provided, but all units have kitchens, and you're just one block from Main Street.

Food is an important part of a stay at the elegant **Merrill Inn** (343 Main St. E., 613/476-7451 or 866/567-5969, www.merrillinn.com, $220-299 d), a 13-room lodging in an 1878 brick Victorian. Not only does the inn have a fine restaurant (5:30pm-9pm Tues.-Sat.), but you get a copious breakfast buffet, as well as afternoon tea or lemonade with freshly baked cookies. The guest rooms, spread out over three floors, are all different, but all are furnished with antiques and period pieces; some have fireplaces, and the Fireplace Suite even has a working wood-burning one.

At the **Waring House Inn** (395 Sandy Hook Rd., 613/476-7492 or 800/621-4956, www.waringhouse.com, $124-299 d), the inn, garden-view restaurant, and lively **Barley Room Pub** (with music several nights a week) are in the 1860s stone farmhouse; the guest rooms upstairs are cozy but tiny. Rooms are more spacious in two newer lodges, furnished with classic pieces from the local Gibbard Furniture company. The stone Vineyard View cottage ($299 d) overlooks the gardens. Also on the property are a cooking school and the **Folkworks Studio Gallery** (613/471-0346, www.danielis.ca), where you can chat with artist Robert Danielis. Rates include full breakfast.

Under the same ownership as the Waring House, the upscale ★ **Claramount Inn & Spa** (97 Bridge St., 613/476-2709 or 800/679-7756, www.claramountinn.com, $189-239 d) is a sunny yellow Colonial Revival mansion built in 1906. The seven spacious suites in the main inn have antiques, large soaker tubs, and some fireplaces; three suites in the neighboring carriage house have a more rustic country style. You can swim in the heated saltwater pool year-round (it has a retractable roof). Rates include breakfast; in the evenings, the chef at **Clara's Restaurant** (dinner $22-37), overlooking the harbor, emphasizes local ingredients in contemporary dishes.

Once a church parsonage, the stately limestone Victorian that houses **The Manse** (10 Chapel St., 613/476-1006 or 877/676-1006, www.themanse.ca, $189-259) is now a boutique bed-and-breakfast. Decorated in rich burgundies and browns, the seven upscale guest rooms are filled with deluxe amenities, from gas fireplaces, iPod docks, and plush robes to refillable water bottles. Outside, sipping drinks beside the kidney-shaped saltwater pool, surrounded by manicured gardens, you'd never know you're just off Picton's Main Street.

Camping

Sandbanks Provincial Park (County Rd. 12, 613/393-3319, www.ontarioparks.com, late Apr.-mid-Oct., $17 per vehicle, tent sites $40-44, electrical sites $46-50) has 549 campsites in five campgrounds, including 174 sites with electricity. The prime sites are at Camper's Beach, right on the lake in the Outlet River Campground. Eager campers often book these sites five months in advance. From Richardson's Campground, it's a short walk to Sandbanks Beach and a slightly longer walk to the Dunes Beach. All the campgrounds have central showers and flush toilets.

The park also has two cottages, with kitchens and linens, for rent. The **Maple Rest Heritage House** ($312) is a four-bedroom, four-bath brick Victorian home that sleeps eight. The smaller lakeside **Jacques Cottage** ($170) can sleep up to six; the small master bedroom upstairs has a double bed, an adjacent open loft space has two twins, and there's a sleep sofa in the living room. Book either cottage—well in advance—through the Ontario Parks reservation service (519/826-5290 or 888/668-7275, www.ontarioparks.com).

FOOD

As you travel around the county, you'll see farm stands on many local roads. Many county regulars make a beeline for **Schroedter's Farm Market** (1492 Hwy. 62, at Hwy. 1, Bloomfield, 613/393-2823) for one reason: freshly made doughnuts.

Near the Black River Cheese Company, **Vicki's Veggies** (81 Morrison Point Rd., off County Rd. 13, Milford, 613/476-7241, www. vickisveggies.com) is a self-service stand selling organically grown vegetables. Vicki's supplies many local restaurants and sells her wares at Toronto's Evergreen Brickworks market. Tomatoes are a highlight in season; Vicki's host an annual **heirloom tomato festival** in September.

Be on the lookout for **Picnic PEC** (613/920-6934), a pink food truck that parks at wineries around the region, dishing out interesting sandwiches like a tofu *bánh mì* with Sriracha mayo. Check their twitter feed (www.twitter.com/PICNICPEC) to find their current location.

Wellington

With a mix of sleek black candlelit tables and wide board pine floors (plus friendly knowledgeable staff), ★ **East and Main Bistro** (270 Main St., 613/399-5420, www. eastandmain.ca, lunch noon-2:30pm, dinner 5:30pm-9pm Wed.-Sun. Feb.-Dec., lunch $11-14, dinner $19-29) feels both stylish and totally relaxed. The menu also walks that hip-homey line; the fresh pickerel might come with roasted potatoes and a caper brown butter sauce, while the locally raised chicken might be stuffed with goat cheese and spinach. Sweets like a warm fruit crumble or classic crème brûlée provide a comforting conclusion. The wines are local, of course.

Bloomfield

An old-fashioned "from scratch" pastry shop, **Just Sweets Retro Bakery** (3 Corey St., 613/393-5365, call for seasonal hours) bakes cupcakes, butter tarts, individual lemon Bundt cakes, and delicious date squares, among other goodies. It's cash only (as they say, "How retro is that?").

A casual café by day, **Agrarian Bistro** (275 Main St., 613/393-0111, www.agrarian-pec.ca, 9am-9pm Mon.-Fri., 11am-9pm Sat.,

10am-9pm Sun., dinner $14-27) morphs into a more upscale dining space at night. Local flavors take the simple fare up a notch—arugula and feta salad includes Ontario peaches, the pickerel was caught in the Bay of Quinte, and even grilled cheese goes upscale with smoky cheddar and farm-fresh greens. On the lower level, a retail **Cheese Market** (11am-5pm Mon.-Thurs., 11am-6pm Fri., 10am-6pm Sat., 10am-5pm Sun.) sells cheeses from near and far, and the **Speakeasy** pub has live music most Friday-Saturday nights.

Picton

Looking like an old-time sweet shop, with white wainscoting, a tin ceiling, and turquoise walls, the **Regent Café** (222 Main St., 613/476-9833, www.regentcafe.ca, 9am-5pm Thurs.-Tues., $4-9), adjacent to the theater of the same name, is a cheerful spot for breakfast, coffee, or a pre-theater bite. The menu includes breakfast burritos, sandwiches, pizzas, and pastries, and yes, the coffee they brag about is good. Wi-Fi is free.

Even if you're not staying at the ★ **Merrill Inn** (343 Main St. E., 613/476-7451 or 866/567-5969, www.merrillinn.com, 5:30pm-9pm Tues.-Sat. Feb.-Dec., $25-36), book a table in their cozy garden-level dining room for some of the county's most interesting food. Start with their signature salad—baby spinach and greens topped with local cheddar, apples, and spicy-sweet pecans—or perhaps smoked trout with a cabbage and radish slaw. Entrées might include local perch topped with lemon aioli; the kitchen takes great care with the accompanying vegetables, too. For the sweet finale, you might sample a trio of bite-size pastries.

Bustling, casual, and modern, the **Blumen Garden Bistro** (647 Hwy. 49, 613/476-6841, www.blumengardenbistro.com, from 5pm Wed.-Mon., $22-32) takes influences from chef-owner Andreas Feller's Swiss-German background and sprinkles them into interesting contemporary dishes. The pork tenderloin might come with wild leek spaetzle, or the gnocchi might be topped with braised rabbit and oyster mushrooms. If anything with a chocolate brownie—more like a rich and delicious flourless cake—is on the menu, save room.

INFORMATION AND SERVICES

Prince Edward County Chamber of Tourism and Commerce (116 Main St., Picton, 613/476-2421 or 800/640-4717, www.prince-edward-county.com) can provide event listings, maps, wine-touring guides, and other information for planning a county visit. The county tourism association also operates several seasonal information kiosks, including **Bloomfield Information Kiosk** (Bloomfield Town Hall, 289 Main St., lower level, 613/393-2796), **Wellington Information Kiosk** (Lakeshore Farms, 467 Main St. W.), and **Hillier Information Kiosk** (The County Way Restaurant, Hwy. 33 at County Rd. 1).

Cooking Classes

With its emphasis on local food, perhaps it's not surprising that the county has several cooking programs to help you learn to use local ingredients. All post upcoming class schedules on their websites. **From the Farm Cooking School** (www.fromthefarm.ca) offers private cooking classes by reservation only (Wed.-Thurs. and Sat. Apr.-Nov., $115 pp) for groups of four to eight that include lunch and a sampling of local wine. The **Waring House Cookery School** (613/476-7492 or 800/621-4956, www.waringhouse.com, $115 pp), at the Waring House Inn, offers a variety of cooking classes, which typically run three hours (including a meal), in their large commercial kitchen. Topics might include fall vegetables or bistro desserts. **Chef Michael Hoy** (613/476-3811, www.chefmichaelhoy.com, $75-95 pp), who has run kitchens at restaurants around the county, also offers three-hour cooking classes.

GETTING THERE AND AROUND

Prince Edward County is 215 kilometers (135 miles) east of Toronto. Take Highway 401 east to either exit 522 (Wooler Rd. S.) or exit 525 (Hwy. 33, Trenton). You need a car to get to around the county.

From Kingston, you can either take Highway 401 west to exit 566 (Marysville) and continue south on Highway 49, or follow the slower but shore-hugging Loyalist Parkway (Hwy. 33) to Adolphustown and then take the 10-minute **Glenora-Adolphustown Ferry** (www.mto.gov.on.ca, 6am-1:15am daily, free). The ferry leaves from the Adolphustown side at 15 minutes before and 15 minutes after the hour; it departs Glenora on the hour and the half-hour. From late June through mid-October, a second ferry runs 10:15am-7:30pm, so that a boat departs from each terminal every 15 minutes.

The main road across the county is Highway 33, the Loyalist Parkway, which becomes "Main Street" in Wellington, Bloomfield, and Picton. If you're coming to Picton from the west, it's faster to cut across on Highway 1 east from Consecon, which rejoins Highway 33 just west of Picton.

If you'd rather not drive while you're wine-tasting, contact **The Culinary Adventure Company** (647/955-8357 or 877/317-4870, www.culinaryadventureco.com). They offer one-day "Uncork the County" wine tours, including round-trip transportation from Toronto, breakfast, lunch, and a dozen tastings at four different wineries. Tours run on selected Saturdays April to November.

Kingston

On June 15, 1841, Kingston became the first capital of the fledgling nation of Canada. If you're interested in history, it's worth exploring this city of 150,000, midway between Toronto and Montreal. There's a 19th-century fort, a majestic city hall, the oldest continuously running public market in Ontario, and well-regarded Queen's University, founded the same year that Kingston took on its capital-city duties.

Kingston is sometimes nicknamed "The Limestone City" for its many well-preserved stone structures (some of which are now inns or B&Bs) that date to the 1800s. Located on Lake Ontario at the southern end of the Rideau Canal, Kingston's waterfront is an important part of its heritage, too, and it makes the present-day city even more pleasant, whether you're strolling the eight-kilometer (five-mile) waterfront trail or looking across the water from your hotel window. Yet even with all this history, there's nothing stuffy about this entertaining little city. It's compact and easy to walk around, with eclectic, contemporary restaurants, casual cafés, and leafy parks.

SIGHTS
★ Fort Henry

Standing majestically on a point overlooking Kingston and the St. Lawrence River, **Fort Henry** (1 Fort Henry Dr., at County Rd. 2, 613/542-7388, www.forthenry.com, 9:30am-5pm daily mid-May-early Sept., adults $17, seniors and ages 6-12 $14) was built in the 1830s to protect the town, the nearby royal dockyards, and the mouth of the adjacent Rideau Canal. Kingston was a major stop on the supply routes between Montreal, Ottawa, and points farther west, making it a strategic location for the British. British troops were stationed at the fort until 1870.

Today, you can tour the restored fort to learn more about the history of Kingston—and

Canada—in the 1800s and visit the soldiers' barracks, the officers' quarters, and the fort's schoolroom, kitchen, and other facilities. Costumed interpreters portray soldiers, as well as schoolteachers, soldiers' wives, and other civilian residents of the fort. Start your visit with the high-tech historical exhibits in the multimedia **Discovery Centre,** then either explore the fort on your own or take a 50-minute guided tour, which departs several times daily (9:45am-4pm).

When planning your visit, check the daily schedule (available online or at the fort) for other activities. You might train as a British soldier, become a student (circa 1867) at "Victorian school," or participate in the trial of a misbehaving private. Try to attend the summer **Sunset Ceremonies** (adults $17, seniors and ages 6-12 $14), when "soldiers" perform precision military maneuvers, accompanied by period military music and gun salutes, culminating in fireworks over the harbor. This event takes place at 8pm most Wednesdays and Saturdays in July-August; call or check the fort's website for exact dates.

In the fall, Fort Henry transforms into **Fort Fright** (7pm-10pm Thurs.-Sat. early-mid.-Oct., 7pm-10pm daily mid-late Oct., $15 pp, includes parking), an elaborate haunted house with shaking coffins, ghouls that jump out at you, and other creepy effects, plus Halloween-themed performances.

On a large patio overlooking downtown Kingston and the lake, you and your little soldiers can refuel at the **Battery Bistro** (613/530-2550, www.foodandheritage.com, 11:30am-3:30pm daily mid-May-late June, 11:30am-9pm daily late June-Aug., 11:30am-3:30pm Sun.-Thurs. and 11:30am-7:30pm Fri.-Sat. Sept.). On summer evenings before the Sunset Ceremonies, dine by candlelight in the **Fort Henry Officers' Mess** (613/530-2550, www.foodandheritage.com, reservations

Kingston

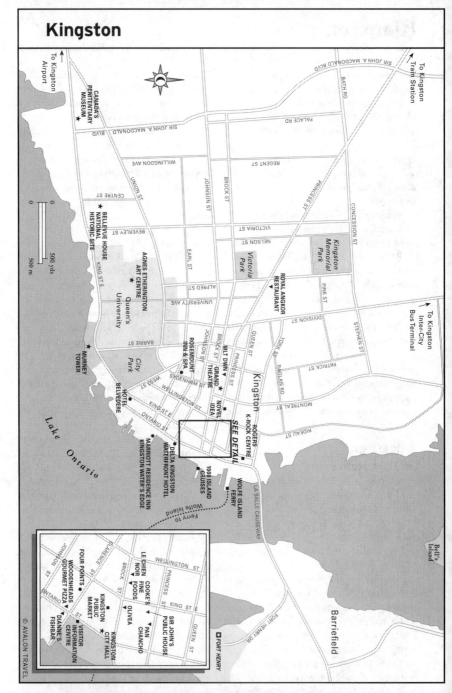

To Kingston Airport

To Kingston Train Station

To Kingston Inter-City Bus Terminal

SIR JOHN A. MACDONALD BLVD
BATH RD
PALACE RD
WILLINGDON AVE
REGENT ST
BROCK ST
JOHNSON ST
UNION ST
CENTRE ST
VICTORIA ST
NELSON ST
CONCESSION ST
BEVERLEY ST
EARL ST
ALFRED ST
UNIVERSITY AVE
PINE ST
DIVISION ST
STEPHEN ST
QUEEN ST
YORK ST
RAGLAN RD
PATRICK ST
MONTREAL ST
RIDEAU ST
KING ST E
BARRIE ST
JOHNSON ST
BROCK ST
PRINCESS ST
SYDENHAM ST
WELLINGTON ST
WEST ST
KING ST E
ONTARIO ST

★ CANADA'S PENITENTIARY MUSEUM

★ BELLEVUE HOUSE NATIONAL HISTORIC SITE

★ AGNES ETHERINGTON ART CENTRE

Queen's University

City Park

★ MURNEY TOWER

● HOTEL BELVEDERE

ROSEMOUNT INN & SPA ●

MLT DWN ▼
GRAND THEATRE ★
NOVEL IDEA ■

ROYAL ANGKOR RESTAURANT ★

Victoria Park

Kingston Memorial Park

Kingston

ROGERS K-ROCK CENTRE ■

SEE DETAIL

● DELTA KINGSTON WATERFRONT HOTEL

● MARRIOTT RESIDENCE INN KINGSTON WATER'S EDGE

1000 ISLAND CRUISES

WOLFE ISLAND FERRY

Ferry to Wolfe Island

Lake Ontario

LA SALLE CAUSEWAY

FORT HENRY DR

Bell's Island

Barriefield

■ FORT HENRY

0 500 yds
0 500 m

Detail inset:

JOHNSON ST
CLARENCE ST
BROCK ST
PRINCESS ST
WELLINGTON ST
KING ST E
QUEEN ST
ONTARIO ST

FOUR POINTS ●

WOODENHEADS GOURMET PIZZA ▼

LE CHIEN NOIR ▼

COOKE'S FINE FOODS ▼

KINGSTON PUBLIC MARKET

OLIVEA ▼

PAN CHANCHO ▼

SIR JOHN'S PUBLIC HOUSE ▼

DIANNE'S FISHBAR ■

VISITOR INFORMATION CENTRE

KINGSTON CITY HALL

© AVALON TRAVEL

the "punishment room" at Canada's Penitentiary Museum

required) on traditional and not-so-traditional foods.

Fort Henry is 2.5 kilometers (1.5 miles) east of downtown Kingston. If you don't have a car, catch Kingston Transit Bus no. 12 (Princess St. near King St. E.), which will drop you off at the top of the fort road.

Kingston City Hall

Built in the 1840s when Kingston was the first capital of Canada, **Kingston City Hall** (216 Ontario St., 613/546-0000, www.cityofkingston.ca) is both a working government building and a National Historic Site. One of the building's highlights is Memorial Hall, with its arched ceiling, 12 stained-glass windows, and massive portrait of Sir John A. Macdonald, the Kingston resident who became Canada's first prime minister.

Take a **guided tour** (10am-4pm daily July-Aug., 10am-4pm Mon.-Fri. mid-May-June and Sept., free) to learn more about City Hall's history and architecture. You can also explore the building on your own year-round;

pick up a tour brochure at the City Hall reception desk.

Murney Tower

In the 1840s, the British built four small fortifications along the Kingston waterfront, which are known as the Martello Towers. The British copied these stocky round towers from a similar French structure constructed on Mortella Point on the island of Corsica (Martello is apparently a corruption of Mortella). Kingston's Martello Towers are among only 13 similar fully intact structures in the world.

One of these fortifications, the 1846 **Murney Tower** (King St. W., at Barrie St., 613/572-5181, www.kingstonhistoricalsociety.ca, 10am-5pm daily mid-May-early Sept., adults $5, seniors and students $4, families $12) is open to the public. A cannon still points out from the tower's narrow windows, and inside, a small historical museum describes the lives of the 19th-century soldiers and their families who lived in the tower.

Canada's Penitentiary Museum

Opposite the maximum-security Kingston Penitentiary, which was an active correctional facility until 2013, is a quirky, fascinating, and sobering museum about the region's prison past. Housed in the former Kingston Pen's warden's residence is **Canada's Penitentiary Museum** (555 King St. W., 613/530-3122, www.penitentiarymuseum.ca, 9am-4pm Mon.-Fri., 10am-4pm Sat.-Sun. May-Oct., donation). The museum includes a "punishment room," which displays various disciplinary measures used over the years—from the strapping board that inmates were strapped to, to be paddled (used as recently as 1969), to The Box, a creepy casket-like container used for solitary confinement in the 1840s. You can peek into actual jail cells, and in the "contraband room" you'll see all manner of handmade weapons and devices used for attempted escapes. Some of the volunteer guards are former corrections staff who can tell you about life on the inside. This is not your everyday tourist attraction, but definitely worth seeing.

Bellevue House National Historic Site

The former home of Sir John A. Macdonald, Canada's first prime minister, the **Bellevue House National Historic Site** (35 Centre St., 613/545-8666, www.pc.gc.ca, 10am-5pm daily July-early Sept., 10am-5pm Thurs.-Mon. late May-June and early Sept.-mid-Oct., adults $3.90, seniors $3.40, ages 6-16 $1.90) is a sprawling 20-room white stucco mansion that Macdonald, his wife, Isabella, and their infant son rented in 1848. Macdonald hoped that the peaceful atmosphere of this country house, located about 1.5 kilometers (one mile) from central Kingston, would improve Isabella's poor health.

Unfortunately, the Macdonalds' son died shortly after they moved into the house. Isabella continued to ail (she may have suffered from tuberculosis), and Macdonald found himself in financial trouble. The family left Bellevue House after only one year, relocating to a smaller and less costly home in town. A few of the Macdonalds' possessions remain at Bellevue House, although most of the furnishings are other pieces from the 1840s. On weekends in July-August, costumed guides lead 90-minute guided tours (1:30pm Sat.-Sun., adults $7.80, seniors $7.30, ages 6-16 $5.80), sharing details about Macdonald, his family, and the home.

Agnes Etherington Art Centre

On the Queen's University campus, the contemporary **Agnes Etherington Art Centre** (36 University Ave., 613/533-2190, www.agnes.queensu.ca, 10am-4:30pm Tues.-Fri., 1pm-5pm Sat.-Sun. May-Aug., 10am-4:30pm Tues.-Wed. and Fri., 10am-9pm Thurs., 1pm-5pm Sat.-Sun. Sept.-Apr., adults $5, seniors and students $3, children under 18 free, all admission free Thurs.) mounts exhibits of works by artists from Canada and around the world. On the third Thursday of every month, you can take a free 45-minute guided tour of the current exhibitions.

ENTERTAINMENT AND EVENTS

First opened in 1879, the **Grand Theatre** (218 Princess St., 613/530-2050, www.kingstongrand.ca) now hosts numerous theatrical, dance, musical, and other productions every year by local, national, and international performers. For rock concerts, sports events, ice shows, and other big productions, head to the **Rogers K-Rock Centre** (1 The Tragically Hip Way, 613/650-5000, www.rogersk-rockcentre.com).

Every year on or around June 15, Kingston celebrates **First Capital Day** (www.cityofkingston.ca), commemorating the city's role as Canada's first capital. Clowns, contortionists, crooners, and all manner of street performers take over downtown during the **Kingston Buskers Rendezvous** (www.kingstonbuskers.com, July).

SHOPPING

Princess Street, between Ontario and Sydenham Streets, is the main downtown shopping district, with local and chain clothing shops, cafés, and other boutiques, including independent bookstore **Novel Idea** (156 Princess St., 613/546-9799, www.novelideabooks.ca, 9:30am-9pm Mon.-Fri., 9:30am-6pm Sat., noon-5pm Sun.), which carries a good selection of both fiction and nonfiction.

One block south of Princess, Brock Street has a few interesting shops, as well, including **Cooke's Fine Foods** (61 Brock St., 613/548-7721, www.cookesfinefoods.com, 9:30am-5:30pm Mon.-Sat.), which opened in 1865. It still has the original counters and tin ceiling, and its shelves are packed with coffees, jams, cheeses, chocolates, and other specialty foods.

ACCOMMODATIONS

If you like staying in inns or B&Bs in stately historic buildings, you'll enjoy staying in Kingston. Downtown Kingston also has several business- and family-friendly chain hotels. The **Delta Kingston Waterfront Hotel** (1 Johnson St., 613/549-8100 or 888/548-6726, www.deltahotels.com, $189-259 d) and the **Marriott Residence Inn Kingston Water's Edge** (7 Earl St., 613/544-4888, www.marriottresidenceinnkingston.com, $189-249 d) are on the waterfront; the **Four Points by Sheraton** (285 King St. E., 613/544-4434 or 800/325-3535, www.fourpointskingston.com, $190 d) is centrally located as well.

Want to know what it was really like to be a soldier in 1800s' Kingston? You won't be issued a musket or army rations, but you can spend the night at **Fort Henry** (1 Fort Henry Dr., at County Rd. 2, 613/542-7388, www.forthenry.com, $200 for up to four people, $50 for each additional person). The billets are basic—you have a cot with a mattress and not much else—and you'll need to bring a sleeping bag, pillow, and flashlight. The fort has modern washroom facilities, including hot showers, although you have to walk across the open courtyard to reach them from the guest quarters, so come prepared for the weather.

Conveniently located between downtown and the Queen's campus, the **Hotel Belvedere** (141 King St. E., 613/548-1565 or 800/559-0584, www.hotelbelvedere.com, $129-259 d), built in 1880 as a private home, is traditionally appointed without feeling frilly or formal. Many of the 20 antiques-filled rooms, in sizes that vary from snug to spacious, have little nooks and crannies; a set of stairs might lead into a closet, or a kitchenette might hide behind the door. Rates include Wi-Fi, parking, and a light continental breakfast (English muffin, juice, tea or coffee) served in your room or in the high-ceilinged guest parlor.

Guests are encouraged to mingle at the ★ **Rosemount Inn & Spa** (46 Sydenham St., 613/531-8844, www.rosemountinn.com, $175-299 d), whether it's over afternoon tea in the lounge, on the spacious front porch, or at breakfast, where a set menu is served around the community table. The nine rooms in the main inn, a stone villa built in 1850, are all different, but throughout the building you'll find leaded-glass windows, oriental rugs, and four-poster beds. Two suites in the adjacent coach house are more modern; one two-level unit has a living area and a bedroom and bath upstairs.

FOOD

For a small city, Kingston has a large selection of good places to eat, from basic international joints to upscale contemporary dining rooms. Most are clustered downtown around Princess, King, and Ontario Streets.

Bakeries and Cafés

Crave a focaccia, muffin, or scone? At **Pan Chancho Bakery and Café** (44 Princess St., 613/544-7790, www.panchancho.com) the bakery (7am-6pm Mon.-Sat., 7am-5pm Sun.) sells scrumptious fresh baked goods to go, while the sit-down café (7am-4pm daily, $8-16) whips up pastries or egg dishes in the morning, and salads, cheese plates, or creative world-rambling entrées later in the day.

Ooze into tiny **MLT DWN** (292 Princess St., 613/766-1881, www.mltdwn.com, 11am-10pm Mon.-Thurs., 11am-3am Fri.-Sat., 11am-10pm Sun., $8-14) for grilled cheese sandwiches with a gourmet twist. The beef brisket comes on rye with provolone, gruyère, caramelized onions, and arugula, while the roasted veg is topped with goat cheese, provolone, portobello, peppers, and greens. To live out your childhood food fantasies, order macaroni and cheese on white bread.

Asian

Kingston has lots of Southeast Asian eateries, serving Cambodian and Thai food. Just out of downtown is the bare-bones but welcoming **Royal Angkor Restaurant** (523 Princess St., 613/544-9268, www.royalangkor.ca, 11am-3pm and 5pm-9pm Mon.-Thurs., 11am-3pm and 5pm-10pm Fri., 4pm-10pm Sat., 4pm-9pm Sun., $9-12). Try the Samlaw Khmer, a hot-and-sour mix of chicken, shrimp, long beans, and tomatoes flavored with tamarind and

Bon Echo Provincial Park

Combining a striking outdoor setting with interesting aboriginal history, **Bon Echo Provincial Park** (16151 Hwy. 41, RR 1, Cloyne, 613/336-2222, www.ontarioparks.com or www.bonechofriends. ca, early May-mid-Oct., $14.50 per vehicle) is worth the trip, whether for a day or longer. The park is 100 kilometers (60 miles) northwest of Kingston and 130 kilometers (80 miles) northeast of Peterborough, located roughly between Toronto and Ottawa.

ABORIGINAL PICTOGRAPHS

The park's centerpiece is **Mazinaw Rock,** jutting 100 meters (325 feet) out of Mazinaw Lake and now preserved as a National Historic Site. On the front surface of the predominantly granite rock are 260 aboriginal pictographs.

Unlike the aboriginal markings at Petroglyphs Provincial Park, which were carved into the rock, the Bon Echo pictographs were drawn or painted onto the rock face. But as at Petroglyphs, the exact date of the drawings, which include turtles, canoes, and underwater creatures, is unknown. Estimates put them at somewhere between 300 and 900 years old.

You can see the Bon Echo pictographs only from the water. In July and August, the 26-seat **Wanderer Ferry** (round-trip adults $8, under age 12 $4) runs 45-minute tours across the lake to the pictographs. The ferry departs several times a day on Saturday-Sunday, Tuesday, and Thursday from the docks near the park visitors center. Another way to reach the pictographs is by canoe or kayak. You can't disembark at this section of the rock, but you can paddle near the drawings. Rent canoes and kayaks at the lagoon.

ON TOP OF THE ROCK

If you're atop Mazinaw Rock, you can't see the pictographs; the rock is too steep to hike or climb down. But you can hike the 1.5-kilometer (0.9-mile) **Cliff Top Trail** to a lookout on the rock's summit; in the fall, you'll have a great vista across the reds, golds, and greens of the surrounding forests. The trail is steep, but there are stairs in the steepest sections.

Like the pictographs, the Cliff Top Trail is accessible only from the water. The **Mugwump**

---

basil; the Golden Chicken, with peanuts and lemongrass; or the Kako Khmer, chicken with green papaya, jackfruit, and eggplant.

Contemporary

The exposed brick walls, tin ceiling, and rust-hued banquettes say "traditional bistro," and you'll find plenty of traditional bistro fare at ★ **Le Chien Noir** (69 Brock St., 613/549-5635, www.lechiennoir.com, 11:30am-11pm daily, lunch $12-27, dinner $17-38), from omelets to burgers to steak frites. But chef Derek Macgregor uses lots of local products and pushes the bistro envelope, too, topping his *poutine* with duck confit and a triple-cream brie, or dressing up his scallops with deep-fried bone marrow. You'll be equally at home here in jeans or a little black dress.

Italian

Decked out with stone walls, wooden tables, and a searingly hot pizza oven, **Woodenheads Gourmet Pizza** (192 Ontario St., 613/549-1812, www.woodenheads.ca, 11:30am-midnight daily, $10-25) is wildly popular for its eponymous pies, as well as salads and fusion variations on classic Mediterranean fare (calamari Mumbai-style, anyone?). The pizzas range from traditional tomato-and-cheese to the creative Citta (topped with brie, prosciutto, and caramelized onions) to quirky combos like the Nonna Mela, with blackened chicken, cheddar cheese, and apple butter.

At the friendly, bustling trattoria **Olivea** (39 Brock St., 613/547-5483, www.olivea. ca, 11:30am-2:30pm and 5pm-10pm Mon.-Fri., 11:30am-10pm Sat.-Sun. May-Sept.,

Ferry (Fri.-Mon. and Wed. late June-early Sept., Sat.-Sun. mid-May-late June and early Sept.-mid-Oct., round-trip adults $4, under age 12 $3) will shuttle you from the lagoon to the start of the trail. You can also canoe across from the lagoon to the trailhead.

BEACHES AND HIKING TRAILS

You can swim in Mazinaw Lake from either **Main Beach** or **North Beach.** North Beach is sandy and good for kids, although the water tends to be a little colder. Take a short hike to **The Narrows,** a point just across a narrow section of water from the rock. You can't see the pictographs from here, but at sunset, the setting sun reflects its colors on Mazinaw Rock.

The park has several other hiking trails, ranging from the easy one-kilometer (0.6-mile) **Bon Echo Creek** route to the rugged 17-kilometer (10.5-mile) **Abes Loop.**

PRACTICALITIES

Bon Echo has 532 **campsites** spread out over several areas, including 333 tent sites ($40-44), 169 electrical sites ($46-50), and 30 backcountry sites (adults $10, ages 6-17 $4.75). There are also six yurts ($98) and four rustic cabins ($142) that sleep up to five. Sawmill Bay is designed primarily for tent camping; there are five walk-in sites directly on Upper Mazinaw Lake, and other sites within a short walk of North Beach. Some sites in the Fairview Campground are near, but not on, the lake. Across Highway 41 from Mazinaw Lake, the Hardwood Hill Campground is a wooded area high up on a hill and feels much more secluded than the lakeside campgrounds. The drawback is that you're farther from the lake. Also on this side of the park is a series of canoe-in backcountry campsites on Joeperry and Pearson Lakes.

If you don't want to camp, rent the **Cabin on the Hill** ($170), an 1870s log cabin that's been updated with electricity, indoor plumbing, and a kitchen. It's a short walk from North Beach and has great views of the rock. The cabin has one bedroom, plus two sleeper sofas in the living room.

The park has no food concessions, although on summer weekends, there's usually a lunchtime **barbecue** (noon-2pm Sat.-Sun.). There's a small market in the village of Cloyne, about a 10-minute drive south of the park, and a larger grocery in Northbrook, farther south on Highway 41.

11:30am-2:30pm and 5pm-10pm Tues.-Fri., 11:30am-10pm Sat.-Sun. Oct.-Apr., $9-25), with a wall of windows facing Market Square, the Italian-Mediterranean menu includes salads, pastas in both full and half portions, and more substantial plates like Ligurian seafood stew or chicken under a brick. The salad with buttery tuna confit, white beans, and arugula pairs well with one of the pastas, perhaps penne with a spicy tomato-based *arrabbiata* sauce.

Pubs

In the 1850s, John A. Macdonald had his law office in the downtown building that now houses **Sir John's Public House** (343 King St. E., 613/766-9296, www.foodandheritage.com, 11:30am-late Mon.-Sat., 10:30am-late Sun., $9-20), part Scottish pub and part homage to Canada's first prime minister. The drink menu features many Scotch whiskeys as well as domestic and international beers and ciders. The basic pub fare has a Scottish twist, such as bangers and mash (sausages with mashed potatoes) and fish-and-chips. You can even sample the classic haggis, though here it's fried into more palatable fritters and served with a tangy piccalilli sauce.

Seafood

The bright-orange awnings reel in crowds to **Dianne's Fishbar** (195 Ontario St., 613/507-3474, www.dianneskingston.com, from 11:30am daily, $8-34), a bustling fish restaurant with sidewalk seating. Though much of the seafood swims in from afar, the kitchen tries to use sustainable species in south-of-the-border dishes like Pacific cod ceviche, fish tacos, roasted halibut with pineapple salsa, or blackened Ontario trout. Local beer and a long list of tequilas keep fish fans feeling liquid.

Groceries and Markets

The **Kingston Public Market** (Springer Market Square, King St. E., between Brock St. and Clarence St., www.kingstonpublicmarket.ca, 6am-6pm Tues., Thurs., and Sat. Apr.-Oct.), behind City Hall, is the oldest market in Ontario, in operation since 1801. Selling local produce and prepared foods that change with the seasons, most of the market's action is between 8am and 3pm.

INFORMATION AND SERVICES

Located in the former train station, the accommodating **Tourism Kingston Visitor Information Centre** (209 Ontario St., 613/548-4415 or 888/855-4555, www.tourism.kingstoncanada.com, 10am-4pm daily Jan.-mid-May, 9:30am-6pm Sun.-Wed., 9:30am-7pm Thurs.-Sat. mid-May-June, 9:30am-8pm Sun.-Wed., 9:30am-9pm Thurs.-Sat. July-early Sept., 9:30am-5pm Sun.-Wed., 9:30am-6pm Thurs.-Sat. early Sept.-mid-Oct., 10am-4pm Sun.-Thurs., 10am-5pm Fri.-Sat. mid-Oct.-Dec.) is in Confederation Park opposite City Hall. The information center has **free Wi-Fi** and two computers with **free Internet access.**

GETTING THERE
Air

From the small **Kingston/Norman Rogers Airport** (YGK, 1114 Len Birchall Way, 613/389-6404 www.kingstonairport.ca), eight kilometers (five miles) west of the city center, **Air Canada** (www.aircanada.com) flies to Toronto several times a day. Although the closest major international airports are **Ottawa Airport** (YOW, 1000 Airport Pkwy., Ottawa, 613/248-2000, www.ottawa-airport.ca) and **Syracuse Hancock International Airport** (SYR, 1000 Col. Eileen Collins Blvd., Syracuse, NY, 315/454-4330 www.syr-airport.org), there are more flight options

and direct transportation via Toronto's **Pearson Airport** (YYZ, 6301 Silver Dart Dr., Mississauga, 416/247-7678 or 866/207-1690, www.torontopearson.com).

Megabus (866/488-4452, www.megabus.com) runs several daily buses between Pearson Airport and Kingston (3.5 hours, one-way adults $50). From Ottawa Airport to Kingston, you'll either need to rent a car or go from the airport to Ottawa's train or bus station and then continue to Kingston on VIA Rail or Greyhound bus.

Train

VIA Rail's Toronto-Ottawa and Toronto-Montreal trains both stop at the **Kingston Train Station** (1800 John Counter Blvd., 888/842-7245, www.viarail.ca). The station is 6.5 kilometers (four miles) northwest of downtown. It's a short cab ride, or you can take Kingston Transit Bus no. 18.

Bus

From the **Kingston Inter-City Bus Terminal** (1175 John Counter Blvd., 613/547-4916), **Greyhound** (800/661-8747, www.greyhound.ca) operates several daily buses to Ottawa (2.75 hours, one-way adults $18-39, seniors and students $18-35, ages 2-11 $18-29). **Megabus** (866/488-4452, www.megabus.com) runs buses throughout the day between Kingston and Toronto (2.75-3 hours, one-way $22-64) and from Kingston to Montreal (3-3.25 hours, one-way $27-64). From the bus terminal to downtown (five kilometers, three miles), either take a cab or catch Kingston Transit Bus no. 2 or no. 18.

Car

Kingston is 265 kilometers (165 miles) east of Toronto via Highway 401. If you're coming from the west, the easiest way to reach downtown Kingston is to take exit 615 and follow Sir John A. Macdonald Boulevard south for about six kilometers (3.7 miles). Turn left onto King Street, which will pass the Queen's University campus and continue toward downtown.

From Ottawa, 195 kilometers (123 miles) northeast of Kingston, the fastest route is to follow Highway 416 south to Highway 401 west. Exit Highway 401 at Highway 15 (exit 623) and continue south to Highway 2. Turn right (west) onto Highway 2. You'll pass Fort Henry and then cross the bridge into downtown Kingston.

GETTING AROUND

You can explore Kingston without a car, since the city's downtown is compact and easy to walk around. You can also walk from the Queen's University campus to downtown (about 1.5 kilometers, 0.9 miles). If you do have a car, consider leaving it at your hotel when you're exploring downtown, since parking can be limited.

Kingston Transit (www.cityofkingston. ca, adults $2.75, seniors and ages 6-18 $2.50, day pass $7.25), the city's public bus system, can take you to most visitor destinations. Use the "Trip Planner" feature on the website to plot your route.

Walking Tours

Canadian history comes alive on the one-hour theatrical walking tour, **In Sir John A.'s Footsteps** (www.sirjohnehroadshow.com, 2pm and 4pm daily July-early Sept., adults $12, seniors, students, and kids over age 5 $9, ages 1-5 $6, families $30) in which actors and musicians guide you through Kingston's historic district, highlighting sights important to the city during the time that Sir John A. Macdonald, Canada's first prime minister, lived and worked here. Tours depart from the Visitor Information Centre (209 Ontario St.).

You can take a **self-guided audio tour** on the same theme that Kingston writer Arthur Milnes created in partnership with the city of Kingston. Download a podcast or MP3 audio file of the narration accompanying the tour from the City of Kingston website (www.cityofkingston.ca). You can even choose your narrators: one tour features former Canadian prime minister Jean Chrétien and former speaker of the House of Commons Peter Milliken, while another version is narrated by hockey players Don Cherry and Jim Dorey. The visitors center can give you pamphlets for several other self-guided historic walking tours around town.

Boat Tours

To see Kingston from the water, take one of the **1000 Islands Cruises** (1 Brock St., 613/549-5544 or 800/848-0011, www.1000islandscruises.ca, early May-mid-Oct., call or check the website for schedules) that depart from the pier at the foot of Brock Street, near Confederation Park. The 90-minute Discovery Cruises (adults $26, kids $13) introduce you to local history while cruising along the waterfront from Fort Henry to the Kingston Penitentiary. The three-hour Heart of the Islands trip combines a Kingston waterfront tour with a cruise around the westernmost Thousand Islands.

Food Tours

Young entrepreneur and Queen's grad Julia Segal launched **Kingston By Fork** (613/888-2327, www.kingstonbyfork.com, June-mid-Sept., call or check the website for tour schedule) to introduce visitors to the flavors of her adopted hometown. Her company offers two different food walks, An Edible Escapade (adults $25, seniors and students $20), a two-hour sampling tour with stops at local shops for chocolate, cheese, Italian food, Indian snacks, and more, and a Homegrown Eats Tour (adults $45, seniors and students $40), a guided one-hour food walk through the Kingston Public Market and some downtown food venues, followed by lunch at a local restaurant. Reservations are recommended.

VICINITY OF KINGSTON
Wolfe Island

Wolfe Island (www.wolfeisland.com) is an easy day trip from Kingston. Measuring 32 kilometers (20 miles) long, and up to 11 kilometers (seven miles) wide, it's the largest of the Thousand Islands. You can see the island's wind turbines as you look across Kingston harbor.

Most day-trippers head to the beach at **Big Sandy Bay** (www.bigsandybay.ca, adults $8, ages 6-17 $3) on the island's southwest corner. It's a 1.3-kilometer (0.8-mile) walk from the parking area to the beach. Bicycles aren't allowed on the walking trail, so cyclists must lock their bikes at the trail gatehouse. The beach is open year-round but staffed only during the summer; in the off-season, leave a donation in the box on the trail gate.

Cycling is a popular way to tour the island. You can rent a bicycle from **Cycle Wolfe Island** (1291 Main St., Marysville, 613/385-2240, cyclewolfeisland@gmail.com, http://cyclewolfeisland.blogspot.com, $15-25), located three blocks from the ferry dock; call or email to reserve. The Wolfe Island website includes a map of island cycling routes.

The Wolfe Island Business and Tourism Association runs a seasonal **Tourist Information Centre** (Main St., Marysville, 613/385-1875, www.wolfeisland.com, May-Oct.) that can help you get oriented. The 20-minute **Wolfe Island Ferry** (www.wolfeisland.com, free) transports passengers, bicycles, and cars between Kingston (Ontario St. at Barrack St.) and the island year-round. There's also a seasonal car ferry (www.hornesferry.com, May-Oct.) from the United States, leaving from Cape Vincent, New York; passports are required.

Frontenac Provincial Park

You don't have to venture far from Kingston to get into the wilderness. The 5,200 hectares (12,849 acres) of **Frontenac Provincial Park** (6700 Salmon Lake Rd., Sydenham, 613/376-3489, www.ontarioparks.com or www.frontenacpark.ca, $14.50 per vehicle) begin less than an hour's drive north of the city. Situated on the southernmost projection of the Canadian Shield, Frontenac has a Northern Ontario landscape that doesn't require a long trek to the north. It's a popular spot for **day-hiking,** with more than 160 kilometers (100 miles) of trails ranging in length from 1.5 to 21 kilometers (0.9-13 miles).

The park's 22 lakes make for good canoeing. Although rentals aren't available in the park, you can rent a canoe from nearby outfitters such as **Frontenac Outfitters** (6674 Bedford Rd., Sydenham, 613/376-6220 or 800/250-3174, www.frontenac-outfitters.com, 9am-5pm Mon.-Fri., 8:30am-5pm Sat.-Sun. Apr.-Oct., $40-55 per day), south of the park entrance. To work on your outdoor skills, take one of the park's **wilderness skills workshops,** offered year-round, including kayaking, snowshoeing, fishing, wilderness navigation, winter camping, and more. For some workshops, there's no fee beyond the park admission, while others have an added charge.

Frontenac has no car camping sites, but there are 48 backcountry **campsites** (adults $12, ages 6-17 $5) throughout the park, accessible either on foot or by canoe. Reservations are recommended on weekends from May to October; contact the **Ontario Parks Reservations Service** (888/668-7275, www.ontarioparks.com, reservation fee online $11, by phone $13).

The park entrance is north of the village of Sydenham, 40 kilometers (25 miles) north of Kingston. From Kingston, take Sydenham Road/Frontenac County Road 9 north for about 20 kilometers (12.5 miles). Turn left onto County Road 5 into Sydenham and watch for the park sign on your right, directing you to County Road 19. From here, it's a winding 13-kilometer (eight-mile) drive to Salmon Lake Road, which enters the park.

The Thousand Islands and the St. Lawrence

The region known as the Thousand Islands extends roughly 80 kilometers (50 miles) from Kingston to Brockville, straddling both sides of the St. Lawrence River, which divides Canada and the United States. The "thousand" is more of an estimate; officially, this area has 1,864 islands. On some islands, you'll see a single home or cottage, while others support year-round communities. To be counted among the Thousand Islands, an island must be above water year-round and have at least two living trees. Two-thirds of the islands are in Canadian waters, although the overall area of the Thousand Islands is split equally between Canada and the United States.

The Thousand Islands are part of the **Frontenac Arch Biosphere Reserve** (www. frontenacarchbiosphere.ca), a United Nations designation designed to protect and promote "globally significant ecological features." The Biosphere Reserve is a 270,000-hectare (667,000-acre) region, rather than a single site, bounded roughly by the towns of Gananoque, Brockville, and Westport, and the area surrounding Frontenac Provincial Park. The Frontenac Arch's significant feature is a ridge of ancient granite that's part of the Canadian Shield, more commonly associated with the rugged landscape of the Canadian north than with Southern Ontario's flatter topography.

Long part of traditional Iroquois and Mohawk territory, the region along the St. Lawrence River's northern banks linked its fortunes to U.S.-Canadian relations. During and after the American Revolution in the late 1700s, Loyalists (American colonists who remained loyal to the British crown) fled across the border into Canada. Many of these Loyalists settled along the St. Lawrence in towns like Brockville, Prescott, and Morrisburg, which still have historic sites reflecting the Loyalist legacy.

Many attractions in the Thousand Islands are seasonal, operating from May through mid-October.

GANANOQUE AND VICINITY

The town of Gananoque—pronounced "Gan-uh-NOCK-way"—is the gateway to the Thousand Islands region. You can learn more about the area's history at the small **Arthur Child Heritage Museum** (125 Water St., 613/382-2535 or 877/217-7391, www.1000islandsheritagemuseum.com, 10am-6pm daily May-Oct., donation) near the waterfront, where the exhibits trace the region's development, from its original First Nations inhabitants, the War of 1812, to the "Golden Age" of the Thousand Islands in the late 1800s, when the region became a popular tourist destination for wealthy Americans.

For views across the Thousand Islands, ride the elevator to the top of the **1000 Islands Tower** (Hill Island, www.1000islandstower. com, 9am-6pm daily May-mid-Oct., adults $10, ages 6-12 $6), which has three observation levels. The Tower, on Hill Island, is located between the Canadian and U.S. spans of the Thousand Islands International Bridge, 20 kilometers (12.5 miles) east of Gananoque and 40 kilometers (25 miles) west of Brockville. It's in Canadian territory, so you don't need your passport if you're coming from the Ontario side. From Highway 401, take exit 661 (Bridge to USA/Hill Island). If you're coming from the U.S. side, follow I-81 to the bridge and clear Canadian customs (remember your passport), and you'll see the tower on the right.

★ Thousand Islands Boat Tours

The best way to appreciate the Thousand Islands is from the water. The **Gananoque Boat Line** (280 Main St., 613/382-2144 or 888/717-4837, www.ganboatline.com,

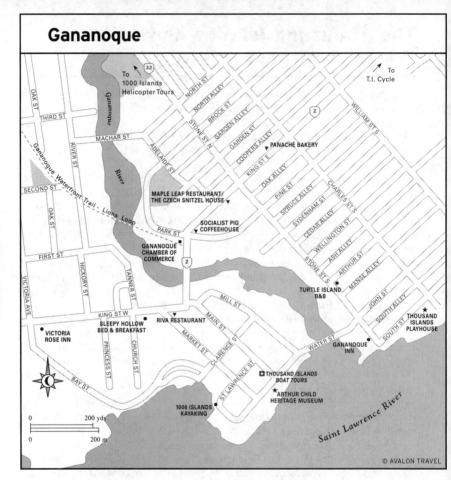

Gananoque

© AVALON TRAVEL

May-mid-Oct.) operates 1-hour, 2.5-hour, and 5-hour cruises around the islands, leaving from the Gananoque waterfront. The one-hour trips (10:30am, noon, 1:30pm, 3pm, 4:30pm, and 7pm daily late June-early Sept., call or check the website for spring and fall schedule, adults $24, seniors $22, ages 6-12 $13, family $61) are primarily nature tours, cruising around some of the islands closest to shore, with commentary about their flora and fauna.

The 2.5-hour tours (10:30am, 12:30pm, 1:30pm, 3:30pm, and 5pm daily late June-early Sept., call or check the website for spring and fall schedule; adults $36, seniors $33, ages 6-12 $14, family $86) include recorded commentary about the history and development of the islands, giving you a more detailed picture of who has lived on various islands, past and present. These tours cruise past, but don't stop at, Boldt Castle.

Boldt Castle

A highlight is a visit to **Boldt Castle** (Heart Island, NY, www.boldtcastle.com, 10am-7:30pm daily late June-Aug., 10am-6:30pm early May-late June and Sept., 10am-5:30pm early-mid-Oct., adults $8.50, ages 6-12 $6). George C. Boldt, owner of New York City's Waldorf Astoria Hotel, began constructing the grandiose 120-room stone castle in 1900 in honor of his wife, Louise. For several years, a crew of more than 300 worked on building the castle. Unfortunately, Louise died suddenly in 1904, and George ordered that all work be halted. He never returned to the property. The castle was abandoned until 1977, when the Thousand Islands Bridge Authority acquired and began restoring the property, which is now available for tours.

The **Gananoque Boat Line**'s Boldt Castle tours (5 hours, 10am and 3pm daily late June-early Sept., call or check the website for spring and fall departures, adults $46, seniors $41, ages 6-12 $18, families $109) depart the Gananoque docks; the cruise includes a two-hour stopover at Boldt Castle. Admission to Boldt Castle is not included in the boat-tour prices.

If you want to tour Boldt Castle but you're short on time, trips run by the **Rockport Boat Line** (23 Front St., Rockport, 613/659-3402 or 800/563-8687, www.rockportcruises.com, daily late June-early Sept., Sat.-Sun. late May-late June and early Sept.-mid-Oct., adults $32, seniors $28, ages 5-12 $12, families $75) take 3.5 hours, including two hours to explore the castle. They depart from the town of Rockport, which is closer to the castle,

19 kilometers (12 miles) east of Gananoque. Departures from Rockport are generally at 10:30am, 12:30pm, and 2:30pm, but call or check the website to confirm seasonal variations. Rockport Boat Line offers a variety of shorter island cruises as well.

Note that Heart Island, where Boldt Castle is located, is in the United States. Coming from Canada, you're crossing an international border and you must have a valid passport.

Helicopter Tours

As beautiful as the Thousand Islands are from the water, they're even more striking from the air, which you can see on a flight with **1000 Islands Helicopter Tours** (88 County Rd. 32, 613/382-3888 or 855/855-4354, www.1000islandshelicoptertours.com). Opt for a 10-minute island overview ($99 pp), add a loop over Boldt Castle on an 18-minute tour ($149 pp), or take a 30-minute flight ($199 pp) that takes in Boldt Castle as well as Singer Castle, which Frederick Gilbert Bourne, president of the Singer Sewing Machine Company, built in the early 1900s.

Sports and Recreation

A fun way to explore the Thousand Islands is by kayak. **1000 Islands Kayaking** (110 Kate

The best way to see the Thousand Islands is on a boat tour.

St., 613/329-6265, www.1000islandskayaking. com, May-Oct., half-day single $45, tandem $75, full-day single $55, tandem $95) rents kayaks and leads guided trips (half day, 9am-noon or 1pm-4pm, adults $85, kids $65; full-day, 9am-4pm, adults $135, kids $85). They'll tailor an excursion to your interests and abilities, whether you want to learn about the history or natural life of the islands or get a good workout. They accept walk-ins, but if you have specific interests or requests, give them a call in advance. They also rent camping gear (handy if you'd like to camp in the Thousand Islands National Park), offer guided multiday paddling tours, and teach kayaking lessons, including a one-day introduction to paddling.

You can cycle between Gananoque and Brockville along the pretty 37-kilometer (23-mile) section of the **Waterfront Trail** (www.waterfronttrail.org), a paved, gently rolling route that parallels the Thousand Islands Parkway. **T.I. Cycle** (711 King St. E., Gananoque, 613/382-5144, www.ti-cycle.com) rents bicycles ($10 per hour, $30-40 per day) April through October.

Entertainment and Events

From May through October, the well-regarded **Thousand Islands Playhouse** (185 South St., 613/382-7020 or 866/382-7020, www.1000islandsplayhouse.com), a professional company established in 1982, presents 7-10 plays in repertory in two riverfront theaters. The deck of the Springer Theatre, overlooking the river, must be one of the prettiest theater lobbies anywhere.

Accommodations

Gananoque has several inns and B&Bs in historic buildings around the center of town. If you're looking for chain motels, they're jumbled together on King Street East.

In many First Nations legends, North America was called Turtle Island. Ted and Chris, owners of the **Turtle Island B&B** (415 Stone St. S., 613/382-7261 or 855/382-7261, www.turtleislandbb.com, $119 d), chose this name for their relaxed lodging, where they display their collection of aboriginal arts and crafts. The three air-conditioned guest rooms in this 1922 brick Victorian are simple but cozy, with quilt-topped beds and First Nations prints on the walls. Fresh-baked scones and Belgian waffles are among the breakfast specialties.

It's easy to spot the **Sleepy Hollow Bed & Breakfast** (95 King St. W., 613/382-4377 or 866/426-7422, www.sleepyhollowbb.ca,

view of the Thousand Islands via helicopter

$110-180 d), a Victorian "painted lady" decked out in yellow, purple, and green. This rambling 1905 home still has its original tin ceiling and oak wainscoting on the first floor. Upstairs, the seven guest rooms are homey and a bit old-fashioned, with period furnishings. There's a pool table for guests, and you can make yourself at home in the octagonal dining room, where owners Don and Marion Matthews serve a full hot breakfast. Wi-Fi is included in the rates.

A grand 1873 brick mansion surrounded by gardens, the **Victoria Rose Inn** (279 King St. W., 613/382-3368 or 888/246-2893, www.victoriaroseinn.com, May-Oct., $159-265 d) was originally the summer residence of Gananoque's first mayor. The main level has high ceilings, arched windows, and the original oak floor. Stylish guest units (some with fireplaces) are here and on the second and third floors, furnished with antiques and creamy beige linens. The Tower Suite has a whirlpool tub in the top-floor turret. Rates include coffee, tea, and cake in the morning, but not a full breakfast.

Gananoque's only waterfront hotel is the **Gananoque Inn** (550 Stone St. S., 613/382-2165 or 888/565-3101, www.gananoqueinn.com, $189-400) with 53 rooms in several different buildings. Some of the traditional rooms in the 1896 main inn have verandas overlooking the water. The newer annex units are large and more upscale, some with whirlpool tubs and fireplaces. The small spa offers the expected range of massages, facials, and other treatments, and the inn has two restaurants: the more formal river-view **Watermark** (from 5pm daily July-Oct., dinner $23-30) and the mellow **Muskie Jake's Tap and Grill** (daily year-round, call for seasonal hours, $12-15).

Food

If you don't want to dine at one of the inns, wander along King Street East to find more casual eateries. You're close enough to Kingston that you could head there for more dining choices.

Stop into **Panaché Bakery** (162 King St. E., 613/382-1412, www.panachebakery. ca, 8am-5:30pm Mon.-Fri., 8am-5pm Sat., 10am-4pm Sun.) for breakfast, a light lunch, or a snack. They bake fresh muffins (try the cranberry walnut), scones, mini quiches, and breads, and they make up a few sandwiches, too.

Get a cup of coffee and check your email (there's free Wi-Fi) at the quirky **Socialist Pig Coffeehouse** (21 King St. E., 613/463-8800, www.thesocialist21pig.com, 7am-10pm Mon.-Thurs., 7am-11pm Fri., 8am-11pm Sat., 8am-11pm Sun. summer, call for off-season hours), where the counter is made from a stack of books. They dish out sandwiches, interesting salads like quinoa with kale, beets, and goat cheese, burritos, and other light meals (11am to 9pm).

Part Canadian diner and part Eastern European schnitzel parlor, the homey **Maple Leaf Restaurant/The Czech Snitzel House** (65 King St. E., 613/382-7666, www. mapleleafrestaurant.ca, 11am-9:30pm Tues.-Sat., 10am-9:30pm Sun. May-mid-Oct., $10-22) serves homemade borscht, spaetzle, and delicious schnitzel in either chicken or pork varieties alongside burgers, omelets, and deli sandwiches.

Modern Italian fare is on the menu at **Riva Restaurant** (45 King St. W., 613/887-2487, www.rivarestaurant.ca, 11:30am-2:30pm and 5pm-10pm Sun.-Thurs., 11:30am-2:30pm and 5pm-11pm Fri.-Sat., lunch $9-19, dinner $12-25), a classy multiroom space where exposed brick walls and wide-board floors offset more contemporary finishes. Choose from salads, pizzas, and pastas, like the gnocchi with short-rib *ragù* or linguine alla carbonara (bacon-cream sauce), as well as veal marsala or steak.

Information and Services

The **Gananoque Chamber of Commerce and Visitors Services Centre** (10 King St. E., 613/382-3250 or 800/561-1595, www.1000islandsgananoque.com and www. travel1000islands.ca, 8am-8:30pm daily late June-early Sept., 9am-5pm daily mid-May-late

June and early Sept.-mid-Oct., 10am-4pm Tues.-Sat. mid-Oct.-mid-May) can provide information about the town and the surrounding area. The **Thousand Islands International Tourism Council** (800/847-5263, www.visit1000islands.com) is another source of information about the islands on both the Canadian and U.S. sides of the border.

Getting There and Around

Gananoque is 30 kilometers (19 miles) east of Kingston, 290 kilometers (180 miles) northeast of Toronto, and 160 kilometers (100 miles) south of Ottawa. If you're traveling east on Highway 401, take exits 645 or 647; heading west, take exits 645 or 648. The prettiest route between Gananoque and Brockville is the 52-kilometer (32-mile) Thousand Islands Parkway, which hugs the shore parallel to Highway 401. Note that the parkway is not the same road as Highway 2, which also parallels Highway 401.

While you don't need a car within Gananoque—it's a short walk among downtown, the waterfront, and many of the accommodations—there's no convenient bus or train service into town.

THOUSAND ISLANDS NATIONAL PARK

The first Canadian national park east of the Rockies, **Thousand Islands National Park** (613/923-5261 or 888/773-8888, www.pc.gc.ca, late May-mid-Oct.) was established in 1904 to encompass more than 20 islands in the St. Lawrence River. On the mainland, stop into the park's **Mallorytown Landing Visitors Centre** (1121 Thousand Islands Pkwy., Mallorytown, 613/923-5261, 10am-4pm Sat.-Sun. late May-early June, 10am-4pm Thurs.-Mon. early June-early Sept., parking $6 per vehicle), between Gananoque and Brockville, to learn more about the region's natural and cultural history.

Three short easy **walking trails,** ranging from 750 meters (0.5 miles) to 1.1 kilometers (0.7 miles), start at the Visitors Centre.

For additional hiking options, head to the park's **Jones Creek area** (1270 Thousand Islands Pkwy.), east of the Visitors Centre, off the Thousand Islands Parkway. West of the Visitors Centre, closer to Gananoque, you can hike at the **Landon Bay Centre** (302 Thousand Islands Pkwy., 613/382-2719).

If you don't have your own boat, the best way to explore the park islands is to rent a kayak or book a paddling tour with **1000 Islands Kayaking** (110 Kate St., Gananoque, 613/329-6265, www.1000islandskayaking.com). The **Misty Isles Lodge** (25 River Rd., Lansdowne, 613/382-4232, www.mistyisles.ca) has boat rentals and offers tours as well.

The park has 61 rustic **campsites** ($15.70) on several of the islands; 36 can be reserved through the **Parks Canada reservation service** (877/737-3783, www.reservation.pc.gc.ca, reservation fee online $11, by phone $13.50), while the remainder are first-come, first-served. You need a boat, a canoe, or a kayak to access these island campsites. You can also stay in an **oTENTik** (www.reservation.pc.gc.ca, $90), a park-managed platform tent that sleeps up to six. There are three oTENTiks on McDonald Island and two on Gordon Island (both islands have composting toilets but no running water), and several more near the Mallorytown Landing Visitors Centre, which has restroom facilities.

BROCKVILLE AND VICINITY

As you wander through the town of Brockville, on the St. Lawrence River at the east end of the Thousand Islands, you'll notice a number of grand Victorian homes, though none is grander than the mansion that local resident George Fulford built at the turn of the 20th century.

★ Fulford Place

Entrepreneur and politician George Taylor Fulford (1852-1905) made his fortune hawking "Pink Pills for Pale People." He had bought the rights to these pills, a simple iron supplement, for $53.01, and successfully marketed his wonder drug as he traveled the world in the late 1800s.

Fulford used the considerable proceeds to build **Fulford Place** (287 King St. E., 613/498-3003, www.heritagetrust.on.ca, adults $6, seniors, students, and kids over age 6 $5), an opulent 35-room Edwardian mansion overlooking the St. Lawrence River, where he lived with his wife Mary White Fulford (1856-1949) and their three children. The house was completed in 1901, but sadly, Fulford enjoyed the fruits of his labors for just a few years. In 1905, he became the first Canadian to die in an automobile accident.

The 1,900-square-meter (20,000-square-foot) home is made of marble and filled with all sorts of sumptuous details—Honduran mahogany ceilings, silk wallpaper, and the original stained-glass windows. Many of the furnishings on view belonged to the Fulford family. Frederick Law Olmsted, who designed New York's Central Park, landscaped the Fulford Place gardens.

The schedule for Fulford Place **tours** (generally 11am-4pm daily late June-early Sept., 11am-4pm Tues.-Sun. late May-late June, last tour at 3:10pm; 1pm Tues.-Thurs., 11am-4pm Sat.-Sun. Sept., 1pm Tues.-Thurs., noon-4pm Sun. Oct.-Dec.) changes seasonally, and it's a good idea to call or check the website to confirm tour hours.

Fulford Place is just east of downtown Brockville on King Street, which becomes Highway 2 on either end of town.

Homewood Museum

One of the oldest houses in Ontario, a Georgian-style stone home built in 1799-1800 is now the **Homewood Museum** (Hwy. 2, Maitland, 613/498-3003, www.heritagetrust.on.ca, 10am-4pm Wed.-Sun. mid-June-early Sept., adults $3, under age 16 $1.50, combination ticket with Fulford Place $6). Seven generations of the Jones family lived here, and unlike many historic homes, all the furnishings belonged to the family, including the four-poster bed, the china and silver, and the early 19th-century surgical tools. The

original owner, Solomon Jones (1756-1822), was a Loyalist and the area's first physician. Guides take you on 30- to 45-minute tours of the house.

The Homewood Museum is located just east of the town of Maitland, between Brockville and Prescott. From Highway 401, take the Maitland exit and go south to Highway 2. Turn east onto Highway 2, and continue about two kilometers (1.25 miles) to the house.

Many members of the Jones family are buried in the **Blue Church Cemetery,** where numerous graves date to the late 1700s and early 1800s. The cemetery is also the final resting place of Barbara Heck, a founder of the Methodist Church. You'll find the graveyard three kilometers (1.8 miles) east of Homewood on Highway 2.

Sports and Recreation

Hundreds of ships were sunk in the St. Lawrence River over the past several centuries, and many of these wrecks are now accessible to scuba divers. **Dive Brockville** (12 Water St. E., 613/345-2800, www.divebrockville.com) can organize dives and supply you with gear.

Accommodations and Food

It's okay to sleep in church—at least if you're staying at the **Green Door Bed-and-Breakfast** (61 Buell St., 613/341-9325, www.greendoorbb.com, $125-150 d), a 1928 former Pentecostal tabernacle that welcoming hosts Lynne and Peter Meleg converted into a funky B&B. The common spaces are striking, with 4.5-meter (15-foot) ceilings and original arched windows. The former altar is now a library. Breakfasts might include ricotta pancakes or poached eggs served on a bed of spinach. The four compact guest rooms are full of character, and two apartments are available in an adjacent 1890s house.

Pick up a coffee and pastry at the long-standing **Tait's Bakery** (31 King St. W., 613/342-3567, www.taitsbakery.net, 7am-5pm Mon.-Fri., 7am-5pm Sat. summer, call for off-season hours). For a light lunch, try **Boboli** (32 King St. W., Brockville, 613/498-2957), which makes homemade soup and deli sandwiches on freshly baked bread.

At the **Georgian Dragon Ale House** (72 King St., 613/865-8224; 11am-11pm Mon.-Thurs., 11am-2am Fri., 9am-2am Sat., 9am-11pm Sun., $10-15), a traditional English pub, you can hang out over a beer, a burger, or a hearty Guinness pie. On weekends they serve good-value breakfast specials.

Information and Services

For more information about the Brockville area, contact the **Brockville and District Chamber of Commerce Tourism Office** (10 Market St. W., 613/342-4357 or 888/251-7676, www.brockvilletourism.com, 8am-5pm daily late May-mid-June, 8am-6pm daily mid-June-early Sept., 8:30am-4:30pm Mon.-Fri. early Sept.-late May).

Getting There and Around

Brockville is 55 kilometers (35 miles) northeast of Gananoque and 110 kilometers (68 miles) south of Ottawa via Highway 401 or Highway 2.

VIA Rail (888/842-7245, www.viarail.ca) trains run to Brockville Station (141 Perth St.) from Toronto (3.25-3.75 hours; one-way adults $73-84, ages 2-11 $38-42), Kingston (0.75 hour; one-way adults $23-34, seniors and students $21-31, ages 2-11 $17-20), and Ottawa (1.25 hours, one-way adults $29-47, ages 2-11 $20-23). The train station is about one kilometer (0.6 miles) northwest of downtown.

Megabus (866/488-4452, www.megabus.com) stops in Brockville from Kingston (one hour, one-way $14-23), Montreal (2.5 hours, one-way $39-50), and Toronto (4 hours, $34-52). The bus drops you in the parking lot of the Food Basics store (3049 Jefferson Dr.), north of Highway 401, about two kilometers (1.2 miles) from downtown. Since the Megabus depot is on the north side of Highway 401, and downtown is on the south, take a cab rather than trying to walk.

It's easiest to explore the region if you have a car, but Brockville's downtown area is compact and walkable. Fulford Place is 1.5 kilometers (0.9 miles) east of downtown.

PRESCOTT

Settled by the British in 1787, the town of Prescott became a military post to defend Canada's border. Fort Wellington, now the **Fort Wellington National Historic Site** (370 Vankoughnet St., at King St., 613/925-2896, www.pc.gc.ca, 10am-5pm daily July-early Sept., 10am-5pm Thurs.-Mon. late May-June and early Sept.-mid-Oct., adults $3.90, seniors $3.40, ages 6-16 $1.90, families $9.80), was built during the War of 1812 to protect shipping routes along the St. Lawrence River from U.S. attack. Nowadays, guides in period costumes demonstrate 19th-century games, crafts, open-hearth cooking, and rifle and cannon handling. The Visitors Centre's exhibits fill in more details about the fort's role during War of 1812, and in summer, you can take a guided tour of the fort (1:30pm Sat.-Sun. July-Aug., adults $7.80, seniors $7.30, kids $5.80).

MORRISBURG
★ Upper Canada Village

Walk back into the 1860s when you enter the gates of **Upper Canada Village** (13740 County Rd. 2, 613/543-4328 or 800/437-2233, www.uppercanadavillage.com, 9:30am-5pm daily early May-early Sept., 9:30am-5pm Wed.-Sun. early Sept.-late Sept., adults $18, seniors $16, ages 6-12 $12), one of Ontario's largest and best-preserved historic villages.

Not only do costumed interpreters staff all the village buildings, going about their business as 19th-century millers, shopkeepers, tavern-keepers, and bakers, they'll enthusiastically tell you about life on the cusp of the Industrial Revolution, as Upper Canada was transforming from farm country to a more mechanized society. In the woolen mill, staff operate original carding and spinning machines, powered by a water turbine that replaced the "old" technology of the spinning wheel. In the grist mill, staff grind grains that the village bakers use to bake bread, and in the saw mill, they're splitting logs with their newfangled machines. There's a cheese factory and a school, a dressmaker and a village doctor, a tinsmith, a print shop, a blacksmith, even a farm, complete with live animals.

Start in the multimedia Discovery Centre, which puts the village into its historical context. The story begins with the original First Nations inhabitants (you can listen to audio clips in the Mohawk language) and continues with the Loyalists who settled here after the U.S. Revolutionary War. More exhibits explain the region's ongoing development from the Industrial Revolution into the 20th century. Kids have plenty of special activities, too. They can dress in traditional garb, learn to milk a cow, and ride along the village canal on a horse-drawn barge.

You can easily visit Upper Canada Village on a day trip from Ottawa, 80 kilometers (50 miles) to the northwest. Pick up Highway 31, which continues south all the way to Morrisburg. Turn left (east) on County Road 2; the village is 11 kilometers (6.8 miles) to the east.

From Gananoque, 110 kilometers (68 miles) to the west, follow Highway 401 to exit 758 (Upper Canada Rd.), go south, then turn left on County Road 2. From there, it's two kilometers (1.25 miles) east to the village.

Upper Canada Bird Sanctuary

Every fall, thousands of geese pass through the **Upper Canada Bird Sanctuary** (5591 County Rd. 2, Ingleside, 613/537-2024, www.stlawrenceparks.com, trails daily year-round) as they migrate south for the winter. At this 9,000-hectare (22,000-acre) preserve of woods, marsh, pastures, and waterways, you might also see great blue heron, wild turkeys, hawks, ducks, and a wide variety of common and less common birds. Even if you're not a birder, the sanctuary is a pleasant for a walk or hike, with eight kilometers (five miles) of self-guided nature trails; in winter, the trails are open for cross-country skiing. The Visitors

Centre (mid-May-late Oct.) has nature exhibits about the area.

The sanctuary is 14 kilometers (nine miles) east of Morrisburg, off County Road 2, near Ingleside. From Highway 401, take exits 758 or 770.

Entertainment and Events

While you're in town, take in a show at the **Upper Canada Playhouse** (12320 County Rd. 2, 613/543-3713 or 877/550-3650, www.uppercanadaplayhouse.com, Apr.-Dec.), a professional theater company that presents several comedies and other light plays every year. The theater is a former toothbrush factory.

Accommodations and Food

Sleep like a pioneer at **Upper Canada Village** (613/543-4328 or 800/437-2233, www.uppercanadavillage.com). Montgomery House ($175), a 19th-century log cabin, looks rustic, but inside, between the log walls and wide pine floors, are a living room with couches and a TV, a double Murphy bed, a full kitchen, and two baths. Upstairs under the eaves are six single beds. Linens are provided, but there's no Internet. The larger Guest House ($275) is a restored farmhouse with a main-floor living area, a country kitchen, a TV/DVD, a computer with Internet access, and a washer-dryer. Three bedrooms upstairs sleep eight total.

Along County Road 2 near Upper Canada Village are a couple of basic motels, including the **Riverside Motel** (13339 County Rd. 2, 613/543-2162 or 877/885-5078, www.stayriverside.ca, $85-99), which has air-conditioning and free Wi-Fi.

About 10 kilometers (six miles) west of Upper Canada Village in the town of Morrisburg is the lavishly decorated ★ **Russell Manor B&B** (36 1st St., 613/543-3871 or 866/401-7472, www.russellmanorbb.com, $115-150 s, $125-160 d). Starting from the upscale parlor with cream-hued rugs and overstuffed sofas, owners Michael Burton (the interior decorator) and Ron Currie (the breakfast chef) have created an elegant, romantic retreat in their 1870s manor house. Upstairs are three two-room suites with separate sitting areas, Victorian furnishings, voluminous draperies, and fine linens; a fourth room is a snug studio overlooking the garden.

Part curio store, part art gallery, and part old-time coffee shop, the **Basket Case Cafe** (27 Main St., 613/543-0002, 10am-6pm Tues.-Sun., $5-7), in a strip mall on County Road 2, is as crammed with stuff as your grandmother's attic. But no matter, they cook up tasty breakfasts, soups, sandwiches, and pies.

Camping

The **St. Lawrence Parks Commission** (613/543-4328 or 800/437-2233, www.parks.on.ca), which operates Upper Canada Village and the Bird Sanctuary, also manages several campgrounds in the Morrisburg area. As a camper you'll receive two free passes that you can use at either Upper Canada Village or at Fort Henry in Kingston; campers can purchase up to four additional tickets at 25 percent off the regular rates by showing your camping receipt at the ticket offices. Contact the Parks Commission or use their online reservation service to reserve a campsite (reservation fee $11.43 plus tax).

The 300-site **Riverside-Cedar Campground** (13180 County Rd. 2, 613/543-3287, mid-May-mid-Oct., tent sites $32-34, electrical sites $37-44, cabins $89-103), along the St. Lawrence River, is closest to Upper Canada Village. Five cabins are available for rent. If you don't have your own tent or RV, you might consider the **instant camping service** ($40-43)—a preassembled tent that sleeps up to six on a raised wooden platform; just bring sleeping bags or bed linens.

The 69-site **Upper Canada Migratory Bird Sanctuary Campground** (5781 Country Rd. 2, Ingelside, 613/537-2024, mid-May-mid-Oct., tent sites $32-36, electrical sites $39-43) is on the bird sanctuary grounds. Campsites have both water and electricity. The campground has showers, and there is a swimming beach along the river.

Getting There and Around

From Ottawa, County Road 31 runs 80 kilometers (50 miles) south to Morrisburg. Following the speedier Highway 416 to Highway 401 is longer (120 kilometers, 75 miles), but it will take you about the same amount of time. Morrisburg is 140 kilometers (87 miles) northeast of Kingston along Highway 401. **VIA Rail** (www.viarail.ca) trains from Toronto or Ottawa stop in Brockville (west of Morrisburg) and in Cornwall (east of Morrisburg), but you really need a car to get around the area.

Ottawa

Look for ★ to find recommended sights, activities, dining, and lodging.

Highlights

★ **Parliament Tours:** Any visit to Ottawa should begin on Parliament Hill, in the ornate complex of copper-roofed buildings that houses Canada's national legislature. Dozens of special events, including a nightly summer sound-and-light show and the nation's biggest Canada Day celebration, also take place in front of Parliament (page 249).

★ **Changing the Guard:** Complete with red-coated, fur hat-wearing guards, this daily summer procession on Parliament Hill echoes

its namesake ceremony at Buckingham Palace (page 253).

★ **Canadian War Museum:** The exhibitions in this striking contemporary museum west of Parliament Hill manage to put a human face on the grim periods of war throughout Canada's history (page 254).

★ **Rideau Canal National Historic Site:** Not only is the Rideau, which stretches from Ottawa south to Kingston, the oldest continuously operating canal in North America, in winter the Canal's Ottawa section transforms into the world's largest skating rink (page 256).

★ **National Gallery of Canada:** Designed by Canadian architect Moshe Safdie, the country's national art gallery has a particularly fine collection of Canadian works, including Inuit art. Wander out back for great city views, too (page 258).

★ **ByWard Market:** Named for both a food market and its surrounding neighborhood, this Ottawa district is foodie central, whether you're looking for a picnic lunch, a five-star meal, or a classic BeaverTails snack (page 260).

★ **Canadian Museum of History:** You can learn almost anything you want to know about Canadian history and culture in this massive—and fascinating—museum, in a distinctive curved building on the Gatineau side of the Ottawa River (page 285).

★ **Gatineau Park:** This 361-square-kilometer (89,000-acre) green space in the Quebec hills just a short drive from Ottawa is the city's backyard—for hiking, cycling, swimming, cross-country skiing, snowshoeing, or just relaxing (page 286).

C anada's national capital brims with pomp and grandeur. Parliament, the Supreme Court, the homes of Canada's prime minister and governor general—along with numerous grand museums—are here. In summer, you can even

take in the daily Changing the Guard ceremony, the iconic fur hats and red uniforms echoing the similar famous ritual at London's Buckingham Palace. History comes alive in current-day Ottawa.

Yet Ottawa isn't all about revolutions and representatives. It's an active, outdoorsy city, where residents are frequently out on foot, on skates, or on the water. The Rideau Canal, the oldest continuously operating canal in North America, transforms in winter into the world's largest skating rink. Across the river from downtown is Gatineau Park, a sprawling nature reserve crisscrossed with trails for hiking, snowshoeing, and cross-country skiing.

Ottawa also knows how to party. The city hosts the nation's biggest Canada Day celebration every July 1, and throughout the year, there's one festival after another. Even in frigid February, Ottawa's long-running winter festival—known as Winterlude—draws thousands of visitors from near and far.

Straddling the border with Quebec, this metropolitan area of more than one million people is one of Canada's most bilingual cities. It may not be as francophone as Quebec City or Montreal, but you'll hear plenty of French, not just in government buildings but all around.

If you think that Ottawa's bureaucratic culture means that its food is equally bland, think again—Ottawa is an unexpectedly foodie destination. The city has a branch of Le Cordon Bleu culinary school, where you can take a workshop or have a classic French meal. The capital also has a growing number of innovative restaurants, where you can taste the latest creations when you've had your fill of history, culture, and the outdoors.

PLANNING YOUR TIME

Ottawa is a year-round destination. As long as you're prepared for serious cold (bring heavy coats, long underwear, warm hats, boots, and

---

Previous: Changing the Guard ceremony on Parliament Hill; Canada's national Parliament Building in Ottawa. **Above:** a favorite Ottawa snack.

Ottawa

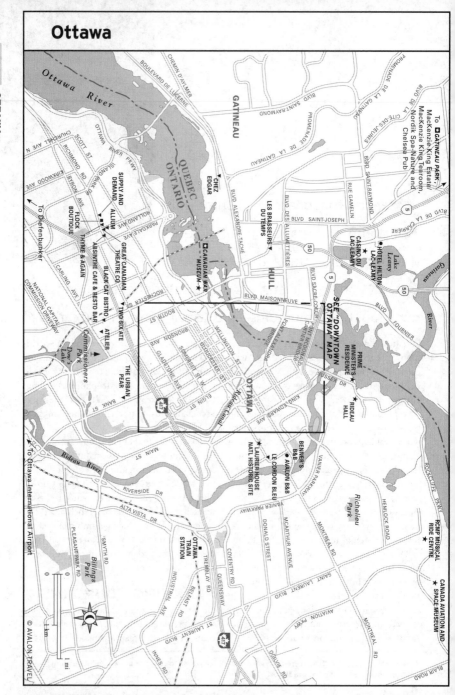

Ottawa River

BOULEVARD DE LUCERNE

CHEMIN D'AYLMER

GATINEAU

To ☆ GATINEAU PARK,
Mackenzie King Estate/
Mackenzie King Tearoom,
Nordik Spa–Nature and
Chelsea Pub

PROMENADE DE LA GATINEAU

BLVD DE LA GATINEAU

CITÉ DES JEUNES

BLVD SAINT-RAYMOND

QUEBEC
ONTARIO

CHEZ
EDGAR

BLVD ALEXANDRE TACHE

BLVD SAINT-RAYMOND

RUE GAMELIN

BLVD DE LA CARRIÈRE

CHURCHILL AVE N

SCOTT ST

RICHMOND RD

KIRKWOOD AVE

BYRON AVE

RICHMOND AVE

OTTAWA RIVER PKWY

ISLAND PARK DR

HOLLAND AVE

PARKDALE AVE

ROCHESTER ST

SUPPLY AND
DEMAND
ALLIUM

FLOCK
BOUTIQUE

THYME & AGAIN

ABSINTHE CAFE & RESTO BAR

GREAT CANADIAN
THEATRE CO.

BLACK CAT BISTRO

TWO SIX ATE

ATELIER

☐ CANADIAN WAR
MUSEUM ★

LES BRASSEURS
DU TEMPS ▼

BLVD DES ALLUMETTIÈRES

BLVD SAINT-JOSEPH

HULL

BLVD SACRÉ-COEUR

BLVD MAISONNEUVE

50

5

CASINO DU
LAC-LEAMY

● HOTEL HILTON
LAC-LEAMY

Lake
Leamy

50

BLVD FOURNIER

Gatineau River

To Diefenbunker

CARLING AVE

NATIONAL CAPITAL
COMMISSION DRIVEWAY

Commissioners
Park

Dow's
Lake

BANK ST

THE URBAN
PEAR

BOOTH ST

BRONSON AVE

WELLINGTON ST

SOMERSET ST

GLOUCESTER ST

GLADSTONE AVE

ELGIN ST

SEE "DOWNTOWN
OTTAWA" MAP

417

OTTAWA

Rideau Canal

KING EDWARD AVE

PONT MCDONALD–
CARTIER BRIDGE

ALEXANDRA BRIDGE

SUSSEX DR

PRIME
MINISTER'S
RESIDENCE

RIDEAU
HALL ★

To Ottawa International Airport

Rideau River

RIVERSIDE DR

ALTA VISTA DR

MAIN ST

SMYTH RD

PLEASANT PARK RD

Billings
Park

PLEASANT PARK RD

INDUSTRIAL AVE

TREMBLAY RD

BELFAST RD

ST LAURENT BLVD

INNES RD

OTTAWA TRAIN
STATION

COVENTRY RD

QUEENSWAY

COLONEL BY DR

DONALD STREET

MCARTHUR AVENUE

MONTREAL RD

VANIER PARKWAY

VANIER PARKWAY

BENNER'S
B&B

● AVALON B&B

LE CORDON BLEU ●

LAURIER HOUSE
NATL HISTORIC SITE ★

Richelieu
Park

HEMLOCK ROAD

ROCKCLIFFE PKWY

SAINT LAURENT BLVD

AVIATION PKWY

OGILVIE RD

MONTREAL RD

RCMP MUSICAL
RIDE CENTRE ★

CANADA AVIATION AND
SPACE MUSEUM ★

ROCKCLIFFE PKWY

BLAIR ROAD

0   1 km

0   1 mi

© AVALON TRAVEL

417

mittens), a winter visit means fewer crowds at Parliament, the museums, and other attractions (though some reduce their hours in the winter months). In spring, the capital shakes off its winter chill as a rainbow of colorful flowers bloom, particularly during the annual Canadian Tulip Festival. And if you want the best weather, schedule your visit during the crisp, clear days of fall.

Still, it's summer when Ottawa really comes alive. Sure, the days can be hot and sticky, but the streets and museums fill with visitors, and every morning, crowds gather for the Changing the Guard ceremony on Parliament Hill. Vendors set up their stalls around the ByWard Market, and one festival after another livens up the summer calendar.

If you have two or three days, you can take in many of Ottawa's highlights: tour the **Parliament** buildings; visit the **National Gallery of Canada** and the **Canadian Museum of History;** stroll, cycle, or (in winter) skate along the **Rideau Canal;** and wrap up with a wander through the **ByWard Market** district to snack on a beaver tail (the city's iconic fried-dough treat), or have dinner at one of the many contemporary restaurants.

With four or five days, you can explore the capital in greater depth. If you're interested in government, politics, or the official life, tour **Rideau Hall** (the governor general's residence) and the **Supreme Court.** You'll have more time to explore the shops around the ByWard Market or venture farther from downtown to shop and eat in the up-and-coming Wellington West neighborhood. If you're visiting with kids, don't miss the **Canadian Museum of Nature** or an afternoon outdoors in **Gatineau Park.** Or head west of the city to the **Diefenbunker,** a quirky—and somber—museum that takes you back to Canada's Cold War era.

Sights

Ottawa's main attractions are clustered in the city center on either side of the Rideau Canal. Parliament Hill and the main downtown district are west of the canal; the ByWard Market, the National Gallery of Canada, and the Royal Canadian Mint are east of the canal. Gatineau, across the Ottawa River from downtown, is where you'll find the Canadian Museum of History and Gatineau Park. With so many major museums, Ottawa can induce a sort of museum fatigue, so balance your sightseeing with more relaxing pursuits. A walk along the Rideau Canal or through the ByWard Market district can help revive flagging energy.

Some of Ottawa's most interesting neighborhoods aren't known for their sights, but they're still worth exploring. Head for Chinatown and Little Italy, both southwest of downtown, to browse the markets or look for a meal. The funky Glebe neighborhood, which runs along Bank Street south of downtown, and Wellington West, on the city's west side, are both fun districts to ramble through for shopping and eating.

PARLIAMENT HILL

Any visit to Ottawa should begin on **Parliament Hill** (111 Wellington St., at Metcalfe St.), the legislative headquarters of Canada's national government. Even if you're not interested in the work of the federal policy wonks, the strikingly ornate complex of copper-roofed Parliament buildings above the Ottawa River is worth visiting for its architectural glamour alone.

★ Parliament Tours

The **Centre Block Guided Tour** (www.parl.gc.ca, generally 9am-4:30pm daily July-Apr., 9am-7:30pm daily May-June, free) takes you through the main Parliament building, which opened in 1920 after a fire destroyed most of the original structure. These 20- to 60-minute tours typically begin in the foyer

Downtown Ottawa

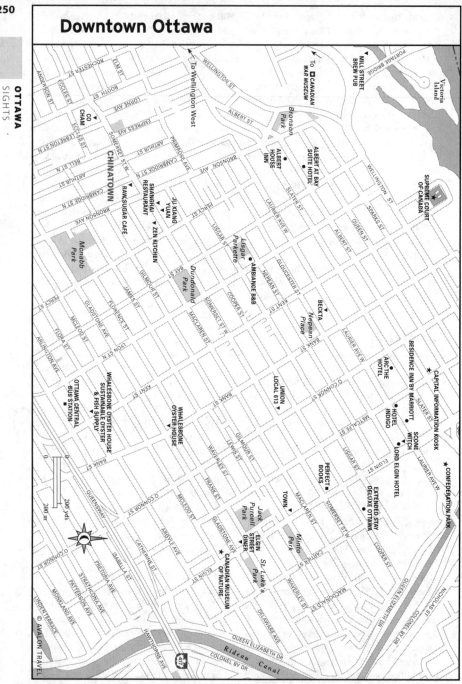

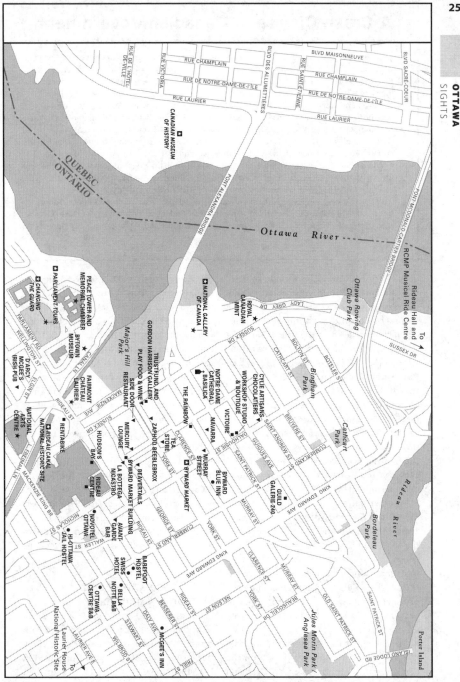

QUEBEC
ONTARIO

Ottawa River

RUE DE L'HÔTEL DE VILLE
RUE VICTORIA
RUE CHAMPLAIN
RUE DE NOTRE-DAME-DE-L'ÎLE
RUE LAURIER
RUE DES ALLUMETTIÈRES
BLVD DES ALLUMETTIÈRES
BLVD MAISONNEUVE
RUE CHAMPLAIN
RUE SAINTE-ÉTIENNE
RUE DE NOTRE-DAME-DE-L'ÎLE
RUE LAURIER
BLVD SACRÉ-COEUR

CANADIAN MUSEUM OF HISTORY

PONT ALEXANDRA BRIDGE

PONT MACDONALD-CARTIER BRIDGE

To
Rideau Hall and
RCMP Musical Ride Centre

Ottawa Rowing Club Park

LADY GREY DR

SUSSEX DR

Rideau River

Bordeleau Park

Porter Island

Jules Morin Park / Anglesea Park

ISLAND LODGE RD

OLD SAINT PATRICK ST

SAINT PATRICK ST

PEACE TOWER AND MEMORIAL CHAMBER
PARLIAMENT TOURS
CHANGING THE GUARD

PARLIAMENT HILL

WELLINGTON ST
BYTOWN MUSEUM
D'ARCY MCGEE'S IRISH PUB
ELGIN ST
NATIONAL ARTS CENTRE
FAIRMONT CHÂTEAU LAURIER
CANAL LOCKS
MACKENZIE AVE
RIDEAU ST
SUSSEX DR
RENTABIKE
RIDEAU CANAL NATIONAL HISTORIC SITE
MACKENZIE KING BR
THE MALL LIT

Major's Hill Park

ROYAL CANADIAN MINT

NATIONAL GALLERY OF CANADA

TRUSTFUND, AND GORDON HARRISON GALLERY
PLAY FOOD & WINE
SIDE DOOR RESTAURANT

CLYLE ARTISANS CHOCOLATIERS
WORKSHOP STUDIO & BOUTIQUE
NOTRE DAME CATHEDRAL BASILICA
VICTOIRE
NAVARRA

THE RAINBOW

TEA STORE
MERCURY LOUNGE
ZAPHOD BEEBLEROX
CLARENCE ST
YORK ST
MURRAY STREET
BYWARD MARKET
BYWARD BLUE INN
GUILD GALERIE 240

HUDSON'S BAY
LA BOTTEGA NICASTRO
BEAVERTAILS
BYWARD MARKET BUILDING

RIDEAU CENTRE

AVANT-GARDE BAR
NOVOTEL OTTAWA
HI-OTTAWA JAIL HOSTEL

NICHOLAS ST
WALLER ST
GEORGE ST
CUMBERLAND ST
RIDEAU ST
KING EDWARD AVE
YORK ST
CLARENCE ST
MURRAY ST
BEAUSOLEIL DR
NELSON ST
CATHCART ST
BOLTON ST
SAINT ANDREW ST
DALHOUSIE ST
SAINT PATRICK ST
GUIGUES AVE
BRUYÈRE ST
CUMBERLAND ST
BOTELER ST

Bingham Park
Cathcart Park

BARREFOOT HOSTEL
SWISS HOTEL
BELLA
NOTTE B&B
OTTAWA CENTRE B&B
MCGEE'S INN

BESSERER ST
DALY AVE
STEWART ST
WILBROD ST
WILBROD ST
FRIEL ST
LAURIER AVE E

To
Laurier House
National Historic Site

A Crash Course in Canadian Government

Your visit to Ottawa will mean more if you know something about the workings of the Canadian government. The federal government has three branches: executive, legislative, and judicial. Canada's **prime minister** is the country's chief executive, and **Parliament,** the national legislature, makes Canada's federal laws.

Parliament is made up of two bodies: the House of Commons, whose 308 members are elected, and the Senate, in which—unlike the U.S. Senate—the 105 legislators are appointed. Each House of Commons member, known as a Member of Parliament or MP, represents a geographically based "riding" or district. They're elected to five-year terms. Senators can come from anywhere in the country. They can remain on the job until they reach age 75.

When a bill is introduced in Parliament, majorities in both the House of Commons and the Senate must approve it. The governor general, who is the British monarch's representative in Canada, then gives final approval—known as "royal assent"—to a bill before it becomes law.

Want to know more? The Parliament website (www.parl.gc.ca) is an excellent resource for information about the Canadian legislative system. And if you visit Parliament Hill in Ottawa, plan to tour the House of Commons and Senate Chambers and, if you can, arrange to watch a legislative session in action.

of the House of Commons, include an overview of Canada's parliamentary process, and, if Parliament isn't in session, visit the green **House of Commons chamber,** the color of which is modeled on the British House of Commons, and the red **Senate chamber.** Also on the tour is the gorgeous **Library of Parliament,** a circular Gothic Revival structure at the back of the Centre Block, which dates to 1876. It's one of the only parts of the original Parliament buildings that survived the devastating 1916 fire (an employee closed the library's thick iron doors, saving it from the flames). Bedecked with elaborate wood carvings and ironwork, the library houses over one million books.

Another option is the 30- to 40-minute **East Block Guided Tour** (www.parl.gc.ca, 10am-4:30pm, July-Aug., free), which explores the 1860s building east of the Centre Block, which now houses legislative offices. The tour visits three rooms that have been restored to their 19th-century functions, including the office of the governor general, the office of Canada's first prime minister, and the Privy Council chamber.

To take either Parliament building tour, you must reserve a ticket in person on the day you want to tour. Tickets are available

beginning at 9am, and they're issued for particular times during the day. The first tours of the day are generally less crowded, so arrive early if you can. On a busy summer day, you might show up in the morning and find that the first available tour is late in the afternoon, so be prepared to adjust your schedule. Tour lengths vary depending on what's going on in the buildings; tours don't enter the Senate or House of Commons chambers when Parliament is in session. Expect airport-style security screening before you enter the building.

Between mid-May and early September, make your tour reservations at the **Capital Information Kiosk** (90 Wellington St., 9am-6pm), opposite Parliament Hill. Between early September and mid-May, arrange your Centre Block tour at the **Visitor Welcome Centre** inside the Centre Block, at the base of the Peace Tower.

The Peace Tower and Memorial Chamber

In the middle of Parliament's Centre Block is the landmark Peace Tower, bedecked with gargoyles and ornate stonework, its clock face visible from blocks away. Completed in 1927, the tower is dedicated to the Canadian soldiers who died in World War I. Bells in the tower chime every quarter hour, and the tower also houses a carillon, with 53 bells ranging in size from 4.5 kilograms (10 pounds) to more than 10,000 kilograms (over 22,000 pounds). From the Parliament lawn, you can listen to **free carillon concerts** (11am-noon daily July-Aug., noon-12:15pm daily Sept.-June).

Take an elevator to the Peace Tower's **observation deck** (generally 9am-7:30pm mid-May-early Sept., 9am-3:30pm early Sept.-mid-May, free) for expansive views of the surrounding area, as well as an up-close look at the carillon's bells. You can go up in the Peace Tower at the end of the Centre Block tours, or ascend the tower without taking a tour. Tickets aren't required, but expect lines, particularly in summer. Go up first thing in the morning to avoid the crowds.

Also in the tower is the Memorial Chamber, a chapel-like space lined with stained-glass windows, memorializing Canadian veterans. The chamber houses seven **Books of Remembrance** containing the names of Canadian men and women who died serving in the armed forces. Daily at 11am, during the **Turning of the Page ceremony,** a page is turned in the Books of Remembrance, so that each name is visible at least once a year. Family members of the dead can make reservations to attend the ceremony by email (memorial-souvenir@parl.gc.ca); the public can view the ceremony from the chamber's entryway.

Parliament Visitor Galleries

When Parliament is in session, visitors are welcome to watch the action from the Visitor Galleries in either the Senate or the House of Commons. The schedule varies, so check the Parliament website (www.parl.gc.ca) for hours. Seating in the galleries is first-come, first-served; go to the Capital Information Kiosk (90 Wellington St.) or Visitor Welcome Centre if you want to attend.

If you're Canadian, you can email or write to your Member of Parliament in advance of your visit to request a seat in the galleries.

You'll then get a seat ahead of visitors who just turn up that day. Look up your MP's contact information on the Parliament website.

A popular time to visit the galleries is during the 45-minute **Question Period,** when the opposition is allowed to question the government. When Parliament is in session, Question Period in the House of Commons is usually held 2:15pm Monday-Thursday and at 11:15am Friday. The Senate Question Period takes place Tuesday-Thursday, but times vary.

You must remain quiet in the galleries—no talking is allowed—so don't bring the kids until they're old enough to sit without chatting.

★ Changing the Guard

If you're visiting Ottawa between late June and August, don't miss the Changing the Guard ceremony (www.parl.gc.ca, 10am daily, free) on the lawn in front of the Parliament buildings. Dressed in ceremonial red coats and tall fur hats recalling their British counterparts at London's Buckingham Palace, the guards march in formation, accompanied by a military band. Most of the young guards are college or university students who are also Canadian armed forces reservists (cool summer job, eh?).

The ceremony takes place rain or shine. Be on the lawn by 9:45am—earlier if you want a front-row view. Before and after the ceremony, the guards march along Wellington and Elgin Streets, where it's often easier to get close-up photos. Consider watching the full ceremony one day and taking more photos on the street the next.

Parliament Grounds

Visitors are welcome to explore the Parliament grounds, which are dotted with statues and monuments, including the **Centennial Flame** on the walkway leading to the Centre Block. It was first lit on January 1, 1967, honoring Canada's 100th birthday. Each of the twelve segments represents one of the provinces and territories (as of 1967). Do you know which current territory is missing? That would be Nunavut, which became Canada's third territory in 1999.

One monument to look for, east of the Centre Block, is *Women Are Persons!*, honoring five female reformers. In 1916, Emily Murphy was appointed a magistrate in the city of Edmonton, the first female magistrate in the British Empire. However, many people protested her appointment, arguing that under the British North America Act of 1867—Canada's founding document—only a qualified "person" could hold public office, and a woman was not legally a person. Murphy, along with Henrietta Muir Edwards, Louise McKinney, Nellie McClung, and Irene Parlby, eventually took the "Persons Case" to Canada's Supreme Court—and lost. They persisted, appealing to the Privy Council in Britain, which finally ruled in 1929 that, yes, women were persons, too.

To guide your explorations, pick up *Discover the Hill: Outdoor Self-Guiding Booklet* in the Visitor Welcome Centre or the **Capital Information Kiosk** (90 Wellington St., 613/239-5000 or 866/811-0055, www.pch.gc.ca, 10am-6pm daily).

Parliament Sound and Light Show

Return to Parliament Hill in the evening for *Mosaika* (613/239-5000 or 866/811-0055, www.mosaika-sl.ca, 10pm daily July-mid-Aug., 9:30pm daily mid-late Aug., 9pm daily Sept., weather permitting, free), a nightly 30-minute sound and light show that illuminates Canada's history and culture, with Parliament as its backdrop. Bring a chair and a blanket if you can.

DOWNTOWN

Extending west and south of Parliament Hill is Ottawa's downtown. Besides the many office and government buildings, several museums and attractions are downtown, as well as numerous hotels. The southern section of downtown, below Lisgar Street, is known as Centretown.

Supreme Court of Canada

With its headquarters a short walk west of Parliament Hill, the **Supreme Court of Canada** (301 Wellington St., 613/995-4330 or 888/551-1185, www.scc-csc.gc.ca, 9am-5pm daily May-Aug., 9am-5pm Mon.-Fri. Sept.-Apr., free) is the country's highest court. Every year, the court hears 80 to 100 cases that it considers to have "national importance," on appeal from the federal and provincial courts. Nine judges sit on Canada's Supreme Court. By law, three justices must come from Quebec, and by convention, the remainder of the court includes three justices from Ontario, two from western Canada, and one from the Atlantic provinces.

Designed by Montreal architect Ernest Cormier (who later worked with the team designing the United Nations Headquarters in New York), the current court building was completed in 1941. From May through August, free 30-minute **tours** of the building are offered, with English-language tours starting on the hour, and French tours on the half-hour. Reservations aren't required. Between September and April, tours run Monday through Friday only, and you must book in advance by completing the online reservation request form on the court's website (www.scc-csc.gc.ca). Tours include an overview of Canada's judicial system, interesting historical tidbits about the court and the justices, and a walk through several rooms, including the court chambers.

The Supreme Court hears cases during three sessions each year, in winter (generally mid-Jan.-Mar.), spring (Apr.-June), and fall (mid-Oct.-Dec.). No sessions are held July-September. If you want to see the Supreme Court in action, you can; **court hearings** are open to the public on a first-come, first-served basis. Sessions normally begin at 9:30am Monday-Friday, and a second daily session is sometimes held starting at 2pm. Check the **court website** (www.scc-csc.gc.ca) for a schedule.

★ Canadian War Museum

A museum of military history could easily

be dreary or downright depressing. Yet the engaging contemporary **Canadian War Museum** (1 Vimy Pl., 819/776-7000 or 800/555-5621, www.warmuseum.ca, 9:30am-6pm Mon.-Wed. and Fri.-Sun., 9:30am-8pm Thurs., June-early Sept., 9:30am-5pm Mon.-Wed. and Fri.-Sun., 9:30am-8pm Thurs. early Sept.-May, adults $13, seniors $11, students $10, ages 3-12 $8, family $32; free admission 4pm-8pm Thurs., parking $5 per hour or $12.50 per day), located on LeBreton Flats, west of Parliament Hill, is neither. The exhibitions put a human face on periods of war, illustrating not just the conflicts but also the societal issues of the times.

The four main galleries that make up the museum's permanent collection are organized chronologically. The first covers warfare on Canadian soil from the earliest days through 1885, including aboriginal conflicts, European conquests, and the War of 1812. The second (1885-1931) illustrates Canada's involvement in the South African War and World War I, while the third (1931-1945) addresses World War II. The fourth gallery begins in 1945 and continues to the present day. Through 2019, the museum is hosting a series of special exhibits exploring various aspects of World War I and World War II, emphasizing their effects on Canadian society. And because a war museum couldn't exist without tanks and airplanes, the LeBreton Gallery houses a large collection of military vehicles and artillery.

The building itself, which opened in 2005, has some interesting design features. Its plant-covered "green roof" is one of the largest in North America. Notice the windows on the north peak, where Morse Code spells out "Lest We Forget." The lead architect, Vancouver-born Raymond Moriyama, also designed Toronto's Bata Shoe Museum.

You can buy a combination ticket (adults $20, seniors $17, students $15, children $12, family $50) good for both the War Museum and the Canadian Museum of History, which is across the Ottawa River in Gatineau. The War Museum is two kilometers (1.2 miles) west of the Parliament buildings. Bus no. 8, toward Gatineau, travels west on Albert Street and stops in front of the museum.

Canadian Museum of Nature

As you walk into this castle-like Tudor Gothic structure, built in the early 1900s as Canada's first national museum building, notice the **mosaic of a bull moose** on the floor of the entrance hall. Its prominent private

the Canadian War Museum

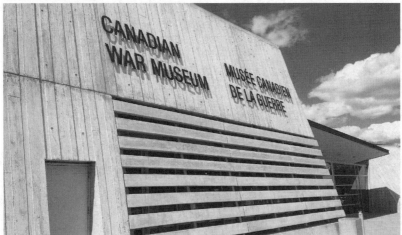

parts apparently created a stir among proper Ottawans in the museum's early days.

Anatomically correct moose mosaics aside, the **Canadian Museum of Nature** (240 McLeod St., 613/566-4700 or 800/263-4433, www.nature.ca, 9am-6pm Sat.-Wed., 9am-8pm Thurs.-Fri. June-early Sept., 9am-5pm Tues.-Wed. and Fri.-Sun., 9am-8pm Thurs. early Sept.-May, adults $12.50, seniors and ages 13-17 $10.50, ages 3-12 $8.50, free admission 5pm-8pm Thurs.), a natural history museum that focuses primarily on Canadian species, is great fun for the kids. Besides the ever-popular dinosaur skeletons, highlights include the Animalium, which houses a creepy collection of live tarantulas, hissing cockroaches, giant snails, and scorpions; a 19.8-meter (66-foot) blue whale skeleton; and the Mammal Gallery, where classic 1950s dioramas of polar bears, moose, bison, and other Canadian beasts are paired with state-of-the-art computer-based activities. The Discovery Zone has more hands-on things to do.

The museum isn't just for children, particularly during the monthly **Nature Nocturne** events, an age-19-and-over evening of music, food, and special events. The glass box that tops the entranceway is known as the Queen's Lantern, with great views over downtown from the top floor. Opened in 2010, it replaced the museum's original tower, which had to be dismantled back in 1916 when it began sinking into the ground.

THE RIDEAU CANAL

The Rideau Canal is more than a Canadian National Historic Site and a UNESCO World Heritage Site. In many ways, this rambling waterway and adjacent green spaces where both residents and visitors can stroll, boat, or skate is also the heart of Ottawa. Bordering the canal, just east of Parliament Hill, are two sights worth seeing if you're interested in Ottawa's heritage: the Bytown Museum and the Fairmont Château Laurier hotel.

★ Rideau Canal National Historic Site

Running 202 kilometers (126 miles) from Kingston to Ottawa, the Rideau Canal (www.pc.gc.ca) is North America's oldest continuously operating canal. After the War of 1812 between the United States and Britain, Canadians were concerned that the St. Lawrence River—a vital shipping channel between Montreal and the Great Lakes—would be vulnerable to another U.S. attack,

This moose mosaic greets visitors at the Canadian Museum of Nature.

since the Americans controlled the river's southern banks. In 1826, led by Lieutenant Colonel John By, work began on the canal that would eventually connect the Ottawa region to Lake Ontario through a series of lakes, rivers, and canals linked by 24 lock stations that allow boats to navigate its changing water levels. More than 1,000 people died constructing the canal, many of whom contracted malaria working along the swampy canal route. After six years of construction, the canal opened in 1832.

The Ottawa section of the canal runs from the Ottawa River southward, separating downtown from the ByWard Market. Between mid-May and mid-October, you can watch boats transit through the **Ottawa Locks;** the lock station closest to downtown is just north of Wellington Street, between Parliament Hill and the Fairmont Château Laurier.

Bytown Museum

To learn more about the history of Ottawa and the construction of the Rideau Canal, visit the **Bytown Museum** (1 Canal Lane, 613/234-4570, www.bytownmuseum.com, 10am-5pm Fri.-Wed., 10am-8pm Thurs. mid-May-mid-Oct., 11am-4pm Tues.-Sun. mid-Oct.-mid-May, adults $6.50, seniors and students $4.50,

ages 5-12 $3, families $15; free admission 5pm-8pm Thurs.) located in Ottawa's oldest stone building, next to the Ottawa Locks. It's built on the site where the construction of the Rideau Canal began back in 1826.

Start your visit with a 20-minute video about the canal's history and check out the working model of the locks. Upstairs, exhibits trace Ottawa's development from its early days as rough-and-tumble Bytown (it was renamed Ottawa in 1855, for the Odawa, an Anishinaabe people indigenous to the area) until it became Canada's capital (in 1857) and beyond. The admission price includes a self-guided audio tour.

If you're visiting with children, look for the "scratch and sniff" cards illustrating local history (guess what the one about horses smells like?). Kids can also dress up in period costumes and play Victorian-era games.

Fairmont Château Laurier

Looming above the Rideau Canal, the **Fairmont Château Laurier** (1 Rideau St., 613/241-1414 or 866/540-4410, www.fairmont.com/laurier), built in 1912, is a grand hotel that's almost as recognizable a part of the Ottawa skyline as the nearby Parliament buildings. Even if you don't stay here, stroll

the Rideau Canal, North America's oldest continuously operating canal

through the upscale lobby with its original marble floor and dark woodwork, or splurge on traditional afternoon high tea in **Zoe's Lounge** (613/241-1414, 2pm-5pm Mon.-Fri., noon-5pm Sat.-Sun., reservations required, adults $32-39, children $22).

BYWARD MARKET DISTRICT AND VICINITY

Home to one of Canada's oldest and largest public markets, the ByWard Market District encompasses the main market building, outdoor vendors, and the surrounding neighborhood, bounded roughly by Sussex Drive and St. Patrick, Cumberland, and George Streets. Whether your taste runs to museums, galleries, boutiques, or all manner of food shops and restaurants, you can easily spend days sampling the wares in and around the ByWard Market. South of the market area, the residential neighborhood of Sandy Hill is home to the University of Ottawa (www.uottawa.ca), the capital's largest educational institution, and other attractions dot the neighborhoods to the east.

★ National Gallery of Canada

It's hard to say which makes a more notable landmark at Canada's national art gallery, the **National Gallery of Canada** (380 Sussex Dr., 613/990-1985 or 800/319-2787, www.gallery.ca, 10am-5pm Fri.-Wed., 10am-8pm Thurs., May-Sept., 10am-5pm Tues.-Wed. and Fri.-Sun., 10am-8pm Thurs. Oct.-Apr., adults $12, seniors and students $10, ages 12-19 $6, under age 12 free, family $24, free admission 5pm-8pm Thurs.). Is it the airy granite, glass, and steel building itself, which opened in 1988, designed by Canadian architect Moshe Safdie? Or is it the gigantic spider that sits on the museum's front plaza? The spider, a bronze sculpture known as *Maman,* by French American artist Louise Bourgeois (1911-2010), guards the museum entrance, standing over nine meters (30 feet) high.

Inside, the museum houses the country's largest visual-arts collection. A good place to start is in the **Canadian art galleries,** which are organized chronologically and include a significant number of works by the Group of Seven, early 20th-century Canadian landscape artists; look for paintings by Lawren Harris (1885-1970), A. Y. Jackson (1882-1974), and Tom Thomson (1877-1917), among others. More contemporary works include paintings by First Nations artist Norval Morrisseau (1932-2007). Also visit the serene **Rideau Chapel,** a 19th-century chapel from Ottawa's

Bytown Museum is in Ottawa's oldest stone building.

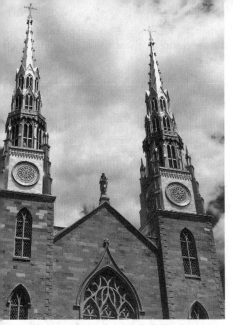
the spires of Notre Dame Cathedral Basilica

fashion would have been perceived in various works.

The museum hosts concerts, films, and other special events throughout the year as well. Check their website or phone for schedules and other details. If all this culture makes you hungry, head for the museum cafeteria. The menu runs to typical sandwiches and salads, but the view across the Ottawa River—to Parliament Hill on one side and the Canadian Museum of History on the other—is one of the best in town.

Notre Dame Cathedral Basilica

Opposite the National Gallery, the twin spires of Ottawa's oldest surviving church, **Notre Dame Cathedral Basilica** (385 Sussex Dr., 613/241-7496, www.notredameottawa.com, 11:30am-6pm Mon., 10am-6pm Tues.-Sat., 8am-8:30pm Sun., free), glint in the afternoon sun. If you think that North America has few churches to rival Europe's cathedrals, stop into this grand Gothic structure, built between 1841 and 1885, with its arched columns, stained-glass windows, and elaborate pipe organ. Visitors are welcome to attend church services (call or check the website for schedules), explore the architecture, or simply take sanctuary for a few moments of quiet contemplation.

Royal Canadian Mint

As the queen ages, what happens to her portrait on the country's coins? If you're interested in this and other pecuniary trivia, visit the **Royal Canadian Mint** (320 Sussex Dr., 613/993-8990 or 800/276-7714, www.mint.ca, 9am-5pm daily, Mon.-Fri. adults $6, seniors $5, ages 5-17 $3, family $15, Sat.-Sun. adults $4.50, seniors $3.75, ages 5-17 $2.25, family $11.25). Although Canada's regular circulation coins are no longer made at this Ottawa facility (production moved to Winnipeg in 1976), the mint still manufactures investment and collection coins, military medals, and Olympic medals.

The only way to see the mint is by taking a

Convent of Our Lady of the Sacred Heart that was saved from demolition in 1972 and reconstructed in its entirety within the museum.

Other highlights are the **Inuit art collection** and the always-surprising **contemporary art** exhibits. There are also comprehensive **photography** and **European** art galleries. In addition to the permanent collections, the museum typically mounts a major exhibition every summer, as well as 12 to 14 smaller exhibits throughout the year.

One strategy for tackling such a large museum is to visit for a short time (perhaps on Thursday evening when admission is free) to get your bearings, and then return for a longer visit. Or take a one-hour **guided tour** (613/998-8888 or 888/541-8888, $7); call for tour topics and for reservations, which are required. To guide your own explorations, rent an **audio guide** ($6); one specialized audio program adds historical perspective to works in the Canadian art galleries, while another focuses on how

30-minute tour, where guides explain the production process, and you can look down on the surprisingly low-tech machines. Medals from the 2010 Winter Olympics, held in Vancouver, are also on display. Tours run frequently throughout the day; call for seasonal schedules. Make a reservation, particularly in the summer, and visit Monday to Friday to see the mint in full operation. On the weekend, admission prices are lower, but the production lines are shut down, so you don't see as much.

Oh, and about the queen? Over the years, the portrait of Queen Elizabeth II that appears on Canada's coins has aged along with Her Majesty. Notice, though, that on newer coins, the monarch isn't wearing her crown. She apparently requested the crown-free likeness, so she'd appear more like a regular person.

★ ByWard Market

Lieutenant Colonel John By, who led the construction of the Rideau Canal, also designed the ByWard Market and its surrounding streets back in the 1820s. He specified that George and York Streets should both be extra wide to accommodate the horse-drawn carriages that brought goods to the market.

The centerpiece of the ByWard Market neighborhood is the **main market building** (55 ByWard Market Square, 613/562-3325, www.byward-market.com, free), with shops selling snacks, light meals, and souvenirs; there's also a **visitor information office** and restrooms. The more interesting part of the market, though, is outside, when vendors set up stalls (generally late April or May through October) to sell produce, prepared foods, and other goodies. You'll find dozens of small shops around the market building as well.

As you wander the market area, make sure to explore the **courtyards** just east of Sussex Drive, from George to St. Patrick Streets. They house restaurants, shops, and cafés that aren't easily visible from the main streets.

Laurier House National Historic Site

Two of Canada's prime ministers lived in a Sandy Hill mansion that's now the **Laurier House National Historic Site** (335 Laurier Ave. E., 613/992-8142, www.pc.gc.ca, 10am-5pm daily July-early Sept., 10am-5pm Thurs.-Mon. late May-June and early-Sept.-mid-Oct., adults $3.90, seniors $3.40, ages 6-16 $1.90, family $9.80

Canada had no official prime minister's residence when Sir Wilfrid Laurier took office in 1896; a group of friends and supporters raised money to build this home, where Laurier lived from 1897 until his death in 1919. When Laurier's wife, Zoe, passed away in 1921, she bequeathed the house to William Lyon Mackenzie King, Laurier's successor as Liberal Party leader. Mackenzie King, who became prime minister that same year, moved into the house (after extensive renovations) in 1923 and lived there until he retired from politics in 1948. Guides in period costume are on hand throughout the house, which is furnished with many of Laurier's and Mackenzie King's belongings.

Laurier House is just over two kilometers (one mile) east of Parliament Hill. If you don't want to walk, catch OC Transpo bus no. 5, which stops in front of the house.

Rideau Hall

Owing to Canada's history as part of the British Empire, the British monarch is still Canada's official head of state. Since the queen presumably has more to do than worry about day-to-day governance of Britain's former colonies, however, Canada's governor general acts as the queen's representative in Canada. In practice, it's the prime minister who runs the government in Canada, and the governor general's role is largely ceremonial. It's fitting, then, that the governor general's residence, **Rideau Hall** (1 Sussex Dr., 613/991-4422 or 866/842-4422, www.gg.ca, free), is a suitably ceremonial mansion, set in parklike grounds northeast of the ByWard Market.

The free 45-minute **tours of Rideau Hall** (10am-4pm Sat.-Sun., by reservation 10am-4pm Mon.-Fri. May-late June,

10am-4:30pm daily late June-early Sept., noon-4pm Sat.-Sun., by reservation 10am-4pm Mon.-Fri. early Sept.-Oct., by reservation 10am-4pm daily Nov.-Apr.) explore the history of the building—built in sections from 1838 through 1940—and visit some of the grand public spaces. Imagine attending a soiree in the majestic ballroom or in the candy-striped Tent Room, where the pink fabric-draped ceiling resembles a circus tent! Tours are offered year-round, and reservations are advised. November through April, tours are by reservation only; call to book one. The grounds are open daily from 8am until one hour before sunset; pick up a brochure at either entrance gate to guide your wanderings around the property. Also on the grounds is a **skating rink** (noon-5pm Sat.-Sun. Jan.-mid-Mar.) that's open for public skating on winter weekends, weather permitting.

To reach Rideau Hall from downtown or the ByWard Market, catch **OC Transpo bus no. 9** (www.octranspo.com) on weekends, check the schedule before heading out, since service can be infrequent. En route to Rideau Hall, you might catch a glimpse of the prime minister's residence (24 Sussex Dr.), but it's not open to the public.

RCMP Musical Ride

Canada's red-coated, Stetson-wearing Mounties, officially known as the Royal Canadian Mounted Police (RCMP), are the country's national police force. But a small group of Mounties have an additional duty: performing with the **RCMP Musical Ride** (www.rcmp-grc.gc.ca/mr-ce). With a troop of 36 horses and riders, the Musical Ride is a cavalry drill team, executing intricate formations choreographed to music. Between May and October, the Musical Ride is frequently on tour in other parts of Canada, but they do perform periodically in Ottawa; check their website for the performance schedule.

Even when the Musical Ride is on the road, you can tour the **RCMP Musical Ride Centre** (RCMP Rockcliffe Stables, 1 Sandridge Rd., 613/741-4285, www.rcmp-grc.gc.ca/mr-ce, 9am-3:30pm daily May-Aug., 10am-1:30pm Tues. and Thurs. Sept.-Apr., free) to meet the horses and learn more about the performing troupe. From Parliament Hill or the Rideau Centre, OC Transpo bus no. 7 will drop you near the stables.

Canada Aviation and Space Museum

If you're a fan of flying, zoom over to the

The RCMP Musical Ride tours the world from its Ottawa base.

hangar-like **Canada Aviation and Space Museum** (11 Aviation Pkwy., 613/993-2010, www.aviation.technomuses.ca, 9am-5pm daily May-early Sept., 10am-5pm Wed.-Mon. early Sept.-Apr., adults $13, seniors and students $10, ages 3-12 $8, families $30, free admission 4pm-5pm daily) that houses Canada's largest collection of civilian and military aircraft, illustrating aviation history from the early 20th century to the present.

Want a bigger thrill? Strap on your goggles and take a **flight tour** (613/316-7229, 9am-5pm daily May-Oct., $65-160 pp) over Ottawa in a vintage Waco UPF-7, an open cockpit biplane that dates to around 1939. Or book a **helicopter tour** (613/447-5662, 9am-5pm daily May-Oct., $200-300 per flight for up to 3 people) over Parliament Hill or Gatineau.

The museum is 6.5 kilometers (four miles) east of Parliament Hill. From downtown, catch an OC Transpo bus eastbound to Hurdman (buses no. 94, 95, 96, 97, 98, and 99), then change to bus no. 129 to the museum.

Entertainment and Events

Ottawa may not have as active a nightlife scene as larger cities like Toronto or Montreal, but as the nation's capital, its arts venues not only promote local artists but also feature Canadian performers from across the country. And with dozens of festivals year-round, there's almost always something going on.

NIGHTLIFE

The ByWard Market area is entertainment central, full of bars, pubs, and music venues. Oddly named nightclub **Zaphod Beeblebrox** (27 York St., 613/562-1010, www.zaphods.ca) offers music nightly, a mix of DJs and up-and-coming bands. Music generally starts around 8pm or 9pm. Check the website or call for daily schedules. **The Rainbow** (76 Murray St., 613/241-5123, www.therainbow.ca, hours vary) books local, national, and international blues acts, with some R&B and jazz thrown in. DJs at **Mercury Lounge** (56 ByWard Market Square, 613/789-5324, www.mercurylounge.com, hours vary) play electronic, house, jazz, funk, and anything with "soul."

For cocktails and eclectic tacos (perhaps Korean pulled pork or Bajan-style fish), find your way to the chic **Side Door Restaurant** (18b York St., 613/562-9331, www.sidedoorrestaurant.com, hours vary), a loungey space inside a stone heritage building; the entrance is literally the side door, on Clarendon Court, off York Street. Try the sake mojito or drinks ($10) like the electric lemonade (tequila, lemon, and vanilla syrup). If you're watching your loonies, come for the happy-hour specials, 4:30pm-6:30pm Sunday-Friday.

Local socialists—and socialites—say "*da*" to the eclectic mix of Soviet propaganda posters, local art, and vast menu of Russian-themed drinks (how about a Red Square or a Proletarian Omelet?) at the appropriately named **Avant-Garde Bar** (135½ Besserer St., at Dalhousie St., 613/321-8908, www.avant-gardebar.ca, 5:30pm-2am Tues.-Sat.). If you're hungry, share a bourgeois fish plate or a bowl of Siberian *pelemeni* (dumplings).

In Chinatown, the **Shanghai Restaurant** (651 Somerset St. W., 613/233-4001, www.shanghaiottawa.com, 11:30am-2pm and 4:30pm-10pm Tues.-Thurs., 11:30am-2pm and 4:30pm-1am Fri., 4:30pm-2am Sat., 4:30pm-10pm Sun.), a typical Chinese eatery by day, morphs into a quirky club on weekend nights when the owners' son, a drag queen who goes by the name China Doll, hosts a Saturday karaoke night and other events. Also in Chinatown, the **Raw Sugar Café** (692 Somerset St. W., 613/216-2850, www.rawsugarcafe.com, café hours 10am-7pm daily, event schedules vary) runs eclectic events including experimental music, readings, and DJ nights.

Feeling the Chill of Canada's Cold War

"Attention! Warning! Take cover immediately!" As the radio announcer issues this urgent alert, the air raid siren begins to wail. Is there an incoming bomber heading straight for Ottawa? No, but at the **Diefenbunker, Canada's Cold War Museum** (3911 Carp Rd., Carp, 613/839-0007 or 800/409-1965, www.diefenbunker.ca, 11am-4pm daily year-round, ticket sales 10:30am-3:30pm daily, adults $14, seniors $13, students $10, ages 6-18 $8, family $40), the drama and fears of the Cold War are very much alive.

Built in 1961 as a safe haven for government officials, this four-level underground bunker in the countryside outside of Ottawa was designed to survive a five-megaton bomb—more than 200 times stronger than the bomb dropped on Nagasaki during World War II. The bunker could house 500 people for up to 30 days following a nuclear attack. Fortunately, the potential nuclear catastrophe never occurred, but the bunker remained staffed and ready for use until 1994. The underground shelter, with 9,290 square meters (100,000 square feet) of living space, is now an unusual museum that vividly illustrates the Cold War era.

You can explore the Diefenbunker on your own, with the complimentary iPod **Diefenguides** (a self-guided audio tour available 11am-2:30pm daily), or with the free **Diefen-app** (an audio-video guide for mobile devices that you can download before your visit). However, it's definitely worth taking a **guided tour** (60-90 minutes, 11am and 2pm Mon.-Fri., 11am Sat.-Sun., included with admission). As you enter the bunker through a 92-meter (300-foot) blast tunnel, your guide will ask each group to imagine that it's 1962 and you're joining others who've already taken refuge after a nuclear attack. You will experience a simulated decontamination procedure and medical exam before making your way through the warren of underground chambers.

The tour visits the war cabinet room, where elected officials would have plotted their strategies, as well as the prime minister's bedroom, the CBC emergency broadcast studio, and even the Bank of Canada vault designed to store 800 tons of gold. There's a recreation room with table tennis and pool tables, since you'd want to get some exercise while confined underground for 30 days. Also in the Diefenbunker are models of public fallout shelters, a cafeteria, black rotary-dial phones, huge IBM computers, and other artifacts of the era.

Tours are appropriate for children of elementary school age and older; younger children may find it unsettling. The temperature in the underground museum is a cool 17-19°C (63-66°F) year-round, so bring a sweater or light jacket. It's a good idea to call and confirm guided tour availability before making the trip to the site. You will need a car to visit the Diefenbunker, a 30-40-minute drive west of downtown Ottawa. Take Highway 417 west to Carp Road then continue north on Carp Road for 12 kilometers (7.5 miles) through the village of Carp to the Diefenbunker entrance.

On a sunny afternoon, sip an Ontario-brewed beer overlooking the river at the **Mill Street Brew Pub** (555 Wellington St., 613/567-2337, www.ottawa.millstreetbrewpub.ca, 11am-10pm Mon., 11am-11pm Tues., 11am-midnight Wed., 11am-1am Thurs., 11am-2am Fri., 10:30am-2am Sat., 10:30am-10pm Sun), west of downtown near the Canadian War Museum. Local bands entertain on Thursday evening.

Check the **Ottawa Xpress** (www.ottawaxpress.ca) or **Ottawa Citizen** (www.ottawacitizen.com) for listings and reviews of the latest hotspots.

THE ARTS

The capital's major arts venue is the **National Arts Centre** (NAC, 53 Elgin St., 613/947-7000 or 866/850-2787, www.nac-cna.ca, box office 10am-9pm Mon.-Sat., additional hours on Sun. performance days). It's home to English- and French-language theater, the NAC Orchestra, and a dance series. The NAC also hosts numerous festivals and special events.

To avoid paying service changes, buy your tickets for NAC events in person at the box office. You can purchase tickets online or by phone from **Ticketmaster** (www.ticketmaster.ca, 888/991-2787), but you'll pay a service fee. See the NAC website for more details on buying tickets. Full-time students ages 13 to 29 can purchase last-minute **Live Rush tickets** (www.liverush.ca) to NAC theater, music, and dance events for only $12. Live Rush tickets are on sale between 10am the day before the show until 6pm on show day. Students with a valid student ID can also purchase advance tickets at a 50 percent discount in-person at the NAC box office.

For a meal or snack before or after the show, visit the NAC restaurant, **Le Café** (613/594-5127, 11:30am-2pm and 5pm-9pm Mon.-Sat., 11:30am-2pm Sun. late May-early Sept., 11:30am-2pm and 5pm-9pm Mon.-Fri., 5pm-9pm Sat. early Sept.-late May). The restaurant stays open until 11pm on show nights, and it opens for dinner on Sunday when there are Sunday performances. The vibrantly colored mural above the café is *Homage to RFK*, by Canadian contemporary artist William Ronald (1926-1998).

Outside the NAC, look—or listen— for **Oscar's Corner** (Elgin St. and Albert St.), a larger-than-life-size bronze statue of Canadian jazz great Oscar Peterson, created by Canadian sculptor Ruth Abernethy. Recordings of Peterson's music play at the site, making it seem as if the musician (1925-2007) is still tinkling away on his piano. A popular photo op: sit on the bench beside Peterson's likeness.

Theater

Every year, the **National Arts Centre English Theatre** (www.nac-cna.ca/en/englishtheatre) typically presents five plays in the main 800-seat theater and three plays in the 290-seat studio theater, ranging from classics to contemporary Canadian works. They also produce family plays and other special presentations.

Established in 1975, the professional **Great Canadian Theatre Company** (GCTC, 1233 Wellington St. W., 613/236-5196, www.gctc.ca, adults $35-49, seniors and students $35) performs several contemporary plays each year, focusing on works by Canadian playwrights or with Canadian content. The first Sunday of each production's run is a pay-what-you-can performance; be at the box office at noon to buy a ticket (donation) for the 2pm show. In addition to the main-stage productions, smaller local companies present works in the black box studio theater.

For a good yarn, from January to June the **Ottawa Storytellers** (613/322-8336, www.ottawastorytellers.ca) present monthly

Ottawa's major theater venue is the National Arts Centre English Theatre.

professional storytelling performances at the National Arts Centre's Fourth Stage; check their website for performance dates and ticket prices. On the first Thursday of every month, they host a story-swap and open-mike night (Public Service Alliance of Canada Bldg., 233 Gilmour St., 7pm-9:30pm, free) with tales by professional and amateur storytellers.

Music

The **National Arts Centre Orchestra** (www.nac-cna.ca/en/orchestra), directed by noted conductor and violinist Pinchas Zukerman, performs in the NAC's 2,323-seat Southam Hall. Concerts are typically held September through June.

Big-name rock, pop, county, and other musicians perform at the **Canadian Tire Centre** (1000 Palladium Dr., 613/599-0100, www.canadiantirecentre.com). The arena is a 30-minute drive (25 kilometers, 16 miles) west of downtown via Highway 417. **OC Transpo Connexion bus no. 403** (www.octranspo. com) will take you from downtown to the arena in about 45 minutes.

Dance

Canadian and international ballet and contemporary dance companies perform as part of the **NAC Dance Series** (www.nac-cna.ca/ dance) at the National Arts Centre. The roster has included the National Ballet of Canada, the Royal Winnipeg Ballet, the Alvin Ailey American Dance Theatre, the Joffrey Ballet, and many other well-known and lesser-known troupes.

FESTIVALS AND EVENTS

Ottawa seems to host one festival after another, particularly during the summer months. The biggest events are the Canada Day festivities, celebrating the nation's birthday on July 1, and the winter festival known as Winterlude; make your travel arrangements in advance if you'll be in town for either of these.

For a complete calendar or more information about the festivities listed here, check online at **Ottawa Festivals** (www.ottawa-festivals.ca) or **Ottawa Tourism** (www.ottawatourism.ca).

Spring

More than one million tulips herald the beginning of spring during the annual **Canadian Tulip Festival** (613/567-5757 or 800/668-8547, www.tulipfestival.ca, May). The festival runs for about two weeks, with most events in Major's Hill Park (Mackenzie Ave., behind the Fairmont Château Laurier) or at Commissioners Park (Preston St. and Queen Elizabeth Dr.) near Dows Lake, south of downtown. Besides the opportunity to tiptoe through the tulips, the festival includes free concerts, garden parties, kids' programs, and fireworks.

Billed as "Canada's largest independent literary celebration," the semiannual **Ottawa International Writers Festival—Spring** (613/562-1243, www.writersfestival.org, Apr.-May) offers author readings, lectures, book launches, poetry cabarets, and other literary events at several venues around the city. Some events are free; others require tickets.

Summer

Are you a theater buff? Sample some of Canada's best contemporary theater productions during the **Magnetic North Theatre Festival** (613/947-7000, ext. 719, or 866/850-2787, ext. 719, www.magneticnorthfestival. ca, June). The festival is held in Ottawa every other year, at venues around town; in the alternate years, the event travels to other Canadian cities. The **Canada Dance Festival** (www. canadadance.ca, June) presents several days of contemporary dance performances, featuring dancers from across Canada.

Although Quebec observes all of Canada's national holidays, the province has its own *Fête Nationale* (www.tourismeoutaouais. com or www.fetenationale.qc.ca, June), also known as Saint-Jean-Baptiste Day, which Ottawa-Gatineau celebrates with a big outdoor concert featuring Quebecois musicians. Held in conjunction with Canada's National

Aboriginal Day, the **Summer Solstice Aboriginal Arts Festival** (613/564-9494, www.ottawasummersolstice.ca, June) showcases aboriginal artists, musicians, and dancers, with lots of kids' activities.

It's been called "Canada's biggest party"—the annual **Canada Day Celebrations** (819/997-0055 or 866/811-0055, www.canadaday.gc.ca, July 1), which include scads of free activities, including official ceremonies, street performers, and concerts; past headliners have included the Barenaked Ladies and Serena Ryder. A highlight is the nighttime fireworks show on Parliament Hill.

Summer also brings a number of music events to town, including the **Ottawa International Jazz Festival** (613/241-2633, www.ottawajazzfestival.com, June-July), **Ottawa BluesFest** (613/247-1188 or 866/258-3748, www.ottawabluesfest.ca, July), and **Ottawa Chamberfest** (613/234-6306, www.chamberfest.com, July-Aug.).

Ottawa's Greek community welcomes visitors to join in **GreekFest** (613/225-8016, ext. 234, www.ottawagreekfest.com, Aug.), a 10-day party of music, dancing, and of course, food. Culminating in a huge Pride Parade and outdoor concert, the **Capital Pride Festival** (613/252-7174, www.capitalpride.ca, Aug.) has been celebrating Ottawa's gay, lesbian, bisexual, and transgendered community since 1986.

Fall and Winter

Like the spring version of this book festival, the **Ottawa International Writers Festival—Fall** (613/562-1243, www.writersfestival.org, Oct.) hosts readings, book talks, lectures, and other events for the literarily inclined. In the world's coldest national capital (a dubious honor that both Moscow and Ottawa claim), what can you do but embrace the long winter? Ottawa does just that during **Winterlude** (613/239-5000 or 800/465-1867, www.pch.gc.ca/winterlude, Feb.), a midwinter festival of outdoor fun that takes place on several February weekends. You'll find an ice sculpture competition, skating on the Rideau Canal, North America's largest outdoor snow playground, and other outdoor events. Bring your mittens! During **Black History Month** (www.blackhistoryottawa.org, Feb.), lectures, concerts, and other special events celebrating the African Canadian experience take place around town.

Shopping

Ottawa's small but growing cohort of local fashion designers sells their wares at boutiques around town. The city also has an active art scene, with contemporary galleries for browsing (and buying). Besides the venues listed here, visit the shops in the major museums for unique souvenirs, books, jewelry, and children's gifts.

SHOPPING DISTRICTS

Far livelier than it seems from its uninviting stone exterior, the **Rideau Centre** (50 Rideau St., 613/236-6565, www.rideaucentre.net, 9:30am-9pm Mon.-Fri., 9:30am-6pm Sat., 11am-5pm Sun.) is a large mall housing popular North American chain stores, including yoga-wear shop Lululemon, clothing retailers like the Gap and Roots, and fast-food outlets like Tim Hortons and Starbucks. It's on the east side of the Rideau Canal, near the Fairmont Château Laurier. Across the street from the Rideau Centre is a branch of the **Hudson's Bay** (73 Rideau St., 613/241-7511, www.thebay.com, 9:30am-9pm Mon.-Fri., 9:30am-6pm Sat., 10am-6pm Sun.) department store.

The streets around the **ByWard Market** are happy hunting grounds for shoppers looking for unique boutiques. West of the market building, **Sussex Drive** is lined

locally made goods at the ByWard Market

One of Ottawa's most unusual gallery spaces is **Guild Galerie 240** (240 Guigues Ave., 613/680-0866, www.galerie240.com, noon-6pm Wed.-Sun.), which artist-owner Brenda Gale Warner runs in her 1870 wood-frame home, east of the ByWard Market. Warner shows her own work and that of other contemporary artists based in Ottawa and farther afield.

Several galleries have set up shop in Wellington West. On the first Thursday of the month, you can visit them all during the **Wellington West 1st Thursdays Art Walk** (www.wellingtonwest.ca, 5pm-9pm Thurs., free); get a list of participating galleries on the website.

BOOKS AND MAGAZINES

Downtown, **Perfect Books** (258A Elgin St., 613/231-6468, www.perfectbooks.ca, 10am-9pm Mon.-Fri., 10am-6pm Sat., noon-5pm Sun.) is a friendly independent bookshop with a knowledgeable staff.

with high-end clothing shops. East of the market, head to **Dalhousie Street** for more eclectic, and more affordable, fashion and housewares.

Outside the city center, the increasingly trendy **Wellington West** district is another spot to find interesting boutiques, food shops, and cafés. Start around the intersection of Wellington and Holland and continue west along Wellington Street. From downtown, it's about a 10-minute drive or 15-minute bus ride; take OC Transpo bus no. 86 to the corner of Holland and Wellington Streets.

ART GALLERIES

A number of contemporary art galleries are clustered around the ByWard Market, including the **Gordon Harrison Gallery** (495 Sussex Dr., 613/746-6853, www.gordonharrisongallery.com, 10am-6pm Wed. and Sat.-Sun., 10am-8pm Thurs.-Fri.), which showcases the work of landscape painter Gordon Harrison, as well as works by other contemporary Canadian landscape artists.

CLOTHING AND ACCESSORIES

Focusing on wearable clothing by Canadian female designers, with roughly half their stock made in Ottawa, the funky **Workshop Studio and Boutique** (242 Dalhousie St., 613/789-5534, www.workshopboutique.ca, 10am-6pm Mon.-Wed., 10am-8pm Thurs.-Fri., 10am-6pm Sat., noon-5pm Sun.), near the ByWard Market, also carries accessories, purses, jewelry, and gifts.

The same owners operate **Flock Boutique** (1275 Wellington St. W., 613/695-0834, www.flockboutique.ca, 10am-6pm Mon.-Wed., 10am-8pm Thurs.-Fri., 10am-6pm. Sat., noon-5pm Sun.), carrying similarly eclectic Canadian-made clothing in the Wellington West neighborhood.

Another creative boutique for dresses, jewelry, and other goods for women, **Victoire** (246 Dalhousie St., 613/321-1590, www.victoireboutique.com, 10am-6pm Mon.-Wed. and Sat., 10am-8pm Thurs.-Fri., noon-5pm Sun.) describes its style as "Rock 'n' Roll tea party . . . loved by rebel girls with good manners everywhere." In addition to this ByWard Market-area shop, they have a second store in Wellington West (1282-B Wellington St. W., 613/421-0089, 10am-6pm Mon.-Wed. and Sat., 10am-8pm Thurs.-Fri., noon-5pm Sun.).

You've gotta love the cheeky spirit of a boutique named **Trustfund** (493 Sussex Dr., 613/562-0999, www.trustfundboutique.com, 10am-6pm Mon.-Wed., 10am-9pm Thurs.-Fri., 10am-6pm Sat., noon-6pm Sun.). Do you need your own trust fund to afford the au courant, and not inexpensive, fashions for men and women? No, but it wouldn't hurt.

GOURMET TREATS

Watch the chocolate makers at work at **Cylie Artisans Chocolatiers** (204 Dalhousie St., 613/695-8887, www.cyliechocolat.com, 10am-6pm Wed.-Sun.), crafting beautiful bonbons that look more like art than food. Purchase a gift box for a fortunate friend—or treat yourself.

Sports and Recreation

PARKS

With the park-lined Rideau Canal running through town, Ottawa feels like a green city. Downtown, you can relax in **Major's Hill Park** (Mackenzie Ave.), behind the Fairmont Château Laurier, or in **Confederation Park** (Elgin St. and Laurier Ave.), which hosts Canada Day festivities, as well as Winterlude events. The bigger **Commissioners Park** (Preston St. and Queen Elizabeth Dr.) is near Dows Lake, south of the city center. The region's largest green space is **Gatineau Park** (33 Scott Rd., Chelsea, 819/827-2020 or 800/456-3016, www.ncc-ccn.gc.ca), in the hills on the Quebec side of the Ottawa River.

SUMMER SPORTS
Cycling

The Ottawa-Gatineau region has more than 220 kilometers (137 miles) of cycling paths as part of the **Capital Pathway** network (www.ncc-ccn.gc.ca). The paths that are most accessible from the central city include the **Rideau Canal Pathway,** a flat paved trail that runs for eight kilometers (five miles) on either side of the canal; the 31-kilometer (19-mile) **Ottawa River Pathway** that takes you from Parliament Hill west to the Canadian War Museum and beyond; and the 12-kilometer (7.5-mile) paved **Rideau River Pathway,** which begins near Rideau Hall and follows the Rideau River south. Get cycling maps online at www.ncc-ccn.gc.ca or from the **Capital Information Kiosk** (90 Wellington St., 613/239-5000 or 866/811-0055, www.pch.gc.ca, 10am-6pm daily).

On **Sunday Bikedays** (www.ncc-ccn.gc.ca, late May-early Sept.), the city closes a number of roads to cars, creating additional cycling, in-line skating, running, and walking routes. In Ottawa, sections of the Sir John A. Macdonald Parkway, Colonel By Drive, and Rockcliffe Parkway become bikeways; in Gatineau Park, it's the Gatineau, Champlain, and Fortune Lake Parkways. Note that the Gatineau routes are hilly.

You can rent bicycles from **RentABike** (2 Rideau St., at Colonel By Dr., 613/241-4140, www.rentabike.ca, 9am-5pm daily mid-Apr.-Oct. 9am-7pm daily early July-late Aug., $10-15 per hour, $40-70 per day), at the Plaza Bridge near the Rideau Canal. **CycleHop** (www.cyclehop.com) launched a public bike-sharing system in Ottawa, after taking over from bankrupt operator Capital BIXI. Check their website for rental locations and other details.

Rafting

Prefer to do your exploring by water? You can enjoy a gentle rafting adventure without even leaving the city on a trip with **Ottawa**

City Adventures (844/688-7238, www.ottawacityadventures.com, adults $49, ages 6-12 $39). This family-friendly three-hour excursion, which starts at Britannia Beach west of the city center, runs three short rapids with lots of peaceful float time in between, before ending near the Canadian War Museum. Call or check their website for seasonal schedules and transportation options.

Yoga

Join hundreds of fellow downward-doggers for **Parliament Hill Yoga** (613/230-6633, www.lululemon.com, noon-1pm Wed. May-Sept., free), a one-hour open-air yoga class on the lawn in front of the Parliament buildings. Sponsored by the local Lululemon athletic-wear store, the free noontime classes, offered on Wednesday in summer, are open to everyone, regardless of your yoga experience.

WINTER SPORTS

Even Ottawa's frigid winters don't keep locals indoors, and if you visit during the colder months, you should get outside, too. Skating on the Rideau Canal is a don't-miss experience. For cross-country skiing and snowshoeing, head for the trails in **Gatineau Park** (33 Scott Rd., Chelsea, 819/827-2020 or 800/456-3016, www.ncc-ccn.gc.ca).

The world's largest ice-skating rink, the **Rideau Canal Skateway** (613/239-5000 or 866/811-0055 information, 613/239-5234 ice conditions, www.ncc-ccn.gc.ca, generally Jan.-early Mar., free) stretches 7.8 kilometers (4.8 miles), beginning just south of Wellington and Rideau Streets and continuing beyond Dows Lake. You can rent skates at several points en route. Closest to downtown, **Capital Skates** (613/238-0134, www.capitalskates.ca, generally 10am-10pm daily, last rental 8pm, $17 for 1st 2 hours) is on the east side of the canal, between the Mackenzie King and Laurier Bridges; farther south is a second location on the west side of the canal near the intersection of the Queen Elizabeth Driveway and Fifth Avenue (6pm-10pm Fri., 10am-10pm Sat.-Sun., last rental 8pm). Skate rentals are also available at **Dows Lake Pavilion** (1001 Queen Elizabeth Dr., 613/232-1001, ext. 5, www.dowslake.com, 9:30am-10pm Mon.-Fri., 9am-10pm Sat., 9am-9pm Sun., last rentals 1 hour before closing, adults $13 1st hour, $18 for 2 hours, $8 per additional hour, children $9 1st hour, $12 for 2 hours, $6 per additional hour). Locals recommend bringing a backpack to carry your shoes as well as water

A popular cycling route follows the Ottawa River.

and snacks. Check the ice conditions before heading out, too, since even a brief stretch of warmer temperatures can unexpectedly close the canal to skaters.

It may seem rather sedate after cruising along on the canal, but you can also skate at the **Rideau Hall Ice Rink** (1 Sussex Dr., 613/991-4422 or 866/842-4422, www.gg.ca, noon-5pm Sat.-Sun. Jan.-mid-Mar., free), on the grounds of the governor general's residence.

SPECTATOR SPORTS

The Senators aren't just Parliamentarians— they're also the capital's National Hockey League team. The **Ottawa Senators** (www. ottawasenators.com) play at the **Canadian Tire Centre** (1000 Palladium Dr., 613/599-0140, www.canadiantirecentre.com),

25 kilometers (16 miles) west of downtown off Highway 417, about a 30-minute drive. The **OC Transpo** (www.octranspo. com) Connexion bus no. 403 makes the 45-minute trip between downtown and the Canadian Tire Centre when there are hockey games or other events at the arena. The regular hockey season runs October to April.

The **Ottawa Redblacks** (613/599-3267 or 877/788-3267, www.ottawaredblacks. com), which played their inaugural season in the professional Canadian Football League in 2014, take to the field at **TD Place** (1015 Bank St.) from June through October. The city's professional soccer team, **Ottawa Fury FC** (613/599-3267 or 877/788-3267, www.ottawafuryfc.com), also play at TD Place from July through October.

Accommodations

Accommodations in Ottawa include hostels, bed-and-breakfasts, boutique hotels, and major chain lodgings. Many hotels are located downtown, within walking distance of Parliament Hill. The ByWard Market neighborhood has several hotels and B&Bs. You'll find more B&Bs south and east of the market in residential Sandy Hill.

Perhaps because the federal government attracts businesspeople and bureaucrats for long-term stays, the capital has numerous suite hotels, many of which are comfortable for families, even if you're visiting for just a day or two. Not only do you have more space, you can save money on food, since all have kitchen facilities. In addition to the suite hotels listed below, try **Premiere Executive Suites** (www.premieresuites.com), which rents studio, one-, and two-bedroom apartments around town for short-term stays.

DOWNTOWN

Many of Ottawa's larger hotels, as well as several small inns and B&Bs, are located in the city center, within a short walk of Parliament Hill.

Under $100

The ambience of the **Ambiance B&B** (330 Nepean St., 613/563-0421 or 888/366-8772, www.ambiancebandb.com, $89-109 s, $99-129 d, suite $160 d) is that of a private home. Built in 1904, this brick Victorian has a snug parlor with an overstuffed sofa and gas fireplace; a three-course breakfast is served around the common dining room table. Upstairs, two of the homey guest rooms share a bath; the other two are en suite. Just like at home, guests can help themselves to complimentary (nonalcoholic) drinks, or use the fridge and microwave. Wi-Fi is included.

$100-150

Built in 1875 as a private residence, the red brick **Albert House Inn** (478 Albert St., 613/236-4479 or 800/267-1982, www.albertinn.com, $129-195 d) is now a 17-room Victorian-style guesthouse downtown. Sure, some of the rooms are a bit old-fashioned, but they're well kept, with en suite baths, flat-screen TVs, and free Wi-Fi. First- and second-floor units have high ceilings that make them feel spacious, and guests are welcome to relax in the bay-windowed parlor. Rates include a full cooked-to-order breakfast. Children under age 10 are not allowed.

There's nothing flashy about the apartment-style **Extended Stay Deluxe Ottawa** (141 Cooper St., 613/236-7500, www.extendedstayhotels.com, $129-174 d) on a Centretown side street, but it covers the basics: comfortable studio and one-bedroom suites, with fully equipped kitchens and free Wi-Fi. There's no restaurant or pool, but they do have a fitness center and hot tub, and you're just a block from the shops and restaurants on Elgin Street.

Built around an open atrium in a historic six-story building, the **Hotel Indigo** (123 Metcalfe St., 613/231-6555 or 877/846-3446, www.hotelindigo.com, $135-244 d) appeals to travelers looking for boutique style without the sky-high price. For a chain hotel, it feels surprisingly individual: in the 106 guest rooms, a floor-to-ceiling mural covers one wall, and the quilt covers are bright floral prints. You've got all the modern amenities, from flat-screen TVs, mini fridges, and coffeemakers to complimentary Internet access. Indigo guests share the fitness room and indoor pool with the Residence Inn by Marriott next door.

$150-200

The spacious one- and two-bedroom suites at the **Albert at Bay Suite Hotel** (435 Albert St., 613/238-8858 or 800/267-6644, www.albertatbay.com, 1-bedroom $149-214 d, 2-bedroom $239-279 d) are a good deal for families or couples traveling together. Even the smallest of the 197 traditionally furnished units are over 74 square meters (800 square feet)—more than double the size of many hotel rooms—and all have full kitchens. There's no pool, but the fitness room overlooks the rooftop terrace. Local phone calls and Wi-Fi are included.

Starting with a glass of sparkling wine at check-in, ★ **ARC The.Hotel** (140 Slater St., 613/238-2888 or 800/699-2516, www.arcthe-hotel.com, $159-259 d), a stylish 112-room boutique property, makes you feel welcome. The guest rooms, with cream-colored upholstery and dark wood furniture, have a Zen feel, with Egyptian cotton linens and Keurig coffeemakers adding a luxurious touch. The smallest rooms, dubbed "intimate queens," are intimate; the king-bed units will give you more space. If a workout in the 24-hour fitness center doesn't sufficiently relax you, you can unwind over a cocktail in the lounge.

In a stately stone building with a green copper roof, the traditionally elegant ★ **Lord Elgin Hotel** (100 Elgin St., 613/235-3333 or 800/267-4298, www.lordelgin.ca, $149-275 d), built in 1941, is an Ottawa institution, with an excellent location near Parliament Hill. Of the 355 guest rooms with classic Biedermeier-style furnishings and free Wi-Fi, some of the nicest are the corner units overlooking the National Arts Centre. Sip cocktails in the gracious lobby lounge; on the lower level are a lap pool, hot tub, and fitness room. The hotel welcomes families and frequently offers discounts that make it an excellent value.

An ample breakfast buffet, an indoor lap pool and fitness facility, free Wi-Fi, and a guest laundry are among the features that make the 177-room **Residence Inn by Marriott** (161 Laurier Ave. W., 613/231-2020 or 877/478-4838, www.marriottresidenceinnottawa.com, $179-249) popular with both road warriors and traveling families. The studios, with a king bed and queen sofa bed, are about the size of typical hotel rooms, but the one- and two-bedroom suites are quite large, especially the corner units; all have kitchens. The hotel hosts twice-weekly happy hours where guests can mingle.

BYWARD MARKET DISTRICT AND VICINITY

The ByWard Market district and the adjacent Sandy Hill neighborhood (south of Rideau St.) have lots of lodging choices, from hostels,

B&Bs, and small hotels to big chain properties. Sandy Hill is primarily residential, surrounding the University of Ottawa, between the Rideau Canal and the Rideau River.

Under $100

Even if you don't usually stay in hostels, have a look at the **HI-Ottawa Jail Hostel** (75 Nicholas St., 613/235-2595 or 866/299-1478, www.hihostels.ca, $34-39 dorm, $39 s, $88-108 d), where some beds are in cells of the 19th-century former Carleton County Gaol (jail). The cells feel claustrophobic and noisy, with heavy grates on the doors and transom windows open to the hallways. More standard dorms and shared-bath doubles lack the cellblock ambiance, but rumors of ghosts abound. Guests share the kitchen or hang out in Mugshots, the pub. Rates include Wi-Fi, breakfast, and a jail tour.

The **Barefoot Hostel** (455 Cumberland St., 613/237-0336, www.barefoothostel.com, $34-37 dorm) is Ottawa's coolest budget lodging. Inside this red brick building near the ByWard Market, the common area with bright blue walls has space for lounging, with a flat-screen TV and computers for guest use. While there's no room to spare in the four dorms, each with four bunks, they're cheery, with wood floors and individual lockers. Guests share two modern baths. Would-be chefs, take note: the kitchen has a microwave, fridge, and toaster, but no stove. The hostel is under the same ownership as the Swiss Hotel next door.

$100-150

Unlike many fussy Victorian B&Bs, the four rooms at the **Avalon Bed-and-Breakfast** (539 Besserer St., 613/789-4334 or 866/557-5506, www.avalonbedandbreakfast.com, $95-125 d) mix a few traditional furnishings with cool, contemporary pieces. The sleek, airy Pewter room, done in silver and white, has a private balcony, and all the rooms in this brick half-duplex, on a residential street in the east end of Sandy Hill, have en suite baths, wood floors, flat-screen TVs, and large windows.

The location is a bit out of the way, but rates include parking as well as a full breakfast.

The other half of the Sandy Hill townhouse that houses the Avalon B&B is a bed-and-breakfast as well: **Benner's B&B** (541 Besserer St., 613/789-8320 or 877/891-5485, www.bennersbnb.com, $95-130 d). The three rooms, all with private baths, have modern appointments; the largest, the King Loft, has exposed brick walls, a king bed, and a sitting area in front of an electric fireplace.

Owner and avid traveler Janis King is happy to swap travel tales with guests at the **Ottawa Centre Bed & Breakfast** (62 Stewart St., 613/237-9494, www.ottawacenterbnb.com, $105-135 d), in her 1901 brick home a short hop from the University of Ottawa campus. Though the appointments seem formal—the living room has a curved entryway and ornate wood mantel, the dining room is filled with antiques and silver pieces—King makes her guests feel at home. Upstairs, the three bedrooms, with en suite baths, have tall windows, oriental rugs, and other traditional furnishings. Rates include full breakfast, parking, and Wi-Fi.

Perhaps some of the rooms in the modest, European-style **ByWard Blue Inn** (157 Clarence St., 613/241-2695 or 800/620-8810, www.bywardblueinn.com, $141-181 d) should have been named "ByWard View," since the sunny, top-floor front units—the inn's nicest—have tiny terraces with views toward Parliament Hill. The rest of the 46 rooms in this six-story building, just east of the ByWard Market, are more basic (and viewless; the cheapest are small and dark), but all have fridges, microwaves, and free Internet access. Rates include continental breakfast.

Plenty of homey touches grace the three-story **McGee's Inn** (185 Daly Ave., 613/237-6089 or 800/262-4337, www.mcgeesinn.com, $118-198 d), including the hand-carved cherry mantel in the parlor. Built in 1886, as the home of Privy Council member John McGee, this family-run inn has 14 guest rooms. Some are small, others quite large—but all have private baths and antique or period furnishings.

Several have original wood fireplaces, some have whirlpool tubs for two, and a couple have private porches. Parking, Internet access, and a full breakfast are included. While the inn is not specifically child-focused, kids under 12 stay free.

Co-owner Oscar Duplancic often serenades guests on the grand piano during breakfast at the aptly named **Bella Notte B&B** (108 Daly Ave., 613/565-0497 or 866/562-9569, www.bellanottebb.com, $138-158 d); Oscar and his wife, Lillian, are both professional musicians. Besides the high-ceilinged dining room with a marble fireplace, one of the nicest spaces is the cozy sitting room upstairs. The three guest rooms are simpler, with carpeted floors. The largest is the third-floor unit with sloped ceiling; another has a private balcony. The brick row house, built in 1868, was once home to Sir Alexander Campbell, one of Canada's founding fathers.

$150-200

One of Ottawa's top midrange lodgings is the 22-room ★ **Swiss Hotel** (89 Daly Ave., 613/237-0335 or 888/663-0000, www.swiss-hotel.ca, $148-228 d). From the exterior of the 1872 stone building, you'd never know that inside, the petite but stylish rooms are a riot of color balanced with crisp white duvets. Every room has an iPad to use, flat-screen TV, and free Wi-Fi. Owner Sabina Sauter, who has run the inn since the mid-1980s, is a tornado of enthusiasm, tending to guests' needs. Breakfast ($15) includes homemade Swiss muesli, as well as freshly baked breads, cheeses, fruits, eggs, and more.

Handy to the ByWard Market and walking distance to Parliament Hill, the 282-room **Novotel Ottawa** (33 Nicholas St., 613/230-3033 or 855/677-3033, www.novotelottawa.com, $165-215 d) was built in the 1980s, but updates—from flat-screen TVs, free Wi-Fi, and MP3 alarm clocks in the guest rooms to a revamped restaurant and bar—have kept it feeling modern and fresh. Adults can choose their preferred pillow style, while kids get free breakfast and a welcome kit with activities. The pool and fitness room, shared with an adjacent property, can seem cramped when crowded.

$200-300

Ottawa's landmark hotel, the castle-like ★ **Fairmont Château Laurier** (1 Rideau St., 613/241-1414 or 866/540-4410, www.fairmont.com/laurier-ottawa, $219-439 d), has a perfect location between the Rideau Canal and the ByWard Market and prides itself on service. Some of the traditionally elegant rooms are smallish, but others are quite spacious, and the public spaces, including the Renaissance-style ballroom with 5.5-meter (18-foot) ceilings, are very upscale. The art deco pool still has its original brass heat lamps. Before booking a stay, join the President's Club, Fairmont's complimentary frequent-stay program, since members get free Internet access.

Food

Ottawa's reputation as a bland, beige bureaucrats' burg is changing, and no more so than in its dining scene. Imaginative contemporary fare, small plates, and an increasing international influence are all making Ottawa an inspired choice for foodies.

DOWNTOWN

While the downtown area is filled with nondescript breakfast and lunch spots catering to local office workers or famished visitors, you can find a more interesting meal if you walk a few blocks south or west of Parliament Hill.

Bakeries and Cafés

The **Scone Witch** (150 Elgin St., 613/232-2173, 7am-8pm Mon.-Sat., 8am-4pm Sun., scones from $2) casts its spell on lovers of the humble biscuit. Lemon poppy seed? Currant ginger? Orange cranberry? It's hard to choose a favorite flavor, so you might have to sample more than one. At midday, try a sconewitch—a sandwich served on a freshly baked scone.

Whether you've got the midnight munchies, crave breakfast at 3pm, or need to refuel with a plate of meatloaf, a burger, or gooey *poutine*, the **Elgin St. Diner** (374 Elgin St., 613/237-9700, www.elginstreetdiner.com, 24 hours daily, $6-14) is your place. It's not gourmet, but it's wholesome, and they're open 365 days a year. If your kids can't find something they like here, send them home.

Contemporary

A dark, skinny room lined with a stainless-steel bar, neighborhood bistro ★ **Town** (296 Elgin St., 613/695-8696, www.town-lovesyou.ca, lunch 11:30am-2pm Wed.-Fri., dinner 5pm-10pm Sun.-Thurs. and 5pm-11pm Fri.-Sat., lunch $14-18, dinner $16-28) feels both homey and hip—a spot where you could dine solo, bring a date, or hang out with your pals. Italian-influenced

sharing plates constitute most of the seasonally changing menu, where you might find marinated smelts on toast, zucchini salad three-ways (grilled, puréed, and stuffed with ricotta), or fresh tagliatelle with peas, spinach, and lemon confit.

Ottawa may be a northern capital, but cheeky **Union Local 613** (315 Somerset St. W., 613/231-1010, www.union613.ca, lunch 11:30am-2pm Mon.-Fri., dinner 5:30pm-10pm daily, late-night menu 10:30pm-2am Wed.-Sat.) proudly serves "inauthentic Southern food." The menu meanders from good ol' plates like juicy fried chicken with pepper vinegar or smoked pork loin with black-eyed peas to wilder dishes like duck hearts with avocado and ancho sauce. Sip your way through the long list of bourbons and whiskeys or quaff a pungent house-made ginger beer.

Seafood

Love oysters? The **Whalesbone Oyster House** (430 Bank St., 613/231-8569, www.thewhalesbone.com, lunch 11:30am-2pm Mon.-Fri., dinner 5pm-10pm Sun.-Wed., 5pm-11pm Thurs.-Sat., lunch $12-25, dinner $26-45) has 'em, shucking several varieties every day from North America's East and West Coasts. Yet it's not just bivalves that has Ottawa seafoodies swimming into this laid-back Centretown joint, with its sturdy wooden tables and exposed brick walls; the menu includes a variety of fresh fish in intriguing preparations, like scallop ceviche with figs and red onion or lobster paired with saffron-scented polenta.

If you just want fresh fish without any fancy trappings (like tables and chairs), the same owners run the nearby **Whalesbone Oyster House Sustainable Oyster & Fish Supply** (504A Kent St., 613/231-3474). It's primarily a fish market, but they also sell a Brownbag Lunch (11am-2pm Tues.-Fri., 11am-3pm Sat., $8-12) with fish sandwiches to go.

Ottawa for Foodies

You don't have to be a top chef to take a class at Le Cordon Bleu Ottawa.

It wasn't so long ago that you'd never hear "foodie" and "Ottawa" in the same sentence, unless that sentence was "Foodies lament the Ottawa culinary scene." No more. Ottawa has a rapidly growing food culture that encourages culinary innovation and the use of local ingredients. To learn more about the culinary landscape in Ottawa's neighborhoods, book an entertaining food walk with **C'est Bon Epicurean Adventures** (613/722-8687 or 613/291-9155, www.cest-boncooking.ca). Their most popular tour is the 2.5-hour Tastes of the ByWard Market ($55) that includes food shops, cafés, and restaurants around the market area. They offer similar tours of Chinatown, Little Italy, and Wellington West, as well as cooking courses.

Even if you're not planning to become the top chef at a gastronomic temple, you can still take a cooking class at **Le Cordon Bleu Ottawa** (453 Laurier Ave. E., 613/236-2433 or 888/289-6302, www.cordonbleu.edu), the only Canadian branch of the famed French culinary school. Half-day, full-day, and multiday programs in French regional cuisine, knife skills, chocolate making, and more are offered for culinary enthusiasts; previous cooking experience is not required.

Savvy Company (613/728-8926, www.savvycompany.ca) organizes some of Ottawa's most informative and entertaining evenings. Cheese tastings are led by their in-house "cheese sommelier" and there are also wine tastings and multicourse dinners where guests mingle with local food producers. Great fun!

As you're exploring Ottawa's food shops, look for the **Savour Ottawa** (613/699-6850, ext. 13, www.savourottawa.ca) logo. Savour Ottawa is an organization whose mandate is to promote local food and support Ottawa's development as a culinary destination. Member businesses must meet minimum standards for using local food. Their website is also a useful resources for learning about eating local in Ottawa.

If you like your local ingredients more liquid, look for beers from the Ottawa region's more than 20 **microbreweries,** including Beaus All Natural, Beyond the Pale, Big Rig, Broadhead, Cassel, Dominion City, HogsBack, Kichesippi, and Turtle Island. Or take a **Brew Donkey Tour** (613/864-3659, www.brewdonkey.ca), where your guide will clue you into the local beer scene as you stop for tastings at several pubs and breweries.

BYWARD MARKET DISTRICT AND VICINITY

Despite its touristy vibe, the **ByWard Market** (55 ByWard Market Square, 613/244-4410) is still a working food market, with vendors setting up produce and other market stalls around the main market building from late April or early May through October.

This part of town is also home to many of the city's contemporary (and often high-end) dining rooms. Murray Street, particularly the stretch between Parent Avenue and Dalhousie Street, is locally known as "Gastro Alley" for its numerous restaurants.

Bakeries and Cafés

Taking its name from the flat, oblong tail of Canada's official animal, **BeaverTails** (69 George St., 613/241-1230, www.beaver-tailsinc.com) cooks up Ottawa's signature pastry: slabs of whole-wheat dough served hot from the fryer. You can slather them with all sorts of ridiculously sweet toppings, like chocolate hazelnut spread or Oreo cookies, but the simplest choices are best: cinnamon sugar, with or without a squeeze of lemon. There's another BeaverTails stand along the Rideau Canal—a popular spot to take a break while skating.

Breathe deeply when you enter the **Tea Store** (53 York St., 613/241-1291, www.teastore.ca, 9am-7pm Sun.-Wed., 9am-8pm Thurs.-Sat.), the better to take in the spicy, fruity, and earthy aromas of more than 200 varieties of tea. This peaceful tea shop and café makes a flavorful chai latte, which you can pair with pastries like tea-scented scones.

To pick up a sandwich on the run, or to gather picnic supplies, squeeze into **La Bottega Nicastro** (64 George St., 613/789-7575, www.labottega.ca, 9am-6pm Mon.-Wed. and Sat., 9am-8pm Thurs.-Fri., 11am-5pm Sun.), a jam-packed (or make that pasta-, cheese-, and *salumi*-packed) Italian deli and food shop. Choose your meat, cheese, bread, and toppings at their sandwich bar for custom-made panini ($6).

Contemporary

Craving a whole pig's head? Nose-to-tail bistro **Murray Street** (110 Murray St., 613/562-7244, www.murraystreet.ca, lunch 11:30am-2:30pm Mon.-Fri., 11am-2:30pm Sat.-Sun., dinner 5:30pm-10pm daily, lunch $12-18, dinner $18-30) will roast a pig's head for you and 10 of your porcine-craving pals (48 hours' notice required). You can also pig out on the pig's foot croquette or the barbecue-glazed pork shoulder confit. If you just want to graze, belly up to the charcuterie bar (11:30am-midnight daily) for a glass of wine and some smoked duck breast or rabbit liver mousse. It's a friendly joint, but vegans? Uh-uh.

You know a place called **Play Food and Wine** (1 York St., 613/667-9207, www.play-food.ca, noon-2pm and 5:30pm-10pm Mon., noon-2pm and 5:30pm-11pm Tues.-Thurs., noon-2pm and 5:30pm-11:45pm Fri., noon-11:45pm Sat., noon-10pm Sun., small plates $12-19) can't be too formal. The kitchen sends out a fun assortment of small plates designed to share. Wines by the taste, glass, or bottle include options from Ontario and farther afield. Owner Stephen Beckta conceived Play as a more casual sibling to his high-end **Beckta** (226 Nepean St., 613/238-7063, www.beckta.com, 5:30pm-10pm daily, $28-39) downtown; he also runs **Gezellig** (337 Richmond Rd., 613/680-9086, www.gezelligdining.com, 11:30am-2pm and 5:30pm-10pm Mon.-Sat., 10am-2pm and 5:30pm-10pm Sun., $26-35), a well-regarded neighborhood bistro in a former bank west of the city center.

Classic French cooking is alive and well at **Signatures** (453 Laurier Ave. E., 613/236-2499 or 888/289-6302, www.signaturesrestaurant.com, 11:30am-1:30pm and 5:30pm-9:30pm Wed.-Fri., 5:30pm-9:30pm Sat., lunch $29, dinner $25-33), the white-tablecloth restaurant at Le Cordon Bleu, the famous culinary school's only Canadian facility, set in an 1874 Sandy Hill mansion. Yet Canadian ingredients have their place, too; the fish paired with squid ink spaetzle might be arctic char, and the pepper-crusted steak au poivre could be made with Alberta beef. The gracious staff tempers French formality with Canadian affability.

Spanish

At **Navarra** (93 Murray St., 613/241-5500, www.navarrarestaurant.com, lunch noon-2pm Tues.-Fri., dinner 5:30pm-10pm Mon.-Sat., brunch 10:30am-2:30pm Sun., lunch $16-21, dinner $18-34), Ottawa-born, Mexico-raised chef-owner René Rodriguez (seen on Food Network's *Top Chef Canada*) cooks up imaginative Spanish-Basque fare, with some Mexican flavors and his own eclectic inspirations thrown in. Salt cod croquettes with spicy-sour tomato relish, slow-braised lamb sauced with hibiscus mole, and smoked, confit, and roasted pig cheeks in an achiote reduction all make their way onto the original menu. The wine list, with plenty of by-the-glass options, is sourced from Ontario, Spain, and around the globe.

CHINATOWN, LITTLE ITALY, AND THE GLEBE

Ottawa's Chinatown (www.ottawachinatown.ca) is not strictly Chinese, particularly when it comes to eating. The neighborhood is home to a large concentration of Vietnamese eateries alongside Chinese, Korean, Japanese, even Middle Eastern options, as well as Ottawa's most distinctive vegetarian dining room. Somerset Street West, between Bay and Rochester Streets, is Chinatown's Main Street; you'll find restaurants both east and west of the colorfully painted Chinatown Gateway arch. OC Transpo bus no. 2 runs from downtown along Somerset through Chinatown.

Little Italy, along Preston Street southwest of downtown, still has traditional red-sauce restaurants, but it's the more modern, non-Italian dining rooms that make the area worth an eating stop. Buses no. 3 or 14 will get you to the vicinity of Little Italy. In the Glebe, centered along Bank Street south of downtown, food options include a mix of hip-grunge cafés, natural foods eateries, and contemporary restaurants. Buses no. 1 and 7 travel along Bank Street from downtown.

Asian

The cheapest meal in town may be a *bánh mì* (Vietnamese sandwich) from **Co Cham** (780 Somerset St. W., 613/567-6050, 10:30am-9pm Tues.-Sat., 10:30am-7pm Sun., $3-8), where the bus fare to get here will cost more than your lunch. At this barebones Chinatown storefront, you can choose from several combinations of meat, pickled carrots and daikon, and fresh herbs on a bun—all for only $3 each. The menu includes other Vietnamese classics, too, from *pho* (noodle soup) to *bun* (rice noodles with meat, bean sprouts, and herbs). To drink, opt for tea or a fruit shake.

Unlike many Chinatown eateries that serve Cantonese fare, no-frills **Ju Xiang Yuan** (641 Somerset St. W., 613/321-3669, 11am-11pm Sun.-Thurs., 11am-midnight Fri.-Sat., $8-16) cooks up hearty, often spicy dishes of China's north. Specialties include stew-like hot pots and skewers of barbecued meats, from cumin-scented lamb to grilled squid to more exotic chicken hearts. An interesting appetizer is the tofu with chef sauce, a plate of cold bean curd tossed with an addictive garlic seasoning. Don't be shy about asking for recommendations or scouting out what other tables are eating.

Contemporary

Splat! Yolko Uno. The Alien. The menu names alone are (almost) worth a visit to chef-owner Marc Lepine's **Atelier** (540 Rochester St., 613/321-3537, www.atelierrestaurant.ca, 5pm-10pm Tues.-Sat., prix fixe $110 pp, reservations essential), Ottawa's first restaurant to experiment with molecular gastronomy techniques, where dinner is an elaborate 12-course tasting menu that has flush foodies all a-flutter. The kitchen will make modifications for "allergies, strong dislikes, and vegetarians" but otherwise, you get whatever wildly inventive dishes are on the evening's menu. Ottawa beige and bland? Not in this atelier.

One of the city's long-standing highly

regarded restaurants, the ★ **Black Cat Bistro** (428 Preston St., 613/569-9998, www.blackcatbistro.ca, 5pm-10pm Mon.-Sat., $20-36) serves French-inspired contemporary fare in a smart-casual Little Italy space. You might start with the foie gras torchon with brown butter and hazelnuts or the scallop *crudo* (cured with lime and cilantro), before moving on to steelhead trout almandine, roast chicken with corn spaetzle, or classic *steak frites*. Save room for the *chocolat pavé* or a fruit tart.

It's not just the name that's clever at **Two Six Ate** (268 Preston St., 613/695-8200, www.twosixate.com, 4pm-2am Wed.-Mon., small plates $11-16), an easygoing bistro in a Little Italy Victorian, with rough plastered walls and aged wood floors. The always-changing, designed-to-share dishes are equally engaging. You might sup on *arancini* made of roasted beet risotto and smoked mozzarella; toasts topped with cold smoked tuna, pickled onion, and olive dust; or surf and turf, featuring grilled calamari, sausage, and deliciously sweet tomatoes. No need to dress up; just bring your appetite for sampling. Night owls: The kitchen stays open till 2am.

A narrow sliver of a space with a sunny terrace just off Bank Street, **The Urban Pear** (151 2nd Ave., 613/569-9305, www.theurbanpear.com, 11:30am-2:30pm and 5:30pm-9pm Tues.-Thurs., 11:30am-2:30pm and 5:30pm-10pm Fri., 10am-3pm and 5:30pm-10pm Sat., 10am-3pm and 5:30pm-9pm Sun., $20-25) is an unpretentious neighborhood bistro, where you could turn up in anything from jeans to a little black dress. Serious cooking showcases lots of local ingredients. Dishes like a salad of honey-roasted squash and fried barley, duck breast with braised shiitake and oyster mushrooms, and a Stilton-topped burger on a house-made brioche have all appeared on the frequently changing menu.

Vegetarian

Zen Kitchen (634 Somerset St. W., 613/233-6404, www.zenkitchen.ca, 5pm-9pm Sun.-Thurs., 5pm-10pm Fri.-Sat., dinner $19-22) is an intimate Chinatown space serving imaginative vegetarian fare. The world-roving menu changes regularly, but meaty, panko-crusted seitan cutlets in a blueberry teriyaki sauce and a Thai-style vegetable curry paired with red lentil fritters are among the entrées. Finish on a sweet note with the seasonal fruit tart topped with coconut whipped "cream" or the chocolate cake with a spicy chili-chocolate sauce. For a complete vegan

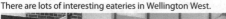

There are lots of interesting eateries in Wellington West.

extravaganza, opt for the multicourse tasting menu ($58 pp).

WELLINGTON WEST

Even though it's just a short ride west of downtown, you won't see many tourists in the Wellington West neighborhood. What you will find is lots of interesting eating. Several cafés make good refueling stops if you're browsing the boutiques, and contemporary dining rooms serve up inventive food to a mostly local clientele.

Bakeries and Cafés

Thyme and Again Take Home Food Shop (1255 Wellington St. W., 613/722-6277, www.thymeandagain.ca, 8am-8pm Mon.-Fri., 9am-6pm Sat., 10am-5pm Sun.) is part café and part takeout shop, carrying sandwiches, prepared foods, and luscious pastries. On the second floor, the small **Exposure Gallery** (613/722-0093, ext. 225, www.exposure-gallery.info) shows work by emerging local artists.

Contemporary

Yes, you can sample the namesake green spirit at the **Absinthe Café and Resto Bar** (1208 Wellington St. W., 613/761-1138, www.absinthecafe.ca, 11:30am-2pm and 5:30pm-10pm Mon.-Fri., 5:30pm-10pm Sat.-Sun., lunch $14-16, dinner $23-31); try "Death in the Afternoon" (absinthe and sparkling wine) or opt for a tasting flight of three absinthe varieties. Food options include traditional *steak frites*, but you might also find bacon-wrapped pork tenderloin served with creamed kale or ravioli stuffed with wild mushrooms and parmesan. The candlelit dining room is decorous enough for a business meal yet relaxed enough for a night on the town.

Roast duck breast served with coconut-curried corn is just one of the original dishes that might grace the oak tables at **Allium** (87 Holland Ave., 613/792-1313, www.alliumrestaurant.com, lunch 11:30am-2pm Tues.-Fri., dinner 5:30pm-9:30pm Mon., 5:30pm-9pm Tues.-Thurs., 5:30pm-10pm Fri.-Sat., lunch $12-16, dinner $25-30), a smart-casual bistro decorated with modern art. Come for the popular Monday tapas night to sample a changing assortment of small plates ($8-15), from smoked fish cakes with Brussels sprout slaw to steak tartare with Sriracha mayo. The restaurant is one block north of Wellington Street.

The black seahorses on the wallpaper give chic ★ **Supply and Demand** (1335 Wellington St. W., 613/680-2949, www.supplyanddemandfoods.ca, 5pm-9:30pm Sun.-Mon., 5pm-10pm Tues.-Sat., $15-23) a fanciful feel, yet this übermodern kitchen plays with its food in a serious way—with top-notch results. Bring friends to this bustling brasserie, the better to sample your way through the artistically plated seafood-centric dishes. Start with something from the menu's "raw and marinated" category, perhaps buttery tuna *crudo* in a lemon-truffle oil with chips of black puffed rice.

Information and Services

Visitor Information

For planning a trip to Ottawa, the best source for up-to-the-minute information is **Ottawa Tourism** (150 Elgin St., Suite 1405, www.ottawatourism.ca, 613/237-5150 or 800/363-4465, 8:30am-4:30pm Mon.-Fri.). Their comprehensive website lists scores of details about the city's sights, activities, and current events. Once you arrive, pick up visitor information or get your questions answered at the **Capital Information Kiosk** (90 Wellington St., 613/239-5000 or 866/811-0055, www.pch.gc.ca, 10am-6pm daily).

Media and Communications

Ottawa's daily newspapers are the **Ottawa Citizen** (www.ottawacitizen.com) and **Ottawa Sun** (www.ottawasun.com). Check **Ottawa Xpress** (www.ottawaxpress.com), an arts-and-entertainment weekly, for extensive listings of things going on around town. **Ottawa Magazine** (www.ottawamagazine.com), published monthly in print and available online, also covers the arts, restaurants, and things to do.

Transportation

GETTING THERE
Air

Ottawa International Airport (YOW, 1000 Airport Pkwy., 613/248-2000, www.ottawaairport.ca) is 15 kilometers (nine miles) south of downtown. **Air Canada** (888/247-2262, www.aircanada.ca) has nonstop flights to Ottawa from most major Canadian cities, U.S. destinations that include Boston, New York, Washington, Ft. Lauderdale, and Orlando, as well as London (UK) and Frankfurt. **WestJet** (800/538-5696, www.westjet.com) flies to several Canadian and U.S. destinations, and **Porter Airways** (888/619-8622, www.flyporter.com) has flights to Toronto's City Airport, Halifax, and Moncton. Several U.S. carriers, including **Delta** (800/221-1212, www.delta.com), **United** (800/864-8331, www.united.ca), and **US Airways** (800/428-4322, www.usairways.com), serve Ottawa as well. Ottawa is also a departure point for travels to Canada's far north. **Air North** (800/661-0407, www.flyairnorth.com) connects Ottawa to Yellowknife, and **Canadian North** (800/661-1505, www.canadiannorth.com) flies between Ottawa and Iqaluit.

The least expensive way to get downtown from the airport is by public transit. Catch OC Transpo **bus no. 97** (613/741-4390, www.octranspo.com, adults $3.45 or two bus tickets, ages 6-11 $1.85 or one bus ticket) outside the arrivals area; it will take you downtown in 30-35 minutes. The bus runs about every 20 minutes during the day and every 30-60 minutes at night. Bus tickets ($1.55 each) are cheaper than the cash fare; buy tickets at the Ground Transportation Desk in the arrivals area. A taxi from the airport to the downtown area will cost $30-35.

Train

If you're traveling to Ottawa from Toronto or Montreal, the train is a fast, efficient option. **VIA Rail** (200 Tremblay Rd., 888/842-7245, www.viarail.ca) has several trains a day to both Toronto (4-4.5 hours, one-way adults $49-144, ages 2-11 $49-72) and Montreal (2 hours, one-way adults $37-76, ages 2-11 $31-37). The Ottawa-Toronto trains all stop in Kingston (2 hours, one-way adults $46-96, ages 2-11 $35-49), and certain trains stop in Brockville, Belleville, and Cobourg.

Ottawa's VIA Rail station is five kilometers (three miles) southeast of the city center. By public transit, the trip between the train station and downtown takes about 15 minutes. Catch **bus no. 95** (613/741-4390, www.octranspo.com, adults $3.45 or two bus tickets, ages 6-11 $1.85 or one bus ticket), which has frequent service (except late at night). A taxi from the train station to downtown will cost about $10-15, depending on traffic conditions.

Bus

Ottawa's **Central Bus Station** (265 Catherine St., 613/238-6668) is south of downtown on the edge of the Glebe neighborhood. **Greyhound** (www.greyhound.ca) runs most of the bus routes in and out of Ottawa, including service to Montreal (2.5 hours, one-way adults $17-38, ages 2-11 $17-29), Toronto (5-6 hours, one-way adults $35-84, ages 2-11 $35-63.50), Kingston (2.5-2.75 hours, one-way adults $17-38.50, ages 2-11 $17-30), North Bay (4.5-5.5 hours, one-way adults $80-99, ages 2-11 $60-74), and Sudbury (6.5-7.5 hours, one-way adults $57-94, ages 2-11 $57-70). Greyhound also runs several buses daily between Ottawa and Montreal's Trudeau International Airport (2 hours, one-way adults $17-38, ages 2-11 $17-29).

Between Ottawa and either Montreal or Toronto, the train is more comfortable than the bus, but the buses travel more frequently. To go downtown from the Central Bus Station by public transit, walk two blocks east to Bank Street and catch northbound **bus no. 1** or **bus no. 7** (613/741-4390, www.octranspo.com, adults $3.45 or two bus tickets, ages 6-11 $1.85 or one bus ticket).

Car

Ottawa is located in Eastern Ontario on Highway 417. It's closer to Montreal (2-2.5 hours by car) than it is to Toronto (about a five-hour drive). From Montreal to Ottawa (200 kilometers, 125 miles), take Autoroute 40 west until it meets Highway 417 at the Ontario-Quebec provincial border.

From Toronto to Ottawa (450 kilometers, 280 miles), the most straightforward route is to follow Highway 401 east, past Kingston and Brockville, then turn north on Highway 416, which joins Highway 417 just south of Ottawa. A more scenic route would be to pick up Highway 7 east of Toronto and follow it northeast until it meets Highway 417. You could also take Highway 401 east to Kingston, then meander north on Highway 15, through the small towns along the Rideau Canal.

From Kingston to Ottawa (200 kilometers, or 125 miles), it's about two hours by car. From the east gate of Algonquin Park to Ottawa, it's about 240 kilometers (150 miles), but the roads aren't fast, so allow 3.5 hours. Take Highway 60 east to Highway 17 east, which will join Highway 417 as you continue east into Ottawa.

GETTING AROUND

The majority of Ottawa's attractions are clustered around the downtown area, so it's easy to get around on foot. You can even walk across the bridge to the Canadian Museum of History in Gatineau (although to reach Gatineau Park and other Gatineau destinations, you'll need to have wheels of some sort). The city's comprehensive bus system is useful if you're traveling farther afield, or if you need to rest your feet.

Bus

Ottawa's public transit system, **OC Transpo** (613/741-4390, www.octranspo.com), includes an extensive network of buses that travel through the city center and out to the suburbs. Most buses operate 6am-midnight Monday-Saturday and 7am-11pm Sunday; service is frequent on weekdays, with buses running every few minutes at peak times, but less so on weekends. Bus no. 97 between the airport and downtown operates 24 hours daily. Many buses that run into or out of downtown use the Transitway, a dedicated lane for buses only.

You can either pay cash (with exact change) when you enter the bus or pay with a bus ticket. It's less expensive to use bus tickets, but

Following the Rideau Canal

A relaxing day or weekend trip between Kingston and Ottawa is to follow the route of the Rideau Canal. The canal runs 202 kilometers (126 miles), with 47 locks and several interesting small towns along the way. Highway 15 is the main north-south route through the canal region. You can see many of the region's highlights in the triangle of three towns: Smiths Falls, Perth, and Westport. The website for the **Rideau Heritage Route Tourism Association** (www.rideauheritageroute.ca) has additional information about the Rideau region.

SMITHS FALLS

Stop in Smiths Falls (www.smithsfalls.ca) to learn more about the Canal's history. Parks Canada's **Rideau Canal Visitors Centre** (34 Beckwith St. S., 613/283-5170, www.pc.gc.ca, 9am-4:30pm daily late May-early Sept., donation) is housed in a 19th-century former mill, where exhibits detail the canal's construction (1826-1832) and its subsequent role in the region's development. Check out the Smiths Falls Locks nearby, too.

Smiths Falls' **Heritage House Museum** (11 Old Sly's Rd., 613/283-6311, www.smithsfalls.ca/heritagehouse, 10:30am-4pm daily May-Dec., 10:30am-4pm Mon.-Fri. Jan.-Apr., adults $4.50, seniors $4, ages 6-18 $3.50, families $14) exhibits regional history in an 1860s Victorian home. If you have kids in tow, they'll only be interested in the house's curiosity: a two-story privy. And no, you don't want to sit on the lower level.

Smiths Falls is 75 kilometers (47 miles) southwest of Ottawa and 95 kilometers (59 miles) northeast of Kingston, along Highway 15.

PERTH

Many of the Scottish stonemasons who built the Rideau Canal settled in Perth, leaving a legacy of elegant stone homes, including **Inge-Va** (66 Craig St., 613/498-3003, www.heritagetrust.on.ca, 10am-4pm Wed.-Sun. mid-June-Aug., adults $3, ages 6-16 $1.50), an 1823 late-Georgian stone residence that is also the site of an archaeological mystery. When archaeologists excavated the site of a privy used by the Radenhurst family, who lived at Inge-Va in the mid-1800s, they were surprised to find thousands of pieces of dishes and glasses. Apparently, the family had thrown out all of their kitchenware. Historians speculate that they may have desperately hoped to stop the spread of infectious diseases that claimed 5 of their 10 children.

A unique way to explore the town is with **Perth Through the Ages** (877/283-1283, www.classictheatre.ca, Wed.-Sun. late June-Aug., adults $12, under age 13 free), a theatrical walking tour through the region's history, created in conjunction with Perth's Classic Theatre Festival. While the specific tour varies annually, costumed actors lead you around town and back in time, where you might learn about the Last Duel (an infamous 1833 shootout between two feuding law students) or Perth's role in creating the record-breaking Mammoth Cheese. Call or check the website for performance details and schedules.

Murphys Point Provincial Park (2243 Elm Grove Rd./County Rd. 21, 613/267-5060, www.ontarioparks.com or www.friendsofmurphyspoint.ca, $14.50 per vehicle) tells the story of a different heritage. The Silver Queen Mine was a mica mine that operated from 1903 to 1920 in what is now the park, with the minerals shipped out along the Rideau Canal. In summer, you can tour

you must purchase tickets in advance, before you board the bus. Many convenience stores, drugstores, and groceries around Ottawa sell bus tickets, including Loblaws, Mac's Milk, Pharma Plus, Quickie, and Shoppers Drug Mart. You can also buy tickets or get bus information at Rideau Center—the **OC Transpo Sales and Information Centre** (50 Rideau St., 8:30am-9pm Mon.-Fri., 9:30am-6pm Sat., 11am-5pm Sun.) is on the third floor—or inside Ottawa City Hall (110 Laurier Ave., 8:30am-5pm Mon.-Fri.).

the former mine and learn more about life as an early 20th-century miner. Murphys Point also has 20 kilometers (12.5 miles) of hiking trails and a 160-site campground (tent sites $40-44, electrical sites $46-50, rustic cabin or yurt $142). The park is 19 kilometers (12 miles) south of Perth, via County Roads 1 and 21.

Perth and surrounding communities are one of Ontario's major **maple syrup-producing** areas. Maple sugaring season, when syrup producers tap their trees and turn sap into syrup, takes place in March and April. Several producers welcome visitors and operate seasonal restaurants, where you can learn about the syrup-making process and (more importantly) taste the maple goodies. **Wheelers Pancake House and Sugar Camp** (1001 Highland Line, McDonalds Corners, Lanark Highlands, 613/278-2090, www.wheelersmaple.com, 9am-3pm daily) is open year-round, while favorite maple-season destinations, open in March and April, include **Temple's Sugar Bush** (1700 Ferguson's Falls Rd./County Rd. 15, Lanark, 613/253-7000, www.templessugarbush.ca) and **Fulton's Pancake House and Sugar Bush** (399 Sugar Bush Rd., Pakenham, 613/256-3867, www.fultons.ca).

With exposed brick walls, a wood bar, and a locally focused food and drink menu, **The Masonry Restaurant and Market** (8 Wilson St. E., 613/466-0505, www.themasonry.ca, 11am-3pm Sun.-Tues., 11am-9pm Wed.-Thurs., 11am-10pm Fri.-Sat., lunch $13-18, dinner $18-40) is a worthy destination for a meal or Ontario microbrew. You can get sandwiches, like a roasted squash and goat cheese panini, to go, too.

Classic album covers, from Bob Marley to the Beatles, decorate the walls of **The Hungry 7** (34 Dufferin St., 613/466-0692, 11am-9pm Tues.-Sun., $10-17), a self-described "modern diner" on Highway 7. It's run by two former Ottawa chefs who are cooking up burgers, sandwiches (try the grilled veggie), pastas, and pot pies for Perth locals and hungry travelers.

Perth and District Chamber of Commerce (34 Herriott St., 613/267-3200 or 888/319-3204, www.perthchamber.com) can give you more information about the region. Perth is off Highway 7, a scenic alternative route connecting Toronto and Ottawa. It's also 20 kilometers (12 miles) west of Smiths Falls via Highway 43.

WESTPORT

One of the prettiest towns in the Rideau region is Westport, perched on the shores of Upper Rideau Lake, 30 kilometers (18 miles) southwest of Perth, along Highway 10. Stroll around town, or head up the ridge overlooking both the town and the lake to the 325-hectare (800-acre) **Foley Mountain Conservation Area** (off Hwy. 10, 613/273-3255, www.rvca.ca, dawn-dusk daily, $6 per vehicle). Several hiking trails wend through the woods; the lookout at Spy Rock has the best views.

A traditional family-run country inn, **The Cove Inn** (2 Bedford-on-the-Water, 613/273-3636 or 888/268-3466, www.coveinn.com, $130-180 d) has nine simple, well-kept guest rooms in the 1872 main building, which was originally a private home, and six additional rooms in the Victorian-style 1876 Fredenburgh House across the street. The **Cove's water-view dining room** (11:30am-8pm Sun.-Thurs., 11:30am-8:30pm Fri.-Sat., lunch $11-15, dinner $12-30) serves pub-style dishes—burgers or hot turkey sandwiches—as well as more substantial dinner fare, with live music several nights a week.

Cash fares are $3.45 for adults, $1.85 ages 6-11. Bus tickets cost $1.55, and most regular trips require two tickets for adults ($3.10) and one ticket ($1.85) for kids. Whether you pay cash or use a ticket, get a transfer from the driver when you board the bus. It's your proof of payment, and it's valid for 90 minutes if you transfer to another route.

If you're going to use the buses several times in one day, buy a **DayPass** ($8.10), good for unlimited trips on the day that you purchase it. Buy the pass directly from the bus driver when you board; you need exact change. The DayPass is a great deal on weekends, when the whole family (two adults and up to four kids under 12) can travel all day on a single DayPass. Use the Travel Planner on the **OC Transpo website** (www.octranspo.com) to figure out what bus to take and when the buses run.

Downtown, many east-west buses run on Albert Street going westbound and Slater Street going east; some lines instead stop on Wellington Street, near Parliament. Going north-south, buses run on Elgin and Bank Streets. On the east side of the Rideau Canal near the ByWard Market, Rideau Street, around Rideau Centre, is a main transit point for buses heading in many directions.

Light Rail

Ottawa has a limited light rail system, the **O-Train** (613/741-4390, www.octranspo.com, $3.45). The single north-south line currently has only five stations that are not conveniently located for reaching most of Ottawa's visitor attractions. The city has begun construction on an expanded light rail network, with service through the downtown area, scheduled to open in 2017 or 2018. Get updates at www.confederation-line.ca.

Taxi

You can usually find taxis near major attractions and hotels, and at the airport, train station, and bus depot. Taxi stands are also located at several points throughout downtown. Taxis are metered. Local companies include **Blue Line Taxi** (613/238-1111, www.bluelinetaxi.com) and **Capital Taxi** (613/744-3333, www.capitaltaxi.com).

Car

Highway 417, also known as the Queensway, is the region's main east-west highway. A network of parkways winds along the rivers and the canal. If you're driving in the city center, pay attention to the many one-way streets. Wellington Street runs east-west in front of Parliament, while Elgin and Bank Streets are main north-south streets downtown. On the east side of the Rideau Canal, Sussex Drive heads north, skirting the ByWard Market neighborhood, and continuing toward Rideau Hall, the governor general's residence. Rideau Street is the main east-west road between the canal and the Rideau River.

Parking can be a challenge in downtown Ottawa. On-street parking is limited to a maximum of three hours between 7am and 7pm, so park in a lot if you'll be longer. Most lodgings charge extra—sometimes a lot extra—for parking, so ask before you book. On Saturday and Sunday, **parking is free** downtown at on-street parking meters and in city-owned parking lots. The free parking zone is bounded by Wellington Street on the north, the Rideau Canal on the east, Catherine Street on the south, and Bronson Avenue on the west. City parking lots in this area include 212 Gloucester Street and 234-250 Slater Street, both between Bank and Kent Streets. Check the city website (www.ottawa.ca) for additional parking information. Between November 15 and April 1, you cannot park overnight on city streets (between 1am and 7am) when Environment Canada forecasts a snow accumulation of seven centimeters or more. To find out if an overnight parking ban is in effect, call the city information line at 311.

Tours

A fun, family-friendly way to explore Ottawa is on an **Urban Quest** (613/853-2886, www.urbanquest.com, year-round, $10 pp), where you solve a series of clues that lead you from place to place. You can do a quest with any number of people, but most are designed for two to four. Typically lasting around 1.5 hours, quests end at a mystery restaurant where you can have lunch or dinner (not included in the quest fee).

Plunge into the Ottawa River on the **Lady Dive Amphibus Tour** (office 613/524-2221 or ticket kiosk 613/223-6211, www.ladydive.

com, May-mid-Oct., adults $31, seniors and students $28, ages 6-12 $21, under age 6 $11, families $87), which combines a circuit of the city's main attractions with a river cruise in an amphibious vehicle. Buy your ticket online or at their kiosk at Sparks and Elgin Streets.

With **Ottawa Walking Tours** (613/799-1774, www.ottawawalkingtours. com, over age 10 $15, under age 11 free), you get a two-hour guided historical walk around the city's main attractions. Tours depart from the Terry Fox statue opposite Parliament Hill (90 Wellington St., at Metcalfe St.). Advance reservations are required; tour schedules are posted on the website.

Gatineau

Cross the Ottawa River from downtown, and you enter the district of Gatineau in the province of Quebec. You're still in metropolitan Ottawa, but it can feel as if you've wandered into another country. While much of Ottawa's population is bilingual, once you enter Gatineau, the first language is definitely French. Several bridges connect this Quebec region, known as the Outaouais (pronounced "oo-ta-WAY"), with the rest of metropolitan Ottawa.

Before a municipal amalgamation back in 2003, Gatineau's downtown area was previously the city of Hull, and some people still use the older name. If an address is located in "Hull," head for downtown Gatineau.

SIGHTS

It's worth crossing the bridge to Quebec for one of the region's best museums: the Canadian Museum of History. Ottawa's largest green space, Gatineau Park, is also on the Quebec side, as is a lovely Nordic-style day spa and a lively casino.

★ Canadian Museum of History

Canada's most-visited museum is the **Canadian Museum of History** (100 Laurier St., 819/776-7000 or 800/555-5621, www.historymuseum.ca, 9:30am-6pm Fri.-Wed., 9:30am-8pm Thurs. May-mid-Oct., 9:30am-5pm Fri.-Wed., 9:30am-8pm Thurs.

Canadian Museum of History

mid-Oct.-Apr., adults $13, seniors $11, students $10, ages 3-12 $8, families $32, IMAX theater adults $7, seniors $6, students $5, ages 3-12 $4, families $23, free admission 4pm-8pm Thurs., parking $5 per hour, $12.50 per day), a massive showcase of human history and culture displaying both its comprehensive permanent collections and regularly changing temporary exhibitions.

Opened in 1989 on the banks of the Ottawa River, the building is one of Ottawa's most distinctive structures, notable for its curved, undulating walls. Alberta-born architect Douglas Cardinal, who is of Métis heritage (his other credits include the Smithsonian Institution's National Museum of the American Indian in Washington DC), was responsible for the museum's design.

A good place to start is in the **First Peoples** galleries. Besides containing one of the world's largest collections of totem poles, the exhibits trace the history of Canada's ab-original communities. Look for the sculpture *Spirit of Haida Gwaii* by noted First Nations artist Bill Reid (1920-1998).

As this book went to press, the museum was creating a new **Canadian History Hall** to occupy roughly half of the building's permanent exhibit space. The hall will include six zones, each representing a different phase of Canadian civilization from more than 15,000 years ago until modern times. This new gallery is expected to open in 2017; check the museum website or phone for updates.

Included with the regular admission are two "museums within the museum": the **Canadian Children's Museum** and the **Canadian Postal Museum.** There's an IMAX theater for a supplemental fee. If you plan to visit the Museum of History and the Canadian War Museum, buy a combination ticket (adults $20, seniors $17, students $15, children $12, families $55), good for both museums.

To walk to the history museum from the Ottawa side of the river, cross the Alexandra Bridge near the National Gallery of Canada. To reach the museum by boat, board the **Au**

Feel de l'Eau Aqua Taxi (819/329-2413, www.aufeeldeleau.ca, one-way adults $5, children $4, round-trip adults $9, children $6, cash only) at the dock near the Rideau Canal's Ottawa lock; it's on the river behind the Bytown Museum.

By bus, take bus no. 8 from Albert Street downtown to the Museum of History stop. You can also catch the **Société de Transport de l'Outaouais** (www.sto.ca) bus no. 77 (Magnus) on Wellington Street at Metcalfe, and get off at Maisonneuve/Papineau, which is about a five-minute walk to the museum. From the ByWard Market area, take STO bus no. 31 (Parc de la Montagne) from Rideau Street at Cumberland to Allumettières/Laurier, also about a five-minute walk from the museum.

★ Gatineau Park

When Ottawans want to escape the city, they head for their backyard—this 361-square-kilometer (89,000-acre) green space in the Gatineau Hills—for hiking, cycling, picnicking, canoeing, or just relaxing.

Start at the **Gatineau Park Visitors Centre** (33 Scott Rd., Chelsea, 819/827-2020 or 800/456-3016, www.ncc-ccn.gc.ca, 9am-5pm daily May-Oct., 10am-4pm Mon.-Fri., 9am-5pm Sat.-Sun. Nov.-Apr.), for maps and tips from the staff to plan your explorations. The park also has a seasonal **Welcome Area** (Gamelin Blvd. at Gatineau Pkwy., June-mid-Oct.) where you can stop for information.

Gatineau Park has 165 kilometers (103 miles) of **hiking** trails. The 2.5-kilometer (1.5-mile) Pink Lake Trail circles the lake of that name. Head for the Champlain Lookout for views across the Ottawa Valley, and walk the 1.3-kilometer (0.8-mile) Champlain Trail. Download a trail map from the www.ncc-ccn.gc.ca website, or pick up a free copy at the Visitors Centre or in Ottawa at the **Capital Information Kiosk** (90 Wellington St., 613/239-5000 or 866/811-0055, www.pch.gc.ca, 10am-6pm daily).

You can swim in several of the park's lakes, including Meech, Philippe, and La Pêche

the "Arc de Triomphe" in the gardens of the Mackenzie King Estate

pass at the Visitors Centre or at any of the park's 15 departure points.

In February, thousands of skiers race in the annual **Gatineau Loppet** (819/778-5014, ext. 232, www.gatineauloppet.com), the largest cross-country ski event in Canada. Even if you're not a marathon ski racer, you can join one of the Loppet's recreational events, including a mini two-kilometer (1.2-mile) course for kids and their parents, with stops for cookies and hot chocolate.

There is no public transportation to Gatineau Park. The Visitors Centre is a 20- to 30-minute drive from downtown Ottawa.

Nordik Spa-Nature

If "steam, soak, and be soothed" is your mantra, you'll be in heaven at North America's largest Nordic-style spa, **Nordik Spa-Nature** (16 chemin Nordik, Chelsea, 819/827-1111 or 866/575-3700, www.lenordik.com, 9am-11pm Sun.-Thurs., 9am-midnight Fri.-Sat., $50 Mon.-Thurs., $59 Fri.-Sun., massages and other services extra), where the seven baths of varying temperatures are outdoors amid the trees. You alternate between hot and cold treatments; there are eight saunas, an infinity pool, even a saltwater float pool. Several areas are silent—the better for relaxation—while others are set up for socializing. With a restaurant and lounge on-site, you can easily spend an entire day. Children under age 16 are not allowed.

Casino du Lac-Leamy

Gambling, as well as concerts, shows, and several restaurants, is another reason to cross the bridge and visit Gatineau's swanky **Casino du Lac-Leamy** (1 Blvd. du Casino, 819/772-2100 or 800/665-2274, www.casino-du-lac-leamy.com, 24 hours daily).

The **Société de Transport de l'Outaouais** (STO, 819/778-8327, www.sto.ca) bus no. 21 travels from downtown Ottawa to the casino. The casino supplies free bus tickets to guests at many downtown hotels; ask the concierge at your lodging. **Au Feel de l'Eau Aqua Taxi** (819/329-2413, www.

Lakes (parking $11 per vehicle). At Philippe and La Pêche Lakes, you can rent canoes and kayaks ($20 for 1.5 hours, $25 for 2 hours, $30 for 3 hours).

Also in the park is the **Mackenzie King Estate** (819/827-2020, 10am-5pm Mon. and Wed.-Fri., 11am-6pm Sat.-Sun. mid-May-mid-Oct., parking $9 per vehicle), the country home of William Lyon Mackenzie King, Canada's 10th prime minister. You can tour the estate's several cottages and lush gardens (there's even an "Arc de Triomphe"), or stop for a sandwich, salad, or afternoon tea at the **Mackenzie King Tearoom** (819/827-3405, 11am-5pm Mon.-Fri., 11:30am-6pm Sat.-Sun. mid-May-mid-Oct., $14-22).

The park is open all year. Fall is one of the best times to visit Gatineau Park, when the leaves change color; come midweek to avoid the leaf-peeping crowds. In October, the park hosts its **Fall Rhapsody,** with a variety of special events. In winter, you can hike, snowshoe, or cross-country ski; purchase a trail

aufeeldeleau.ca) runs a shuttle boat between downtown and the casino.

ACCOMMODATIONS AND FOOD

If you can't drag yourself away from the black-jack tables, or if you just want a comfortable place to stay in Gatineau, you can crash at the **Hôtel Hilton Lac-Leamy** (3 Blvd. du Casino, 819/790-6444 or 866/488-7888, www.hilton. com, $249-389 d), where original works by glass artist Dale Chihuly decorate the lobby. Besides the 349 modern rooms, the hotel has indoor and outdoor pools, a fitness center, tennis courts, a large spa, several restaurants, and three bars. Parking is free in the outdoor lot.

Hearty pub food—burgers, pasta, and a don't-miss duck confit grilled cheese sandwich—will fill your belly, while the friendly vibe and beers on tap will cheer your soul at the **Chelsea Pub** (238 Old Chelsea Rd., Chelsea, 819/827-5300, www.chelseapub.ca, 11:30am-midnight Mon.-Fri., 11am-midnight Sat., 11am-11pm Sun., $12-17). Established as a tavern in 1875, it's one of several casual eateries near the Gatineau Park Visitors Centre.

Microbrewery **Les Brasseurs du Temps** (170 rue Montcalm, 819/205-4999, ext. 1, www.brasseursdutemps.com, 11:30am-midnight Sun.-Tues., 11:30am-1am Wed., 11:30am-2am Thurs.-Sat., $12-22) brews a variety of beers that you can order along with their international pub fare, from sandwiches to fish-and-chips to *poutine*. They even try to make beer drinking educational with an exhibit on the history of brewing in the Outaouais.

Tiny **Chez Edgar** (60 rue Bégin, 819/205-1110, www.chezedgar.ca, 10am-6:30pm Tues.-Fri., 10am-5pm Sat., 9:30am-5pm Sun.) is a popular purveyor of contemporary comfort food for lunch and weekend brunch: pastries, soups, creative sandwiches, and salads.

PRACTICALITIES

Ottawa and Gatineau have separate bus systems. Some Ottawa (OC Transpo) buses go to Gatineau, but Gatineau's own bus system, **Société de Transport de l'Outaouais** (STO, 819/778-8327, www.sto.ca), operates within Gatineau and between Gatineau and downtown Ottawa; the STO website has route maps and a trip planner. The regular STO adult cash fare is $3.90. You can purchase an STO day pass, called *La Passe-temps,* for $8.50, good for unlimited travel for one day. Regular OC Transpo bus tickets are not accepted on the STO system. However, you *can* use an OC Transpo DayPass on STO buses. Taxi companies serving Gatineau include **Crown Taxi** (819/777-1645) and **Regal Taxi** (819/777-5231).

For information about Gatineau, contact **Outaouais Tourism** (103 Laurier St., 819/778-2222 or 800/265-7822, www.tourismeoutaouais.com). For more food-centric stops in Gatineau and vicinity, check out the **Outaouais Gourmet Way** (www.outaouaisgourmetway.com), an interactive directory of regional food experiences.

Cottage Country, Algonquin, and the Northeast

Look for ★ to find recommended sights, activities, dining, and lodging.

Highlights

★ **Muskoka Wharf:** Learn how steamships helped develop tourism around the Muskoka Lakes at this Gravenhurst development that includes a historic boat museum, and cruise the lake on a traditional steamship (page 297).

★ **Canoeing in Algonquin Provincial Park:** Ontario's largest provincial park is one of the province's best destinations for canoeing, whether you're paddling on the numerous lakes and rivers or taking a multiday trip across the backcountry (page 311).

★ **Science North:** Sudbury's cool, contemporary science museum is filled with "please touch" exhibits that are particularly ecofriendly (page 319).

★ **Temagami:** This lake region is one of the most accessible places in the north for canoe trips, whether you're a novice or experienced paddler (page 321).

★ *Polar Bear Express* **Train:** Go where no roads go on this rail trip north to James Bay, where you can explore the Cree First Nations communities of Moosonee and Moose Factory Island (page 324).

F or a getaway to the outdoors, head north to Ontario's Cottage Country and to the woodland region that extends northeast, all the way to James Bay.

The Muskoka Lakes region north of Toronto has long been a popular weekend getaway for families to escape to their summer cottages or stay at lakeside resorts. Muskoka Cottage Country begins just 100 kilometers (60 miles) north of Toronto and is centered around the towns of Gravenhurst, Bracebridge, and Huntsville. Dotted with inland lakes, ski hills, and waterfront towns along Lake Muskoka and numerous smaller lakes, this region offers plentiful opportunities for outdoor adventure and relaxation. The area's top attraction is Algonquin Provincial Park, one of Ontario's largest protected green spaces; visit for a day or a week and take a short hike, paddle across an inland lake, or set out on a multiday wilderness adventure.

Beyond Algonquin, smaller parks like Arrowhead Provincial Park are great for families looking to camp, hike, or swim, while farther north, the lakes and forests surrounding Temagami make it a prime destination for canoe trips.

While the northeast is a natural choice for outdoor adventures, it's ripe for cultural explorations, too. Aboriginal people have lived in Northern Ontario for thousands of years, and many First Nations welcome visitors who want to learn about their culture and traditions. If you venture north to the remote communities of Moosonee and Moose Factory Island on the shores of James Bay, you can explore the culture of the Cree First Nation, one of Canada's largest aboriginal groups.

Northeastern Ontario also has a large francophone population, so don't be surprised to see bilingual signs or hear *"Bonjour"* and *"Merci."* The city of Sudbury is particularly bilingual; it's Canada's third-largest French-speaking community outside Quebec. In some northern towns, you'll find French Canadian influences in the food, with *tourtière* (meat pie) and *poutine* (french fries topped with cheese curds and gravy) almost as common as burgers and fries.

Looking for outdoor adventure? Cultural adventure? Just plain adventure? Then head north.

Previous: canoeing on Ontario's northern lakes; Algonquin's Killarney Lodge. **Above:** The world's largest Muskoka chair welcomes visitors to Gravenhurst.

Cottage Country, Algonquin, and the Northeast

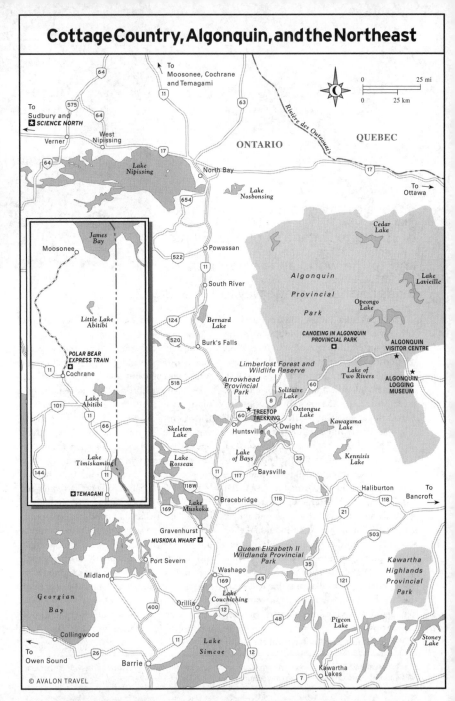

© AVALON TRAVEL

PLANNING YOUR TIME

This region is packed with outdoor activities, but many Cottage Country and northeastern attractions don't begin operation until mid- or late May and close in mid-October, after the Canadian Thanksgiving weekend. July and August are the busiest travel months; fall is the best time to visit, when the foliage is most dramatic.

A weekend trip could take you to the Muskokas and **Algonquin** for a relaxing outdoor getaway. You'd want at least a long weekend to take a canoe trip in **Temagami** or to explore the cities of North Bay or Sudbury. With several days to spare, you could travel to Cochrane, then take the *Polar Bear Express Train* onward to the Cree communities of **Moosonee** and **Moose Factory Island.**

Muskoka Cottage Country

With more lakes than you can count, the Muskoka region is one of Ontario's vacation lands. For many Ontarians, Muskoka is Cottage Country, a place to escape from the city, where your obligations are nothing more than to sit on the porch of your cottage and relax. Even people who don't have cottages of their own (or friends with cottages who invite them for weekends) head to Cottage Country to stay in B&Bs, hotels, or the many cottage resorts that dot the lakes.

The Muskoka region, north of Toronto, encompasses the towns of Gravenhurst, Bracebridge, and Huntsville, among others, extending northwest to Georgian Bay and northeast to Algonquin Provincial Park. Tourism to Muskoka began in earnest in the 1800s when steamboats transported visitors across the lakes. These days, nearly all the steamboats are gone (except for a couple used for sightseeing cruises), but the visitors continue to come. And if you're looking for a place to get outdoors, whether to hike, canoe, or just sit on the porch, you should, too.

BARRIE

Barrie isn't really part of the Muskoka region, but you'll likely pass through the city on your way north. Even though it's 105 kilometers (65 miles) north of Toronto, it feels

the mantra for summer in Ontario

Muskoka Lakes

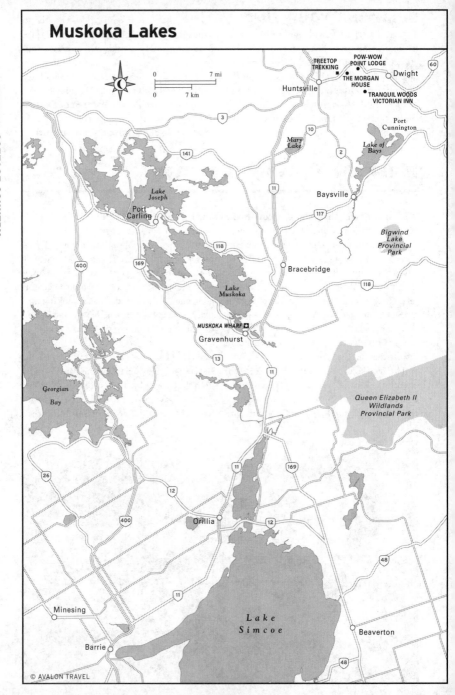

like an extension of the metropolitan area (and people do commute daily from Barrie to Toronto), rather than the start of a cottage holiday. Still, it's a handy spot to break up your drive, whether to have a bite to eat or to stay for a day or two. And if you're continuing north from Barrie, stop in the town of Orillia to tour the former home of noted Canadian humorist Stephen Leacock. Barrie spreads out along the shore of Lake Simcoe, so even in the heart of the city, you can stroll along the lake. Dunlop Street is the main downtown thoroughfare; most sights and shops are on or around Dunlop.

Barrie has a small but worthwhile art museum, the **Maclaren Art Centre** (37 Mulcaster St., 705/721-9696, www.maclarenart.com, 10am-5pm Mon.-Fri., 10am-4pm Sat.-Sun., adults $5), which exhibits work by established Canadian and emerging regional artists. Half of the building was Barrie's original public library, built in 1917; the other half is an airy contemporary addition. If you're looking for a gift for an arty friend, browse the jewelry and works by local artists in the gallery shop.

You can cruise the lake on the *Serendipity Princess* (Bayfield St., at Simcoe St., 705/728-9888, www.midlandtours.com, June-Sept., adults $26, seniors $24, students $21, ages 5-14 $16, families $68), a paddle-wheel boat that offers daily summer sightseeing excursions. Boats depart from the Barrie Town Dock.

If you're heading north and need outdoor gear, stop at the Barrie outpost of **Mountain Equipment Co-op** (61 Bryne Dr., 705/792-4675, www.mec.ca, 10am-7pm Mon.-Wed., 10am-9pm Thurs.-Fri., 9am-6pm Sat., 11am-5pm Sun.), a Canadian chain that stocks clothing, camping equipment, and other supplies. You must be a member to make a purchase, but anyone can join by paying the $5 lifetime membership fee. The Barrie store is just off Highway 400 (exit 94, Essa Rd.).

Accommodations

Several chain motels cluster along Hart Drive (take the Dunlop St. exit from Hwy. 400), in an area that has nothing much to recommend it except views of the highway. Closer to downtown, you'll find B&Bs and small inns.

Owners Pam and Bob Richmond have set up a separate wing for guests on the second floor of their 1911 brick Georgian-style home east of downtown. The **Richmond Manor B&B** (16 Blake St., 705/726-7103, www.bbcanada.com, $80 s, $110 d) has two large, traditionally furnished guest rooms with peekaboo views of Kempenfelt Bay. A shared bath is located between the rooms, and across the hall is a guest lounge with a TV and DVD player. Breakfast is a formal affair, served on fine china in the stately dining room.

Catering to business travelers and people relocating to the Barrie area, the **Harbour View Inn** (1 Berczy St., 705/735-6832, www.harbourviewinn.ca, $129-349) has six rooms and suites—some with lake views—in a brick Victorian just east of downtown. While the accommodations aren't large, they all have kitchenettes, with a microwave, a mini fridge, a coffeemaker, a toaster, and dishes; some have sleep sofas to accommodate an extra guest.

Food

One of Ontario's largest and longest-running farmers markets, the year-round **Barrie Farmers Market** (Collier St. at Mulcaster St., www.barriefarmermarket.com, 8am-noon Sat.) has been operating since 1846. Selling seasonal produce, prepared foods, yummy baked goods, and crafts, the market is outside City Hall May to October; it moves inside City Hall from November to April.

Some of Barrie's most interesting food isn't downtown—it's in the strip malls and industrial parks off Highway 400. A good example is **Cravings Fine Food** (131 Commerce Park Dr., 705/734-2272, www.cravingsfinefood.ca, 9am-6pm Mon.-Tues., 9am-7pm Wed.-Fri., 9am-5pm Sat.), a café and gourmet shop that sells beautifully crafted (and scrumptious) pastries, sandwiches, salads, and other prepared foods, perfect for a quick meal on the road or to take north to the cottage.

If you love butter tarts, find your way to

the strip mall that houses **The Sweet Oven** (75 Barrie View Dr., Suite 103A, 705/733-9494, www.thesweetoven.com, 10am-6pm Mon.-Sat.), which makes these tasty tarts ($2, or $10 for six) in numerous varieties. Flavors like peanut butter, mint, or chai are novelties, but the classics—plain, pecan, or raisin—are the best.

Information and Services
You can pick up all sorts of information about Barrie and the surrounding region at the helpful **Tourism Barrie Visitor Information Centre** (205 Lakeshore Dr., 705/739-9444 or 800/668-9100, www.tourismbarrie.com, 9am-5pm Mon.-Fri., 10am-4pm Sat. Sept.-June, 9am-5pm Mon.-Fri., 10am-4pm Sat.-Sun. July-Aug.), located on the south side of Lake Simcoe. Tourism Barrie also staffs a seasonal **Downtown Information Kiosk** (Bayfield St. at Simcoe St., 9am-7pm daily May-mid-Oct.).

The provincially run **Ontario Travel Information Centre** (21 Mapleview Dr. E., 705/725-7280 or 800/567-1140, www.ontario-travel.net, 8am-8pm daily June-Aug., 8:30am-4:30pm daily Sept.-May), just off Highway 400, can help with travel questions about Barrie and points north.

Getting There and Around
From Toronto, both **Ontario Northland** (800/461-8558, www.ontarionorthland.ca, 90 minutes, adults $25 one-way) and **Greyhound** (800/661-8747, www.grey-hound.ca, 90 minutes, adults $9-31 one-way) run frequent buses to the Barrie Bus Terminal (24 Maple Ave., 705/739-1500) downtown. Ontario Northland buses continue north from Barrie to Gravenhurst, Bracebridge, Huntsville, North Bay, Temagami, and Cochrane; another travels toward Parry Sound and Sudbury.

Simcoe County Airport Service (137 Brock St., 705/728-1148 or 800/461-7529, www.simcoecountyairportservice.ca, one-way $68 for 1 person, $96 for 2, $122 for 3, $147 for 4) runs door-to-door van service from Toronto's Pearson Airport to Barrie.

Barrie Transit (705/739-4209, www.barrie.ca, $3), the city's bus service, can take you around town if you don't have a car. Get a transfer when you board, since it's good for 75 minutes, and parents, take note: up to three elementary school kids ride free with a paying adult.

Many car rental companies have Barrie offices, including **Avis** (www.avis.com), **Budget** (www.budget.ca), **Discount Car Rentals** (www.discountcar.com), and **Enterprise Rent-A-Car** (www.enterpriserentacar.ca).

ORILLIA
Though his day job was as a political science professor at Montreal's McGill University, Stephen Leacock (1869-1944) became famous as a writer and humorist. He published 35 humorous books, including *Sunshine Sketches of a Little Town* (1912) and *Arcadian Adventures of the Idle Rich* (1914).

In 1928, Leacock built a summer house near Old Brewery Bay in the town of Orillia. The home, which was his permanent residence following his retirement from McGill in 1936 until his death 12 years later, is now the **Stephen Leacock Museum** (50 Museum Dr., 705/329-1908, www.leacockmuseum.com, 10am-4pm daily June-Sept., 10am-4pm Mon.-Fri. Oct.-May, adults $5, seniors $4, students $3, kids $2). Some parts of the house are nearly as Leacock left them, including the sunroom with his worktable and his living room facing the lake. On the main floor are signed portraits of Leacock that noted photographer Yousuf Karsh took in 1941.

Orillia is 40 kilometers (25 miles) northeast of Barrie via Highway 11.

GRAVENHURST
You know you've arrived in Cottage Country when you pass by the **world's largest Muskoka chair** (1170 Muskoka Rd. S.), at the south end of town. What's a Muskoka chair, you ask? It's the laid-back wooden porch

chair that most Americans call an Adirondack chair. This symbol of relaxation gives you a clue of what Gravenhurst is all about.

Gravenhurst's main attractions are at **Muskoka Wharf** (www.discovergravenhurst. com), the lakefront development where you can tour a boat museum or cruise the lake in a traditional steamship. The town is also the birthplace of Norman Bethune, a Canadian doctor who became wildly famous in China, where he's still considered a hero long after his death.

Gravenhurst Opera House (295 Muskoka Rd. S., 705/687-5550 or 888/495-8888, www.gravenhurstoperahouse.com), built in 1901, hosts concerts, plays, and films. **Music on the Barge** (Gull Lake Rotary Park, Brock St. at Bethune Dr., 7:30pm Sun. mid-June-mid-Aug.) has brought toe-tapping summer concerts, from big band to Dixieland to folk, to the waterfront since 1959.

★ Muskoka Wharf

The Muskoka Lakes Navigation Company opened in 1866, and during its heyday operated the largest fleet of inland lake steamships in North America. The ships carried passengers and freight across the Muskoka Lakes, providing service where the railroads didn't reach and roads either didn't go or were difficult to navigate. More than 100 lakeside hotels once operated in the Muskokas, and the guests all arrived by steamship.

One of these ships, the **RMS *Segwun,*** built in 1887 and used as an official Royal Mail Ship, remains North America's oldest operating steamship. **Muskoka Steamships** (185 Cherokee Lane, 705/687-6667 or 866/687-6667, www.realmuskoka.com, mid-June-mid-Oct., adults $21-50, kids $12.50-36) offers 1- to 4-hour sightseeing cruises on the *Segwun,* departing from their Muskoka Wharf docks.

Back on land, explore the region's steamship traditions at the creatively designed **Muskoka Boat & Heritage Centre** (275 Steamship Bay Rd., 705/687-2115, www.realmuskoka.com, 10am-6pm Mon.-Fri., 10am-4pm Sat.-Sun. mid-June-mid-Oct., 10am-4pm Tues.-Sat. mid-Oct.-mid-June, adults $7.75, seniors $5.75, kids $3.75, families $18.75), filled with multimedia exhibits. In a recreated lakeside hotel, the owner welcomes you (in a video) and you can pretend that you're holidaying in the 19th century. Another exhibit is a recreated steamship that you can go aboard. Also visit the Grace and Speed Boathouse, North America's only in-water

Muskoka Boat & Heritage Centre in Gravenhurst

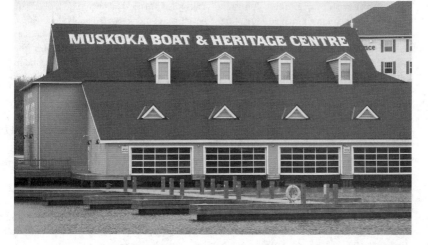

exhibit of working antique boats, with up to 20 spiffy craft on view. If you show your tickets from a Muskoka Steamships cruise, admission to the museum is free.

Bethune Memorial House National Historic Site

Gravenhurst-born surgeon Henry Norman Bethune (1890-1939) became a legendary physician, known largely for a brief tour of service on the other side of the world.

In 1938, after China and Japan went to war, Bethune traveled to China to tend to the injured, and after he arrived at the front, the legend of the foreign doctor's commitment to the Chinese began to spread. Bethune implemented a medical education program and established mobile medical facilities, including an operating theater that two mules could carry. After less than two years in the country, however, Bethune accidentally cut his finger while performing an operation, developed an aggressive form of blood poisoning, and died within the month. Chinese leader Mao Zedong wrote an essay, "In Memory of Norman Bethune," which became required reading for Chinese students and helped solidify Bethune's status as a hero in China.

The **Bethune Memorial House National Historic Site** (235 John St. N., 705/687-4261, www.pc.gc.ca, 10am-4pm daily July-mid.-Oct., 10am-4pm Wed.-Sun. June and mid-late Oct., adults $3.90, seniors $3.40, ages 6-16 $1.90, families $9.80) comprises two buildings: a modern museum that recounts Bethune's history, and the 1880 home where Bethune was born. Visit on a weekday if you can, when the house's diminutive rooms are less crowded and staff have more time to explain Bethune's legacy.

Tree Museum

One of Cottage Country's most offbeat attractions is this outdoor art gallery outside Gravenhurst. No, the **Tree Museum** (1634 Doe Lake Rd., 705/684-8185, www.thetree-museum.ca, dawn-dusk daily May-Oct., free) isn't a museum of trees—it's a gallery outside in an 80-hectare (200-acre) woodland with imaginative sculptures and other eclectic works among the trees. Be prepared for lots of walking along the sometimes muddy paths. It's one kilometer (0.6 miles) from the parking area to the first sculpture, and another 1.2 kilometers (0.75 miles) to the center of the site; return the way you came. The museum has no restrooms or other facilities, so bring water and a snack.

To get to the Tree Museum, follow Highway 11 north past Gravenhurst, then exit at Doe Lake Road (Muskoka Rd. 6). Go east about eight kilometers (five miles) till you see museum signs on your right.

Accommodations

The **Residence Inn by Marriott** (285 Steamship Bay Rd., 705/687-6600 or 866/580-6238, www.marriott.com, $165-419 d) is located at Muskoka Wharf, overlooking Lake Muskoka. The 106 modern suites with kitchen facilities include studios with sleeper sofas and larger units with one or two bedrooms. Rates include buffet breakfast, parking, and Wi-Fi.

You won't be bored at **Taboo Resort** (1209 Muskoka Beach Rd., 705/687-2233 or 800/461-0236, www.tabooresort.com, mid-Feb.-Oct., $299-639 d), set in the woods on Lake Muskoka north of town. There's a private beach, four outdoor heated pools, golf, tennis, a spa, canoes, kayaks, and stand-up paddleboards, plus several restaurants and bars. The prime picks of the 101 guest rooms, done in sleek satiny woods, are right above the lake. Thirty individually decorated condos, with two to four bedrooms, are scattered around the property, although most don't have lake views.

Food

Though it looks a bit twee, with floral café curtains and blue-and-white china, the **Blue Willow Tea Shop** (900 Bay St., Muskoka Wharf, 705/687-2597, www.bluewillowtea-shop.ca, 11am-4pm Tues.-Thurs., 11am-8pm

Fri.-Sat., 11am-3pm Sun., $7-16) makes a good lakeside rest stop at Muskoka Wharf. They serve soups, salads, and sandwiches at lunch, along with a large selection of black, green, and fruit teas. Midafternoon, take a tea break with a scone or slice of cake, or settle in for traditional high tea ($23 pp).

You'll be fed well at the **Well Fed Deli** (150 Hotchkiss St., 705/684-9355, www.wellfedinc. com, 8am-3pm Mon., 8am-5pm Tues.-Fri., 10am-3pm Sat.), a diminutive downtown shop serving sandwiches (they roast their own turkey, beef, and peameal bacon), seasonal salads, and fresh-baked pastries. Most business is take-out, since there are just two sidewalk tables out front.

Information and Services

Muskoka Tourism (800/267-9700, www. discovermuskoka.ca) provides information about Gravenhurst and the rest of the Muskoka Lakes region. They operate a travel information center on Highway 11 south of Gravenhurst in the town of Kilworthy. Both the **Gravenhurst Chamber of Commerce** (www.gravenhurstchamber.com) and the **Town of Gravenhurst** (www.discover-gravenhurst.com) provide visitor information online.

Getting There and Around

Gravenhurst is 180 kilometers (112 miles) north of Toronto and 75 kilometers (47 miles) north of Barrie. From Toronto, take Highway 400 north to Barrie, then continue north on Highway 11 into Gravenhurst.

From Toronto's Bay Street Station, **Ontario Northland** runs several daily buses to **Gravenhurst Station** (150 2nd St. S., 705/687-2301 or 800/461-8558, www.ontarionorthland.ca, 2.5-2.75 hours, one-way adults $41.20, seniors and students $35, ages 2-11 $20.55). **Northern Airport Shuttle** (705/474-7942 or 800/461-4219, www.northernairport.com, 2 hours, one-way adults $83) makes two scheduled trips a day in each direction between Toronto's Pearson Airport and Gravenhurst.

Exploring Gravenhurst is easiest if you have a car, although you can walk between Muskoka Wharf and the town center. The nearest car rental offices are in Bracebridge.

BRACEBRIDGE

Like many Muskoka towns, Bracebridge's tourism industry dates to the late 1800s, when visitors from Toronto arrived by train and boat. Most of the old-time resorts are gone, but the town's main street, Manitoba Street, has an old-timey feel that makes for a pleasant stroll. Bracebridge is a good base for exploring the region—it's an easy drive to Gravenhurst or Huntsville and to other towns along the surrounding lakes. With comfortable B&Bs and excellent restaurants, it's also a spot where you can just unwind.

Since the lakes are an important part of the Muskoka experience, get out on the water with **Lady Muskoka Cruises** (300 Ecclestone Dr., 705/646-2628 or 800/263-5239, www.ladymuskoka.com, noon Sat.-Sun. May-June, noon daily July-Aug., noon Sat.-Sun. and Wed. Sept.-mid-Oct., adults $29.20, seniors $27.43, students $22.12, ages 5-12 $14.60), which operates sightseeing boats on Lake Muskoka. Cruises depart at noon.

Bracebridge's own microbrewery, **Muskoka Brewery** (1964 Muskoka Beach Rd., 705/646-1266, www.muskokabrewery.com, 11am-5pm Mon.-Tues., 11am-6pm Wed.-Thurs., 11am-7pm Fri., 11am-5pm Sat., noon-4pm Sun. May-Oct., call for off-season hours), welcomes visitors to their shop. You can also tour the brewery (1:30pm, 2:30pm, and 3:30pm Thurs.-Sat.).

A Bracebridge summer tradition is the free **Bandshell Concert Series** (Memorial Park, Manitoba St., www.bracebridge.ca) on Thursday evenings from June through early September.

Accommodations

Sandy Yudin has run **Century House B&B** (155 Dill St., 705/645-9903, www.bbmuskoka.com/centuryhouse, $70-80 s, $80-100 d), the 1855 brick farmhouse she shares with her husband, Norman Yan, for two decades, and knows how to make guests feel at home. The three traditional B&B rooms are furnished with quilts and wicker chairs and have all the essentials—comfortable beds, reading lamps, bathrobes—but no extraneous frills; they share two baths. Sandy's a great cook, serving multicourse breakfasts with fresh fruit, eggs, smoked trout, and toast with homemade marmalade. The B&B is a 15-minute walk to Manitoba Street's shops and restaurants.

Although it's just a short walk from the town center, the **Bay House Bed-and-Breakfast** (2 Dominion St., 705/645-7508, www.bbmuskoka.com/bayhouse, $128-168 d) feels like a cottage in the woods. The three lower-level guest rooms are done in cheery pastels. The largest has an electric fireplace and four-poster bed, while the Garden Room opens onto the patio. Jan and Peter Rickard are experienced innkeepers who are full of tips for things to do, although after their hearty breakfasts (which might include lemon ricotta pancakes or eggs hollandaise), you may be tempted just to soak in the outdoor hot tub.

Food

You can have a sandwich at **Marty's "World Famous" Café** (5 Manitoba St., 705/645-4794, www.martysworldfamous.com), but the shop's self-proclaimed fame is for the gooey caramel butter tarts. Just heed their advice not to eat these runny pastries in your car, or, as they warn, "You'll end up wearing them!"

A friendly joint for hanging out and sipping a microbrew, **The Griffin Gastropub** (9 Chancery Lane, 705/646-0438, www.thegriffinpub.ca, 4pm-midnight Wed., noon-2am Thurs.-Sat., $12-18) serves inventive pub grub, including addictive risotto balls, bison burgers, and sticky toffee pudding. Live folk, rock, blues, or jazz usually starts around 9pm Thursday through Saturday. The pub is at the top of a narrow alleyway, off Manitoba Street.

Don't be put off by the strip mall

setting; there's serious sushi savvy at the chic **Wabora Fusion Japanese Restaurant** (295 Wellington St. N., 705/646-9500, www.waborasushi.com, 11am-11pm daily, $8-20). The cavernous room has both an artfully arranged cocktail bar and a well-lit sushi bar where the chefs craft wildly imaginative *maki* rolls, like the Bracebridge (salmon, crab, asparagus, and gobo wrapped in cucumber with lemon-*ponzu*-caramel sauce) or the Spicy Cottage (shrimp tempura, crab, spicy tuna, greens, mango, and avocado in a rice paper roll). The straight-up *nigiri* are first-rate, too.

Colorful original artwork seems to pop from the walls at ★ **One Fifty Five** (155 Manitoba St., 705/645-1935, www.onefiftyfive.ca, lunch 11:30am-2:30pm Tues.-Sat., dinner 5pm-9:30pm Tues.-Sun., lunch $11-16, dinner $19-29), Bracebridge's white-tablecloth restaurant. The menu is colorful, too, with choices like crispy chicken *piccata* with grilled vegetable orzo or maple-cured rainbow trout. For dessert, it's hard to choose between the warm flourless chocolate cake and the lemon tart topped with fresh berries.

Information and Services

Tourism Bracebridge (1 Manitoba St., 705/645-8121 or 866/645-8121, www.tourismbracebridge.com) provides information about the area. Find more trip-planning details online at **The Heart of Muskoka** (www.theheartofmuskoka.com).

Getting There and Around

Bracebridge is 195 kilometers (121 miles) north of Toronto and 18 kilometers (11 miles) north of Gravenhurst. From Toronto, take Highway 400 north to Barrie, then continue north on Highway 11 to Bracebridge.

Ontario Northland (705/646-2239 or 800/461-8558, www.ontarionorthland.ca, 3 hours, one-way adults $44.50, seniors and students $37.75, ages 2-11 $22.20) buses from Toronto's Bay Street Station stop at the Riverside Inn (300 Ecclestone Dr.). Buses continue to Huntsville, North Bay, Temagami, and points farther north. **Northern Airport Shuttle** (705/474-7942 or 800/461-4219, www.northernairport.com, 2.25 hours, one-way adults $87) makes two scheduled trips a day in each direction between Toronto's Pearson Airport and Bracebridge.

Bracebridge is fairly compact and walkable, but to explore the Muskoka region further, you need your own vehicle.

Huntsville and Vicinity

Located just west of Algonquin Provincial Park, the attractive town of Huntsville is a favorite destination in its own right, with lots of outdoor activities, good places to eat, and a cute downtown. But it's also close enough to Algonquin that you can easily stay in town and make day trips into the park.

SIGHTS AND RECREATION

Start your Huntsville visit walking around downtown, looking for the **Group of Seven Outdoor Gallery** (www.groupofsevenoutdoorgallery.ca), more than 80 colorful wall murals that decorate town buildings. The murals are replicas of works by the Group of Seven artists who worked in Canada in the early 1900s.

Muskoka Heritage Place

If you're interested in the history of the Muskoka region, there's a lot to see at **Muskoka Heritage Place** (88 Brunel Rd., 705/789-7576, www.muskokaheritageplace.org, 10am-4pm daily mid-May-mid-Oct., last admission 3pm, adults $16.55, seniors $14.90, ages 3-12 $11.20). Your first stop should be in the **museum** (10am-4pm daily mid-May-mid-Oct., 10am-4pm Mon.-Fri. mid-Oct.-mid-May), which traces the region's roots from the early First Nations people, through the first European contact, the fur trading and lumber eras, and the evolution of the Muskokas as a tourist destination. More fun for kids is the **pioneer village** (mid-May-mid-Oct.), where wandering around the 20 restored buildings takes you back to the period between 1880 and 1910. Costumed interpreters demonstrate blacksmithing, woodworking, and other trades. You can explore a trapper's cabin, a one-room schoolhouse, and a First Nations encampment.

Catch a ride on the **Portage Flyer** steam train (100 Forbes Hill Dr., departs at noon, 1pm, 2pm, and 3pm Tues.-Sat. July-Aug., check the website for off-season schedule, adults $5.70, seniors $5.10, ages 3-12 $3.50), which ran from 1904 to 1959 in nearby Dwight along the world's smallest commercial railroad. It operated on a 1.8-kilometer-long (1.125-mile) narrow-gauge track as a portage, ferrying supplies and travelers across a sliver of land between Peninsula Lake and Portage Bay. The train trip runs about 30 minutes and includes a stop at the **Rail Museum,** a re-creation of a 1920s train station, where you can learn more about the role of railroads and steamboats in the Muskokas' development. If you're a train enthusiast, note that the steam engine pulls the train only in July and August; in spring and fall, a diesel locomotive does the work, to help preserve the steam engine's life.

Muskoka Heritage Place is just a few minutes' drive from downtown Huntsville. From Main Street, go south on Brunel Road. The train depot is a short distance from the main entrance; watch for the signs.

Arrowhead Provincial Park

Through far smaller and less well known than nearby Algonquin, the four-season **Arrowhead Provincial Park** (451 Arrowhead Park Rd., 705/789-5105, www.ontarioparks.com/park/arrowhead, $14.50 per vehicle), on Arrowhead Lake 10 kilometers (six miles) north of Huntsville, is a

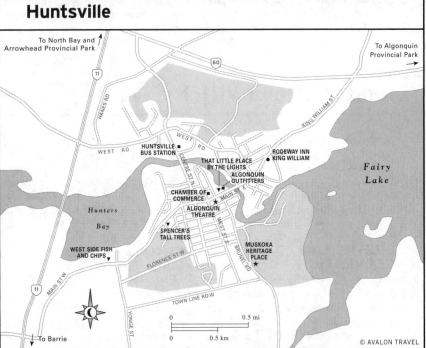

Huntsville

To North Bay and
Arrowhead Provincial Park

To Algonquin
Provincial Park

Fairy Lake

HUNTSVILLE BUS STATION
RODEWAY INN KING WILLIAM
THAT LITTLE PLACE BY THE LIGHTS
ALGONQUIN OUTFITTERS
CHAMBER OF COMMERCE
ALGONQUIN THEATRE
SPENCER'S TALL TREES
MUSKOKA HERITAGE PLACE
WEST SIDE FISH AND CHIPS

Hunters Bay

WEST RD
HANES RD
CENTRE ST N
KING WILLIAM ST
MAIN ST E
WEST ST S
BRUNEL RD
FLORENCE ST W
TOWN LINE RD W
YONGE ST
MAIN ST W

0   0.5 mi

0   0.5 km

To Barrie

© AVALON TRAVEL

family-friendly outdoor destination with lots to do year-round. If you purchase a day-use pass at either Arrowhead or Algonquin, you can use that pass in both parks.

For day **hiking,** Arrowhead has 15 kilometers (nine miles) of easy-to-moderate trails, including the 5.3-kilometer (3.3-mile) Arrowhead Lake Trail that circles the lakeshore. A short walk from the parking lot on Roe Campground Road leads to the **Big Bend Lookout,** which overlooks the winding Big East River. Arrowhead Lake has several **swimming** beaches, and the waters here and on smaller Mayflower Lake are calm spots for **paddling.** You can rent canoes, kayaks, stand-up paddleboards, and bicycles (including fat-tire trail bikes) at the Beach Information Building in July-August and from the main park office in the spring and fall. In winter, Arrowhead's hiking paths become cross-country ski trails; ski rentals are available. The park also floods a road to

create a groomed 1.3-kilometer (0.8-mile) **ice-skating trail** through the woods.

Limberlost Forest and Wildlife Reserve

An excellent, less-visited hiking destination is the privately owned **Limberlost Forest and Wildlife Reserve** (S. Limberlost Rd., 705/635-1584, www.limberlostlodges.com, 9am-5pm daily, free), where more than 70 kilometers (44 miles) of trails circle many of the property's 20 lakes as they crisscross the forested 4,045-hectare (10,000-acre) reserve. Check the website or ask at the reserve office for the extremely detailed *Master Trail Guide,* which tells you about each of the trails and their notable features; it also includes trail maps.

From Huntsville, follow Highway 60 east for about 10 kilometers (six miles), then turn left (north) onto Limberlost Road (Muskoka Rd. 8). Continue another nine kilometers (5.6

miles), and turn right onto South Limberlost Road and follow it for three kilometers (1.8 miles) to the reserve entrance. The gates of the reserve look imposing, but pull up and they'll slide open.

Treetop Trekking

In a wooded park east of Huntsville, this adventure company (1180 Hwy. 60, 705/788-9000 or 855/788-9009, www.treetoptrekking.com, mid-Mar.-Oct., adults $64, ages 12-15 $54, ages 9-11 $47) offers three-hour outdoor experiences that include up to seven **zip lines** and multiple **aerial ropes courses** ranging 3 to 21 meters (10 to 70 feet) high. A highlight (or terror-inducer) is the Tarzan jump, a controlled leap from a platform high in the trees. Phone for reservations, which are required; they'll try to accommodate same-day requests. Kids under age 16 must be accompanied by an adult, and the website details age, height, and weight requirements. Ask about family discounts.

ENTERTAINMENT AND SHOPPING

The **Algonquin Theatre** (37 Main St. E., 705/789-4975 or 877/989-4975, www.algonquintheatre.ca) stages concerts, plays, and lectures, featuring performers from near and far. The **Huntsville Festival of the Arts** (705/789-4975, www.huntsvillefestival.on.ca) brings concerts, art workshops, and other events to venues around town; many are outdoors and free. For ticketed events, buy tickets online, by phone, or in person at the Algonquin Theatre.

Shops along Huntsville's Main Street sell outdoor gear, artwork, and souvenirs. **Algonquin Outfitters Huntsville** (86 Main St. E., 705/787-0262 or 800/469-4948, www.algonquinoutfitters.com, 9:30am-6pm Mon.-Wed., 9:30am-8pm Thurs.-Fri., 9am-6pm Sat., 11am-4pm Sun. July-early Sept., 10am-6pm Mon.-Fri., 9am-5pm Sat., 11am-4pm Sun. early Sept.-June) stocks outdoor clothing and camping supplies and rents canoes, kayaks, and bikes.

They also have a store closer to Algonquin Park, **Algonquin Outfitters Oxtongue Lake** (1035 Algonquin Outfitters Rd., Dwight, 705/635-2243 or 800/469-4948, www.algonquinoutfitters.com, 8am-6pm Mon.-Thurs., 8am-7pm Fri.-Sun. July-early Sept., 9am-5pm Mon.-Thurs., 8am-6pm Fri.-Sat., 9am-6pm Sun. May-June and early Sept.-mid-Oct., 9am-5pm daily mid-Oct.-Apr.) that has canoe, kayak, and bike rentals. They offer

paddling at Arrowhead Provincial Park

guided canoe and kayak trips in and around Algonquin Park, too.

ACCOMMODATIONS

Lodgings in and around Huntsville range from basic in-town motels to B&Bs hidden in the woods, cottage colonies, and upscale resorts. Many accommodations are off Highway 60 east of town. Closer to Algonquin's West Gate, in the tiny town of Dwight, more lodgings cluster around Oxtongue Lake.

Huntsville

The 32-unit **Rodeway Inn King William** (23 King William St., 705/789-9661 or 888/995-9169, www.kingwilliaminn.com, $129-189 d) is the nicest of the in-town motels, upgraded with crisp white linens, newer furnishings, and mini fridges. The standard rooms, with either two doubles or one double and one queen, are slightly smaller but otherwise similar to the queen rooms, which have one queen and a sleep sofa. The largest rooms are kings with a whirlpool tub. Wi-Fi is included.

East of Huntsville

A stay at **The Morgan House** (83 Morgans Rd., 705/380-2566 or 866/311-1727, www.morganhousewoolworks.ca, $100-110 d), a bed-and-breakfast in a comfortable stone country home, is like a holiday with good friends on their mostly organic farm. Co-owner Pam Carnochan, a wool artist, welcomes guests on the screened-in porch or in the parlor with its overstuffed furniture. Upstairs, the two simple guest rooms, with traditional quilts on the beds, share one large bath. Breakfast includes homemade baked goods and eggs from the farm's hens. Families are welcome.

A suburban home set amid gardens, and, yes, tranquil woods, the **Tranquil Woods Victorian Inn** (50 North Portage Rd., 705/788-7235, www.tranquilwoods.ca, $130-145 d) is Victorian in style, but it's in a newly built house with high ceilings and an airy feel. Personable owners Judy and Dan offer touring tips while serving a hearty breakfast. The largest of the three guest rooms is on the main floor, with a private patio. Upstairs,

the Red Oak room has a sleigh bed and Victorian furnishings, while the red-walled Scarlett Maple room is more country cottage.

Over breakfast at the ★ **Pow-Wow Point Lodge** (207 Grassmere Resort Rd., 705/789-4951 or 800/461-4263, www.powwowpointlodge.com, $290-450 pp for 2 nights), staff ring a bell and announce the day's activities, such as sandcastle contests and swimming races, just like at summer camp. There's a lakeside beach for swimming and canoeing, tennis courts, and shuffleboard. Accommodations include basic lodge rooms and cottages and more updated units, but all feel homey. Owners Doug and Dee Howell have run the lodge since 1989, and many guests return year after year. Rates include three ample meals; rates for kids and teens are discounted.

You won't be bored at the classy **Deerhurst Resort** (1235 Deerhurst Dr., 705/789-6411 or 800/461-4393, www.deerhurstresort.com, $239-719 d, resort fee $25 per room), with activities such as golf, tennis, trail rides, and zip-lining. The lake has water slides, trampolines, and all kinds of watersports. In winter, there's cross-country skiing and ice-skating. Accommodations include standard hotel rooms and 1- to 3-bedroom condos with full kitchens. The main dining room, serves contemporary fare with local ingredients; several more casual eateries are scattered around the property. A high-energy musical show, performed several nights a week in summer and fall, is great fun.

Dwight and Oxtongue Lake

The cheapest beds near Algonquin are at the laid-back **Wolf Den Hostel and Nature Retreat** (4568 Hwy. 60, Oxtongue Lake, 705/635-9336 or 866/271-9336, www.wolfdenbunkhouse.com, year-round, $27 dorm, $45-85 s, $68-85 d, $90-125 cabins). Located between Dwight and the West Gate, the property's main lodge has a shared kitchen, a large lounge, and guest rooms. Two log bunkhouses have an eight-bed dorm upstairs and rooms for four to five on the main level. Baths are central and shared. There's no meal service, so bring your own provisions.

A small cluster of lodgings sits along Oxtongue Lake, just off Highway 60, about a 10-minute drive from Algonquin's West Gate. It's a pretty setting, although the proximity of Highway 60 and its traffic noise can be bothersome. Under the same ownership as the Bartlett Lodge in Algonquin Park, **The Pines Cottage Resort** (1032 Oxtongue Lake Rd., Dwight, 705/635-2379, www.algonquinparkaccommodations.com, mid-May-mid-Oct., $170-250) has family-friendly one- and two-bedroom cottages with fully equipped kitchens in the woods above Oxtongue Lake, where there's a sandy beach. Rates include the use of canoes and kayaks.

More modern, but a little closer to Highway 60, the year-round **Blue Spruce Resort** (4308 Hwy. 60, Dwight, 705/635-2330, www.bluespruce.ca, $142-339) has both hotel-style suites and stand-alone 1- to 3-bedroom cottages, all with kitchens. There are tennis courts, a swimming beach, coin-operated laundry, and Wi-Fi.

Camping

Arrowhead Provincial Park (451 Arrowhead Park Rd., 705/789-5105, www.ontarioparks.com, mid-May-mid-Oct., tent sites $40, electrical sites $46) has three campgrounds with a total of 378 campsites, 185 with electrical service. The Roe Campground is the most secluded, and the forested Lumbly Campground—with no electrical sites—is closest to the lakes and feels the most rustic. The large East River Campground accommodates RVs and also has five camping cabins ($142); the cabins are heated and sleep up to five. The campgrounds all have central flush toilets and showers.

FOOD
Huntsville

Two of the best spots for picnic supplies or a meal to go are located on Highway 60, just east of town, and both have similar names. The **Farmer's Daughter** (118 Hwy. 60, 705/789-5700, www.fresheverything.ca, 8am-6pm Mon.-Wed., 8am-7pm Thurs.-Fri., 8am-6pm Sat., 8am-5pm Sun.) is a combination prepared food counter, bakery, and gourmet market. They sell fresh produce, sandwiches made to order, and fancy fixings like smoked fish pâté and homemade jams. Their baked goods, including the addictive trail mix bars, are excellent.

Across the road, the **Butcher's Daughters** (133 Hwy. 60, 705/789-2848, www.butchersdaughters.ca, 9am-6pm Mon.-Sat., 10am-4pm Sun. July-Aug., 9am-6pm Mon.-Sat. June and Sept., 9am-6pm Tues.-Sat. Oct.-May, $4.50-8) makes good deli sandwiches, interesting soups, and salads. There's a small seating area, or you can take your food to go.

For many Ontarians, a trip to Cottage Country isn't complete without a stop at the old-style, family-friendly **West Side Fish and Chips** (126 Main St. W., 705/789-7200, www.westsidefishandchips.com, 8am-8pm daily, $5-17) for a hearty plate of halibut and chips and a gooey slice of coconut cream pie. They're always busy, but you can amuse yourself with trivia game cards while you wait.

You know **That Little Place by the Lights** (76 Main St. E., 705/789-2536, www.thatlittleplacebythelights.ca, 9am-9pm Mon.-Sat., 11am-4pm Sun., lunch $5-14, dinner $12-15)? It's a cozy Italian trattoria masquerading as a touristy ice cream parlor and coffee shop. The sauces for the pastas and pizzas are homemade (try the spicy linguini puttanesca with olives, capers, anchovies, and peppers), and the salads are simple but fresh. It's family friendly, too, especially if you promise the kids gelato for dessert.

The long-running **Spencer's Tall Trees** (87 Main St. W., 705/789-9769, www.spencerstalltrees.com, 5pm-close Mon., 11:30am-2pm and 5pm-close Tues.-Fri., 5pm-close Sat., call for seasonal hours, lunch $11-21, dinner $18-49) is set in a heritage house amid, yes, tall trees. In the several dining nooks, you can sup on classics like venison with spaetzle, veal Oscar (topped with crab), or pickerel in a maple-thyme-butter sauce. Lunch options range from salads and sandwiches to pastas. To finish with something sweet, try the chocolate pâté or a seasonal fruit crumble.

Dwight and Oxtongue Lake

The perpetual lines attest to the popularity of **Henrietta's Pine Bakery** (2868 Hwy. 60, Dwight, 705/635-2214, www.henriettaspine-bakery.net, 9am-5pm Mon.-Sat., 10am-4pm Sun. May-mid-Oct.), where specialties include sticky buns and a highly recommended scone-like cranberry pastry called the Muskoka cloud. Come early in the day, since they close when the goodies sell out.

INFORMATION AND SERVICES

The **Huntsville/Lake of Bays Chamber of Commerce** (8 West St. N., 705/789-4771, www.huntsvilleadventures.com), just off Main Street, can provide more information about events and things to do in the Huntsville-Algonquin region.

GETTING THERE
Car

Huntsville is 215 kilometers (133 miles) north of Toronto and 35 kilometers (22 miles) north of Bracebridge. From Toronto, take Highway 400 north to Barrie, then continue north on Highway 11 to Huntsville.

Bus

Ontario Northland (705/789-6431 or 800/461-8558, www.ontarionorthland.ca, 3.75-4 hours, one-way adults $54.50, seniors and students $46.25, ages 2-11 $27.25) operates buses from the Toronto Central Bus Station to **Huntsville Bus Depot** (77 Centre St. N.), which is one kilometer (0.6 miles) north of Main Street. Buses continue from Huntsville to North Bay, Temagami, Cochrane, and other northern destinations.

To get to Huntsville directly from Toronto's Pearson airport, you can take the **Northern Airport Shuttle** (705/474-7942 or 800/461-4219, www.northernairport.com, 2.75 hours, one-way adults $91), which runs two daily trips in each direction.

GETTING AROUND

While it's easy to get to Huntsville without a car, exploring the region around town, including Algonquin Park, is difficult without your own wheels. If you don't have your own car, you can take the bus to Huntsville, then rent a car to explore Algonquin. **Enterprise Rent-A-Car** (174 Main St. W., 705/789-1834 or 800/736-8222, www.enterpriserentacar.ca) and **Discount Car Rentals** (8 Ott Dr., 705/788-3737, www.discountcar.com) have Huntsville locations.

Algonquin Provincial Park

If you visit only one of Ontario's many outdoor destinations, the province's first provincial park is an excellent choice. Measuring 763,000 hectares (1.9 million acres), immense **Algonquin Provincial Park** (705/633-5572, www.ontarioparks.com or www.algonquin-park.on.ca) stretches across a wide swath of Northeastern Ontario. Covered with hardwood and coniferous forests, the region was a major logging area in the 1800s, and many visitors are surprised to learn that limited logging is still allowed in the park. When the park was created in 1893, it wasn't to bring a halt

to logging, but rather to protect the region's wildlife. The park's earliest tourists arrived by train, disembarking at a rail depot near Cache Lake and staying in a nearby hotel. In the 1930s, Highway 60 was built across Algonquin's southern sections, and as more tourists came by road, rail service was discontinued. The prevailing wisdom was that eliminating train service would keep the park more "natural."

Highway 60 is still the main access route for visitors entering the West Gate from Huntsville (or Toronto) or the East Gate from Ottawa. If your time is limited, pick a few stops—perhaps a paddle at Canoe Lake, hiking one or two of the shorter trails—and spend an hour at the exhibits in the park Visitors Centre. Despite the park's popularity, you can find quiet trails and canoe routes to explore even if you stay near Highway 60. But Algonquin offers ample opportunities to get out into the wilderness, too; most of the park's vast backcountry is reachable only by canoe. Algonquin Park is open year-round, although many park services and sights operate only from April or May until mid-October.

SIGHTS

The park's main sights are listed from west to east along Highway 60, the direction you'll reach them coming from Toronto or elsewhere in the Muskokas. Distances are from the park's West Gate, so a sight at "Km. 20" is 20 kilometers east of the West Gate. From Ottawa, Peterborough, and the Kawarthas, or from elsewhere in Eastern Ontario, enter the park from the East Gate (at Km. 56) and follow these locations in reverse.

West Gate (Hwy. 60, Km. 0)

At Algonquin's western entrance, staff can help you get oriented and provide information about things to do, particularly helpful if your time is limited. All visitors must purchase a park permit ($17 per vehicle) and display it on the dashboard. Permits are available at the East and West Gates and at the Algonquin Park Visitors Centre. If you're driving across the park on Highway 60 without stopping, you don't need a permit; but if you stop anywhere in the park, even to use a restroom, you must have a permit or risk being fined.

If you're spending several days in the park or visiting multiple parks, consider purchasing an **Ontario Parks seasonal pass,** which allows unlimited day visits to any Ontario provincial parks. You can buy a summer-only pass (valid Apr.-Nov., $107.50), a winter-only pass (Dec.-Mar., $70), or a full-year pass (Apr.-Mar., $150.50).

Canoe Lake (Hwy. 60, Km. 14.1)

The history of Canoe Lake is inextricably linked to the mysterious disappearance of the painter Tom Thomson (1877-1917), a member of the Group of Seven artists who lived and worked in Ontario in the early 1900s. Beginning in 1912, Thomson spent several

You can kayak or canoe on Algonquin's Canoe Lake.

Algonquin Provincial Park

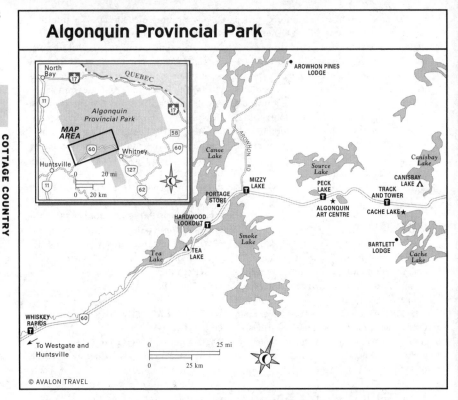

© AVALON TRAVEL

years painting in Algonquin Park, mostly on and around Canoe Lake. Thomson was last seen on July 8, 1917, in the vicinity of Canoe Lake—and then he vanished. His overturned canoe was found behind the lake's Wapomeo Island, and several days later, his body was pulled from the lake. The exact circumstances of his death remain a puzzle that has never been solved. In his memory, the **Tom Thomson memorial cairn** was erected in 1930 on one of Thomson's favorite Canoe Lake campsites. The cairn is accessible only by canoe.

The **Portage Store** (Hwy. 60, Km. 14.1, 705/633-5622, www.portagestore.com, late Apr.-mid-Oct.) on Canoe Lake rents canoes and can give you tips on where to go, including how to get to the Thomson cairn. They also offer half-day and full-day guided paddles.

Algonquin Art Centre (Hwy. 60, Km. 20)

The **Algonquin Art Centre** (705/633-5555, www.algonquinartcentre.com, 10am-5pm daily June-mid-Oct.) has a small gallery (donation) that shows changing exhibits of works by artists who have an Algonquin connection. The center also offers drop-in art activities (10:30am-4:30pm daily July-Aug., $10-25) for both children and adults.

Cache Lake (Hwy. 60, Km. 23.5)

Cache Lake was once the center of activity in Algonquin Park. From the 1890s, when the park was first established, until the 1950s, this lake area had a rail depot—Algonquin Park Station—as well as a large hotel. All that remains today, aside from the lovely lake itself, is a short historical walking trail, where several

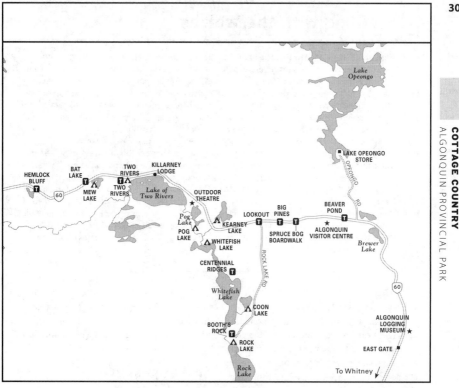

signs with historical photos along a wooded path tell you about the area's interesting past.

Lake of Two Rivers (Hwy. 60, Km. 31)

Lake of Two Rivers is a busy place. In addition to the large **Two Rivers Campground** (705/633-5572), there's a snack bar, a grocery store, and mountain bike rentals. East of the campground, **Killarney Lodge** (Lake of Two Rivers, Hwy. 60, Km. 33.2, 705/633-5551 or 877/767-5935, www.killarneylodge.com) is set on the Lake of Two Rivers. Just east of the lodge is a public swimming beach.

Algonquin Visitors Centre (Hwy. 60, Km. 43)

Even if you've entered the park from the west, it's worth stopping into the **Algonquin Visitors Centre** (9am-5pm daily late Apr.-Oct., 9am-4pm Mon.-Fri., 9am-5pm Sat.-Sun. Nov.-late Apr., daily hours during holiday weeks) to learn more about the park. Start by watching a 12-minute film about the park's history and natural features, then visit the exhibit area, which covers these topics in more detail. In summer, many interpretive programs are based at the Visitors Centre. A shop sells detailed park maps and guides as well as books about wildlife, camping, and the outdoors. There's a basic cafeteria (spring-fall), and free Wi-Fi.

What's the best feature of the Visitors Centre? It's the deck out back, which overlooks a wide swath of park territory and helps you appreciate Algonquin's expanse. There's another overlook from the short **Fire Tower Trail,** a boardwalk that leads to a reconstructed cupola, the lookout at the top of a fire tower.

Howling with the Wolves

One of the many animals that live in the Algonquin Provincial Park wilderness is the wolf. And one of the most popular (and eeriest) activities at Algonquin Park is the Wolf Howl. These events typically attract more than 1,500 visitors, who assemble at the park's Outdoor Theatre (Hwy. 60, Km. 35.4) for a presentation about wolves and their habitat. Then everyone gets in their cars and drives caravan-style to a designated spot where park naturalists have heard a wolf pack on the previous night. Once everyone is in place, the naturalists begin a sequence of howls—hoping that the wolves will respond with howls of their own. Sometimes they do, and sometimes they don't, but if you're lucky enough to hear the wolf pack howling, it's a unique experience.

The Wolf Howls are typically held during August, occasionally the first week of September, the only time of year when wolves are likely to remain in one place for days at a time. The howls are held once a week, at 8pm Thursday, and last about three hours. Check event bulletin boards throughout the park, or phone the **Visitors Centre** (613/637-2828) to confirm if the week's Wolf Howl will be held. Howls are canceled if no wolves are in an area along Highway 60 or if the weather is inclement, so you generally won't know till the day of the event whether it will take place. Updates on the Wolf Howls are also posted on the **Friends of Algonquin Park website** (www.algonquinpark.on.ca), where you can sign up to receive an email update on the week's Wolf Howl.

Algonquin Logging Museum (Hwy. 60, Km. 54.5)

Logging was an important part of Algonquin's heritage. Learn more about that history and about the delicate balance between industry and preservation at the **Algonquin Logging Museum** (9am-5pm daily late June-mid-Oct., free). You can watch a short video about Algonquin's logging history, but the most interesting parts of this museum are outdoors.

As you follow a walking trail through a recreated logging camp, you can see how loggers cut and squared the trees, hauled them across the lakes, and drove them through water chutes to transport them to the cities. You can climb aboard an "alligator," a steam-powered tugboat used to haul logs. The trail also takes you past a working log dam and chute, a restored blacksmith shop, a locomotive, and a classic 1950s truck. There are enough things to touch and climb on that kids may enjoy it, even if they don't appreciate the historical angle.

East Gate (Hwy. 60, Km. 55.8)

Like the West Gate, Algonquin's eastern entrance has an information office that sells the required park permits ($17 per vehicle), provides park maps, and offers suggestions about things to see and do. If you're driving east toward Ottawa, you can use the restrooms here before hitting the road.

SPORTS AND RECREATION
Bicycling

Algonquin Park has two cycling trails that are easy to reach from Highway 60. The relatively flat, family-friendly 16-kilometer (10-mile) **Old Railway Bike Trail** follows the route of a former rail line between Cache Lake and the Rock Lake Campground. The trail passes the campgrounds at Mew Lake, Lake of Two Rivers, Kearney Lake, Pog Lake, Whitefish Lake, and Coon Lake. The more challenging **Minnesing Mountain Bike Trail** (Hwy. 60, Km. 23, late-June-mid-Oct.) includes four hilly loops of 4.7, 10.1, 17.1, and 23.4 kilometers (2.9, 6.3, 10.6, and 14.5 miles). The trail is often quite muddy in June and July.

You can rent bikes at the **Two Rivers Store** (Hwy. 60, Km. 31.4, 705/633-5622) and the **Opeongo Store** (Lake Opeongo, 6.2 km/3.9 miles north of Km. 46.3, 613/637-2075 or 888/280-8886, www.algonquinoutfitters.com).

★ Canoeing

Algonquin Park is one of Ontario's most popular destinations for canoeing. Not only can you paddle on the park's numerous lakes and rivers, but Algonquin also has more than 2,000 kilometers (1,240 miles) of canoe routes across the backcountry, ideal for overnight or multiday canoe trips. A useful planning resource is the *Canoe Routes of Algonquin Provincial Park Map* (www.algongquin-park.on.ca, $5), which you can order online or purchase at any of the park stores or information centers. It details all the lakes, access points, portages, and campsites across Algonquin.

Within the park, you can rent canoes at the **Portage Store** (Canoe Lake, Hwy. 60, Km. 14.1, www.portagestore.com) and the Opeongo Store (6.2 km/3.9 miles north of Km. 46.3), run by **Algonquin Outfitters** (613/637-2075 or 888/280-8886, www.algon-quinoutfitters.com). Both outfitters offer shuttle services to take you and your canoe to various launch points. Many outfitters outside the park will rent canoes with car-top carriers.

Both the Portage Store and Algonquin Outfitters offer guided canoe day trips. The Portage Store runs a full-day trip (9:30am-4:30pm daily late June-early Sept., 9:30am-4:30pm Tues., Thurs., and Sat.-Sun. mid-May-late June and early Sept.-early Oct., adults $60, under age 14 $30) on Canoe Lake, which includes an orientation about the park, basic canoe instruction, and a day-long paddle with a stop for a picnic lunch. In July and August they also offer a half-day trip (1pm-5pm, adults $36, under age 14 $18). Reservations are advised for both trips.

From their Opeongo Store, Algonquin Outfitters offers a guided half-day Costello Creek trip (Mon.-Fri. mid-May-Oct., $70 for 2 people, $47 pp for 3, $35 pp for 4). They also run a full-day guided canoe trip (9am Mon.-Fri. mid-May-Oct., $150 pp for 2, $100 pp for 3, $75 pp for 4) departing from their Oxtongue Lake store. Reservations are required for all trips. Ask about discounts for kids and teens.

Hiking

All along the Highway 60 corridor are trails for day hikes, ranging from an easy boardwalk path to strenuous all-day excursions. More experienced hikers can tromp along more than 140 kilometers (87 miles) of backpacking trails through the park's interior.

The most accessible park trails:

- **Whiskey Rapids** (Km. 7.2, 2.1 km/1.3 miles, moderate)
- **Hardwood Lookout** (Km. 13.8, 0.8 km/0.5 miles, moderate)
- **Mizzy Lake** (Km. 15.4, 11 km/7 miles, moderate)
- **Peck Lake** (Km. 19.2, 1.9 km/1.2 miles, moderate)
- **Track and Tower** (Km. 25, 7.7 km/4.8 miles, moderate)
- **Hemlock Bluff** (Km. 27.2, 3.5 km/2.2 miles, moderate)
- **Bat Lake** (Km. 30, 5.6 km/3.5 miles, moderate)
- **Two Rivers** (Km. 31, 2.1 km/1.3 miles, moderate)
- **Centennial Ridges** (Km. 37.6, 10 km/6 miles, strenuous)
- **Lookout** (Km. 39.7, 1.9 km/1.2 miles, moderate)
- **Big Pines** (Km. 40.3, 2.9 km/1.8 miles, moderate)
- **Booth's Rock** (Km. 40.5, 5.1 km/3.2 miles, moderate)
- **Spruce Bog Boardwalk** (Km. 42.5, 1.5 km/0.9 miles, easy)
- **Beaver Pond** (Km. 45.2, 2 km/1.2 miles, moderate)

Trail guides, with more details about each of these hikes, are available at the trailheads (spring to fall) and online (www.algonquin-park.on.ca).

Winter Sports

If you want to try dogsledding, these outfitters can get you out on the Algonquin trails. **Voyageur Quest** (416/486-3605 or 800/794-9660, www.voyageurquest.com) offers one-day, weekend-long and multiday dogsledding trips (Dec.-Mar., weather permitting). **Snow Forest Adventures** (705/783-0461, www.snowforestadventures. ca, late Dec.-Mar.) runs half-day (adults $150 pp) and full-day ($250 pp) dogsledding trips that depart from the Sunday Lake dogsledding trails (Hwy. 60, Km. 40). No experience is necessary, and kids under 12 can ride with a paying adult for $50 (half-day) and $100 (full-day).

Algonquin Park has three areas that offer trails for cross-country skiing. At the West Gate, the groomed **Fen Lake Ski Trail** has four loops, ranging 1.25-13 kilometers (0.75-8 miles). One kilometer (0.6 miles) west of the East Gate, the groomed **Leaf Lake Trail** has routes measuring 5 to 51 kilometers (3-32 miles) in length. For more challenging wilderness skiing, head to the **Minnesing Trail** (Hwy. 60, Km. 23), where four ungroomed loops range 4.7 to 23.4 kilometers (3-14.5 miles). For snowshoeing, you can explore nearly anywhere in the park, including any of the hiking trails along Highway 60. Snowshoes are not allowed on the cross-country trails.

In winter, you still need to purchase a park permit ($17 per vehicle). Also make sure you have ample time to get off the trails before dark, and wear warm clothes, particularly hats, gloves, boots, and multiple layers appropriate for your outdoor activity.

Outfitters

A number of outfitters, both within and outside Algonquin Park, can help you organize canoeing, camping, and hiking trips; rent you the gear you need; or take you on a guided journey. Some even organize dogsledding excursions. **Algonquin Outfitters** (800/469-4948, www.algonquinoutfitters.com) has locations throughout the Muskoka region, including the Opeongo Store on Lake Opeongo within the park, Oxtongue Lake outside the West Gate, and Huntsville. They offer a variety of guided or self-guided trips, including half-day, full-day, and multiday canoe and kayak excursions. Located on Canoe Lake, the **Portage Store** (Hwy. 60, Km. 14.1, 705/633-5622, www.portagestore.com, late Apr.-mid-Oct.) organizes canoe trips and offers half-, full-, and multiday guided paddles. Outside the East Gate, **Opeongo Outfitters** (29902 Hwy. 60, Whitney, 613/637-5470 or 800/790-1864, www.opeongooutfitters.com, mid-Apr.-mid-Oct.) can rent gear for a multiday canoe trip, including a canoe, tent, a pack, a sleeping bag, food, cooking utensils, and other supplies. You can also rent a kayak or canoe for the day.

Voyageur Quest (416/486-3605 or 800/794-9660, www.voyageurquest.com) organizes several different Algonquin excursions, such as three- to seven-day canoe trips (including trips designed for families), a moose photography safari, and winter dogsledding trips. **Northern Edge Algonquin** (888/383-8320, www.northernedgealgonquin. com) runs a stand-up paddling safari and yoga retreat; a weekend of hiking, canoeing, and wildlife spotting; and a multiday canoe adventure across Algonquin's remote backcountry. Run by the Algonquin First Nation of Wolf Lake, **Algonquin Canoe Company** (705/981-0572 or 866/889-9788, www.algonquincanoe.com) offers guided daylong and multiday canoe trips as well as cultural tours, including a weekend of traditional drumbuilding and drumming. **Snow Forest Adventures** (705/783-0461, www.snowforestadventures.ca) offers half-day and full-day dogsledding trips, from late December through March, weather permitting.

ACCOMMODATIONS AND FOOD

If you want to stay within the park, you can choose from three upscale lodges (which also operate restaurants), rustic former ranger cabins, yurts, or camping. The lodges, cabins, and most of the campgrounds are open spring to fall. In winter, you can camp at Mew Lake, off Highway 60, or out in the backcountry. The park cafeterias and snack bars also operate seasonally.

Park Lodges

With hiking, swimming and canoeing, there's plenty to do at **Arowhon Pines** (Arowhon Rd., 705/633-5661 or 866/633-5661, www. arowhonpines.ca, late May-mid-Oct., $205-450 pp). The private cabins have a queen bed, lounge area, and private deck. The less-expensive shared cabins have a private room and bath, but share the lounge space with guests. Lodging rates include breakfast, lunch, and dinner as well as use of all the recreational facilities. To reach Arowhon Pines, follow Highway 60 to Km. 16, then turn north onto Arowhon Rd., which winds through the woods to the lodge.

Getting to **Bartlett Lodge** (Cache Lake, 705/633-5543 or 866/614-5355, www.bartlettlodge.com, mid-May-late Oct.) is half the fun; the lodge is accessible only by boat. When you turn off Highway 60 at Km. 23.5, call the lodge, which will send their water taxi. Some of the lakeside one- to three-bedroom cabins ($179-265 pp) date to the early 1900s. Studio units ($165-199 pp) are in a historic log cabin. Rates include buffet breakfast and a multicourse dinner. The lodge also offers a "glamorous camping" option in a furnished **platform tent** ($105-135 pp, including breakfast); a washroom with showers is in an adjacent building.

Killarney Lodge (Lake of Two Rivers, Hwy. 60, Km. 33.2, 705/633-5551 or 866/473-5551, www.killarneylodge.com, mid-May-mid-Oct., $189-379 pp) is the easiest park lodge to reach, just off Highway 60. With no TVs, radios, or phones, the 25 log cottages are set in the woods, with neat knotty-pine or rough-hewn log interiors. The "one-bedroom" cabins are one room with a king or queen bed; the "two-bedroom" cabins have two rooms, one with a king bed, a second with twin beds. Many cottages are right on the lake, and each comes with its own canoe. Rates include three meals a day.

Ranger Cabins

Algonquin has 14 **Ranger Cabins** (mid-Apr.-mid-Oct., $63-138) that offer indoor camping. They're rustic log structures without running water or electricity where rangers patrolling the park would overnight. You can reach five by car, at Rain Lake, Bissett Creek Road, Kiosk, and two cabins at Brent; others are in the backcountry. Equipped with a table and chairs, a wood stove, and an outdoor toilet,

a cottage at Algonquin's Killarney Lodge

most cabins have bunks but not mattresses, so bring a sleeping pad and a sleeping bag, along with any cooking supplies you want. The Friends of Algonquin Park website (www.algonquinpark.on.ca) has detailed descriptions of each cabin.

Camping

Algonquin is a popular destination for campers, with the largest number of campsites—more than 1,300—of any Ontario provincial park. **Reserve your campsite** (519/826-5290 or 888/668-7275, www.ontarioparks. com/reservations, tent sites $40-44, electrical sites $50, reservation fee online $11, by phone $13) in advance, particularly for summer and fall weekends. Eight of the front-country campgrounds are accessible by car near Highway 60. Most are seasonal, opening in late April or mid-May and closing between early September and mid-October. Only the Mew Lake campground is open year-round.

The front-country campgrounds:

- **Tea Lake** (Km. 11.4, 42 sites) has showers and flush toilets.

- **Canisbay Lake** (Km. 23.1, 242 sites) has secluded campsites, swimming beaches, showers, flush toilets, and laundry facilities.

- **Mew Lake** (Km. 30.6, 131 sites), which has central flush toilets, showers, and laundry, also has seven yurts ($98), available year-round. The yurts, which sleep six, are furnished with two sets of bunk beds (a double below and a single above), a table and chairs, a propane barbecue, cooking utensils, and dishes. They have electric lights and heating. You still need to bring sleeping bags or other bedding, as well as food and other personal items.

- **Two Rivers** (Km. 31.8, 241 sites) is the most centrally located, and frequently the most crowded. It has a beach, a laundry, flush toilets, and showers.

- **Pog Lake** (Km. 36.9, 286 sites) has secluded campsites and central showers, laundry, and flush toilets.

- **Kearney Lake** (Km. 36.5, 103 sites) has two beaches, showers, and flush toilets.

- **Coon Lake** (6 kilometers south of Km. 40.3, 48 sites) has a beach and pit toilets.

- **Rock Lake** (8 kilometers south of Km. 40.3, 121 sites) has two beaches, showers, flush toilets, and laundry.

Algonquin has three more drive-in campgrounds (late Apr.-mid-Oct.) farther north. **Achray** (45 sites), **Brent** (30 sites), and **Kiosk** (22 sites) campgrounds are all accessible from Highway 17 but far more secluded than the Highway 60 camping areas. Achray and Kiosk have flush toilets, and Achray also has a yurt, but none of these three campgrounds has showers.

Algonquin Park also has numerous **backcountry campgrounds** (adults $12, ages 6-17 $5); most are accessible only by canoe. The Friends of Algonquin Park (www. algonquinpark.on.ca) has detailed information to help plan a trip into the backcountry. Several outfitters also organize backcountry trips.

East of the Park

A short drive outside the park's East Gate, the **Couples Resort** (139 Galeairy Lake Rd., Whitney, 866/202-1179, www.couplesresort. ca, $246-838 d), on the waterfront, is unabashedly romantic. Some of the large rooms have four-poster beds, hot tubs or whirlpool baths, and wood-burning fireplaces. Enjoy the seasonal outdoor heated saltwater pool, play billiards or table tennis, take a sauna, or use the fitness room and spa. Midweek specials can reduce the rates significantly. Rates include breakfast and a semiformal five-course dinner; for the evening meal, jeans, shorts, and sandals are forbidden, and men must wear a dress shirt with a collar.

Food

If you're not a lodge guest, you can still come for a meal in the dining room at **Arowhon Pines** (Arowhon Rd., 705/633-5661 or 866/633-5661, www.arowhonpines.ca, late

May-mid-Oct.), where meals are fixed-price: breakfast (8am-10am, $25 pp), weekday lunch (12:30pm-2pm, $35 pp), weekend lunch buffet (12:30pm-2pm, $50 pp), and an abundant multicourse dinner (6:30pm only, $75 pp). The dining room doesn't have a license to serve alcohol, but you can bring your own.

The **Bartlett Lodge Dining Room** (Cache Lake, 705/633-5543 or 866/614-5355, www.bartlettlodge.com, mid-May-late Oct.) is open to nonguests for breakfast ($17.50 pp) and in the evening, when an elaborate five-course prix-fixe dinner ($65 pp) is served; kids have a three-course dinner option ($25 pp). The dining room isn't licensed to serve alcohol, but you can bring your own.

The main lodge building at **Killarney Lodge** (Lake of Two Rivers, Hwy. 60, Km. 33.2, 705/633-5551 or 866/473-5551, www.killarneylodge.com, mid-May-mid-Oct.) dates to 1935 and now houses the dining room, open to nonguests and serving hearty, fixed-price, three-course menus at lunch (noon-2pm daily, $25) and dinner (5:45pm-7:30pm daily, $60). If you're not a lodge guest, reservations are advised for dinner. Also, the dining room keeps slightly shorter hours in May-June, so phone to confirm.

You can get casual meals at the **Portage Store** (Canoe Lake, Hwy. 60, Km. 14.1, 705/633-5622, www.portagestore.com), which serves breakfast, lunch, and dinner daily late April-mid-October, and at the **Sunday Creek Café** (Hwy. 60, Km. 63, 613/637-1133), the basic cafeteria in the Algonquin Visitors Centre. A seasonal snack bar sells sandwiches and ice cream at the **Two Rivers Store** (Hwy. 60, Km. 31.4).

INFORMATION AND SERVICES

For questions about Algonquin Park, phone the **Algonquin Park Information Office** (705/633-5572, 8am-4pm daily). You can also get visitor information at the park's West Gate, East Gate, and Visitors Centre. Online, the best source of information is the **Friends of Algonquin Park** (www.algonquinpark.on.ca). **Ontario Parks** (www.ontarioparks.com) will give you an overview of the park facilities but doesn't provide as much detail.

Mobile phones do work in Algonquin Park, if you're within about three kilometers (two miles) of Highway 60. There are dead spots, though, and outside this zone, don't count on picking up a phone signal. Within the park, three stores sell camping supplies (including mosquito repellent, rain ponchos, and basic first aid) and a small selection of groceries. The **Portage Store** (Km. 14.1) is on the west end of Highway 60 at Canoe Lake, the **Two Rivers Store** (Km. 31.4) at the Lake of Two Rivers Campground is at roughly the midway point on Highway 60, and the **Opeongo Store** is to the east, a short drive north of Km. 46.3.

GETTING THERE
Car

Algonquin's West Gate is 45 kilometers (28 miles) east of Huntsville via Highway 60. The East Gate is five kilometers (three miles) west of the town of Whitney. From Toronto (270 kilometers, or 168 miles), the most direct, if most heavily trafficked, route is to take Highway 400 north to Highway 11 north, which will take you to Huntsville, where you can take Highway 60 to the West Gate.

An alternate route from Toronto takes you to the East Gate. Go east on Highway 401, then pick up Highway 115 to Peterborough; from there, take Highway 28 north to Bancroft, Highway 62 north to Maynooth, then Highway 127 north to Highway 60, which will bring you to the park's East Gate. While this route sounds more complicated, it's clearly marked; it's about 310 kilometers (190 miles) from Toronto. From Ottawa, it's 240 kilometers (150 miles) to the East Gate; take Highway 417/17 west to Highway 60.

You can buy gas at the Portage Store (Km. 14.1, early May-mid-Oct.). Otherwise, the nearest gas stations are in Oxtongue Lake and Dwight west of the park, and in Whitney to the east.

Bus

The **Parkbus** (800-928-7101, www.parkbus. ca) provides direct bus service from Toronto to Algonquin (one-way adults $60, seniors and students $54, ages 2-12 $30, round-trip adults $85, seniors and students $77, ages 2-12 $43). It's an excellent nonprofit initiative designed to get people out of the city—and out of their cars—by offering transportation to a growing number of national parks and Ontario provincial parks. The bus runs on selected weekends throughout the summer season. The bus departs from several points in Toronto, including 30 Carlton Street (between Yonge St. and Church St., 1 block from the College subway station) and Dufferin Street at Bloor Street West, which is at Dufferin subway station. The Parkbus can also take you from Ottawa to Algonquin. You can catch the bus in downtown Ottawa from the Rideau Centre (50 Rideau St.) or west of downtown at the Mountain Equipment Co-op store (366 Richmond Rd.).

You can get off the bus at several points, including the Wolf Den Hostel near Oxtongue Lake, the West Gate, the Portage Store at Canoe Lake, Lake of Two Rivers Campground, Pog Lake, and the Algonquin Outfitters store on Lake Opeongo. These locations either have accommodations (you can camp at Lake of Two Rivers or Pog Lake, or bunk at the Wolf Den), or they're departure points for outfitters who organize guided trips. The Parkbus works with several outfitters, so you can buy an all-inclusive trip if you prefer.

GETTING AROUND

There is no public transportation within Algonquin Park. If you arrive on the **Parkbus** (800/928-7101, www.parkbus.ca), you can camp at Lake of Two Rivers or Pog Lake, which are both centrally located and have hiking, cycling, and canoeing options nearby, so it's feasible to do without a car. You can also arrive by bus and do a canoeing or hiking trip that you've booked through an outfitter; the bus will drop you at one of several outfitters' locations.

Otherwise, unless you're comfortable bicycling or hiking long distances, you need a car to explore the park. The most convenient place to rent a car in the vicinity of the park is in Huntsville.

North Bay to James Bay

Traveling north from Algonquin Provincial Park or northeast from the Ottawa Valley, the towns get farther apart and the forests get denser. Mining and logging have historically formed the backbone of local economies here, but tourism, particularly outdoor adventure and ecotourism, is a growing business. From the city of North Bay, it's a short trip to the lake town of Temagami, which has excellent canoe-trip options. Farther north, you can board the train for a unique journey to First Nations communities along James Bay.

For more regional travel details, contact **Northeastern Ontario Tourism** (2009 Long Lake Rd., Unit 401, Sudbury, 705/522-0104 or 800/465-6655, www.northeasternontario.com).

NORTH BAY
Sights

On May 28, 1934, quintuplets were born to Oliva and Elzire Dionne, a French Canadian couple living in Corbeil, outside North Bay. These five identical girls—the now-famous Dionne Quintuplets—became an immediate media sensation. By an act of Parliament, they were removed from their parents, who already had five other children under age seven, and designated wards of the Ontario government, which built an "observation playground" where the quints lived—in view of more than three million visitors—until 1943. Although they were eventually returned to their family, the transition to normal life was difficult, and their treatment eventually drew public indignation. The house where the quints were born, which was moved to its current location adjacent to North Bay's Regional Tourist Information Centre east of downtown, is now the **Dionne Quints Museum** (1375 Seymour St., 705/472-8480 or 888/249-8998, www.northbaychamber.com, 9am-7pm daily July-Aug., 9am-5pm Mon.-Fri. and 10am-4pm Sat.-Sun. mid-May-June and Sept.-mid-Oct., adults $3.75, seniors and ages 13-18 $3.25, ages 5-12 $2.25, families $11), filled with memorabilia about their lives and information about their complicated history.

The **Heritage Railway and Carousel** (Memorial Dr., 4pm-dusk Fri., 10am-dusk Sat.-Sun. mid-May-late June, 10am-dusk daily late June-early Sept., 10am-dusk Sat.-Sun. early Sept.-mid-Oct., $2) is an old-time miniature train and merry-go-round that will appeal to kids. In the former train station, the **Discovery North Bay Museum** (100 Ferguson St., 705/476-2323, www.discoverynorthbay.com, 10am-6pm Tues.-Fri., 8am-3pm Sat., adults $7, seniors and students $6, ages 5-12 $5) has model trains and other changing exhibits. Lake Nipissing is a short walk from downtown, and you can explore the lake on a sightseeing cruise aboard the ***Chief Commanda II*** (200 Memorial Dr., 705/494-8167 or 866/660-6686, www.georgianbaycruise.com, mid-May-early Oct., adults $32, seniors and students $29, youth 13-16 $22, kids 5-12 $16).

Accommodations and Food

Chain motels line Lakeshore Drive south of the city center, including **Super 8 North Bay** (570 Lakeshore Dr., 705/495-4551, www.super8.com, $100-135 d). Off Highway 11, there's **Hampton Inn North Bay** (950 McKeown Ave., 705/474-8400 , www.hamptoninn.hilton.com, $118-159 d) and **Holiday Inn Express & Suites North Bay** (1325 Seymour St., 705/476-7700, www.ihg.com/holidayinnexpress, $121-159 d).

Main Street has several eateries, including the vegetarian-friendly **Cedar Tree Lebanese Restaurant** (183 Main St. E., 705/472-2405, www.cedartreelebaneserestaurant.com, 11am-8pm Mon.-Sat., $5-18), which serves tasty falafel, tabbouleh, *shawarma,* and other Middle Eastern classics.

Information and Services

North Bay's **Regional Tourist Information Centre** (1375 Seymour St., at Hwy. 11,

North Bay's Heritage Carousel

Nipping into Nipissing

The big woods of Algonquin give way to farm country as you drive north on Highway 11, then turn west toward the small village of Nipissing (pronounced "NIH-pih-sing"). Nipissing is attracting modern-day pioneers who are simultaneously getting back to the land and welcoming visitors into their lives. It's a funky, little-touristed destination for a weekend getaway.

Pop in for a quick look through the quirky **Nipissing Museum** (Hwy. 654 at Hwy. 534, 705/724-2938, 10am-4pm Tues.-Sun. mid-June-early Sept., donation), and you may find you're there for an hour or more. The museum was a labor of love for the local resident nicknamed "Museum Joe," who assembled several buildings packed with artifacts reflecting life in Nipissing since the early 1900s. There's the dress of a local woman who met with British royalty, the cash register from the general store, a wide variety of household items, and scads of photos.

The family-run **Board's Honey Farm** (6866 Hwy. 534, 705/729-2939 or 888/363-2827, www. boardshoneyfarm.com, 10am-5pm May-Oct.), between Nipissing and Restoule, houses more than 300 colonies of bees and sells a variety of homemade honeys and honey products. On Thursday in July and August, you can take a guided tour of the beekeeping operations (1:30pm); otherwise, explore the gardens, walking trails, and hives on your own.

Continue west of Highway 534 to quiet **Restoule Provincial Park** (705/729-2010, www. ontarioparks.com), where you can swim in the lake and perhaps spot deer, moose, or other wildlife nearby.

WHERE TO STAY AND EAT

Staying at the **Piebird Bed & Breakfast** (113 Chapman's Landing Rd., 705/724-1144, www. piebird.ca, $125-150 d) is like escaping to a laid-back farm run by your cool, socially conscious friends. Upstairs in the 100-year-old farmhouse are three country bedrooms, two with queen beds and one with a single. They share a bath with an old claw-foot tub; there's also a solar shower outside. A separate cottage on the property ($165) has a full kitchen and bath.

Piebird owners Sherry and Yan, who grow their own vegetables, share their love of organic farming with guests. They serve vegetarian breakfasts, and they'll prepare lunches and dinners by reservation. Even if you're not staying here, you can book a meal if your group includes at least four (or if you're able to join an existing group). They also organize workshops about vegetarian food, herbs, canning, and other topics related to organic and local food, and they host periodic concerts, including the annual **Picnic and Garden Concert,** a day of music and outdoor eating; check their website for details.

GETTING THERE

Nipissing is 340 kilometers (210 miles) north of Toronto and 110 kilometers (68 miles) beyond Huntsville. Turn off Highway 11 at Highway 534 and continue west for about 13 kilometers (eight miles). For Nipissing Village, go north on Highway 654; Highway 534 continues west toward Restoule.

705/472-8480 or 888/249-8998, www.cityofnorthbay.ca, 9am-7pm daily July-Aug., 9am-5pm Mon.-Fri. and 10am-4pm Sat.-Sun. mid-May-June and Sept.-mid-Oct., 9am-5pm Mon.-Fri. and 10am-2pm Sat.-Sun. mid-Oct.-mid-May) can assist with information about the area.

Getting There and Around

At the junction of Highways 11 and 17, North Bay is roughly equidistant to Toronto and Ottawa (355 kilometers, or 220 miles), and 130 kilometers (80 miles) east of Sudbury. **Ontario Northland** (www.ontarionorthland.ca) has bus service to Toronto, while **Greyhound** (www.greyhound.ca) runs buses to Sudbury and Ottawa. The **bus station** (100 Station Rd., 705/495-4200) is east of downtown, near Highway 17.

You really need a car to explore North Bay.

Local rental agencies include **Avis** (705/476-9730, www.avis.com), **Enterprise** (705/840-7777, www.enterprise.com), and **National** (705/474-3030, www.nationalcar.com).

SUDBURY

Sudbury reveals its charms slowly. This industrial city of 160,000 is ringed with the belching smokestacks and rocky pits of its many active mines. Yet if you find yourself here, en route to Sault Ste. Marie, Manitoulin Island, Killarney Provincial Park, or wilderness spots farther north, it's worth exploring. The city's science museum is a don't-miss sight if you have children in tow, and the compact downtown has a handful of interesting restaurants and galleries, including **Artists on Elgin** (168 Elgin St., 705/674-0415, www.artistsonelgin.ca, 10am-5pm Mon.-Sat.), which features local artists' work.

★ Science North

Kids (and their parents) could easily spend a day or more at Sudbury's cool, contemporary science museum, **Science North** (100 Ramsey Lake Rd., 705/523-4629 or 800/461-4898, www.sciencenorth.ca, 9am-6pm daily late June-early Sept., 10am-4pm daily early Sept.-Dec., call or check the website for hours winter-spring; adults $25, seniors and ages 13-17 $23, ages 3-12 $21).

Built into a massive rock on the edge of Ramsey Lake (you enter the exhibit halls through a tunnel blasted from the bedrock), this year-round hands-on museum is packed with "please touch" exhibits, focusing on the environment, animals, the human body, and more. In the Nature Exchange, kids can bring in something they've found—a plant, a rock, a bug—learn something about it, and exchange it for something in the museum's collection. Many exhibitions highlight the wildlife, plants, geology, and ecology of Northern Ontario.

Admission packages including Science North and the on-site IMAX theatre or planetarium are available, as are combination tickets to Science North and Dynamic Earth.

Dynamic Earth

In a region where mining, primarily for nickel and copper, is such a big part of the local economy, it's no surprise that a major attraction is the high-tech mining museum **Dynamic Earth** (122 Big Nickel Rd., 705/523-4629 or 800/461-4898, www.dynamicearth.ca, Mar.-Oct., call or check the website for winter hours, adults $20, seniors and ages 13-17 $18, ages 3-12 $16).

A highlight is the 45-minute Underground Tour through a simulated mine, where you walk through 100 years of mining technology, from the dark, narrow tunnels of the early 1900s to the more high-tech mines of today. It's a rather promotional pitch for the mining industry but still makes for an interesting tour. Another fun exhibit is the Mining Command Centre, where you use computers to drill or smash rocks and track mine activities (you can even spy on the Underground Tour groups). Outside, the **Big Nickel,** a really big 13-ton replica of a 1951 Canadian five-cent piece, symbolizes the importance of nickel production to Sudbury's, and Canada's, economy.

Dynamic Earth operates in conjunction with Science North, and you can buy a combination ticket to both; the two attractions are about five kilometers (three miles) apart.

Entertainment and Events

Sudbury hosts a variety of arts festivals, including **Northern Lights Festival Boreal** (www.nlfbsudbury.com, July), a long-running music fest on Ramsey Lake; the **Cinéfest Sudbury International Film Festival** (www.cinefest.com, Sept.), and the **Sudbury Jazz Festival** (www.jazzsudbury.ca, Sept.). A unique food-and-music party is the **Canadian Garlic Festival** (www.ukrseniors.org, Aug.), sponsored by the Ukrainian Seniors Centre; bring your own breath mints.

Accommodations

The "artisan" at the **Artisan Upstairs Guesthouse** (318 Jeanne D'Arc Ave., 705/674-4387, www.artisanupstairs.com,

$100 s, $130 d), on a residential street east of downtown, is co-owner Pete Lautenschlager, who carved much of the furniture and woodwork in these two second-floor guest rooms. Popular with couples and business travelers, the bedrooms have sponge-painted walls and private baths. Guests can use the fully equipped kitchenette and relax on the deck overlooking the nearby woods. Rates include full breakfast.

The **Southbay Guesthouse Sudbury** (1802 Southbay Rd., 705/859-2363, www.southbayguesthouse.com) has an enviable waterfront location in a private home on Ramsey Lake. The larger Luna de Miel suite ($155 d) has a king bed, two-person whirlpool tub, and a fireplace, while the queen-bed Sunrise suite ($139 d) opens onto a lakeside deck. Rates include breakfast. The same family runs Manitoulin Island's Southbay Guesthouse.

Among the nicest of Sudbury's many chain motels along Regent Street south of downtown is the 121-room **Hampton Inn-Sudbury** (2280 Regent St., 705/523-5200, www.sudburyontario.hamptoninn.com, $127-159 d), which makes both business travelers and vacationing families feel at home. The beds are topped with crisp white duvets, and kids will appreciate the indoor pool.

Food

Head downtown around Durham Street for a selection of restaurants and cafés. A seasonal **farmers market** (233 Elgin St., 705/674-4455, www.greatersudbury.ca/market, 8am-2pm Sat., 10am-2pm Sun., late June-Oct.) operates outside the downtown rail station.

The name is fitting at **Café Petit Gateau** (149 Durham St., 705/222-2233, www.cafepetitgateau.com, 9am-5pm Tues.-Fri., 10am-4pm Sat.), a tiny shop that bakes a changing assortment of cookies, scones, cakes, and other sweets to pair with tea or espresso drinks. **Fromagerie Elgin** (5 Cedar St., at Elgin, 705/675-1000, www.fromagerieelgin.ca, 10am-9pm Mon.-Sat., 11am-3pm Sun., $6-12) is part cheese shop and part café, where patrons settle into the long wooden table for cheese plates, sandwiches, and daily-changing soups. They host art exhibits and regular live music nights, too; call for schedules. At **Leinala's** (272 Caswell Dr., 705/522-1977), a traditional Finnish bakery, it's difficult to choose among the delicious sweet breads and fresh-cooked doughnuts, including their specialty, jelly pigs (glazed and filled with jam). It's in a strip mall off Regent Street, south of downtown.

A chill downtown spot for vegetarians and their nonveg companions is the **Laughing Buddha** (194 Elgin St., 705/673-2112, www.laughingbuddhasudbury.com, 11am-2am daily), a café-bar that hums till the wee hours. Whether you want herbal tea or booze, a Treehugger Salad (a hearty bowl of romaine, tomatoes, mushrooms, raisins, and cashews) or a Swiss and Sow (a ham and cheese sandwich), the laid-back staff will oblige.

Information and Services

Sudbury Tourism (200 Brady St., 705/674-4455, ext. 7718, or 866/451-8252, www.sudburytourism.ca) has details about the city on its website.

Getting There

Sudbury is well served with air, train, and bus connections, but all its transportation terminals are inconveniently located outside the city center.

Air

The **Greater Sudbury Airport** (YSB, 5000 Air Terminal Dr., Garson, 705/693-2514 or 855/359-2972, www.flysudbury.ca) is 25 kilometers (15 miles) northeast of downtown. **Air Canada** (www.aircanada.com) flies to Toronto's Pearson Airport, but you can sometimes find better deals on **Porter Airlines** (www.flyporter.com) to Toronto's City Airport. **Bearskin Airlines** (705/693-9199 or 800/465-2327, www.bearskinairlines.com) serves Ottawa, Sault Ste. Marie, and Thunder Bay.

From the airport to in-town hotels, **Sudbury Cab** (705/626-7968, www.

sudburycab.com) runs both shared-van shuttles ($40-60) and taxis ($50-73). You must book shuttles at least one day in advance.

Train

VIA Rail's transcontinental Toronto-Vancouver train stops two or three days a week at **Sudbury Junction** (2750 Lasalle Blvd., 705/524-1591), 10 kilometers (six miles) northeast of the city center. The Sudbury-Toronto leg (one-way adults $64-103) takes 7-8 hours. Note that the only trains using the **Sudbury Downtown Station** (233 Elgin St.) travel to the town of White River, between Sault Ste. Marie and Thunder Bay.

Bus

From Sudbury's **Intercity Bus Terminal** (854 Notre Dame Ave., 705/524-9900), three kilometers (1.9 miles) north of downtown, **Ontario Northland** (www.ontarionorthland.ca) runs buses to Toronto (5.5-6 hours, one-way adults $73.15, seniors and students $62.20, children $36.60) and north to Cochrane (6 hours, one-way adults $74.25, seniors and students $63.10, children $37.10). **Greyhound** (www.greyhound.ca) connects Sudbury with Sault Ste. Marie (4.5 hours, one-way adults $54-86) and Toronto (5-5.5 hours, one-way adults $46-97). A taxi from the bus station to downtown will cost about $15.

Car

Sudbury is at the intersection of Highway 69 to Toronto and Highway 17, which goes west to Sault Ste. Marie and east to North Bay and Ottawa. The city is 390 kilometers (242 miles) north of Toronto, a five- to six-hour drive. Sudbury is 90 minutes north of Killarney Provincial Park and about the same distance to Manitoulin Island's swing bridge.

Getting Around

Although the city center is compact and walkable, Sudbury's attractions are all outside downtown. You can get around by bus (if you're patient) or taxi, but having your own wheels is more convenient. **Greater

Sudbury Transit (705/675-3333, www.greatersudbury.ca) runs the city's bus network. Local cab companies include **Lockerby Taxi** (705/522-2222, www.lockerbytransportation.com) and **Aaron Taxi** (705/523-3333, www.aaronservices.ca/taxi). **Avis** (www.avis.ca), **Enterprise** (www.enterpriserentacar.ca), and **Budget** (www.budget.ca) are among Sudbury's car rental options.

★ TEMAGAMI

If you love to canoe or hike, Temagami, a wilderness region dotted with lakes large and small, makes a great getaway. Outdoor adventurers flock here in summer, increasing the population from 1,000 to over 10,000. Paddlers will find scores of opportunities for multiday canoe trips. If it's winter in the outdoors you crave, Temagami can oblige, with snowshoeing, cross-country skiing, and dogsledding. Local outfitters help organize active trips.

The town's name, pronounced "Teh-MAW-gah-mee," is an Ojibwa word, roughly translated as "Deep Water by the Shore," a fitting moniker for this lake country.

Sights

For an expansive aerial view of the surrounding lakes and forests, climb the 30-meter (100-foot) **Temagami Fire Tower** ($3). At 396 meters (1,300 feet) above sea level, it's the highest point on Yonge Street (Hwy. 11), which runs more or less all the way to Toronto (and at one time was named the longest street in the world).

Two kilometers (1.2 miles) south of town, **Finlayson Point Park** (24 Finlayson Park Rd., off Hwy. 11, 705/569-3205, www.ontarioparks.com, late May-late Sept., $14.50 per vehicle) has two small sandy swimming beaches on Lake Temagami. You can also rent canoes or explore the park's hiking trails. A museum has exhibits about the park's natural environment.

A vast protected wilderness surrounds Temagami, with a network of backcountry parks. The largest is **Lady Evelyn

Smoothwater Provincial Park (www.ontarioparks.com) to the northwest. Exploring this rugged region isn't for outdoor novices; you need backcountry camping, white-water canoeing, and other wilderness skills. Contact local outfitters for information about backcountry trips.

Sports and Recreation

Smoothwater Wilderness Lodge (705/569-3539 or 888/569-4539, www.smoothwater.com) can organize canoe, kayak, or hiking adventures. The **Temagami Outfitting Company** (6 Lakeshore Dr., 705/569-2595, www.icanoe.ca) runs an outdoor gear store and plans canoe, kayak, and hiking trips. **Lakeland Airways** (705/569-3455, www.lakelandairways.ca) can take you into the wilderness surrounding Temagami by floatplane. They'll even strap your canoe to the plane and drop you off on a remote lake.

Another way to explore is by houseboat, which you can pilot along the interconnected lakes that wind through the region. Contact **Leisure Island Houseboat Rentals** (705/569-3261, www.leisureislandhouseboats.com) or **Three Buoys Houseboat Rentals** (705/569-3455, www.threebuoyshouseboats.ca) for rentals.

For winter excursions, contact **Wolf Within Adventures** (705/840-9002, www.wolfwithin.ca), which runs dogsledding expeditions with a team of Alaskan huskies.

Accommodations and Food

Temagami's best place to stay is the ★ **Smoothwater Wilderness Lodge** (Smoothwater Rd., off Hwy. 11, 705/569-3539 or 888/569-4539, www.smoothwater.com, $30 dorm, $140 d, packages available). The rustic petite doubles and bunkhouse are comfortable, staff are friendly and knowledgeable, and family-style breakfasts ($15) and dinners ($55) feature local ingredients. Adventures include paddling on the property's lake and multiday canoeing and camping excursions. In winter, you can snowshoe or cross-country ski on 50 kilometers (31 miles) of trails. Lounge

Climb the Temagami Fire Tower for views of the surrounding lakes.

lakeside or in the Gathering Hall with comfy sofas, books, and games. Smoothwater is 14 kilometers (8.7 miles) north of Temagami.

Shops and restaurants are clustered along Highway 11 and on Lakeshore Drive, bordering Lake Temagami. Although the sign at this roadside stand says **B&D Burgers** (6731 Hwy. 11, $2.50-12), everyone calls it "The Chip Shop," because that's what you should order: chips (french fries), specifically the French Canadian specialty known as *poutine*. You can get a hamburger, hot dog, or fried fish, if you must, but it's the mounds of fries topped with gooey cheese and brown gravy that keep the picnic tables packed. When they ask if you want "shredded or curds" on your *poutine*, they're inquiring about the cheese; to be authentic, you want curds.

Camping

Finlayson Point Park (Finlayson Park Rd., off Hwy. 11, 705/569-3205, www.ontarioparks.com, late May-late Sept., tent sites $35-40, electrical sites $40-46) has 117 campsites, many right on Lake Temagami. The campground has showers, flush toilets, and laundry facilities. The park also rents a two-bedroom **cabin** ($170) with log furniture and an electric fireplace; it has no plumbing, but it's a short walk to the washrooms.

Campers are welcome to pitch a tent on the lawn at **Smoothwater Wilderness Lodge** (705/569-3539 or 888/569-4539, www.smooth-water.com, $15); you can use the restrooms and showers in the bunkhouse.

Practicalities

The **Temagami Chamber of Commerce Information Centre** (7 Lakeshore Dr., 705-569-3344 or 800/661-7609, www.temagamiinformation.com) can give you information about the area. Temagami is 455 kilometers (285 miles) north of Toronto and 100 kilometers (60 miles) north of North Bay. **Ontario Northland** (www.ontarionorth-land.ca) operates two buses a day between Toronto and **Temagami station** (Hwy. 11, 705/569-3310, 8 hours, one-way adults $104.40, seniors and students $88.75, children $52.25) and from Temagami on to Cochrane (5-5.25 hours, one-way adults $73.35, seniors and students $62.40, children $36.70).

COCHRANE

The main reason to come to Cochrane is to leave again. This windswept town with a remote, almost Wild West feel, is the starting point for the *Polar Bear Express* train that runs north toward James Bay, at the edge of the Arctic.

While Cochrane isn't far enough north to support arctic wildlife, the town capitalizes on its polar bear connection as the home of the small **Polar Bear Habitat and Heritage Village** (1 Drury Park Rd., 705/272-2327 or 800/354-9948, www.polarbearhabitat.ca, 9am-5pm daily May-Oct., 10am-4pm daily Nov.-Apr., adults $16, seniors $14, students $12, ages 5-11 $10, families $45), a polar bear sanctuary and research facility. A highlight for visitors is swimming with the bears—on the other side of a clear enclosure. Because the

bear population at the sanctuary fluctuates, check the status before making a special trip; in 2014 there were two bears in residence. Also on the grounds is a modest one-street heritage village and a snowmobile museum.

If you still have time to kill, visit the **Tim Horton Museum** (7 Tim Horton Dr., off 4th St. E., 705/272-5084, call for hours, $2), inside the Tim Horton Event Centre, 2.5 kilometers (1.6 miles) east of the station. Born in Cochrane in 1930, Horton played 22 seasons in the National Hockey League, but he's equally well known as the founder of the ubiquitous Canadian doughnut shop chain that bears his name.

For visitor information, look for the giant polar bear. Chimo, an 11-meter (35-foot) bear statue (its name is an Inuit word meaning "welcome"), greets visitors outside the **Town of Cochrane Information Centre** (3 3rd Ave./Hwy. 11, 705/272-4926, www.town.cochrane.on.ca).

Accommodations and Food

Cochrane's accommodations are clustered near the train station, with additional chain motels on Highway 11 south of town. Behind a grim stone facade is Cochrane's most upscale lodging, the **Best Western Swan Castle Inn** (189 Railway St., 705/272-5200 or 800/265-3668, www.bestwesternontario.com, $130-150 d), which has 39 middle-of-the-road rooms and a helpful staff. Rates include continental breakfast.

You can roll out of bed and onto your train from the **Station Inn** (200 Railway St., 705/272-3500 or 800/265-2356, www.ontarionorthland.ca, $105-115 d), with 23 smallish rooms above the depot. The **coffee shop** ($5-16) serves three meals daily, from eggs and sandwiches to pastas and pork chops. The low-rise **Commando Motel** (80 7th Ave. S., 705/272-2700, www.commandomotel.com, $65 s, $70 d) is another option, with free Wi-Fi, one block from the station.

To rustle up some grub, your best bet is the **J.R. Bar-B-Q Ranch** (63 3rd Ave., 705/272-4999, 11am-9pm Mon.-Sat., 3pm-8pm Sun.),

Where's the Factory on Moose Factory?

The James Bay region in Northern Ontario has been traditional Cree territory for thousands of years. More recently (in the 17th century, that is), the Hudson's Bay Company established Ontario's first English-speaking settlement on Moose Factory Island, just south of James Bay. Traders came to the island in 1673, which makes Moose Factory Ontario's oldest fur-trading community.

It was this fur-trading heritage that gave the island its unusual name. The "Moose" referred to the Moose River, where the island is located, but there wasn't (and still isn't) a factory on the island, at least in the modern sense of the word. In the 17th century, the chief agent at a fur-trading post was called a "factor." And the place where a factor worked was called a "factory."

Today, little of this fur-trading era remains on Moose Factory Island. On Front Street, near the Quickstop Convenience Store, is the **Hudson's Bay Staff House** that was once part of the Hudson's Bay Post. A more permanent legacy, perhaps, is the island **cemetery** (Pehdabun Rd.) where some of these early settlers were laid to rest.

where the family-friendly room, decorated with saddles and trophy fish, feels like the love child of a cowboy and a north-woods fisherman. The hearty barbecued ribs (half rack $18, full rack $24) are worth hooting over, and the menu includes ample portions of barbecue chicken, burgers, steaks, and pizza.

Getting There and Around

Cochrane is off Highway 11, 725 kilometers (450 miles) north of Toronto and 375 kilometers (235 miles) beyond North Bay. *Polar Bear Express* passengers who've arrived in Cochrane by car can leave their vehicles in the station parking lot during their journey north.

Cochrane Station (200 Railway St., 705/272-4228) is both the train station and the depot for **Ontario Northland** buses from Toronto (www.ontarionorthland.ca, 12-13 hours, one-way adults $160.75, seniors and students $136.65, ages 2-11 $80.35), a long haul via Huntsville, North Bay, and Temagami. Cochrane has no public transit, but you can easily walk around the small town.

★ *POLAR BEAR EXPRESS* TRAIN

You won't see polar bears en route (it's still too far south), nor is the Ontario Northland train particularly "express," yet this 299-kilometer (186-mile) **rail journey** (800/265-2356, www.ontarionorthland.ca, 5 hours, Sun.-Fri. July-Aug., Mon.-Fri. Sept.-June, one-way adults $59.25, seniors and students $50.40, children $29.65) gives you a fascinating glimpse of life in the north. From Cochrane, the train chugs through stands of birch and poplar toward swampier lowlands dotted with skinny, green-tufted black spruce before pulling into the predominantly Cree community of Moosonee, where you can also visit nearby Moose Factory Island, another Cree settlement.

It's not a luxury train, but there's a dome car with broader views of the surrounding terrain, a dining car, an entertainment car (where local bands often perform), and a family car, offering activities and movies to help kids pass the time. You can rent a worthwhile audio tour ($15) that provides background about the region, points out highlights of Moosonee and Moose Factory Island, and introduces you to Cree culture.

Many people take the *Polar Bear Express* from Cochrane, make a quick tour of Moosonee and Moose Factory Island, and return the same night. If you have time, though, stay at least one or two nights in the north to better experience Cree culture.

In July and August, day-trippers have almost four hours to walk around Moosonee and Moose Factory before the southbound train departs. The rest of the year, the train's tourism amenities are discontinued, and the southbound train leaves three hours after the northbound train arrives, making a day trip less feasible.

Practicalities

The **Polar Bear Express** train departs Cochrane at 9am and reaches **Moosonee Station** (705/336-2210) about five hours later. The return train leaves Moosonee at 6pm in July-August and at 5pm September-June.

Advance reservations are recommended; pay for your tickets at least three days in advance and receive a 10 percent discount. Family discounts may be available for at least one adult and one child traveling together.

Moosonee and Vicinity

If you look at a map of Northeastern Ontario, you'll notice one important thing is missing: roads. The only way to reach the remote area around James Bay, which has a predominantly First Nations population, is by rail or air.

The *Polar Bear Express* train travels to Moosonee, a town of about 3,500 near James Bay. The Moosonee area has two main settlements: the dusty frontier town of Moosonee itself on the mainland, and the island of Moose Factory in the Moose River just offshore. Local websites with information about

the region include the **Moose Cree First Nation** (www.moosecree.com) and the town of **Moosonee** (www.moosonee.ca).

Moosonee's main street is 1st Avenue, which runs from the train station to the river, where you can catch a water taxi to Moose Factory Island. Stop first at the **Railway Car Museum** (1st St., July-Aug., free), opposite the station, to check out the exhibits about the area's culture and history. Down the street is **Northern College** (1st St., 705/336-2913, www.northernc.on.ca, 8am-4pm Mon.-Fri., free), where displays of indigenous crafts, including leather and beadwork, line the hallways.

Moose Factory Island

Home to 2,700 people, Moose Factory is 4.8 kilometers (three miles) long and 3.2 kilometers (two miles) wide; the Moose Cree First Nation Reserve occupies much of the island.

The island's main attraction is the **Cree Cultural Interpretive Centre** (Pehdabun Rd., 705/658-4619, ext. 265, www.moosecree.com, 9am-5pm Sun.-Fri. July-Aug., off-season by appointment, adults $10, under age 12 $5), which has well-designed exhibits about Cree culture, language, traditional medicine, and food. Outside the building, you can peek

native script on the Railway Car Museum, Moosonee

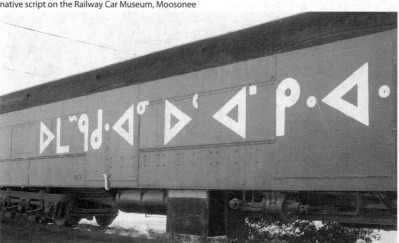

into several tepees. Located on the island's east side, the center is about a 30-minute walk from the Cree Village Ecolodge or from the town docks. The waterfront views along Pehdabun Road are lovely.

In summer, the Cree Village Ecolodge can arrange **boat trips** from Moose Factory to nearby Fossil Island and up to James Bay, 15 kilometers (nine miles) to the north, weather and tides permitting.

The whole island seems to gather at the **Moose Cree Complex** (Mookijuneibeg Dr.), part shopping mall and part community center. There's a grocery store, a pharmacy, a coffee shop, a bank, and a post office, and residents often sell homemade baked goods or crafts. The building also houses the **Moose Cree Tourism Office** (705/658-4619, ext. 265).

Accommodations and Food

Opposite the docks in Moosonee, the friendly **Polar Bear Lodge** (705/336-2345, $115 d) has 27 barebones rooms—half have one double bed, the remainder have two—and a **restaurant** (year-round) that serves three meals a day. In July and August, they run a free shuttle to and from the train station. On 1st Street are the **Northern Store** (a large

grocery), a bank, and the post office. Note the Cree script on signs around town.

It's much nicer to stay on Moose Factory Island, where the Moose Cree First Nation run the ★ **Cree Village Ecolodge** (Hospital Dr., 705/658-6400 or 888/273-3929, www.creevillage.com) on the banks of the Moose River. The 20 rustically comfortable rooms have organic cotton bedding, birch blinds, and Wi-Fi, and the staff help arrange tours. The lodge's showpiece is the dining room—the best place to eat in the area—with a soaring ceiling and a multistory wall of windows facing the water. The kitchen uses traditional First Nations ingredients in its bison chili, baked pickerel, venison, and other dishes ($17-33).

In a teepee opposite the Ecolodge, you'll often find Cree women cooking bannock—a traditional biscuit-like bread—over an open fire. Hours are irregular, so if you see the fire going, stop for a snack. For a casual meal, join the locals at the **Moose Cree Complex Coffee Shop** (Mookijuneibeg Dr., 8am-7pm Mon.-Sat., 9am-7pm Sun., $6-12) for bacon and eggs, sandwiches, and other diner-style chow.

The **Northern Store** (Moose Cree Complex, Mookijuneibeg Dr., 705/658-4552, 10am-6pm Mon.-Wed. and Sat., 10am-8pm

the Moose Cree First Nation run the Cree Village Ecolodge

Thurs.-Fri.) is a well-stocked grocery store, although prices—as in many northern towns—are significantly higher than they are down south. You can also pick up provisions at **G. G.'s Corner** (Center Rd., 705/685-4591, 11am-9pm daily) or **Quickstop Convenience** (Front St., 705/658-4086, noon-7pm daily).

Getting Around

From Moosonee's train station, it's about a 15-20-minute walk to the docks; a taxi will cost about $6. In summer, **water taxis** ($15 pp) cross the river between Moosonee and Moose Factory Island in 10-15 minutes. Boats typically wait at the docks on both the Moosonee and Moose Factory sides. The Cree Village Ecolodge has its own dock, on the opposite side of the island from the main public dock, so be sure to tell the boatman if you're heading to the lodge.

In midwinter, the river freezes solid enough to support an **ice road** between Moose Factory and the mainland; taxis and other vehicles can drive across. During the fall "freeze-up" and spring "break-up" periods, when the river is too icy for boats to cross but not solid enough for cars, the only way on and off Moose Factory Island is by helicopter.

Taxis typically meet trains arriving in Moosonee. For a cab on Moose Factory Island, call **Creeway** (705/658-5256) or **Northway** (705/658-4131).

Georgian Bay

With Caribbean-blue water, dramatic rock formations, and a network of red-and-white lighthouses standing guard along the shore, some of Ontario's most spectacular scenery surrounds Georgian Bay. If you're looking

for a getaway to the outdoors, whether for exhilarating adventure or relaxing by the water, head to this eastern finger of Lake Huron.

Measuring 320 kilometers (200 miles) long and 80 kilometers (50 miles) wide, Georgian Bay is dotted with more than 30,000 islands and some of the finest scuba diving in the north. The region has three national parks, several large provincial parks, ski slopes, and canoe routes, as well as the world's longest freshwater beach. It's a hugely popular destination for hikers, too, encompassing the northern portions of the Bruce Trail, Canada's longest hiking route.

You won't want to miss the stunning Bruce Peninsula, with its unusual rock formations, offshore islands, and network of hiking trails. Georgian Bay Islands National Park is the gateway to the 30,000 Islands region, and splurging on a floatplane tour over the water nearby is a new level of thrill. Winter

sports enthusiasts should head to the Blue Mountains, Ontario's top ski and snowboarding region; the surrounding area draws foodies, too, with numerous top-notch restaurants. If you prefer history and culture with your outdoor adventures, the towns of Midland, Penetanguishene, and Parry Sound will oblige.

Another superlative outdoor destination, Killarney Provincial Park lures paddlers and hikers to its shores studded with pink granite and its trails lined with pines. You can hike the challenging trail to The Crack for views across the hills, or simply spend a morning canoeing on a peaceful inland lake.

On Manitoulin Island, the Great Spirit Circle Trail is a leader in aboriginal tourism, offering experiences in music, dance, traditional medicine, hiking, and more that introduce visitors to First Nations culture and heritage. The world's largest freshwater island, Manitoulin has long sandy beaches,

---

Previous: Killarney Provincial Park; South Baymouth. **Above:** canoeing on Killarney's George Lake.

Look for ★ to find recommended sights, activities, dining, and lodging.

Highlights

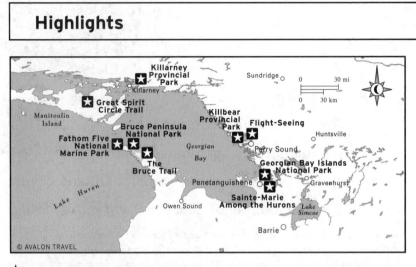

★ **Bruce Peninsula National Park:** This national park is among Ontario's most beautiful settings. Its intricate rock formations, turquoise waters, and more than 40 species of orchids draw hikers, kayakers, and other nature lovers (page 338).

★ **The Bruce Trail:** This iconic Canadian hiking route stretches 845 kilometers (525 miles) from the Niagara region to the end of the Bruce Peninsula (page 339).

★ **Fathom Five National Marine Park:** Best known for its distinctive "flowerpot" rock formations and for the shipwrecks where you can snorkel or explore by boat, this national marine conservation area also has some of the finest scuba diving in North America (page 341).

★ **Sainte-Marie Among the Hurons:** This historic village "reimagines" the first European settlement in Ontario, where French Jesuits lived and worked with the indigenous Wendat people in the 1600s (page 362).

★ **Georgian Bay Islands National Park:** Of the thousands of islands that dot Georgian

Bay, 63 are protected in this island national park. Visit for a day of hiking and swimming, or stay in a quiet cabin by the shore (page 368).

★ **Flight-Seeing:** The most thrilling way to take in Georgian Bay's 30,000 Islands is on a floatplane tour. Soar above the bay by day or take a romantic sunset flight—complete with champagne (page 372).

★ **Killbear Provincial Park:** This waterfront area near Parry Sound offers granite cliffs, sandy beaches, and a lovely destination for hiking, canoeing, swimming, and camping (page 375).

★ **Killarney Provincial Park:** Escape to the wilderness of this vast and dramatic park, with its rugged white dolomite ridges, pink granite cliffs, pine forests, and crystal-clear lakes (page 377).

★ **Great Spirit Circle Trail:** Explore aboriginal culture on Manitoulin Island, the world's largest freshwater island. Take a guided "Mother Earth" nature hike or a workshop on traditional dance, drumming, or food, and stay on a First Nations reserve (page 382).

Georgian Bay

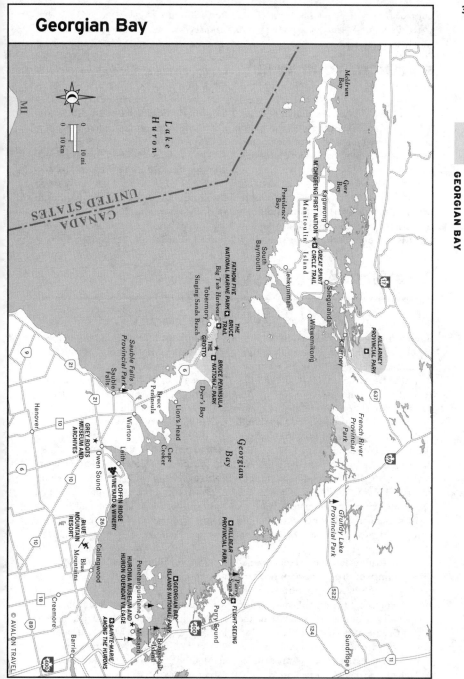

© AVALON TRAVEL

quiet roads for cycling, and—like much of this waterside region—plenty of spots to sit and simply enjoy the bay.

PLANNING YOUR TIME

Many attractions and services around Georgian Bay don't begin operation until mid- or late May and close in mid-October, after the Canadian Thanksgiving weekend. One exception is the Blue Mountains, which draws winter visitors for skiing and snowboarding.

For a long weekend, do a quick tour of the **Bruce Peninsula,** ski or snowboard at **Blue Mountain,** pair a visit to **Midland**'s historic sights with a day trip to **Georgian Bay Islands National Park,** or base yourself in

Parry Sound and explore the nearby provincial parks. You can easily spend 4-5 days on the Bruce Peninsula, particularly if you want to hike sections of the Bruce Trail and snorkel or scuba-dive in the **Fathom Five National Marine Park.**

An excellent way to explore the region is by following the **Georgian Bay Coastal Route,** a complete loop around the bay. From May to October you can take a ferry between the Bruce Peninsula and **Manitoulin Island,** then continue to **Killarney Provincial Park,** the Georgian Bay Islands, Midland, **Wasaga Beach,** and the Blue Mountains. Although you could cover most of this route in a week, you'll have more time for outdoor activities if you can spend at least 10 days.

The Bruce Peninsula

With limestone cliffs, crystal blue waters, forested hiking trails, and even a wide variety of orchids, the Bruce Peninsula's striking natural scenery is the main reason to visit this finger of land that juts out between Lake Huron and Georgian Bay. The must-see attractions are its two national parks—Bruce Peninsula National Park and Fathom Five National Marine Park—at the peninsula's north end, around the town of Tobermory. Yet beyond these natural attractions, it's the friendly, low-key atmosphere that draws vacationers. Though the region attracts plenty of visitors, it hasn't lost its small-town warmth, with people greeting each other on the street and on the trail.

For pre-trip research, check out the detailed **County of Bruce Tourism website** (www.explorethebruce.com), with extensive information about the Bruce Peninsula and surrounding communities. Also pick up the useful **Grey-Bruce Official Visitor Map** (www.explorethebruce.com) at information centers around the region; it shows both major and minor roads across the peninsula.

TOBERMORY

To explore Bruce Peninsula National Park and the Fathom Five National Marine Park, it's most convenient to base yourself in Tobermory, a pretty waterfront town at the northern tip of the Bruce Peninsula. Highway 6, the peninsula's main north-south road, ends in Tobermory.

National Park Visitors Centre

Start your visit at the **National Park Visitors Centre** (120 Chi Sin Tib Dek Rd., 519/596-2233, www.pc.gc.ca, 9am-5pm Sun.-Mon. and Thurs.-Fri., 8am-5pm Sat. mid-May-late June, 8am-8pm daily late June-early Sept., 9am-5pm Thurs.-Mon. early Sept.-mid-Oct., national park admission fee adults $5.80, seniors $4.90, children $2.90, families $14.70, for information about both Bruce Peninsula National Park and Fathom Five National Marine Park. Watch a short film about the area's highlights and explore exhibits about local ecology. Then climb the 112 steps up the 20-meter (65-foot) **Lookout Tower** for views across the peninsula and the nearby islands.

In summer, park staff offer a variety of

The Bruce Peninsula

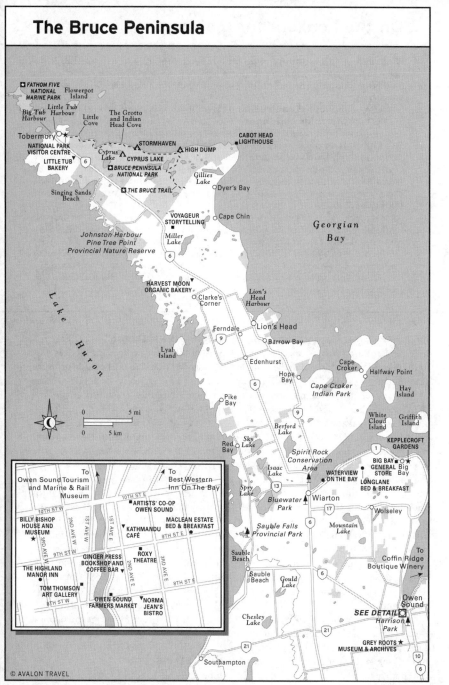

FATHOM FIVE NATIONAL MARINE PARK
Flowerpot Island
Big Tub Harbour
Little Tub Harbour
Little Cove
The Grotto and Indian Head Cove
CABOT HEAD LIGHTHOUSE
Tobermory
NATIONAL PARK VISITOR CENTRE
LITTLE TUB BAKERY
Cyprus Lake
STORMHAVEN
CYPRUS LAKE
HIGH DUMP
BRUCE PENINSULA NATIONAL PARK
Gillies Lake
THE BRUCE TRAIL
Dyer's Bay
Singing Sands Beach
VOYAGEUR STORYTELLING
Cape Chin
Georgian Bay
Johnston Harbour Pine Tree Point Provincial Nature Reserve
Miller Lake
HARVEST MOON ORGANIC BAKERY
Clarke's Corner
Lion's Head Harbour
Lake Huron
Ferndale
Lion's Head
Barrow Bay
Lyal Island
Edenhurst
Cape Croker
Halfway Point
Hope Bay
Cape Croker Indian Park
Hay Island
Pike Bay
White Cloud Island
Griffith Island
Red Bay
Sky Lake
Berford Lake
Spirit Rock Conservation Area
KEPPLECROFT GARDENS
Isaac Lake
BIG BAY GENERAL STORE
Big Bay
Spry Lake
WATERVIEW ON THE BAY
LONGLANE BED & BREAKFAST
Bluewater Park
Wiarton
Wolseley
Sauble Falls Provincial Park
Mountain Lake
Sauble Beach
To Coffin Ridge Boutique Winery
Sauble Beach
Gould Lake
Owen Sound
SEE DETAIL
Harrison Park
Chesley Lake
GREY ROOTS MUSEUM & ARCHIVES
Southampton

0 5 mi
0 5 km

Owen Sound detail

To Owen Sound Tourism and Marine & Rail Museum
To Best Western Inn On The Bay
10TH ST E
ARTISTS' CO-OP OWEN SOUND
10TH ST W
MACLEAN ESTATE BED & BREAKFAST
BILLY BISHOP HOUSE AND MUSEUM
2ND AVE W
1ST AVE W
1ST AVE E
KATHMANDU CAFÉ
9TH ST E
9TH ST W
3RD AVE W
GINGER PRESS BOOKSHOP AND COFFEE BAR
ROXY THEATRE
3RD AVE E
THE HIGHLAND MANOR INN
8TH ST E
TOM THOMSON ART GALLERY
2ND AVE E
8TH ST W
OWEN SOUND FARMERS MARKET
NORMA JEAN'S BISTRO

© AVALON TRAVEL

On the Lookout for Lighthouses

What is it about lighthouses that draw people like a beacon? If you're a lighthouse lover, the Lake Huron and Georgian Bay coasts are prime territory for lighthouse touring. Many of the region's lighthouses were built in the mid- to late 1800s or early 1900s during the heyday of Great Lakes shipping.

On Lake Huron, visit the **Chantry Island Light** (www.chantryisland.com) near Southampton and the **Kincardine Lighthouse** (www.sunsets.com), a lighthouse-turned-museum near Kincardine's downtown. The Bruce Peninsula has several lighthouses, including the **Big Tub Lighthouse** in Tobermory, the **Cabot Head Lighthouse and Museum** (www.cabothead.ca), the **Lion's Head Lighthouse** on Lion's Head Beach, and the **Cape Croker Lighthouse** at the tip of Cape Crocker, a First Nations reserve. On Flowerpot Island in the Fathom Five National Marine Park, you can visit the **Flowerpot Island Light Station.** One of the most picturesque light stations is the **Killarney East Lighthouse,** on the bay near Killarney Provincial Park.

Today the lonely job of lighthouse keeper has generally gone the way of the dodo bird, as most lighthouse operations are automated. For a glimpse of old-fashioned lighthouse-keeping life, book a stay at **Cabot Head Lighthouse,** where you can spend a week as part of the assistant light keeper's program (late May-mid-Oct.). It's a working holiday where you help greet visitors to the lighthouse, assist in the gift shop, and pitch in with some housekeeping duties. For reservations or more information, complete the form on the **Friends of Cabot Head** website (www.cabothead.ca). The lighthouse stays are quite popular, so make plans well in advance.

---

interpretive programs, including guided hikes and children's activities. If you plan to camp on Flowerpot Island in the Fathom Five Marine Park, or to scuba-dive in any of the park territory, you must register at the Visitors Centre before heading out. The Visitors Centre is the northernmost point on the Bruce Trail. Check out the "sculpture" made from hikers' worn boots in the lobby and the **Bruce Trail Cairn** marking the end of the Bruce Trail. If you've hiked the entire trail, this is the spot to take your photo. Two hiking trails start at the center. It's an easy 800-meter (0.5-mile) walk to the **Little Dunks Bay Lookout.** The 4.8-kilometer (three-mile) **Burnt Point Loop Trail** meanders through the forest (with some rough, rocky patches) to Georgian Bay, where you can look out over the Fathom Five islands.

The Visitors Centre is a 10-minute walk from Tobermory's Little Tub Harbour along a flat, partly paved section of the Bruce Trail. By car, look for the park sign on Highway 6, just south of town.

Little Tub Harbour

Most of Tobermory's shops and services cluster around Little Tub Harbour. Boats to the Fathom Five islands leave from Little Tub, as do sightseeing cruises around Tobermory and the Fathom Five islands.

The two-hour Great Blue Heron glass bottom boat tour, run by **Blue Heron Tours** (519/596-2999, www.blueheronco.com, late June-early Sept., adults $36, seniors $34, ages 6-16 $27) on a 125-passenger ferry, sails to Big Tub Harbour, where you can see two 19th-century shipwrecks close to the surface, and continues around Russel Island, Cove Island, the Otter Islands, and Flowerpot Island. Another option, for the same price, is a two-hour sunset cruise (May-mid-Oct.). **Bruce Anchor Cruises** (519/596-2555 or 800/591-4254, www.bruceanchorcruises.com, adults $28, seniors $26, ages 6-16 $19) also offers two-hour tours that follow a similar route aboard a 47-passenger glass-bottom Zodiac.

Big Tub Harbour

Tobermory has a second port area, known as

Big Tub Harbour. The first lighthouse at Big Tub was constructed in 1885 to guide ships safely into port. The present-day **Big Tub Lighthouse,** a hexagonal tower that was automated in 1952, still performs that role at the harbor's mouth. The lighthouse isn't open to the public, but you can walk around the exterior and along the rocky shore. You can also swim or snorkel here.

The remains of two 19th-century ships lie in the shallow water of Big Tub Harbour. The *Sweepstakes,* a two-masted schooner, ran aground near Cove Island Lighthouse in 1885; the boat was towed to Big Tub Harbour, where it sank. The steamer *City of Grand Rapids* caught fire in 1907 while docked in Little Tub Harbour. The boat was towed out of the harbor to prevent the fire from spreading to other nearby ships; the burning ship then drifted into Big Tub Harbour and sank there.

You can see the shipwrecks on one of the boat tours out of Tobermory or on several of the Flowerpot Island boats. Snorkeling and scuba diving are allowed around the wrecks, but only at designated times, since boat traffic in the area can be heavy. Check with the **National Park Visitors Centre** (519/596-2233, www.pc.gc.ca) for details.

Entertainment and Shopping

Looking for a unique way to spend an evening? Storytellers and gregarious hosts Leslie Robbins-Conway and Paul Conway welcome visitors to their country home near Tobermory for **Voyageur Storytelling: Country Supper Storytelling Concerts** (56 Brinkman's Rd., Miller Lake, 519/795-7477, www.voyageurstorytelling.ca, 6pm-10:15pm Tues., Thurs., and Sat. mid-June-early Sept.; adults $46, seniors and students $42, children $36), pairing a multi-course home-cooked meal with a storytelling performance. Expect stories, poems, music, interesting conversation, and good fun.

At the annual **Orchid Festival** (www.orchidfest.ca, late May), you can join guided orchid-viewing walks, take flower drawing or photography workshops, or learn more about the peninsula's orchid population. Check the website for a schedule, or stop into festival headquarters at **National Park Visitors Centre** (120 Chi Sin Tib Dek Rd., Tobermory, 519/596-2233).

Most of the shops around Little Tub Harbour sell T-shirts and other ordinary souvenirs. One exception is **Circle Arts** (14 Bay St., 519/596-2541, www.circlearts.com, 10am-5:30pm daily mid-May-mid-Oct.), a fine-art

Big Tub Lighthouse, Tobermory

gallery showcasing prints, paintings, sculpture, photographs, jewelry, textiles, one-of-a-kind furniture, and other works crafted by Canadian artists, many of whom have ties to the Bruce Peninsula. You might find anything from a $15 ceramic candleholder to a $20,000 painting.

Accommodations

Motels and B&Bs cluster around, or within walking distance of, Little Tub Harbour. Other accommodations dot Highway 6 south of town; if you don't want to take your car everywhere, try to stay near the harbor. In July and August and on holiday weekends, even basic motel rooms go for over $100; it's a good idea to book in advance, or at least arrive early in the day. The **Tobermory Chamber of Commerce** website (www.tobermory.com) lists local accommodations with last-minute availability.

Inside this nondescript vinyl-sided house about a 15-minute walk from Little Tub Harbour is the surprisingly stylish **Molinari's B&B** (68 Harpur Dr., 877/596-1228, www.themolinaris.com, $125 d). Owners Maria and Bob, who relocated from Montreal after falling in love with the Bruce Peninsula during scuba-diving visits, decorated the three contemporary guest rooms in richly hued textiles and outfitted then with microwaves, fridges, coffeemakers, and small flat-screen TVs. Guests take breakfast in the sleek industrial kitchen; there's no other common space, though, so it's not a sit-around-and-chat kind of lodging.

The friendly **Blue Bay Motel** (32 Bay St., 519/596-2392, www.bluebay-motel.com, May-mid-Oct., $110-160 d), right above Little Tub Harbour, has 16 basic but comfortable rooms with fridges, coffeemakers, and updated linens; the best are the second-floor units with water views (the first-floor rooms face the parking lot). There's also a large three-bedroom suite with a full kitchen. You can borrow one of the motel bicycles to tool around the area.

The **Maple Golf Inn** (22 Maple Golf Crescent, 519/596-8166, www.maplegolfinn.ca, from $125 d, $200 suite), in a suburban home looking onto the Cornerstone Golf Club, is popular with hikers, since there's an access point to the Bruce Trail nearby. Hosts Jill and Lawrence Stewart serve a full breakfast to guests who stay in two comfortable main-floor rooms decorated in a modern country style, with quilts, wood floors, and private baths. Downstairs, a family-friendly basement suite, which sleeps up to five, has two bedrooms and a separate living room.

Looking for a true getaway? At ★ **E'Terra** (www.eterra.ca, $800-1,075 d), a sumptuous wood and stone manor hidden in the woods, the owners won't divulge the address until you make a reservation. Four of the six guest rooms are two-story suites, and all have French linens and heated flagstone floors. Guests can unwind in the spacious living room or in the cozy third-floor library and take a sauna or a dip in the saltwater pool. You could drive to Tobermory in just a few minutes, but why would you want to leave?

Food

Most of Tobermory's dining options are in or near Little Tub Harbour or along Highway 6. In a little house just south of town, **Little Tub Bakery** (4 Warner Bay Rd., at Hwy. 6, 519/596-8399, 9am-6pm Mon.-Fri. summer, call for off-season hours) is justifiably famous for their gooey butter tarts. The cinnamon rolls and freshly baked pies are also delicious. You can pick up a sandwich or homemade pizza for a picnic.

Surprised to find a vegetarian-friendly eatery on a golf course? **Ancient Cedars Café** (Cornerstone Golf Club, 7178 Hwy. 6, 519/596-8626, www.ancientcedarscafe.com, 9am-9pm Tues.-Sat. and 9am-4pm Sun.-Mon. summer, call for off-season hours, $8-12) does dish out burgers and steak sandwiches made from locally raised beef, but the menu also features vegan *bulgogi,* a barbecue seitan sandwich, and a tasty sweet potato and black bean burrito.

The owners of Molinari's B&B

operate **Molinari's Espresso Bar and Italian Restaurant** (53 Bay St., 519/596-1228, www.themolinaris.com, May-Oct.), cooking up breakfast, lunch, and dinner, including Italian sandwiches, salads, and pastas.

Several places in Tobermory serve fish-and-chips, but you can't miss the bright blue and yellow facade of **The Fish and Chip Place** (24 Bay St. S., 519/596-8380, www.thefishandchipplace.com, lunch and dinner daily late May-mid-Oct., call for seasonal hours, $7-12). The small menu includes the eponymous whitefish and french fries; their fish taco won't put any Baja joints out of business, but this far north of the border, it will do. On a sunny afternoon, particularly if you've been hiking, a beer on the deck is a perfect reward.

Information and Services

The **Tobermory Chamber of Commerce Information Centre** (Hwy. 6, just south of Little Tub Harbour, 519/596-2452, www.tobermory.com) can provide maps and information about attractions, lodging, and services. You can also park your car here for the day at no charge. **County of Bruce Tourism** (www.explorethebruce.com) has extensive information about Tobermory and the rest of the Bruce Peninsula.

The **Foodland Market** (9 Bay St., 519/596-2380, 7am-9pm daily) at Little Tub Harbour stocks basic supplies for picnics or camping and also has a coin laundry.

Getting There
Car

Tobermory is approximately 300 kilometers (186 miles) northwest of Toronto, about a four-hour drive, weather and traffic permitting. Parking around Little Tub Harbour is restricted to two hours. If you're planning a longer stay in town, or heading out on a boat tour, leave your car in one of the free long-term parking lots. There's one at the Tobermory Chamber of Commerce Information Centre on Highway 6, two smaller lots on Head Street (between the Information Centre and Little Tub Harbour), and another on Legion Street, west of Highway 6.

Bus

Without a car, the most convenient way to travel from Toronto to Tobermory, Bruce Peninsula National Park, or other points on the peninsula is on the **Parkbus** (800/928-7101, www.parkbus.ca, one-way adults $60, seniors and students $54, ages 2-12 $30, round-trip adults $86, seniors and students

freshly baked tarts from Little Tub Bakery

$77, ages 2-12 $43), which operates on selected weekends. The bus departs from several points in Toronto, including 30 Carlton Street (between Yonge St. and Church St., subway: College), and Dufferin Street at Bloor Street West (subway: Dufferin). On the Bruce Peninsula, the Parkbus drops off and picks up at stops in Wiarton, Lion's Head, the National Park's Cypress Lake campground, and Tobermory; check the website for details.

If you can't arrange your schedule to ride the Parkbus, the other bus option is to connect through Owen Sound. **Greyhound** (800/661-8747, www.greyhound.ca) can get you to Owen Sound from Toronto and points farther afield. From Owen Sound to Tobermory, **First Student Canada bus service** (2180 20th St. E., Owen Sound, 519/376-5712, www.tobermory.com, one-way adults $34, seniors and ages 4-12 $32) runs one bus a day in each direction Friday-Sunday and holiday Mondays July through early September. The schedule is timed to connect with the Manitoulin Island ferry.

Ferry
The **MS *Chi-Cheemaun* Ferry** (information 519/376-6601, reservations 800/265-3163, www.ontarioferries.com, mid-May-mid-Oct.), nicknamed "The Big Canoe," runs between Tobermory and South Baymouth on Manitoulin Island. The crossing takes about two hours, and the ship accommodates 638 passengers and 143 cars. The ferry cuts out several hours of driving time compared to the road route between Southern Ontario and Manitoulin. Reservations are advised, particularly if you're taking a car. The **Tobermory ferry terminal** is at 8 Eliza Street (519/596-2510).

Getting Around
Without a car, you can easily walk around Tobermory or to the National Park Visitors Centre, catch a boat to Flowerpot Island, and take other short hikes in the area. Some hotel or B&B owners will drop you at the trailhead for a day hike, so inquire when making

exploring The Grotto at Bruce Peninsula National Park

lodging reservations. **Thorncrest Outfitters** (7441 Hwy. 6, 519/596-8908, www.thorncrest-outfitters.com) runs a shuttle service for hikers or paddlers (they'll also transport your canoe or kayak) between Tobermory and Cyprus Lake, Dyer's Bay, or Lion's Head.

★ BRUCE PENINSULA NATIONAL PARK
Intricate rock formations. Caribbean-blue water. Centuries-old trees. Inland lakes. More than three dozen types of orchids. **Bruce Peninsula National Park** (www.pc.gc.ca, open year-round, $11.70 per vehicle), which encompasses 156 square kilometers (60 square miles) spread over several parcels of land, protects these natural features that are unique in Ontario. The park is at the northern tip of the Bruce Peninsula near the town of Tobermory.

The Grotto and Indian Head Cove
The park's most visited sights are the Grotto, a waterside cave, and the adjacent Indian

Head Cove, and with good reason. Through centuries of erosion, the waters of Georgian Bay have sculpted the area's soft limestone cliffs, leaving dramatic overhangs, carved rocks, and underwater caves, such as the Grotto. At Indian Head Cove, the rocks are sculpted into pillars, narrower at the bottom and wider at the top, resembling smaller versions of the "flowerpots" in the Fathom Five National Marine Park. Particularly on bright sunny days, the contrast between the brilliant blue-green bay, the polished white rocks along the shoreline, and the layered rock cliffs is striking.

You can climb down to sea level to explore the cave-like Grotto, but even if scrambling down steep rocks isn't your thing, you can still view the Grotto from above. At Indian Head Cove, the rock formations are on the pebbly beach, so no climbing is required. You can swim in Georgian Bay, although the water is cold year-round.

It's a moderate hike to the Grotto from the day-use parking area near the **Cyprus Lake Park Office** (Cyprus Lake Rd., off Hwy. 6, 519/596-2263), where several trails lead to Georgian Bay. Once at the shore, head north along the rocky shore to Indian Head Cove and then to the Grotto. Allow about 30-45 minutes to walk each way from the parking area. You must stop at the park office to pay a day-use parking fee ($11.70 per car) before you set out. There are restrooms at the Cyprus Lake office and near the Grotto, but no other services, so bring whatever food and water you need.

Cyprus Lake

From the Cyprus Lake day-use parking area (Cyprus Lake Rd., off Hwy. 6), you can walk down to the lake in just a few minutes. There's a sandy beach with somewhat warmer water than in chilly Georgian Bay, as well as picnic tables. The **Cyprus Lake Trail** follows the lakeshore. A mostly flat, 5.2-kilometer (3.2-mile) loop trail, it's a popular spot for bird-watching. Paddlers looking for a calm body of water to canoe or kayak can head out into Cyprus Lake. In winter, you can snowshoe along Cyprus Lake and on to the Grotto. Park at the Cyprus Lake main gate, then follow the Cyprus Lake Trail to the Georgian Bay Trail.

There are no boat rentals at the lake, but in Tobermory, **Thorncrest Outfitters** (7441 Hwy. 6, 519/596-8908, www.thorncrestoutfitters.com) rents canoes and kayaks and can transport them to the lake. They also offer a number of full- and half-day guided paddling trips at various locations on the northern Bruce Peninsula.

★ The Bruce Trail

Serious hikers often plan their holidays to hike the **Bruce Trail** (www.brucetrail.org), doing sections of this 845-kilometer (525-mile) route in two-day, three-day, or weeklong increments. They return to the trail until they've completed the entire route from the Niagara region to Tobermory. Yet you don't have to be an indomitable whole-trail hiker to enjoy the Bruce Trail. You can easily take day hikes along the trail, in and around Bruce Peninsula National Park.

From the Grotto, the Bruce Trail extends along Georgian Bay in both directions. If you continue to the west, you can hike all the way to Tobermory (18 kilometers, 11 miles). Between the Grotto and Little Cove (12.6 kilometers, 7.8 miles), the trail is quite difficult, with very rocky terrain, but you're rewarded with sweeping views of Georgian Bay. From Little Cove to Tobermory (5.4 kilometers, 3.4 miles), the trail flattens out and wends through the cedar forest.

Heading east from the Grotto along the bay, the Bruce Trail hugs the shore to Stormhaven (2.4 kilometers, 1.5 miles), where there's a primitive camping area and restroom. The trail then gets more difficult for the next 9.5 kilometers (six miles) to the High Dump camping area.

Because many sections of the Bruce Trail are quite rugged, get details about your route before you set out. The staff at the Cyprus Lake Park Office or the National Park Visitors

The Bruce Trail

One of Canada's iconic outdoor experiences is a hike along Ontario's Bruce Trail, an 845-kilometer (525-mile) hiking route that extends from the Niagara region to the tip of the Bruce Peninsula. How long does it take to complete the whole trail? If you hiked eight hours a day, covering about 30 kilometers (19 miles), it would take you roughly a month to hike end to end. However, unless you're an experienced hiker, this pace will likely be much too fast. And while some hikers do the entire trail straight through, far more end-to-end hikers complete the trail in a series of shorter excursions over several months or years.

The Bruce Trail runs from the Niagara region to the Bruce Peninsula.

Some sections of the trail are flat and easy, while others are quite rugged—get information about your route before you set out. A good source of trail information is the **Bruce Trail Conservatory** (905/529-6821 or 800/665-4453, www.brucetrail.org), a nonprofit committed to protecting and promoting the trail. They have a free online overview map, and you can download detailed maps of individual trail sections ($3 per map). If you're serious about hiking the entire trail, consider purchasing the **Bruce Trail Reference** ($37), available on the conservatory website or through Canadian bookseller Chapters/Indigo (www.chapters.indigo.ca). Many Canadian libraries stock the guide, too. It's updated regularly—and there are changes and additions to the trail—so check for the most recent edition.

If you'd like to find hiking companions or join in group hikes, check out one of the nine Bruce Trail clubs, which help maintain the trail and arrange group activities in different regions. The **Peninsula Bruce Trail Club** (www.pbtc.ca) organizes hikes throughout the year on the Bruce Peninsula and publishes guides to peninsula day hikes. You can get a list of all the trail clubs from the Bruce Trail Conservatory website. The Bruce Trail Conservatory website includes a list of campgrounds that are accessible to the trail, as well as B&Bs and inns that welcome trail hikers. Many innkeepers whose lodgings are close to the trail will pick up or drop off hikers at nearby trailheads.

Another option for hikers who don't want to camp or lug gear is the **Home-to-Home B&B Network** (888/301-3224, www.hometohomenetwork.ca). Stay at any lodgings in this network of B&Bs, located between Wiarton and Tobermory, and hike to your next destination. The B&B owners will move your luggage to your next lodging. In the morning, you'll have a hot breakfast before beginning the day's hike. Reservations are required at least two weeks in advance.

Centre can help match a hike to your ability level.

Singing Sands Beach

On the west side of the peninsula, Singing Sands Beach (Dorcas Bay Rd.) looks like it's part of a completely different natural environment than the rocky eastern shores—and it is. The flat, sandy beach spreads out around Dorcas Bay with vistas out across Lake Huron; it's a popular swimming spot. A short boardwalk trail loops around an adjacent marsh, and the three-kilometer (1.9-mile) **Forest Beach Loop Trail** is another easy walk that's good for bird-watching.

Camping

Within Bruce Peninsula National Park, **Cyprus Lake Campground** (Cyprus Lake Rd., mid-Apr.-mid-Oct. $23.40, mid-Oct.-Apr.

$15.70) has 232 drive-in campsites in three camping areas. All border Cyprus Lake and have restroom facilities with flush toilets and cold-water taps, but no showers. No electrical or sewer hookups are available. There are showers at Little Tub Harbour in Tobermory, about 15 kilometers (nine miles) north of Cyprus Lake. Ten furnished **yurts** (May-mid-Oct., $120), with outdoor propane barbecues, are available at Cyprus Lake. A central heated washroom with flush toilets and showers is located a short walk from the yurts. Between May and mid-October, you can reserve campsites and yurts through the Parks Canada Campground Reservation Service (877/737-3783, www.pccamping.ca). Reservations are advised, particularly during July and August. From mid-October to April, campsites are first-come, first-served.

Also in the park are two primitive backcountry campgrounds ($9.80 pp): **Stormhaven** and **High Dump.** Stormhaven is 2.4 kilometers (1.5 miles) east of the Grotto along Georgian Bay. High Dump is 9.5 kilometers (six miles) east of Stormhaven, or eight kilometers (five miles) from the parking area at Crane Lake (from Hwy. 6, take Dyer's Bay Rd. east to Crane Lake Rd.). To reach either area, you need to backpack in along the Bruce Trail. You must register at the Cyprus Lake Park Office (Cyprus Lake Rd., off Hwy. 6) before heading out. Between May and October, register by phone (519/596-2263) or in person at the office; the rest of the year, register at the self-service kiosk outside the office.

Stormhaven and High Dump each have nine sites with tent platforms and a composting toilet. No water is available, so bring your own or purify the water from the bay. Outside the park, the closest accommodations are in Tobermory.

Information and Services

For general information about Bruce Peninsula National Park, phone or visit the **National Park Visitors Centre** (120 Chi Sin Tib Dek Rd., Tobermory, 519/596-2233, www.pc.gc.ca). Between May and October, you can also contact the **Cyprus Lake Park Office** (Cyprus Lake Rd., off Hwy. 6, 519/596-2263).

★ FATHOM FIVE NATIONAL MARINE PARK

One of three national marine conservation areas in Canada, **Fathom Five National Marine Park** (519/596-2233, www.pc.gc.ca) includes 22 islands in Georgian Bay off the northern end of the Bruce Peninsula. Formed over 400 million years ago, these rocky islands are composed primarily of dolomite, a type of limestone. The main attractions for visitors are the distinctive rock formations known as "flowerpots." Narrow at the bottom and wider at the top, these rock stacks resemble massive stone pots. While the waves have slowly worn away the softer limestone on the pillars' lower end, the harder dolomite tops have survived, creating the unusual shape. Access to the park is by boat from the town of Tobermory.

More than 20 shipwrecks lie within the park's territory, making it a popular destination for scuba divers. In fact, the park gets its name from William Shakespeare's play *The Tempest*, in which the following lines describe the father of Ferdinand, who is feared dead in a shipwreck:

Full fathom five thy father lies;
Of his bones are coral made;
Those are pearls that were his eyes:
Nothing of him that doth fade
But doth suffer a sea-change
Into something rich and strange.
Sea-nymphs hourly ring his knell
Hark! now I hear them, ding-dong, bell.

A fathom is a unit of measure roughly equal to 1.8 meters (six feet), so "fathom five" is nine meters, or about 30 feet—a long way down!

Scuba Diving and Snorkeling

While you might not think of such a northern location as a prime scuba destination, Fathom Five has some of the world's best freshwater diving. Not only is the water generally clear, but the combination of underwater cliffs, caves, and other geological formations, along with the more than 20 shipwrecks in the area, give divers plenty to explore.

All divers must register in person in Tobermory at the **National Park Visitors Centre** (120 Chi Sin Tib Dek Rd., 519/596-2233, www.pc.gc.ca, national park admission fee adults $5.80, seniors $4.90, children $2.90). The park charges divers a daily fee of $4.90 pp in addition to the park admission fee and the cost of boat transportation. If you're planning to dive at least four days, buy an annual divers' pass ($19.60).

Several companies in Tobermory run single-day and multiday dive trips to the Fathom Five islands and surrounding areas. They also offer scuba lessons and gear rentals. Contact **Divers Den** (3 Bay St., 519/596-2363, www.diversden.ca), **G+S Watersports** (8 Bay St. S., 519/596-2200, www.gswatersports.net), or **Tobermory Aquasports** (7037 Hwy. 6, 519/596-8474, www.tobermoryaquasports.com). While not all the shipwrecks are visible to snorkelers, some are, and you'll see them much more clearly than you would from a glass-bottom boat. Divers Den offers two-hour (adults $52, kids $28, families $135)

and four-hour (adults $64, kids $32, families $72) snorkeling tours; they provide guidance, snorkeling gear, and the thick warm wetsuits you'll need to swim in the chilly water. G+S Watersports runs similar snorkeling excursions.

Flowerpot Island

Unless you have your own boat, only one of the park's 22 islands is accessible to visitors: Flowerpot Island, named for the two towering rock pillars known as the "flowerpots." These rock stacks sit waterside on the island's eastern shore.

Tour boats from Tobermory dock at Beachy Cove on the east side of Flowerpot Island. The island isn't large, at about two square kilometers (0.77 square miles), so it's only about a 15-minute walk from Beachy Cove to the first **small flowerpot,** which is seven meters (23 feet) high, and a few minutes farther to the **large flowerpot,** which stands 12 meters (40 feet) high. From the flowerpots, you can follow the **Loop Trail,** passing a small cave. The path up to the cave is easy to miss; it's on the left just beyond the flowerpots. You can't go inside the cave, but you can peer into the entrance.

Beyond the cave, the Loop Trail continues

snorkeling for shipwrecks off the Bruce Peninsula

to the **Flowerpot Island Light Station** on the island's northeast tip. The first lighthouse on the island went into service in 1897; in the 1960s, the original light was replaced with a steel lighthouse tower that's still flashing its beacon today. You can walk out to the tower and to an adjacent observation deck with a view across Georgian Bay. Near the light station is the light keeper's house, which contains a small museum (July-Aug.).

To return to Beachy Cove from the lighthouse, either backtrack along the trail past the flowerpots or continue on the Loop Trail up and over the bluffs in the middle of the island. This latter section of the Loop Trail is more rugged; park staff advise allowing at least an extra hour to return via this route.

If you can tolerate cold water (or wear a wetsuit), you can swim or snorkel off Flowerpot Island. The beaches are rocky, so wear protective footwear. The best swimming spots are near Beachy Cove or around the flowerpots. In either location, be alert for boat traffic.

Camping

Camping is your only option if you want to spend the night on Flowerpot Island. The park accepts **camping reservations** (519/596-2233, ext. 221) each year beginning in early May. The **Flowerpot Island Campground** ($9.80 pp) has six basic tent sites, all a stone's throw from the shore and a 5- to 10-minute walk from the Beachy Cove boat dock. There's a composting toilet nearby but no showers or running water. Bring your own water or purify the bay water for drinking. No supplies are available on the island. Parks Canada cautions that campers should bring enough food, water, and warm clothing to last extra days, since boat service back to the mainland can be canceled if the weather turns bad.

Information and Services

Park staff are frequently on duty at Flowerpot Island's Beachy Cove during the summer. Otherwise, get information at the **National Park Visitors Centre** (120 Chi Sin Tib Dek Rd., 519/596-2233, www.pc.gc.ca, 9am-5pm Sun.-Mon. and Thurs.-Fri., 8am-5pm Sat. mid-May-late June, 8am-8pm daily late June-early Sept., 9am-5pm Thurs.-Mon. early Sept.-mid-Oct.) before you leave Tobermory.

A small volunteer-run snack bar near the lighthouse is open during the summer, but hours are erratic. There are restrooms at Beachy Cove between the ferry dock and the campground, and near the lighthouse. It's almost worth hiking to the light station just to use the **Loo with a View,** with its vistas across the bay.

Getting There

The national park does not run its own boats; instead, it works with two private companies that offer boat trips to Flowerpot Island from mid-May to mid-October. Sailing schedules vary seasonally, so check their websites or phone for details. Also confirm when the last boats leave Flowerpot Island to return to the mainland, and get back to the dock at Beachy Cove in plenty of time. You don't want an unexpected overnight stay!

Both **Blue Heron Tours** (Little Tub Harbour, 519/596-2999, www.blueheronco.com) and **Bruce Anchor Cruises** (519/596-2555 or 800/591-4254, www.bruceanchorcruises.com) run boats from Little Tub Harbour to Beachy Cove and offer these island shuttles combined with shipwreck-viewing tours. If you just want to get to Flowerpot Island, Blue Heron's jet boat (round-trip adults $34, seniors $32, ages 6-16 $25) shuttles you between Little Tub Harbour and Beachy Cove in 15 minutes. For a few dollars more, you can add a brief ride through Big Tub Harbour to look at the remains of two shipwrecks on the 25-minute island shuttle and shipwrecks tour (round-trip adults $40, seniors $37, ages 6-16 $30). You don't see much—the wrecks look like shadows under the water—but it's as close as you can get to the sunken ships without snorkeling or scuba diving. You can see the shipwrecks more clearly on the glass bottom boat tour (adults $40, seniors $37, ages 6-16 $30) en route to

Flowerpot Island. Bruce Anchor Cruises can also take you to Flowerpot Island with stops to view the shipwrecks (adults $37, seniors $35, ages 6-16 $29). They operate different boats with varying schedules, so check to see what's most convenient for you.

You must pay the national park admission fee (adults $5.80, seniors $4.90, children $2.90) in addition to the price for the boat trips. Park admission includes access to Flowerpot Island and to the National Park Visitors Centre in Tobermory.

DYER'S BAY

Unlike many of the Bruce Peninsula's lighthouses, which you can see only from the exterior, at the **Cabot Head Lighthouse** (806 Cabot Head Rd., Miller Lake, 519/795-7780, www.cabothead.ca, 10am-7pm daily late May-mid-Oct., donation $3), you can venture inside. The lower levels of the red-and-white wooden structure are a museum with exhibits about local marine history. Climb up to the observation tower for a light keeper's view out across the bay. The original Cabot Head Lighthouse began operation in 1896. It remained in use until 1968, when it was torn down and replaced with the current light, which is an automated beacon. The lighthouse

is about 40 kilometers (25 miles) southeast of Tobermory, about a 45-minute drive. From Highway 6, go east on Dyer's Bay Road.

LION'S HEAD

Lion's Head is a friendly little village on Georgian Bay in the approximate north-south midpoint of the Bruce Peninsula. You can stroll or swim at the beach, browse the village shops, or have a beer in the local pub. With its central location, Lion's Head is a convenient base for exploring the peninsula, particularly if you want to visit sights beyond the Tobermory area.

Set on the bay at the mouth of Lion's Head harbor, **Lion's Head Lighthouse** is a re-creation of the original light station built here in 1903. Students at the local high school constructed the current lighthouse in 1983, using plans for the original structure. The lighthouse is particularly photogenic, with the bay and the cliffs of the Niagara Escarpment as a backdrop.

On the south side of town, **Lion's Head Provincial Park** (519/389-9056, www.ontarioparks.com, free) is known for its "potholes," deep, cylindrical holes carved by erosion into the limestone rocks. It's about a 20-minute walk along a flat section of the Bruce Trail to

Lion's Head Lighthouse

two of the large potholes. The trail continues toward Georgian Bay, where it becomes more difficult as it hugs the cliffs. The reward for the climb up and along the tops of the rocks is a spectacular view of the cliffs and the bay. This section of the trail isn't recommended for small children, as the trail veers quite close to the cliffs. Access to the potholes trail is from Moore Street; the trail starts opposite 128 Moore Street. The park has no restrooms or other services.

The **Central Bruce Peninsula Chamber Of Commerce** (2866 Hwy. 6, Ferndale, 519/793-3178, www.centralbrucepeninsula. ca, daily July-Aug., Sat.-Sun. mid-May-June and Sept.-mid-Oct.) runs a seasonal visitor information center on Highway 6 at Highway 9 (the Lion's Head turnoff). The rest of the year, staff answer questions by phone. Lion's Head is about 250 kilometers (160 miles) north of Toronto. There's no public transportation to or around the area.

Accommodations and Food

Big rooms, a beachside location, reasonable rates, and a warm welcome from owner Barbara Grison and her staff are the reasons to stay at the **Lion's Head Beach Motel and Cottages** (1 McNeil St., 519/793-3155, www. lionsheadbeachmotelandcottages.ca, $89-115 s, $105-125 d). Although the family-friendly motel rooms won't win any design prizes, they're well maintained, larger than average, and include kitchenettes. The newer two- and three-bedroom cottages ($125-260) would be even more comfortable if you've brought Grandma or the kids.

If you're not a regular at **The Lion's Head Inn & Restaurant** (8 Helen St., 519/793-4601, www.lionsheadinn.ca, 11am-11pm daily May-Oct., 4pm-9pm Wed.-Sat. Nov.-Apr., $10-20), you may feel like one after you've stopped for a beer in this convivial pub. The food is a notch above basic bar grub and includes burgers, pasta, fish-and-chips, and steaks. Built as a boardinghouse in 1879, the inn has three simple guest rooms upstairs ($80-120 d), two with a shared bath and one with a private bath.

In the center of Lion's Head village, **Marydale's Restaurant** (76 Main St., 519/793-4224, 8am-8pm daily summer, 8am-7pm daily fall-spring, $7-15) serves substantial breakfasts and simple home-style fare year-round.

It's worth visiting the small **Lion's Head Farmers Market** (1 Forbes St., 9am-noon Sat. late May-mid-Oct.) just for its open-air setting right on Lion's Head Beach. Vendors sell produce, muffins, other baked goods, and crafts. Pull off Highway 6 at the **Harvest Moon Organic Bakery** (3927 Hwy. 6, 519/592-5742, www.harvestmoonbakery.ca, 9am-4:30pm Wed.-Sun. July-Aug., 9am-4:30pm Thurs.-Sun. May-June and Sept.-Oct.) for butter tarts, hearty potato-filled pasties, or homemade multigrain bread. Besides sampling the treats that come out of this riotously colorful little house, you can stroll around the quirky sculpture garden (free). The bakery is about 10 minutes north of Ferndale, on the west side of the highway.

WIARTON AND VICINITY

Wiarton sits on Colpoys Bay, an inlet off Georgian Bay, with the cliffs of the Niagara Escarpment towering above the water. Highway 6, the peninsula's main north-south route, runs straight through town, where it's called Berford Street. While its year-round population is under 2,500, Wiarton has all the basic services you need, including a 24-hour grocery store. Many of Wiarton's limestone or brick buildings downtown date to the mid-1800s; the village was incorporated in 1880, and the railroad reached the area the following year. The former railroad station is now the town's information center.

Two fingers of land jutting into Georgian Bay on either side of Wiarton are worth exploring. To the north, Cape Crocker is a First Nations reserve; to the east, you can head toward the village of Big Bay, visiting caves, gardens, and an ice cream shop en route. Wiarton's most famous resident may be **Wiarton Willie,** a weather-forecasting groundhog. Similar to the American

Punxsutawney Phil, Wiarton Willie comes out of his burrow annually on Groundhog Day (Feb. 2). If he sees his shadow, Canada's winter will last another six weeks; if he doesn't, spring is supposedly on the way. For much of the year, you can view Willie in his pen outside the Wiarton branch of the Bruce County Public Library (578 Brown St., at William St.). Local sculptor Dave Robinson crafted a 4.5-ton limestone statue of the town's notable groundhog. *Willie Emerging* sits near the beach in **Bluewater Park** (William St.). Also in the park is Wiarton's former train station, an ornate wooden building built in 1904 and moved to its present site in 1971.

East of Wiarton, in the hamlet of Big Bay, you can stroll among the irises, lilacs, poppies, and lavender in the peaceful privately owned **Kepplecroft Gardens** (504156 Grey Rd. 1, Big Bay, 519/534-1090, www.keppelcroft. com, 10am-5pm Wed.-Sun. May-mid-Oct., donation $3). With a Zen garden, a woodland garden, and rock sculptures, Kepplecroft Gardens are part of a regional network of private gardens, known as the **Rural Gardens of Grey and Bruce Counties** (www.ruralgardens.ca), that are open to visitors. The website lists gardens hours and locations; you can also pick up a *Rural Gardens* map at any of the information centers on the Bruce Peninsula.

Wiarton celebrates its weather-forecasting groundhog during the annual **Wiarton Willie Festival** (519/534-5492, www.wiartonwillie.com), a winter carnival that includes a parade, fireworks, concerts, pancake breakfasts, sleigh rides, and, of course, Willie's prediction for the end of winter. The festival takes place for several days around Groundhog Day (Feb. 2).

Stop into the **Wiarton Information Centre** (Bluewater Park, 519/534-3111, www. visitwiarton.ca, May-early Sept.) in the former train station. You can also get visitor information from the **Town of South Bruce Peninsula** (315 George St., 519/534-1400 or 877/534-1400, www.southbrucepeninsula.com, 8:30am-4:30pm Mon.-Fri.), or the **County of Bruce Tourism** (578 Brown St.,

519/534-5344 or 800/268-3838, www.explorethebruce.com). Wiarton is about 220 kilometers (137 miles) northwest of Toronto. There's no public transportation in the area, so it's difficult to explore without a car.

Cape Croker

Part of the Saugeen Ojibway First Nations territory, the 6,000-hectare (14,825-acre) Cape Croker Peninsula juts out into Georgian Bay north of Wiarton. The peninsula's Ojibwa name, Neyaashiinigmiing, means "a point of land nearly surrounded by water," and the name is apt—except for a sliver of land connecting the peninsula to the mainland, it's ringed by the waters of the bay. Cape Croker is a pretty spot for a drive or hike, particularly on the north side of the peninsula with views across the water to the limestone bluffs of the Niagara Escarpment. You can drive out to the **Cape Croker Lighthouse,** built in 1902 on the tip of the cape, but the interior isn't open to the public, and the setting, behind a chain-link fence, isn't that picturesque.

Near the mainland end of the peninsula, the **Cape Croker Indian Park** (519/534-0571, www.capecrokerpark.com, $10 per vehicle) has a lovely beach and hiking trails as well as a campground. The park is also the site of the annual **Cape Croker Powwow** (www. nawash.ca, late Aug., $5), where you can experience the music, dance, and other traditions of the local First Nations community. Visitors are welcome at the powwow as long as they are respectful of local customs. Ask permission before taking photos or videos, and leave the beer at home—the powwow is an alcohol-free event.

Accommodations and Food

In the late 1990s, Evan LeBlanc and Dave Peebles bought a basic roadside motel overlooking Colpoys Bay, and they've steadily upgraded the property that is now the three-story **Waterview on the Bay** (501205 Island View Dr., 519/534-0921 or 877/534-0921, www.waterview.ca, Apr.-Oct., $100-160 d). The 21 rooms include simple rooms with two double beds and a fridge and the "luxury suites," with whirlpool tubs, sleigh beds, and expansive bay views. Also on the property are five two- or three-bedroom cottages ($200-250). There's a swimming pool and a sandy beach. The Waterview is family-friendly, pet-friendly, and just overall friendly.

Bonnie Howe and Phil Howard purchased a farm east of Wiarton and opened **Longlane Bed & Breakfast** (483078 Colpoy's Range Rd., 519/534-3901, www.longlane.ca, $90 s, $110 d), where they raise cattle and chickens and grow their own vegetables. Upstairs in the 1902 farmhouse, the three guest rooms are decorated with quilts and country curtains. Guests share two baths, as well as a sitting area with a TV, and in the morning, they tuck into hearty farm breakfasts around the communal kitchen table. The owners will shuttle hikers to the Bruce Trail nearby.

Wiarton's best restaurant, the **Green Door Café** (563 Berford St., 510/534-3278, www.thegreendoorcafe.com, 11am-3pm Sun.-Tues., 11am-8pm Wed.-Sat. late June-Aug., 11am-3pm Sun.-Wed., 11am-8pm Thurs.-Sat. Sept.-late June, $5-14) looks like a small-town coffee shop, where local retirees stop in for cups of joe and grilled cheese sandwiches. At this unassuming eatery, though, the straightforward sandwiches and hearty main dishes are well prepared from fresh ingredients. Try the delicious, garlicky Caesar salad or the meaty cabbage rolls.

Tiny **Big Bay General Store** (250854 Big Bay Sideroad at Grey Rd. 1, 519/534-4523, daily late May-early Sept., Sat.-Sun. spring and fall), east of Wiarton, doesn't stock many groceries, but they do serve delicious homemade ice cream. They make more than 80 different flavors, with 10 to 12 available at a time. Call to confirm open hours before making a special trip.

Camping

Owned and operated by the Chippewas of Nawash First Nation, the **Cape Croker Indian Park** (519/534-0571, www.capecrokerpark.com, early May-mid-Oct., $29-39)

has an enviable waterfront location on Sydney Bay. The 210-hectare (520-acre) property has 315 campsites with showers, flush toilets, laundry facilities, a swimming beach, and canoe rentals. Prime waterfront sites look across to the cliffs of the Niagara Escarpment, while other sites are tucked into the woods. A small camping cabin with two bunks ($65) is also available. Definitely reserve in advance for the August powwow, and you may want to book ahead for the popular waterfront sites, for the cabin, or for holiday weekend stays.

SAUBLE BEACH

On Lake Huron at the south end of the Bruce Peninsula, Sauble Beach is a full-fledged beach-holiday town. This sun-and-fun community has burger stands and soft-serve ice cream shops, T-shirt sellers and bikini boutiques, and, oh, yes, a sandy lakeshore beach that seems to go on and on. The world's second-longest freshwater beach, Sauble Beach (Lakeshore Dr.) is a flat paradise of sand that extends for 11 kilometers (nearly seven miles); only Wasaga Beach, east of Collingwood, is longer. The early French explorers who traversed this area named it La Rivière au Sable ("River to the Sand") for the nearby Sauble River, but by the end of the 19th-century, the town was known as Sauble Beach for its major geographical asset.

Since the water is fairly shallow, Sauble Beach is a good choice for families with younger kids. The atmosphere in July and August can be rather honky-tonk, but the farther you go from the heart of town, the easier it is to find a peaceful spot to lay your towel. And despite the summer crowds, the beach is undeniably beautiful, and sunsets over the lake can be spectacular. Outside summer high season, you'll sometimes have the fine golden sand almost to yourself. Beach parking is available in lots right on the sand and along Lakeshore Road. Prepare for epic summer traffic jams. The **Sauble Beach Sandfest** (Lakeshore Blvd., www.saublebeach.com) takes place the first weekend of August and turns the beach into a giant outdoor sand sculpture gallery, drawing both professional and amateur sand sculptors.

Sauble Beach has a large assortment of standard beach motels and cottages. The **Sauble Beach Information Centre** (672 Main St., 519/422-1262, www.saublebeach. com, 9am-5pm Mon.-Fri., 10am-3pm Sat.) has information about cottage rentals and lists of area accommodations. If you prefer a more peaceful atmosphere, you could stay in Wiarton, about 20 kilometers (12.5 miles) from Sauble Beach, and come to the beach during the day. Restaurants in town, which are clustered along Main Street and on 2nd Avenue North (one block east of the beach), tend to serve burgers, pizza, and other eat-and-run fare.

Sauble Beach is about 220 kilometers (137 miles) northwest of Toronto via Highways 6/10. After you pass through Owen Sound, continue on Highway 6 to Bruce Road 8, which heads west into Sauble Beach.

Sauble Falls Provincial Park

About one kilometer (0.6 miles) north of Sauble Beach, the small provincial **Sauble Falls Provincial Park** (Sauble Falls Pkwy./ County Rd. 13, 519/422-1952, www.ontario-oparks.com, late Apr.-Oct., $14.50 per vehicle)

couldn't feel more different than the frenzied tourist crush of the nearby town. Although it does get busy in summer, it still feels like an escape into the woods.

The petite waterfalls along the Sauble River that give the park its name descend in tiers, almost like an aquatic wedding cake, over a staircase of dolomite limestone. You can watch the falls from a small viewing platform or along either side of the river; it's a lovely spot for a picnic. In spring and fall, you may see salmon and rainbow trout attempting to swim upstream over each ledge of the falls. You can also go canoeing or kayaking on a stretch of the Sauble River that winds through the park. Canoe and kayak rentals (daily mid-June-early Sept., Sat.-Sun. early Sept-mid-Oct., call for fall hours) are available off Sauble Falls Parkway just north of the river.

Sauble Falls Provincial Park has 152 campsites (tent sites $35-40, electrical sites $40-46). In both the East Campground and the larger, radio-free West Campground, the nicest sites front the Sauble River. Both areas have flush toilets and showers; the West Campground has laundry facilities. Reserve campsites up to five months in advance though the **Ontario Parks Reservations Service** (888/668-7275,

Sauble Falls Provincial Park

www.ontarioparks.com, reservation fee online $11, by phone $13).

OWEN SOUND

It's hard to imagine that this small community of about 22,000 was once known as "Chicago of the North." From 1885 through 1912, when the Canadian Pacific Railway (CPR) made Owen Sound the terminus of its steamship line, the town's port was the busiest in the upper Great Lakes. Many of the town's Victorian homes and buildings date to this era. Alas, in 1912, the Canadian Pacific Railway moved its shipping operations farther east to Port McNicoll, Ontario, which had better rail connections, thus ending Owen Sound's glory years.

For a small city, Owen Sound has a large number of museums and historic attractions. To stroll through the town's history, pick up the *Historic Downtown Walking Tour* brochure at the **Owen Sound Tourist Information Centre** (1155 1st Ave. W., 519/371-9833, www.owensound.ca). Many grand homes, built in the late 1800s, are along 1st Avenue West, while Victorian-era commercial buildings still stand along 2nd Avenue East.

Owen Sound was a destination for formerly enslaved people who came north along the Underground Railroad. To learn about this heritage, follow two self-guided tours of sites that were important to African Canadians. Pick up brochures about these tours—*The Freedom Trail,* a 10-kilometer (six-mile) walking or cycling tour, and the *Owen Sound Underground Railroad Driving Tour*—at the **Owen Sound Tourist Information Centre** (1155 1st Ave. W., 519/371-9833, www.owensound.ca) or on the website.

Grey Roots Museum and Archives

If you think that a museum about a region's roots is a musty trove of papers and old tools, think again. The contemporary **Grey Roots Museum and Archives** (102599 Grey Rd. 18, 519/376-3690 or 877/473-9766, www.

greyroots.com, 10am-5pm daily late May-mid-Oct., 10am-5pm Tues.-Sat. mid-Oct.-late May, adults $8, seniors $6, ages 5-12 $4, families $20) showcases the history and culture of Owen Sound and the surrounding region with cool multimedia features that include films, radio stories, and computer-based displays.

Start in the Grey County gallery, where the permanent "Grey Roots" exhibit introduces you to the people who settled the region—from the local First Nations to early pioneers to notable citizens such as Agnes Macphail, a Grey County native who became Canada's first woman elected to Parliament. Other galleries host temporary and traveling exhibitions; recent exhibits have focused on "Saints and Sinners" (how alcohol influenced Grey County's development), letters between local soldiers and their families during the Great War (World War I), and Victorian-era death and mourning customs.

If you have kids in tow, explore **Moreston Heritage Village** (11am-4:30pm daily June-early Sept.), the on-site pioneer village that's staffed by costumed volunteers. Watch the blacksmith at work, visit the 1850s log cabin, or check out the schoolhouse. The museum is located about seven kilometers (4.4 miles) south of downtown.

Tom Thomson Art Gallery

Artist Tom Thomson (1877-1917) grew up outside Owen Sound in the town of Leith. A member of the Group of Seven—notable Canadian landscape artists of the early 20th century—Thomson is best known for the paintings he created in Algonquin Park between 1912 and 1917, until his death, reportedly by drowning, in Algonquin's Canoe Lake. The small, modern **Tom Thomson Art Gallery** (840 1st Ave. W., 519/376-1932, www.tomthomson.org, 10am-5pm Mon.-Sat., noon-5pm Sun. late May-mid-Oct., 11am-5pm Tues.-Fri., noon-5 Sat.-Sun. mid-Oct.-late May, donation $5) mounts changing exhibits of work by Thomson and other Ontario artists.

Billy Bishop Home and Museum

Owen Sound native William Avery Bishop (1894-1956), a fighter pilot with the British Royal Flying Corps, became one of the most decorated Canadians serving in World War I. Bishop's childhood home, in a restored Victorian mansion, is now the **Billy Bishop Home and Museum** (948 3rd Ave. W., 519/371-0031, www.billybishop.org, 10am-5pm Mon.-Sat., noon-5pm Sun. late May-mid-Oct., 11am-5pm Tues.-Fri., noon-5 Sat.-Sun. mid-Oct.-late May, donation $5) that includes artifacts from Bishop's life and from World Wars I and II, with an emphasis on aviation history.

Owen Sound Marine and Rail Museum

Located in Owen Sound's former Canadian National Railway station (the station's waiting room now houses the Owen Sound Tourist Information Centre), the **Owen Sound Marine and Rail Museum** (1155 1st Ave. W., 519/371-3333, 10am-5pm Mon.-Sat., noon-5pm Sun. late May-mid-Oct., call for off-season hours, donation) commemorates the region's glory days as a ship and rail hub in the late 1800s. There are ship models and railroad exhibits; outside, you can climb on board a restored caboose.

Harrison Park and the Black History Cairn

Owen Sound was one of the northernmost stops on the Underground Railroad, the network of safe houses that protected slaves fleeing from the United States in the 1800s.

The **Black History Cairn** (www.owensound.ca), located in **Harrison Park** (2nd Ave. E.), memorializes the journey of enslaved people into the north. This outdoor sculpture includes eight tiles inlaid in the ground, incorporating quilt patterns that represented coded messages to escaping slaves—according to legend, the patterns were originally sewn into quilts. One pattern symbolizes the North Star, which guided slaves to freedom; a

Canadian aviator Billy Bishop grew up in this Owen Sound home.

log cabin symbol indicates a safe house; another is a sailboat, signifying a water crossing. Around the tiles is a stone structure representing the ruins of a church, with windows looking toward the Sydenham River. According to Bonita Johnson de Matteis, the artist who designed the cairn, newly freed people might have looked out similar church windows in Owen Sound as they gave thanks for their freedom. Johnson de Matteis herself is a descendent of a slave who escaped from the United States and settled in Owen Sound.

Harrison Park is located off 2nd Avenue East, south of downtown. Once you arrive in Harrison Park, to find the Black History Cairn, walk north from the parking area near the Harrison Park Inn; the cairn is just past the playground. The park is a lovely spot for a picnic, and it's crisscrossed with trails for hiking, running, and cycling; it also has three playgrounds, as well as canoe rentals.

Coffin Ridge Boutique Winery

In the rolling hills east of town, with views to

Georgian Bay, the small-batch **Coffin Ridge Boutique Winery** (599448 2nd Concession N., Annan, 519/371-9565, www.coffinridge.ca, 11am-6pm Mon.-Sat., 11am-5pm Sun. summer, call or check the website for off-season hours) cultivates 10 hectares (25 acres) of cold-climate grapes that are made into drinkable one-of-a-kind wines. Sample what's on offer at the tasting bar, or have a glass with a cheese and charcuterie plate overlooking the vineyard. In the restroom, videos of *The Munsters,* the quirky 1960s TV monster show, play up the coffin theme.

Entertainment and Shopping

The historic downtown **Roxy Theatre** (251 9th St. E., 519/371-2833 or 888/446-7699, www.roxytheatre.ca), built in 1912, hosts live theater and musical performances throughout the year.

The first weekend in August, Owen Sound's annual **Emancipation Celebration Festival** (Harrison Park, 2nd Ave. E., www.emancipation.ca) recalls the struggles of the formerly enslaved people who traveled the Underground Railroad to freedom in Canada. First held in 1862, it's the longest continuously running emancipation festival in North America. Events include a speaker's forum, music, and a picnic.

From photography to metalwork to jewelry, the **Owen Sound Artists' Co-op** (279 10th St. E., 519/371-0479, www.osartistsco-op.com, 9:30am-5:30pm Mon.-Sat.) displays and sells the work of its roughly 40 member artists, all from the local area.

Accommodations

Owen Sound's lodging options range from chain motels (primarily along Highway 6/10 on the town's east side) to Victorian-style bed-and-breakfasts.

The most romantic inn in town is the ★ **Highland Manor** (867 4th Ave. A W., 519/372-2699 or 877/372-2699, www.high-landmanor.ca, no children under 14, $120 s, $170 d), a grand brick mansion on a shady residential street. Guests can browse books about the area in the library and take their elaborate breakfasts in the formal dining room. Upstairs, the guest rooms have working fireplaces and antique furnishings. Owners Linda Bradford and Paul Neville are passionate about local history, and they're a wealth of information about things to do nearby.

In a circa-1900 Victorian home, **MacLean Estate Bed & Breakfast** (404 9th St. E., 519/416-5326, www.macleanestate.com, $109-129 d) retains period details like original leaded-glass windows and pocket doors, but there's nothing stuffy about the welcome you get from owners Jamie Heimbecker and Matthew MacLean, who've updated the B&B with air-conditioning, HDTV, DVD players, and fast Wi-Fi. The largest of the second-floor guest rooms has a turret and a private bath; the other two share a large bath. Staying here includes a full breakfast and lots of local tips; Jamie grew up nearby and is tapped into the local community.

Although it's out of the town center on a charmless stretch of road, and most of its 100 rooms are standard chain accommodations, the **Best Western Inn on the Bay** (1800 2nd Ave. E., 519/371-9200 or 800/780-7234, www.bestwesternontario.com, $140-240 d) does have rooms overlooking Georgian Bay and a hot tub facing the waterfront.

Food

If you'd like to wander and check out food options, head downtown to 2nd Avenue East, between 10th and 7th Streets. The year-round **Owen Sound Farmers Market** (114 8th St. E., 519/371-3433, www.owensoundfarmers-market.ca, 8am-12:30pm Sat.) sells baked goods, crafts, and seasonal produce.

Ginger Press Bookshop and Café (848 2nd Ave. E., 519/376-4233, www.gingerpress.com, bookshop 9:30am-6pm Mon.-Fri., 9am-2pm Sat., café 9:30am-2pm Mon.-Fri., 9am-noon Sat., $5-12) is part bookstore and part casual café, serving soup, sandwiches, and other light meals. Fresh-pressed apple ginger juice is their specialty. Wi-Fi is free.

At the eclectic **Kathmandu Café** (941 2nd

Ave. E., 519/374-0500, www.kathmanducafe. ca, generally 11am-9pm Mon.-Sat., call to confirm hours, $15-25), local ingredients join Asian and global influences to create curries and other world-beat dishes.

Named in homage to Norma Jeane Mortenson, better known as the actress Marilyn Monroe, **Norma Jean's Bistro** (243 8th St. E., 519/376-2232, 11:30am-10pm Mon.-Sat., $12-27) has been a downtown fixture since 1984. Though the menu looks fairly standard—pastas, sandwiches, chicken, steak—the creative kitchen livens things up with seasonal ingredients and as many surprising twists as a Hollywood flick.

Information and Services

The **Owen Sound Tourist Information Centre** (1155 1st Ave. W., 519/371-9833 or 888/675-5555, www.owensound.ca), which shares a building with the Marine and Rail Museum, is full of information about attractions and lodgings around town. The regional tourism association, **Grey County Tourism** (102599 Grey Rd. 18, 519/376-3265 or 877/733-4739, www.visitgrey.ca), has a helpful information desk in the lobby of the Grey Roots Museum.

Getting There and Around

Owen Sound is 190 kilometers (120 miles) northwest of Toronto, about a 2.5-hour drive via Highways 6 and 10. **Greyhound Bus Lines** (City Transit Centre, 1020 3rd Ave. E., 519/376-5375 or 800/661-8747, www.greyhound.ca) runs one direct bus daily in each direction between Toronto and Owen Sound (about 4 hours, $36-59 pp). The **Grey Bruce Airbus** (800/361-0393, www.greybruceairbus.

com, adults $75 one-way, $136 round-trip) operates four trips daily in each direction between Toronto's Pearson Airport and the Owen Sound Days Inn (950 6th St. E.).

The majority of Owen Sound's roadways are numbered streets and avenues (streets run east-west, avenues run north-south). The Sydenham River divides the east and west sides, so a "west" address, such as the Tom Thomson Gallery on 1st Avenue West, is west of the river, while an "east" address is east of the river.

Owen Sound's attractions are clustered in two main areas—around downtown and south of the center. The main downtown shopping street is 2nd Avenue East, south of 10th Street and east of the river. From downtown, you can continue south on 2nd Avenue East to reach Harrison Park and the Grey Roots Museum. Owen Sound has a walkable downtown core. You can get around town during the day on **Owen Sound Transit** buses (Downtown Transit Terminal, 1020 3rd Ave. E., 519/376-3299, www.owensound. ca, adults $2.50, students $2, under age 5 free), which operate 6:30am-6pm Monday-Friday and 9am-4pm Saturday. The useful Crosstown loop bus circles between downtown and Harrison Park.

To explore the surrounding towns or farther up the Bruce Peninsula, it's much easier to have your own wheels. It's about a 45-minute drive to Wiarton and 75-90 minutes to Tobermory. Several major car rental companies have offices in Owen Sound, including **Enterprise Rent-A-Car** (www.enterpriserentacar.ca), **Thrifty Car Rental** (www. thrifty.com), and **Discount Car Rentals** (www.discountcar.com).

Collingwood and the Blue Mountains

The Blue Mountain Resort, just outside the town of Collingwood, is Ontario's top ski destination. If you're expecting the Alps or the Rockies, you may chuckle when you see the size of the "mountains" here, but these rolling hills have enough terrain to keep most skiers or snowboarders occupied for at least several days. Besides the winter snow-sports season, the busiest times are midsummer (for mountain biking, hiking, golfing, and other outdoor activities) and fall weekends, when the trees blaze with color.

Collingwood (population 19,000) serves skiers and other outdoor adventurers with grocery stores, movie theaters, and excellent restaurants; it's a good base for exploring the region. If your goal is skiing, snowboarding, or other active pursuits, it's most convenient to stay in the Village at Blue Mountain, the resort area at the mountain base.

BLUE MOUNTAIN RESORT

Owned by resort giant Intrawest, **Blue Mountain Resort** (108 Jozo Weider Blvd., 705/445-0231 or 877/445-0231, www.bluemountain.ca) is a car-free village, where casually upscale restaurants, bars, and outdoor clothing shops line the pedestrian streets. You can easily walk from village lodgings to the lifts; if you stay in one of the village condo developments, a free shuttle will pick you up.

Blue Mountain Activity Central (705/443-5522) acts as an activity concierge for guests. Staff keep a schedule of regular events, including free guided hikes or snowshoe tours, sleigh rides, scavenger hunts, toboggan tours, and more, plus activities for kids and teens. They also book activities both on and off the mountain. Prices for many mountain activities are discounted for guests staying in Blue Mountain Village lodgings.

Special events take place at Blue Mountain nearly every weekend from July through early October and on select weekends during the rest of the year. Highlights include the **May Long Weekend Music and Fireworks** (late May), **Salsa at Blue Festival** (late June), **Village Beach Party** (early Aug.), and **Apple Harvest Festival** (early Oct.).

Skiing and Snowboarding

Blue Mountain Resort began life as a winter sports mecca and now has 15 lifts serving 42 trails. At 720 vertical feet, it's not a tall mountain, nor does it get buried in snow like western resorts, but an extensive snow-making operation supplements the average annual snowfall of 280 centimeters (110 inches). The winter season typically starts in December and runs through March. Come midweek to avoid the crowds.

Lift tickets (adults $64, seniors and ages 6-17 $44) are good for either day skiing (9am-4:30pm) or afternoon-night skiing (12:30pm-10pm). If you just want to ski in the evening (4:30pm-10pm), when 30 of the trails are open, tickets are adults $39, seniors and ages 6-17 $34. Ski and snowboard rentals, lessons, and kids camps are all available. For snowboarders, a **terrain park** (9am-9pm daily) has its own chairlift. To access the park, you must purchase a one-time $10 park pass in addition to your lift ticket.

Mountain Biking

From spring through fall, mountain bikers take over the trails at Blue Mountain Resort. The lifts are open to bikers 10am-8pm daily late June-early September, 10am-5pm Friday-Sunday late May-late June, and 10am-5pm Friday-Sunday early September-mid-October. Daily trail passes are $6 (no lift access), $15 (one lift access), or $38 (unlimited lift access). You can rent bikes and safety gear. A variety of guided mountain-biking options are available for youth, teens, adults, and families, both novice and experienced riders.

Collingwood and the Blue Mountains

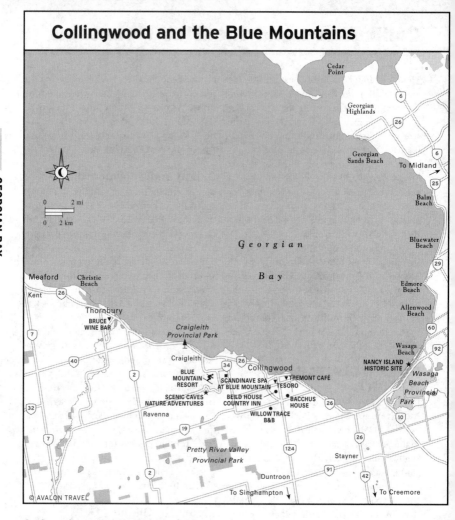

Swimming and Water Sports

The year-round **Plunge Aquatic Centre** (200 Gord Canning Dr., 705/444-8705, www.plungebluemountain.ca, adults $15, ages 3-12 $12, families $42) adjacent to the Westin Trillium House, entertains waterlovers with indoor and outdoor swimming pools, several water slides, rope swings, hot tubs, and a water playground for toddlers. Schedules vary seasonally, but in general, Plunge is open daily in summer and winter, weekends only in spring and fall.

Admission tickets are good for a three-hour period.

In summer, Blue Mountain Resort maintains a **beach** (Blue Mountain Activity Central, 705/443-5522) on Georgian Bay, open only to resort guests. A complimentary 10-minute shuttle ride will take you from the village to the beach.

Mountain Coaster

Thrill-seekers should head for the **Ridge Runner Mountain Coaster** (daily

Wild Winter Adventures

Ontario may not have the towering mountains of western Canada, but that doesn't mean you can't take to the slopes. Not only do the Georgian Bay and Cottage Country regions north of Toronto have several spots for downhill skiing and snowboarding, but there are plenty of opportunities for cross-country skiing, snowshoeing, dogsledding, and other winter adventures. The Ottawa Valley region, a short drive from the nation's capital, is the other major Ontario destination for winter sports.

Blue Mountain Resort (705/445-0231 or 877/445-0231, www.bluemountain.ca) is the largest downhill ski resort in Ontario and offers mountain biking and other outdoor sports when the snow season ends. Closer to Toronto, **Horseshoe Resort** (1101 Horseshoe Valley Rd., Barrie, 705/835-2790 or 800/461-5627, www.horseshoeresort.com), north of Barrie off Highway 400, has downhill skiing and snowboarding, fat-tire snow biking, tubing, snowshoeing, and ice-skating in winter, plus golf, mountain biking, treetop trekking, among other summer activities.

For more places to ski or snowboard, check the **Ontario Snow Resorts Association** (www.skiontario.ca) or make tracks to these mountain resorts:

- **Calabogie Peaks Resort** (30 Barrett Chute Rd., Calabogie, 613/752-2720 or 800/669-4861, www.calabogie.com)

- **Dagmar Ski Resort** (1220 Lake Ridge Rd., Uxbridge, 905/649-2002, www.skidagmar.com)

- **Hidden Valley Highlands Ski Area** (1655 Hidden Valley Rd., Huntsville, 705/789-1773 or 800/398-9555, www.skihiddenvalley.on.ca)

- **Hockley Valley Resort** (793522 3rd Line EHS, Mono, 519/942-0754 or 866/462-5539, www.hockley.com)

- **Lakeridge** (790 Chalk Lake Rd., Uxbridge, 905/649-2058, www.ski-lakeridge.com)

- **Mount Pakenham** (577 Ski Hill Rd., Pakenham, 613/624-5290, www.mountpakenham.com)

- **Mount St. Louis Moonstone** (24 Mount St. Louis Rd., Coldwater, 705/835-2112, www.mountstlouis.com)

- **Searchmont Ski Resort** (103 Searchmont Resort Rd., Searchmont, 705/781-2340, www.searchmont.com)

mid-May-Oct., Sat.-Sun. mid-Dec.-Mar., over age 12 $15 per ride, ages 3-12 $6 per ride), which twists and turns from the top of the Glades area through the trees and down to the village. One or two people can ride together in each car, and riders control the car's speed. For specific operating hours, which vary seasonally, check with Blue Mountain Activity Central (705/443-5522, www.bluemountain.ca).

Summer Activities

Two different ropes courses test your agility and balance. On the family-friendly **Woodlot Low Ropes** (daily mid-May-Oct., over age 12 $25, ages 6-12 $20), navigate three routes at different heights, crossing beams, ropes, suspended logs, and other swaying aerial elements. The tougher **Timber Challenge High Ropes** (daily mid-May-Oct., over age 12 $59) comprises seven different courses that take you more than 15 meters (50 feet) above the forest floor.

Another activity for the adventurous, the **Wind Rider Triple Zips** (daily mid-May-Oct., over age 12 $15, ages 10-12 $12) includes two 122-meter (400-foot) zip lines. Three lines run in parallel, letting you zip with friends or family members. On the **Apex Bagjump** (daily mid-May-Oct., over age 12 $15, ages 8-12 $12), you free-fall from four increasingly higher platforms into a puffy airbag on the ground.

Still want more things to do? Hiking, tennis, golf, miniature golf, indoor rock climbing, mountaintop Segway tours, and riding the **Blue Mountain Gondola** (late May-mid-Oct., over age 12 $15, under age 12 $12) are among the many other mountain activities.

Accommodations

Blue Mountain Village has several hotel and condominium properties, and just outside the village are additional condo and townhouse complexes. You can book lodgings through **Blue Mountain Central Reservations** (877/445-0231, www.bluemountain.ca). When booking, ask whether the lodging is ski-in, ski-out or within walking distance of the lifts. Winter room rates typically start at about $150 d, and a variety of lodging and lift ticket packages are available.

The **Blue Mountain Inn** was the village's original lodging, and while it's starting to show its age, it offers moderately priced accommodations. You can walk to the Century Express chair lift. For more style, the boutique **Mosaïc** has 163 contemporary suites, ranging from studios to three-bedroom units. The smaller units have kitchenettes, and the larger suites, some of which are multilevel townhouses, have full kitchens. There's a fitness center as well as a year-round outdoor pool and hot tub. It's not as close to the lifts as the **Weider Lodge** or the **Grand Georgian**—both slightly older, well-appointed condo hotels—but the rooms are more stylish and you can walk to the gondola in a few minutes.

The village's most upscale lodging, a short walk from the gondola, is the **Westin Trillium House** (220 Gord Canning Dr., 705/443-8080 or 800/937-8461, www.westin-bluemountain.com, $195-550 d), designed like a grand Georgian Bay lodge. The 222 spacious units, including standard guest rooms and one-, two-, and three-bedroom suites, have modern furnishings in ski-lodge beiges and browns, as well as TV/DVDs and kitchenettes. There's a 24-hour gym, year-round outdoor pool, sauna, and hot tubs. If you're too tired to walk downstairs to the restaurant or lounge, you can order from room service.

Food

Food in the village tends toward either fare to fuel up fast and get back on the slopes or simple but hearty pub-style eats. For more dining options, head to the nearby towns of Thornbury to the west or Collingwood to the east. Start your day with coffee and pastry at the **Royal Majesty Espresso Bar Bakery**

Georgian Bay views from the Blue Mountain Gondola

(190 Jozo Weider Blvd., 705/812-3476, www.royalmajesty.ca, generally 7am-9pm daily), or stop in later for soup or a sandwich. Free Wi-Fi.

The local outpost of a Toronto-based restaurant group, **Oliver and Bonacini Café Grill** (Westin Trillium House, 220 Gord Canning Dr., 705/444-8680, www.oliver-bonacini.com, 7am-10pm daily, lunch $13-27, dinner $15-42) is one of the best places to eat in the village. The contemporary dishes—chopped salad with romaine, arugula, pickled squash, and pumpkin seeds; shrimp linguine with almond pesto; pork chops with spice-roasted sweet potatoes and apple chutney—are both crowd-pleasing and creative.

It's worth the 20-minute drive to ★ **Bruce Wine Bar and Kitchen** (8 Bruce St., Thornbury, 519/599-1112, www.brucewinebar.ca, 11:30am-close Tues.-Sun., $15-28), which emphasizes local ingredients in its imaginative sharing plates, wood-fired pizzas, and entrées. The pies range from traditional to unusual; try the excellent version topped with smoked trout, pea sprouts, cherry tomatoes, and pickled onions. While the entrées change regularly, they always include a "daily beast" (perhaps duck, rabbit, or venison) and sustainable seafood. The wine list highlights Canadian labels and by-the-glass options; the vibe at the rustic wood tables or along the bar is welcoming and informal.

Information and Services

Blue Mountain Resort is 170 kilometers (105 miles) northwest of Toronto and 11 kilometers (7 miles) west of Collingwood, off Highway 26. Depending on traffic and weather conditions, it's about a two-hour drive from metropolitan Toronto. For resort information or reservations, contact **Blue Mountain Resorts** (108 Jozo Weider Blvd., 705/445-0231 or 877/445-0231, www.bluemountain.ca); you can also get information from the **Blue Mountain Village Association** (705/444-7398, www.bluemountainvillage.ca).

Getting Around

If you're staying in the Village at Blue Mountain, you don't need a car. The village is car-free (and ringed with parking lots where you can leave yours). A free **resort shuttle** (www.bluemountain.ca) loops through the village daily every 15-20 minutes between 8am and 10:30pm. Outside of these hours, call for a pickup by dialing extension 8280 on any resort phone.

COLLINGWOOD

While many people come to Collingwood to ski or snowboard at nearby Blue Mountain, it's also a pleasant spot for a weekend getaway, even if you're not mountain-bound. The Collingwood area draws gourmets to its many first-rate restaurants. The **Georgian Trail** (www.georgiantrail.ca) is a flat, 34-kilometer (21-mile) rail trail for hiking and cycling that runs west from Collingwood to the towns of Thornbury and Meaford, passing several beaches en route. In winter, it's a cross-country ski and snowshoeing trail.

To soothe those post-adventure sore muscles, sink into the outdoor baths at the **Scandinave Spa at Blue Mountain** (152 Grey Road 21, Blue Mountains, 705/443-8484 or 877/988-8484, www.scandinave.com, 10am-9pm daily, $50, Wed. $40), which offers a Scandinavian-style "bath experience." First, warm up in one of the Finnish saunas, steam baths, or outdoor hot tubs. Then immerse yourself in a chilling plunge pool. After recovering in a relaxation area, repeat the process until you feel totally tranquil; the average stay is 2-4 hours. The experience is even more magical when snow falls on the hot pools. Bathing suits are required, and you must be at least 19 years old.

For several days in July, Collingwood is overrun with Elvis Presley lookalikes. The annual **Collingwood Elvis Festival** (866/444-1162, www.collingwoodelvisfestival.com) features a parade and more than 100 tribute concerts; it ranks among the world's largest Elvis festivals.

Scenic Caves Nature Adventures

Located in the hills outside Collingwood, **Scenic Caves Nature Adventures** (260-280 Scenic Caves Rd., 705/446-0256, www.sceniccaves.com, 9am-8pm daily late-June-early Sept., call or check the website for spring and fall hours, adults $23, seniors $21, ages 3-17 $19) is a sprawling outdoor playground. Walking trails wind through the woods, and you can explore a network of underground **caves** (try to squeeze through "Fat Man's Misery," a narrow rock channel). A highlight is a stroll across the 126-meter (413-foot) **suspension bridge**, one of Ontario's longest suspension footbridges, with panoramic views across Georgian Bay. Admission rates include access to the caves, suspension bridge, and walking trails.

At 777-meters (2,550-feet) long, the **Thunderbird Twin Zip Line** (adults $48, seniors $46, ages 10-17 $44) is Canada's longest twin zip line, with two zip lines side-by-side and vistas across the Blue Mountains and Georgian Bay. Tickets for the Twin Zip Line include access to the caves, suspension bridge, and trails.

Another option is a three-hour guided ecotour (adults $95, seniors and ages 10-17 $85), which includes a short hike to the suspension bridge, followed by a treetop canopy tour through the trees on a network of narrow wooden bridges. You'll also tour the caves and whiz through the air on two zip lines, including a 305-meter (1,000-foot) plunge from the top of the Niagara Escarpment.

In winter, the park is open for cross-country skiing and snowshoeing (9am-5pm daily Dec.-Mar., full-day pass: adults $19 weekend, $15 weekday, seniors and ages 6-17 $15 weekend, $13 weekday). You can even snowshoe across the suspension bridge. Ski and snowshoe rentals are available.

Allow a minimum of two hours to explore the site, but you can easily spend most of the day. Wear running or hiking shoes. There's a small snack bar, but for more variety, pack your own picnic lunch.

Accommodations

A number of Collingwood's restored Victorian homes are now inns or B&Bs, and in the hills around town, you'll find more small accommodations. Contact the **Collingwood Area Bed-and-Breakfast Association** (www.bbcanada.com) for additional lodging options. Motels are clustered west of town along Highway 26.

crossing the suspension bridge at Scenic Caves Nature Adventures

The **Beild House Country Inn** (64 3rd St., 705/444-1522 or 888/322-3453, www.beildhouse.com, $140-150 d) is just a block from Collingwood's main downtown street, but it has the faded charm of a country estate. The parlor, with its dark woodwork and chintz sofas, and the dining room, where elaborate multicourse dinners are served by candlelight, recall its glory days as a private residence. The 11 guest rooms are romantic in a cozy, if slightly fussy, Victorian style. Rates include full breakfast and afternoon tea. If you're not staying at the inn, you can have dinner ($55-65) with advance reservations.

The four guest rooms at romantic **Bacchus House** (142 Hume St., 705/446-4700, www.bacchushouse.ca, call for rates) are decorated with a wine theme: the purple Pinot Noir Suite has an ornate four-poster bed, and the Cabernet Sauvignon Suite has a claw-foot tub. Common spaces in this 1880 yellow-brick Victorian include the living room, with a fireplace, a deck with a hot tub, and the dining room where a full breakfast is served. Only the location on a busy street mars the elegance of this upscale lodging; the golden-hued Chardonnay Suite at the rear of the house is the quietest.

Set on a six-hectare (15-acre) property with gardens, walking trails, a swimming pool, and a gaggle of ducks and hens, the **Willow Trace B&B** (7833 Poplar Side Rd., 705/445-9003, www.collingwoodbedandbreakfast.com, $130-155 d) feels like a rural getaway, yet it's only a five-minute drive from downtown. The rooms are bright and modern, with two upstairs and one that's family-friendly on the lower level facing the gardens. Among the breakfast options that co-owner and chef Philip Tarlo, who runs the B&B with his wife, Leanne Calvert, prepares are cinnamon french toast, customized omelets, or a full English breakfast.

Food

Collingwood's restaurants range from the foodie to the ardently epicurean. Most are located on or near Hurontario Street in the town center.

Hidden in a lane downtown, **Tesoro** (18 School House Lane, 705/444-9230, www.tesororestaurant.ca, 11am-11pm Mon.-Sat. fall-spring, 11am-10pm Mon.-Sat. winter., lunch $9-20, dinner $15-35), with its sturdy pine tables and vibrant red chairs, is the sort of welcoming, casual Italian eatery everyone would like to have in their neighborhood. There's a long list of creative pizzas (try the Tre Funghi, with black olives and three types of mushrooms), as well as updated versions of Italian classics like penne *arrabbiata* (pasta with spicy sausage and hot peppers), chicken parmigiano, or lasagna.

In an 1889 former hotel, the classy **Tremont Café** (80 Simcoe St., 705/293-6000, www.thetremontcafe.com, 10am-11pm Wed.-Mon., lunch $11-16, dinner $16-36), with a curved bar, white-painted woodwork, and floor-to-ceiling windows, invites lingering, with daytime coffee, evening drinks, and lunch (11am-3pm) and dinner (5:30pm-9:30pm) in between. On the plate, expect well-crafted dishes with lots of seasonal ingredients: a lemon-tahini-dressed veggie bowl, hearty salads, or shrimp tacos mid-day, and heartier fare, from short ribs with harissa and wilted greens to duck confit paired with parsnip purée, for supper.

One of Ontario's most distinctive dining destinations is ★ **Eigensinn Farm** (449357 Concession Rd. 10, Singhampton, 519/922-3128, www.stadtlanderseigensinnfarm.com), which draws well-heeled gourmets from far and wide. Chef-owner Michael Stadtlander, with his wife and business partner, Nobuyo, accommodate no more than a dozen diners nightly, creating extravagant eight-course tasting menus ($275-300). And that's not including wine; the restaurant has no liquor license, so guests bring their own. The restaurant's schedule can be as wildly personal as the dining experience, so make reservations well in advance. It's about 13 kilometers (eight miles) south Collingwood via County Road 124.

The owners of Eigensinn Farm run the nearby **Haisai Restaurant & Bakery** (794079 County Rd. 124, Singhampton, 705/445-2748, www.haisairestaurantbakery.com, no credit cards). The bakery (11am-4pm Fri.-Sun.) sells freshly baked breads and pastries, along with a selection of prepared foods. The restaurant (11am-3pm Fri.-Sun.) serves imaginative pizzas, dim sum, and other dishes with locally sourced ingredients.

Information and Services

The **Georgian Triangle Tourist Association** (45 St. Paul St., 705/445-7722 or 888/227-8667, www.visitsouthgeorgianbay.ca) runs a visitor information center that provides information about the Collingwood-Blue Mountain region. **Greyhound Bus Lines** (800/661-8747, www.greyhound.ca) operates one daily bus in each direction between Toronto and Collingwood (3 hours); the same buses also go on to Blue Mountain. In town, the buses depart from Collingwood's **Transportation Centre** (22 2nd St., 705/445-7095). On the mountain, buses stop at the **Blue Mountain Inn** (www.bluemountain.ca).

Getting There and Around

Simcoe County Airport Service (705/728-1148 or 800/461-7529, www.simcoecountyairportservice.ca) runs regular vans from Toronto's Pearson Airport to Collingwood and the Blue Mountain Resort. Prices vary depending on the number of people in your party. From Pearson Airport to Collingwood, the one-way price is $97 for one person, $130 for two; to Blue Mountain, it's $109 for one, $143 for two. **Colltrans** (705/446-1196, www.collingwood.ca, 6:30am-9pm Mon.-Fri., 7am-6pm Sat., 9am-5pm Sun., $2) is the town's public transportation service, with several routes around the community and between Collingwood and Blue Mountain.

VICINITY OF COLLINGWOOD

Several small towns around Collingwood, including Thornbury and Meaford to the west and Creemore to the south, are worth exploring for their galleries, shops, and restaurants. Wasaga Beach, the world's longest freshwater beach, is also an easy day trip from Collingwood.

Creemore

This village of about 1,300 people makes a great day trip if you're looking for that elusive "small-town charm." The main downtown street—Mill Street—is lined with art galleries, cafés, and shops, ready-made for wandering and browsing. Creemore's main attraction is the **Creemore Springs Brewery** (139 Mill St., 705/466-2240 or 800/267-2240, www.creemoresprings.com, 10am-6pm Mon.-Sat., 11am-5pm Sun.), started in 1987 by three beer-loving guys who retired to the area and decided they needed a hobby. The brewery produces several varieties of beer, including their signature Creemore Springs Premium Lager. Free 30-minute tours, offered several times a day year-round, wrap up with a beer tasting.

The **Mad and Noisy Gallery** (154 Mill St., 705/466-5555, www.madandnoisy.com, 11am-5pm Mon.-Fri., 10am-5pm Sat., noon-4pm Sun. summer, call for off-season hours) is neither—it's named for the two rivers that meet near Creemore. It showcases high-quality work of painters, sculptors, photographers, and other artists, most of whom hail from the Southern Georgian Bay area. The **Maplestone Gallery** (142 Mill St., 705/520-0067, www.maplestonegallery.com, 11am-5pm Thurs.-Fri., 10am-5pm Sat., 11am-4pm Sun.) is unique in Canada for displaying only contemporary mosaic art. Many of the works are surprisingly ornate and, not surprisingly, beautiful. Want to learn to create mosaics yourself? The gallery runs periodic workshops for beginners.

Mill Street has several cafés, bakeries, and restaurants, as well as the **100 Mile Store** (176 Mill St., 705/466-3514, www.100milestore.ca), a local grocery that sources its products—from produce and meats to snacks, cheeses, and ice cream—within 100 miles of town.

The sign outside **Creemore Kitchen** (134 Mill St., 705/466-2900, www.creemorekitchen.ca, lunch 11am-2:30pm, dinner from 5:30pm Wed.-Mon., $8.50-28) says, "Seasonal. Local. Good Food," and that's what you get at this modern country kitchen in a cute country house. At lunch, try one of the sandwiches, like the Asian-inspired pork belly with pickled carrots on a steamed bun, and in the evening, your options might include Filipino-style spring rolls with onion-tomato jam, a seasonally changing pasta, or fried chicken with biscuits and gravy. There's a **bakery** (11am-4pm) if you'd like something sweet.

When you're done shopping and snacking, venture east of Mill Street to find the **Creemore Jail** (Library St., between Elizabeth St. and Caroline St.). This diminutive stone structure, built in 1892, claims to be the smallest jail in North America.

Creemore is about 30 kilometers (19 miles) southeast of Collingwood. Take Highway 26 east from Collingwood to Highway 42 south; then go west on Highway 9 into Creemore and turn left onto Mill Street.

Wasaga Beach

The Wasaga area had a part in the War of 1812, through a trading ship called the *Nancy*. Built in 1789, the *Nancy* was pressed into service as a British supply vessel. In 1814, American troops attacked the *Nancy* on the Nottawasaga River. The ship sank, and over the next century, the silt and sand flowing through the river collected around the ship's hull, preserving the remains and forming an island around the boat.

The *Nancy* was excavated in the 1920s, and today, at the **Nancy Island Historic Site** (119 Mosley St., 705/429-2728, www.wasagabeachpark.com, 10am-6pm daily mid-June-early Sept., 10am-6pm Sat.-Sun. late May-mid-June and early Sept.-mid-Oct.), you can see the *Nancy*'s hull, watch a video about her story, and join in as park staff reenact elements of the *Nancy*'s history. Also on the site is the **Wasaga Beach Welcome Centre**, which has information about the *Nancy* and

the surrounding area, a small museum, and a replica of an 1884 lighthouse that once stood near Collingwood's harbor.

Along Georgian Bay, **Wasaga Beach Provincial Park** (11 22nd St. N., 705/429-2516, www.ontarioparks.com, 8:15am-10pm daily Apr.-mid-Oct., Apr.-late June and early Sept.-mid-Oct. $20 per vehicle, late June-early Sept. $16-20) is the world's longest freshwater beach. This stretch of sand extends for 14 kilometers (nearly nine miles) and is divided into eight different sections, each with a different personality. Beaches 1 to 4 are closer into town and have more restaurants, shops, and other services; they're also more crowded and honky-tonk. As you move farther from the town center—to beaches 5 and 6 to the south and New Wasaga and Allenwood Beaches to the north—the sand becomes less populated and more peaceful. Because the beach is flat and the bay is shallow, Wasaga is a popular destination for families.

Although most people come for the beach, Wasaga also has 50 kilometers (31 miles) of hiking trails. The park service leads guided hikes on selected Wednesdays in July and August. In winter, there are 30 kilometers (19 miles) of trails for cross-country skiing. Access the trail network from the **Wasaga Nordic Centre** (101 Blueberry Trail, 705/429-0943, 9am-5pm daily mid-Dec.-mid-Mar., adults $13, ages 6-17 $6).

The **Town of Wasaga Beach** (705/429-3844, www.wasagabeach.com) and the **Wasaga Beach Chamber of Commerce** (705/429-2247 or 866/292-7242, www.wasagainfo.com) are good sources of information about accommodations and services in the Wasaga area, which includes the usual assortment of modest beach motels, plus privately run campgrounds (the provincial park has no camping facilities). The Chamber can provide details about cottage rentals. Located about 20 kilometers (12.5 miles) east of Collingwood, Wasaga Beach is an easy day trip; take Highway 26 to Highway 92.

Midland and Parry Sound

The peninsula on Georgian Bay's southwestern side that houses the towns of Midland and Penetanguishene played an important role in Ontario's early history. Long populated by First Nations people, in the 1600s a site near present-day Midland became the region's first European settlement, when a group of French Jesuits established a village. Several interesting historic sites, particularly the well-designed Sainte-Marie Among the Hurons, illuminate the region's past. The area retains a strong French and First Nations heritage.

Like other areas around Georgian Bay, the Midland region has its share of beautiful outdoor destinations, particularly Wye Marsh in Midland and the large Awenda Provincial Park in Penetanguishene. It's also a gateway to the 30,000 Islands region of Georgian Bay, some of which are protected in Georgian Bay Islands National Park. You can visit Georgian Bay Islands National Park in a day trip from Midland or Penetanguishene; it's less than an hour's drive to Honey Harbour, where the boat to the park islands departs.

North along Georgian Bay is Parry Sound, a pleasant community that's both a cultural destination and a base for outdoor activities; the ruggedly beautiful Killbear Provincial Park nearby draws travelers to its shores and waterfront campgrounds.

MIDLAND

The largest community along this part of Georgian Bay, Midland (population 17,000) still retains a low-key small-town feel along King Street, the main downtown street. The town has begun to sprawl out from the center, with malls and other developments, and its sights are spread around the area, but it's a convenient base for exploring the region's historic and outdoor attractions.

As you walk around downtown Midland, look for the 34 wall **murals** (www. downtownmidland.ca). One mural, painted on silos along Midland Harbor, depicts a Jesuit priest and a Wendat indigenous person at Sainte-Marie; it is reportedly the largest outdoor historic mural in North America. Pick up a mural map at the harbor-front **Midland Visitor Information Centre** (165 King St., 705/527-4050 or 855/527-4050, www. midland.ca, 9am-8pm daily May-Sept.).

★ Sainte-Marie Among the Hurons

In 1639, a group of French Jesuit missionaries began constructing a community near present-day Midland, establishing the first European settlement in Ontario. Their goal was to bring Christianity to the indigenous Wendat people, whom they called the "Hurons." The Jesuits worked with the Wendat for 10 years, until hostilities worsened between the Wendat and the nearby Iroquois people. After two priests were killed in skirmishes with the Iroquois, the Jesuits abandoned the settlement and burned it to the ground to protect it from desecration. Centuries later, in 1930, Pope Pius XI canonized the murdered priests, Jean de Brébeuf and Gabriel Lalemant.

What you see today at the fascinating historic village **Sainte-Marie Among the Hurons** (Hwy. 12 E., 705/526-7838, www. saintemarieamongthehurons.on.ca, 10am-5pm daily mid-May-mid-Oct., 10am-5pm Mon.-Fri. late Apr.-mid-May and late Oct., adults $12, seniors $10, students $10.50, ages 6-12 $9.25) is a "reimagination" of the 17th-century settlement. Because the Jesuits left no records, historians can only theorize what the community actually looked like. It wasn't until the 1940s and 1950s that archeologists began excavating the area, providing clues to the village's history and structure.

Sainte-Marie was reconstructed replicating French construction styles of the period.

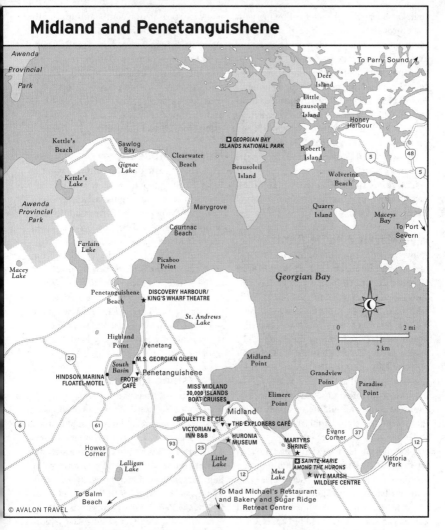

Midland and Penetanguishene

Surrounded by a high wooden fence, the settlement has 25 buildings in three main areas. The **North Court** was the mission's primary living and working quarters, including a cookhouse, chapel, carpentry shop, a chicken run, and stables. The **South Court,** where supplies arrived following an 800-mile canoe journey from Quebec, has a reconstructed waterway with working locks. The third section of the settlement was the **Native Area,** where a church, a longhouse, a hospital, and other

structures illustrate the mix of French and Wendat building styles and cultures.

You can easily spend several hours exploring the settlement. Start your visit with the 15-minute movie that introduces the site's history. In summer, costumed guides staff the village buildings, demonstrating elements of village life, from cooking to blacksmithing to Wendat storytelling. In spring or fall, when fewer staff are on duty, pick up the audio guide ($3 summer, free spring and fall) to help understand the site. Following your walk through the village, you can explore museum exhibits that provide more background and history about the settlement.

Sainte-Marie Among the Hurons organizes special events throughout the year. Highlights include the annual **Aboriginal Festival** (June), which honors the Wendat heritage with traditional dancing, music, games, and crafts, and the **First Light Festival** (late Nov.), which lights up the Sainte-Marie site with more than 3,000 candles.

The site is five kilometers (three miles) east on Highway 12 from the intersection of Highway 93.

Wye Marsh Wildlife Centre

A lovely spot to enjoy the outdoors is the nature center and marshlands at **Wye Marsh Wildlife Centre** (16160 Hwy. 12 E., 705/526-7809, www.wyemarsh.com, 9am-5pm daily, adults $11, seniors and students $8.50, ages 4-12 $8, families $30) on Midland's east side, next to Sainte-Marie Among the Hurons. The visitors center has exhibits about local ecology, and kids enjoy the live animal presentations, but the real action is outdoors on the network of walking trails. Rent an audio guide about the plants and wildlife, or simply follow the interpretive signs; climb the observation tower for views over the marsh.

The marsh is a nesting habitat for **trumpeter swans,** and one highlight of a visit here is the chance to observe these majestic birds. You can canoe or kayak on the channels that wind through the marsh, and guided canoe excursions ($8 pp) are offered. In winter, there are 22 kilometers (14 miles) of groomed trails for cross-country skiing and 10 kilometers (six miles) of snowshoeing trails. Ski ($15) and snowshoe rentals ($5-10) are available. A variety of other nature programs are offered throughout the year.

Martyrs' Shrine

Across the highway from Sainte-Marie Among the Hurons, the 1926 **Martyrs' Shrine** (16163 Hwy. 12 W., 705/526-3788, www.martyrs-shrine.com, 8am-9pm daily mid-May-mid-Oct., over age 11 $5, up to $20 per vehicle), with its two soaring spires, honors the memory of the two Jesuits who worked at Sainte-Marie but died in a 1649 Iroquois raid. Roman Catholic mass is held several times a day, and you can stroll the gardens and walkways. The site draws religious pilgrims from all over the world.

Huronia Museum

Exploring the **Huronia Museum** (549 Little Lake Park, 705/526-2844, www.huronia-museum.com, 9am-5pm daily May-Oct., 9am-5pm Mon.-Fri. Nov.-Apr., adults $10, seniors $7, ages 5-17 $5), an old-fashioned regional history museum, feels like a treasure hunt. You might find everything from washtubs to wheelchairs, sewing machines to the Slenderizer (an old-time exercise machine). Most of the hodgepodge of artifacts dates from the 1800s and 1900s. Also on the site is the Huron Ouendat Village, a modest re-creation of a 16th-century First Nations settlement.

Sports and Recreation

The Midland-Penetanguishene peninsula is surrounded by water, but many of the beaches are private. One exception is the small, sandy **Balm Beach** (www.visitbalmbeach.com) on Georgian Bay, a pretty spot to watch the sunset. From Midland, take Highway 25/Balm Beach Road directly west to the water. The **Miss Midland 30,000 Islands Boat Cruises** (705/549-3388, www.midlandtours.com, mid-May-mid-Oct., adults $28, seniors $26, students $21, ages 5-14 $15) are two-hour tours around Georgian Bay Islands National Park and some of the other islands in the 30,000 Islands region. Cruises depart from the Midland Town Dock at the foot of King Street.

Accommodations

Midland has the usual selection of chain motels, clustered along King Street near Highway 12 or on Yonge Street off Highway 93. Try the **Best Western Highland Inn** (924 King

St., 705/526-9307 or 800/461-4265, www.bestwesternmidland.com) or the **Midland Comfort Inn** (980 King St., 705/526-2090 or 888/274-3020, www.comfortinn.com). For more bed-and-breakfast options, check the website of the **Southern Georgian Bay B&B Association** (www.southerngeorgian-baybb.com).

You feel like part of the family when you stay at **The Victorian Inn Bed & Breakfast** (670 Hugel Ave., 705/526-4441 or 877/450-7660, www.victorianinn.ca, $119-149), a bright-yellow house with a wraparound porch. Two of the three homey guest rooms, with quilt-topped beds, have en suite baths; the larger Royal Suite has a separate sitting area and a private bath across the hall. Well-traveled owners Peter and Kim Hakkenberg have filled the dining room, where they serve a full breakfast, with mementos of their journeys. Children under age 12 are not permitted.

Set amid marshlands south of Midland, the peaceful ★ **Sugar Ridge Retreat Centre** (5720 Forgets Rd., Wyebridge, 705/528-1793 or 866/609-1793, www.sugarridge.ca, $149 s or d, includes breakfast) offers yoga retreats and other workshops. Owners Liz and Kurt Frost have 10 sturdy, simply furnished cabins, which sleep up to four, in the fields around the main lodge, a contemporary Zen-style retreat center with an airy yoga studio and large dining room. Cabins have no plumbing, phones, or Internet; restrooms, showers, and Wi-Fi are available in the lodge, where breakfast is served. Guests are welcome to join in **yoga classes** (nonguests $15).

Food

For places to eat in Midland, wander along King Street downtown. At **Ciboulette et Cie** (248 King St., 705/245-0410, www.ciboulet-teetcie.ca, 8am-6am Mon.-Thurs. and Sat., 8am-7pm Fri., 10am-4pm Sun.), a cheerful café and takeout shop (the name is French for "Chives and Co."), the day starts with freshly baked scones and other pastries. Creative sandwiches and delicious ready-to-eat salads, perhaps Brussels sprout slaw or roasted sweet potatoes with cranberries, make a quick lunch.

With its walls of books, maps, and photos of faraway lands, **The Explorers Cafe** (345 King St., 705/527-9199, www.theexplorerscafe.com, noon-10pm Tues.-Sat., lunch $10-17, dinner $21-32) resembles a Victorian-era adventurer's residence. The menu wanders the world, too, from Indian curry to Argentinean steak to East African-style shrimp. Despite the international emphasis, there's usually a "100-mile meal," with most ingredients locally sourced. Although the restaurant is right downtown, you may need a compass to find it, since it's set back from the main road; look for their signboard on King Street.

Craving Texas-style barbecue pork ribs? Jerk chicken? Barbecue brisket? Head for the little yellow bungalow, about 10 minutes south of Midland, that houses **MAD Michael's Restaurant and Bakery** (8215 Hwy. 93, Wyebridge, 705/527-1666, www.madmichaels.com, noon-8pm Thurs.-Sun. May-mid-Oct., lunch $9-20, dinner $15-25). This isn't any ordinary barbecue shack; chef "Mad" Michael White smokes ribs in his outdoor kitchen, bakes bread, and in his spare time, crafts rustic wood furniture. Save room for a slice of homemade pie.

Practicalities

The **Midland Visitor Information Centre** (165 King St., 705/527-4050 or 855/527-4050, www.midland.ca, 9am-8pm daily May-Sept.), near the waterfront downtown, has lots of information about the region. The Midland-Penetanguishene area is about 160 kilometers (100 miles) from Toronto. From Highway 93, take Highway 12 east, then turn left onto King Street for downtown Midland or continue east on Highway 12 to Sainte-Marie Among the Hurons, the Martyrs' Shrine, and Wye Marsh. You need a car to explore the attractions around the region.

PENETANGUISHENE

Smaller than nearby Midland, the town of Penetanguishene (population 9,300) has a strong French heritage; roughly 16 percent of the residents speak French as their first language. Penetanguishene's main attractions are the restored naval base at Discovery Harbour and the sprawling Awenda Provincial Park, which has the region's best beaches. Penetanguishene Harbor is also the departure point for the area's most interesting 30,000 Islands cruise.

Discovery Harbour

Ahoy, matey! Climb aboard the replicas of two majestic 18th-century British sailing vessels, the HMS *Bee,* a supply schooner, and the HMS *Tecumseth,* a warship, at **Discovery Harbour** (93 Jury Dr., 705/549-8064, www. discoveryharbour.on.ca, 10am-5pm daily July-early Sept., 10am-5pm Mon.-Fri. late May-June, adults $7, seniors and students $6.25, ages 6-12 $5.25), a restored naval base that the British built following the War of 1812 to protect the Upper Great Lakes region from future American attacks. While only one original building remains (the 1845 Officers' Quarters), the reconstructed site reflects naval and military life here in the 1800s. Guides in period costumes conduct tours of the 19 historic buildings and demonstrate various aspects of sailors' lives, including cooking, rope

work, and games. Also on-site is the HMS. *Tecumseth* Centre, which houses the original hull of this 1815 warship, as well as exhibits about and artifacts from Penetanguishene during the War of 1812.

30,000 Island Cruises

What makes the island cruises special on the **MS *Georgian Queen*** (705/549-7795 or 800/363-7447, www.georgianbaycruises. com, May-mid-Oct., adults $20-27, seniors $18-24, ages 5-14 $9-11, families $49-65) is the onboard commentary that the companionable captain provides. As you cruise out of Penetanguishene Harbor and out among the 30,000 Islands, Captain Steve will not only point out the sights, but he'll tell you who lives on what island (many are private), which properties are for sale and at what price, and how locals manage to build homes, transport goods, and spend summers on these isolated chunks of rock. The 1.5- to 3.5-hour cruises depart from the Town Docks at the foot of Main Street. Take one of the longer cruises if you can, since the shortest excursions stay around the harbor.

Awenda Provincial Park

Fronting Georgian Bay 11 kilometers (seven

tall ships at Discovery Harbour

miles) northwest of Penetanguishene, the 2,915-hectare (7,200-acre) **Awenda Provincial Park** (Awenda Park Rd., off Concession Rd. 16 E./Lafontaine Rd. E., 705/549-2231, www.ontarioparks.com, $14.50 per vehicle) is a beautiful destination for hiking and swimming. One of central Ontario's largest parks, Awenda is in a transition zone between north and south, making it home to a diverse array of plants and trees, as well as roughly 200 bird species and many reptiles and amphibians. In summer, park staff offer nature programs, theatrical productions, and other special events; call the park office or check online with **Friends of Awenda** (www.awendapark.ca) for schedules.

The park has approximately 30 kilometers (19 miles) of multiuse trails. The most popular is the easy **Beach Trail,** which connects the park's four beaches. Off the Beach Trail, you can follow the easy, one-kilometer (0.6-mile) **Beaver Pond Trail,** most of which is along a boardwalk, to an area that had extensive beaver activity. Longer park trails include the **Robitaille Homestead Trail,** a three-kilometer (1.9-mile) round-trip trail past ancient sand dunes that begins in the day parking lot near Bear Campground; the five-kilometer (three-mile) **Wendat Trail,** which starts near Kettle's Lake; and the 13-kilometer (eight-mile) **Bluff Trail,** which circles the campgrounds and connects the camping areas to the beach.

Some of the area's nicest swimming spots are within the provincial park, which has four beaches along Georgian Bay. **First Beach,** closest to the parking area, is a sheltered, family-friendly sand beach that also has rocks for the kids to climb. You can continue along the beach trail to **Second Beach; Third Beach,** which has particularly soft sand; and eventually to the more secluded **Fourth Beach.** It's about two kilometers (1.25 miles) from First to Fourth Beach.

You can also swim at **Kettle's Lake,** an inland lake with an easy boardwalk trail to the water. The lake is a calm spot for canoeing, particularly for beginning paddlers; in summer, canoe rentals are available. Around the lake, you might see otters, beavers, loons, or great blue herons. Awenda is open year-round, and you can cross-country ski here in winter.

Entertainment

Located at Discovery Harbour, the **King's Wharf Theatre** (97 Jury Dr., 705/549-5555, www.draytonentertainment.com) is a professional summer theater that produces several plays every year from June to early September.

Accommodations and Food

Catering primarily to boaters and their guests, the **Hindson Marina Floatel-Motel** (79 Champlain Rd., 705/549-2991, www.hindsonmarina.com, $125-179 d) is a floating lodging, right on the docks on the west side of Penetanguishene Harbor. The three rooms and one two-room suite are ordinary motel units, but you can't get much closer to the water than this. Entrance is through the marina gates.

Awenda Provincial Park's **Stone Cottage** (Awenda Park Rd., off Concession Rd. 16 E., 888/668-7275, www.ontarioparks.com, May-Oct., reservation fee online $11, by phone $13, late June-early Sept. $1,040 per week, May-June and Sept.-Oct. $150 per night) has a spacious terrace above the water and a huge living room with a stone fireplace and windows facing the bay. One bedroom has a double bed and two bunks, the other twin beds. It has no running water; drinking water is provided, and there's an outhouse but no shower. Bring sleeping bags or linens, food, and cooking gear. Make reservations well in advance.

Up the hill from Penetanguishene harbor, **Froth Café** (102 Main St., 705/549-7199, www.frothcafe.com, 8am-6pm Tues.-Sat., 9am-4pm Sun.) is convenient for breakfast, lunch, or a sightseeing coffee break. The menu is simple: scones, bagels, french toast, and omelets in the morning ($2-8); salads and sandwiches ($8-11), including a warm chicken panini, at midday. Jazz on the stereo and local art on the walls make it feel cool and arty, and Wi-Fi is free.

Camping

The six campgrounds at **Awenda Provincial Park** (Awenda Park Rd., off Concession Rd. 16 E./Lafontaine Rd. E., 888/668-7275, www.ontarioparks.com, mid-May-mid-Oct., reservation fee online $11, by phone $13, tent sites $40, electrical sites $46) are set amid maple and oak forests, so the 333 shaded sites feel comparatively private. All the camping areas have flush toilets and showers, and three have laundry. None of the campgrounds is on the water. The Snake, Wolf, and Deer Campgrounds are closest to the bay, but it's still a long walk. Bring bicycles if you can.

Practicalities

The **Penetanguishene Tourist Information Centre** (2 Main St., 705/549-2232, www.penetanguishene.ca, 9am-6pm daily May-Aug., 10am-6pm daily Sept.-Oct.) is at the town docks. The Midland-Penetanguishene area is about 160 kilometers (100 miles) from Toronto. Highway 93 connects Midland to Penetanguishene, where it becomes Main Street.

★ GEORGIAN BAY ISLANDS NATIONAL PARK

Georgian Bay is dotted with at least 30,000 islands. Some are not much more than a big rock jutting out of the water, while others are substantial enough to house entire communities. A visit to **Georgian Bay Islands National Park** (705/527-7200, www.pc.gc.ca), established in 1929 and encompassing 63 islands across Georgian Bay, is perhaps the easiest way to sample the island experience.

With numerous hiking trails, beaches, and campgrounds as well as a visitors center, Beausoleil Island, the largest of the park's islands, is the most accessible area. Parks Canada runs a seasonal boat service from Honey Harbour to Beausoleil to take day-trippers to the island (in fact, the boat is named

DayTripper). To reach islands other than Beausoleil Island, you need to have your own boat, make arrangements with a local outfitter, or hire a water taxi.

While experienced kayakers and canoeists can explore the park islands on their own, the park service advises extreme caution due to the frequently heavy boat traffic and the many rocks just under the surface that can surprise the unwary. The park has partnered with **White Squall Paddling Centre** (19 James St., Parry Sound, 705/746-4936, www.whitesquall.com) to offer guided kayak trips to some of the park's northern islands.

Honey Harbour is the jumping-off point to visit the park. It's about 168 kilometers (104 miles) northwest of Toronto and 35 kilometers (22 miles) northwest of Midland, the nearest major town. If you don't have a car, you can ride the convenient **Parkbus** (800/928-7101, www.parkbus.ca, adults $57 one-way, $82 round-trip, seniors and students $52 one-way, $74 round-trip, ages 2-12 $29 one-way, $41 round-trip) from Toronto to Honey Harbour on selected summer weekends. The bus departs from several points in Toronto, including 30 Carlton Street (between Yonge St. and Church St., subway: College) and Dufferin Street at Bloor Street West (subway: Dufferin).

Georgian Bay Islands National Park is technically open year-round, but park services, including boat transportation between Honey Harbour and Beausoleil Island, operate only between mid-May and mid-October.

Beausoleil Island

The main destination for visitors exploring Georgian Bay Islands National Park is this 11-square-kilometer (4.2-square-mile) island, 15 minutes by boat from the Parks Canada marina in Honey Harbour. A unique feature of Beausoleil Island is that it encompasses two different natural environments. The northern part of the island is typical of the Canadian Shield, which extends into Northern Ontario, with its rocky shoreline and its windblown juniper and pine forests. On Beausoleil's southern half, you'll see more hardwood trees,

That's a Lot of Islands

Many people outside Ontario know about the Thousand Islands, the chain of islands along the St. Lawrence River in the eastern part of the province. After all, there's even a salad dressing with the Thousand Islands name. Yet the Georgian Bay region has far more than just a thousand isles. Depending on who's counting, Georgian Bay is dotted with at least 30,000 islands. It's one of the world's largest freshwater archipelagoes. Some of these islands are hardly more than specks of bare rock, while others are quite substantial. Manitoulin Island, which measures 2,765 square kilometers (1,067 square miles) on the bay's northern side, is the largest freshwater island in the world.

What created these many different islands? During the ice age, more than 10,000 years ago, glaciers covered what is now Canada. According to one theory, the movement of these glaciers compressed and reshaped the land, fashioning the distinctive landscape of islands and coves that today surrounds Georgian Bay.

UNESCO has recognized the unique geography of the Georgian Bay region and its islands, designating 347,000 hectares (857,455 acres) of the shoreline between the Severn and French Rivers as the **Georgian Bay Biosphere Reserve** (705/774-0978, www.gbbr.ca). One of 15 such reserves in Canada, it's home to more than 100 species of at-risk animals and plants, including the eastern wolf, the lake sturgeon, and the Massasauga rattlesnake. The biosphere's mission is to assist in the conservation of these species and to support education and sustainable development in the region.

The 30,000 Islands are a mix of public and private lands. Some, like the 63 islands of **Georgian Bay Islands National Park** (705/526-9804, www.pc.gc.ca) or **Fathom Five National Marine Park** (519/596-2233, www.pc.gc.ca), are government-protected natural areas. Many others are privately owned, with a cottage or two offering their owners a waterfront getaway. Visitors to this island region can cruise around the bays and harbors, explore the island parks, and even soar above the islands by floatplane. So come back again; to tour even a fraction of these 30,000 islands will take years of exploring.

especially maples, beech, oak, and birch, and land that's grassy or marshy rather than rocky. The best sandy beaches are on the southern end, but you can swim almost anywhere that looks inviting. Bring your own food, water, and anything else you need (hiking shoes, swim suit, towel, and insect repellent). While park rangers are on duty on Beausoleil Island from spring to fall, there are no snack bars or other services.

Beausoleil Island has about a dozen marked hiking trails, including the 6.9-kilometer (4.3-mile) Huron path that runs between the island's north and south and the 2.5-kilometer (1.5-mile) loop around pretty Fairy Lake. Most are for hikers only, but mountain bikes are allowed on two of the routes. For trail details, pick up the free park *Visitor Guide* at any of the park offices or at the Beausoleil welcome center.

Parks Canada runs the **DayTripper** boat

(705/526-8907, adults $15.70, seniors $13.45, ages 6-16 $11.70) to transport visitors from Honey Harbour to Beausoleil Island. The *DayTripper* makes the 15-minute trip several times a day in July and August and Friday through Tuesday in the spring and fall. The *DayTripper* rates include park admission. Phone for reservations, which are advised.

Two privately owned water taxis also shuttle visitors from Honey Harbour to the park's islands: **Georgian Bay Water Services** (705/627-3062, www.gbws.ca) and **Honey Harbour Boat Club** (705/756-2411, www.hhbc.ca). If you take a water taxi to Beausoleil, park admission is adults $5.80, seniors $4.90, and ages 6-16 $2.90.

Accommodations and Food

Within the national park, you can camp or stay in one of the camping cabins. Otherwise, you'll need to sleep on the mainland.

Camping

Beausoleil Island has nine campgrounds. The largest is **Cedar Spring Campground** (705/526-8907, $25.50, reservation fee $9.80 per campsite), near the boat dock, with 56 tent sites and six family-friendly two-bedroom camping cabins (sleeps up to 5, $160), as well as flush toilets and showers.

In addition to the cabins at Cedar Spring, four lovely secluded **cabins** ($140) overlook the shore at **Christian Beach.** Sleeping two adults, the cabins come with a queen bed, a table and chairs, barbecues, and solar-powered electricity. Park staff transport your gear from the *DayTripper* dock and provide water; the cabins have no plumbing, but there's a composting toilet nearby. Consider bringing or renting a mountain bike, which will give you more flexibility in exploring the island. It's a 1.8-kilometer (1.2-mile) walk from the Cedar Spring boat dock.

If you don't have camping gear or don't want the hassle of transporting it, ask about the park's **equipped camping service** (705/526-8907, reservations required, $55). You get a large prospector tent that staff set up before you arrive, with cots or sleeping pads, along with a dining shelter, a table and chairs,

a propane stove, and a water container. Bring sleeping bags or bedding, food, cooking gear, and other personal items.

The island's remaining primitive campgrounds ($15.70) are first-come, first-served with either pit or composting toilets. Campers must bring their own water:

- **Honeymoon Bay** (13 sites), at the island's northernmost end
- **Chimney Bay** (6 sites)
- **The Oaks** (7 sites)
- **Sandpiper** (8 sites)
- **Tonch North** (4 sites)
- **Tonch East** (7 sites)
- **Tonch South** (7 sites)
- **Thumb Point** (8 sites)

Outside the Park

The village of Honey Harbour, where the park boat dock is located, has a handful of seasonal places to stay and eat. Port Severn is a blink-and-you'll-miss-it town off Highway 400's exit 153, just south of the Honey Harbour turnoff, but it has the nicest lodging in the vicinity of the national park. If you want to stay somewhere with more food and entertainment options, sleep in the Midland area and spend the

Christian Beach cabins in the Georgian Bay Islands National Park

day in the national park; it's about an hour's drive.

The closest lodging to the park, **Delawana Inn Resort** (42 Delawana Rd., Honey Harbour, 888/557-0980, www.delawana.ca) has been a summer camp-like property since the 1890s. New owners purchased the resort and resumed limited operations in 2014, while renovations were underway and new programming was in development. Call or check the website for an update.

The **Rawley Resort and Spa** (2900 Kellys Rd., Port Severn, 705/538-2272 or 800/263-7538, www.rawleyresort.com) feels like a waterfront estate, particularly as you sit in the dining room, looking across the manicured lawns to the water. The restaurant is rather formal, serving classic dishes such as veal scaloppini, grilled steak, or roasted Alaskan halibut, with live jazz several nights a week. Accommodations are spread over several buildings and range from upscale guest rooms, to large one- or two-bedroom suites, to two-story loft units overlooking the water. There's an outdoor pool and a small beach.

Information and Services

The administrative office of **Georgian Bay Islands National Park** (705/527-7200, info. gbi@pc.gc.ca, 8am-4pm Mon.-Fri.) is located in Midland. You can phone or email for information year-round. The park service runs a **Welcome Centre** (9:30am-5pm Sun.-Thurs., 9am-7pm Fri., 9am-6pm Sat. July-Aug., 9:30am-5pm Sun.-Tues., 9am-7pm Fri., 9am-6pm Sat. mid-May-June and Sept.-mid-Oct.) on Beausoleil Island, near the Cedar Spring Campground.

At the **Lock 45 Port Severn Welcome Centre** (175 Port Severn Rd. N., Port Severn, 705/538-2586, mid-May-mid-Oct.), off Highway 400's exit 153 between Midland and Honey Harbour, Parks Canada staff provides information about park and area activities. The Welcome Centre is located on the 386-kilometer (240-mile) **Trent-Severn Waterway** that connects Lake Ontario with Georgian Bay; the lock station has a small exhibit area about the waterway and the lock system, and you can watch boats transiting the lock.

PARRY SOUND

Fronting Georgian Bay, Parry Sound is a jumping-off point for exploring the 30,000 Islands region, which dots the waters just offshore. It's a popular destination for kayaking, whether you're just getting started or you're an experienced paddler. For a relatively small community (the year-round population is about 6,000), Parry Sound has a surprisingly robust cultural life, drawing music lovers in particular to the beautifully designed performing arts center.

Parry Sound's most famous native son may be hockey player Bobby Orr, whose legacy lives on in the **Bobby Orr Hall of Fame** (Charles W. Stockey Centre for the Performing Arts, 2 Bay St., 705/746-4466 or 877/746-4466, www.bobbyorrhalloffame.com, 10am-5pm Tues.-Sat., 11am-4pm Sun. July-early Sept., 10am-5pm Wed.-Sat. early Sept.-June; adults $9, seniors and children $6, families $25). The first-floor exhibits document Orr's legendary National Hockey League career, beginning in 1962, when the Boston Bruins recruited him for their junior team at age 14. If you have kids in tow, they'll likely head upstairs to play the hockey skills games.

30,000 Islands Cruises

Off the Parry Sound coast, Georgian Bay is dotted with thousands of islands, and one of the best ways to explore this coastal region is on a cruise. The 550-passenger *Island Queen* (9 Bay St., 705/746-2311 or 800/506-2628, www.islandqueencruise.com), which bills itself as Canada's largest sightseeing boat, runs a three-hour cruise (1pm daily June-mid-Oct., adults $38, ages 6-12 $19) that passes Killbear Provincial Park and circles a number of the islands. In July and August, there's also a two-hour morning cruise (10am daily July-Aug., adults $28, ages 6-12 $14) that sticks closer to shore and the inner islands, where you can catch glimpses of cottages and vacation homes.

After years of service as Niagara Falls' *Maid of the Mist*, the **MV *Chippewa III*** (Spirit of the Sound Schooner Co., Seguin River Parkette, off Bay St., 705/746-6064 or 888/283-5870, www.spiritofthesound.ca, July-Aug.) tours the waters off Parry Sound. They offer a variety of island cruises, including a two-hour afternoon cruise (adults $26, under age 17 $13), a sunset cocktail cruise (adults $30, under age 17 $15), and a dinner cruise (adults $60, under age 15 $4 per year). They also run trips to **Henry's Fish Restaurant** (705/746-9040, mid-May-Sept.) on Frying Pan Island (adults $38, under age 17 $19), combining a cruise with a stop for a fish-and-chips lunch.

★ Flight-Seeing

Touring the 30,000 Islands by boat is a lovely way to spend an afternoon, but seeing the islands by air is an entirely different thrill. Run by husband-and-wife pilots Keith and Nicole Saulnier, **Georgian Bay Airways** (11A Bay St., 705/774-9884 or 800/786-1704, www.georgianbayairways.com, May-Oct.) flies Cessna floatplanes that take off from Parry Sound Harbor and soar over the nearby islands. Seeing the islands from above gives you a much clearer picture of their number and diversity; some are barely more than a boulder in the bay, while others support entire towns. Keith and Nicole know the region well and can tell you all about the islands below.

The basic tour runs 25-35 minutes (adults $103-135), or you can opt for a variety of special flights, from a sunset champagne flight ($310 per couple) to a fish-and-chips meal at **Henry's Fish Restaurant** (705/746-9040, mid-May-Sept.) on Frying Pan Island. They've hosted in-flight marriage proposals, and even a wedding, so if you have something special in mind, let them know.

Canoeing and Kayaking

The Parry Sound area is an excellent starting point for canoe or kayak tours, and one well-established local outfitter has two locations to help you get out on the water. The **White Squall Paddling Centre** (53 Carling Bay Rd., Nobel, 705/342-5324, www.whitesquall.com, 9am-5:30pm Sat.-Thurs., 9am-8pm Fri. Apr.-Aug., 9am-5:30pm daily Sept.-mid-Oct.), on Cole Lake, rents canoes and kayaks, offers lessons that including stand-up paddleboarding, and organizes a variety of day-trips as well as multiday kayak tours. It's located off Highway 559 en route to Killbear Provincial Park.

In downtown Parry Sound, the **White**

The M.V. *Chippewa III* cruises the waters near Parry Sound.

Squall Outdoor Gear Store (19 James St., 705/746-4936, www.whitesquall.com, 9:30am-5:30pm Mon.-Thurs. and Sat., 9:30am-8pm Fri., 11am-4pm Sun. summer) is primarily a gear shop, but you can get information about rentals and trips here, too.

Entertainment and Shopping

The hub of cultural life in Parry Sound—indeed, in this entire region of Ontario—is the **Charles W. Stockey Centre for the Performing Arts** (2 Bay St., 705/746-4466 or 877/746-4466, www.stockeycentre.com). This striking contemporary building, right on the bay and built of local timber and stone, hosts concerts, lectures, and other events year-round. Parry Sound's major cultural event, held at the Stockey Centre, is the annual **Festival of the Sound** (42 James St., 705/746-2410 or 866/364-0061, www.festivalofthesound.ca). Since 1979, this classical-music festival has been drawing Canadian and international musicians and music lovers for three weeks of concerts in July and August.

Accommodations

Parry Sound has several B&Bs and small inns located between downtown and the harbor. The nicest spots to relax at the homey and well-located **40 Bay Street Bed & Breakfast** (40 Bay St., 705/746-9247 or 866/371-2638, www.40baystreet.com, $150-200 d) are the two sunporches overlooking the harbor. The Bay Room, the smallest of the three cozy guest quarters (all with private baths), has expansive harbor views, too. The Retreat Room's special feature is the oversize bath, and the Garden Room lives up to its name with a private deck facing the flower-filled yard. No kids under age 11.

You have plenty of space to unwind at **Victoria Manor Bed & Breakfast** (43 Church St., 705/774-1125, www.victoria-manorbb.ca, $108 d), constructed in 1907, with a traditional parlor, cozy book-lined library, and large screened porch. Upstairs, three comfortable guest rooms have individual touches: the Blue Room has a private deck,

the Red room has an antique washbasin, and the bay-windowed Pink Room features an elaborately quirky lamp. Though the rooms share one large bath, guests sign up for their morning shower time to minimize congestion. The B&B is a short walk from downtown.

Built in 1882 (with a 1950s addition), the rambling 11-room **Bayside Inn** (10 Gibson St., 705/746-7720 or 866/833-8864, www.ps-baysideinn.com, $128-143 d) is conveniently located near downtown. The well-turned-out rooms, done in a modern country style, all have air-conditioning, flat-screen TVs, Wi-Fi, and refrigerators. For families, ask for a room with two sleeping areas separated by a divider. Free coffee and tea are available every morning, and guests can have breakfast for a small additional charge (continental $4, full breakfast $8).

Though rustic on the outside, the six units (in three cabins) overlooking the river at the **Log Cabin Inn** (9 Little Beaver Blvd., at Oastler Park Dr., 705/746-7122, www.log-cabininn.net, $150 d) are country-contemporary inside, with a king or two queen beds, fireplaces, and modern baths. Rates include continental breakfast, and packages including breakfast and dinner in the upscale restaurant are available. The property is three kilometers (1.9 miles) south of town.

Food

The downtown area, around the intersection of Seguin and James Streets, has several basic places to eat. Along the harbor, Bay Street has a couple of seasonal eateries, open in the summer and fall.

Families and couples, visitors and locals, even the occasional visiting hockey team all turn up at **Wellington's Pub and Grill** (105 James St., 705/746-1333, www.wellingtonspubandgrill.com, $10-25), a friendly pub-restaurant downtown decorated with black-and-white photos from Parry Sound's past. From salads to steaks to succulent schnitzel, the food is straightforward but tasty, and the bar stocks plenty of local brews.

For more gourmet dining, head south of

Two More Georgian Bay Parks

Traveling along Highway 69 north of Parry Sound, you'll find two more provincial parks that are worth a stop for an afternoon, a weekend, or more: Grundy Lake and French River.

GRUNDY LAKE PROVINCIAL PARK

The family-friendly outdoor destination **Grundy Lake Provincial Park** (20400 Hwy. 522, Britt, 705/383-2286, www.ontarioparks.com, mid-May-mid-Oct., $14.50 per vehicle) is filled with lakes, and not just the one that gives the park its name. The forests, wetlands, rocky shores, and sandy beaches feel less wild, at least in the front country, than in the parks fronting Georgian Bay, but Grundy Lake has a gentle beauty and plenty to do.

The park's **Interpretive Centre** at Smokey Point offers summer nature programs, guided hikes, and other activities for kids. You can swim from sandy Main Beach on Grundy Lake and from the seven other **beaches** around the park, and the calm waters make for peaceful canoeing and kayaking. Though the park doesn't rent boats, **Grundy Lake Supply Post** (Hwy. 69 at Hwy. 522, Britt, 705/383-2251, www.grundylakesupplypost.com, 8am-9pm daily July-early Sept., 8am-5pm Mon.-Sat., 9am-5pm Sun. mid-May-June and early Sept.-mid-Oct.) does, and they'll deliver **canoes** ($30-35 per day) and **kayaks** ($30 per day) to the park.

For **hiking**, the park has several moderate trails. The 2.5-kilometer (1.5-mile) Gut Lake Trail follows the rock-lined shore that's part of the Canadian Shield, while the 1.5-kilometer (0.9-mile) Swan Lake Trail wanders through the marshlands around Swan Lake. On the 3.6-kilometer (2.25-mile) Beaver Dams Trail, you'll see the dams that give the path its name; park staff report that hikers have spotted deer, grouse, and even moose on this trail.

Campers can choose from 586 sites across nine **campgrounds** (tent sites $40-44, electrical sites $46-50). Most have sites on or near a lakeshore, with showers, flush toilets, and laundry facilities nearby. Grundy Lake offers Ontario Parks's **Learn to Camp** program on several summer weekends. The park provides tents, air mattresses, a camp stove, cooking equipment, and firewood, and staff teach you the basics for getting started outdoors, from pitching a tent to building a campfire. Grundy also runs two-hour **Learn to Fish** programs, where you learn fundamental fishing skills and then go out to catch your own.

town to the **Log Cabin Inn** (9 Little Beaver Blvd., at Oastler Park Dr., 705/746-7122, www.logcabininn.net, lunch $8-15, dinner $23-40), where you can sample apple-wood-smoked pork chops, pan-seared pickerel, or filet mignon in, yes, a log cabin. Don't expect pioneer hardship, though; the solid log structure with a soaring ceiling overlooks the river, with a fireplace, twinkling candles, and a lengthy wine list setting the mood.

Information and Services

Georgian Bay Country Tourism (70 Church St., 705/746-1287 or 888/229-7257, www.gbcountry.com) can provide information about the Parry Sound region. Parry Sound is 222 kilometers (138 miles) northwest of Toronto along Highway 400/69. It's 163 kilometers (101 miles) south of Sudbury via Highway 69, and 170 kilometers (105 miles) from Killarney.

Getting There and Around

Ontario Northland (800/461-8558, www.ontarionorthland.ca) runs three buses daily in each direction between Toronto and Parry Sound (3.5 hours, adults $53) and between Parry Sound and Sudbury (2-2.5 hours, adults $37). Buses stop at Richard's Coffee (119 Bowes St., 705/746-9611), about 1.8 kilometers (1.1 miles) east of downtown. Two or three times a week, **VIA Rail** (888/842-7245, www.viarail.ca) runs the *Canadian* between Vancouver and Toronto; it stops at Parry Sound Train Station (70 Church St.), about one kilometer (0.6 miles) north of downtown,

Grundy Lake is 85 kilometers (53 miles) north of Parry South and about 20-minutes' drive south of the Highway 637 turnoff for Killarney Provincial Park.

FRENCH RIVER PROVINCIAL PARK

The French River, which runs 110 kilometers (68 miles) from Lake Nipissing to Georgian Bay, was an aboriginal trading route for thousands of years before the first French explorers and missionaries arrived in the early 1600s. The river became an important passage for the fur trade in the 1700s and early 1800s. **French River Provincial Park** (705/857-1630, www.ontarioparks.com) incorporates part of this territory, and it's a good place to take a break along Highway 69. The park **Visitors Centre** (daily July-Aug., Sat.-Sun. late-May-June and Sept.-mid-Oct., $2), in an interesting modern building, has a *Voices of the River* exhibit about the area's history, particularly the mix of First Nations, French, and English cultures.

A short walk from the Visitors Centre, a suspension bridge soars over the French River. It's the **world's largest snowmobile bridge**, measuring 156 meters (512 feet) long, built in 2005 by the French River Snow Voyageurs Snowmobile Club. The bridge has great views up and down the river. The four-kilometer (2.5-mile) **Recollet Falls Trail,** which starts at the Visitors Centre, follows the French River Gorge to the waterfall, a route that First Nations people, fur traders, and other explorers would have traveled centuries ago. If you want to stay a while, the park has 230 backcountry campsites. There's no road access to any of the sites, so you need to backpack or paddle in.

French River Provincial Park is about 15 minutes' drive from Grundy Lake. It's 90 kilometers (56 miles) north of Parry Sound and 65 kilometers (40 miles) south of Sudbury.

NO CAR, NO PROBLEM

If you don't have a car, or if you don't want the hassle of driving, check the schedule for the **Parkbus** (800/928-7101, www.parkbus.ca, adults $60 one-way, $86 round-trip, seniors and students $54 one-way, $77 round-trip, ages 2-12 $30 one-way, $43 round-trip), which can take you from Toronto directly to either of these parks on selected weekends.

GEORGIAN BAY
MIDLAND AND PARRY SOUND

but the schedule is much less convenient than the bus. Parry Sound's attractions are clustered along the harbor, a short walk from downtown. For taxi service, try **Parry Sound Taxi** (705/746-1221).

★ KILLBEAR PROVINCIAL PARK

With pink granite cliffs, windblown pines, and several long sandy beaches along Georgian Bay, **Killbear Provincial Park** (35 Killbear Park Rd., Nobel, 705/342-5492, www.ontarioparks.com, $14.50 per vehicle) is a spectacular location for outdoor activities such as hiking, canoeing, and swimming. Lesser known than Ontario's "destination" provincial parks like Algonquin or Killarney, Killbear is less than an hour's drive from Parry Sound, which makes it an easy day trip. If you'd like to stay longer, Killbear's campgrounds are the third largest in the Ontario provincial park system; only Algonquin and The Pinery have more campsites.

The park **Visitors Centre** (705/342-5492, 10am-5pm daily mid-May-mid-Oct.) has exhibits about the geology, natural history, and cultural history of the Killbear area. Particularly popular with the kids (well, with most of them) are the snake exhibits; in summer, naturalists give "snake talks" where you can learn about and touch local reptiles. In July and August, you can join in guided hikes, slide shows, kids' activities, and or other interpretive programs. Be sure to walk around to the back of the Visitors Centre for great views of Georgian Bay.

Killbear is home to the endangered Massasuaga rattlesnake. While it's not likely you'll see one, if you do come upon a rattlesnake near the campgrounds or along the road, notify a park staff member, who will relocate the snake to a less-traveled area. Don't try to pick up or move the snake yourself.

The park is officially open mid-May through mid-October, but in the off-season, you can walk in for winter hiking, cross-country skiing, or snowshoeing.

Sports and Recreation

Several easy hiking trails run through the park, making Killbear pleasant for novice hikers. Heading along the shoreline out to the far end of the park, the **Lighthouse Point Trail** is an easy one-kilometer (0.6-mile) route that passes a 1904 lighthouse. The 3.5-kilometer (2.2-mile) **Lookout Point Trail** goes through the forest to a lookout above Georgian Bay. For the bayside views of the park's pink granite rocks, follow the **Twin Points Trail,** a 1.6-kilometer (1-mile) path loop from the day-use parking area. A six-kilometer (3.7-mile) walking and cycling trail runs from the park entrance past several of the campgrounds to Lighthouse Point.

Killbear's three kilometers (1.9 miles) of sandy beaches include a popular swimming beach at the day-use area. You can swim near most of the campgrounds as well. **Harold Point,** with both a sand beach and rocky cliffs, is a pretty spot to watch the sunset.

Surrounded by water on three sides, Killbear is popular for canoeing and kayaking. The most sheltered waters are near the park's day-use area. Canoe and kayak rentals are not available inside the park, but you can rent boats by the day from nearby outfitters from mid-May to mid-October, including **Killbear Park Mall** (495 Hwy. 559, Nobel, 705/342-5747, www.killbearparkmall.com, canoes $24, single kayaks $29, double kayaks $45, stand-up paddleboards $29) and **The Detour Store** (401 Hwy. 559, Nobel, 705/342-1611, www.thedetourstore. ca, canoes $22-28, single kayaks $25-30,

double kayaks $35-40). **White Squall Paddling Centre** (53 Carling Bay Rd., Nobel, 705/342-5324, www.whitesquall. com), off Highway 559 en route to Killbear, rents a variety of canoes ($42-47 per day), kayaks (single $24-50 per day, double $33-72 per day), and stand-up paddleboards ($24-33 per day), and runs a shuttle service to deliver boats to locations in and around the park.

Camping

Killbear Provincial Park (35 Killbear Park Rd., Nobel, 705/342-5492, www.ontarioparks.com, tent sites $40-44, electrical sites $46-50) has seven different campgrounds, with a total of 880 campsites, most within a five-minute walk of the shore. All the campgrounds, except for the more remote 55-site Granite Saddle area, have restrooms, showers, and laundry facilities. About one-quarter of the sites have electrical hookups. Among the prime sites are the waterfront campsites fronting the beach at **Kilcoursie Bay.** Other campgrounds with waterfront sites include **Beaver Dams, Harold Point,** and **Lighthouse Point.**

Killbear's campgrounds book up early, so make reservations well in advance through **Ontario Parks Reservation Service** (888/668-7275, www.ontarioparks.com, reservation fee online $11, by phone $13). You can make reservations up to five months before your stay.

Information and Services

Contact the **Killbear Provincial Park office** (35 Killbear Park Rd., Nobel, 705/342-5492, www.ontarioparks.com) or check online with **Friends of Killbear** (www.friendsofkillbear. com) for more information. Several small stores along Highway 559 stock food and other provisions. For a better selection, do your shopping in Parry Sound.

Getting There and Around

By road, Killbear Provincial Park is 35

kilometers (22 miles) northwest of Parry Sound, about a 45-minute drive. From Parry Sound, take Highway 69 north to Nobel, where you pick up Highway 559 west to the park. There's no public transportation to or around the park, so you'll need to come by car.

Killarney

Located on Georgian Bay south of Sudbury, Killarney ranks among Ontario's most beautiful natural destinations. This wilderness park juts out into the bay with white dolomite ridges and pink granite cliffs providing a striking backdrop for hiking, canoeing, and kayaking.

★ KILLARNEY PROVINCIAL PARK

One of Ontario's premier outdoor destinations, **Killarney Provincial Park** (Hwy. 637, Killarney, 705/287-2900, www.ontarioparks.com, $14.50 per vehicle) is known for its striking scenery, particularly the white quartzite and pink granite cliffs that dominate the hilly ridges throughout the park. Dense pine forests surround more than 40 crystal blue lakes, and the park is home to approximately 100 bird species. Killarney's rolling hills are what remains of the La Cloche Mountains. Worn down over millions of years, the La Cloche range once had peaks taller than the present-day Rockies. Today, white rocks peek out through the woods near the peaks, and the granite cliffs that surround many of the lakes and the shores of Georgian Bay glow with a pinkish cast, particularly in the early-morning and late-afternoon sun.

At 645 square kilometers (250 square miles), Killarney is tiny compared to mammoth Algonquin Provincial Park. Yet it feels more remote, with secluded wilderness territory just a short hike or paddle away. This wilderness naturally takes some effort to reach. The park is located off Highway 69 between Parry Sound and Sudbury. Within the park, services are limited and camping is the only accommodations option, although lodgings,

restaurants, and services are located nearby in the village of Killarney.

For most Killarney visitors, the first stop is **George Lake** (off Hwy. 637), where the main park office and campground are located. You can swim or canoe here, and it's the starting point for two of the park's hiking trails. At the **Killarney Park Observatory** (George Lake), evening astronomy programs are held regularly in summer. The park hosts other summer events, from nature presentations to concerts, at the George Lake Amphitheatre. Get schedules from the park office or the **Friends of Killarney Park** (www.friendsofkillarneypark.ca).

Killarney Provincial Park is open year-round, but many businesses in the village close from mid-October to May. And at any time of year, be prepared for sudden storms and rapid weather changes. Even if it's sunny when you head out in the morning, a storm can blow in by afternoon.

Beaches

Killarney's most accessible swimming beaches are two sandy stretches along George Lake. The main beach at **George Lake** is in the day-use area; it's a launching point for canoes and kayaks, so just watch for paddling traffic. **Second Beach** is in the George Lake Campground. You can also swim in the park's numerous interior lakes and rivers.

Canoeing and Kayaking

George Lake is the park's most popular spot for short canoe excursions. You can easily paddle for an hour or two, appreciating the striking scenery, with pink granite cliffs surrounding sections of the lake. **Bell Lake,** on the park's east side, is another good canoeing spot. From the Bell Lake Road turnoff from Highway 637—21 kilometers (13 miles) east of George Lake or 38 kilometers (24 miles) west of Highway 69—it's about nine kilometers (5.5 miles) farther to the lake. Other kayaking destinations include **Chikanishing Creek** (Chikanishing Rd., off Hwy. 637) and areas along Georgian Bay.

Killarney Outfitters (1076 Hwy. 637, 705/287-2828 or 888/222-3410, www.killarneyoutfitters.com) and **Killarney Kanoes** (Bell Lake, 705/287-2197 or 888/461-4446, www.killarneykanoes.com) rent canoes and kayaks at both George and Bell Lakes.

With more than 40 lakes throughout the park, Killarney is a launching point for multiday canoe trips. Killarney Outfitters offers a trip-planning service ($95) that includes suggesting a route, arranging for permits, and preparing a detailed trip plan. They provide gear packages ($84-95 pp per day) for multiday canoe or kayak trips, including canoe or kayak rental, camping gear, and cooking equipment. Another service is a shuttle for canoeists whose excursions start at one point and end at another. Killarney Kanoes can also outfit you for a multiday canoe, kayak, or backpacking adventure.

Based in Parry Sound, the **White Squall Paddling Centre** (705/746-4936 or 705/342-5324, www.whitesquall.com) is another outfitter that organizes multiday kayak trips in the Killarney area.

Hiking

Killarney Provincial Park isn't really a beginner's hiking destination, but the park rates several of the trails "moderate," suitable for people who can manage some steep sections and rocky terrain. Hiking times are estimates only; it's a good idea to talk with park staff before you head out.

Across the highway from the George Lake park office, you can pick up the **Granite Ridge Trail,** which winds through the forest and climbs up to two lookout points, one overlooking Georgian Bay and the other onto the rocky cliffs of La Cloche Range. Allow 1 to 1.25 hours for this moderate two-kilometer (one-mile) loop trail. The longer **Cranberry Bog Trail** (four kilometers, 2.5 miles) starts in the George Lake Campground; the trailhead is near site no. 101. As the name suggests, it passes through bogs and marshes, and then goes along A. Y. Jackson Lake, named for one of the Group of Seven artists. Allow about two hours round-trip.

A short hike that gives you beautiful views of Georgian Bay's rocky shores is the **Chikanishing Trail.** Allow 1 to 1.5 hours for this three-kilometer (1.9-mile) loop that involves some scrambles across massive granite boulders (best save this hike for a dry day, as the rocks can be slippery when wet). The trailhead is at the end of Chikanishing Road, off Highway 637 about two kilometers (1.2 miles) west of George Lake.

For great vistas across the La Cloche Mountains, climb up through the boulders of **The Crack,** a challenging but rewarding trail. This six-kilometer (3.7-mile) route has difficult, rocky sections, and the trail is not a loop, so you must return the same way you came in. Pick up the trail off Highway 637, seven kilometers (4.3 miles) east of the George Lake park office. Save this hike for a clear day to appreciate the awesome views. The trail to The Crack is part of the 100-kilometer (62-mile) **La Cloche Silhouette Trail,** a difficult backpacking route that will take many hikers at least seven days.

On the east side of the park, the **Lake of the Woods Trail** is a 3.5-kilometer (2.2-mile) loop around Lake of the Woods; part of the route crosses a beaver dam. The trail starts from Bell Lake Road, which is off Highway 637, about 21 kilometers (13 miles) east of George Lake or 38 kilometers (24 miles) west of Highway 69.

Art Programs

If Killarney's natural setting inspires you to make art, look for details about the **Artist-in-Residence Program.** Created by the Friends of Killarney Park, this summer program brings an established artist to the park to work and offer classes to visitors. Check with the park office or the Friends of Killarney Park website (www.friendsofkillarneypark.ca) for details about these art experiences.

Skiing and Snowshoeing

The park has more than 30 kilometers (19 miles) of trails for cross-country skiing and snowshoeing. The trails all start at the George Lake Park Office, which also offers snowshoe rentals. You can usually expect plenty of snow December through March.

Camping

Killarney's car-camping area is the **George Lake Campground** (July-mid-Oct. $44, mid-Oct.-June $35), which has 128 campsites, with flush toilets, showers (July-mid-Oct.), and laundry facilities, but no electricity. The most secluded spots are near Second Beach, along Blue Heron Circle, although those sites are also the farthest from the showers.

To reserve a campsite, contact **Ontario Parks Reservations** (888/668-7275, www.ontarioparks.com, reservation fee online $11, by phone $13) up to five months in advance; early reservations are recommended, particularly for summer weekends. Campsites can be

reserved from May to October; the rest of the year, sites are first-come, first-served.

The George Lake Campground also has six **yurts** (year-round, reservations required, $98). Aluminum-framed yurts sleep up to six, have two bunk beds with a double lower and single upper bunk, a table and chairs, and electric heat. The adjacent deck has a propane-fueled barbecue and a bear-proof box for storing your food. It's a few-minutes' walk from the yurt parking area (spring-fall); each yurt has a cart for hauling your gear. In winter, so you must ski or snowshoe 500 meters (0.3 miles) from the front gate. Toilets and water taps are located near the parking area.

For a true wilderness experience, head for one of Killarney's year-round **backcountry campsites** (705/287-2900, www.ontarioparks.com, adults $12, ages 6-17 $5.10). You can hike in to 33 of these sites; another 140 backcountry campsites are accessible only by canoe.

Killarney Kanoes (Bell Lake, 705/287-2197 or 888/461-4446, www.killarneykanoes.com) rents tents, sleeping bags, and other camping gear.

The Village of Killarney

About 500 people live in the village of

view from the top of The Crack trail at Killarney Provincial Park

Killarney, which is on the harbor 10 kilometers (six miles) west of the provincial park. Until 1962, when Highway 637 was built between Killarney and Highway 69, the only way to get to the village was by water (or in winter, across the ice to Manitoulin Island). Killarney was originally known by its Ojibwa name, Shebahonaning, and many present-day residents have aboriginal roots.

Most of the town's lodgings and services are located on or near Channel Street, named for the Killarney Channel, which the street follows. The nicest time to stroll along the waterfront is in the early evening, as the sun begins to set. The land you see directly across the channel is George Island. Formerly a logging area, the island is now primarily wilderness. You can hike around the island on the 7.5-kilometer (4.7-mile) **George Island Trail,** which is rated moderate to difficult; make sure you have sturdy hiking boots and enough food and water for the day. Both the **Killarney Mountain Lodge** (705/287-2242, www.killarney.com) and the Sportsman's Inn (705/287-9990, www.sportsmansinn.ca) arrange boat transportation to and from George Island.

Originally built in 1868 and rebuilt in 1909, the **Killarney East Lighthouse** (Ontario St.) is at the mouth of the channel on the east side of the village. You can hike or swim nearby, and it's especially pretty just before sunset.

Accommodations and Food

None of the places to stay in the village of Killarney are particularly upscale, but most are comfortable enough and have restaurants or pubs. Many accommodations and other services close between mid-October and early May.

Opposite the harbor, **The Pines Inn** (36 Channel St., 705/287-1068, www.bbcanada.com, year-round, $90-95 s or d) is a comfortable, old-time lodge with a busy pub and restaurant. Upstairs, the six simple guest rooms with quilt-covered beds share two baths; washbasins in the rooms help minimize the wait. Owners Paul and Adele Malcew offer a warm welcome, with Paul serving cold beer behind the bar and Adele cooking bacon-and-eggs breakfasts, burgers, grilled fish, and other home-style fare. Even if you're not staying here, stop in for a drink and a chat; the pub is a local hangout.

At the **Sportsman's Inn** (37 Channel St., 705/287-9990 or 877/333-7510, www.sportsmansinn.ca, mid-May-mid-Oct.) on the harbor, there are several different room types, from plain rooms in a separate motel building ($109 d) to more upscale units overlooking the waterfront ($159 d) to large two-bedroom suites ($320 d). The main dining room serves straightforward traditional fare, from grilled chicken to whitefish to steak ($20-29), while the pub sticks with nachos, burgers, and other basics.

A holiday at the waterfront ★ **Killarney Mountain Lodge** (3 Commissioner St., 705/287-2242 or 800/461-1117, www.killarney.com, mid-May-mid-Oct., $75 s, $150 d with breakfast, $120-195 pp with breakfast and dinner, $135-195 pp with 3 meals), with rustic pine-paneled rooms and cabins, a pool, games, and canoes, feels summer camp. The dining room serves three basic meals daily, and there's live music (from 9pm Tues.-Sun.) in the window-lined **Carousel Bar.** TV and Wi-Fi are in the main lodge, but rooms have no phones, TVs, or Internet access. The owners also operate Killarney Outfitters store and guide service; ask about packages including activities.

Lines are legendary at **Herbert Fisheries** (21 Channel St., 705/287-2214, lunch and dinner daily June-Aug., Fri.-Sun. May and Sept.-early Oct.), which serves first-rate fish-and-chips (from $16) on the waterfront.

Information and Services

When you arrive in the Killarney area, stop at the **Killarney Provincial Park** main office (Hwy. 637, 705/287-2900) at George Lake to pick up the free park information guide and ask questions of the park staff. The **Friends of Killarney Park Store** (George Lake Campground, 705/287-2800, www.

friendsofkillarneypark.ca, year-round) sells park guides, maps, books, and other souvenirs; they have a second location at Bell Lake. You can also order canoeing and hiking guides online—a boon for trip planning.

The useful website of **Friends of Killarney Park** (www.friendsofkillarneypark.ca) has information about park events, hiking trails, and other activities. The Friends also run an online forum, where you can post questions about hiking and canoe trips and read trip reports from others who have explored the park.

The **Killarney Outfitters Store** (1076 Hwy. 637, 705/287-2828 or 888/222-3410, www.killarneyoutfitters.com, 8am-8pm daily July-Aug., 8am-5pm daily spring and fall) is located between the village and the main park entrance at George Lake. They sell outdoor clothing and camping supplies; rent canoes and kayaks ($37-59) as well as other gear; and can arrange a variety of outdoor excursions. **Pitfield's General Store** (7 Channel St., 705/287-2872) sells basic groceries and snacks year-round. They also have a coin laundry.

Getting There and Around
Car

Killarney is 425 kilometers (265 miles) northwest of Toronto, about a 5-6-hour drive. Sudbury is the closest city, about a 90-minute drive to the north; Parry Sound is two hours' drive to the south. The only road into Killarney is Highway 637, which is off Highway 69 between Parry Sound and Sudbury. From the Highway 69/637 interchange, it's 67 kilometers (42 miles) to the village of Killarney, about an hour by car.

While the village of Killarney is only about 20 nautical miles from the eastern tip of Manitoulin Island, there's no public boat service between the two. By car, it's a three-hour drive from Killarney to Little Current (220 kilometers, 137 miles). From Killarney, return to Highway 69 and travel north toward Sudbury; then take Highway 17 west to Espanola, where you pick up Highway 6 south, which crosses the bridge to Manitoulin.

Bus

Without a car, the simplest way to travel from Toronto to Killarney is on the **Parkbus** (800/928-7101, www.parkbus.ca, one-way adults $64, seniors and students $58, ages 2-12 $32, round-trip adults $92, seniors and students $83, ages 2-12 $46), which operates on selected weekends in summer and fall. The bus departs from several points in Toronto, including 30 Carlton Street (between Yonge

Killarney Mountain Lodge has plenty of spots to relax.

St. and Church St., subway: College) and Dufferin Street at Bloor Street West (subway: Dufferin). The Parkbus picks up and drops off at three points in the Killarney area: Bell Lake, George Lake (at the park headquarters and main campground), and in the village of Killarney. The Parkbus also works with local outfitters to offer all-inclusive packages, including transportation and lodging; get details on the website.

Otherwise, it's not easy to get to Killarney without a car. **Ontario Northland** (www. ontarionorthland.ca) buses between Parry Sound and Sudbury will stop at Highway 637, but you're still an hour's drive from town or the park. **Killarney Outfitters** (705/287-2828 or 888/222-3410, www.killarneyoutfitters.com) can provide a shuttle ($130 one-way) from the bus stop into town, which is pricey unless you can split the cost among travelers.

Manitoulin Island

Bordered by Lake Huron to the west and Georgian Bay to the east, Manitoulin isn't Canada's largest island (that distinction belongs to Baffin Island). Yet Manitoulin is still tops for its size: It's the largest freshwater island in the world.

Don't expect to make a quick loop around Manitoulin in a couple of hours. Measuring 2,765 square kilometers (1,067 square miles), with good but meandering roads, Manitoulin is a place for leisurely exploration. One of the most significant things to explore is the island's aboriginal culture. Manitoulin and the surrounding mainland region are home to eight First Nations, collectively known as the Anishinaabe people. An innovative aboriginal tourism association, the **Great Spirit Circle Trail,** offers a variety of cultural programs to introduce visitors to local First Nations traditions. The First Nations communities hold traditional **powwows** that welcome visitors, too.

Because the island is so large, consider your interests in deciding where to stay. If you're interested in aboriginal culture, base yourself on the island's eastern half, where you'll be close to more First Nations attractions. For the best beaches, head south; the nicest sandy spot is Providence Bay on the south shore. And if you're looking for a remote getaway, go west, where villages like Gore Bay and Meldrum Bay have comfortable inns.

Scientists believe that millions of years ago, Manitoulin was connected by land to the Bruce Peninsula. Today, the only land access is from the north, via Highway 6, where a "**swing bridge**"—similar to a drawbridge, except that it swings sideways instead of lifting—links the island to the mainland.

If you're coming from Toronto and Southern Ontario, the most direct route to Manitoulin is by boat. From mid-May to mid-October, a ferry runs between Tobermory, on the Bruce Peninsula, and South Baymouth, on the southeast corner of Manitoulin Island. The island's high season mirrors the ferry schedule, so when the ferry docks for the winter, many Manitoulin lodgings close and restaurants shut down or reduce their hours.

SIGHTS

Just across the swing bridge onto the island is the town of **Little Current.** The small downtown runs along Water Street, with a handful of shops for browsing. You can also stroll along the harbor, which fronts Lake Huron's North Channel, watching the sailboats and the occasional cruise ship.

★ Great Spirit Circle Trail

Based in M'Chigeeng, the **Great Spirit Circle Trail** (5905 Hwy. 540, 705/377-4404 or 877/710-3211, www.circletrail.com), an aboriginal tourism association, offers a

Manitoulin Island

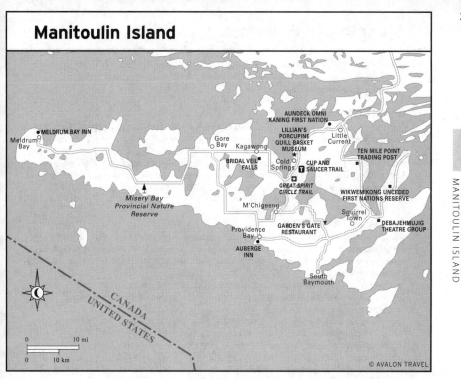

number of activities to introduce visitors to First Nations traditions, and several nearby attractions focus on aboriginal culture. The M'Chigeeng First Nation (the *m* is silent) is 34 kilometers (21 miles) southwest of Little Current and 78 kilometers (48 miles) northwest of South Baymouth.

The Great Spirit Circle Trail offers programs that include one- to two-hour introductions to indigenous herbal medicines, First Nations crafts, storytelling, traditional drumming, longer guided hiking, horseback riding, or canoe experiences. Programs are typically available between late May and early October; call or check the website for details and to make arrangements.

At the **Ojibwe Cultural Foundation and Museum** (15 Hwy. 551, 705/377-4902, www.ojibweculture.ca, 9am-6pm Mon.-Fri., 10am-4pm Sat., noon-4pm Sun. mid-June-Sept., 9am-4:30pm Mon.-Fri. Oct.-mid-June, adults $7.50, seniors and students $5), exhibits

focus on First Nations history and contemporary aboriginal arts.

Opposite the Ojibwe Cultural Foundation, the **Immaculate Conception Church** (Hwy. 551, 705/377-4985, donation) mixes First Nations and Roman Catholic religious traditions. The round structure with a conical roof recalls a traditional tepee; on the bright blue front door, a yellow sun with four rays in the shape of a cross is an indigenous people's religious symbol. Inside, look for other aboriginal paintings and carvings.

Part shop and part gallery, **Lillian's Porcupine Quill Basket Museum** (5950 Hwy. 540, 705/377-4987, www.lillianscrafts.ca, 10am-6pm Mon.-Fri., 10am-5pm Sat.-Sun., free) displays a local First Nations craft: baskets and boxes intricately woven from colorful porcupine quills. Make sure you see the exhibits done by master craftspeople in the back room. The front room sells more typical aboriginal souvenirs.

Planning to Powwow

One of the most interesting ways to experience aboriginal culture is to attend a traditional pow-wow, a festival that encompasses dance, music, and food. And one of Ontario's best places to find powwows is on Manitoulin Island.

WHERE TO POWWOW

Manitoulin's largest and longest-running powwow is the **Wikwemikong Cultural Festival and Powwow** (www.wikwemikongheritage.org), held annually in early August on the Wikwemikong Reserve on the island's east side. Most of Manitoulin's other First Nations communities hold annual traditional powwows, as well, including the **Aundeck Omni Kaning** (June), **Sheguiandah** (July), and **M'Chigeeng** (late Aug. or early Sept.). Get a powwow schedule and details about any of these events from the **Great Spirit Circle Trail office** (705/377-4404 or 877/710-3211, www.circletrail.com).

POWWOW ETIQUETTE

Traditional powwows are generally open to the public, and most are free, although donations are accepted. Competition powwows often charge admission of $10-15. A master of ceremonies leads the powwow and explains the various dances and ceremonies. You can purchase food and traditional crafts on-site.

During certain ceremonial songs or dances, photography and video recording are prohibited; the master of ceremonies will usually explain when these ceremonies are taking place. At other times, you may take photos or videos, but it's polite to ask for permission first, particularly when you're photographing a dancer in traditional regalia. Because many believe that the regalia (which should never be called "costumes") have their own spirit, and frequently are handmade or passed down from an ancestor, you should never touch the regalia, either. Powwows are alcohol-free events.

To learn more about powwow customs and etiquette, request a copy of the Great Spirit Circle Trail's ***Powwow Guide*** (705/377-4404 or 877/710-3211, www.circletrail.com).

Miigwetch (Thank you)!

Kagawong

Heading west from M'Chigeeng on Highway 540, you reach Kagawong, a cute village whose Ojibwa name means "where mists rise from the falling waters." It's a fitting moniker, since the town's main attraction is **Bridal Veil Falls,** where you can splash under the waterfall. Stairs lead from a parking area down to the falls, and a walking path follows the riverbank from the falls into the village.

If you need a break after playing in the falls, don't worry—there's chocolate. **Manitoulin Chocolate Works** (160 Main St., 705/282-0961, www.manitoulinchocolate.ca, 9am-6pm Mon.-Sat., 11am-5pm Sun. July-Aug., 10am-5pm Tues.-Sat., 11am-4pm Sun. May-June and Sept.-Dec.) crafts chocolates and other confections in a former village blacksmith shop. They sell coffee, tea, and hot chocolate, too.

Sheguiandah and Wikwemikong

South of Little Current along Highway 6, stop at the **Viewpoint at Ten Mile Point,** where vistas stretch east across Sheguiandah Bay. Adjacent to the viewpoint, the **Ten Mile Point Trading Post and Gallery** (12164 Hwy. 6, Sheguiandah, 705/368-2377) looks like a standard souvenir shop, but amid the T-shirts and trinkets are high-quality works, from jewelry to leather to prints, by First Nations artists. They also carry a large selection of books about Manitoulin and First Nations culture, including books for kids.

Hiking

overlooking the cliffs from the Cup and Saucer Trail

One of Manitoulin's most popular hikes is the **Cup and Saucer Trail** (Hwy. 540 at Bidwell Rd., dawn-dusk daily mid-May-mid-Oct.), which climbs the Niagara Escarpment to spectacular lookouts from the 70-meter (230-foot) cliffs. This 12-kilometer (7.5-mile) route is divided into several shorter trails, including the optional two-kilometer (1.2-mile) adventure trail, which takes hikers up and down ladders and along narrow ledges to a viewpoint overlooking the North Channel. The trailhead is 18 kilometers (11 miles) west of Little Current, just north of M'Chigeeng.

A fascinating way to explore the Cup and Saucer Trail is on a **Mother Earth Nature Hike,** (2.5-3 hours, $40 pp) led by an aboriginal guide, who will help you identify local plants and understand how they're used in aboriginal medicine and cooking. Contact the **Great Spirit Circle Trail** (705/377-4404 or 877/710-3211, www.circletrail.com) to book.

Legend has it that, back in the 1880s, a farmer was cutting down grass in southwest Manitoulin when two men approached and asked the place's name. "Misery," the hot, tired farmer called it, and the name stuck. Today, it's the antithesis of misery for hikers who stroll the 15 kilometers (nine miles) of trails in the **Misery Bay Provincial Nature Reserve** (400 Misery Bay Park Rd., 705/966-2315, www.ontarioparks.com and www.miserybay.org, 10am-5pm daily July-Aug., 10am-5pm Sat.-Sun. mid-May-June and Sept.-mid-Oct., adults $2, ages 6-17 $1). The park visitors center has exhibits about the area's geological and natural features, which include its wetlands and its alvar ecosystem, a rare type of flat rock landscape found primarily in the Great Lakes region. You can follow a 1.3-kilometer (0.8-mile) trail to a **swimming beach.** The Misery Bay turnoff is 35 kilometers (22 miles) west of Gore Bay along Highway 540.

On the peninsula jutting out from Manitoulin's eastern shore is the **Wikwemikong Unceded First Nations Reserve**—"unceded" because the group never agreed to any treaty that would give title of its land to the government. It's Canada's only officially recognized unceded aboriginal reserve. The Wikwemikong offer a variety of tours and cultural experiences, including walking tours and canoe excursions. Contact the **Wikwemikong Tourism Information Center** (888/801-9422, www.wikwemikong.ca) for details.

If you visit during July or August, don't miss a production by the **Debajehmujig Theatre Group** (office: 8 Debajehmujig Lane, 705/859-2317, www.debaj.ca). They perform works with aboriginal themes in the ruins of Wikwemikong's Holy Cross Mission and host other theater, music, and art events at their **Debajehmujig Creation Centre** (43 Queen St., Manitowaning, 705/859-1820).

Beaches

Although Manitoulin is ringed with beaches, the best sandy spots are on the south shore, west of South Baymouth. And the best of the best? **Providence Bay Beach,** a long strip of soft sand along Lake Huron, backed by swaying grasses and a boardwalk trail. The beach's Harbour Centre building (spring-fall) has restrooms, a small exhibit area about the local history and environment, and, wonder of wonders, an espresso bar, **Huron Island Time,** run by the owners of the nearby Auberge Inn. It serves coffee, pastries, locally made hot dogs, and ice cream; you can rent kayaks, canoes, bicycles, and beach chairs here as well.

In eastern Manitoulin, off Highway 6 between Sheguiandah and Manitowaning, is the largest of the island's 108 freshwater lakes, Lake Manitou.

ACCOMMODATIONS AND FOOD

Manitoulin lodgings include cottages, B&Bs, small inns, and summer camp-style resorts. No chains or megaresorts have set up shop yet. It's a good idea to book ahead, especially in July and August. Manitoulin isn't a fine-dining destination—it's much easier to find burgers and fish-and-chips than a gourmet meal—but most towns have someplace to get a bite.

Little Current

The Great Spirit Circle Trail runs the 57-room **Manitoulin Hotel and Conference Centre** (66 Meredith St. E., 705/368-9966 or 855/368-9966, www.manitoulinhotel.com or www.circletrail.com, $139-229 d), near the swing bridge. The expansive lobby overlooking the channel is modeled after a First Nations gathering place, and the guest rooms are decorated with light wood furnishings and First Nations' motifs. Amenities include Keurig coffeemakers, flat-screen TVs, and free Wi-Fi.

Both sailors and landlubbers wash into the **Anchor Inn** (1 Water St., 705/368-2023, www.anchorgrill.com, 7am-11pm daily July-Aug., call for off-season hours, lunch $5-15, dinner $8-25) for a beer or for chow that ranges from burgers and sandwiches to steaks and fish plates. Upstairs, the inn has several simple rooms ($50-70 d) and apartments ($80-90 d), although light sleepers should note that rooms over the bar can be noisy, particularly on weekends when bands are playing.

The take-out counter at **Island Jar** (15 Water St., 705/368-1881, 9am-5:30pm

summer fun on Providence Bay Beach

Stay in a teepee on Manitoulin Island.

Mon.-Fri., 9am-5pm Sat.), a small organic grocery, whips up freshly made smoothies, sushi, salads, and sandwiches from pulled pork to hummus. Have coffee and check your email at **Loco Beanz** (7 Water St., 705/368-2261, 7am-5pm Mon.-Sat., 8am-3pm Sun. summer), a cheery café with free Wi-Fi.

Aundeck Omni Kaning

On this First Nations reserve off Highway 540, five kilometers (three miles) west of Little Current, **Endaa-aang "Our Place"** (705/368-0548, www.aokfn.com) rents four well-kept cabins in parklike grounds near the North Channel waterfront. The wood-paneled cabins sleep six, with a double bedroom, a twin-bed room, and a living room with a sofa bed; they have full kitchens as well as decks with barbecues. Also on the property are **tepee rentals.** The tepees sleep eight but are unfurnished. Bring sleeping bags and other camping gear; restrooms are nearby.

Guests can use the reserve's beach along the North Channel, but it's otherwise not open to the public. For reservations, contact "Our Place" directly, or book through the **Great Spirit Circle Trail** (705/377-4404 or 877/710-3211, www.circletrail.com).

M'Chigeeng

The **Great Spirit Circle Trail** (705/377-4404 or 877/710-3211, www.circletrail.com) has several **tepees** (June-Sept., $40) on their M'Chigeeng property where visitors can stay. Washrooms are a short walk away, and you can rent cots or sleeping bags.

A convenient place to eat before or after you visit the Circle Trail or the Ojibwe Cultural Foundation, **Season's Family Restaurant** (Hwy. 551, 705/377-4344, 7am-7:30pm Mon.-Sat., $5-15) serves bacon and eggs, sandwiches, and other family-style dishes.

South Baymouth and Tehkummah

The closest accommodations to the ferry terminal, the **Southbay Gallery and Guesthouse Manitoulin** (14-15 Given Rd., South Baymouth, 705/859-2363, www.southbayguesthouse.com, May-Sept., $110-169 d) has several guest rooms (two with private baths), with stocky wooden furniture, in two different buildings. The property also includes a self-contained guest cottage, a hot tub, and an art gallery-shop. The same family runs the Southbay Guesthouse in Sudbury.

One of the island's best restaurants is in the countryside 26 kilometers (16 miles) north of South Baymouth. In a house at the end of a garden path, ★ **Garden's Gate Restaurant** (312 Hwy. 542, Tehkummah, 705/859-2088 or 888/959-2088, www.gardensgate.ca, lunch and dinner Tues.-Sun. June, lunch Tues.-Sun. and dinner daily July-Aug., dinner Tues.-Sun. May and Sept.-Oct., lunch $13-15, dinner $16-23), with its floral tablecloths and cozy screened porch, looks grandmotherly, but the food—updated country fare made with fresh local ingredients—is first-rate. Fish is a specialty, and the menu always includes vegetarian options. Save room for the homemade pie.

Providence Bay

A five-minute walk from Providence Bay Beach, the ★ **Auberge Inn** (71 McNevin St., 705/377-4392 or 877/977-4392, www.aubergeinn.ca, year-round, $40 dorm, $95 d), the island's only hostel, is a friendly place with three bunk beds in a dorm and two private rooms, one with a double bed and one with a queen bed and two bunks. Guests share a large bath upstairs. Convivial owners Alain Harvey and Nathalie Gara-Boivin offer great tips and rent bicycles, kayaks, or canoes. Rates include self-serve continental breakfast and Wi-Fi. Nathalie is also a certified yoga teacher, who offers occasional weekend yoga retreats.

What's a day at the beach without fish-and-chips? **Lake Huron Fish and Chips** (20 McNevin St., 705/377-4500, late May-Sept.) is just inland from Providence Bay. Take a peek into their tiny **West Backline Gallery** next door to see what's on view.

Gore Bay

One of Manitoulin's most elegant accommodations is **The Queen's Inn Bed-and-Breakfast** (19 Water St., 705/282-0665, www.thequeensinn.ca, May-Dec., $110-130 s, $135-160 d), overlooking the harbor in Gore Bay. Built in the late 1800s, this Victorian manor has a formal antiques-filled parlor and a saloon-turned-breakfast-room where a hot morning meal is served. On the second and third floors are eight Victorian-style guest rooms, five with private baths. Sit on either of the two verandas to enjoy the harbor views.

Buoys Eatery (1 Purvis Dr., off Water St., 705/282-2869, www.buoyseatery.com, lunch and dinner daily June-Sept., Wed.-Sun. Oct.-May, $9-18) looks like an ordinary fish shack (albeit with a lovely deck), but the two specialties make it worth the stop: fish and wedges (broiled or fried local whitefish paired with thick slices of roasted potato) and pizzas with either traditional or out-of-the-ordinary toppings; the Greek Obsession sports *tzatziki* sauce, gyro meat, feta cheese, and olives.

Meldrum Bay

To get way, way away from it all, book a stay at the family-run **Meldrum Bay Inn** (25959 Hwy. 540, 705/283-3190 or 877/577-1645, www.meldrumbayinn.com, year-round, $140-170 d), in an 1878 wood-frame building with a wide front porch, overlooking the water on Manitoulin's far west end. Seven simple rooms share two baths; rates include continental breakfast. The home-style dining room (late May-mid-Sept., entrées $18-27) specializes in local whitefish and barbecue ribs. Meldrum Bay is 167 circuitous kilometers (104 miles) from South Baymouth and 134 kilometers (83 miles) from Little Current; allow at least two hours from the island's east side.

INFORMATION AND SERVICES

Just over the swing bridge, stop into the **Manitoulin Tourism Association Welcome Centre** (70 Meredith St. E./Hwy. 6, Little Current, 705/368-3021, www.manitoulintourism.com), where obliging staff provide maps and brochures, book ferry reservations, and offer advice about things to do and places to stay. Their website is an excellent resource for planning your island visit; it has a good map with descriptions of Manitoulin's various communities. If you arrive on the ferry, pick up maps and brochures at the **ferry terminal information center** (41 Water St., South Baymouth, 705/859-3161).

For information about aboriginal tourism on Manitoulin, contact the **Great Spirit Circle Trail** (5905 Hwy. 540, M'Chigeeng, 705/377-4404 or 877/710-3211, www.circletrail.com). The **Wikwemikong Tourism Information Center** (888/801-9422, www.wikwemikong.ca) can tell you about activities on the Wikwemikong Reserve.

GETTING THERE
Ferry

From Toronto or other Southern Ontario destinations, the quickest way to Manitoulin is by ferry from the Bruce Peninsula. The **MS *Chi-Cheemaun* Ferry** (800/265-3163, www.ontarioferries.com, mid-May–mid-Oct., one-way adults $16.50, seniors $14.25, ages 5-11 $8.25, cars $27.75-45)—its Ojibwa name means "The Big Canoe"—makes the two-hour run between Tobermory and South Baymouth several times daily. Discounts are available for families and for same-day returns. Make a reservation if you're taking a car; a $15 reservation fee applies to many sailings.

Car

By road, it's a long slog—about 510 kilometers (320 miles) from Toronto to Manitoulin. After taking Highway 400/69 north toward Sudbury, it's still 90 minutes farther on Highway 17 west and Highway 6 south to Manitoulin's **swing bridge.** In summer, every hour on the hour (dawn-dusk), the bridge swings sideways to allow boats to pass underneath, halting road traffic for 15 minutes. The bridge is only one lane, so even when it's open, traffic alternates in each direction. Don't be in a rush to make the crossing.

GETTING AROUND

Highway 6 runs along the island's east side between Little Current and South Baymouth, passing Sheguiandah and Wikwemikong en route. From Little Current, Highway 540 goes west to M'Chigeeng, Kagawong, Gore Bay, and Meldrum Bay. From South Baymouth to M'Chigeeng, take Highway 6 north to Highway 542 west, then, at Mindemoya, pick up Highway 551 north to M'Chigeeng. To Providence Bay, turn south onto Highway 551. For Gore Bay, continue west on Highway 542.

Manitoulin has no public transportation. If you're an avid cyclist able to ride fairly long distances, **bicycling** is a reasonable way to tour the island. From South Baymouth, it's 30 kilometers (19 miles) to Providence Bay and 62 kilometers (39 miles) to Little Current. For cycling tips, check with the **Manitoulin Tourism Association** (705/368-3021, www.manitoulintourism.com) or with the owners of the **Auberge Inn** (71 McNevin, Providence Bay, 705/377-4392 or 877/977-4392, www.aubergeinn.ca).

Lake Superior

Biggest, deepest, longest—Northern Ontario is a place of geographical superlatives, and the region encompassing Lake Superior is no exception. Not only is Superior the deepest of the five great lakes, it is the largest body of fresh

water in the world. No wonder it's frequently called an inland sea. Unless you taste the salt-free water as you listen to the waves crashing on the shores of this immense lake, which stretches 560 kilometers (350 miles) from end to end and 260 kilometers (160 miles) across, you'd swear you were looking out across the ocean.

Lake Superior's land borders include not just Ontario, but the U.S. states of Minnesota, Wisconsin, and Michigan, and a popular driving route circles the lake on both sides of the international boundary. On the Ontario shores, connected by the Trans-Canada Highway, two cities bookend the Lake Superior region: Sault Ste. Marie to the east and Thunder Bay in the west. While each has several worthwhile attractions and a diverse cultural heritage stretching from the aboriginal peoples to more recent immigrant Italians, Scandinavians, and Asians, it's the landscape and outdoor activities outside

the metropolitan areas—on land and on the water—that make Lake Superior special.

From Sault Ste. Marie, you can take a one-day rail journey into the wilderness of Agawa Canyon. North and west of the Sault, the shores of Lake Superior are lined with spectacular beaches, canoe or kayak routes, and rocky cliffs crisscrossed with hiking trails, many in beautiful provincial parks and in Ontario's largest national park. From Thunder Bay, you can make day trips into nearby parks to wander amid waterfalls, canyons, and dramatic foliage, especially when the autumn leaves turn red and gold.

Lake Superior figures prominently in art and literature, from paintings by Canada's Group of Seven to the 19th-century epic poem, *The Song of Hiawatha*, that Henry Wadsworth Longfellow set "By the shores of Gitche Gumee" (from the lake's Ojibwa name, *Gichigami*). Whether on foot, with a paddle, or behind the wheel, or with your own camera,

---

Previous: Kakabeka Falls, west of Thunder Bay; the *Wawa Goose* sculpture outside the Wawa Visitor Information Centre. **Above:** Lake Superior Provincial Park.

Look for ★ to find recommended sights, activities, dining, and lodging.

Highlights

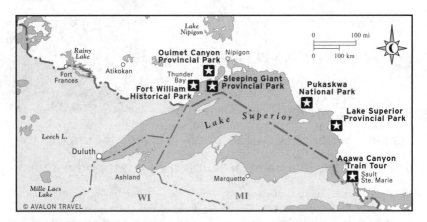

★ **Agawa Canyon Tour Train:** A car-free day trip into the northern wilderness, this rail journey is particularly spectacular during the fall foliage season (page 396).

★ **Lake Superior Provincial Park:** One of Ontario's most beautiful outdoor destinations, this provincial park extends along the eastern shore of the world's largest body of fresh water. You'll find sandy beaches, rocky coves, rugged hiking trails, and even ancient rock paintings (page 400).

★ **Pukaskwa National Park:** Explore First Nations culture at Ontario's largest national park, which caters both to outdoors newcomers and to experienced adventurers with hiking and paddling amid stunning Lake Superior terrain (page 404).

★ **Fort William Historical Park:** Journey back to the time of the voyageurs and their aboriginal trading partners at this recreated early-1800s fur-trading post near Thunder Bay (page 412).

★ **Sleeping Giant Provincial Park:** Jutting into the lake across the harbor from Thunder Bay, this craggy, forested park has more than 100 kilometers (60 miles) of hiking trails, including the challenging "Top of the Giant," which rewards hikers with expansive cliff-top vistas (page 417).

★ **Ouimet Canyon Provincial Park:** Carved by natural forces over millions of years, Ouimet Canyon spans a 150-meter (495-foot) gorge with jagged cliffs on either side and lookout points high above the canyon floor (page 419).

Lake Superior

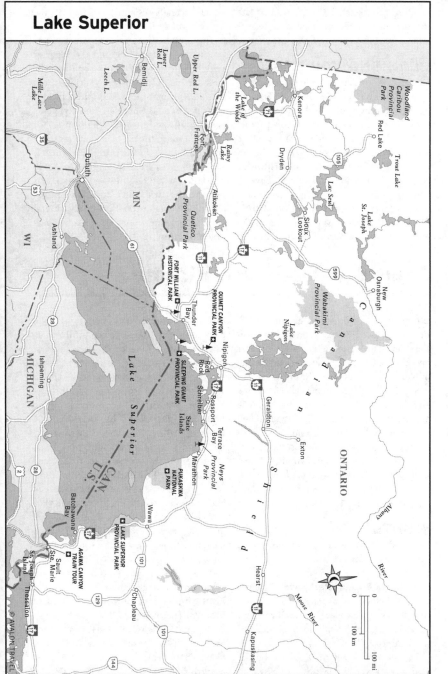

© AVALON TRAVEL

paintbrush, or sketchpad, you too can explore the rock-lined shores and wooded landscapes around Longfellow's "shining Big-Sea-Water."

PLANNING YOUR TIME

Distances between northern destinations are long, and it's a full day's drive from Toronto to even the nearest points in the Lake Superior region. If your time is short, consider flying to Thunder Bay or Sault Ste. Marie. Once you've arrived near Lake Superior, you can explore either **Sault Ste. Marie** or **Thunder Bay** and the nearby parks in a long weekend. Allow at least four or five days to take in the sights along **Lake Superior's North Shore** and at least 7 to 10 days if you'd like to do the full **Lake Superior Circle Route,**

which encompasses both the Canadian and U.S. sides of the lake.

July and August are the most popular months for travel in the Lake Superior region, when everything is open and the weather is mild. Consider visiting in autumn (Sept.-mid-Oct.) when the foliage is at its peak and the bugs are (mostly) gone. Avoid May and June, when both the black flies and mosquitoes are at their most active. And if you do travel in the frequently snowy months from November to April, note that many lodgings and restaurants outside the cities shut down except for those catering to cross-country skiers, snowshoers, snowmobilers, or other outdoor adventurers.

Sault Ste. Marie and Vicinity

With an Ojibwa community here for centuries, and a French Jesuit mission established in 1668, Sault Ste. Marie, on the St. Mary's River opposite the U.S. city of the same name, is one of North America's oldest European settlements. Its riverside location helped it become an important fur-trading post in the 1700s and eventually an industrial city of 75,000 people. While "the Sault" (pronounced "soo") has several interesting museums, the best attractions take you out of town, including a train tour to Agawa Canyon, a drive north along the shores of Lake Superior, or a day trip east to St. Joseph Island.

SIGHTS

Most of the Sault's attractions are downtown between Queen Street East and the river. Stroll the riverfront boardwalk and take a break in **Roberta Bondar Park,** which honors Canada's first woman astronaut, a Sault native who flew aboard the space shuttle *Discovery* in 1992. The park pavilion hosts frequent summer concerts.

In 1895, the Sault canal opened on the St. Mary's River, the last link in a system

of Canadian waterways connecting Lake Superior to the Atlantic Ocean. At the time, it was the world's longest lock and the first in Canada to operate on electric power. Although the original lock was replaced in the 1990s, recreational boaters now pass through a smaller lock within the historic one. At the **Sault Ste. Marie Canal National Historic Site** (1 Canal Dr., 705/941-6262, www.pc.gc. ca, 10am-8pm Mon.-Fri. mid-May-June, 10am-8pm daily July-early Sept., 8:30am-4:30pm Mon.-Fri. early Sept.-mid-Oct., free), you can explore exhibits about the lock and the region's shipping history; the visitors center is housed in the original powerhouse. Tours of the site ($2.90-5.80), which includes five historic structures, are available on request.

Two unusual historic buildings and a modern heritage center constitute the **Ermatinger-Clergue National Historic Site** (831 Queen St. E., 705/759-5443, www. ecnhs.com, 9:30am-4:30pm daily mid-Apr.-Nov., adults $10, seniors and kids 6 and older, $8). In the Heritage Discovery Centre, a worthwhile 20-minute film illustrates the

Sault Ste. Marie

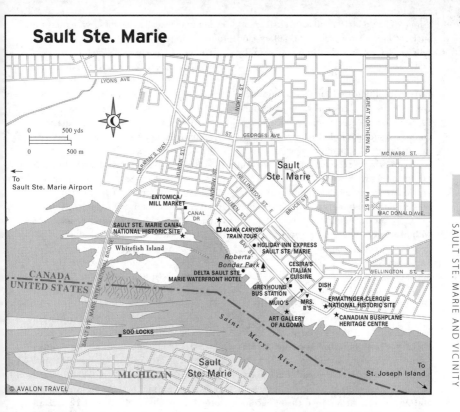

Sault's history, first as a fur-trading outpost and later as an industrial community, bringing to life the stories of the two businessmen whose residences now sit on the site. The stately, Georgian-style Old Stone House, built in 1814, was home to wealthy fur trader Charles Oakes Ermatinger, his Ojibwa wife, Mananowe (Charlotte), and their 13 children. Next door is the Clergue Blockhouse, a replica of a frontier fort cantilevered above a former gunpowder magazine. Francis Hector Clergue, an industrialist and (ultimately failed) entrepreneur, had this odd structure built in 1895 as his home and office. Costumed interpreters guide you through both buildings and explain about 19th-century local life.

Small rugged aircraft known as bush planes traditionally provided a vital transportation link throughout Northern Ontario, offering access to regions with few roads. At

the **Canadian Bushplane Heritage Centre** (50 Pim St., 705/945-6242 or 877/287-4752, www.bushplane.com, 9am-6pm daily mid-May-mid-Oct., 10am-4pm daily mid-Oct.-mid-May; adults $12, seniors $11, students $7, children $3), in a cavernous former air service hangar, you can learn about the importance of these planes past and present and have some fun, too. Climb aboard several of the 25 historic airplanes, check out exhibits on fighting forest fires, or take a video flight tour of Agawa Canyon.

The waterfront **Art Gallery of Algoma** (10 East St., 705/949-9067, www.artgalleryofalgoma.ca, 9am-5pm Tues. and Thurs.-Sat., 9am-9pm Wed., noon-5pm Sun., adults $5, students $3) has three galleries with rotating contemporary art exhibits that showcase established and emerging regional artists. Among the permanent collection are works by

Group of Seven artists and aboriginal artists such as Norval Morrisseau. The gallery shop sells jewelry, cards, and other pieces, many by Northern Ontario artists.

Does a millipede tickle? Find out at **Entomica** (35 Canal Dr., www.entomica. com, Wed-Sun., check the website for hours, $2), a hands-on insectarium, where staff encourage visitors to hold the bugs—if you're not squeamish about creepy-crawlies. They've got common and exotic insects from near and far, including stick bugs, giant cockroaches, and Malaysian rhinoceros beetles (with a proboscis that resembles its mammalian namesake). Entomica shares a building with the **Mill Market** (705/257-9658, www.millmarket.ca), a farmers market (3pm-7pm Wed., 8am-2pm Sat.), and a flea market (11am-3pm Sun.).

★ Agawa Canyon Tour Train

In 1918, artists Lawren Harris, J. E. H. MacDonald, and Frank Johnston rented a boxcar to travel and paint along the Algoma Central Railway, which runs north from Sault Ste. Marie into the Agawa Canyon and beyond. These painters, along with several colleagues who later joined them, became known as the Group of Seven, creating and exhibiting the works that these wilderness sojourns inspired.

You don't have to travel by boxcar to explore the same scenery that motivated these artists. Book a seat on the **Agawa Canyon Train** (Algoma Central Railway, 129 Bay St., 705/946-7300 or 800/242-9287, www.agawa-canyontourtrain.com, daily late June-mid-Oct., summer adults $90, seniors $78.50, ages 6-18 $42, ages 2-5 $37, fall adults $110, seniors $110, ages 6-18 $73.50, ages 2-5 $51), a one-day trip into the wilderness.

Agawa Canyon is tiny compared to Arizona's Grand Canyon or Mexico's Copper Canyon, but with a river winding amid the trees and below the rock walls, it's an attractive—and car-free—destination. The most popular times for the trip are the last two weeks of September and the first week of October, when fall colors are typically at their peak.

After the train pulls out of Sault station at 8am, beginning the four-hour, 184-kilometer (114-mile) ride north, the city's mills and factories give way to forests, hills, and lake after lake. At Mile 92, the train crosses a curved trestle bridge over the Montreal River; near Mile 102, look left and you can see all the way to Lake Superior. You can take in the

The Agawa Canyon Tour Train readies for its early morning departure.

"engineer's view," too; cameras mounted on the engine periodically project onto monitors inside the coaches. Recorded commentary tells you about other scenic spots en route.

Passengers disembark at the canyon, where they have about 90 minutes to explore before the return train leaves. The prettiest hike climbs 320 steps up the **Lookout Trail** (30-40 minutes round-trip), the best vantage point for photos over the canyon. The flatter **Bridal Veil Falls Trail** (30 minutes round-trip) goes to the 68.5-meter (225-foot) waterfall of the same name. As you walk back from the falls, take the path across the train tracks (carefully) to follow the **Black Beaver Falls Trail** to a second, smaller waterfall. If you don't dawdle, you should have time to see both the lookout and the falls.

The train's dining car begins serving breakfast shortly after the morning departure and is open for lunch until late afternoon. You're also welcome to bring your own food to eat en route or picnic at the canyon. However, you may prefer to eat on the train and use the relatively brief canyon stopover to explore. The train gets you back to Sault Ste. Marie around 6pm.

ACCOMMODATIONS

The city's most upscale lodging is the river-front **Delta Sault Ste. Marie Waterfront Hotel** (208 St. Mary's River Dr., 705/949-0611 or 888/713-8482, www.deltahotels.com, $129-249 d), where many of the 195 contemporary rooms, with mini fridges, flat-screen TVs, and free Wi-Fi, have water views. The fitness center, pool, and restaurant overlook the river.

If you have a car, an excellent-value lodging for both families and business travelers is **Algoma's Water Tower Inn** (360 Great Northern Rd., 705/949-8111 or 888/461-7077, www.watertowerinn.com, $116-135 d). Although the surroundings are typically suburban, once you're inside, it feels like a mini resort, particularly in the Aqua Spa, with its indoor pool and indoor-outdoor hot tubs.

Among the mid-range chain hotels downtown, the renovated 115-room **Holiday Inn Express Sault Ste. Marie** (320 Bay St., 705/759-8200, www.ihg.com/holidayinnexpress, $121-204 d) is a short walk from the Agawa Canyon train station and the waterfront. Other chain hotels line Great Northern Road, including the **Fairfield Inn** (633 Great Northern Rd., 705/253-7378, www.marriott.com, $119-159) and the newer **Microtel Inn & Suites** (724 Great Northern Rd., 705/450-2423 or 800/337-0050, www.microtelinn.com, $115-160).

FOOD

Dining options are plentiful around Queen Street East downtown and amid Great Northern Road's strip malls. The city has a large Italian population, which makes Italian eating a good choice; finding the best pizza is a competitive sport.

Dish (740 Queen St. E., 705/946-3474, 8am-5pm Mon.-Fri., 10am-4pm Sat., $4-6), a loungey espresso bar-café, may be downtown's coolest place to hang out. Besides coffee drinks and fruit smoothies, they serve soups, salads, and creative sandwiches, like pesto chicken or roasted red pepper hummus. Wi-Fi is free.

Popular with everyone from young folks on dates to old folks on pensions, ★ **Muio's** (685 Queen St. E., 705/254-7105, www.muios.com, 7am-close daily, lunch $5-11, dinner $10-24) is so retro, it's hip. The must-have dish is the "broasted" chicken (the Sault's version of Southern fried), which comes as chicken on a bun or as a heaping platter with potatoes and salad or coleslaw. The ravioli is another favorite, and other options include pizza, burgers, and steaks. Breakfast is served as well.

With its dark wainscoting and white tablecloths, **Cesira's Italian Cuisine** (133 Spring St., 705/949-0600, www.cesiras.com, lunch 11am-3pm Tues.-Fri., dinner 5pm-9pm Tues.-Sat., lunch $8-18, dinner $13-35), in an old house downtown, has a faded elegance that belies the great value of its traditional Italian fare, particularly the inexpensive specials, like the $11 lunch features. The handmade pastas are excellent.

LAKE SUPERIOR
SAULT STE. MARIE AND VICINITY

Among pizza partisans, popular picks include **Mrs. B's** (76 East St., 705/942-9999, 11am-10:30pm Mon.-Thurs., 11am-11:30pm Fri.-Sat., 1pm-7pm Sun., $7-27) in a bright red building downtown, and **Fratelli's** (522 Great Northern Rd., 705/256-1313, www.giovannisrestaurant.ca, 11am-11pm Mon.-Sat., 11am-10pm Sun., $8-29), which also makes tasty *panzarotti,* Ontario's version of a calzone.

INFORMATION

The helpful crew at **Tourism Sault Ste. Marie** (99 Foster Dr., 705/759-5442 or 800/461-6020, www.saulttourism.com), and their equally informative website, can clue you into things to do in the Sault. For more information about the region surrounding Sault Ste. Marie, contact the **Algoma Kinniwabi Travel Association** (334 Bay St., 705/254-4293 or 800/263-2546, www.algomacountry.com).

GETTING THERE AND AROUND

The Ontario Sault is across the river from its Michigan namesake. Michigan's I-75 crosses the International Bridge into the Canadian Sault's downtown. Remember that passports are required for travel between the United States and Canada. Within Ontario, it's an easy 3.5-hour drive between Sault Ste. Marie and Sudbury, 300 kilometers (186 miles) to the east. The Sault is roughly equidistant (700 kilometers, or 435 miles) between Toronto and Thunder Bay.

From **Sault Ste. Marie Airport** (YAM, 475 Airport Rd., 705/779-3031, www.saulttairport.com), 20 kilometers (12 miles) west of downtown, **Air Canada** (www.aircanada.com) and **Porter Airlines** (www.flyporter.com) fly to Toronto. **Bearskin Airlines** (www.bearskinairlines.com) has flights to Thunder Bay.

The **Greyhound Bus Station** (73 Brock St., 705/949-4711 or 800/661-8747, www.greyhound.ca), off Queen Street East downtown, has buses to Sudbury (4.5 hours, $54-86), Toronto (11 hours, $65-143), and Thunder Bay (9.5-10 hours, $105-183), among other destinations.

The city's attractions are clustered in the walkable downtown, so if you stay downtown, you don't need a car. The 25-kilometer (15-mile) **John Rowswell Hub Trail,** for pedestrians and cyclists, loops through the city center connecting all the main sights. However, to explore Lake Superior Provincial

Finding the best pizza is a competitive sport in Sault Ste. Marie.

Planning a Lake Superior Circle Tour

Circumnavigating Lake Superior is a 2,000-kilometer-plus (1,300-mile) road trip that not only runs through some of Ontario's most dramatic scenery, it also crosses through the U.S. states of Minnesota, Wisconsin, and Michigan. Whether by car, on a motorcycle, or even by bike, it's an epic but manageable journey.

On the Ontario side, Thunder Bay is just an hour's drive from the U.S. border, while the city of Sault Ste. Marie is just across the International Bridge from its U.S. namesake. In between you'll find small towns but far more forests, wooded parks, and beaches. The U.S. shores are more developed, including the cities of Duluth (Minnesota) and Marquette (Michigan), though you'll still find plenty of open spaces along the way.

For more information about planning a Lake Superior Circle Tour, contact the **North of Superior Tourism Association** (www.nosta.on.ca). Duluth-based *Lake Superior Magazine* (www.lakesuperior.com) features lots of regional destinations online and in its print publications. Several Moon guides (www.moon.com) to the Midwestern United States cover Lake Superior territory, including *Moon Michigan* by Laura Martone, *Moon Wisconsin* by Thomas Huhti, and *Moon Minnesota* by Tricia Cornell.

Park or other day-trip sights, you'll need your own wheels. All the major car rental companies have offices in Sault Ste. Marie.

ST. JOSEPH ISLAND

The second-largest freshwater island in the world after Manitoulin, rural St. Joseph is dotted with farms, beaches, and two tiny villages. It's a leisurely day-trip from the Sault.

The island's main attraction is the **Fort St. Joseph National Historic Site** (Fort Rd., 705/246-2664, www.pc.gc.ca, 9:30am-5pm daily June-mid-Oct., adults $3.90, seniors $3.40, children $1.90, families $9.80). The British built the fort in the 1790s; the Americans burned it to the ground during the War of 1812. What remains are the excavated ruins of the fort buildings, from the powder magazine to the kitchen to a surprisingly intact chimney. The Visitors Centre exhibits explain about life in this remote outpost and the alliances between the British and the First Nations; guided tours are available ($4). The fort is on St. Joseph's southwestern tip, 37 kilometers (23 miles) from the bridge onto the island.

North of the fort, stop to stroll around lovely **Adcocks' Woodland Gardens** (4757 5th Side Rd., 705/246-2579, www.adcockswoodlandgardens.com, dawn-dusk daily, donation), part cultivated grounds and part wild woods.

You can get a bite to eat in the villages of Richards Landing and Hilton Beach. Have a burger or a sandwich on homemade bread at the homey **Dry Dock Restaurant** (Marks St., Hilton Beach, 705/246-0850, 8am-8pm daily, $5-15), decorated with lighthouse paraphernalia.

The St. Joseph turnoff from Highway 17 is 45 kilometers (28 miles) east of Sault Ste. Marie.

BATCHAWANA BAY

Batchawana Bay Provincial Park (Hwy. 17, 705/882-2209, www.ontarioparks.com, mid-May-mid-Oct., $11.25 per vehicle), on Lake Superior 70 kilometers (44 miles) north of the Sault, has a long sandy beach that's a pleasant place to swim or lounge by the lake.

Even lovelier is the smooth stretch of sand backed by dunes and trees at **Pancake Bay Provincial Park** (Hwy. 17, 705/882-2209, www.ontarioparks.com, early May-mid-Oct., $14.50 per vehicle), 10 kilometers (6.2 miles) farther north. Hikers may want to follow the **Edmund Fitzgerald Lookout Trail** (Lookout Trail Rd.) to a viewing platform above the section of the lake where the SS *Edmund Fitzgerald* sank in 1975; allow two to three hours to hike the seven-kilometer (4.4-mile) trail. The trailhead is across the highway from the rest of the park, two kilometers (1.2 miles) to the north.

A popular place for **camping** (tent sites $40-44, electrical sites $46-50), Pancake Bay has 328 campsites along the water; try to book a lakefront site or one up in the Hilltop Campground, as others are quite close to the highway. The campground has showers, flush toilets, and laundry facilities, as well as five **yurts** ($98) that each sleep six. Reserve campsites and yurts through the **Ontario Parks Reservations Service** (888/668-7275, www.ontarioparks.com, reservation fee online $11, by phone $13).

For a bite to eat in Batchawana Bay, try the hearty fare at **Voyageurs' Lodge and Cookhouse** (Hwy. 17, 705/882-2504, www.voyageurslodge.com), including burgers, *tourtière* (Quebec meat pie), and traditional baked beans with bannock. They're especially busy Friday evenings for their weekly fish fry. If you can't bear to get back on the road after stuffing yourself on the blueberry crisp pie, check into one of the motel rooms. The Voyageurs' store sells essentials, booze, and delicious, supersize apple fritters.

★ LAKE SUPERIOR PROVINCIAL PARK

One of Ontario's most beautiful outdoor destinations, **Lake Superior Provincial Park** (Hwy. 17, 705/856-2284, www.ontarioparks.com or www.lakesuperiorpark.ca, mid-May-late Oct., $14.50 per vehicle) stretches 115 kilometers (72 miles) along Lake Superior's eastern shore. As you sit on a sandy beach or scramble up the rocky cliffs, you could be forgiven for thinking you were actually at the ocean, as surf crashes onto the rocks and the steely blue-gray water disappears into the horizon, with no land in sight.

For park information, contact the main park office, located in the northern half of the park near Red Rock Lake, or the **Agawa Bay Visitors Centre** (705/882-2026, 9am-8pm daily mid-June-early Sept., 9am-5pm

LAKE SUPERIOR

SAULT STE. MARIE AND VICINITY

road sign at the Voyageurs' Lodge and Cookhouse

daily mid-May-mid-June and early Sept.-mid-Oct.). If you're coming from the north, pick up a park brochure and map at the Wawa Visitor Information Centre (Hwy. 17 at Hwy. 101, Wawa).

The Lake Superior region famously inspired the Group of Seven landscape painters in the early 1900s. Find your own inspiration with the **Art in the Park** programs, which include painting, printmaking, and photography workshops, ranging from an hour to a weekend. Throughout the summer, park staff regularly offer guided hikes, kids' programs, and other activities. Get program details from the Visitors Centre or the website of the Friends of Lake Superior Park (www.lakesuperiorpark.ca).

Sights

At the south end of the park, stop at the well-designed modern **Agawa Bay Visitors Centre** (705/882-2026, 9am-8pm daily mid-June-early Sept., 9am-5pm daily mid-May-mid-June and early Sept.-mid-Oct.) to learn more about Lake Superior, which is not just the largest, deepest, and coldest of the Great Lakes—it's the largest body of freshwater in the world. Other exhibits illustrate the lake's legendary storms, including the one that sank the freighter SS *Edmund Fitzgerald* in 1975, immortalized in Ontario-born singer Gordon Lightfoot's ballad "Wreck of the Edmund Fitzgerald." The knowledgeable staff here can help you plan your time in the park. Wi-Fi is available by donation.

A few kilometers north of Agawa Bay, a short (0.5-kilometer, 0.3-mile) but steep and rocky trail leads to the **Agawa Rock Pictographs** (mid-May-mid-Sept.), red ocher graphics that Ojibwa people painted on a lakefront rock face several hundred years ago. Park staff are usually on hand in July and August to tell you more about the aboriginal people and their history. The rocky shore here is especially beautiful. Because you have to scramble out onto slippery rocks to see the pictographs, you can visit only when the lake is calm; otherwise, the surf can crash dangerously onto the rocks.

Continuing north is **Katherine Cove,** with a sheltered beach of fine white sand that is a pretty picnic spot. If the surrounding trees were palms instead of evergreens, you could imagine that you were in the Caribbean. The terrain changes again at **Old Woman Bay,** approaching the park's northern boundary. Evergreen hills rise and fall around the bay, and waves often pound the broad sandy beach.

Recreation

Hikers will find a wide variety of terrain, ranging from easy paths like the two-kilometer (1.2-mile) **Crescent Lake Trail,** the longer six-kilometer (3.7-mile) but still fairly flat **Pinguisibi-Sand River Trail,** or the rugged 65-kilometer (40-mile) **Coastal Trail** that extends from Agawa Bay north beyond Gargantua Harbour; allow five to seven days to hike the entire coastal route, and you can do sections as day-hikes. Pick up hiking information and maps at the park office or the Agawa Bay Visitors Centre.

You can swim in Lake Superior if you're hardy; the surf is often strong, and even in August the average surface temperature is a chilly 14.5°C (58°F). Head for one of the more sheltered bays to find warmer water. The park also has several interior lakes, which are warmer, calmer places to swim or boat. You can rent **canoes** (mid-June-early Sept., $10 per hour, $30 per day) at Agawa Bay, Rabbit Blanket Lake, and Crescent Lake,

the trail to the Agawa Rock Pictographs

and from the Red Rock Park Office near Mijinemungshing Lake.

Camping

The park has 226 campsites in three different areas. To camp beside Lake Superior, book a site at the park's largest and most popular camping area, **Agawa Bay Campground** (mid-May-mid.-Oct., tent sites $40-44, electrical sites $46-50), where the premium sites are right on the beach. Agawa has showers, flush toilets, laundry facilities, and an outdoor amphitheater offering summer nature programs. In the park's northern half, on a smaller interior lake, you can camp at the **Rabbit Blanket Lake Campground** (mid-May-late Oct., tent sites $40, electrical sites $46), which has flush toilets, showers, and laundry facilities. To reserve campsites at Agawa Bay and Rabbit Blanket Lake, contact the **Ontario Parks Reservations Service** (888/668-7275, www.ontarioparks.com, reservation fee online $11, by phone $13).

Near the park's southern boundary, the rustic 20-site **Crescent Lake Campground** (mid-June-mid-Sept., $35 tent sites), with a lakeside swimming beach, has vault toilets, but the nearest running water is at Agawa Bay. Reservations aren't possible at Crescent Lake. The park's 200 **backcountry campsites** (mid-May-Oct., adults $11, ages 6-17 $5) are accessible on foot or by canoe.

If you don't want to camp, the closest accommodations are south of the park in Batchawana Bay or to the north in Wawa.

Outfitters

Naturally Superior Adventures (705/856-2939 or 800/203-9092, www.naturallysuperior.com) is based at the Rock Island Lodge, near Wawa. Rent kayaks, take kayaking lessons, or sign up for day hikes or canoe or kayak excursions. In July and August, they arrange **stand-up paddleboarding** sessions at Rabbit Blanket Lake. They can also organize multiday adventure trips in the park and around the Lake Superior region.

Headquartered south of the park in Goulais River, **Caribou Expeditions** (705/649-3540 or 800/970-6662, www.caribou-expeditions.com) focuses on water-based adventures, including kayak or canoe rentals and guided tours, lodge-to-lodge kayaking trips, and wilderness excursions.

Getting There

Highway 17 from Sault Ste. Marie to Wawa bisects Lake Superior Provincial Park; you can tour the park on a day-trip from either town. From the Sault, it's 140 kilometers (87 miles)—less than two hours by car—to the Agawa Bay Visitors Centre, and another 64 kilometers (40 miles) from Agawa Bay to Old Woman Bay.

WAWA

Wawa is an Ojibwa word meaning "wild goose," so it's fitting that the chief landmark in this community is the 8.5-meter-tall (28-foot-tall) **Wawa Goose,** created by sculptor Dick Vandercliff. The goose perches outside the **Wawa Visitor Information Centre** (Hwy. 17 at Hwy. 101, www.wawa.cc, 8am-8pm daily July-Aug., 9am-5pm daily mid-May-June and Sept.-mid-Oct.), south of town. After taking your obligatory goose photo, head inside to pick up information about the Lake Superior region or check your email (there's free Wi-Fi).

With an interpretive display about the local First Nations, the large **Sandy Beach** fronts Lake Superior south of town; take Michipicoten River Village Road west off Highway 17 and follow the beach signs. In town, there's an attractive beach on **Wawa Lake.**

The best place to stay near Wawa is ★ **Rock Island Lodge** (800/203-9092, www.rockislandlodge.ca, mid-May-early Nov., $98-114 d). The four rooms don't have phones or TVs, but they do have private baths, Wi-Fi, and awe-inspiring views of Lake Superior. Out on the deck, the lake is so close that you're practically in the water. Rates include breakfast, and staff will prepare lunch and dinner on request, or you can use the lodge kitchen to cook your own meals.

Winnie the Pooh's Ontario Roots

The wilderness outside the tiny Ontario town of White River may have been the original home of a beloved children's literary icon: Winnie the Pooh. Legend has it that, during World War I, a Canadian army veterinarian named Harry Colebourn purchased an orphaned bear cub from an Ontario trapper when the train on which his regiment was traveling made a stopover in White River. Colebourn named the bear for his hometown, Winnipeg. Colebourn brought "Winnie" to England as his regiment's mascot and eventually gave her to the London Zoo. It was there that writer A. A. Milne and his son Christopher first met the bear that was to inspire Milne's famous stories.

Located 95 kilometers (60 miles) west of Wawa, White River has commemorated its honey-loving bear connection by building a public **park** (Hwy. 17) with a children's playground and a statue of Winnie. The **White River Heritage Museum** (200 Elgin St., 807/822-2657, www.whiteriver.ca, 10am-6pm Tues.-Sat. May-Sept.) has a collection of Pooh memorabilia.

Should you want to stop in this Pooh bear-loving community, grab a bite at **Catz Family Restaurant** (200 Hwy. 17, 807/822-2121, 6am-10pm daily, $7-15), which serves "good ol' northern comfort food," from burgers to pierogi to a hearty hot turkey sandwich. The 29 simple, well-maintained guest rooms at the family-run **White River Motel** (Hwy. 17, 807/822-2333 or 800/822-5887, www.whiterivermotel.com) have fridges, coffeemakers, and Wi-Fi. The 43-room **Continental Motel** (217 Hwy. 17, 807/822-2500 or 800/822-3616, www.continentalmotel.ca) across the road also has a restaurant.

Between Wawa and Lake Superior Park, the **Best Northern Motel** (150 Hwy. 17, 705/856-7302 or 800/434-8240, www.bestnorthern.ca, $78-92 s, $85-99 d, $135 cottages) is an updated motel with 11 guest rooms, all with microwaves, refrigerators, coffeemakers, and flat-screen TVs, as well as three two-bedroom cottages. It's right off the highway, however, so beware of road noise. The main lodge has a sauna, a rec room with a pool table, and a **restaurant** ($11-29) that serves Polish specialties along with more standard burgers, fish, and steaks.

Next door, **Kinniwabi Pines International Restaurant** (106 Hwy. 17, 705/856-7226, 8am-9pm daily, lunch $8-13, dinner $16-25) offers a world-roaming menu of Caribbean, Chinese, and Canadian dishes. Breakfast is also served.

You'll find more basic motels and eateries in town, along Mission Road and Broadway Avenue, Wawa's main streets. The **Wawa Motor Inn** (118 Mission Rd., 705/856-2278 or 800/561-2278, www.wawamotorinn.ca, $81-144 d) has adequate rooms in their main motel block and in a rustic "log village" set back from the road. They also have several two-bedroom cottages ($195-235).

Wawa is 230 kilometers (145 miles) north of Sault Ste. Marie.

Lake Superior's North Shore

The Trans-Canada Highway runs along Lake Superior's northern shore, lined with boreal forests and rocky evidence of the Canadian Shield. The road dips and rises, gently curving toward or away from the lake, with "wow"-inducing landscapes and water vistas surprising you as you round a bend or crest a hill. One of Ontario's most beautiful driving routes, this section of the Trans-Canada connects Wawa to the city of Thunder Bay and beyond, with stopover towns and several national and provincial parks along the way.

A 10,000-square-kilometer (3,900-square-mile) section of Lake Superior forms the **Lake Superior National Marine Conservation Area** (807/887-5467, www.pc.gc.ca), the marine equivalent of a Canadian national park. Beginning east of Terrace Bay, the conservation area encompasses the lake and its islands west to the Sibley Peninsula (home of the Sleeping Giant) and south to the U.S. border. When its establishment is finalized, it will become the largest protected freshwater area in the world.

While the conservation area doesn't have a visitors center or official facilities, Parks Canada staff work with local communities and First Nations to develop programs for visitors, host special events, and promote the region's numerous land- and water-based recreational activities, such as hiking, wildlife viewing, cross-country skiing, canoeing, kayaking, sailing, fishing, scuba diving, and even surfing on the lake. Outfitters in Wawa, Terrace Bay, Rossport, Nipigon, and Red Rock can organize all manner of outdoor trips.

You can make the 485-kilometer (300-mile) drive from Wawa to Thunder Bay in a leisurely day, but plan to stop off along the way. You could spend weeks here before you'd run out of outdoor adventures. Except in the cities of Sault Ste. Marie and Thunder Bay, the Lake Superior region has little in the way of public transportation. While **Greyhound** (www.greyhound.ca) does provide bus service to towns along Lake Superior's North Shore, it's not really practical to explore without a car unless you've arranged with an outfitter for local transportation.

★ PUKASKWA NATIONAL PARK

The largest national park in Ontario spreads across Lake Superior's northeastern reaches, encompassing 1,878 square kilometers (725 square miles) of northern forest and Great Lake coastline, home to moose, woodland caribou, wolves, and bears. Pronounced "PUCK-a-saw," **Pukaskwa National Park** (off Hwy. 627, Heron Bay, 807/229-0801, www. pc.gc.ca, late May-mid-Oct., adults $5.80, seniors $4.90, ages 6-16 $2.90, or $14.80 per vehicle) draws both novice outdoorspeople and experienced adventurers who come to hike or kayak amid Lake Superior's dramatic terrain. The park also offers interesting programs to introduce visitors to the region's First Nations culture.

In summer, the waterside **Hattie Cove Visitors Centre** (9am-4pm daily July-Aug.) is a hub of activity, with daily interpretive programs, from art workshops to guided hikes to presentations about the park's Prescribed Fire program for maintaining the health of its forests. Check out the colorful wall mural that's full of First Nations symbols. The center has free Wi-Fi.

Park cultural interpreters run unique programs at the **Anishinaabe Camp,** which has several traditional First Nations wigwams and other structures near the Visitors Centre. Staff demonstrate and explain aspects of Ojibwa culture, including traditional medicines, drumming, and ceremonies, sharing not just aboriginal heritage but present-day life and teachings of the First Nations communities who make their home in this Ontario region.

Get a program schedule from the Visitors Centre or by contacting the park office.

Hiking

Pukaskwa has lots of choices for day hikes of varying levels of difficulty:

- **Beach Trail** (1.5 km, easy): Follows the boardwalk along the Lake Superior shore.
- **Manitou Miikana** (2 km, moderate): Known as the "Spirit Trail," this route overlooks the lake and the Pic River dunes.
- **Southern Headland Trail** (2.2 km, moderate): Rocky shores, pine forests, and lake views.
- **Bimose Kinoomagewnan** (2.6 km, moderate): An interpretive trail around Halfway Lake, highlighting the Ojibwa people's Seven Grandfather Teachings. Park cultural interpreters lead periodic guided hikes on this trail; check with the park office for schedules.
- **White River Suspension Bridge** (18 km round-trip, moderate): This demanding but popular full-day hike leads to a suspension bridge 23 meters (75 feet) above Chigaminqinigum Falls.

For experienced backcountry hikers who want a multiday adventure, the park's **Coastal Hiking Trail** runs 60 kilometers (37 miles) one-way through rugged wilderness terrain. Refer to the Coastal Hiking Trail Trip Planner, available on the park website (www.pc.gc.ca), for more details about backcountry hiking.

Kayaking

Pukaskwa's offshore waters aren't a beginner kayaking or canoeing destination, since Lake Superior's weather and water conditions can be changeable and challenging. Unless you're an experienced kayak tripper, consider working with a local outfitter to plan your paddling adventure. **Naturally Superior Adventures** (705/856-2939 or 800/203-9092, www.naturallysuperior.com) offers guided sea kayaking trips along the Pukaskwa coast. The park publishes a detailed Coastal Paddling Route Trip Planner, available online, to help you prepare for a paddling journey.

Camping

Hattie Cove Campground (late May-early Sept. tent sites $25.50, electrical sites $29.40, May and Sept.-mid-Oct. tent sites $15.70, electrical sites $19.60) has 67 well-spaced wooded sites. The 29 electrical sites are all in the larger south loop area; tent campers may prefer the

hiking along the rocks in Pukaskwa National Park

Once a POW Camp, Now a Park

If you were looking for a remote encampment to sequester prisoners of war, you'd want a place where your charges would be unlikely to escape, right? Maybe you'd choose a region with sandy soil too soft to tunnel out, bounded by a huge frigid lake that's too rough to flee in a makeshift boat. Perhaps you'd consider the wilds of Northern Ontario, on the shores of Lake Superior. In fact, the Lake Superior region did house German POWs during World War II. The site of one POW camp, known as Camp 100, is now **Neys Provincial Park** (807/229-1624, www.ontarioparks. com, mid-May-mid-Sept., $11.25 per vehicle).

German prisoners were sent to Canada when European POW camps began to run out of capacity. Chosen for its remote location and for the difficulty it would pose for an attempted escape, Neys Camp 100 housed high-ranking German officers. It was an active POW camp from 1941 to 1946, accommodating 650 prisoners at its peak. Many were allowed to work at nearby logging camps, which were short-staffed because of the war. In 1948, after all the prisoners had been repatriated to Germany, Neys began receiving new residents—Japanese Canadians who had been interned during the war. Neys became a temporary relocation facility, housing these displaced Japanese Canadians until they were reunited with their families or found more permanent homes.

Neys has a place in art history, as well. Lawren Harris, A. Y. Jackson, and other members of the Group of Seven painted along the Lake Superior shore in and around the present-day provincial park. Harris painted views looking out to Pic Island, a vista that you can still see today. You can learn more about Neys' heritage in the park's Visitors Centre. This lakeside park has a long sandy swimming beach and several easy to moderate hiking trails, including the one-kilometer (0.6-mile) Under the Volcano Trail along the rocky shoreline, and the two-kilometer (1.2-mile) Lookout Trail that climbs up to viewpoints over the park.

For campers, Neys has 144 wooded, well-spaced **campsites** (tent sites $35, electrical sites $40). Areas 1, 2, and 3 all have sites near the Lake Superior shore, while Area 4 is close to the Little Pic River. Only Area 2 has a full-service comfort station with flush toilets, showers, and laundry facilities.

Neys Provincial Park is off Highway 17, 30 kilometers (19 miles) west of Marathon and 55 kilometers (35 miles) east of Terrace Bay.

quieter north loop. Both areas have comfort stations with hot showers and flush toilets. The park does not accept advance reservations for Hattie Cove sites. In spring and fall, some campground facilities, including restrooms, are closed; campsite fees are reduced accordingly.

Backpackers traveling the Coastal Hiking Trail can set up camp at primitive backcountry sites along the route, which are equipped with a tent pad, privy, fire pit, and bear box. To manage the number of campers in the park's wilderness, advance reservations are required for backcountry camping; call the park office to book.

Practicalities

Pukaskwa National Park is approximately 410 kilometers (255 miles) northwest of Sault Ste.

Marie and 310 kilometers (195 miles) east of Thunder Bay. It's located off Highway 17, the Trans-Canada Highway, 180 kilometers (115 miles) west of Wawa. Take the Heron Bay exit onto Highway 627 and follow it 15 kilometers (nine miles) to the park entrance.

You can pick up basics at the convenience stores in the Pic River First Nation (www.pic-river.com), bordering the park on Highway 627. The nearest town with lodging, restaurants, and other services is **Marathon** (www.marathon.ca), eight kilometers (five miles) west of the Highway 627 turnoff.

TERRACE BAY, SCHREIBER, AND THE SLATE ISLANDS

Overlooking Lake Superior, the town of Terrace Bay (population 1,800) grew from the

Terrace Bay is a gateway to the Lake Superior National Marine Conservation Area.

also live on the islands, which offer lots of adventures for kayakers and hikers.

Sights and Recreation

The **Terrace Bay Lighthouse** (Simcoe Plaza, off Hwy. 17, Terrace Bay, 8am-10pm Mon.-Fri., 9:30am-9pm Sat.-Sun., free) never guided any ships ashore. The town built this 15-meter (50-foot) lighthouse-style tower as replica of the lighthouse on the nearby Slate Islands; sitting at 68 meters (224 feet) above sea level, the Slate Island Light is considered the tallest lighthouse on the Great Lakes. The replica lighthouse is a lookout tower, with views over the town to the lake.

About one kilometer (0.6 miles) west of town, a short walkway leads to a viewing platform above pretty **Aguasabon Falls** (Hwy. 17, Terrace Bay, www.terracebay.ca/falls), pronounced "AUG-was-saw-bin," which cascade 30 meters (100 feet) into a deep gorge.

Although Lake Superior's water never gets that warm, you can walk, sun, or even swim at the beach. Wide, sandy **Terrace Bay Beach** (Beach Ave.) is a five-minute drive south of Highway 17. **Schreiber Beach,** three kilometers (1.9 miles) from that town's center, is a little harder to find, but its secluded shores, lined with pink-tinged stones, are worth seeking out. From Scotia Street in downtown Schreiber, take the underpass on Subway Street beneath the railroad tracks, then turn right to follow steep Isbester Drive until it ends just above the beach.

Hikers can explore sections of the challenging, 52-kilometer (32-mile) **Casque Isles Trail** (www.voyageurtrail.ca) that connects Terrace Bay, Schreiber, and Rossport. You can pick up the trail near Terrace Bay Beach or Schreiber Beach.

The two largest Slate Islands, Patterson and Mortimer, along with several smaller islands and their surrounding waters, make up **Slate Islands Provincial Park** (www.ontarioparks.com), which currently has no visitor facilities. Several outfitters run day trips or overnight trips to the Slates. Departing from Terrace Bay or Rossport, the **Bluebird**

surrounding woods; for decades, its main employer has been a pulp mill. It's now a jumping-off point for exploring the Lake Superior National Marine Conservation Area, and it has enough services to make it a handy stop as you're traveling across the lake's North Shore.

Workaday Schreiber, in the hills 15 kilometers (nine miles) west of Terrace Bay, started as a railroad town, when crews building the Canadian Pacific Railway in the 1880s set up camp here. Still a rail freight hub, it's now home to about 1,000 people, with a good diner and a secluded beach to lure you off the highway.

A collection of rocky islands in Lake Superior, 13 kilometers (eight miles) off the coast of Terrace Bay, the Slate Islands are home to the largest known herd of predator-free woodland caribou. In the early 1900s, during particularly cold winters when Lake Superior froze all the way to the islands, caribou crossed from the mainland, where they have remained and thrived. Beavers, red foxes, snowshoe hares, and other small mammals

Charter Boat (807/824-3353, www.bluebird-charterboat.com, $120 per hour for 1-6 people) runs sightseeing tours to the Slates and other Superior islands. Wawa-based **Naturally Superior Adventures** (705/856-2939 or 800/203-9092, www.naturallysuperior.com) offers guided kayak trips in the Slate Islands.

Accommodations and Food

Terrace Bay has several basic roadside motels. The **Norwood Motel** (Hwy. 17, Terrace Bay, 807/825-3282, $75 d) looks straight from the 1950s, pink bath tile and all, but the rooms have microwaves, mini fridges, free Wi-Fi, and (surprise!) Keurig coffeemakers.

Although they face a gas station, many rooms at the **Drifters Imperial Motel** (Hwy. 17, Terrace Bay, 807/825-3226 or 877/825-1625, www.driftersimperialmotel.ca, $79-99 d) have been updated with woodsy log furnishings and free Wi-Fi. Adjacent to the motel, the friendly **Drifters Restaurant** (807/825-3226, 11am-10pm daily, lunch $5-13, dinner $12-25) specializes in Italian dishes and also serves burgers, steaks, and salads, including a meal-size spinach salad with feta cheese and figs.

You can buy snacks and groceries at **Costa's Foods** (Simcoe Plaza, Terrace Bay, 807/825-4501, www.costasfoods.ca, 9am-6pm Mon.-Fri., 8:30am-5:30pm Sat.). Also in the plaza are a liquor store, a bank, a post office, a bakery, and a Chinese restaurant.

Look for the Esso station to find **Voyageurs Restaurant** (Hwy. 17, Schreiber, 807/824-2452, www.voyageuresso.ca, 7am-9:30pm daily, lunch $4-14, dinner $12-22), a convenient pit stop with all-day breakfast, soups, sandwiches, and Italian dishes.

Practicalities

Terrace Bay is on Highway 17, 260 kilometers (160 miles) west of Wawa and 225 kilometers (140 miles) east of Thunder Bay. Schreiber is 17 kilometers (11 miles) west of Terrace Bay. The **Terrace Bay Tourist Information Centre** (1008 Hwy. 17, 807/825-3315, ext. 235, or 800/968-8616, www.terracebay.ca, late May-Sept.) can provide lots of information about the Lake Superior North Shore and has free Wi-Fi. The town of Terrace Bay offers free Wi-Fi that you can pick up around Simcoe Plaza.

ROSSPORT

The waterside hamlet of Rossport is another worthwhile stopover along Lake Superior's North Shore. Watch carefully for the exit, though, or you'll easily blow right past the

Schreiber Beach

Rainbow Falls Provincial Park

tiny town, which is home to fewer than 100 souls. You can hike, swim, canoe, or kayak in a nearby provincial park, or use the village as a launching point for Slate Islands trips. Unlike many North Shore communities, which have only simple roadside motels, Rossport has several bed-and-breakfasts.

To the west of Rossport, the towns of Nipigon and Red Rock have cultural or natural attractions to draw you off the highway, and they're also starting points for lake excursions.

Sights and Recreation

Tiny **Rossport Museum** (Main St., July-Aug.), housed in a Canadian Pacific Railroad caboose, has exhibits on the area's rail and marine history.

For a short hike along the Lake Superior shore, follow the 1.5-kilometer (0.9-mile) **Rossport Coastal Trail.** Some sections are close enough to Highway 17 that you can hear the cars whiz by, but the lake views make up for it. It's a linear trail, so you need to return

the way you came. The trailhead is at the east end of Rossport village.

Eleven kilometers (seven miles) east of Rossport, **Rainbow Falls Provincial Park** (Hwy. 17, spring-summer 807/824-2298, fall-winter 807/825-3403, www.ontarioparks.com, mid-May-mid-Oct., $11.25 per vehicle) has several popular hiking trails, including the three-kilometer (1.9-mile) Rainbow Falls trail, which follows a boardwalk down 180 steps to a bridge, with views of the falls along the way; across the bridge, the trail turns more rugged as it climbs to a viewpoint with vistas to Lake Superior. The 52-kilometer (32-mile) **Casque Isles Trail** (www.voyageurtrail.ca), linking Terrace Bay and Rossport, also passes through the park. You can swim, or rent canoes and kayaks, in a sheltered cove at East Beach; West Beach has a small swimming area as well.

Experienced scuba divers head out from Rossport to explore the **wreck of the Gunilda,** a steam yacht that hit a shoal off the coast and sank in 1911. Lying 81 meters (265 feet) beneath Lake Superior's surface, the ship is considered one of the most intact freshwater wrecks in the world. **Discovery Charters** (807/824-3323, www.discoverycharters.ca) organizes dive trips to the *Gunilda* and other nearby shipwrecks.

Accommodations and Food

Rossport's most distinctive place to stay is the **Serendipity Gardens Guest House** (807/824-2890, www.serendipitygardens.ca, $100 d), with four guest rooms in a unique dome-like building. Choose one of the upstairs units with Gothic-inspired arched windows; all the handcrafted wood-paneled rooms have queen beds and kitchenettes. Rates include "breakfast in a box" (yogurt, a muffin, and juice). The same owners run **Serendipity Gardens Café** (222 Main St., 807/824-2890, 11am-9pm daily, call for off-season hours, $12-30), which serves salads, sandwiches, and home-style dinners; baked lake trout is a specialty. Check in for the Guest House is at the café.

Other B&Bs in town include the four-room **Willows Inn B&B** (116 Main St., 807/824-3389 or 877/825-1275, www.bbcanada.com, $90-110 d) and the three-room **Island Shores Bed & Breakfast** (440 Main St., 807/824-1182, www.bbcanada.com, $100-130 d).

Camping

Rainbow Falls Provincial Park (Hwy. 17, spring-summer 807/824-2298, fall-winter 807/825-3403, www.ontarioparks.com, tent sites $35, electrical sites $40) has two camping areas, both with showers and flush toilets. Eight kilometers (five miles) east of Rossport, the **Rossport campground** (mid-May-mid-Oct.) has 36 sites on a lakeside point; although they're not very shaded, several are right on Lake Superior. The larger **Whitesand Lake campground** (mid-May-late Sept.), along with the rest of the park's facilities, is 11 kilometers (seven miles) east of Rossport, where most of the 97 sites are set among the pines. For views of Whitesand Lake, book a site in the Lakeside camping area.

Practicalities

Rossport is just off Highway 17, 37 kilometers (23 miles) west of Terrace Bay and 190 kilometers (118 miles) east of Thunder Bay.

Based in Rossport, **Superior Outfitters** (807/824-3314, www.kayakrossport.ca) rents kayaks and canoes, offers kayak day-trips (July-Aug., $95 pp), and organizes multiday kayak excursions to the Slate Islands and other Lake Superior destinations. In addition to offering shipwreck scuba diving trips, **Discovery Charters** (807/824-3323, www.discoverycharters.ca) runs 1.5- to 4-hour boat tours ($50-80 pp) of the islands around Rossport and out to the Slate Islands.

NIPIGON

In 1941, American author Holling C. Holling penned a tale of an aboriginal boy living in the Ontario highlands near Nipigon, who carves a figure in a small canoe and sends him off to try to reach the ocean. Calling him *Paddle to the Sea,* the boy sets the canoe in the snow, and when spring comes, the little boat begins its journey down a stream into Lake Superior. The intrepid wooden canoe survives encounters with beavers and boys, freighters and frozen winters, even a tumble over Niagara Falls, before finally reaching the Atlantic.

The town of Nipigon has brought Paddle's journey back to life in its **Paddle to the Sea Park,** a children's playground with interpretive panels recounting parts of the Paddle story. The main section of the park is downtown behind the public library, and like Paddle, the park itself continues toward the water, with sections near the town marina.

Nipigon is 72 kilometers (45 miles) west of Rossport on Highway 17. Between Rossport and Nipigon, watch for the viewpoint markers and pull over at the **Kama Bay Lookout** for spectacular Lake Superior views.

Nipigon-based **Epic Adventures** (807/887-1008, www.epicadventures.ca) offers guided hiking, kayaking, mountain biking, snowshoeing, and cross-country skiing tours, ranging from two hours to a full day ($25-185 pp), and also leads multiday multisport outdoor trips along the Lake Superior North Shore.

RED ROCK

The village of Red Rock lost many jobs when the local paper mill closed, but the town is developing its tourism infrastructure. Head for the Nipigon Bay shore and the **Red Rock Marina and Interpretive Centre** (7 Park Rd., www.redrocktownship.com, 8am-8:30pm daily) to check out the high-tech interactive exhibits about the region.

Every summer, the town hosts **Live from the Rock** (www.livefromtherockfolkfestival.com, Aug.), a weekend-long folk festival. Also nearby, the Red Rock Indian Band, an Ojibwa First Nation, welcomes visitors to its annual powwow, the **Opwaaganasining Traditional Gathering** (www.rrib.ca, July); the Pays Plat First Nation hosts the **Pawgwasheeng Powwow** (www.ppfn.ca, July).

In the Red Rock Marina, the **Marina Restaurant** (7 Park Rd., 807/886-2606, 8:30am-8:30pm Sun.-Thurs., 8:30am-9:30pm Fri.-Sat., call for off-season hours, $8-12) dishes up burgers, sandwiches, and hot meals with a warm welcome. If lasagna is the daily special, don't pass it up.

Nipigon River Adventures (807/621-6342, www.nipigonriveradventures.com) can organize fishing, kayaking, mountain biking, rock climbing, hiking, sailing, and other trips in the Lake Superior National Marine Conservation Area. They accommodate guests at their Red Rock-area **Lodge** ($90 s, $135 d, with meals $120 s, 200 d).

To reach Red Rock, exit Highway 17 south of Nipigon onto Highway 628 and follow it into the village.

Thunder Bay and Vicinity

The largest city on Lake Superior's Canadian shores, Thunder Bay is a natural starting point for exploring this lake region, whether you're spending a weekend, circling the lake, or stopping off on a cross-Canada road trip. Once a key fur-trading post, Thunder Bay is still an important trade location. Its port, one of the world's largest grain-handling facilities, draws major ships transporting cargo along the Great Lakes and the St. Lawrence. The forest industry, with its pulp and paper mills, dominated the economy for many years, supplemented more recently with jobs in tourism, health care, education, and other service industries.

The present-day city of Thunder Bay, with a population of just under 110,000, grew out of two nearby towns: Fort William to the south and Port Arthur to the north. In 1970, after decades of debate, the towns, along with several smaller surrounding communities, amalgamated into the city of Thunder Bay. The city's main downtown is now the northern one, around Water Street, Red River Road, and Marina Park. A smaller downtown district in former Fort William centers at Arthur and May Streets. Strip malls and big box stores occupy much of the area between these two districts, creating a suburban strip inside the city rather than around the outskirts.

From Thunder Bay, you can set out on all manner of outdoor adventures. Three provincial parks—Sleeping Giant, Ouimet Canyon, and Kakabeka Falls—are within an hour's drive of the city, and opportunities for hiking, kayaking, sailing, and other sports abound.

SIGHTS

An interesting historic neighborhood to explore is the **Bay & Algoma Historic District.** Once a center of the region's Scandinavian community, Bay Street still houses the Finnish Labour Temple with its well-loved Hoito Restaurant, a Scandinavian deli, and gift shops selling Scandinavian products and souvenirs. Around the corner, Algoma Street is morphing into a funkier strip, with a juice bar, tea purveyor, yoga studio, and other eclectic shops.

Prince Arthur's Landing

A public park extending along the lakeside marina, **Prince Arthur's Landing** (Marina Park, Water St., www.thunderbay.ca) is filled with outdoor sculptures and ways to enjoy the outdoors. Since opening in 2011, the park has become a hub of activity and a major step toward reclaiming the city's formerly industrial lakeshore.

The park's most distinctive feature is its diverse collection of **public art,** which you'll encounter as you explore the grounds. On the patio of the Water Garden Pavilion (which houses Bight Restaurant) are the graceful giant water droplets of *Traveller's Return* by Andy Davies. In the aboriginal culture-inspired Spirit Garden, a series of panels on the *Celebration Circle,* by Randy Thomas and Roy

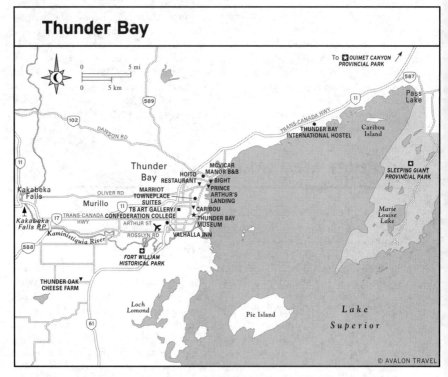

Thunder Bay

To ⊕ OUIMET CANYON PROVINCIAL PARK

0   5 mi
0   5 km

589

102

DAWSON RD

587

Pass Lake

TRANS-CANADA HWY

THUNDER BAY INTERNATIONAL HOSTEL

Caribou Island

11

Thunder Bay

MCVICAR
MANOR B&B
HOITO
RESTAURANT

BIGHT
PRINCE ARTHUR'S LANDING

⊕ SLEEPING GIANT PROVINCIAL PARK

Kakabeka Falls

11

OLIVER RD

Murillo

MARRIOT TOWNEPLACE SUITES

CARIBOU

Marie Louise Lake

Kakabeka Falls P.P.

17

11

TRANS-CANADA HWY

TB ART GALLERY/ CONFEDERATION COLLEGE

ARTHUR ST

THUNDER BAY MUSEUM

Kaministiquia River

ROSSLYN RD

VALHALLA INN

588

⊕ FORT WILLIAM HISTORICAL PARK

THUNDER OAK CHEESE FARM

Loch Lomond

Pie Island

Lake Superior

61

© AVALON TRAVEL

Thomas, incorporates images from the artists' Ojibwa culture. Throughout the park, literary quotes are etched into stones, on walls, and other unexpected locations; one example is *Round Dance,* by Sarain Stump, set into the ground on Pier 2: "Don't break this circle / Before the song is over / Because all of our people / Even the ones long gone / Are holding hands."

Three kilometers (1.9 miles) of trails for **walking** and **cycling** wind along Lake Superior's lakeshore. Daredevils demonstrate their skills in the **skateboard park,** and in the Water Garden, kids play on the **splash pad** (it's a **skating rink** in winter). One section of the park is designated as the **International Tai Chi Park** (www.pengyoutaiji.ca), where morning tai chi practitioners perform their graceful moves on the yin-yang practice pad.

In the **Baggage Building Arts Centre** (11am-5pm Tues.-Sun.), in a former freight shed, there's a small gallery and gift shop as well as periodic art workshops. Prince Arthur's Landing has a regular schedule of movies, concerts, and other special events, including the weekly **Summer in the Parks concerts** (6pm-9pm Wed. July-Aug.). Find out what's happening by checking the website of **Tourism Thunder Bay** (www.thunderbay.ca).

★ Fort William Historical Park

How many beaver pelts does it take to buy a wool blanket or a musket? At **Fort William Historical Park** (1350 King Rd., 807/473-2344, www.fwhp.ca, 10am-5pm daily mid-May-Sept., mid-June-mid-Aug. adults $14, seniors and students $12, ages 6-12 $10, mid-May-mid-June and mid-Aug.-Sept. adults $12, seniors and students $11, ages 6-12 $9), a family-friendly living history site on the banks of the Kaministiquia River, you travel back to the fur-trading days of the early 1800s.

the fort itself, which has been reconstructed to represent life in 1815-1816. **Tours** of the fort, its 40-plus buildings, and its working farm run 60-90 minutes. You might start at the wigwams in the aboriginal encampment outside the fort, where costumed interpreters expand on First Nations life. Within the fort, you can visit the canoe shed, where the vessels that carried traders and their goods were built, or the fort doctor's office, where your guide might demonstrate instruments used for pulling teeth or administering enemas. Another stop is the trading post, piled high with furs, where you learn the trade value of various pelts.

In summer, you can talk with interpreters representing Scottish fur traders, French voyageurs, Ojibwa and Métis people, farmers, and others who "live" at the fort. You might also ride down the river in a **voyageur canoe.** Fewer hands-on activities are available in spring and fall, when admission prices drop slightly. The fort hosts special events throughout the year, including the **Anishnawbe Keeshigun Aboriginal Festival** (July) and the **Voyageur Winter Carnival** (Feb.).

An on-site **canteen** (lunch $8-12) serves rib-sticking voyageur beef stew and French Canadian pea soup as well as more modern sandwiches and pizzas. To reach Fort William, which is south of Thunder Bay Airport, follow Highway 61 south, then turn west onto Broadway to the park.

Museums

Thunder Bay Museum (425 Donald St. E., 807/623-0801, www.thunderbaymuseum.com, 11am-5pm daily mid-June-early Sept., 1pm-5pm Tues.-Sun. early Sept.-June, adults $3, ages 6-17 $1.50, families $8, free admission Tues.) recounts the region's history through a series of small rooms, each reflecting a particular business or social organization: a school, a post office, a medical office, a shoemaker, a real estate office. Rotating exhibits showcase area architecture, military history, and music.

Focusing on regional artists, including

a voyageur guide at Fort William Historical Park

Fort William served as the inland headquarters of the North West Company, a fur-trading company based in Montreal that was established in 1783 as a rival to the Hudson's Bay Company. Not a military outpost, Fort William was set up in 1803 as a trading post. It served as a rendezvous point between voyageurs—French Canadian traders who traveled several weeks by canoe from Quebec, bringing goods from eastern Canada and Europe—and the traders and their First Nations allies from the west who arrived bringing beaver pelts and other valuable furs. The fort was a vital link in Canada's fur trade for over a decade. However, in 1821, the North West Company, facing stiff competition from the Hudson's Bay Company, merged with its rival. Trade routes shifted, and the fort's importance began to decline, until it closed permanently in the 1880s.

At the fort **Visitors Centre,** a short film introduces the history of the North West Company and its relationship with the region's First Nations. Visitors then proceed to

Finland on the Lake

Beginning in the 1870s and continuing until World War I, immigrants from Finland settled in the Thunder Bay area. Some came to Canada seeking land to farm, and more found work in Northern Ontario's burgeoning lumber and railroad industries. Subsequent waves of immigration—after World War I and later in the 1950s—continued to increase the number of Finnish settlers in and around Thunder Bay. At one time, the Thunder Bay region housed the largest community of Finns outside of Finland. Today, roughly 12,000 local residents claim Finnish ancestry.

For visitors, the region's Finnish culture remains most accessible in two places: the restaurant and the sauna. Both locals and travelers have long flocked to eateries like **Hoito Restaurant** (314 Bay St., 807/344-7081, www.finlandiaclub.ca) and the **Scandinavian Home Restaurant** (147 Algoma St. S., 807/345-7442, www.scandihs.com) for Finnish pancakes—plate-size hotcakes that are slightly thicker than a French crepe. Another locally popular treat is *pulla,* a cardamom-scented coffee bread, which you can find at Finnish bakeries and shops like the **Scandinavian Delicatessen** (307 Bay Str., 807/344-3632), across the street from The Hoito, which sells other traditional food products from Finland, Sweden, Norway, and Denmark. The Scandinavian custom of smoking fish continues at the family-run **Fish Shop** (960 Lakeshore Dr., 807/983-2214, www.thefishshop.ca), where you can purchase ready-to-eat smoked trout, whitefish, and salmon.

In Finland, saunas are an important element of the culture, providing both health benefits and social relaxation. In Thunder Bay, you can enjoy an in-town steam—solo, with friends, or with family members—at **Kangas Sauna** (379 Oliver Rd., 807/344-6761, www.kangassauna.ca). While it may not have the same cachet as a log sauna out in the woods, it has been providing locals with private sauna sessions for decades, and you'll still sweat plenty. Saunas at Kangas rent for 90 minutes and include use of the communal hot tub. Prices vary depending on the number of people and the size of the sauna: small ($17 for 1 person, $23 for 2, $33 for 3, $48 for 4), medium ($24 for 1, $29 for 2, up to $63 for 5), and large ($24 for 1, $29 for 2, up to $71 for 6). Saunas include a changing room and shower. You can rent towels ($4). Bathing suits aren't required (just lock your sauna door), although you have to wear suits in the hot tub. And if you haven't had your fill of Finnish pancakes, the on-site restaurant serves 'em by the plateful.

aboriginal artists, the **Thunder Bay Art Gallery** (Confederation College Campus, 1080 Keewatin St., www.theag.ca, noon-8pm Tues.-Thurs., noon-5pm Fri.-Sun., adults $3, seniors and students over age 11 $1.50, free admission Wed.) changes the displays in its three small exhibit rooms several times a year.

ACCOMMODATIONS

Built from unusual red stone, the grand Victorian manor housing the ★ **McVicar Manor B&B** (146 Court St. N., 807/344-9300, www.bbcanada.com, $105-145 s, $120-160 d) retains its high ceilings, imposing dining room, and curved turret. Owners Dorothy and Tom Walch have created a comfortable atmosphere for guests, where you can help yourself to tea, linger over breakfast, or peruse local menus. Upstairs, two of the

spacious antiques-filled guest rooms have en suite baths; the third has a private bath down the hall. On a residential street, the B&B is a short walk from downtown. Wi-Fi is free.

There's nothing picturesque about the surroundings of the **Marriott Towneplace Suites** (550 Harbour Expressway, 807/346-9000, www.marriott.com, $118-269 d), overlooking the parking lot of a big box store. Still, as one of Thunder Bay's newer chain motels, this family-friendly five-story property covers the essentials: colorful modern studio, one-, and two-bedroom suites with full kitchens, granite counter tops, flat-screen TVs, and free Wi-Fi; a modest complimentary breakfast; a compact pool and fitness facility; and a central location.

Convenient if you're traveling by air or exploring the attractions surrounding Thunder

a lighthouse in Thunder Bay harbor

Plan to attend the annual **Savour Superior Food and Drink Festival** (www.savoursuperior.com, Sept.) to sample what's new and local from around the region. The rest of the year, visit the **Thunder Bay Country Market** (Dorothy Dove Bldg., Canadian Lakehead Exhibition grounds, off Memorial Ave., 807/622-1406, www.thunderbaycountrymarket.com, 8am-1pm Sat. year-round, 4pm-7pm Wed. late May-early Sept.) for local products, such as elk jerky, homemade pickles, and baked goodies; look for **Boreal Birch Syrup** (www.birchsyrup.ca)—an alternative to maple—and for several varieties of gouda from **Thunder Oak Cheese Farm** (807/628-0175 or 866/273-3329, www.cheesefarm.ca).

Originally opened to offer reasonably-priced meals to Finnish bush workers when they came to the city (an average dinner in the 1930s cost 25 cents), ★ **Hoito Restaurant** (314 Bay St., 807/344-7081, www.finlandiaclub.ca, 8am-7pm daily, breakfast $5-11, lunch and dinner $6-19) has become a Thunder Bay breakfast tradition, especially for its crepe-like Finnish pancakes, served plain or piled high with eggs, bacon, or ham. Expect weekend brunch lineups, but don't expect high style; the restaurant is on the lower level of the 1910 Finnish Labour Temple, with all the atmosphere of a church basement.

Like the Hoito around the corner, the **Scandinavian Home Restaurant** (147 Algoma St. S., 807/345-7442, www.scandihs.com, 7am-3pm Mon.-Fri., 7am-2:30pm Sat., 9am-2pm Sun., $5-14) was established as part of a support network for Scandinavian immigrants. These days, families, visitors, and old-timers all pack this cheery Viking-themed diner for substantial all-day breakfasts and a mix of home-style and Scandinavian specialties, like the salted salmon sandwich and *mojakka* (Finnish beef stew). Of course, they've got Finnish pancakes, too.

Squeezed into a tiny storefront,

Bay, the **Valhalla Inn** (1 Valhalla Inn Rd., 807/577-1121 or 800/964-1121, www.valhallainn.com, $125-255 d) is adjacent to the city's airport. Recent renovations have upgraded this 262-room older property with white duvets, electrically equipped desks, and free Wi-Fi. Make sure to request an updated room. Restaurants on-site include the Runway 25 steakhouse, the more casual all-day Timbers, and a Starbucks café.

Eighteen kilometers (11 miles) east of downtown, between Thunder Bay and Sleeping Giant Provincial Park, the privately run **Thunder Bay International Hostel** (Longhouse Village, 1594 Lakeshore Dr., Shuniah, 807/983-2042, www.thunderbayhostel.com, $25 pp) has been hosting guests since 1973, in two adjacent houses surrounded by pines. There are no dorms here; accommodations are in simple private singles and doubles, with shared baths and kitchen facilities. Well-traveled owner Lloyd Jones has filled this homey residence with mementoes of his global journeys.

vegetarian-friendly **Growing Season Juice Collective** (201 Algoma St. S., 807/344-6869, www.growingseason.ca, 11am-7pm Mon.-Sat., $6-12) serves fresh-pressed juices and smoothies, sandwiches with locally made Thunder Oak gouda, and rice bowls. Try the sesame-ginger dressed Living Salad with greens, baked tofu, avocado, and sprouted lentils.

Its wallpaper adorned with photos of silvery trees, **Silver Birch** (28 N. Cumberland St., 807/345-0597, www.thesilverbirchrestaurant.com, 11am-2pm and 5pm-10pm Tues.-Fri., 5pm-10pm Sat., lunch $12-15, dinner $18-32) hums with quiet conversation and emphasizes northern ingredients, in dishes like bacon-wrapped pickerel glazed with birch syrup or garlicky Caesar salad topped with bannock croutons and elk sausage chips. You can drink a "Birch Bark Canoe"—Crown Royal whiskey with birch beer.

Choose a seat overlooking the waterfront or on the patio at lively ★ **Bight** (2201 Sleeping Giant Pkwy, Unit 100, 807/622-4448, www. bightrestaurant.ca, 11:30am-10pm Sun.-Mon., 11:30am-11pm Tues.-Wed., 11:30am-midnight Thurs., 11:30am-1am Fri.-Sat., lunch $12-18, dinner $14-41) in Marina Park. The world-rambling bites range from Ukrasian wontons (pierogi gone Asian) to Thai quinoa salad, but closer-to-home flavors like the green apple salad (with spinach, hazelnuts, goat cheese, and paper-thin fruit), magenta-hued beet gnocchi with almond pesto, and straight-up steaks are good picks, too.

Excellent pizza from the wood-burning oven, seasonal specialties like fresh corn salad or pumpkin ravioli, and internationally inspired entrées—perhaps Korean-style steak with kimchi fried rice, *piri piri* chicken, or maple-glazed pheasant paired with a chard-gouda gratin—make contemporary **Caribou Restaurant & Wine Bar** (727 Hewitson St., 807/628-8588, www.caribourestaurant.com, lunch Thurs.-Fri., dinner daily, $16-33) a long-running favorite for dinner with family or friends. Save room for the light and flavorful lemon *pot de crème*.

INFORMATION AND SERVICES

For the scoop on the city's arts and entertainment scene, check out *The Walleye* (www.thewalleye.ca), the local alternative arts and culture publication. **Tourism Thunder Bay** (www.thunderbay.ca) runs two local visitor information centers that are both attractions as well: On a hill east of the city, the **Terry Fox Tourist Information Centre** (off Highway 11/17, 1 km/0.6 miles east of Hodder Ave., 807/983-2041 or 800/667-8386, 8:30am-7pm daily mid-June-early Sept., 9am-5pm daily Sept.-mid.-June) looks out across Lake Superior to the Sleeping Giant, but it's worth stopping to see the 2.7-meter (nine-foot) bronze **statue of Terry Fox**. A young British Columbia man, Fox embarked on a cross-Canada run in 1980 to raise money for cancer research, after losing his own leg to the disease. He unfortunately had to stop his "Marathon of Hope" as he neared Thunder Bay, after running 5,342 kilometers (3,339 miles). Though Fox succeeded in raising more than $24 million, his own cancer had returned and would end his life at age 22 on June 28, 1981.

Downtown near Marina Park, the distinctively shaped **Pagoda Information Centre** (Water St. at Red River Rd., 807/684-3670, 10am-6pm Tues.-Sat. June-early Sept.) claims to be Canada's oldest continuously operating tourism office, dating back to 1909.

Tours

To experience Lake Superior from the water, book a cruise with **Sail Superior** (807/628-3333, www.sailsuperior.com), which offers several 90-minute sailing tours of Thunder Bay harbor (daily mid-May-mid-Oct., adults $49, students $39, under age 11 $25), departing from Marina Park. They also run half-day excursions to the Welcome Islands ($395 for up to 8 people) and organize other day or overnight sailing trips.

For a unique perspective on the islands of Lake Superior and the topography of the Sleeping Giant, take a 20- to 30-minute flight-seeing tour with **Wilderness North** (807/983-2047 or 888/465-3474, www.wildernessnorth.com, $99-129). You fly in a classic bush plane, a De Havilland Beaver, built in 1953.

GETTING THERE
Air

The **Thunder Bay International Airport** (YQT, 100 Princess St., off Hwy. 61, 807/473-2600, www.tbairport.on.ca) is southwest of the city center. **Air Canada** (www.aircanada.com) and **Westjet** (www.westjet.com) fly to Thunder Bay from Toronto's Pearson Airport and from Winnipeg; **Porter Airlines** (www.flyporter.com) has flights from Toronto City Airport. **Bearskin Airlines** (www.bearskinairlines.com) flies between Thunder Bay and Sault Ste. Marie and to several towns in Northwestern Ontario. **Wasaya Airways** (www.wasaya.com) flies to several northern communities.

Bus

Buses run to the Thunder Bay **Greyhound Bus Station** (815 Fort William Rd., 807/345-2194, www.greyhound.ca) from Sault Ste. Marie (10 hours, $105-183), Toronto (21-22 hours, $113-287), and Winnipeg (9.5 hours, $95-142).

Car

Thunder Bay is approximately 700 kilometers (435 miles) northwest of Sault Ste. Marie and the same distance east of Winnipeg. It's 80 kilometers (50 miles), along Highway 61, from the U.S. border near Grand Portage, Minnesota. From Toronto to Thunder Bay is 1,375 kilometers (860 miles)—a two-day drive. If you're interested in exploring Thunder Bay, Lake Superior, and other points in Northwestern Ontario, consider flying to Thunder Bay and either renting a car or arranging with one of the local outfitters for onward transportation. All the major car rental companies have Thunder Bay offices.

GETTING AROUND

Highway 11/17, the Trans-Canada Highway, skirts the western side of Thunder Bay. From the east, Hodder Avenue will take you toward downtown and the Marina. The Harbour Expressway runs east-west from the Trans-Canada to Fort William Road, close to the lakeshore.

Thunder Bay's attractions are scattered throughout the surrounding region, making it challenging to explore without a car. Within the city, you can get to many destinations on buses run by **Thunder Bay Transit** (807/684-3744, www.thunderbay.ca, $2.65).

★ SLEEPING GIANT PROVINCIAL PARK

From Thunder Bay's waterfront, you can see a hulking forested peninsula looming just offshore. If you look closely, and use your imagination, you can glimpse in the peninsula's terrain, the reclining profile of a gigantic humanlike figure, its arms crossed over its chest. The Ojibwa have many legends surrounding the creation of this Sleeping Giant, which they call Nanabijou, the Spirit of the Deep Sea Water. In one tale, Nanabijou was turned to stone after the location of the peninsula's rich silver deposits was disclosed to outsiders. Regardless of its origin, this craggy neck of land with cliffs rising 240 meters (780 feet) above the lake has become one of Lake Superior's most iconic outdoor destinations.

An hour's drive east of Thunder Bay on the Sibley Peninsula, the vast **Sleeping Giant Provincial Park** (Pass Lake, 807/977-2526, www.ontarioparks.com, $14.50 per vehicle) offers lots of opportunities for visitors to enjoy the outdoors. The park's boreal forest is home to moose, wolves, deer, foxes, and lynx. You can fish for yellow perch and northern pike in several inland lakes; in the park's largest lakes, you might catch walleye or smallmouth bass, too. Birders, take note: more than 200 avian species have been spotted in the region.

Near the park's northern entrance, **Thunder Bay Lookout**—atop some of Ontario's highest cliffs—has views across the lake to the city of Thunder Bay. If you're not afraid of heights, peer through the slatted lookout platform to the cliffs and rocky shores below. The nine-kilometer (5.5-mile) gravel and dirt road to the lookout can be steep and pot-holed in sections, but once you arrive in the parking lot, the lookout is only a minute's walk away.

The **Visitors Centre** and park information office are at Marie Louise Lake, near the park's south end, where the main campground is also located.

Hiking

Sleeping Giant has more than 100 kilometers (60 miles) of hiking trails that range from easy lakeside strolls to challenging daylong or multiday adventures. Because weather along Lake Superior can change rapidly, always carry raingear and warm clothing, even if the sun is shining when you set out.

The park's signature hike is the **Top of the Giant**, a 22-kilometer (14-mile) round-trip climb across the peninsula's southern sections to scenic lookouts across Lake Superior. Starting from the Kabeyun South trailhead, this route follows several different trails. The Kabeyun Trail leads past Tee Harbour, where it meets the Talus Lake Trail;

from there, you continue toward the Top of the Giant, where an additional two-kilometer (1.25-mile) steady climb leads you to one of Ontario's highest lookout points. Park staff caution that you shouldn't attempt this tough hike unless you're in good physical condition, but dramatic views are the hiker's reward.

A far easier path is the **Sea Lion**, a mostly flat, 2.5-kilometer (1.5-mile) walk to the lakeshore, where an unusual rust-tinged, vaguely animal-shaped geological formation jutting into the water gives the route its name. The Sea Lion Trail branches off from the Kabeyun Trail toward the park's southern end. Other day hikes include the family-friendly **Sibley Creek Trail** (1.7 km, 1 mile, round-trip) that starts from the Marie Louise Lake campground; the **Wildlife Habitat Trail** (4.8 km, 3 miles, round-trip), where you might spot deer or even moose; and the **Middlebrun Bay Trail** (10 km, 6 miles, round-trip), which traverses wetlands en route to a sandy beach.

Seasoned backpackers can explore the dramatic 40-kilometer (25-mile) linear **Kabeyun Trail,** which begins at the Thunder Bay Lookout and follows the coast around the Sleeping Giant.

Thunder Bay Lookout, Sleeping Giant Provincial Park

Mountain Biking

Experienced cyclists can tackle several park trails and roads by mountain bike. The Sawyer Bay, Sawbill Lake, Burma, and Pickerel Lake Trails are open to mountain bikers, as is a section of the South Kabeyun Trail to the junction with Talus Lake Trail. Cyclists can pedal the steep rutted road to the Thunder Bay Lookout and the easier route along Marie Louise Drive, which starts from the campground.

Workshops and Programs

In summer, park staff run numerous interpretive programs, including nature walks, campfires, and children's activities. Get details from the Visitors Centre. **Lake Superior Visits** (807/344-9208, www.superiorvisits. com) offers periodic photography workshops in Sleeping Giant Provincial Park, including a one-day photo safari hike and a fall colors photo weekend. The annual weekend-long **Festival of the Giant** (www.thefriendsof-sleepinggiant.ca, Aug.) entertains families with a sand sculpture contest, a barbecue, and lots of kids' activities.

Winter Sports

When the snow falls, the park grooms 50 kilometers (31 miles) of trails for cross-country skiing and snowshoeing. The Visitors Centre remains open as a warm-up lodge and restroom stop for winter adventurers.

Camping

The **Marie Louise Lake Campground** (www.ontarioparks.com, mid-May-mid-Oct., tent sites $40-44, electrical sites $46-50) has 200 campsites, including 85 with electrical service. The campground's comfort stations have hot showers and laundry facilities. It's a short walk to a swimming beach and playground. Also in the campground are five **cabins** (year-round, $169.50). Sleeping six, each cabin has three bedrooms (one with a double bed and two with bunk beds), a kitchen, a bath, and a sun porch. Linens, dishes, and cooking equipment are provided. The park rents three **camping trailers** (May-Oct., $98-142), which also sleep six. Although the trailers have showers, air-conditioning, and TV, you need to bring your own bedding and walk to the nearby campground for toilets.

Book campsites, cabins, or trailers up to five months in advance through the **Ontario Parks Reservation Service** (888/668-7275, www.ontarioparks.com, reservation fee online $11, by phone $13).

Getting There

Because Sleeping Giant's territory spreads across 244 square kilometers (60,300 acres), it's not a quick drive-in, drive-out destination. Plan to spend at least a full day to explore the park. The park turnoff from Highway 17 is Highway 587 south at Pass Lake, 50 kilometers (32 miles) east of Thunder Bay. From there, it's another 30 kilometers (19 miles) south to the Visitors Centre and main campground at Marie Louise Lake.

On your way to or from the park, detour to **The Fish Shop** (960 Lakeshore Dr., 807/983-2214, www.thefishshop.ca, 9am-6pm daily Mar.-Dec.) for excellent smoked trout, whitefish, or salmon—a perfect picnic with some crusty bread and summer tomatoes.

★ OUIMET CANYON PROVINCIAL PARK

Northern Ontario has plenty of places where the forested landscape gives way to more extreme topography. Ouimet Canyon, in the small **Ouimet Canyon Provincial Park** (Ouimet Canyon Rd., Dorion, 807/977-2526, www.ontarioparks.com, mid-May to mid-Oct., $2), is one of those places. Carved by natural forces over millions of years, Ouimet Canyon is a 150-meter (495-foot) wide **gorge** with jagged cliffs on either side. An easy one-kilometer (0.6-mile) loop trail leads to two lookout points, 100 meters (330 feet) directly above the canyon floor.

The canyon is especially striking in the fall when clusters of trees and plants turn gold and red; autumn colors are typically the most vibrant from the second half of September through early October. While it's difficult to tell from above, several varieties of arctic plants, normally found in much more northern regions, thrive on the canyon floor. In part to protect this fragile vegetation, visitors are not allowed into the canyon.

Ouimet Canyon is a day-use park, with no camping facilities. Most visitors come from Thunder Bay or stop off as they're driving along Lake Superior's North Shore. You can combine a stop at Ouimet Canyon with a day at Sleeping Giant Provincial Park. The Ouimet Canyon turnoff from Highway 11/17 is 75 kilometers (47 miles) east of Thunder Bay and 35 kilometers (22 miles) west of Nipigon.

Nearby Sights

The Ouimet Canyon area has two other points of interest.

Off Ouimet Canyon Road, **Eagle Canyon Adventures** (275 Valley Rd., Dorion, 807/857-1475, 10am-6pm daily May-mid-Oct., adults $20, kids over age 3 $10) boasts **Canada's longest suspension bridge,** a 183-meter (600-foot) span high above a canyon. If that's not enough adventure, there's a second 92-meter (300-foot) suspension bridge to cross, as well as a **zip line** ($60) that whizzes you through the air for more than 800 meters (0.5 miles).

Some of the rocks and boulders around the Lake Superior region are rich with amethysts, and **Amethyst Mine Panorama** (500 Bass Lake Rd., 807/622-6908, www.amethystmine. com, 10am-5pm daily mid-May-mid-Oct., 10am-6pm daily July-Aug., over age 5 $8), part working mine and part tourist attraction, is Canada's largest amethyst deposit. The stones were discovered here in 1955, and the mine has been operating since 1960.

Your admission price includes a 5- to 10-minute tour, covering the mine's history and facts about amethyst. What's more entertaining, particularly for the kids, is to dig for your own amethysts in the rock-studded field. If you'd like to keep what you dig up, it's $3 per pound. A gift shop sells amethyst jewelry, decorative stones, and other products.

The turnoff for the mine from Highway 11/17 is at East Loon Road, 55 kilometers (35 miles) east of Thunder Bay. From there, it's about 8 kilometers (5 miles) along a well-marked, mostly dirt road to the mine.

KAKABEKA FALLS PROVINCIAL PARK

Northern Ontario's largest waterfall is located in **Kakabeka Falls Provincial Park** (Hwy.

Ouimet Canyon Provincial Park

More Northern Adventures

Vast—really vast—tracts of wilderness stretch north from Lake Superior to Hudson Bay and west to the Manitoba border. Adventurous travelers could explore for years in this immense region. Thunder Bay is a starting point for many more travels throughout Northwestern Ontario. Here are a few ideas to assist in planning additional adventures:

CANOEING IN QUETICO PROVINCIAL PARK

Known for its world-class wilderness paddling, **Quetico Provincial Park** (108 Saturn Ave., Atikokan, 807/597-2735, www.ontarioparks.com or www.quetico100.com) has more than 2,000 lakes. Much of the immense forested territory in this 4,600-square-kilometer (1,775-square-mile) provincial park is accessible only by canoe.

You can sample Quetico's pine forests, cliffs, waterfalls, and lakes with a stay in the park's Dawson Trail campground, which has 106 car-camping sites. The park's main entrance is off Highway 11, 165 kilometers (103 miles) west of Thunder Bay. To really experience Quetico's terrain, though, you need to get out into the backcountry. Outfitters like **Canoe Canada Outfitters** (807/597-6418, www.canoecanada.com) and **QuetiQuest** (807/929-2266, www.quetiquest. com) can help plan Quetico trips.

NORTHERN WILDERNESS WITH WILDERNESS NORTH

Based in Thunder Bay, outfitter **Wilderness North** (807/983-2047 or 888/465-3474, www. wildernessnorth.com) organizes a number of multiday trips throughout Northwestern Ontario. They own several lodges, accessible only by floatplane, that they use as bases for many trips, and they work with aboriginal guides in the surrounding First Nations communities.

One such adventure, the Path of the Explorer, pairs canoeing and hiking in **Wabakimi Provincial Park** (www.ontarioparks.com)—Ontario's second-largest provincial park—with an excursion by floatplane and canoe to explore ancient First Nations pictographs on the rock faces surrounding Cliff Lake. They can tailor this trip to your paddling background; no prior canoe-tripping experience is required. Check their website or give them a call to discuss these and other wilderness trip ideas with a cultural slant.

WEST TO LAKE OF THE WOODS

With more than 105,000 kilometers (65,000 miles) of shoreline, Lake of the Woods wraps around more than 14,000 islands as it extends from Northwestern Ontario into Manitoba and across the U.S. border into Minnesota. The city of **Kenora** (www.kenora.ca), 500 kilometers (310 miles) west of Thunder Bay via the Trans-Canada Highway, is one starting point for exploring this expansive lake region. You could also base yourself in another Lake of the Woods destination, **Sioux Narrows Provincial Park** (www.ontarioparks.com), for fishing, swimming, sailing, and canoeing.

The **Northwest Ontario Sunset Country Travel Association** (807/468-5853 or 800/665-7567, www.ontariossunsetcountry.ca) has information to help plan a Lake of the Woods adventure.

11/17, Kakabeka Falls, 807/453-9231, www. ontarioparks.com, year-round, $14.50 per vehicle), a 30-minute drive west of Thunder Bay. Viewing platforms and boardwalk paths on both sides of the Kaministiquia River give you excellent vantage points for admiring the 40-meter (130-foot) high falls. Though it's sometimes called the "Niagara of the North,"

Kakabeka is far more modest than its famous southern neighbor; still, it's an impressive cascade of water.

In addition to the boardwalk trail overlooking the falls, Kakabeka has several longer **hiking** routes. The easy Mountain Portage Walking Trail, a 1.25-kilometer (0.75-mile) loop, follows the portage route that early explorers took to bypass the falls. The 2.5-kilometer (1.5-mile) Little Falls Walking Trail is another loop with views along the river and a climb up the Mountain Portage. Upriver from the falls, there's a small beach and riverside **swimming** area. For information about periodic **photography workshops** in Kakabeka Falls Provincial Park, contact **Lake Superior Visits** (807/344-9208, www.superiorvisits.com).

Camping

The park has 169 **campsites** (www.ontarioparks.com, mid-May-mid-Oct., tent sites $40, electrical sites $46) in three campgrounds. The Whispering Hills Campground is in the woods up a steep road from the falls; it has central showers and laundry facilities. Bordering the Kaministiquia River, the Riverside Campground and the adjacent Fern's Edge Campground have vault toilets as well as central flush toilets but no showers.

Practicalities

Kakabeka Falls Provincial Park is 35 kilometers (22 miles) west of Thunder Bay, just off Highway 11/17. Unless you plan to camp, most visitors day-trip from Thunder Bay. If you're taking a quick look at the falls and moving on, pay for parking by the hour instead of buying a full-day pass. The park **Visitors Centre** (late May-mid-Oct.) on the river's west bank, provides information and runs summer interpretive programs.

You'll find basic services, including a couple of places to eat, just east of the park in the village of Kakabeka Falls. For coffee, fresh baked goodies, and light meals, stop into the cabin that houses **Metropolitan Moose Beanery & Café** (4770 Hwy. 11/17, Kakabeka Falls, 807/473-5453).

Background

The Landscape

Covering 1.1 million square kilometers (425,000 square miles), Ontario is nearly as large as France, Italy, and Germany combined. It's not Canada's largest province (Quebec has that distinction), but it's twice as big as Texas, the second-largest U.S. state, and just slightly smaller than Alaska. Ontario's northernmost regions share the same latitude as southern Alaska, while Point Pelee, the southernmost point on the Ontario mainland, is at the same latitude as Northern California's wine country. No wonder, then, that Southern Ontario is a major wine-producing region.

Ontario sits between Manitoba to the west and Quebec to the east, but if you think it's landlocked in the middle of the country, think again. The province borders four of the five Great Lakes—Ontario, Erie, Huron, and Superior—along more than 3,000 kilometers (2,300 miles) of shoreline. Ontario even has over 1,000 kilometers (680 miles) of saltwater shores on its northern boundary with Hudson Bay.

Beyond these major bodies of water, Ontario has nearly 250,000 lakes holding one-third of the world's freshwater, as well as numerous rivers and streams. Of course, the province's most impressive water feature may be Niagara Falls, which thunder down the Niagara River separating Canada from the United States.

GEOGRAPHY

With its granite rock formations and pine forests, the Canadian Shield covers two-thirds of Ontario, extending from Manitoba across the province nearly to Ottawa and to the Thousand Islands farther south. In the far north, in the Hudson Bay lowlands along Hudson and James Bays from Moosonee to Fort Severn, the rocks and pines give way to swamps and meadows.

In the south, in the ecological zone known as the Mixedwood Plain, more lowlands along the Great Lakes are flat farm country, while the woodlands include a mix of deciduous trees and evergreens. Bisecting a 725-kilometer (450-mile) section of Southern Ontario, extending roughly between the Niagara and Bruce Peninsulas, is the Niagara Escarpment, a forested ridge of sedimentary rock that juts above the region's otherwise flatter terrain. The highest point on the escarpment is 510 meters (1,625 feet) above sea level.

CLIMATE

Although Toronto is northwest of Buffalo, Torontonians are quick to point out that the lake effect that dumps piles of snow on their New York State neighbors has a different result in their city. Toronto's position on Lake Ontario's northern shore moderates the winter weather, and the city averages 115 centimeters (45 inches) of snow per year, less than Buffalo can get on a single day. Winter is still cold and frequently snowy—January's average temperatures range from -10°C (14°F) to -2°C (28°F)—but at least you might not always be battling major blizzards if you visit midwinter.

Toronto's spring is fairly short, beginning in late April or May, and summers can turn hot and humid. In July, the average temperatures range from a low of 15°C (59°F) to a high of 27°C (81°F). Fall is a lovely time of year, and the best season to travel across much of the province, particularly in late September and early October when the trees put on their annual autumn color show.

South of Toronto, on the Niagara

Previous: historic buildings in downtown Peterborough; Gut Lake in Grundy Lake Provincial Park.

Ontario's Average Temperatures

These are the average annual temperatures in several of Ontario's cities. Keep in mind that temperatures can fluctuate on a given day. On a typical July day in Toronto, for example, the temperature might be as low as 18°C (64°F) at night to 26°C (79°F) during the day.

City	January	April	July	October
Toronto	-4°C, 25°F	7.5°C, 46°F	22°C, 72°F	10.5°C, 51°F
Niagara Falls	-4.5°C, 24°F	7.5°C, 46°F	22°C, 72°F	10.5°C, 51°F
Ottawa	-10.5°C, 13°F	6°C, 43°F	21°C, 70°F	8°C, 46°C
Windsor	-4.5°C, 24°F	8°C, 46°C	23°C, 74°F	11°C, 52°F
Sudbury	-13.5°C, 8°F	3°C, 38°F	19°C, 66°F	6°C, 43°C

Source: Environment Canada

Peninsula, the Niagara wineries claim that the region's climate is similar to that of France's Burgundy region and Loire Valley, with Lake Ontario again moderating the more extreme winter weather found in nearby New York State. Temperatures are slightly more moderate than in Toronto, too, slightly hotter in summer, not quite as frigid in winter. Niagara's warm summers and temperate autumns are the busiest times here, when tourism is in full swing.

As you travel north of Toronto, into the Muskoka Cottage Country and along Georgian Bay, the slightly cooler summers have made these regions popular with Torontonians escaping the city's heat and humidity. It's still hot midsummer, but at least you can cool off with a swim in the lake. In winter, a snow belt starts north of Toronto around the city of Barrie. It can be snowing in Barrie (and on the ski hills between Barrie and Collingwood) when it's raining or dry in Toronto.

Ottawa residents will maintain, with a certain perverse pride, that their city is the coldest capital in the world. Moscow may also claim that distinction, but there's no disputing that winter in Ottawa—320 kilometers (200 miles) north of Syracuse, New York—can be frigid. While Ottawa may not get the heavy snows that towns like Syracuse do, it's definitely in the snow belt, averaging 235 centimeters (nearly eight feet) of snow per year. Still, the city celebrates its winter weather with the popular Winterlude Festival in February and with lots of outdoor activities. Spring comes late to Ottawa (it might begin to warm in April, but it's not consistently springlike till May), and summers, as in Toronto, are hot and sticky. Fall, as it is throughout Ontario, is one of Ottawa's best seasons.

Across Northern Ontario, winter temperatures, as you'd expect, dip well below freezing, and snowfall is heavy. Summers, though, can be surprisingly hot and humid, with daytime highs above 30°C (86°F). Even along Hudson and James Bays, expect warm temperatures if you're traveling in July and August.

Plants and Animals

PLANTS

Although you might not know it from a downtown Toronto street corner, forests dominate Ontario's landscape, covering more than 60 percent of the province's land. The types of trees you'll find vary from the southern to northern regions.

In the south, along Lake Erie and Lake Ontario and extending to Lake Huron's southeastern shore, deciduous forest is dominant. Trees common to this region include maple, oak, and walnut. You'll find the white trillium, Ontario's official provincial flower, blooming in deciduous forests in late April and early May.

Moving north, the forests become a mix of deciduous and coniferous trees, the former including red maples, sugar maples (accounting for most of the province's maple syrup production), yellow birch, and red oak, and the latter including eastern white pine (Ontario's official provincial tree), eastern hemlock, red pine, and white cedar. This forest region, known as the Great Lakes-St. Lawrence Forest, extends across the central part of the province, along the St. Lawrence River, on the Lake Huron shores, and in the area west of Lake Superior.

If you think of orchids as tropical plants, you may be surprised to learn that more than 40 species of orchids grow on the Bruce Peninsula, which juts into Lake Huron. The best time to see the orchids in bloom is mid-May through early June.

Boreal forest covers most of Northwestern Ontario, covering 49 million hectares (121 million acres). The predominant species here are jack pine and black spruce, as well as white birch, poplar, and balsam fir.

In the far north's Hudson Bay Lowlands, constituting the remaining 25 percent of Ontario's land and bordering the subarctic tundra, trees include black spruce, white spruce, white birch, balsam fir, and balsam poplar. This area is also one of the world's largest expanses of wetlands.

Ontario's provincial government owns more than 90 percent of the province's forests. About one-third is classified as "production forest," meaning that it's available for logging. Although some provincial parks and reserves, like Algonquin Provincial Park, are protected from further development, logging has historically been part of their economy, and limited logging is still allowed.

Even in its urban areas, Ontario is beginning to realize that its trees are an important asset. In Toronto, which currently has an estimated 10 million trees, the city is working toward a goal of increasing its tree canopy from 28 percent to 40 percent by 2057. The city hosts annual tree-planting days and plants free trees on residential streets.

ANIMALS

Southern Ontario is home to the white-tailed deer as well as other small animals, including raccoons, skunks, beavers, red foxes, and gray squirrels. In fall, thousands of monarch butterflies typically pass through the province's southwest, crossing Lake Erie as they migrate south to Mexico. Although butterfly numbers have been fluctuating in recent years, Point Pelee National Park remains one of the best spots to witness the monarch migration. The Point Pelee region is also prime bird-watching territory. More than 370 species of birds have been recorded in the vicinity, and in the spring, thousands of birders come to witness the migration of songbirds returning to the north.

In the Canadian Shield region that covers much of central Ontario, the animals get bigger. While you'll still see foxes, squirrels, and beavers, this region is also home the eastern timber wolf, the gray wolf, white-tailed deer, caribou, Canadian lynx, and black bear. One of the most popular events in Ontario's

Algonquin Provincial Park is the summer **Wolf Howl,** when park naturalists imitate wolf calls and wild wolves may howl in response. Many of the fish that you see on Ontario tables, including pike, lake trout, and walleye, come from this region.

In the far north, caribou, moose, and black bears become more prevalent, and in the extreme northern reaches, including the vast protected territory of Polar Bear Provincial Park (accessible only by air), there's a small population of polar bears. Seals, walruses, and beluga whales can sometimes be spotted off the northern coasts.

History

ABORIGINAL PEOPLES AND THE FIRST EUROPEANS

Archaeologists have found evidence of human settlement in Ontario dating back more than 10,000 years. In the north, early aboriginal people hunted and fished, while farther south, they were the region's first farmers. The province's name, Ontario, comes from an Iroquoian word that's loosely translated as "sparkling water."

The first Europeans to explore Ontario arrived in the early 1600s. French explorer Étienne Brulé sailed along the St. Lawrence River into Lake Ontario in 1610, while his countryman Samuel de Champlain followed in 1615, after overseeing the construction of a fort at what is now Quebec City. British explorer Henry Hudson claimed the Northern Ontario region that now bears his name—Hudson Bay—for Britain in 1611.

A group of French Jesuit missionaries began constructing a community near present-day Midland in 1639, establishing the first European settlement in Ontario. Their mission was to bring Christianity to the indigenous Wendat people, whom they called the "Huron." You can visit a re-created version of this settlement, where the Jesuits worked with the Huron for 10 years. It's now known as Sainte-Marie Among the Hurons.

In 1670, the Hudson's Bay Company was established, when the British monarch granted the company the exclusive trading rights to the land around Hudson Bay. Over the next 100 years, the fur trade flourished across Northern Ontario and the rest of Canada's far north. Aboriginal hunters sold furs to the Hudson's Bay Company in exchange for knives, kettles, and what became the company's signature wool blankets.

FRANCE VS. BRITAIN

Both France and Britain staked claims to territory in present-day North America during the 1600s and 1700s, and battles broke out as the two countries fought over these territorial claims.

During the Seven Years' War (1756-1763), while many conflicts took place in what is now Quebec and Eastern Canada, others were waged in what is now Ontario, along Lake Ontario and in the Niagara region. In 1759 the British defeated the French in Quebec City, during the Battle of the Plains of Abraham, which turned the tide of the war. The Canadian territories became part of the British Empire.

Over the subsequent decades, the British found that their vast colony was difficult to govern. In 1791, the British Parliament passed the Constitutional Act, which divided the territory in two. The region encompassing present-day Ontario became Upper Canada, and what is now Quebec became Lower Canada.

Upper Canada's first capital was the town of Newark, which is now called Niagara-on-the-Lake. In 1793, the capital was moved farther north, away from the volatile American border, to the settlement of York, which eventually grew to become the city of Toronto.

THE UNITED EMPIRE LOYALISTS

In the late 1700s, a wave of immigration to Upper Canada came from south of the border. The 13 British colonies south of Canada declared their independence from Britain, launching the American Revolutionary War, which resulted in the creation of the United States. After the war, many Loyalists—Americans who remained loyal to the British Crown—found that they were no longer welcome in the new United States.

The Loyalists came north to the still-British colony of Upper Canada, where many received land grants from the British government. Many of the early settlers to Eastern Ontario, along the Thousand Islands, in Kingston, in Prince Edward County, and in what is now the Rideau Canal region, were Loyalists, who kept British traditions alive in their new colony.

THE WAR OF 1812

Tensions between Britain and France flared up again in the early 1800s. The British navy eventually set up a blockade, preventing French ships from reaching the Americas and stopping American ships heading for Europe. In North America, where Britain and the United States still had an uneasy relationship in the aftermath of the American Revolution, the shipping blockade became one more significant source of conflict. In 1812, the United States attacked the closest outpost of the British Empire: Canada.

Many battles during the War of 1812, which lasted until 1815, were fought on Ontario soil, in the regions bordering the United States: the Niagara Peninsula, Toronto, the Windsor-Detroit area, and along the St. Lawrence River in Eastern Ontario. The Americans burned the legislative buildings in Toronto; the British in turn attacked Washington DC and set the White House aflame.

The British and American governments eventually negotiated a settlement, and the war officially ended with the Treaty of Ghent, signed on December 24, 1814, and ratified February 16, 1815.

BUILDING CANALS AND WATERWAYS

After the War of 1812, Canadians were concerned that the St. Lawrence River—a vital shipping channel between Montreal and the Great Lakes—could be vulnerable to another U.S. attack, since the Americans controlled the river's southern banks. In 1826, British lieutenant colonel John By arrived on the site of what is now Ottawa and made plans both for a new town—christened Bytown—and for a canal that would run south to Lake Ontario through a series of connected lakes, rivers, and waterways. The canal, which opened in 1832, became the Rideau Canal.

During the same period, entrepreneur William Hamilton Merritt proposed the idea of a canal across the Niagara Peninsula to provide a passage for ships traveling between Lake Ontario and Lake Erie. The Niagara River connected the two lakes, but a significant natural feature prevented the river from becoming a shipping route: the unnavigable Niagara Falls. Construction began on the Welland Canal, which included a series of locks to help ships "climb the mountain"—the Niagara Escarpment—between the two lakes. The canal opened in 1829.

Settlers in Ontario were also looking to improve shipping routes across the central sections of the province. In 1833, the first lock was built on what would eventually become the Trent-Severn Waterway, connecting Lake Ontario with Georgian Bay.

FIRST STEPS TO A UNITED CANADA

Upper and Lower Canada, which had been split apart in 1791, were joined again in 1840 as the Province of Canada. Toronto had been the capital of predominantly British Upper Canada, while Quebec City was the capital of francophone Lower Canada. However, when the two provinces were united, neither would accept the other's capital as the seat of government. As a compromise, the city of Kingston became the first capital of the Province of Canada. But the political wrangling continued, and two years

commemorating the Underground Railroad in Owen Sound

States to freedom in Canada. Following what was known as the Underground Railroad, a network of safe houses and churches that gave shelter to the refugees, the vast majority of those slaves crossed into Canada into what is now Southwestern Ontario. Many remained in the region, with significant settlements in Windsor, Sandwich, Amherstburg, Chatham, Dresden, and Buxton, and many of their descendants live here today.

CONFEDERATION

The Province of Canada was split once again in the 1860s, creating the new provinces of Quebec and Ontario. But this time, these provinces joined with Nova Scotia and New Brunswick to establish a new nation: the Dominion of Canada. The British Parliament passed the British North America Act in 1867, which officially created this fledgling country, joining these four original provinces in confederation on July 1, 1867. Kingston lawyer and politician John A. Macdonald became the first prime minister of the new nation of Canada. Today, Canadians celebrate Confederation on July 1, Canada Day.

ONTARIO'S DEVELOPING INDUSTRIES

In the late 1800s and early 1900s, Ontario began the transition from a primarily agricultural province to a more industrial one. In 1903, a huge silver vein was discovered in Northern Ontario, near the town of Cobalt, launching the mining industry in this region. In Southwestern Ontario, the industry was automobiles; the year after Henry Ford founded the Ford Motor Company, the company set up a manufacturing plant across the river from Detroit, in the Ontario city of Windsor.

During this same era, tourism became important to the Ontario economy as the railroads and steamships ferried visitors to lakeside resorts in the Muskoka region, the Kawarthas, the Thousand Islands, and Niagara Falls. The falls also became a source of hydroelectric power, beginning in 1906.

The province's industrial development

later, the capital was moved to Montreal. In the meantime, the frontier outpost of Bytown that Lieutenant Colonel John By had settled in the 1830s had become the city of Ottawa. By 1857, when the legislature still hadn't been able to agree on a permanent home for the Canadian capital, they referred the problem to the British monarch, Queen Victoria. The queen and her advisors unexpectedly chose the comparatively remote outpost of Ottawa.

Situated between English Upper Canada and French Lower Canada, Ottawa had a relatively central location. But another important factor was that other potential capitals—Toronto, Kingston, and Montreal—were extremely close to Canada's boundary with the United States. Ottawa, in contrast, was at a safer distance from the American border. Since 1857, Ottawa has been the nation's capital.

THE UNDERGROUND RAILROAD

In the mid-1800s, thousands of enslaved African Americans fled from the United

continued throughout the 20th century, during and after both World Wars, and into the 1950s and 1960s. The Toronto subway—Canada's first—opened in 1954, and the Macdonald-Cartier Freeway (Hwy. 401), which crosses the province from Windsor to the Quebec border, opened in 1968. And more recently, an Ontario company helped usher in the smartphone era when the Waterloo-based company formerly known as Research in Motion introduced the BlackBerry.

Government and Economy

GOVERNMENT

Canada has a three-tiered governmental structure, with federal, provincial (or territorial), and municipal governments. The federal government, headquartered in Ottawa, is responsible for foreign policy, national defense, immigration, and other national issues. The provincial governments handle health care, education, policing, and the highways, among other things. Local issues, such as zoning, city police and firefighting, snow removal, garbage, and recycling, are the municipal governments' purview.

Retaining its roots as a British Commonwealth country, Canada is a constitutional monarchy. The country's head of state is officially the monarch of the United Kingdom. That means that the Queen of England is also the Queen of Canada. Although Canada has preserved many of its British influences and traditions, including the summer Changing the Guard ceremony in Ottawa, the monarch's role in Canada is largely symbolic, and it's Canada's **prime minister** who is the country's chief executive.

The queen's official representative in Canada as head of state is the **governor general.** This, too, is largely a ceremonial role. The governor general functions something like a governmental ambassador, officiating at ceremonies, bestowing awards, and opening and closing Parliament sessions. With the prime minister's advice, the queen appoints the governor general for a five-year term.

Parliament is the national legislature, which has two bodies: the elected 338-member House of Commons and the appointed 105-member Senate. The governmental structure at the provincial level parallels that of the federal government. The head of each provincial government is the premier, a position analogous to a U.S. state governor. Each province and territory has its own legislature. Toronto is Ontario's provincial capital; the Legislative Assembly building is in Toronto's Queen's Park.

ECONOMY

In Ontario's early days, the region's economy was based on its natural resources, including timber, fur, and minerals. Logging, trapping, and mining are still important components of Northern Ontario's economy. In cities like Sudbury and Timmins, mines dominate the skyline, and across the north, you'll share the highways with massive logging trucks.

Southern Ontario was formerly agricultural, and while you'll see plenty of farms, orchards, and vineyards, the province's southern sector is now heavily industrial. Manufacturing, particularly in the automotive, pharmaceutical, and aerospace sectors, has been a foundation of Ontario's economy for many years. The province produces more than half of all manufactured goods that are exported from Canada.

As in many other countries, the service industries have become more and more important in Ontario, now accounting for more than 75 percent of the province's economy. Toronto is Canada's financial capital; not only is Canada's major equities market, the Toronto Stock Exchange, based here, but so are the headquarters of scores of banks and financial services companies.

High technology has become a major Ontario business, too. Greater Toronto, the Kitchener-Waterloo region, and Ottawa are major centers for software and hardware development, telecommunications, and biotechnology. Toronto is a hub for Canada's communications industries as well, including TV and film production, broadcasting, publishing, performing arts, design, and advertising.

With more than 30 colleges and universities, education is a significant component of Ontario's economy. Canada's largest university—the University of Toronto—is in Ontario. Other major Ontario universities include York University, Ryerson University, and the Ontario College of Art and Design, all based in Toronto; McMaster University in Hamilton; the University of Waterloo and Wilfred Laurier University in Waterloo; the University of Western Ontario in London; the University of Windsor; Carleton University and the University of Ottawa in the nation's capital; and Queen's University in Kingston.

ENVIRONMENTAL ISSUES

Like many heavily industrialized regions, Ontario has its environmental challenges. Along the lakeshores, particularly sections of Lake Erie, Lake Ontario, and Lake Huron, you'll still see power plants and other reminders of the province's industrial heritage—some still active, some long abandoned. In northern towns like Sudbury and Timmins, where mining remains an important part of the local economy, barren rocky pits mar parts of the landscape, and smoke can darken the skies. Similarly, the logging industry has cut wild swaths across Ontario's north.

Another industrial legacy, unfortunately, is water pollution. The Great Lakes can be plagued with poor water quality, although significant efforts have been made in recent years to clean up the lakes and make them again fit for recreation. Many beaches now have a Blue Flag program in place, where a blue flag identifies areas that are clean and safe for swimming.

As Ontario's cities continue to grow, urban sprawl, increasing traffic, and worsening air quality are challenges to address. These issues are most acute in Toronto, the province's

Kitchener-Waterloo is a high-tech hub.

largest metropolitan area, and in the Golden Horseshoe, the suburban ring around metropolitan Toronto. But Ontario is continuing to promote alternatives to car travel, with increasing options for train, bus, and ferry travel across the province.

People and Culture

Ontario is Canada's most populous province, home to more than 13.5 million people, or nearly 40 percent of Canadians. Most of Ontario's population lives in the cities, with over five million concentrated in the region known as the Golden Horseshoe with Toronto at its center. The Golden Horseshoe extends around the western end of Lake Ontario from the Niagara Peninsula to Toronto's eastern suburbs.

DEMOGRAPHY

Canada's government actively encourages immigration as a way to counterbalance the country's declining birthrate and provide workers for the nation's growing economy. Due to these immigration policies, which began in earnest in the 1970s, Canada's largest cities have become among the most multicultural on the planet. Half of all immigrants to Canada settle in Ontario.

Toronto, in particular, is a city of immigrants. Roughly half of the metropolitan area's residents were born outside Canada, and approximately 100,000 new immigrants move to the city every year. While the majority of Toronto's early settlers were of British origin, immigrants now come from all over the globe. In recent years, Toronto's Chinese community has increased by more than 15 percent, the Indian community by 25 percent, and the Filipino community by over 30 percent.

After English and French, Chinese is the most widely spoken language in Ontario. Ontario also has significant Italian- and German-speaking populations.

RELIGION

Christianity is the major religion in Canada. More than 40 percent of Canadians are Roman Catholic, and about one-quarter are Protestant; in Ontario, Protestants are the predominant religious group, with Roman Catholics a close second. Recent census figures indicate that more than 15 percent of Canadians claim no religious affiliation at all.

Although only about 1 percent of Canada's population, or roughly 350,000 people, is Jewish, Canada has the fourth-largest Jewish population in the world, after Israel, the United States, and France. More than half of Canada's Jews live in Toronto.

Canada's largest non-Christian religious group is Muslim, representing about 2 percent of the population nationwide. In Ontario, Muslim communities are concentrated in the large urban areas of Toronto and Ottawa.

FRENCH LANGUAGE AND CULTURE

Ever since European explorers first landed on Canada's shores, the country was settled by both English- and French-speaking colonists. While many people assume that Quebec is Canada's only French-speaking region, Ontario, in particular, had a large francophone population during colonial times. Even as late as the mid-1800s, more than half of Ontario's population were native French speakers.

Today, English is the first language throughout most of the province of Ontario, and there's no need to brush up on your *bonjour* and *merci* to travel here. However, since the province shares a long border with francophone Quebec, French is widely spoken throughout the region, and Ontario's francophone community is the largest in Canada outside Quebec. Roughly 500,000 Ontario residents, or just under 5 percent of the population, speak French as their first language. More than 60 percent of Ontario's francophones live in the province's eastern and northeastern regions.

Ottawa has a particularly large francophone and bilingual community. In fact, as the capital of bilingual Canada, Ottawa is itself a bilingual city, closer in linguistic mindset—and physical proximity—to Montreal than to Toronto. The Ottawa metropolitan area spans two provinces, Ontario and Quebec. The city of Ottawa is on the Ontario side of the Ottawa River, but on the opposite riverbank is the community of Gatineau in French-speaking Quebec. Residents easily go back and forth across the bridges between the two provinces, many living on one side and working on the other. Reflecting this linguistic diversity, nearly half the population of the Ottawa region is fully bilingual. The government operates in both languages, as do many businesses.

Across the province, Ontario's francophone community continues to grow through immigration, as French-speaking immigrants from Africa, the Caribbean, and Europe have settled here. Today, about 10 percent of Ontario's francophones are members of a visible racial minority.

ABORIGINAL CULTURE

Canada has three officially recognized aboriginal groups: the First Nations, the Inuit, and the Métis. *First Nations* is the modern term for aboriginal people who are neither Inuit nor Métis. The Inuit people live primarily in Canada's far north, while the Métis—descendants of French settlers and their First Nations spouses—have historically settled in the prairies and the west.

Canada's aboriginal peoples—totaling just over one million people—make up about 4 percent of the nation's population. Roughly one-quarter of Canada's aboriginal people, most of whom fall under the "First Nations" designation, live in Ontario.

Ontario's aboriginal people are divided primarily into two groups, based on their linguistic heritage. The Cree, Oji-Cree, Algonquin, Ojibwa, Odawa, Potawatomi, and Delaware, whose historical territory has spread across central and Northern Ontario, speak languages that derive from Algonquian, while the Six Nations people, who are concentrated in the southern part of the province and include the Mohawk, Oneida, Onondaga, Cayuga, Seneca, and Tuscarora, are Iroquoian-speaking.

Some of Ontario's aboriginal

Manitoulin's Immaculate Conception Church combines First Nations and Catholic traditions.

peoples—including the Anishinaabe on Manitoulin Island, the Cree along James Bay, the Ojibwa near Peterborough in Eastern Ontario, and the Six Nations near Brantford and Hamilton—are beginning to open their communities to tourism, offering opportunities for visitors to learn about their cultures while bringing in new revenue.

The Arts

As you travel around Ontario, you can't help but see works by the Group of Seven, Canadian landscape painters who worked primarily in the 1920s and whose works have become associated with Ontario. The original members, Franklin Carmichael, Lawren Harris, A. Y. Jackson, Frank Johnston, Arthur Lismer, J. E. H. MacDonald, and Frederick Varley, were all based in Ontario. Although artist Tom Thomson died (under mysterious circumstances in Algonquin Provincial Park) before the group was officially formed, he worked with most of its members and is normally considered part of the group. The National Gallery of Canada in Ottawa has an extensive collection of Group of Seven works, as do Toronto's Art Gallery of Ontario and McMichael Canadian Art Collection. In Owen Sound, there's a small museum, the Tom Thomson Art Gallery, devoted to Thomson's work.

LITERATURE

Many of Canada's notable contemporary authors live and work in Ontario or have made the province their home. Margaret Atwood, born in Ottawa in 1939, is one of Canada's best-known novelists. She writes on themes including feminism (*The Edible Woman*, 1969), science fiction (*The Handmaid's Tale*, 1985), life in Toronto (*The Robber Bride*, 1993), and ancient Greece (*The Penelopiad*, 2005).

Another of Canada's most notable writers, Carol Shields, was born in the United States but moved to Canada at age 22. She lived in Ottawa, Winnipeg, and Victoria, authoring 10 novels, three collections of short fiction, three volumes of poetry, and four published plays. She won the Pulitzer Prize for *The Stone Diaries* (1993). Her other books include *A Fairly Conventional Woman* (1982), *Larry's Party* (1997), and *Unless* (2002).

Short-story writer and novelist Alice Munro, who was born in and continues to live in Ontario, writes frequently about growing up female in the province's rural communities in the 1940s and 1950s. Among her works are *Lives of Girls and Women* (1971), *Who Do You Think You Are: Stories* (1978), *The View from Castle Rock* (2006), and *Dear Life* (2012). Her stories also appear periodically in *The New Yorker* and *The Atlantic*. Munro won the Nobel Prize in Literature in 2013.

Timothy Findley was born in Toronto and began his professional career as an actor, performing with the Stratford Festival in 1953. He later became the first playwright-in-residence at Ottawa's National Arts Centre and author of more than a dozen novels, including *The Wars* (1977). Sri Lankan-born novelist Michael Ondaatje has lived and worked in Ontario for many years, teaching at the University of Western Ontario, York University, and the University of Toronto. His best-known works, including *The English Patient* (1992) and the more recent *Anil's Ghost* (2000), don't draw on Ontario life, but one of his earlier novels, *In the Skin of a Lion* (1987) is set in 1930s Toronto.

With so many Ontarians hailing from abroad, it's no surprise that many of the province's modern writers deal with immigrant themes. Rohinton Mistry, born in India and now living in Toronto, writes about the Indian and Indian Canadian communities in novels such as *A Fine Balance* (1995) and *Family Matters* (2002). Toronto novelist M. G.

Vassanji also tackles immigrant themes, particularly about Indians and Africans. His books include *No New Land* (1991), *The In-Between Life of Vikram Lall* (2003), and *The Assassin's Song* (2007). Another Toronto writer, Dionne Brand, born in Trinidad in 1953, considers immigrant issues in her works as well, including the 2005 novel *What We All Long For,* as does Barbados-born novelist and memoirist Austin Clarke in books such as *The Meeting Point* (1967), *Storm of Fortune* (1971), and *The Bigger Light* (1975).

Born in Ontario in 1959, Nino Ricci drew on his experiences as an Italian Canadian in his first novel, *Lives of the Saints* (1990). His subsequent books include *In a Glass House* (1993), *Where She Has Gone* (1997), *Testament* (2003), and *The Origin of Species* (2008). One of Ontario's earliest "immigrant" writers was Susanne Moodie, who came with her husband from England in 1832 and settled in Upper Canada, in what is now Ontario. She described their experiences in her autobiographical works, *Roughing It in the Bush; or, Life in Canada* (1852) and the sequel, *Life in the Clearings Versus the Bush* (1853).

Humorist Stephen Leacock offered up a different take on small-town Ontario life in *Sunshine Sketches of a Little Town* (1912), which was among his 35 books of humor. His former home in Orillia, north of Barrie in central Ontario, is now a museum. Ontario-born playwright and novelist Robertson Davies set many of his novels, such as *Fifth Business* (1970) and *What's Bred in the Bone* (1985), in his home province. More recently, novelist Jane Urquhart, who was born in the small Northern Ontario town of Little Long Lac and now lives in the southern part of the province, considers regional themes, in works such as *The Stone Carvers* (2001).

MUSIC

Ontario has contributed many performers to the music and dance worlds. Rock-and-roll legend Neil Young hails from Toronto, as does classical pianist and composer Glenn Gould (1932-1982), where a concert hall in the Canadian Broadcasting Company building bears his name. Singer-songwriter Gordon Lightfoot, born in Orillia, is perhaps best known for "The Wreck of the Edmund Fitzgerald," his ballad about a Lake Superior shipwreck. Stratford's hometown heartthrob is former teen pop sensation Justin Bieber; country singer Shania Twain was born in Windsor and raised in Timmins. The bands Barenaked Ladies and Tragically Hip both have Ontario roots, as do singer-songwriters Alanis Morissette, who was born in Ottawa, and Avril Lavigne, born in Belleville.

THEATER AND FILM

Toronto is a major center for English-language theater, with more than 90 theater venues around the metropolitan region. A number of the city's professional repertory companies focus on Canadian plays. Toronto is also home to a theater landmark. The Elgin and Winter Garden Theatres are Canada's only "double-decker" theater—one auditorium is stacked atop the other—and one of fewer than a dozen ever built worldwide. In Ottawa, the National Arts Centre (NAC) is the theater hub. The NAC has resident English- and French-language companies and often hosts national and international theater troupes and special events.

North America's two largest theater festivals take place in Ontario: the Stratford Festival and the Shaw Festival in Niagara-on-the-Lake. The Stratford productions, which run annually from late April through October, include works by Shakespeare and by many other classical and more contemporary playwrights. Similarly, the Shaw Festival was launched in 1962 to produce works by Irish playwright George Bernard Shaw but now mounts plays by Shaw, his contemporaries, and more modern authors during its annual April-to-October season.

Toronto is often called "Hollywood North" for the number of movies made here. Among the films shot on location in Toronto are *Chicago, Hairspray, The Time Traveler's Wife,*

Mean Girls, Harold and Kumar Go to White Castle, and *Cinderella Man.* To see what's currently filming in the city so you can be on the lookout for the stars, check the lists that the Toronto Film and Television Office publishes on their website (www.toronto.ca/tfto).

Every September, Ontario hosts one of the industry's major film fests: the Toronto International Film Festival. Headquartered in the distinctive glass TIFF Bell Lightbox theater building, the festival screens more than 300 movies from around the world and draws celebrities from across the globe. Ontario has also contributed many actors to Hollywood. Among the many film-industry notables who were born in Ontario are Dan Aykroyd (Ottawa), John Candy (Toronto), Jim Carrey (Newmarket), Ryan Gosling (London), Rachel McAdams (London), Sandra Oh (Ottawa), Catherine O'Hara (Toronto), Christopher Plummer (Toronto), and Martin Short (Hamilton). Even early film star Mary Pickford, who became known as "America's Sweetheart," was actually born in Toronto.

Essentials

Transportation

GETTING THERE
Air

If you're flying to Ontario from abroad, Toronto will likely be your gateway city. The province's largest metropolitan area is also its transportation hub. Ottawa, Canada's national capital, has an international airport as well, with flights from across Canada, several U.S. cities, and some European destinations.

Ontario Airports

Toronto's **Pearson International Airport** (YYZ, 6301 Silver Dart Dr., Mississauga, 416/247-7678 or 866/207-1690, www.torontopearson.com) is Ontario's major airport, with flights from across Canada, the United States, and European and Asian countries. Canadian carriers **Air Canada** (888/247-2262, www.aircanada.ca) and **WestJet** (800/538-5696, www.westjet.com), along with a number of U.S., European, and Asian airlines, fly into Pearson.

Toronto has a second, smaller airport, the **Toronto City Airport** (YTZ, www.torontoport.com), located on the Toronto Islands a short ferry ride from downtown. You can fly here from New York City, Boston, and Chicago, and from several Canadian cities. **Porter Airways** (888/619-8622, www.flyporter.com) is the main carrier serving this airport, although Air Canada also flies here from Montreal.

Ottawa International Airport (YOW, 1000 Airport Pkwy., 613/248-2000, www.ottawa-airport.ca) has flights from most major Canadian cities, U.S. destinations that include Boston, New York, Washington DC, Ft. Lauderdale, and Orlando, as well as London and Frankfurt. **Air Canada** (888/247-2262, www.aircanada.ca) and **WestJet** (800/538-5696, www.westjet.com), along with a number of U.S. airlines, fly to Ottawa.

Most of Ontario's other large cities, including two that are within 90 minutes' drive of Toronto, have airports with flights from other parts of Canada. You can fly nonstop to **Hamilton International Airport** (YHM, 9300 Airport Rd., 905/679-1999, www.flyhi.ca), southwest of Toronto, from Calgary year-round, and spring-fall from Edmonton, Halifax, and Moncton. In the Kitchener-Waterloo area, the **Region of Waterloo International Airport** (YFK, 4881 Fountain St., Breslau, 519/648-2256 or 866/648-2256, www.waterlooairport.ca) has nonstop flights from Calgary and Chicago.

Other regional Ontario airports include:

- **London International Airport** (YXU, 519/452-4015, www.londonairport.on.ca)
- **Windsor International Airport** (YQG, 519/969-2430, www.yqg.ca)
- **Greater Sudbury Airport** (YSB, 705/693-2514, www.flysudbury.ca)
- **Sault Ste. Marie Airport** (YAM, 705/779-3031, www.saultairport.com)
- **Thunder Bay International Airport** (YQT, 807/473-2600, www.tbairport.on.ca)

U.S. Airports

If you're flying to Ontario from the United States, it's worth checking airfares to nearby airports just across the U.S. border. Airline taxes are lower in the United States than in Canada, so airfares may be cheaper, too.

For Toronto and the Niagara region, check the **Buffalo-Niagara International Airport** (BUF, 716/630-6000 or 877/359-2642, www.buffaloairport.com). For Windsor and

---

Previous: Toronto's Union Station is a VIA Rail hub; the MS *Chi-Cheemaun* ferry on Manitoulin Island.

The *Canadian* travels between Vancouver and Toronto.

a quick two-hour ride, there are also several daily trains.

You can purchase train tickets online, by phone, or in person at most stations. VIA Rail fares are cheaper when you buy your tickets in advance. You'll get the lowest fare if you're willing to buy a nonrefundable ticket at least four days before you plan to travel. Fares are typically lowest from mid-October through May. Fares also depend on the class of service. On shorter routes, such as Montreal-Toronto, you can choose between economy and business class. A business-class ticket includes a multicourse meal with cocktails and wine onboard the train; you also get to wait in the more comfortable Panorama lounge, with complimentary drinks and newspapers, in the station. On *The Canadian,* options range from a basic economy seat to several types of sleeping berths and cabins; sleeper tickets include meals as well as access to a shower room and an observation car.

VIA Rail periodically runs last-minute specials on their website, offering significantly discounted rates for travel within the upcoming weeks. If you're planning a lot of train travel, it's worth checking their website, signing up for their newsletter, or following them on Twitter to learn about additional sales and discount offers.

points in Southwestern Ontario, look at flying into **Detroit Metro Airport** (DTW, 734/247-7678, www.metroairport.com).

Train
VIA Rail

Canada's national rail carrier, **VIA Rail** (888/842-7245, www.viarail.ca), can take you to Ontario from across the country. VIA's flagship route, **The Canadian,** crosses Canada from Vancouver to Toronto via Jasper, Edmonton, Saskatoon, and Winnipeg. If you do the trip nonstop, it takes 3.5 days. There are departures three times a week in each direction May through mid-October and twice a week the rest of the year.

From Atlantic Canada, **The Ocean** travels overnight from Halifax to Montreal, where you can make connections for Ottawa, Toronto, or other Ontario destinations. The train runs three days a week in each direction. Between Montreal and Toronto, VIA Rail runs several trains a day; the trip takes five-to-six hours. Between Montreal and Ottawa,

Amtrak

From the United States, American rail carrier **Amtrak** (800/872-7245, www.amtrak.com) has limited service into Ontario, and most routes involve a lengthy layover. The one exception is the train between New York City and Niagara Falls or Toronto, the **Maple Leaf,** which makes the 12.5-hour trip between New York City and Toronto daily, stopping in Niagara Falls along the way.

From Chicago and U.S. points farther west, or from Boston and other northeastern U.S. cities, there's no direct rail service to Toronto or anywhere else in Ontario. Coming from the west, you could take the Amtrak **Wolvervine** train from Chicago to Detroit, where you can cross the border to Windsor to continue your travels or transfer to the Toronto-bound VIA Rail train. Alternatively, you can take the Amtrak **Lake Shore Limited** from Chicago to Buffalo, where you can change to the Maple Leaf or catch a bus to Toronto.

If you're starting your trip in Boston, you can catch the **Lake Shore Limited** westbound to Buffalo and transfer there, or go first to New York City and change to the Maple Leaf. Unless you're a real rail buff (or you're coming from New York City), flying or even taking the bus is more efficient.

Bus
Megabus
Megabus (705/748-6411 or 800/461-7661, www.megabus.com) has some of the best fares and service to Toronto from Montreal and from the eastern United States, including New York City, Syracuse, Washington DC, Baltimore, and Philadelphia. Megabus can also take you to Kingston (from Montreal) and Niagara Falls (from New York City). On some routes, Megabus periodically offers one-way sale fares as low as $1.50, so check the website, particularly if you're flexible with your travel dates.

Note that Megabus allows passengers to travel with only one piece of luggage weighing less than 23 kilograms (50 pounds), plus one small hand-baggage item. There's no option to check additional bags; you'll just be turned away.

Greyhound
Greyhound (www.greyhound.ca) can take you to Toronto from many Canadian and U.S. cities, although you'll frequently have to change buses along the way. They run frequent buses between Montreal and Ottawa; change in Ottawa if you're going on to Toronto. If you're traveling to Ontario from Quebec City, Halifax, and points in Eastern Canada, you transfer in Montreal. Greyhound's long-haul western routes travel to Ontario from Calgary and Winnipeg, stopping in Thunder Bay, Sault Ste. Marie, Sudbury, and Toronto. From Vancouver, you have to change buses in

Calgary. From Edmonton, transfer in either Calgary or Winnipeg.

From the United States, Greyhound runs direct buses to Toronto from New York City (with stops in Syracuse and Buffalo, and on some buses, Niagara Falls), Detroit (stopping in Windsor and London), and Chicago. To reach Toronto from Boston, you need to transfer in Buffalo or Syracuse. From Philadelphia or Washington DC, you need to transfer in New York City.

Detroit-Windsor Tunnel Bus
If you're crossing the border between Michigan and Southwestern Ontario, you can take the **Detroit-Windsor Tunnel Bus** (www.citywindsor.ca). Assuming no traffic or border delays, the trip takes only 15-20 minutes. The buses begin running at 5:30am Monday-Saturday, 8am Sunday, and continue until 12:30am or 1am Monday-Saturday, midnight on Sunday.

Car
Required Documents for Drivers
If you have a valid driver's license from your home country, that license will be valid in Canada for three months. If you're driving over the border from the United States, bring the car's registration forms and proof of insurance. Either carry the insurance policy itself or get a free Canadian Non-Resident Insurance Card from your insurance agent. You must have a minimum of $200,000 combined liability insurance in Ontario.

If you're planning to rent a car in the United States and drive it across the border, confirm with your car rental company in advance that you're allowed to drive out of the country. Make sure you have a copy of the rental contract handy at the border crossing.

If you're driving a borrowed car across the border, bring a letter of permission signed by the owner, even if the owner is a family member. The border agents may not ask for the letter, but you can save some hassles if you have it on hand.

Ontario Land Border Crossings

You can cross the border between the United States and Canada at a number of Ontario points. In the Niagara Falls area, four bridges cross the Niagara River, which separates Ontario from New York State: the **Peace Bridge** (www.peacebridge.com), linking Fort Erie, Ontario, with I-190 from the Buffalo area; the **Rainbow Bridge** (www.niagarafallsbridges.com), which directly links Niagara Falls, Ontario, with Niagara Falls, New York; the **Whirlpool Bridge** (www.niagarafallsbridges.com), north of the Rainbow Bridge, available to NEXUS cardholders only; and the **Queenston-Lewiston Bridge** (www.niagarafallsbridges.com) between Queenston, Ontario, and Lewiston, New York.

Between Michigan and Southwestern Ontario, you can cross from Detroit to Windsor via the **Ambassador Bridge** or the **Detroit-Windsor Tunnel.** The **Blue Water Bridge** (www.bwba.org) connects Port Huron, Michigan, and Sarnia, Ontario. The **International Bridge** connects the cities of Sault Ste. Marie, Michigan, and Sault Ste. Marie, Ontario.

Three international bridges cross the St. Lawrence River between New York State and Eastern Ontario. The **Thousand Islands Bridge** (www.tibridge.com) is a major crossing linking I-81 with Highway 401; the **Ogdensburg-Prescott International Bridge** (www.ogdensport.com) runs between Ogdensburg, New York, and Prescott, Ontario; and the **Seaway International Bridge** (www.sibc.ca) links Massena, New York, and Cornwall, Ontario.

GETTING AROUND
Air

Ontario covers a lot of ground, and when you're traveling from one end to the other, or if your time is limited, consider flights within the province. On shorter, well-traveled routes, like Toronto to Ottawa or Montreal, airfares are often priced competitively with the train or bus. On longer routes or in more remote areas, airfares tend to be high.

Toronto is the hub for flights within Ontario, although Ottawa has convenient air connections as well. **Air Canada Jazz** (888/247-2262, www.flyjazz.ca), Air Canada's regional affiliate, flies between Toronto and Ottawa, Windsor, North Bay, Sudbury, Timmins, Sault Ste. Marie, and Thunder Bay. Ontario routes on **WestJet** (888/937-8538, www.westjet.com) include Toronto to Ottawa

Both a bridge and tunnel connect Windsor to Detroit.

and Toronto to Thunder Bay. Within Ontario, **Porter Airways** (888/619-8622, www.flyporter.com), based at Toronto City Airport on the Toronto Islands, flies between Toronto and Ottawa, Windsor, Sudbury, Sault Ste. Marie, and Thunder Bay.

Bearskin Airlines (800/465-2327, www.bearskinairlines.com) flies across Northern Ontario, including service to Sudbury, Sault Ste. Marie, and Thunder Bay. **Air Creebec** (819/825-8375 or 800/567-6567, www.aircreebec.ca) can take you between Timmins, Moosonee, and points farther north. **Wasaya Airways** (877/492-7292, www.wasaya.com) connects Thunder Bay to several northern communities.

Train

VIA Rail (888/842-7245, www.viarail.ca) runs trains across Southern Ontario. You can travel between Toronto and Niagara Falls, Stratford, St. Marys, London, Windsor, and Sarnia. In the eastern part of the province, VIA Rail trains connect Ottawa, Brockville, Kingston, Belleville, Cobourg, and Toronto. **Ontario Northland** (800/461-8558, www.ontarionorthland.ca) operates the *Polar Bear Express* train from Cochrane north to Moosonee.

GO Transit (416/869-3200 or 888/438-6646, www.gotransit.com) operates a network of commuter trains from Toronto to the surrounding communities, including Oakville, Burlington, Hamilton, Brampton, Barrie, Richmond Hill, and Markham. GO provides seasonal service to Niagara Falls, running weekends and holidays from late May through mid-October, also operating as the Niagara **bike train,** which has a bike rack-equipped baggage car.

Bus

Buses connect most Ontario cities and smaller communities. **Megabus** (www.megabus.com) has direct buses and great prices between Toronto and Niagara Falls and between Toronto and Kingston, with one-way sale fares sometimes going as low as $1.50. **Greyhound** (www.greyhound.ca) has the most extensive bus service across Ontario. It operates regular buses between Toronto and Kitchener, Waterloo, Stratford, London, Windsor, Owen Sound, Collingwood, Blue Mountain, Barrie, Sudbury, and Sault Ste. Marie. Greyhound also runs most of the bus routes in and out of Ottawa, including service to Toronto, Kingston, North Bay, and Sudbury. You can also take Greyhound buses between Sudbury, Sault Ste. Marie, and Thunder Bay.

To travel between Toronto and the Muskoka Lakes or to Ontario towns farther north, **Ontario Northland** (www.ontarionorthland.ca) has regular bus service. Check their schedules if you're going to Barrie, Gravenhurst, Bracebridge, Huntsville, Parry Sound, Sudbury, North Bay, Temagami, or Cochrane. **GO Transit buses** (www.gotransit.com) connect Toronto with surrounding suburbs and towns, including Kitchener, Waterloo, and Hamilton.

Car

If most of your time in Ontario will be in Toronto, Ottawa, or Niagara Falls, you can get around without a car. It's possible to travel to other destinations car-free, and we've detailed car-free options throughout the book. However, for the greatest flexibility in exploring the province, either drive your own vehicle or rent one along the way.

To get information about highway conditions, including winter weather conditions and summer construction status, phone the **Ontario Ministry of Transportation**'s toll-free 24-hour road conditions line (800/268-4686).

Car Rentals

The major North American car rental companies have outlets at Toronto's Pearson Airport, at Ottawa International Airport, and at regional airports around the province. A number of smaller car rental agencies also have offices near Pearson Airport; it's worth comparing their rates to other major companies.

Ontario's cities and most small towns also have at least one or two car rental offices.

Enterprise (800/261-7331, www.enterpriserentacar.ca) has an extensive network of rental offices around Ontario; both **National** (877/222-9058, www.nationalcar.ca) and **Discount Car Rentals** (800/263-2355, www.discountcar.com) have offices in many towns as well.

One strategy that can sometimes save money on car rentals is to take the bus or train from Toronto to your next destination and rent a car from there. Toronto rates are often higher than those in nearby cities such as Kitchener or Hamilton, although at times you'll find better deals in Toronto. Most agencies provide discounts for weekly rentals and additional discounts for rentals of a month or more. Some also offer discounts for members of the Canadian Automobile Association (CAA) or American Automobile Association (AAA).

Driving

Ontario law requires adults and children weighing over 18 kilograms (40 pounds) to wear seat belts with both lap and shoulder belts. Toddlers who weigh 9-18 kilograms (20-40 pounds) must ride in a forward-facing child safety seat, and infants weighing up to 9 kilograms (20 pounds) must travel in a rear-facing infant safety seat.

Most Ontario highways have a speed limit of 100 km/h (62 mph). On the Trans-Canada Highway, the speed limit is typically 90 km/h (56 mph), and country roads have a speed limit of 80 km/h (50 mph).

You can make a right turn at a red light in Ontario (as long as you stop and make sure it's clear), unless it's otherwise posted. Hitchhiking is not allowed on major (controlled access) highways, such as Highway 401. Radar detectors are illegal in Ontario. If the police stop you, officers can confiscate a radar device—and fine you—even if the device is turned off.

Emergency Services

Dial 911 to reach the police, ambulance, or other emergency service if you have an automobile accident, or phone the **Ontario Provincial Police emergency line** (888/310-1122). If you're involved in a car accident where someone is injured or where the estimated property damage is more than $1,000, Ontario law requires you to contact the police and stay at the scene of the accident until the police officers give you the OK to move on.

Boat
Great Lakes Ferries

The **Owen Sound Transportation Company** (www.ontarioferries.com) operates two ferry services on Ontario's Great Lakes. Between April and mid-December, ferries run to Pelee Island, Ontario's southernmost point, from Leamington or Kingsville in Southwestern Ontario.

To travel from Toronto or other points in Southern Ontario to Manitoulin Island, the quickest route is to take the MS *Chi-Cheemaun* Ferry from Tobermory at the tip of the Bruce Peninsula. The ferry runs mid-May to mid-October.

National Park Ferries

Ontario's Georgian Bay Islands National Park is composed entirely of islands, so you can reach the park only by water. Parks Canada (www.pc.gc.ca) runs the ***DayTripper*** boat service from the town of Honey Harbour to the park's Beausoleil Island from late spring through early fall.

One of only three national marine conservation areas in Canada, **Fathom Five National Marine Park** (www.pc.gc.ca) includes 22 islands in Georgian Bay off the northern end of the Bruce Peninsula. Access to the park is by boat from the town of Tobermory. Parks Canada has partnered with two private companies, **Blue Heron Tours** (www.blueheronco.com) and **Bruce Anchor Cruises** (www.bruceanchorcruises.com), which offer several types of boat trips to the park's Flowerpot Island from mid-May through mid-October.

Visas and Officialdom

ENTERING CANADA

For the most up-to-date requirements for visitors coming to Canada, visit **Citizenship and Immigration Canada** (CIC, www.cic.gc.ca).

Important note: If you have a criminal record, including misdemeanors or driving while impaired (DWI or DUI), no matter how long ago, you can be prohibited from entering Canada, unless you obtain a special waiver well in advance of your trip. Refer to the Application Forms and Guides section of the CIC website for additional information.

U.S. Citizens

The United States' Western Hemisphere Travel Initiative (WHTI) requires all travelers to present a valid passport or other approved document when entering the United States from within the Western Hemisphere, including Canada. So while you technically don't need a passport to enter Canada, without one, the United States won't let you back in, which means that Canada won't admit you in the first place. The bottom line: you need a valid passport to enter Canada.

If you are driving over the border, a valid U.S. Passport Card can be used instead of a passport. You can get more information about a U.S. Passport Card, which is not valid for air travel, from the **U.S. State Department** (www.travel.state.gov).

Several U.S. states and Canadian provinces have begun issuing Enhanced Drivers Licenses that can be used as an alternative to a passport or passport card when you're crossing a land border; they're not valid for air travel. As of this writing, U.S. citizens who are residents of Michigan, New York, Vermont, and Washington can apply for Enhanced Drivers Licenses. The **WHTI website** (www.cbp.gov) has more details about Enhanced Drivers Licenses and other border-crossing documents.

Citizens of the United States do not need a visa to visit Canada for stays of less than six months.

Citizens of Other Countries

All other foreign visitors to Canada must have a valid passport, and depending on your nationality, you may also need a visitor visa. British, Australian, and New Zealand citizens don't require a visa, nor do citizens of many European nations. Check with Citizenship and Immigration Canada (CIC, www.cic.gc.ca) to confirm what documents you require.

CUSTOMS

Visitors to Canada can bring a reasonable amount of personal baggage, including clothing, camping and sports equipment, cameras, and computers for personal use. As long as you're at least 19 years old, you can bring in a limited amount of alcoholic beverages duty- and tax-free: up to 1.5 liters of wine or 1.14 liters of other alcohol. Visitors are also allowed to bring in up to 200 cigarettes or 50 cigars. You can bring gifts for friends or family into Canada duty- and tax-free as long as each gift is valued at $60 or less; if it's worth more, you'll have to pay duty and taxes on the excess amount. Alcohol and tobacco don't count as gifts. They're subject to the limits above, even if you're bringing them to give as gifts.

Travelers must declare all food, plants, or animals they bring into Canada. In general, you're allowed to bring food for personal use, although there are some restrictions on fresh fruits, vegetables, meats, and dairy products. You can generally bring your pet cat or dog, too, subject to certain restrictions. Get the latest information from the Canadian government's Be Aware and Declare website (www.beaware.gc.ca).

In general, visitors cannot bring weapons

into Canada. You're specifically prohibited from bringing automatic weapons, sawed-off rifles or shotguns, most handguns, and semi-automatic weapons into Canada. There are some exceptions for hunters, and all visitors must declare any firearms in writing. Check the detailed requirements with the **Canada Border Services Agency** (www.cbsa.gc.ca).

Recreation

NATIONAL PARKS

Ontario is home to five of Canada's national parks: Bruce Peninsula National Park, known for its spectacular rock formations, beaches, and wide range of hiking trails; Georgian Bay Islands National Park, comprising 63 islands large and small; Point Pelee National Park, marking the southernmost point on the Canadian mainland; Thousand Islands National Park, in Eastern Ontario; and Pukaskwa National Park on Lake Superior's north shore. The province also has two national marine conservation areas: Fathom Five National Marine Park and the Lake Superior National Marine Conservation Area.

Parks Canada (888/773-8888, www.pc.gc.ca) is the agency responsible for the country's national parks. You can purchase an annual **Parks Canada Discovery Pass** (adults $67.70, seniors $57.90, ages 6-16 $33.30, family or group $136.40), valid at more than 100 national parks, national marine conservation areas, and national historic sites across the country. The family or group pass is good for up to seven people arriving together at a particular site. If you're going to visit several parks and historic sites during your travels, a Discovery Pass can be a good value.

Tip: If you purchase your Discovery Pass at the beginning of a month, your pass will be valid for 13 months, rather than 12, since the pass expires on the last day of the month in which you bought it. That is, if you purchase your pass on March 1, 2016, it will be valid until March 31, 2017. You can buy a Discovery Pass online or by phone from Parks Canada or in person at any national park or historic site. If you've already bought a day pass to a park or historic site within the past 30 days, you can credit the price of that ticket toward a Discovery Pass.

When you're spending several days in just one park, you're better off purchasing a **seasonal pass** for that particular park. For example, at the Bruce Peninsula National Park, a day pass is $11.70 per vehicle, and a seasonal pass is $49 per vehicle, so the season pass would save you money if you were staying five days or more.

PROVINCIAL PARKS

Ontario also has more than 300 provincially managed outdoor spaces, run by **Ontario Parks** (www.ontarioparks.com). Among the province's most popular parks are Algonquin Provincial Park in Cottage Country near Huntsville, Killarney on Georgian Bay, Lake Superior north of Sault Ste. Marie, Wasaga Beach near Collingwood, and The Pinery on Lake Huron, outside Grand Bend. It's hard to narrow down more favorite parks, but others worth exploring include Sandbanks on Lake Ontario, in Prince Edward County; Awenda, near Midland on Georgian Bay; Killbear and Grundy Lake, also on Georgian Bay, north of Parry Sound; Sauble Falls, on the Bruce Peninsula; and Sleeping Giant, near Thunder Bay.

Daily park entrance fees range $11.50 to $20 per vehicle. If you're going to visit several provincial parks, or if you're going to return to the same park over multiple days, consider purchasing a **provincial park pass** (800/668-9938, www.ontarioparks.com). You can buy a seasonal pass good for unlimited park visits during either the summer (Apr.-Nov., $107.63) or the winter (Dec.-Mar., $70), or an annual pass ($150.57) valid for the entire year. Buy park passes online, by phone, or at most provincial parks.

HIKING

Ontario has plenty of opportunities to hit the trail, whether you're looking to tromp around in the woods or along the lake for an afternoon or set off on a multiday hiking adventure. The **Ontario Trails Council** (www.ontariotrails.on.ca) provides information about trails province-wide.

One of Canada's iconic outdoor experiences is a hike along Ontario's **Bruce Trail** (www.brucetrail.org), an 845-kilometer (525-mile) route that extends from the Niagara region to the tip of the Bruce Peninsula. While some hikers do the entire trail straight through, far more end-to-end hikers complete the trail in a series of shorter excursions over several months or years. And many more hikers use the trail only for day hiking.

The world's longest network of trails, the **Trans-Canada Trail** (www.tctrail.ca) extends—as its name suggests—across the country. Some sections of the trail are urban walks, like parts of Ottawa's **Capital Pathway** (www.ncc-ccn.gc.ca) or Toronto's **Waterfront Trail** (www.waterfronttrail.org). Others, like the **Voyageur Trail** (www.voyageurtrail.ca) in Northern Ontario, are wilderness routes. Check the Trans-Canada Trail website for more hike ideas.

CYCLING AND MOUNTAIN BIKING

Ontario has an extensive network of trails for both road cycling and mountain biking. Some regions of the province, particularly along the lakeshores, are fairly flat. Inland, it's not the Rockies, but you'll find enough rolling hills to get your heart pumping. **Ontario By Bike** (www.ontariobybike.ca) can give you more ideas about where to cycle around the province.

The Niagara region is an excellent spot for cyclists, even if you're a not a hard-core long-distance rider. The **Greater Niagara Circle Route** (www.niagararegion.ca), with more than 140 kilometers (87 miles) of mostly paved cycling trails, loops around the Niagara Peninsula. You can bring your bike from Toronto on the seasonal **bike train,** run by GO Transit (www.gotransit.com).

Running nearly 1,400 kilometers (870 miles), the **Waterfront Trail** (www.waterfronttrail.org) follows the Lake Erie, Lake Ontario, and St. Lawrence River banks, between Windsor and the Quebec border. Another long-distance route, the 450-kilometer (280-mile) mixed-use **Central Ontario Loop Trail** circles from Port Hope on Lake Ontario, through Peterborough and the Kawarthas region, north to Haliburton and Bancroft. Many sections of the **Trans-Canada Trail** (www.tctrail.ca) are also open to cyclists.

Hardwood Ski and Bike (www.hardwoodhills.ca), in the hills northeast of Barrie, has 80 kilometers (50 miles) of mountain bike trails. Some of Ontario's downhill ski resorts become mountain bike meccas in summer, including **Blue Mountain** (www.bluemountain.ca), near Collingwood.

WATER SPORTS

Surrounded by four of the five Great Lakes, with over 200,000 inland lakes large and small, Ontario is a popular destination for all types of water sports. You can go **swimming** in most of these lakes, although the water, particularly in the Great Lakes, can be quite chilly. Pollution or increased bacteria levels can also close beaches temporarily. The **Blue Flag** (www.blueflag.org) program assesses the environmental safety of participating beaches, so swim when the blue flag is flying; their website also lists Ontario's approved Blue Flag beaches.

Ontario is a hugely popular destination for **canoeing** and **kayaking,** whether you want to paddle around a lake for an hour or two or embark on a multiday expedition. The most popular destinations include Algonquin Provincial Park, Killarney Provincial Park, and Temagami. **Stand-up paddleboarding** is growing in popularity throughout Ontario. Look for stand-up paddleboard rentals and lessons at many lake destinations.

For **white-water rafting,** head for the Ottawa River region, west of Ottawa; you can even do a gentle raft trip within the Ottawa city limits. For **scuba diving,** the Fathom Five National Marine Conservation Area, off the Bruce Peninsula, has some of the finest diving in the north; you can **snorkel** here, too.

Ontario may not have oceans or palm trees, but yes, you can go **surfing.** Lake Superior routinely sees waves of 3 to 4.5 meters (10 to 15 feet) that bring out hardy surfers and their boards. Even in midsummer, it's critical to prepare for the cold, though, with thick wetsuits, gloves, hoods, and booties. Thunder Bay is a good place to start your surfing adventure, and many surfers head for Terrace Bay on the lake's north shore.

WINTER SPORTS

Oh, yes, Ontario has plenty of winter weather, so if you like to get outdoors, you'll have plenty of opportunities for winter sports. In winter, you can **ice-skate** almost anywhere in Ontario. Practically every city or town has a rink or a frozen pond where you can strap on your skates. But the best place to skate is on Ottawa's Rideau Canal, which becomes the world's largest rink.

Compared to the snow resorts in the mountains of Western Canada, Ontario's **ski and snowboard** spots are smaller and more modest. But there are plenty of places where you can schuss down the mountain within a short distance of either Toronto or Ottawa. The province's largest ski area is the Blue Mountain Resort, near Collingwood. Other downhill destinations include Horseshoe Resort near Barrie, or Calabogie Peaks and Mount Pakenham near Ottawa.

While Ontario's rolling hills may seem small for downhill skiing or snowboarding, they offer excellent terrain for **cross-country skiing** or **snowshoeing.** A number of the provincial parks remain open in winter for skiers and snowshoers, including Algonquin, Arrowhead (near Huntsville), Awenda (outside of Midland), Killarney (between Parry Sound and Sudbury), The Pinery (on Lake Huron), and Wasaga Beach (near Collingwood). Gatineau Park, near Ottawa, is also a popular cross-country ski destination.

If you ever wanted to learn about **dogsledding** and lead your own team of dogs, you can give it a try in Ontario. Several outfitters offer dogsledding excursions in and around Algonquin Provincial Park, as does Wolf Within Adventures in Temagami.

canoeing and kayaking along the Grand River, southern Ontario

Accommodations and Food

Room rates are listed for high season—generally May or June through September or October, except at the ski resorts or other winter destinations, when high season typically runs from late December through February or March. Even within that time period, rates can fluctuate significantly, depending on the lodging's occupancy, nearby special events, and even the weather, so check current rates before making your plans. You'll need to add the 13 percent HST (harmonized sales tax) to the listed rates.

In Ontario's cities, especially Toronto and Ottawa, accommodations rates tend to be highest midweek when vacationers are competing for lodging space with business travelers. Hotels catering to road warriors will often discount their rates Friday through Sunday. Conversely, in areas that are primarily tourist destinations, including Niagara Falls, the Bruce Peninsula, Georgian Bay, Prince Edward County, and any of the national or provincial parks, weekends are busiest, and you might find lower lodging prices and more availability between Sunday and Thursday.

In most of the province, you'll save money on lodging by visiting in winter. A room for a midwinter weekend in Toronto may cost as much as 50 percent less than that same accommodation in July. However, outside the urban areas, since many attractions close from mid-October through mid-May, accommodations may shut down as well.

ACCOMMODATIONS
Cottage Rentals and Resorts

Throughout Ontario, going to "the cottage" is a long-established summer ritual. Even if you're not fortunate enough to own a country getaway or have friends or family willing to invite you to their cottage, you can still join the throngs of summer cottagers. Many cottages are available for summer rentals, and

cottage resorts—essentially a hotel where you sleep in a cottage but have hotel services like a dining room, water sports, and organized activities for the kids—are also popular. Cottages frequently rent for a minimum of a week, at least in summer, while you can usually book shorter stays at cottage resorts. Weekly rentals most often run Saturday to Saturday.

The Muskoka region north of Toronto is often known simply as Cottage Country, where Huntsville, Bracebridge, Gravenhurst, and the surrounding communities are all magnets for cottagers. You'll also find cottages and cottage resorts around Georgian Bay, along Lake Huron, in the Kawarthas, and pretty much anywhere that there are lakes and woods.

If you're renting a cottage, ask what's included and what's nearby: Do you need to supply your own linens and towels? What appliances—stove, oven, dishwasher, washing machine, clothes dryer—does the cottage have? What types of beds are in each bedroom? Is there a patio or deck? A barbecue? Internet access? A TV? DVD player? Is the cottage on a main road, or at the end of a quiet lane? How far is the nearest beach? Where's the closest grocery store?

Start your hunt for a cottage on the Ontario Tourism website (www.ontariotravel.net), which has a cottage search function where you can search by area, time period, and a range of amenities. Tourism offices and visitors bureaus in most regions can also provide information about cottage rentals in their vicinity.

Bed-and-Breakfasts

Ontario has bed-and-breakfast accommodations in major cities, smaller towns, and out in the country. Some are upscale and modern, with private baths and high-tech amenities like flat-screen TVs, iPod docks, and espresso machines. Others are homey but

Cool Sleeps

Is a bed too boring? If you're looking for an unusual place to lay your head, check out these unique Ontario accommodations.

- You can bed down in a tepee on a First Nations reserve, when you stay at **Endaa-aang "Our Place"** or with the **Great Spirit Circle Trail** on Manitoulin Island.

- At the **HI-Ottawa Jail Hostel,** in the nation's capital, some of the beds are in cells of the 19th-century former Carleton County Gaol. Ditto for the weirdly fun **King George Inn and Spa,** with rooms behind bars in the former Cobourg Jail, east of Toronto.

- Stay in a lighthouse. For a hands-on lighthouse experience, apply to be an assistant light keeper for a week at the **Cabot Head Lighthouse** on the Bruce Peninsula.

- Want to know what it was like to be a soldier in the 1800s? You won't be issued a musket or army rations, but you can spend the night in Kingston's **Fort Henry.**

- The **Sugar Ridge Retreat Centre,** with 10 cabins surrounding a contemporary Zen-style lodge near Midland, may be one of the quietest places you'll ever stay, whether you come for a yoga retreat or simply a peaceful escape.

- Outside the town of Tobermory on the Bruce Peninsula, **E'Terra** is the ultimate hideaway: the phone number is unlisted, the property has no sign, and the owners won't divulge the address until you make a reservation.

more modest—like staying with your aunt and uncle, where the bath is down the hall and you get a bed and a morning meal but not much else.

If a room has an en suite bath, it's in your suite, that is, it's inside your room, for your own use. A private bath can sometimes be en suite, but the term often refers to a bath that's outside of your room but reserved for you only; you might have to walk down the hall, but you won't have to share. A shared bath is just that: a bath used by guests of more than one room. Ask how many guest rooms share each bath; when there are two baths for three guest rooms, you're less likely to have to wait than when six rooms take turns for a single bath.

Wireless Internet access is widely available at Ontario B&Bs, and it's generally included in the rates, but always ask if Wi-Fi is important to you. Some B&Bs will have a computer for guest use; again, if that's something you need, ask. Outside major cities, most B&Bs have parking available. In the cities, they may not, or there may be a parking fee.

Remember that in a bed-and-breakfast, you're usually a guest in the owner's home. Many people enjoy staying at B&Bs, where they can chat with the owner and meet other guests over a cup of coffee or breakfast. Most owners will respect your privacy, but they're also your hosts, who can make recommendations about things to see and do nearby.

Hostels

If your vision of a youth hostel includes crowded, run-down dormitories filled with unwashed backpackers, it may be time to update your perception. Hostels do still tend to draw younger people, but older travelers and families have discovered the benefits of hostel travel, too.

Some hostels, like Toronto's Planet Traveler, are very modern and very wired—with free Wi-Fi, phone booths where you can make calls via Skype, even lockers with electrical outlets to plug in your laptop or phone charger. While others may not be as well outfitted, Internet access (usually Wi-Fi) is standard, as are shared kitchens, laundry facilities, and common areas for lounging and meeting other guests. Hostels often organize local activities, from pub crawls to city tours, to acquaint you with the area and with other travelers.

While the standard hostel accommodations are a shared dorm with bunk beds and shared baths, accommodating anywhere from 4 to 10 travelers, there are lots of variations. Dorms can be female-only, male-only, or mixed, so ask if you have a preference. Many hostels now offer more deluxe rooms that you share with only two or three other people; you're still not getting hotel amenities, but you are getting a little more space. Many have private rooms, with a double bed or two twins, or family rooms, where you share with your family members but no one else. For two or more travelers sharing a room, hostel prices can sometimes approach those of bed-and-breakfasts or lower-end hotels, so shop around. Hostels generally supply sheets, a blanket, and a towel. To prevent bedbug infestation, most prohibit travelers from bringing their own linens.

Many Canadian hostels are affiliated with **Hostelling International** (HI, www.hihostels.com) and offer discounts to HI members. Not only do you get discounts on hostel stays, but you're also eligible for 10 percent off VIA Rail tickets and 25 percent off Greyhound bus travel within Canada. Ontario hostels also provide members with discounts on some tours or museum admissions.

You typically buy a membership from your home country's HI association, which you can do online. For Canadian citizens and residents, **Hostelling International-Canada** (613/237-7884 or 800/663-5777, www.hihostels.ca) sells adult memberships, valid for two years, for $35; junior memberships, for

kids under 18, are free. At **Hostelling International-USA** (301/495-1240, www.hiusa.org), memberships are valid for one year for adults (US$28), seniors 55 and older (US$18), and youths (free). Other international hostel organizations include **YHA England and Wales** (www.yha.org.uk), **Fédération Unie des Auberges de Jeunesse** (France, www.fuaj.org), **YHA Australia** (www.yha.com.au), and **Youth Hostels Association of New Zealand** (www.yha.co.nz). Get a complete list of international chapters from Hostelling International (www.hihostels.com).

For more information about privately run hostels and other budget accommodations in Ontario and across Canada, see **Backpackers Hostels Canada** (www.backpackers.ca).

University Residences

You don't have to be a student or professor to stay in a university residence. Many Ontario universities open their residence halls to visitors during the summer months (generally mid-May through August). Accommodations range from basic dormitory rooms with shared baths down the hall to suites with kitchen facilities that would be comfortable for families. Some residence halls provide breakfast, some give you an option to eat at campus dining facilities, while at others, you're on your own for meals.

Staying in residence is best for independent travelers, since you don't have a hotel staff to help you out, and you won't get room service or other hotel-style frills. The advantage? The cost can be significantly lower than for nearby hotel accommodations, and the locations are often quite central.

- Hamilton: **McMaster Summer Residences** (905/525-9140, http://conference.mcmaster.ca, $58-78)

- Kingston: **Queen's University Residence Halls** (613/533-2223, http://eventservices.queensu.ca, $50-60)

- London: **Western Bed & Breakfast** (University of Western Ontario, University

Dr., 519/661-3476 or 888/661-3545, www.stayatwestern.com, $55-65)

- Niagara-on-the-Lake: **Niagara College Residence** (137 Taylor Rd., 905/641-4435 or 877/225-8664, www.stayrcc.com, 2-bedroom suite $90-140)

- Ottawa: **University of Ottawa Residences** (90 University St., 613/562-5771 or 888/564-4545, www.ottawaresidences.com, $35-99)

- Toronto: **Massey College Residences** (4 Devonshire Pl., at Hoskin Ave., 416/978-2895, www.masseycollege.ca, $62-90)

- Waterloo: **University of Waterloo Residences** (519/888-4567, www.conferences.uwaterloo.ca, $52-73); **Hotel Laurier** (Wilfred Laurier University, 200 King St. N., 519/884-0710, ext. 2771, www.wlu.ca/hotel, $45-80)

Camping

In Ontario, you can camp in many of the national and provincial parks, and in private campgrounds. In addition to sites where you can pitch a tent or park your RV, many national and provincial parks have cabins or yurts to rent (the latter are tentlike structures modeled after the dwellings of nomads in Mongolia, China, and other regions). You usually have to bring your own sleeping bags and linens, as well as cooking supplies, but you don't have to bring or pitch a tent.

You can camp at four of the five Ontario national parks; there are no individual campgrounds at Point Pelee National Park. At Pukaskwa National Parks, campsites are available on a first-come, first-served basis. You can (and should) make campsite reservations if you're planning to camp at the Bruce Peninsula, Georgian Bay Islands, and Thousand Islands National Parks. Book through the **Parks Canada reservation service** (877/737-3783, www.pccamping.ca).

To find a campsite at one of the many campgrounds run by the provincial **Ontario Parks** (888/668-7275, www.ontarioparks.com) agency, search the park reservation website, which not only lists park campgrounds, but also lets you search online for campground availability. For campgrounds that accept reservations, you can book a site up to five months in advance.

For information about Ontario's more than 400 private campgrounds, contact the **Ontario Private Campground Association** (www.campgrounds.org).

Camp in Parks Canada's "oTENTik" style tent cabins in the Thousand Islands.

Learn to Camp, Ontario Style

What if you've never been camping, but you've always wanted to give it a try? Or you camped a couple of times as a kid, but don't have the gear you need now?

Ontario Parks (www.ontarioparks.com) offers a **Learn to Camp** program to help get you started on your outdoor adventure. Park staff teach you the basics, from how to pitch a tent to how to build a campfire. The park provides tents, air mattresses, a camp stove and cooking equipment, firewood, even flashlights; you bring your food, clothes, and other personal items, as well as a sleeping bag or bedding. The program is offered at certain provincial parks on selected dates. Some parks even run two-hour **Learn to Fish** programs, where you learn basic fishing skills, before trying to catch your own fish.

"Roofed accommodations," including cabins, camping trailers, and yurts, are available in a growing number provincial parks. You may still need to bring sleeping bags and other gear, but you don't need to pitch your own tent.

Parks Canada (www.pc.gc.ca) also offers periodic Learn to Camp programs in some national parks, and many parks now offer roofed accommodations, too. In the national parks, these include cabins, yurts, and "oTENTiks," platform tents that are essentially a cabin floor with tent walls. Another alternative, in the Georgian Bay Islands National Park, is an "equipped camping service," in which park staff set up a large tent for you and provide various gear.

FOOD AND DRINK

The "eating local" movement—choosing foods that are grown or produced locally— is sweeping Ontario in a big way. From the biggest cities to many a small town, summer farmers markets have become hugely popular, and many Ontario chefs are sourcing and promoting local products. The **Ontario Culinary Tourism Alliance** (www.ontarioculinary.com) is a good resource for learning more about the province's foods. **Farmers Markets Ontario** (www.farmersmarketsontario.com) lists farmers markets around the province.

While local food is booming, Ontario's long history of immigration has influenced its cuisine, too. Many formerly unknown foods are now routine parts of Ontario meals, sometimes adapted to use locally grown ingredients. You'll find the legacy of Italian immigration in many communities, especially in the Niagara region, in Sault Ste. Marie, and in Thunder Bay; German and Eastern European fare from Kitchener-Waterloo and St. Jacobs west to Lake Huron and south toward Windsor; Scandinavian heritage in the Thunder Bay area; and French Canadian influences in Eastern and Northeastern Ontario and in the Ottawa region. Multiethnic Toronto has historically Italian, Portuguese, Greek, Indian, and Korean neighborhoods, as well as several Chinatowns, and across the city you'll find foods from around the globe.

Regional Specialties

Outside Canada, it's known as Canadian bacon, but in Canada, the thickly sliced cured pork commonly served for breakfast or in sandwiches is called back bacon or **peameal bacon.**

Ontario's numerous lakes yield several varieties of fresh fish, including pickerel and perch. It's baked, grilled, or fried up for fish-and-chips.

Artisanal cheese making is a growing business in Ontario, particularly in Prince Edward County, the Ottawa region, and the region between Kitchener and Lake Huron. Look for Ontario cheeses at farmers markets and specialty cheese shops around the province. One distinctive use of cheese that you'll find both in Ontario's French Canadian communities and across the country is **poutine,** french fries topped with brown gravy and melted cheese curds. Originally from Quebec, *poutine* may sound unappealing, but it is gooey, salty, and savory, and surprisingly addicting.

Central and Eastern Ontario is maple country, so you'll find lots of maple products, including syrup, maple butter, and taffy. In late winter (usually Mar.-Apr.), you can visit **sugar shacks** that tap the sap from maple trees and produce syrup, although most are now large commercial operations rather than little shacks in the woods. Many operate seasonal pancake houses to showcase their maple products. A particular treat is **maple taffy on snow;** hot syrup is poured onto snow, which firms it into taffy that's rolled on a stick. While late winter is the production season, you can purchase Ontario-made maple syrup at farmers markets and groceries year-round.

In late spring and early summer, you'll find strawberries and rhubarb. As the summer goes on, the markets fill with raspberries, blueberries, and peaches, then grapes, apples, and pears. Look for farms where you can pick your own fruit for the absolute freshest produce (as well as fun for the kids).

Panzarotti are Ontario's version of calzone. It's baked dough stuffed with tomato sauce and cheese, often including sausage, peppers, or other toppings typically found on pizza. You'll see *panzarotti* in Sault Ste. Marie (which also has excellent pizza) and anywhere there's a large Italian community.

Summer in Ontario is **fruit pie** time, with strawberry, raspberry, blueberry, peach, apple, and other varieties appearing on bakery and farm-stand shelves as each fruit comes into season. Year-round, in francophone communities, you might see *tourtière,* which is a savory meat pie. Found in many of Canada's First Nations communities, **bannock** is a biscuit-like bread, baked, fried, or grilled over an open fire.

Beaver tails aren't actually the tails of beavers; they're just shaped like them. They're fried slabs of whole-wheat dough topped with cinnamon sugar and a squeeze of lemon (or with all sorts of other sweet toppings). They're an Ottawa tradition, but you can now find them in many parts of Canada and abroad.

If you have only one dessert in Ontario, it should be a **butter tart.** No, it's not a pie shell filled with butter; it's a single-serving pastry filled with a gooey mix of brown sugar, butter, and eggs. The dark-sugar custard filling resembles American pecan pie without the nuts, although butter tarts sometimes have pecans

Ontario is Canada's main wine-producing area.

or raisins added. You can find butter tarts at bakeries across the province.

Ontario Wines

Ontario is Canada's main wine-producing area, with vineyards and wineries concentrated in several areas. The largest is the Niagara region, with more than 100 wineries in and around the town of Niagara-on-the-Lake and in the Twenty Valley, incorporating the towns of Beamsville, Vineland, and Jordan. In Eastern Ontario, Prince Edward County is a growing wine district, and in the southwestern corner of the province is the small wine-producing area known as the **Essex Pelee Island Coast (EPIC) Wine Country** along Lake Erie's North Shore. Most wineries welcome visitors, and you can buy their wines at the winery shops; larger wineries also sell to restaurants and wine stores around the province.

Ontario may be best known for its **ice wine,** a sweet, intense dessert wine that's made from grapes that are allowed to freeze on the vine. The production process is labor-intensive (the frozen grapes must be hand-picked) and very sensitive to temperature variations, which makes ice wine an expensive, if delicious, treat.

The **Wine Council of Ontario** (www.winecountryontario.ca) is a good source of information about Ontario wines and wineries.

Travel Tips

OPPORTUNITIES FOR STUDY AND EMPLOYMENT

To go to school or work in Canada, you must apply for and receive a study or work permit before you enter the country. The government agency responsible for study and work permits is **Citizenship and Immigration Canada** (www.cic.gc.ca). For general information about living and working in Canada, refer to **Living Abroad in Canada** (www.livingabroadincanada.com). For specific information about studying and working in Ontario, also see the **Ontario Ministry of Citizenship and Immigration** (www.citizenship.gov.on.ca).

ACCESS FOR TRAVELERS WITH DISABILITIES

Many, but not all, of Ontario's attractions, hotels, restaurants, entertainment venues, and transportation options are accessible to travelers with disabilities. A useful general resource that provides information about accessible travel to and around Canada is the Canadian government's **Access to Travel** website (www.accesstotravel.gc.ca). It includes helpful details about transportation between and around Ontario cities and towns, as well as general tips and travel resources.

Many Ontario provincial parks offer accessible facilities. Many picnic areas, campsites, and park restrooms, as well as some trails, can accommodate wheelchairs and other mobility aids. Get details on facilities in specific parks from **Ontario Parks** (www.ontarioparks.com).

TRAVELING WITH CHILDREN

Ontario is an extremely family-friendly destination. Not only are there tons of fun things for families to do, there are lots of resources to help support traveling families or make travel more affordable. Many museums and attractions offer free admission for kids under a certain age (often 5 or 6, but sometimes 11 or 12). Many offer discounted family admission rates, which generally include two adults and at least two children.

During the summer (late June-Aug.) and during school holiday periods, including Christmas-New Year's (late Dec.-early Jan.)

and March break (mid-Mar.), many attractions offer kids' camps or other activities for children. Just note that these periods will also be the most crowded times at family-friendly places.

Kids stay free at some major hotels. Other good lodging options for traveling families, besides the typical chain motels, include suite hotels (in cities) and cottages (in more rural areas), which often provide more space for the money, as well as kitchen facilities where you can prepare your own food. Cottage resorts, which offer cottage accommodations as well as the services of a hotel (a dining room, water sports, or other kids' activities), are great fun for families; many specifically target multiple generations traveling together.

Some bed-and-breakfasts don't accept kids, so always ask. One type of B&B that's typically great for kids is a bed-and-breakfast on a farm. There's usually space for kids to run around, as well as animals to look at; children may even be able to help with farm chores.

Many Ontario restaurants have children's menus with burgers, chicken, sandwiches, or other nonthreatening foods. Some will also make smaller portions of regular menu items or prepare a simple pasta dish. Encourage your kids to eat what you're eating, though, since they may surprise you (and themselves) with a new food that they like.

WOMEN TRAVELING ALONE

Overall, Ontario is a relatively safe destination compared to many spots around the world, and women shouldn't hesitate to travel alone. However, exercise caution wherever you go, and particularly in urban areas, avoid venturing out alone late at night or in the wee hours of the morning. If you are out late on your own, don't walk—take a cab. Take your cues from local women, too; if you don't see other women walking or waiting for the bus, that's a clue that maybe you shouldn't either.

An excellent resource for women travelers is **Journeywoman** (www.journeywoman. com), a Toronto-based worldwide website where women travelers can share tips and ask for advice from local women. Another great site for women's travel tips, particularly for solo travelers, is **Wanderlust and Lipstick** (www.wanderlustandlipstick.com).

SENIOR TRAVELERS

The good thing about getting older is that you can often get discounts. Many Ontario attractions, lodgings, and transportation providers offer discounts for seniors. The age of eligibility varies, however; it might be 55, 60, 62, or 65. For seniors who love the outdoors, Ontario Parks offers discounts at the provincial parks, with reduced rates for day-use admission and camping fees.

GAY AND LESBIAN TRAVELERS

Canada is far more welcoming to gay and lesbian travelers than many other destinations. Same-sex marriage is legal in Canada, and Ontario was among the first provinces to make it permissible, in 2003. Ontario's largest gay and lesbian community is in Toronto, and the city's annual Pride Week is one of the biggest gay and lesbian pride celebrations in the world. The hub of the community is the Church and Wellesley neighborhood, known as the Gay Village, although accommodations, restaurants, and other facilities across the city (and indeed across the province) welcome gay travelers. The city also has a newer gay and lesbian neighborhood, dubbed "Queer West," along Ossington Avenue between Dundas Street West and Queen Street West and along Queen Street West between Ossington Avenue and Roncesvalles Avenue.

Resources for gay and lesbian travel to Ontario include:

- **Travel Gay Canada** (www.travelgaycanada.com): The country's gay and lesbian tourism association

- **TAG Approved** (www.tagapproved.com): Gay-friendly hotels and attractions

- **Ontario Tourism** (www.ontariotravel. net): Search for "LGBTQ Travel" for information about accommodations, festivals and events, and other travel tips

- **Tourism Toronto** (www.seetorontonow. com/toronto-diversity): Toronto travel tips and resources, including information about same-sex weddings in the city

- **Ottawa Tourism** (www.ottawatourism. ca): Lists resources and events for LGBT travel in the nation's capital

CONDUCT AND CUSTOMS
Smoking

Smoking is not allowed in any enclosed public space in Ontario. That means you can't smoke in restaurants, bars, offices, stores, sports arenas, casinos, theaters, or other entertainment venues. In hotels, you can smoke in your room only if it's a designated smoking room (which are becoming less and less common); smoking is prohibited everywhere else in the hotel.

So where can you smoke? Smoking is permitted on outdoor patios, but only if there's no roof. You can smoke in your car, unless you're traveling with a child who's under 16. And you're still allowed to smoke outdoors on the sidewalk. You must be at least 19 to purchase cigarettes or other tobacco products in Ontario.

Alcohol

The legal drinking age in Ontario is 19. Liquor, wine, and beer are sold in government-run liquor stores. Because the Liquor Control Board of Ontario operates these stores, they're known by the acronym LCBO. There are separate stores that sell beer called The Beer Store. Driving under the influence of alcohol or drugs is a criminal offense. The law applies not only to cars, but also to boats, snowmobiles, and all-terrain vehicles. You can immediately lose your driver's license for 90 days if you're found to have a blood-alcohol level of more than 0.8 or if you refuse to take a breathalyzer test.

Ontario Holidays

Ontario observes all of Canada's national holidays, as well as additional provincial holidays. Banks, post offices, and government offices are typically closed on major holidays; stores may or may not be open. For example, most stores are closed on Christmas Day but reopen for major sales on Boxing Day.

NATIONAL HOLIDAYS

- New Year's Day (Jan. 1)
- Good Friday
- Easter Monday
- Victoria Day (3rd Mon. in May)
- Canada Day (July 1)
- Labour Day (1st Mon. in Sept.)
- Thanksgiving (2nd Mon. in Oct.)
- Christmas Day (Dec. 25)
- Boxing Day (Dec. 26)

ONTARIO PROVINCIAL HOLIDAYS

- Family Day (3rd Mon. in Feb.)
- Civic Holiday (1st Mon. in Aug.)

Tipping

In restaurants, the expected tip is 15 percent, with 18-20 percent for particularly good service. You should also tip around 15 percent in bars and taxis. Give hotel baggage handlers at least a dollar or two for each bag they carry, and tip concierges in proportion to the services they provide; if they've gotten you seats for a sold-out play or reservations at the booked-for-months restaurant, compensate them for their service. Many people also leave tips of at least $5 per night for hotel housekeeping staff.

Etiquette

Canadians have a reputation for being polite,

and for the most part, that reputation is well deserved. People generally wait patiently in line to board buses and streetcars and give up their seats on public transit to seniors, pregnant women, and anyone with a disability.

The Canadian Human Rights Act prohibits discrimination on the basis of "race, national or ethnic origin, colour, religion, age, sex, sexual orientation, marital status, family status, disability and conviction for which a pardon has been granted." Discrimination still exists, of course, but most Canadians pride themselves on getting along and try to respect other cultures and customs. When you enter a Canadian home, you may be expected to remove your shoes. Many bed-and-breakfasts want you to leave your shoes by the front door, as well.

Health and Safety

Travelers should always carry a basic first-aid kit, including bandages, aspirin or another pain reliever, sunscreen, insect repellent, and an antiseptic or antibiotic ointment. You might want to include an ointment or other product to relieve the itching of mosquito bites; if you're prone to allergic reactions, consider packing an antihistamine as well. If you wear glasses, bring an extra pair. If you take prescription medication, carry a copy of your prescription.

EMERGENCIES

In an emergency, call **911** to reach police, fire, ambulance, or other emergency services. In some remote areas of the province without 911 service, dial 0 and say "This is an emergency" to be transferred to the police. You can also reach the **Ontario Provincial Police emergency line** (888/310-1122).

HEALTH CARE AND INSURANCE

If you become ill or injured while in Ontario, you can go to the nearest hospital emergency room or walk-in health clinic. If you're a resident of another Canadian province, your provincial health plan may not provide health coverage while you're in Ontario. If the plan does provide coverage, it may pay only the amount it would pay for the service in your home province, not what you might be billed in Ontario. Either way, before your trip, it's a good idea to purchase supplemental travel health insurance to cover any unexpected medical costs while you're in Ontario.

If you live outside of Canada, make sure that you have health insurance that will cover you and your family in Canada. You will normally have to pay for the service provided in Ontario and then file a claim with your health insurance provider after you return home.

MOSQUITOES AND BLACK FLIES

Mosquitoes in Ontario may not be a "hazard," but they're surely a major nuisance, particularly from May through August. Try to avoid being outside at dusk or in the early evening when mosquitoes are most active. Outdoors, cover up with long pants and a long-sleeved shirt, and don't forget socks. Using an insect repellent is also a good idea; you can get recommendations from a good outdoors store, like Mountain Equipment Co-op.

Black flies are buzzing, biting insects that live in forested areas, particularly in the late spring, and they're a hugely annoying pest. Across much of Ontario, black flies are worst in May and at least the first half of June; the farther north you go, the later the black fly season. The flies can't bite through clothing, but they can certainly find their way *under* your clothing, especially around your ankles or wrists. Tucking your pants into your socks, while perhaps not the most fashionable solution, will help prevent bites, as will a good insect repellent. Black flies are attracted to darker colors, so wearing lighter hues may help keep them away.

If you're camping, make sure your tent has a screen panel that's not ripped, and always keep the screen closed. The kids may whine when you tell them, for the 100th time, to zip the tent fly, but they'll thank you if it keeps the bugs out of the tent. And even if you're staying indoors, make sure the windows have screens. Ceiling fans or window fans that circulate the air around you make it more difficult for bugs to light.

Information and Services

MONEY

Canada's currency is the Canadian dollar, and like its U.S. counterpart, it's divided into 100 cents. Canadian bills include $5, $10, $20, $50, and $100 denominations. Coins include 5, 10, and 25 cents, and one and two dollars. The gold-colored one-dollar coin is called the loonie, for the picture of the loon on its back. The two-dollar coin is nicknamed the "toonie," since it's equal to two loonies. Throughout this book, prices are listed in Canadian dollars unless otherwise specified.

Major credit cards, including Visa, MasterCard, and American Express, are accepted throughout the province, although some smaller establishments may take payment in cash only. You'll find Automated Teller Machines (ATMs)—which Canadian banks call Automated Banking Machines, or ABMs—in almost every town.

The Bank of Canada (www.bankofcanada.ca), Canada's central bank, publishes the official exchange rate between Canadian dollars and other currencies. You can exchange U.S. dollars, euros, British pounds, Australian dollars, and other major currencies for Canadian dollars at banks across Ontario or at currency exchange dealers in Toronto, Ottawa, and towns near the U.S. border. Most of the Ontario travel information centers around the province can exchange currency. In tourist areas close to the border, like Niagara Falls or the Thousand Islands, some businesses will accept U.S. dollars, although the exchange rate is usually worse than the official rate, and you'll get change back in Canadian funds. You're nearly always better off paying in Canadian currency or using a credit card.

Ontario has a 13 percent sales tax, the **HST,** or harmonized sales tax. Not every purchase a traveler might make is subject to HST, but many are. You don't pay sales tax in Ontario on basic groceries.

COMMUNICATIONS AND MEDIA
Telephone

Across most of Southern and Central Ontario, you must dial the full 10-digit number (the area code plus the seven-digit local number) in order to place a call, even if you're within the same area code. If you're calling from outside Ontario or from a different area code, you must also dial "1" (which is the country code for Canada, the same as for the United States), followed by the 10-digit number.

Toll-free numbers, which you can call for free from a landline and some mobile phones, depending on your plan, begin with the area codes 800, 855, 866, or 877. You must dial "1" before the toll-free number.

Cellular phone service is widely available across Ontario, although you may find dead zones in more remotes areas. If you're going to be making a lot of long-distance phone calls while you're in Ontario, purchasing a pre-paid phone card might save you money. You can buy phone cards at convenience stores, some drug stores, and many grocery stores.

Internet

Internet access is widely available across Ontario. Ontario's major airports have free

Wi-Fi service. VIA Rail offers complimentary Wi-Fi in major Ontario train stations and on board most of their trains in the Windsor-Quebec City corridor, which includes trains to Windsor, London, Toronto, Kingston, Ottawa, and Montreal.

Most hotels, motels, bed-and-breakfasts, and hostels provide Internet access for guests, and many also have a computer you can use. Larger hotels sometimes charge a daily fee for Internet access; it's always a good idea to ask. Many coffee shops and cafés have free Wi-Fi, but they expect that you'll purchase at least a cup of coffee or tea before tapping into the network. Some require you to ask for a password. Some libraries have public Internet access, available free or for a small fee. Visitor information centers may offer free Wi-Fi, or staff can tell you where you can get online.

As you get out of the cities, you may find it a bit harder to get online, although even in fairly remote areas, many accommodations have Internet access for guests. In rural areas, the signal may be less reliable; sometimes you might be able to get online in the lobby or other public space, but not in your room or cottage.

MAPS AND VISITOR INFORMATION

The best source of information about travel in Ontario (in addition to this book, of course) is **Ontario Travel** (www.ontariotravel.net). Created by the Ontario Tourism Marketing Partnership, an agency of the provincial government, this site provide details about things to see and do all across Ontario, including a calendar of upcoming events. The **Canadian Tourism Commission** (www.canada.travel) is the government of Canada's official guide to travel across the country and includes information about travel in Ontario.

If you're a member of either the **American Automobile Association** (AAA, www.aaa.com) or the **Canadian Automobile Association** (CAA, www.caa.ca), you can request free maps of Ontario and its major cities. If you belong to AAA, you can get maps from the CAA, and vice versa.

Ontario Travel Information Centers

The province operates a number of travel information centers that offer travel and visitor information, either by phone or in person. Some are open year-round, while others operate seasonally. The major locations are listed here; you can get a complete list at www.ontariotravel.net.

In Toronto and Central Ontario:

- **Toronto** (Union Station, 65 Front St. W., 416/314-5899, ontariotravel.toronto@ontario.ca)
- **Barrie** (21 Mapleview Dr. E., at Hwy. 400, 705/725-7280 or 800/567-1140, ontariotravel.barrie@ontario.ca)

In the Niagara Region:

- **Niagara Falls** (Rainbow Bridge, 5355 Stanley Ave., 905/358-3221, ontariotravel.niagarafalls@ontario.ca)
- **Niagara-on-the-Lake** (251 York Rd., 905/684-6354, ontariotravel.stcatharines@ontario.ca)

In Southwestern Ontario:

- **Sarnia** (Blue Water Bridge, 1455 Venetian Blvd., 519/344-7403, ontariotravel.sarnia@ontario.ca)
- **Tilbury** (62 Hwy. 401 E., 519/682-9501, ontariotravel.tilbury@ontario.ca)
- **Windsor Park** (Detroit-Windsor Tunnel, 110 Park St. E., 519/973-1338, ontariotravel.windsorp@ontario.ca)

In Eastern Ontario:

- **Bainsville** (22064 N. Service Rd., Hwy. 401, at the Ontario-Quebec border, 613/347-3498, ontariotravel.bainsville@ontario.ca)

In Northwestern Ontario:

- **Sault Ste. Marie** (Sault Ste. Marie International Bridge, 261 Queen St. W.,

705/945-6941, ontariotravel.ssm@ontario.ca)

- **Neebing** (7671 Hwy. 61, south of Thunder Bay, 807/964-2094, ontariotravel.pigeonriver@ontario.ca, mid-May-Oct.)

Regional Tourism Organizations

Tourism agencies in the regions and major cities around Ontario provide detailed information about their districts:

In Toronto and Central Ontario:

- **Tourism Toronto** (416/203-2500 or 800/499-2514, www.seetorontonow.com)
- **Tourism Hamilton** (905/546-2666 or 800/263-8590, www.tourismhamilton.com)

In the Niagara Region:

- **Niagara Falls Tourism** (905/356-6061 or 800/563-2557, www.niagarafallstourism.com)
- **Niagara-on-the-Lake Chamber of Commerce** (905/468-1950, www.niagaraonthelake.com)

In Southwestern Ontario:

- **Waterloo Regional Tourism Marketing Corporation** (519/585-7517 or 877/585-7517, www.explorewaterlooregion.com), including Kitchener-Waterloo, Cambridge, St. Jacobs, and surrounding communities
- **Stratford Tourism Alliance** (519/271-5140 or 800/561-7926, www.visitstratford.ca)
- **Tourism London** (519/661-5000 or 800/265-2602, www.londontourism.ca)
- **Tourism Windsor, Essex, and Pelee Island** (519/255-6530 or 800/265-3633, www.visitwindsoressex.com)

Around Georgian Bay:

- **Bruce Peninsula-County of Bruce Tourism** (519/534-5344 or 800/268-3838, www.explorethebruce.com)
- **Grey County Tourism** (519/376-3265 or 877/733-4739, www.visitgrey.ca), providing information about Owen Sound, Collingwood, and the Blue Mountains
- **Georgian Bay Destination Development Partnership** (www.visitgeorgianbay.com), providing information about the region surrounding Georgian Bay

In Cottage Country:

- **Muskoka Tourism** (705/689-0660 or 800/267-9700, www.discovermuskoka.ca) covering Gravenhurst, Bracebridge, Huntsville, the Muskoka Lakes, and the region surrounding Algonquin Provincial Park
- **Northeastern Ontario Tourism** (705/522-0104 or 800/465-6655, www.northeasternontario.com), covering Sudbury, North Bay, and other Northeastern Ontario communities

In Eastern Ontario:

- **Ottawa Tourism** (613/237-5150 or 800/363-4465, www.ottawatourism.ca)
- **Peterborough and the Kawarthas Tourism** (705/742-2201 or 800/461-6424, www.thekawarthas.ca)
- **Prince Edward County Tourism** (613/476-2421 or 800/640-4717, www.prince-edward-county.com)
- **Tourism Kingston** (613/544-2725 or 866/665-3326, www.tourism.kingstoncanada.com)
- **Thousand Islands International Tourism Council** (800/847-5263, www.visit1000islands.com)

In Northwestern Ontario:

- **Algoma Kinniwabi Travel Association** (705/254-4293 or 800/263-2546, www.algomacountry.com), including Sault Ste. Marie, Wawa, and Lake Superior's North Shore
- **North of Superior Tourism Association** (800/265-3951, www.northofsuperior.org), covering Thunder Bay and vicinity

WEIGHTS AND MEASURES

Canada officially uses the metric system. Distances and speed limits are marked in kilometers, gasoline and bottled beverages are sold by the liter, and weights are given in grams or kilograms. Because the country didn't adopt metric units until the 1970s, however, you'll still occasionally see grocery items measured with pounds or ounces, and older folks, who didn't grow up with the metric system, will sometimes use imperial units.

Electricity in Canada is 120 volts, 60 hertz, the same as in the United States, with the same types of plugs.

Ontario has two time zones. Most of the province, including cities as far west as Thunder Bay, is in the eastern time zone. The westernmost part of the province, on the Manitoba border, is in the Central time zone. Ontario observes daylight savings time. Clocks move forward one hour on the second Sunday in March and turn back one hour on the first Sunday in November.

Resources

Suggested Reading

FICTION

Atwood, Margaret. *Cat's Eye*. Toronto: Mc-Clelland & Stewart, 1988. One of Ontario's most eminent writers, Atwood (www.margaretatwood.ca) has written more than a dozen novels, including this one about a painter who returns to her native Toronto.

Brand, Dionne. *What We All Long For*. Toronto: A. A. Knopf Canada, 2005. A novel about a young Toronto artist from a Vietnamese immigrant family and several of her friends.

Lansens, Laurie. *Rush Home Road*. Toronto: A. A. Knopf Canada, 2002. Set in the fictional town of Rusholme, an all-black community in Southwestern Ontario settled by fugitive slaves, which the author modeled after the village of Buxton, this novel follows their descendants in their rural surroundings.

Munro, Alice. *Lives of Girls and Women*. New York: McGraw-Hill, 1973. A collection of linked stories chronicling a young woman's coming-of-age in small-town Ontario, by the 2013 winner of the Nobel Prize in Literature. For more Ontario stories, check out Munro's *Dear Life* (Toronto: McClelland and Stewart, 2012).

Shields, Carol. *Unless*. Toronto: Random House Canada, 2002. The eldest daughter of an Ontario novelist becomes a mute panhandler in downtown Toronto. Shields (1935-2003, www.carol-shields.com) wrote several other novels set in Ontario or elsewhere in Canada.

FOOD AND WINE

Norton, James and Dilley, Becca. *Lake Superior Flavors: A Field Guide to Food and Drink along the Circle Tour*. Minneapolis: University of Minnesota Press, 2014. A guide to local food along the Lake Superior Circle Route, on both the Canadian and U.S. sides of the lake.

Ogryzlo, Lynn. *Niagara Cooks: From Farm to Table*. Toronto: Epulum Books, 2008. Part cookbook and part local food guide, this book (www.niagaracooks.ca) features the foods and wines of the Niagara region.

Ogryzlo, Lynn. *Ontario Table: Featuring the Best Food from Across the Province*. Toronto: Epulum Books, 2011. A cookbook and agricultural guide (www.ontariotable.com) that highlights local growers, foods, and wines from around Ontario.

Rosen, Amy. *Toronto Cooks: 100 Signature Recipes from the City's Best Restaurants*. Vancouver: Figure 1 Publishing, 2014. A cookbook featuring dishes from many of Toronto's top chefs.

Sanders, Moira, and Elstone, Lori. *The Harrow Fair Cookbook*. Toronto: Whitecap Books, 2011. Recipes, featuring regional produce and products, from Southwestern Ontario's Harrow Fair, one of Canada's oldest country fairs.

NONFICTION

Christmas, Jane. *The Pelee Project: One Woman's Escape from Urban Madness.* Toronto: ECW Press, 2002. A Toronto journalist takes a sabbatical on Pelee Island to reevaluate her life and values, learning something about Canadian island life along the way.

Wilkens, Charles. *Walk to New York: A Journey Out of the Wilds of Canada.* Toronto: Viking Canada, 2004. A 50-something author decides to shake up his life by walking 2,200 kilometers (1,300 miles) across Ontario from Thunder Bay to New York City.

TRAVEL

Bogue, Margaret Beattie. *Around the Shores of Lake Superior: A Guide to Historic Sites.* Waterloo: Wilfred Laurier Press, 2007. As the title suggests, this book provides background about historic sites along Lake Superior.

Brown, Ron. *Top 125 Unusual Things to See in Ontario.* Toronto: Firefly Books, 2014. Author Ron Brown (www.ronbrown.ca) has written more than 20 books about Ontario, including this one about the province's quirkiest attractions. His other recent books include *Rails across Ontario: Exploring Ontario's Railway Heritage* (Toronto: Dundurn Press, 2013) and *Backroads of Ontario* (Toronto: Firefly Books, 2013).

Esrock, Robin, *The Great Central Canada Bucket List: One-of-a-Kind Travel Experiences* (Toronto: Dundurn Press, 2015). Travel writer and adventurer Esrock (www.robinesrock.com) highlights the best travel experiences in Ontario and Quebec.

McGuffin, Gary and Joanie, *Great Lakes Journey: Exploring the Heritage Coast* (Toronto: McClelland & Stewart, 2003) and *Superior: Journeys on an Inland Sea* (Toronto: Boston Mills Press/Firefly Books, 1995). These photo-filled books by husband-and-wife adventurers (www.garyandjoaniemcguffin.com) document their travels through the Northern Ontario wilderness.

Pearen, Shelley. *Exploring Manitoulin,* 3rd edition. Toronto: University of Toronto Press, 2001. Although much of the practical information in this guide to Ontario's Manitoulin Island is dated, it still provides a useful overview of the island's history and culture.

Runtz, Michael. *The Explorer's Guide to Algonquin Park.* Erin, ON: Boston Mills Press, 2008. A detailed guide to Algonquin Provincial Park, one of Ontario's largest protected green spaces.

Internet Resources

GOVERNMENT

Citizenship and Immigration Canada
www.cic.gc.ca
The federal government agency responsible for overseeing visitors and immigrants to Canada, including information about visitor visas, work permits, study permits, and applications for permanent residence.

Government of Ontario
www.ontario.ca
The provincial government website with information for visitors and residents about travel, recreation, money, documents, and more.

PARKS
Ontario Parks
www.ontarioparks.com
Information about, and reservations booking service for, Ontario's more than 330 provincial parks.

Parks Canada
www.pc.gc.ca
The federal government agency that manages the country's national parks and national historic sites.

Parks Canada Campground Reservation Service
www.pccamping.ca
Reservations booking service for Canada's national park campgrounds, including those in Ontario.

TRANSPORTATION
Major Airlines
Air Canada
www.aircanada.com

Porter Airlines
www.flyporter.com

Westjet
www.westjet.com

Trains and Buses
Amtrak
www.amtrak.com
U.S. rail carrier that provides train service to Toronto and Niagara Falls from American cities.

Greyhound Bus Lines
www.greyhound.ca
Provides the most extensive network of bus services across Ontario, as well as buses from the eastern United States to Ontario.

Megabus
www.megabus.com
Operates buses between Toronto and Niagara Falls, Kingston, and Montreal, as well as buses between Toronto and the eastern United States, including New York City, Syracuse, Washington DC, Baltimore, Philadelphia, and Pittsburgh.

OC Transpo (Ottawa)
www.octranspo.com
Ottawa's public transit system, including a Trip Planner routing feature.

Ontario Northland
www.ontarionorthland.ca
Runs buses between Toronto and various points in Northern Ontario, including service to the Muskoka region and the northeast. Also operates the *Polar Bear Express* train from Cochrane to Moosonee.

VIA Rail
www.viarail.ca
Canada's national rail system, which operates trains across the country.

Toronto Transit Commission
www.ttc.ca
Toronto's public transit system, including subways, streetcars, and buses. The website includes a Trip Planner to help you plan the best route to your destination.

TRAVEL
Canadian Tourism Commission
www.canada.travel
The government of Canada's official guide to travel across the country.

Environment Canada
www.weather.gc.ca
Provides weather forecasts and historical weather data for more than 150 locations across Ontario and many more destinations across Canada.

Ethan Meleg Outdoor Photography
www.ethanmeleg.com
For more photographs to inspire your Ontario travels, check out the work by Ontario-based

photographer Ethan Meleg, who shot the cover photo for this edition of *Moon Ontario*.

Festival and Events Ontario
www.festivalsandeventsontario.ca
A guide to festivals and special events around the province, including an annual Top 100 Ontario Festivals list.

Living Abroad in Canada
www.livingabroadincanada.com
Book and website by author Carolyn B. Heller that provides resources and information about relocating to Canada, including immigration details, work and study permits, housing, education, and jobs.

Ontario Culinary Tourism Alliance
www.ontarioculinary.com
An organization that promotes Ontario's food producers and culinary travel destinations.

Ontario Travel
www.ontariotravel.net
Created by the Ontario Tourism Marketing Partnership, an agency of the provincial government, this website provides details about things to see and do all across Ontario.

Ottawa Tourism
www.ottawatourism.ca
Guide to travel in Ottawa, the nation's capital.

Tourism Toronto
www.seetorontonow.com
A guide to festivals and events, things to see and do, and other travel details in and around the city of Toronto.

Visit Niagara Canada
www.visitniagaracanada.com
Travel information for the Niagara Peninsula, including Niagara Falls, Niagara-on-the-Lake, and the Niagara wine country.

Wine Country Ontario
www.winecountryontario.ca
A guide to Ontario's wineries in the province's main wine-producing regions: the Niagara Peninsula, Prince Edward County, and the North Shore of Lake Erie.

Index

List of Maps

Acknowledgments

I could never have completed a project of this magnitude without the support of many people and organizations across Ontario and beyond.

I'm especially grateful for the ongoing assistance of the Ontario Tourism Marketing Partnership, particularly the ever-helpful Helen Lovekin and Kattrin Sieber Duncan.

In Toronto, many thanks to Vanessa Somarriba at Tourism Toronto, Audrey Ooi of Tasty Tours, Dustin Fuhs of LiveToronto, Kerry Connelly, Tracy Ford, Stacey Masson, Cassie Prosper, and Steven Ross. In the Niagara region, thanks to Clark Bernat, Holly Goertzen, Barbara Grumme, Madalena Phillips, Helen Young, and Niagara Falls Tourism.

My gratitude to Minto Schneider of the Waterloo Regional Tourism Marketing Corporation, for her ability to make things happen (and for feeding me well). Both Dana Borcea at Tourism Hamilton and Cathy Rehberg of Stratford Tourism were helpful as always, with lots of news (and good meals) to share in their regions. I'm also grateful to Jenny Shantz in St. Jacobs, Deb Dalziel at Elora Tourism, Heather McEwen at Tourism Brantford, Melissa De Luca at Tourism London, Jamie Kent and the Grand Experiences team, Odette Yazbeck and Jenniffer Anand at the Shaw Festival, and Ruth Klahsen at Monforte Restaurant. More thanks to go to Anne Lukin for sharing her local food knowledge and good company, and to Kathleen Stanley and Roger Dufau, Wilma and Brian Skipper, and Shane Burry who all welcomed me to their lodgings.

In Southwestern Ontario, thank you to Lionel Kernerman at Tourism Windsor, Essex, Pelee Island; Robert and Debbie Honor; Sarah Rupert at Point Pelee National Park; Ann Wilson (Oxley Estate Winery); Shannon Prince (Buxton National Historic Site); Bryan and Anna Walls (John Freeman Walls Historic Site), and to Pina Ciotoli and Adriano Ciotoli of Windsor Eats.

In Eastern Ontario, I appreciated the support of Kelly Jessup and the rest of the team at Peterborough & the Kawarthas Tourism, Ashley Stewart (Prince Edward County), Connie Markle at Tourism Kingston, Deanna Davies and Susan LeClair (St. Lawrence Parks Commission), and Kathrine Christensen (1000 Islands Tourism). Many thanks also to Gina and Bill Stewart, Holly Doughty, and Wolfgang Stichnothe for the hospitality, to Lloyd Graham for the bike ride, and to the 1000 Islands Playhouse, 4th Line Theatre, and Perth Through the Ages for the first-rate productions. Thank you, too, to Scott Ewart and his staff at 1000 Islands Kayaking, and to Dave Kouri and Ewelina Sobala at 1000 Islands Helicopters, for the adventures.

Special thanks to the top-notch Ottawa Tourism team, especially Jantine Van Kregten. Also in the Ottawa-Gatineau region, my gratitude to Ottawa City Adventures, Anne Chardon at Tourisme Outaouais, Nathalie Lalonde and Marianne Trotier (Nordik Spa-Nature), the staff at Gatineau Park, and Geneviève Léveillé (Casino du Lac-Leamy).

Bev Hughes (Georgian Bay Destination Development Partnership) once again worked miracles to show off the best of the beautiful Georgian Bay region. Also around Georgian Bay, my thanks to the staff at the Georgian Bay Islands and Bruce Peninsula National Parks, to the always helpful Explore the Bruce organization, and to Patti Kendall at the Blue Mountain Village Association.

Extra-special thanks to Lynn Bryant for sharing my Georgian Bay adventures and for gamely enduring early-morning animal wake-up calls, cold-water snorkeling, rainy-day moose spotting, many kilometers on the hiking trails, and melted butter tarts.

I appreciated the hospitality of Jamie Heimbecker in Owen Sound, Barbara Grison in Lion's Head, Kelly Levack in Tobermory, Maury and Annabelle East in Killarney, and Peter and Kim Hakkenberg in Midland. I also enjoyed the unique evening of dinner and entertainment with Leslie Robbins-Conway, Paul Conway, and their family of Voyageur Storytelling on the Bruce Peninsula.

On Manitoulin Island, my appreciation to Falcon Migwans and Gladys King of the Great Spirit Circle Trail, Alain Harvey at the Auberge Inn, Shirin Grover at the Meldrum Bay Inn, and Ron Berti of the Debajehmujig Theatre Group. In the Muskoka region, I'm grateful to Laura Kennedy and Kate Hillyar at the Deerhurst Resort and to Jordan Mulligan at Muskoka Tourism.

A giant thank-you to Paul Pepe at Tourism Thunder Bay for introducing me to this striking part of the province. Many thanks, too, to Parks Canada staffers Sylvio (Hoss) Peletier for the lasagna and all the information, Greg Stroud for the regional tips, and Annique Maheu and Jennifer Metherel for showing off beautifully remote Pukaskwa National Park. More thanks to Greg Heroux for the sailing adventure, Krista and Alan Cheeseman for the float plane tour, Dorothy and Tom Walch for the warm welcome, Dean Main for passing on his enthusiasm for Terrace Bay, Frank Trichilo for making me breakfast, and Lois Nuttall for sharing her Thunder Bay knowledge and encouraging me to go to the sauna.

More thanks go to Ian McMillan and Lindsey Ackland of Tourism Sault Ste. Marie and to Carol Caputo of Ontario's Algoma Country.

A special shout-out to the helpful crew at Ontario Parks, especially Lori Waldbrook, Barb Rees, Rick Stronks (Algonquin), Peter Briand (Arrowhead), Denise Anderson and Jessica Schulze (Grundy Lake), Lance Tugwell (Neys), and the staffs at French River, Sleeping Giant, and Lake Superior Provincial Park. Dave Sproule gets particular kudos for hiking with me to "The Crack" at Killarney. Thanks, too, to Judy Hammond and Glenn Cameron (Clear Communications) for continuing to share their park tips and extensive network of connections.

Toasts to all my generous media colleagues at the Travel Media Association of Canada for their suggestions and support, with particular cheers to Lynn Ogryzlo for her warm Niagara welcome (and apologies for things that went bump in the night).

And for the many others across Ontario who provided timely tips and a warm welcome, you have my gratitude.

Many thanks to the awesome team at Avalon Travel, including my editor for this new edition, Erin Raber, my original editor Sabrina Young, Acquisitions Editor Elizabeth Hollis Hansen, Acquisitions Director Grace Fujimoto, Map Editor Kat Bennett, and Darren Alessi for working his magic on the photographs. Special thanks to talented photographer Ethan Meleg for providing the striking cover photo for this edition.

Back home, my appreciation to Michaela and Talia for once again tolerating their mother's ramblings, and to Alan, as always, for his love and his patience for the day when the book would finally be done.

MAP SYMBOLS

▦ Expressway	★	Highlight	✗ Airfield	⚲	Golf Course
▭ Primary Road	○	City/Town	✈ Airport	▣	Parking Area
▭ Secondary Road	◉	State Capital	▲ Mountain	▰	Archaeological Site
------ Unpaved Road	⊛	National Capital	✛ Unique Natural Feature	⚱	Church
- - - - Trail	★	Point of Interest		🛢	Gas Station
⋯⋯ Ferry	•	Accommodation	⟰ Waterfall	⬭	Glacier
▬▬ Railroad	▼	Restaurant/Bar	▲ Park	▨	Mangrove
▥ Pedestrian Walkway	▪	Other Location	🅃 Trailhead	▨	Reef
⬚⬚⬚ Stairs	⋏	Campground	⛷ Skiing Area	▨	Swamp

CONVERSION TABLES

°C = (°F - 32) / 1.8
°F = (°C x 1.8) + 32
1 inch = 2.54 centimeters (cm)
1 foot = 0.304 meters (m)
1 yard = 0.914 meters
1 mile = 1.6093 kilometers (km)
1 km = 0.6214 miles
1 fathom = 1.8288 m
1 chain = 20.1168 m
1 furlong = 201.168 m
1 acre = 0.4047 hectares
1 sq km = 100 hectares
1 sq mile = 2.59 square km
1 ounce = 28.35 grams
1 pound = 0.4536 kilograms
1 short ton = 0.90718 metric ton
1 short ton = 2,000 pounds
1 long ton = 1.016 metric tons
1 long ton = 2,240 pounds
1 metric ton = 1,000 kilograms
1 quart = 0.94635 liters
1 US gallon = 3.7854 liters
1 Imperial gallon = 4.5459 liters
1 nautical mile = 1.852 km

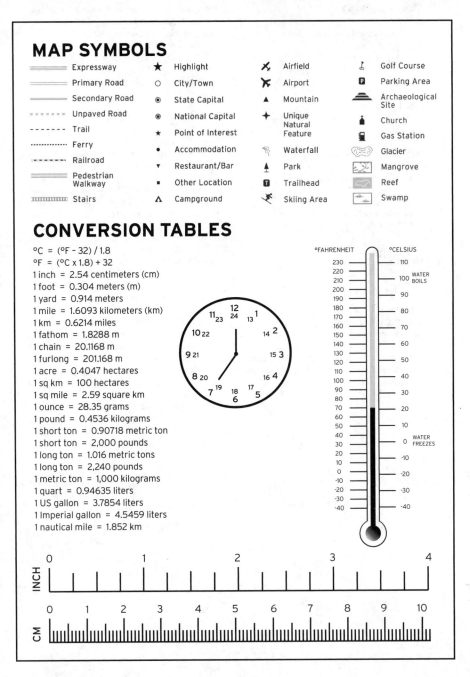

MOON ONTARIO

Avalon Travel
a member of the Perseus Books Group
1700 Fourth Street
Berkeley, CA 94710, USA
www.moon.com

Editor: Erin Raber
Copy Editor: Christopher Church
Graphics and Production Coordinator: Darren Alessi
Cover Design: FaceOut Studios, Charles Brock
Moon Logo: Tim McGrath
Map Editor: Kat Bennett
Cartographers: Chris Henrick, Andrea Butkovic, Stephanie Poulain, Brian Shotwell
Indexer: Greg Jewett

ISBN: 978-1-63121-041-9
ISSN: 2165-4506

Printing History
1st Edition — 2012
2nd Edition — June 2015
5 4 3 2 1

Text © 2015 by Carolyn B. Heller.
Maps © 2015 by Avalon Travel.
All rights reserved.

Some photos and illustrations are used by permission and are the property of the original copyright owners.

Front cover photo: Halfway Rock, Bruce Peninsula National Park © Ethan Meleg
Title page photo: © Carolyn B. Heller
All interior photos © Carolyn B. Heller except page 23 © dreamstime.com; page 27 © Metropolitan Hotels; page 51 Courtesy of the McMichael Canadian Art Collection; page 245 © Peter Spirer/123rf.com

Printed in Canada by Friesens.